PageMaker 6.5
COMPLETE

R. Shamms Mortier

Rick Wallace, et. al

Hayden
Books

PageMaker 6.5 Complete

©1997 R. Shamms Mortier, Rick Wallace, et. al

Library of Congress Catalog Number: 97-78099

ISBN: 1-56830-331-9

Copyright © 1997 Hayden Books

Printed in the United States of America 1 2 3 4 5 6 7 8 9 0

Warning and Disclaimer

ABOUT THE AUTHORS

R. Shamms Mortier, Ph.D., has written over 500 articles on every aspect of computer graphics and animation for dozens of major national and international publications since 1985, and continues as a writer for over a dozen major publications. This is his fourth major book (others include *Desktop Videography*, Michtron Publications, 1988; the graphics section of the *Maclopedia*, Hayden Books, 1996; *Macromedia BackStage Pass*, Ventana Books, 1997). He has also published articles on classroom teaching for the National Department of Education, as well as papers on adult education. He managed the Media Graphics Service at the University of Vermont for 15 years, while teaching courses on graphic design. He operates a graphics and animation studio in Bristol, Vermont (Eyeful Tower Communications) that serves academic, industrial, and regional broadcast clients. He has beta tested software for every major national developer, and continues as a consultant on computer graphics and animation to a number of national and regional enterprises.

Rick Wallace has spent most of his life explaining things to people in one way or another. After 20 years as an award-winning reporter, investigator, and news director in radio and television he discovered computers and a whole new area that needed explaining. He left the news business and became president of a company that produced video tutorials on computers and software. These days his day job is vice president at a crisis management and political campaign firm, using computers to create strategy documents, presentations, television, and radio commercials, and print advertising. By night he writes computer books and so far he has written more than a dozen of them.

Phil Gaskill has a degree in music and a traditional typesetting background, before he moved into the DTP realm. He has been using PageMaker since 1987, and worked at Aldus from 1988 to 1992, before moving to New York. In New York he works as a "freelance book production person," as he puts it, because he is not really sure of what to call what he does. He has written several articles for *Adobe* and *Aldus* magazines, *MacUser* and *MacAddict*. In addition to that, he has written *Real World PageMaker 5.0* for Random House, and has coauthored *Quark XPress: Tips and Tricks* for Peachpit Press.

Richard Romano is a contributing editor to *Digital Imaging* and *Micropublishing News* magazines. He is also a book editor for Micropublishing Press. He has been a PageMaker user since 1985, when it first came out. He graduated from Syracuse University in 1989 and has a certificate in multimedia tehchnology from New York University.

Carla Rose has a degree in fine arts. She has authored or coauthored 18 books on various aspects of computing, including *Maclopedia* and *The Whole Mac*. She has been the senior contributing editor for *Portable Computing Magazine*, and has written for magazines as diverse as the *Atlantic Fisherman, New Yorker,* and *Digital Video.*

Ellen Wixted is seeking an MFA in painting at Indiana University. For eight years prior to that, she was a part of the PageMaker team. Before she left, on her artistic endeavors, she was the Product Marketing Manager, in charge of PageMaker 6.5. Among other things, she was part of the core team responsible for defining the new feature set for PageMaker 6.5. She also has a strong technical writing and editing background.

TRADEMARK ACKNOWLEDGMENTS

All terms mentioned in this book that are known to be trademarks or services marks have been appropriately capitalized. Hayden Books cannot attest to the accuracy of this information. Use of a term in this book should not be regarded as affecting the validity of any trademark or service mark. **Adobe PageMaker** is a trademark of **Adobe Systems Incorporated**. **Extensis** is a trademark of the **Extensis Corporation**.

DEDICATION

This book owes its existence to all of the writers involved, as well as Melanie Rigney, Bront Davis, and Terrie Deemer of Hayden Books. The author also wishes to thank Diane, Ania, Mic, Minky, and Snow for their unqualified and constant support, as well as all of his students through the years.

—R. Shamms Mortier

HAYDEN BOOKS

The staff of Hayden Books is committed to bringing you the best computer books. What our readers think of Hayden is important to our ability to serve our customers. If you have any comments, no matter how great or how small, we'd appreciate your taking the time to send us a note.

You can reach Hayden Books at the following:

Hayden Books
201 West 103rd Street
Indianapolis, IN 46290
317-581-3833

Email addresses:

America Online: Hayden Bks
Internet: hayden@hayden.com

Visit the Hayden Books Web site at http://www.hayden.com

CONTENTS AT A GLANCE

TABLE OF CONTENTS

Introduction

Welcome to PageMaker 6.5 Complete! Our goal in this book is to increase your productivity and to give you the answers to the problems that you encounter in your work. The headings in the chapters will help you quickly find the solutions you are looking for, and all the information you need will be close at hand. The modular structure of the Complete series means less flipping between chapters in order to find all the coverage of a topic; instead, everything you need is right there.

This is a cross-platform book. Where keyboard shortcuts are mentioned, the Macintosh combination appears in parentheses (Command-J) and the Windows combination in brackets [Control-J]. We've made every attempt to cover differences clearly and completely.

Here's a review of the icons you'll encounter as you read PageMaker 6.5 Complete.

Tip

This icon represents a tip, a useful piece of information that will help you get the most out of PageMaker.

Note

Notes include extra information from the author that you will find helpful, like background information that isn't really directly related to the topic at hand but is interesting or useful to know.

Warning

Warnings suggest you stop and think about what you're about to do, because it may cause problems later on. A common warning suggests you save a backup copy before attempting the process described.

This icon indicates features, commands, or tools that are new to PageMaker 6.5.

We hope that you find this book the most exhaustive resource on its topic, and also the easiest to use and navigate. We've tried to put all the information you need right at your fingertips.

Chapter ·········· 1

INTRODUCTION TO PAGEMAKER

Because many of you are upgrading from a PageMaker version earlier than 6.0, whereas others are upgrading from version 6.0 or 6.01, it is important to document the changes in 6.0, 6.01, and 6.5, to give you a better grasp of how extensively PageMaker has been revised.

NEW FEATURES ADDED IN PAGEMAKER 6.5

PageMaker 6.5 includes complete support for Adobe Acrobat 3.0—Export publications directly to Adobe Portable Document Format. (PDF) files, maintaining the design and layout for onscreen and Internet publishing. (PageMaker includes the Acrobat Distiller and Reader—everything you need to create and view PDF files.)

Enhanced HTML Export plug-in—Easily export PageMaker pages or stories into HTML, preserving Hyperlinks and an approximate version of the layout.

Hyperlinks—Hyperlinks palette for authoring Hyperlinks. Browse mode for testing Hyperlinks. Drag-and-drop Hyperlinks from Web browsers into PageMaker.

Image conversion—automatically convert graphics into Web-compatible JPEG or GIF formats when you export files to HTML Color consistency. Get consistent cross-platform color when working in a Web browser thanks to the online publishing color library. And RGB optimizing ensures colors in PDF files look the same as in PageMaker. Design tools quickly create online designs using pre-designed page sizes and templates. Automatic reformatting when page size or orientation changes.

Page Design

Document-wide layers—Set up a single file for multiple versions of a publication, add annotations, and more.

Object masking—Crop text, graphics, and images easily into polygons, ovals, and rectangles.

Automatic layout adjustment—Automatically reposition and resize text blocks, frames, and graphics when you change columns, orientation, or master pages.

Improved Adobe Table 3.0 software—Easily layout text and data in rows and columns, and now include color.

Text and graphics frames—Set up page layout independent of content.

Publishing options—Create a wide variety of documents up to 999 pages each.

Extensive printing features—Enjoy maximum flexibility with support for Adobe PostScript, PCL, and QuickDraw printers. Includes Print Fit view and printer styles, plus the capability to print nonconsecutive pages and reader's spreads, and to designate selected objects as nonprinting.

Professional typographic controls—Set typography to professional standards with point-size dependent tracking, kerning in 0.001 increments, and expanded and condensed type.

Time-saving devices—Streamline the workflow with more than 15 new template designs, instantly define grids with an enhanced Grid Manager Plug-in, impose pages using the Build Booklet Plug-in, and generate an automatic table of contents or index across multiple publications.

Multiple master pages—Specify and apply different page designs within a single publication.

Enhanced Polygon tool— Draw freeform polygons and lines, and edit points on existing polygons.

Link management controls—Reliably track changes to imported text and graphics files.

Text capabilities—Speed text processing with a built-in word processor, spelling checker, and search-and-replace feature.

Improved navigation—Quickly move between pages with new Go Back and Go Forward commands.

Object handling—Automatically align and distribute objects. Combine multiple elements into a unit with a single keystroke, and move or resize an element without having to separate it from the rest of the group. Easily maintain the relationships of layout elements with object locking.

Navigation aids—Automatically create bookmarks and HyperText links for table of contents and index entries in PDF Files.

Automatic layout adjustment—Change page size or orientation and quickly reformat publications for online viewing.

Hyperlinks—Easily author Hyperlinks both within PageMaker and to any URL on the World Wide Web using the new Hyperlinks palette. Then use PageMaker's browse mode to test them.

Smooth Integration with Other Adobe Software

Smooth upgrade path—Directly open PageMaker 4.x, 5.x, and 6.x files.

Drag-and-drop capabilities—Easily share elements among open PageMaker 6.5 publications and between PageMaker and other applications (note that there is no drag-and-drop between a 5.0 document and 6.5).

Adobe Illustrator import—Quickly place Adobe Illustrator files in their native format directly into PageMaker and view high-quality previews onscreen. Macromedia FreeHand files should be saved out as Illustrator files first.

Interactive tabbed palettes—Conserve onscreen space by controlling how palettes are grouped and displayed, just as you do in Adobe Photoshop and Adobe Illustrator.

Hot links—Open Photoshop and Illustrator files from within PageMaker for faster graphics editing.

New standard menus and keyboard shortcuts—Work more efficiently with the entire Adobe family of products.

Clipping paths—Use TIFF clipping paths that you've applied to images in Photoshop.

Photoshop Effects plug-in—Apply special effects 10 to 20 times faster than before.

Extensive technical support—Enjoy 90 days of complimentary technical support for new purchases and 30 days of complimentary support for upgrades (only in the U.S. and Canada).

Adobe Type Manager 4.0—See text more clearly thanks to anti-aliasing on the fly.

Leading-Edge Color Publishing

Multichannel DCS support to and from Photoshop—Separate high fidelity color images, and then edit them in Photoshop using the Channel24 plug-in by VISU Technologies (sold separately).

Support for all leading standards—Output files to any Adobe PostScript language, PCL, or QuickDraw device using any prepress format: DCS 2.0, Scitex CT, CIE Lab TIFF, and OPI.

Integrated automatic trapping and separation—Print professional-quality publications using fully integrated trapping controls. Plus, use built-in controls for printing process and spot-color separations, printing selective inks, and editing the screen angle and screen ruling for spot, process, and high-fidelity inks.

Complete Kodak Photo CD support—Quickly import and auto-sharpen photographic images.

17 color libraries—Use color libraries from companies such as Pantone Inc., Toyo, Focoltone, Trumatch, and DIC.

Color Management status display—Easily track individual colors using the color management display in the Edit Color dialog box.

Extensible color management for device-independent color—Ensure consistent and predictable color throughout your design, proofing, and printing process. PageMaker includes the ICC-compliant Kodak Digital Science Color Management System and support for Apple ColorSync 2.0. Plus, support for the ICC color management profile standard means you can share device profiles between multiple color management systems.

PostScript Level 2—Print separations faster from PostScript Level 2 imagesetters.

Extensive color production features—Easily specify spot or process colors or tints of either (even at the object level); import spot colors from EPS files to the PageMaker palette; convert image formats from RGB to CMYK TIFF for separations; and instantly remove unused colors from a publication file.

Complete high-fidelity color support—Specify, trap, and print color separations for high fidelity colors using the PANTONE® Hexachrome™ color library. Edit high-fidelity color values for maximum flexibility.

Multichannel DCS support to and from Photoshop.

Device independent color management.

Color management status display in the Edit Color dialog box.

Advanced Compatibility with Other Vendors' Products

More extensible plug-in architecture—Create more powerful custom solutions in PageMaker with access to objects, palettes, application events, plug-in private data, and communication between plug-ins.

Complete file compatibility—Share files among the Macintosh, Power Macintosh, Windows 95, and Windows NT 4.0 Workstation versions of PageMaker 6.5.

Save for Service Provider Plug-in—Consolidate and hand off everything your printer needs in a single file.

Right-mouse-button menus—Gain quick access to context-related commands in the Windows 95 and Windows NT 4.0 Workstation versions.

QuarkXPress converter—Convert QuarkXPress files to PageMaker publications.

QuickTime import filter—Enhance PageMaker documents by adding QuickTime movie frames. Or, when exporting into HTML or PDF files, include entire movies for playback.

Plug-in functionality—Simplify tasks using a wide range of plug-ins, including Sort Pages, Align Objects, and Expert Kerning.

Import and export filters—Streamline workflow with dozens of filters, including new filters for ClarisWorks 4.0 and Microsoft Works 4.0 (both for Macintosh only).

Support for OLE 2.0—Work seamlessly with other applications.

Macro capabilities—Use the PageMaker scripting language and a set of enhanced tools to write scripts that automate repetitive tasks, and then access them instantly through the Scripts palette.

Electronic Distribution

PageMaker can export publications to PDF or HTML formats. It includes a free copy of Adobe Acrobat Distiller for creating PDF files that can be distributed, viewed, and printed on most desktop computers.

Text Import

Using a Macintosh, you can import text from the following:

- Microsoft Word, versions 3.0, 4.0, 5.0, and 6.0
- Word for Windows, versions 6.0 and 7.0
- WordPerfect, versions 2.x and 3.0/3.1
- WordPerfect for Windows and DOS, versions 4.2, 5.x, and 6.x
- MacWrite II and MacWrite Pro
- Microsoft Works, versions 2.0, 3.0, and 4.0
- WriteNow, versions 2.x and 3.0
- ClarisWorks, versions 1.0, 2.0, 3.0, and 4.0
- XyWrite III

Using Windows, you can import text from the following:

- WordPerfect, versions 5.x and 6.x
- Microsoft Word for DOS, versions 3.0, 4.0, 5.0, and 6.0
- Word for Windows, versions 2.0, 6.0, and 7.0
- WordStar, versions 3.3, 4.0, 5.0, and 6.0

- Windows Write
- XyWrite III

The PageMaker Story Importer can also import text from PageMaker 5.0 and 6.0 publications, as well as cross-platform (Macintosh/Windows).

Text typed or placed in PageMaker can be exported in these formats:

- ASCII text
- DCA/RFT
- RTF
- Tagged text

If using a Macintosh, you can also export text in these formats:

- Microsoft Word 3.0
- MacWrite II
- WriteNow 2.0 and 3.0 formats
- XyWrite III

If using Windows, you can also export text in WordPerfect 5.0

Graphics Import

PageMaker can import, display, and print black-and-white, grayscale, and color images and illustrations from most drawing, illustration, charting, and image-editing applications. PageMaker has import filters for TIFF files, including RGB, CMYK, and CIE Lab TIFF images, Kodak Photo CD images, EPS graphics, GIF files, Scitex CT, and DCS 1.0 and 2.0 files. PageMaker also imports files compressed in JPEG, LZW, PackBits, and Group 3 (Huffman-type) formats and can read and write OPI comments.

Formats accepted by PageMaker for both Macintosh and Windows include: BMP; CGM; DXF; EMF; PCX; PICT (.PCT); WMF; MacPaint (.PNT); Adobe Illustrator for the Macintosh, versions 5.0, 5.5, and 6.0; Adobe Illustrator for Windows, versions 4.1; and QuickTime.

Under Windows, other formats accepted include ADI, Excel Chart 3.0 and 4.0, GEM, HPGL (.HGL, .PLT), Lotus PIC, and WPG. PageMaker for Windows also accepts files from CorelDRAW!, versions 3.0, 4.0, and 5.0; CorelDRAW! clip art (.CMX); Table Editor 2.1 files; and Tektronix Plot-10 files.

Spreadsheet/Database Import

PageMaker reads and places text and charts produced by the major spreadsheet and database programs. For exact specifications on which specific applications are supported, refer to the PageMaker documents or call Adobe for technical assistance.

By using a Macintosh, you can import files directly from Microsoft Excel 3.0, 4.0 and 5.0. In addition, you can use text and graphics filters to import files from other spreadsheet and database programs.

By using Windows, you can import files directly from Lotus 1-2-3, versions 1.0, 2.0, 3.0, 4.0, and 5.0; Microsoft Excel, versions 4.0, 5.0 and 7.0; and Lotus Symphony, versions 1.0, 2.0, and 3.0. PageMaker for Windows 95 also includes an ODBC import filter and data sources for dBASE, Microsoft FoxPro, Microsoft Access, Microsoft SQL Server, and Paradox. In addition, you can use text and graphics filters to import files from other spreadsheet and database programs.

Networks

On the Macintosh, PageMaker works with AppleTalk and EtherTalk. Using Windows, PageMaker works with Novell netware and other networks supported by Microsoft Windows.

Fonts

On the Macintosh, PageMaker is compatible with Type 1, Adobe Multiple Master, and TrueType fonts. PageMaker also supports type management programs, including Adobe Type Manager, Adobe Type Reunion, and Suitcase.

In Windows, PageMaker is compatible with Windows-supported soft fonts, including Type 1, Adobe Multiple Master, and TrueType. PageMaker also supports such type management programs as Adobe Type Manager.

Plug-ins

Save for Service Provider Plug-in.

Enhanced Grid Manager Plug-in.

Photoshop Effects Plug-in.

Word Counter Plug-in.

SYSTEM REQUIREMENTS

Macintosh/Power Macintosh—Minimum System Requirements

68030 or greater processor, 7.1 or later, 9-inch (PowerBook) or 13-inch or larger monitor (640×480 pixels), CD-ROM drive (3.5-inch disk set available for purchase). RAM: 6MB of RAM available to PageMaker (Macintosh), 9 MB of RAM available to PageMaker (Power Macintosh) Additional RAM required to run Apple System Software.

Enhanced Recommendations

PowerPC processor, 7.5.3 or later, high-resolution, 24-bit screen display, 12MB or more of RAM available to PageMaker (additional RAM required to run Apple System Software), 56MB of free hard-disk space for full installation, PostScript-language printer, 26MB of free hard-disk space for minimum installation. PageMaker supports virtual memory.

Windows 95/Windows NT 4.0 Workstation—Minimum System Requirements

Intel 486 processor, Microsoft Windows 95 or Windows NT 4.0 Workstation operating system, VGA display card, CD-ROM drive (3.5-inch disk set available for purchase). Total RAM installed: 8MB for Windows 95, 16MB for Windows NT 4.0 Workstation. Plus default virtual-memory settings and 26MB of free hard-disk space for minimum installation. PageMaker supports virtual memory.

Enhanced Recommendations

Pentium or greater processor, high-resolution (24-bit or, greater Super VGA) video display card, 24MB or more of RAM installed, 67MB of free hard-disk space for full installation, PostScript-language printer.

Note

PageMaker 6.5 is specifically designed to take advantage of Windows 95 and Windows NT 4.0 Workstation systems.

A TOUR OF THE PAGEMAKER 6.5 INTERFACE

Access to all of the command sets, dialog boxes, and features in PageMaker 6.5 can be activated from the top menu bar, as well as from keyboard equivalents and the onscreen dialog boxes after they are brought to the screen. The first step in bringing all of the command controls into view is from the top menu bar, so this section illustrates the lists of command included in each of the pull-down menu options in PageMaker 6.5. Thorough walk-through for each of the listings is included in the appropriate sections of the book that detail the creative implications involved with these listings. (Hypertext commands, for example, are detailed in sections of the book that deal with Hypertext projects, whereas menu commands that address graphics are detailed in the sections devoted to PageMaker graphics creation and manipulation.) The eight listings in the top menu bar include (left to right): File, Edit, Layout, Type, Element, Utilities, View, and Window. Illustrations of the contents of each of these menu items is given in the following sections. Every dialog box and command interface in PageMaker can be accessed and activated from one of these eight menus.

The File Menu

The PageMaker File menu is dedicated to the global control of PageMaker files and file transfers, as well as the Document Setup and Print commands (see Figure 1.1).

Figure 1.1

The PageMaker File menu.

The Edit Menu

The Edit menu lists features that address separate selections in a PageMaker project. The general commands can be compared to those found in a standard word processor (see Figure 1.2).

Figure 1.2

The Edit menu lists selections that target specific PageMaker items for alteration.

The Layout Menu

The PageMaker Layout menu addresses Page transposition and column guides (see Figure 1.3).

The Type Menu

The Type menu is concerned with every aspect of font usage for your document. Fonts are as important to the overall design of a page as is global element composition. Using the wrong font can detract from a document's overall design so that all the other work you put in to craft the right look is almost wasted. This means not only choosing the correct font, but its size and justification components as well. Text blocks in your documents should appear as a family of elements so that body text across a page or pages attain a similar look, as will headlines and subheads. As a page designer, you are already aware of how important font selection and placement is, and also how necessary it is to have access to all of the needed parameter settings in one place.

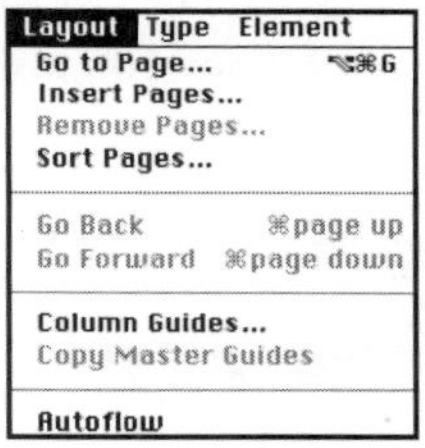

Figure 1.3

The Layout menu.

One potential confusion that you should be aware of is the difference between Style and Type Style in the Type menu listings. Type Style refers to the options that any selected word or text block can illustrate, including: Normal, Bold, Italic, Underline, Strikethru, Outline, Shadow, and Reverse. Style refers to text block style presets, such as Headline, Body text Copy, Caption, and the like. Text Styles are always preset and cannot be customized (for example, you cannot determine the degree to which Boldness is applied to a text block as far as Type Styles are concerned). Styles, on the other hand, can be customized and defined beforehand. Styles can incorporate Type Styles as part of their definition. Type Styles usually are applied more locally than are Styles.

Some page designers prefer to maintain tighter control over every possible parameter of type and font usage in their creations, whereas others are satisfied with leaving the fine tuning to the print house if need be, while concentrating upon the more global aspects of page design. PageMaker allows both possibilities, even to the point of allowing the customization of separate characters. The following figures (1.4 to 1.11) illustrate where to find the command listings accessible from the Type menu.

Figure 1.4

The PageMaker Type menu.

Leading can be added to a selected text block automatically, customized, or by selecting one of the presets in the Leading pull-down menu (see Figure 1.5).

Figure 1.5

The Leading pull-down menu.

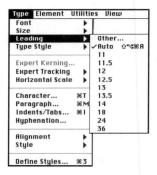

Leading settings vary the amount of space between lines of text in a text block. Tight (smaller) leading settings will make a text block appear darker because of the density of the elements, whereas looser (larger) settings will act to make the text block look more gray at first glance. The default leading is set to Automatic, enabling PageMaker to apply a general leading spacing. A good way to adjust for overhangs and widows (small parts of a text block that hang over into an additional column) is to tighten the leading a bit. That can often compress the text just enough to get it to fit in one contiguous block. Care should be taken as far as making the leading settings too small, however, because this can make the text unreadable or visually displeasing because of the lack of perceivable "air" to breathe. Experimentation is always advised before settling on a final leading amount.

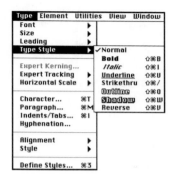

Figure 1.6

PageMaker offers eight selectable Type Styles from the Type Styles menu.

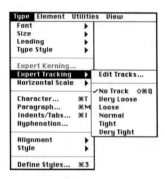

Figure 1.7

The Expert Tracking menu lists six options and has the capability to customize the settings.

Tracking is used to change the spaces between letters in a text block. Tracking can be used to readjust text so that it fits within a proscribed area, or as a design mechanism. As a design mechanism, purposely packing a text block in a smaller space than usual, or in a wider spacing than is expected, is best used on single-line heads. Radical Tracking (meaning very loose or ultra-tight) is seldom used on larger blocks of body copy, since it makes reading more difficult. This rule is sometimes broken, however, and very tight tracking is used in publications that want to achieve radical new design looks. Tracking use is often a compromise between hard and fast rules and experimental design practices.

Figure 1.8

The horizontal scale of the selected text block can be reduced or enlarged by using the Horizontal Scale pull-down menu.

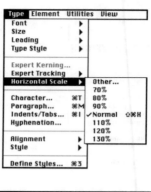

Figure 1.9

Text can be aligned by selecting one of the options in the Alignment pull-down menu.

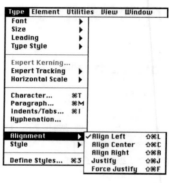

Figure 1.10

Selected text blocks can be targeted for PageMaker styles.

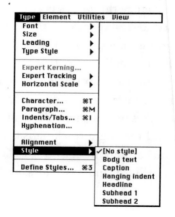

Each PageMaker publication can have its own style components for global text attributes such as body text, captions, hanging indents, heads, subheads, and your personal text block identifiers. Styles can be saved to a file and loaded for application in other documents. Styles can also be applied directly from the Styles palette. The process for customizing a Style is simple:

1. Type a line of text with the font, size, and Type Style attribute desired.

2. Highlight the text block.

3. Go to the Type, Define Styles menu item and save the highlighted text as a named selection. It will then appear in the Style menu for application to any other text block.

Figure 1.11

Customized Styles can be archived with the Define Styles option.

The Element Menu

When it's time to create and transform your graphics, the Element menu is the place to go. The most important items listed here as far as native PageMaker graphics are concerned (rectangles, ovals, polygons, and freeform polygon shapes) are the first three listings: Fill, Stroke, and Fill and Stroke. The first two, Fill and Stroke, enable you to apply basic fills and strokes to selected PageMaker graphic elements. The third item, Fill and Stroke, enables you to create and apply more complex fills and strokes to a selection, including the adjustment of transparent screens of color, overprints, and reversals. PageMaker graphics are usually used in conjunction with text blocks to set them apart from standard body copy, or transformed into frames for either text or graphics.

Frame, which is new in PageMaker 6.5, is important because whatever is attached to a frame is automatically glued inside it, making the maneuvering and placement of framed elements that much easier to move as a group. Because any closed shape can be used as a framed area, frames can be a major design element of a piece. For more specific hints and descriptions concerning Frames, see Chapter 5 "Frames," and also investigate Chapters 8 and 9 ("PageMaker's Drawing Tools" and "Graphics—Magic Tricks and Plug-Ins").

Text wrapping is accessed from this menu. More data on the use of Text wrapping can be found in Chapter 6, "Working with Text." Mask and Unmask, two other selections listed in the Element menu, are explored in Chapter 8, where the Image option is also thoroughly explored. For a view of the dialog interfaces listed under the Element menu, see Figures 1.12 through 1.23.

Figure 1.12

The Element Menu.

Figure 1.13

Pattern fills are accessed through the Fill submenu.

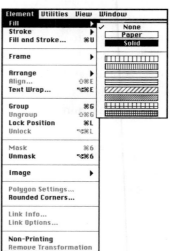

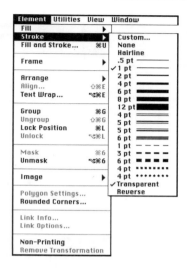

Figure 1.14

The Stroke menu applies line widths to a selected graphic's border or to a line.

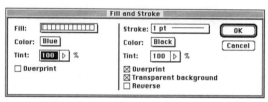

Figure 1.15

Fill and Stroke enables you to control both fills and border strokes.

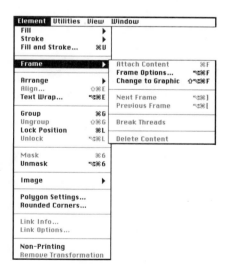

Figure 1.16

The Frame submenu.

Figure 1.17

The Frame Options dialog box is a subset of the Frame menu.

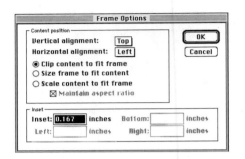

Figure 1.18

Layered PageMaker elements can be moved back and forth by using the Arrange submenu.

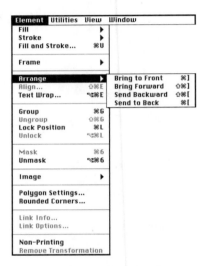

Figure 1.19

The Image submenu lists Image Control (for grayscale images), CMS Source commands, and the path to Photoshop™ Effects.

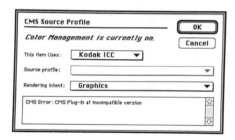

Figure 1.20

The CMS Source Profile command set.

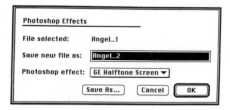

Figure 1.21

Photoshop Effects are applied in this Image submenu.

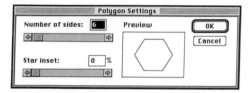

Figure 1.22

The Polygon Settings submenu brings up the customization controls for polygon graphics.

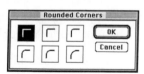

Figure 1.23

Rounded corners can be applied to rectangles and rectangular frames.

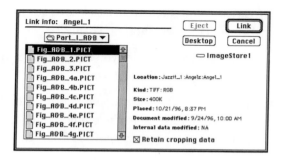

Figure 1.24

Linked data is applied with this Element selection.

Figure 1.25

*Link Options are accessed by
these commands.*

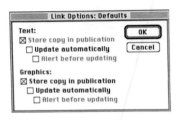

The Utilities Menu

PageMaker Utilities are located in the sixth menu listing (see Figure
1.26). The first listing here is for accessing PageMaker's resident plug-
ins (see Figure 1.27). These include:

◆ **Add Cont'd Line**—Automatically cuts the selected text block
and by one line and slips a new text block at the base of the
selected text block, pointing to the next page in the story
thread. For more information on the use of this plug-in, see
Chapter 6.

◆ **Balance Columns**—Adjusts and equalizes the length of all
columns of the same story on a page. See Chapter 6.

◆ **Build Booklet**—Sorts the pages of small booklets and brochures so
that they impose correctly when folded together and are printed.
See Chapter 14, "The World of Print Publishing".

◆ **Bullets and Numbering**—Automatically numbers or adds your
choice of bulleted dingbats to selected text blocks. See Chapter 6.

◆ **Change Case**—Applies one of five case changes to selected text:
Lower, Upper, Title, Sentence, or Toggle.

◆ **Create Color Library**—Enables you to define your own library
of colors. See Chapters 10 and 11 on color.

◆ **Drop Cap**—Allows for the creation of a drop cap, the size of
which can be set in relation to the number of lines it is to
become at the start of a paragraph. See Chapters 6 and 7.

◆ **EPS Font Scanner**—This plug-in warns you when you try to
print a publication that contains an EPS font not installed on
your system. The default is On. See Chapter 7, "Formatting
Type and Paragraphs."

◆ **Global Link Options**—Allows you to set the place where elements of your publication will be stored.

◆ **Grid Manager (replaces "Guide Manager" in version 6.0)**— You can use this dialog to set column and gutter dimensions, ruler guide parameters, and baseline data. Everything can be saved and loaded for another document. See Chapter 3, "Setting Up Master Pages."

◆ **Keyline**—Draws a keyline box around any object with your selection of Fill and Stroke. See Chapter 14.

◆ **Pub Info**—Gives you feedback concerning the fonts, styles, and other elements in your publication. This is a vital utility to use before sending your work out to a service bureau. See Chapter 15, "Prepress Service Bureaus and Printers."

◆ **Publication Converter**—Enables you to bring in previously saved documents from older versions of PageMaker.

◆ **QuickTime Media**—After placing a frame from a QuickTime movie, you can select it and then access this plug-in. You will then be able to select another frame in the sequence for placement of the page. You can also double-click a placed movie frame to bring up this dialog box.

◆ **Running Headers & Footers**—Allows you to apply header and footer data lines to a pages. See Chapter 7.

◆ **Save for Service Provider**—Double-check all the elements in your publication in this dialog before shipping the document to a service provider. See Chapter 15.

◆ **Update PPD**—Collects data about your printer or imagesetter, and updates the driver to take advantage of any enhancements made. See Chapter 14.

◆ **Word Counter**—This dialog box gives you an accurate reading of the number of characters, words, sentences, paragraphs, text blocks, and stories in your document.

Figure 1.26

The Utilities menu.

Figure 1.27

The Plug-Ins submenu gives you access to all PageMaker specific plug-ins.

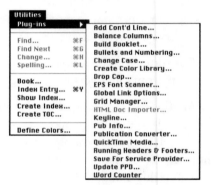

Another three groups of listings are present in the Utilities menu: story editor commands (Find, Find Next, Change, and Spelling), index/TOC commands, and define colors options. Read the following chapters for specific information that relates to the additional Utilities menu options—Chapter 6 for text, Chapter 9 for TOC and indexing, and Chapters 10 and 11 for color information. It should also be noted that the story editor commands can be scripted as of version 6.0. For more information on scripting, see Chapter 13, "Automating PageMaker." Figures 1.28 through 1.32 illustrate various dialog boxes from the Utilities menu.

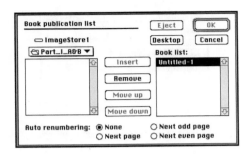

Figure 1.28

The Book publication list dialog box.

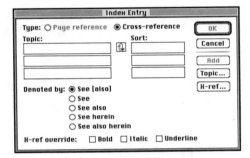

Figure 1.29

The Index Entry dialog box.

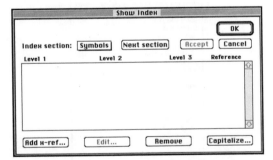

Figure 1.30

The Show Index dialog box.

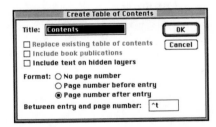

Figure 1.31

The Create Table of Contents dialog box.

Figure 1.32

The Define Colors dialog box enables you to customize PageMaker's palette.

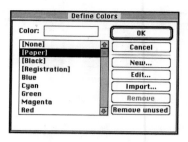

The View Menu

The View menu lists options for customizing PageMaker's display and global controls. The View menu deals with display issues that effect how the PageMaker workspace is configured, and it will differ according to each page designer's working style. For more definitive information on altering PageMaker's display screen, see Chapter 2, "Personalizing PageMaker." Also refer to Figures 1.33 and 1.34.

Figure 1.33

The View menu enables you to shape the PageMaker screen to your own individual work style.

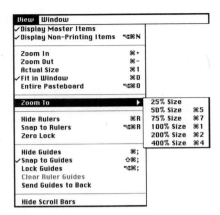

Figure 1.34

The Zoom To control in the View menu.

The Window Menu

The Window menu (see Figure 1.35) is devoted to the display of Page-Maker's workspace and enables you to toggle on or off PageMaker's Toolbox and Control palettes to enhance the way that you work most comfortably.

Figure 1.35

The Window menu lists all PageMaker's command palettes and controls.

The PageMaker toolbox contains all the command icons. The toolbox usually remains toggled on. See Figures 1.36 through 1.45 for illustrations of the dialog boxes in the Windows menu.

Figure 1.36

The PageMaker Toolbox.

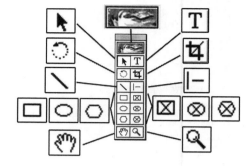

Figure 1.37

The contents of the PageMaker Control palette change according to the tool selected in the Toolbox.

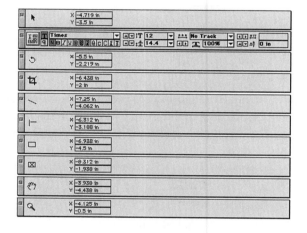

Figure 1.38

The Styles palette and pull-out menu.

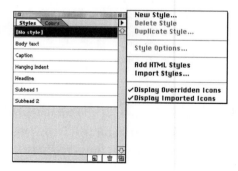

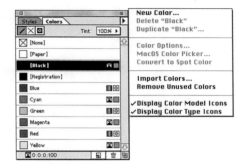

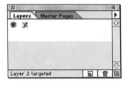

Figure 1.40

The Layers palette.

Figure 1.41

The Master Pages palette.

Figure 1.42

The Hyperlinks palette and pull-out menu.

Figure 1.43

The Scripts palette.

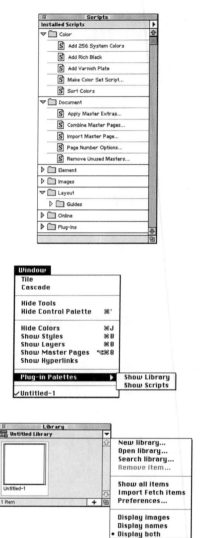

Figure 1.44

The Plug-in Palettes selection accesses the Show Scripts and Library palettes.

Figure 1.45

The Library palette and pull-out menu.

New Features Added in PageMaker 6.0

Adobe PageMaker 6.0 offers more than 50 new features and enhancements for Macintosh and Windows users.

HTML (HyperText Markup Language) Author plug-in (enabling users to export PageMaker publications into HTML format).

The Create Adobe PDF plug-in—Allows PageMaker publications to be saved in Adobe Acrobat Portable Document Format (PDF), complete with automatic HyperText links and article threads.

Color Support Enhancements

Support for the Kodak Precision Color Management System (CMS) and Kodak Photo CD, as well as advanced high-fidelity color printing technologies, such as PANTONE Hexachrome libraries.

Sophisticated automatic trapping, a new Print Fit view, and Printer Styles for enhanced printing and prepress capabilities.

Multiple master pages, object masking, grouping, locking, and alignment and distribution controls.

Compatibility with Adobe Photoshop and Adobe Illustrator software.

Win 32s dynamic linking libraries, enabling Windows users the functionality of 16-bit Windows 3.1 and Windows 95.

Pantone, Inc.'s check-standard trademark for color reproduction and color-reproduction materials.

Versatile Color Publishing—Kodak Precision Color Management System—Delivers accurate and consistent color, from scanning and screen display to proofing and final output.

Support for Multiple Color Management Systems—Enables users to mix and match supported color management systems from different vendors to create a CMS solution that is tailored to their specific needs.

Complete Photo CD Support—Enables users to auto-sharpen, crop, and color-balance Kodak Photo CD images on import, optionally save them to a local disk as CIE Lab TIFF images, and color-manage them directly in PageMaker.

High-fidelity Color Support—Expands the color gamut of process-color printing from PageMaker by allowing users to print separations for more than the standard four process color inks, including support for PANTONE Hexachrome libraries.

PANTONE Hexachrome Libraries—Allows users to select Hexachrome colors from predefined libraries for both coated and uncoated stock.

RGB to CMYK Conversion—Streamlines workflow by letting users convert and separate color TIFF images directly within PageMaker.

Object-level tints—Let users quickly assign tints of an existing color to any object.

Expanded PANTONE Color Libraries—Enables users to specify specialty inks, such as metallics, fluorescents, and pastels.

Remove Unused Colors from Color Palette—Enables users to automatically remove unused colors through the Define Colors or Print dialog boxes.

Support for CIE Lab Color TIFF images—Enables users to import, print, and separate images stored as device-independent color TIFF files.

Quick Edit of Color Names—Enables users to quickly modify color names using a keyboard shortcut (Command + click on the Macintosh, Control+click on Windows).

Choice of None in Color palette—Enables users to remove color from objects with the click of a button in the redesigned Color palette.

Page Design Enhancements

Multiple Master Pages—Offers the capability to specify and apply page designs that include repeating elements, including margins, and column guides, for up to 256 master pages in a single publication.

Group and Ungroup—Simplifies moving or resizing multiple items by combining them into a unit with a single keystroke; elements within a group can be modified without being ungrouped.

Position Lock and Unlock—Gives even more control over page designs, with the capability to prevent locked items from being moved, resized, or deleted.

Object Masking—Allows users to mask text and graphics with any PageMaker-drawn object.

Alignment and Distribution Options—Aligns or distributes page items quickly and easily.

Table Application—Provides powerful capabilities for creating sophisticated, typographically-rich tables.

Arrange Menu—Organizes such features as grouping, aligning, and locking in a format similar to that used by Adobe Photoshop and Adobe Illustrator.

Zoom To tool—Enables users to quickly zoom in on selected areas of a page.

Polygon tool—Provides customizable settings for the number of polygon sides, as well as the degree of inset for quick drawing of geometric objects, such as triangles and starbursts.

Guide Manager for Automatic User-definable Grids—Enables users to specify horizontal and vertical margins and guides to create page grids, including baseline grids; users can save and apply grid designs using libraries.

Bring Forward and Send Backward—Enables objects to be moved forward or backward one layer at a time.

Modified Stacking Order Behavior—Maintains the stacking order of multiple objects when the user selects overlapping elements. The selected element no longer pops to the top of any overlapping objects.

Open Recent Publications—Lists the last eight saved publications so that they can be opened directly from the File menu. This can be compared to the "recent files" item under the Apple menu.

Customizable Workspace—Saves the size and position of open palettes with each file, so when reopened, the publication appears as it was when closed.

Kerning Enhancements—Include improved automatic kerning and support for kerning in 0.001-em increments.

Nonprinting Objects—Enables the user to designate certain objects as nonprinting for fast proofing, working with FPO (for position only) objects, and applying production notes. Nonprinting objects can be displayed or hidden onscreen, and the Nonprinting option can be overridden from within the Print dialog box.

Double-click tools to Set Preferences—Makes it easy to specify tool-specific defaults.

Copy and paste into Find and Change dialog boxes—Streamlines the process of searching for and replacing text by eliminating the need to type into edit fields.

Expanded Options for Finding and Changing Formatting—Provides even more flexible production by allowing users to search for and replace attributes, such as type color and tint, leading method, alignment, and tracking.

Expert Printing and Prepress Control Enhancements

Integrated automatic trapping—Enables sophisticated auto-trap specifications, such as the capability to specify trap width, trapping thresholds, black attributes, and the capability to auto-overprint black text, lines, and fills. Includes built-in defaults and customized settings.

Reader's spreads—Enables users to print facing pages directly from the Print dialog box so that spreads will print as they appear onscreen.

Printer styles—Makes selecting print options foolproof by enabling users to save frequently used printer settings; enables users to bypass Print dialog boxes when using a predefined printer style.

Print Fit View—Helps ensure that pages fit within the dimensions of the selected output device's paper or film by providing onscreen display of the relationship between the page and output medium.

Expanded support for prepress standards—Means PageMaker now supports a wide range of prepress standards, including import of DCS 2.0, Scitex CT, CIE Lab TIFF, and JPEG files, as well as support for OPI 2.0.

Two-way printer communication (Macintosh)—Provides greater flexibility when printing by querying the printer directly to determine available memory and when fonts need to be downloaded, reducing dependence on accurate PPD files.

TIFF Clipping Path Support—Maintains a transparent background in imported TIFF images that have clipping paths, providing more design options.

OPI Reader and Writer—Provide better compatibility with OPI servers, including Adobe Color Central, to improve post-production workflow.

Improved EPS printing performance—Streamlines printing with more efficient printer-memory management than in previous versions; alerts user if fonts in EPS graphic are not available at print time.

Change Color Management Preferences at print time—Enables users to set CMS preferences, change output profiles, or turn off the CMS from within the Print dialog box.

TIFF Image Format Type displayed in link dialog box—See at a glance whether TIFF images are RGB, CMYK, or CIE Lab format.

Extensive Compatibility

Backward Compatibility—Saves publications in PageMaker 5.0 format for file compatibility among workgroups, though you may have to substitute fonts and make other adjustments.

New plug-ins—Provide more choices for custom publishing solutions, including Guide Manager, Align Objects, Scripts palette, and Adobe Photoshop Effects..

Create Adobe PDF plug-in—Makes it easy to create PDF files for on-line distribution. Users can quickly form HyperText links simply by placing items in a table of contents or index in PageMaker.

HTML Author plug-in—Enables users to convert text and inline graphics in PageMaker into HTML format for use on the World Wide Web.

Improved Existing plug-ins—Offer more capabilities and improved interfaces in Running Headers & Footers, Build Booklet, and others.

Features Enhancements

New Filters—Include Photo CD, EMF, TAGS, ClarisWorks (Macintosh), CorelDRAW! 4 and 5 (Windows), CMX (Windows), and ODBC (Windows).

Adobe Photoshop Filters Support—Extends creative options with the capability to apply special effects from Adobe Photoshop plug-ins, such as Kai's Power Tools and Gallery Effects, to images directly in PageMaker. The applied effects suffer some speed drawbacks due to the way PageMaker handles bitmaps, but it can be a time-saver when memory constraints do not allow multiple applications to be opened at the same time. The larger the imported bitmaps, the longer time it will take to apply Photoshop filters from within PageMaker.

Adobe Photoshop Hot Link—Allows fast image editing by launching Adobe Photoshop when a user double-clicks an Adobe Photoshop image in a PageMaker publication.

Adobe Illustrator Hot Link (Macintosh)—Allows fast illustration editing by launching Adobe Illustrator when a user double-clicks an Adobe Illustrator EPS file in a PageMaker publication.

Scripts palette—Makes scripts instantly accessible for automating repetitive publishing tasks.

Custom Scripts and plug-ins for the Story Editor—Automate word processing tasks, such as find/change and spelling verification by using custom scripts and plug-ins to access story editor capabilities.

OLE 2.0 Client Support—Offers linking and embedding of OLE 2.0 objects in PageMaker.

Drag and Drop from OLE 2.0 Applications—Enables users to drag objects from OLE 2.0 server applications, such as Microsoft Word and Excel, directly into PageMaker 6.0.

QuarkXPress File Converter (Macintosh)—Automatically converts QuarkXPress (versions 3.1, 3.2, and 3.3) documents to PageMaker 6.0 publications.

Extra Value CD-ROM Content

Adobe Acrobat Distiller Personal Edition and Reader—For creating PDF files of PageMaker publications for electronic distribution and reading PDF files.

Adobe Photoshop LE (Windows)—The limited edition version of the world's leading image-editing software.

PageMaker 6.0 Multimedia Overview—Highlights of new and enhanced features, as well as expert tips for using PageMaker.

Kodak Photo CD Images and Information—Royalty-free image samples and detailed information on using Photo CD images effectively.

Straight Talk Papers, TechNotes, and PageMaker Tips & Tricks—Detailed technical information useful for professionals and novices.

PageMaker Gallery—An interactive tour of artwork created in PageMaker by professional designers.

Adobe Type On Call—220 Type 1 typefaces that can be unlocked at no charge when users register their Type On Call CD.

Adobe Type Manager—For improving the appearance of Adobe PostScript typefaces at any size.

New Features Added in PageMaker 6.01

ColorSync 2.0 Color Management Standard.

If you have the Apple ColorSync 2.0 Color Management System (CMS) installed, you can use ColorSync as the Color Management System in PageMaker 6.01. When you use the ColorSync 2.0 CMS, you cannot separate bitmapped images into PANTONE Hexachrome colors. (Apple ColorSync 2.0 does not support high-fidelity color.)

Improved RGB to CMYK conversion.

RGB to CMYK conversions now closely match those of Adobe Illustrator 6.0, so that both PageMaker and Illustrator output the same colors when printing and creating Adobe PDF files.

Undocumented Plug-ins

When installed, plug-ins are found in the PageMaker Plug-ins menu in the Utilities menu.

Global Link Options: This plug-in enables you to quickly apply Link Options settings to all linked text and graphics in the current publication. For example, you can specify whether to store each linked graphic outside the publication, or specify to update placed graphic and text files automatically.

Publication Converter: This plug-in enables you to quickly find all PageMaker 4.0 and 5.0 publications on your hard drive (or a mounted network volume) and convert them into PageMaker 6.0 publications. The converted publications are stored in the same folder as the original publication. Optionally, you can specify a PageMaker script that the plug-in should run on each publication after it is converted. You can also find text files with a specified extension; for example, you can locate and translate publications created in PageMaker 6.0 for Windows.

Change Case: This plug-in changes the way the selected text is capitalized. You can use this plug-in, for example, to do the following:

◆ Change all letters to either lowercase or uppercase.

◆ Capitalize only the first letter of every sentence and change all other letters to lowercase.

◆ Capitalize the first letter of every word.

◆ Change (toggle) the case of every letter.

Word Counter: This plug-in calculates the number of characters, words, sentences, and paragraphs in the publication or currently highlighted text. For an accurate count:

◆ The text must have a standard font applied. (Symbol fonts reassign characters that the plug-in assumes designate the end of a word or sentence, such as the comma, colon, and period, and thus might skew the count.)

◆ The text cannot be threaded between a regular page and a master page.

◆ The text must be selected (highlighted) with the text tool to count that text only. If you select text blocks with the pointer tool or have no text selected, the resulting count is for the entire publication.

Pub Info: Identical to the version that shipped with PageMaker 5.0, this plug-in enables you to view or save a report on the current publication. The report includes status information on the linked files, paragraph styles, and fonts necessary to print the publication.

Scripts Palette

Scripts palette comes with several useful scripts installed automatically. (The exact number of scripts depends on the kind of installation you chose when installing PageMaker. More sample scripts are in the Technical Library folder on the Adobe PageMaker 6.0 Deluxe CD-ROM.) Choose Scripts palette from the Windows menu, and click the Scripts folder to view the following folders and scripts:

Color

- ◆ Add 256 System colors—Loads the Color palette with pre-defined colors from the Operating System.

- ◆ Add rich black—Adds the color Rich black to the Color palette. The color definition is 100% process Black; 50% Cyan; and 50% Yellow.

- ◆ Add Varnish plate—Adds a new color to the Color palette for creating varnishes.

- ◆ Remove unused—Removes each color from the publication's Color palette that is not currently applied to text or graphics in the active publication. (An imported color EPS file must be deleted before its unused colors can be removed with this script.)

Layout

The next four scripts add nonprinting ruler guides to indicate the page borders.

- ◆ Edge guides, letter tall
- ◆ Edge guides, letter wide
- ◆ Edge guides, tabloid tall
- ◆ Edge guides, tabloid wide

Plug-ins

Each script in this folder opens the corresponding plug-in installed with PageMaker.

- Add Cont'd Line
- Balance Columns
- Build Booklet
- Bullets & Numbering
- Create Color Library
- Drop Cap
- Guide Manager
- HTML Author
- Keyline
- Open Template
- Running Headers & Footers
- Update PPD

Printing

The following scripts that apply bleeds are set up for letter-tall page size. If you want to use a different page size, you must edit the scripts.

- Add .5 inches (12mm) bleed off bottom extends the selected graphic vertically so that it creates a half-inch bleed off the page. (Not available for Canadian English.)
- Add .5 inches (12mm) bleed off left edge extends the selected graphic to the left so that it creates a half-inch bleed off the left side of the page. (Not available for Canadian English.)
- Add .5 inches (12mm) bleed off right edge extends the selected graphic to the right so that it creates a half-inch bleed off the right side of the page. (Not available for Canadian English.)

◆ Add .5 inches bleed off top extends the selected graphic verti-cally so that it creates a half-inch bleed off the top edge of the page. (Not available for International or Canadian English.)

◆ Export for prepress adds a printer style (a collection of Print dialog box settings) to the PageMaker Printer Style menu. You can use this style as is or edit it to suit your needs. Its settings are defined to create a .SEP file for use in a post-processing application such as Adobe TrapWise. The PPD Color General is specified for the publication.

Text

◆ fi and fl ligature replacement. Finds each instance of the two-letter combinations "fi" and "fl" in the active publication and replaces it with the single ligature character for finer typography.

Styles

Remove default styles. Deletes the default paragraph styles defined for new publications.

Trapping

◆ **95% gray as black**—Lowers the Black Limit value in the Trapping Options dialog box to 95% so that a lighter black (with 95% Process Black in its color definition) is still trapped as a solid black. This enables you to compensate for dot-gain when using low-grade paper stock.

◆ **Overprint all black objects**—Specifies that black text, fills, and lines overprint throughout the publication. Choose Trapping Options from the Utilities menu to manually change the settings back again.

◆ **Overprint black lines and fills**—Specifies that black lines and fills overprint throughout the publication. Choose Trapping Options from the Utilities menu to manually change the settings back again.

◆ **Overprint black text**—Specifies that black text overprints. Choose Trapping Options from the Utilities menu to manually change the settings back again.

◆ **Turn off trapping**—Disables trapping (but not overprinting) for the active publication.

◆ **Turn on trapping**—Enables trapping for the active publication.

Monitor Calibration

For color management purposes, PageMaker 6.01 includes a stand-alone utility that can create a device profile for your monitor: the Kodak Monitor Installer. This utility is installed in the Utilities folder within the RSRC folder.

New PANTONE Hexacrome, Kodak Precision Transforms

Two new Hexachrome Precision Transforms (PTs) offer improved high-fidelity separations compared to those supplied with PageMaker 6.0. The new PTs appear in the Separations Printer pop-up menu in the CMS Setup dialog box in PageMaker. Which PT you select depends upon the following press operating conditions:

◆ Normal SID (Solid Ink Density) produces the clearest, sharpest images and closely matches the SID and dot-gain characteristics of the inks as printed in the PANTONE Hexachrome Color Selector.

◆ High SID has a slightly wider tolerance for heavy inking (especially black) on press. It also produces excellent separations with minimal loss of clarity and sharpness in images.

Note

If you are working on a high-fidelity color project that was started in PageMaker 6.0, your output using the new PTs will be different from the 6.0 output.

Microsoft OLE Components (Power Macintosh systems only)

The Microsoft OLE files installed with PageMaker 6.01 are not required to start PageMaker on a Power Macintosh. However, the OLE files are necessary if you do the following:

◆ Paste or insert using OLE operations in PageMaker, such as the Insert Object command in the Edit menu or the Paste Link option in the Paste Special dialog box.

◆ Import Microsoft Word 6.0 files in their native format.

◆ Use the CheckList utility.

◆ Print publications that contain Adobe Table files that were pasted as OLE objects.

SUMMARY

Starting with version 6.0 and now version 6.5, PageMaker has seen a lot of changes. New features have been added, while others have been enhanced or modified. This chapter gave a basic overview of the new features and menus in PageMaker 6.5. Chapter 2 "Personalizing PageMaker," tells you what you need to do to effectively run PageMaker 6.5 on your computer.

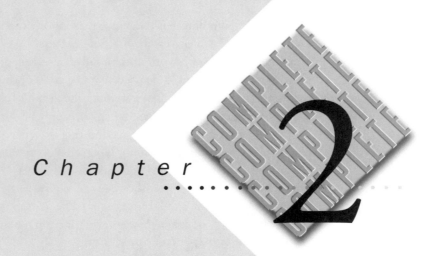

Chapter **2**

PERSONALIZING PAGEMAKER

Although it is possible to run PageMaker 6.5 with as little as 9MB of RAM and a 68030 processor (Mac), or 8MB-16MB and on a 486 (Windows), it is vital to remember that using PageMaker on a non-accelerated system with just the minimum RAM requirements will not allow you to accomplish much. You will be able to design simple flyers and other similar material, and to utilize a minimum of clip art, but that's about it. These days, if your interest is in setting up a studio that offers PageMaker output on a professional basis, you absolutely have to be thinking Power Macintosh or a Pentium system. You should consider a minimum of 48MB of RAM for a Mac or 32MB for a Windows system. The true minimum requirement when graphics is to be a major component of your work is more like 64MB-72MB of RAM and an accelerated system. Why is this so?

Graphics manipulation is the major reason for expanding the memory allocated to PageMaker. Even though PageMaker enables you to manipulate a proxy of your graphics files onscreen, thereby conserving the memory that would be used if you were working with the actual graphics files, the very act of manipulating graphics chews up available memory. This is more the case when you apply Photoshop effects from within PageMaker. One way around this is to use Photoshop (or an equivalent application) for applying effects to bit-mapped images. Applying bitmap effects in PageMaker is really a last resort, and should be used only when Photoshop, or an equivalent image processing application, is not available, because effects applied in PageMaker (even with loads of available memory) function much slower than they do in a real bitmap image application.

Obviously you will have financial concerns when it comes to purchasing an accelerated system, or when you know it's time to add RAM or upgraded acceleration components to your present system. You should also be aware, however, that the DTP industry, and those enterprises that want to become a long-lasting and viable part of it, exist for one major focus: deadlines. Meeting deadlines has everything to do with producing quality work in a minimum amount of time. Faster systems (such as Power Macs and Pentiums) are a necessary requirement in this process. PageMaker is like a finely tuned carburetor. Why would you want to place it in an engine that can't incorporate its potential?

Back to financial considerations. The cost of accelerated systems, and system RAM, continues to drop. If you are developing a business plan for a DTP service or design studio that plans to utilize PageMaker as a major component, make sure it contains a budget for a system (and enough RAM) to allow you to hit the ground running. If you are debating whether to upgrade or replace your existing system, don't hesitate to make it a reality. Faster processing and enough RAM to handle more complex tasks take the frustration out of DTP enterprises, and PageMaker will be capable of functioning as the maximized tool it was intended to be.

Having a good amount of available RAM and a fast system is inversely proportional to a designer's frustration index. Ideas come to a good designer while she is in the middle of the working process, and they must be acted upon immediately before they evaporate. That means you've just got to see the results of a visual alternative as quickly as possible. The last thing a designer needs is slow feedback. Speedy feedback is vital, because that can lead to even more immediate explorations. All of this adds to your education as a designer, a client's appreciation, and your ability to master the intricacies of PageMaker itself.

PAGEMAKER PREFERENCES

PageMaker Preferences are accessed from the File menu (see Figure 2.1). There are four Preference categories: General, Online, Layout Adjustment, and Trapping.

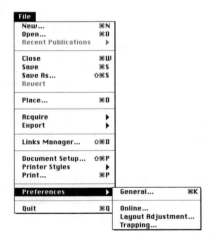

Figure 2.1

The PageMaker Preferences submenu.

The General Preferences dialog box (see Figure 2.2) enables you to set the ruler measurement parameters, "problem" areas in the layout, the apparent resolution of the graphics display, Control palette options, Save options, and Guides options. In addition, you can access three other sub-menus: More, Map fonts, and CMS Setup.

Figure 2.2

*The General Preferences
dialog box.*

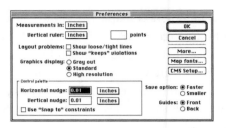

Getting an Intuitive Feel for PageMaker Preferences

The General Preferences dialog box enables you to customize PageMaker parameters according to your way of working as a designer and also according to specific equipment you may have in your studio (or that your service bureau tells you it has). PageMaker remembers the General Preferences settings for the next session, and they remain in place until you alter them.

The first General Preferences screen to greet you enables you to select the standards of measurement for the Horizontal ruler (called Measurements in) and the Vertical ruler. Your Horizontal ruler can have measured increments in Inches, Decimal Inches, Millimeters, Picas, or Ciceros. The Vertical ruler allows any of these choices and one more: Custom. If you select Custom, you can enter a specific number of Points in a neighboring input area. You should consider entering the number 72, as 72 points are equivalent to an inch; however, you might have reason to select another point increment here.

Below this are two checkboxes titled Layout problems. The first is called Show loose/tight lines. If checked, PageMaker will alert you when kerning for a selected block seems too loose or tight so that you can make amends. Checking the second enables PageMaker to notice and report when the reformatting of a paragraph alters the local formatting already set (boldface, italics, and so on). The purpose of being alerted to these potential design problems is to allow you to have more definitive warning when things go amiss. If you have a color monitor, any layout problems discovered are highlighted in yellow.

Below the Layout problems area is a three option listing for your Graphics display: Gray out, Standard, and High resolution. When you import a graphic for placement in a PageMaker document, it will take its cue from the item selected from these three options. Gray out makes it appear as a simple gray box. Standard enables you to discern what the graphic looks like, though aliasing (jagginess) is apparent. High resolution causes the graphic to appear without jagginess at its set resolution. Use the Gray out option when you are adjusting the global look of a document and want to move things around without being hampered by the time it takes a graphic to display. On the other end, if you want as close an approximation as possible of the graphic, perhaps for overlaying a text block in a specific relationship to the graphic, use High resolution. Standard is the default, enabling you to get a good idea of the graphic without the redraw delay (and the memory requirements) that High resolution demands.

At the bottom left of the General Preferences dialog box is an area named Control palette. In it are settings for Horizontal and Vertical nudging, and a checkbox for applying "Snap to" constraints. The settings tell PageMaker that when the Snap to option is checked, any dimension larger than those set horizontally or vertically will initiate PageMaker to pull the selected item within that dimension, as if magnetized by an unseen force. The Default settings are both 0.01 inches, which is usually close enough for most projects when Snap to is turned on.

At the bottom right of the General Preferences dialog box are the choices for Save option (Faster or Smaller) and Guides (Front or Back). Selecting the "Smaller" Save option is generally the best choice, because it maximizes storage space. Guides are best placed in Back, because they can be accidentally grabbed and moved if placed in Front.

More

When you click the More button, a dialog box appears that contains four separate areas: Text, Story Editor, Graphics, and PostScript printing (see Figure 2.3).

Figure 2.3

*The More Preferences
dialog box.*

The Text area has an input size for setting *Greeking*. Greeking, as many of you know, is a way of faking text so that you can see where the text is and how it fills a space, without the unnecessary complication of reading it. Greeking is a useful page design tool. Whatever point size is set here determines the parameter below which text will be Greeked. Greeking comes from the term "it's Greek to me," a way of saying that something is unreadable. There's also a checkbox for automatically turning pages when text is autoflowed onto a page, and another that tells PageMaker to use typographer's quote marks when quotes are used in a text block. Also listed are two options, only one of which can be activated. These enable you to select whether you want to see TrueType fonts displayed with the correct spacing or the correct character shape. Only one of the two is possible due to the display nature of TrueType.

Next are controls for PageMaker's Story Editor, the built in word processor. You can select the Story editor's font and type size, as well as the ability to toggle on or off the style names display and whether typographer's paragraph markings are to be made visible.

The third item grouping enables you to choose whether to set the graphics according to size or resolution, with a resolution of 100% being the default (size can be set through a standard kilobyte option). PageMaker can also alert you when you are ready to store graphics files over any set amount, just so you are aware that your storage space must have that amount (in kilobytes) in reserve.

The last item here is devoted to PostScript printing, and how much memory should be freed for graphics. The settings are Normal or Maximum, with Normal as the default when the situation is tight.

Map Fonts

One of the most dreaded remarks a service bureau can make after you have sent them your stringently designed and deadlined PageMaker file, is "sorry, but we don't have your fonts in our library." For this reason, it is common to call the service bureau beforehand to find out what their font library contains and to send along a disk file of your uncommon fonts along with the job they are used in. But what about the PostScript printer at your side? It has a limited number of fonts available, and you might have used some TrueType fonts in your project. Wouldn't it be nice to preset a font mapping parameter that tells the PostScript printer to use substitute PostScript fonts under certain conditions. This dialog box allows you to configure the exact conditions under which any selected fonts will be substituted for (see Figure 2.4). You can use either the ATM (Adobe Type Manager) or the PANOSE font matching system. The Substitution tolerance is set by a slider that goes from Exact to Loose. Exact substitution will take no prisoners, whereas a looser setting will understand that there is room to compromise. A selected default font is used when the system can't find your definitive choices. You can set all of your font substitution parameters (for every font contained in a document) by using the Font Spellings (how the same font's name is spelled on Mac versus Windows systems) and Exceptions (setting specific font exceptions that take into consideration any missing fonts). (See Figure 2.5.) Using this dialog box is especially useful when you are moving a project between platforms. A help system is included that walks you through the settings in the dialog box (see Figure 2.6).

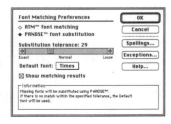

Figure 2.4

The Map Fonts submenu enables you to set the Font matching Preferences (ATM or PANOSE).

The Spellings button in the Map Fonts dialog box opens the Alternate Spellings dialog box, enabling you to edit and set alternate font name spellings so that the appropriate font substitutions can be addressed when necessary (see Figure 2.8).

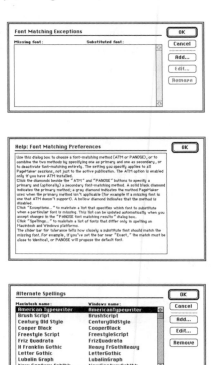

Figure 2.5

The Font Matching Exceptions dialog box allows you to customize font substitutions further.

Figure 2.6

The Help button brings up a text file that tells you exactly what is at stake when font substitutions take place, and how to customize the settings.

Figure 2.7

The Alternate Spellings dialog box.

Color Management System

You can set the parameters for the Color Managment System (CMS) you are using in PageMaker in this secondary dialog box in the General Preferences window (see Figure 2.8). This system lists ColorSync and Kodak as the two options, but your system might have more or different CMS possibilities. Color management can be toggled on or off. When on, all listed components will try to adhere to the CMS settings, and will attempt to display and utilize comparable color settings. It is often a problem in the DTP world, for instance, that the colors as seen on a monitor are very different from those seen on the resulting printed page (reflective color on paper is of a different nature from the colors produced by light emission on a computer monitor). Though it is difficult at best to achieve a 100-percent match between the monitor and a printed page, Color Management Systems can come very close. You can set your monitor to emulate one of the CMS choices (in this case, ColorSync or Kodak), or select none. You can also select whether the CMS is to pay attention to a Composite printer (most medium end printers) or a printer that will handle your color separated pages (higher end printers). Monitor and Printer choices are chosen from a manufacturer's listing. You may also choose whether you want your Composite printer to pay attention to CMS rules, and whether to embed the CMS profiles in your document.

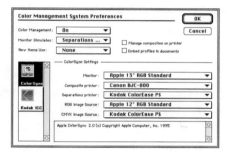

Figure 2.8

The CMS Setup button enables you to select the appropriate Color Management System Preferences, monitor simulation, and other associated parameters.

PAGEMAKER DEFAULTS

Defaults are preset specifications. PageMaker ships with two types of defaults: Publication Defaults and Application Defaults. You can change these defaults to suit your particular needs, either for a specific job or for all your PageMaker work.

Publication Defaults

Publication defaults only apply to the current publication you are working on. You set publication defaults by changing menu and dialog box settings while the publication is active and no object is selected. PageMaker saves the new settings with the publication so that you don't have to reset them the next time you open that specific publication.

Note

You can double-click text and drawing tools in the toolbox to set text and drawing-tool defaults for the publication.

Application Defaults

Application defaults are remembered even after you quit and restart PageMaker. You set application defaults by changing menu and dialog box settings while no publication is open. The settings you specify will apply to every new PageMaker publication you create from scratch.

Other Preferences Dialog Boxes

In addition to the General Preferences settings, PageMaker offers three other Preferences dialog boxes: Online, Layout Adjustment, and Trapping.

The Online Preferences dialog box (see Figure 2.9) enables you to set specific parameters for making a PageMaker document Web active. Among these is the activating of embedded link sources when the Hand tool is selected (making a link change color on a Web page as the hand moves over it), and centering the upper-left of the anchor selection. You might also use the browser to locate your desired download folder and to find the location of the Web browser (Netscape, Internet Explorer, and so on) you will use. For other more definitive data on using PageMaker's Web related tools and processes, see the sections of the book that deal with Web issues directly.

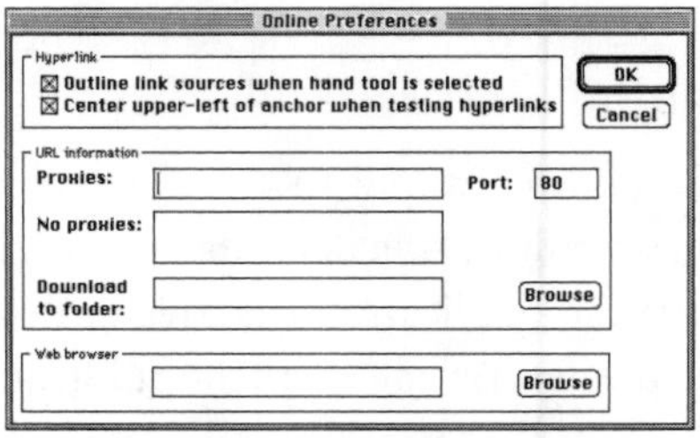

Figure 2.9

Hyperlinks are set using the Online Preferences dialog box.

Layout Adjustment Preferences (see Figure 2.10) enables you to set various parameters for adjusting page elements and ruler guides. Under Adjust page elements, you can choose to activate the resizing of groups and imported graphics. You can also select to ignore object and layer locks (giving you more freedom to manipulate graphics), and to ignore ruler guide alignments (for a less mechanical look when that is desired). Adjust ruler guides may be set as locked or movable. Column and margin alignment can be kept or freed, so that columns and associated margins can be moved as a group or freely.

Figure 2.10

The Layout Adjustment Preferences include the Snap-to parameter setting, Adjust page elements options, and adjust ruler guides options.

The Trapping Preferences dialog box (see Figure 2.11) is used to set specific conditions for Trapping. The issue of trapping is far too complex to allude to lightly, so the reader is advised to turn to the section on trapping issues in Chapter 11 before altering any of the settings in this dialog box.

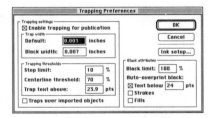

Figure 2.11

All of PageMaker's Trapping settings are set in the Trapping Preferences dialog box.

Clicking the Ink setup... button in the Trapping Preferences dialog box opens the Ink Neutral Density Values dialog box. This is used to set ink options (see Figure 2.12).

Figure 2.12

The Ink Neutral Density Values dialog box.

SUMMARY

Now that you have configured PageMaker to facilitate optimum workflow, let us now turn our attention to setting up master pages.

Chapter **3**

SETTING UP MASTER PAGES

Before you begin placing words and pictures on your PageMaker pages, you need to set up those pages. Page set up includes determining the dimensions of the page, deciding how many columns of type you'll use on each page, and placing elements such as page numbers, headers or footers. To make the job easier, PageMaker 6.5 enables you to create *master pages*, which contain all the repeated elements for the page.

Some things never change; others do change, even though they shouldn't. That's the reasoning behind using master pages. Instead of having to do repetitive tasks, such as placing page numbers on each page, you can do it once and know that every page's number will appear where it is supposed to. More important, from the designer's point of view, using a layout grid and master pages gives your publication a professional, unified look and helps assure that your pages stick to the design you've planned for them. Traditionally, paste-up artists either used preprinted grid sheets or drew the lines they needed in light blue pencil. (Light blue doesn't reproduce when photographed to make a printing plate.) PageMaker makes it even easier to set up a grid. Unlike the preprinted sheets, PageMaker can remove these grid lines when you no longer need them, and, of course, you can hide them for an unobstructed view of the page.

DESIGNING A MASTER PAGE GRID

Setting up a layout grid means thinking ahead about the underlying structure of your pages. What elements will be included on all—or most—of them? Will the text be set in multiple columns or straight across the page? What about illustrations? If your project is a newsletter with several different stories, pictures, or graphic elements on a page, how will you position them to lead the reader through the page without confusion? If you have a grid structure in mind when you set up your pages, you can hang the text and graphics on it and know that your layout will follow the underlying discipline. The layout grid helps you to achieve a fluid and coherent presentation of your message. It also gives you the freedom to break away from the imposed structure occasionally, stepping out of bounds for dramatic effect.

How to Design a Grid

Page design is something art directors and designers spend months, if not years, learning; however, there is no easy way to teach it in a few simple steps. If you have no idea what your publication should look like, start by studying similar ones. Notice how the stories in a newsletter are placed on the page. See whether two equal-sized columns of type look balanced—or boring. Look at margins to see how much space is enough. Think about the purpose of your finished pages. Newsletters often try to mimic newspapers, with multiple columns, and small pictures. Book designers frequently use a single column of type because it's easier to read. If you are doing a corporate report, it needs to be eye-catching, and still readable. Before you start placing grid lines, you need to think out your project very carefully.

Ask yourself these questions:

1. How will this document be printed? Single or double pages? How many? If it's a newsletter, will it use 11×17-inch paper folded in half, or some other size?

2. How much text and how many pictures do I have to work with? Do I want to use multiple columns? If so, how many?

3. Are there headers or footers (an identifying line of type at the top or bottom of the page)? What about the page numbers?

4. What other elements appear on the page? What about headlines? Will some pages be very different from the rest?

After you define the elements and spaces that you will be working with, you can think about the framework that will indicate their positions. The grid is a set of lines to guide you as you place type and graphics. Make a "dummy" of your project to see where you need to position the grid lines (see Figure 3.1).

Figure 3.1

A typical grid and the resulting pages.

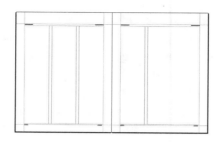

In PageMaker, you impose your layout grid on each of your pages by setting up master pages that include the grid lines. Every item you place on a master page is repeated on every (same side) page in your publication.

PageMaker In the Real World

Dummies for PageMaker

Despite many years of experience with the computer and PageMaker, when I start a project I almost always reach for pencil and paper first. I sketch out a rough "dummy" of the proposed layout, starting with the banner, scribbled text blocks and very rough indications of photos and charts I will use. The dummy not only helps me decide how to lay out the pages, but reminds me to leave space for the table of contents, letters, and monthly columns. It also lets me see whether I have too much "stuff" and need to add more pages, or need to go looking for more material to fill the holes. I like to make up several of these dummies with different layouts, and choose the most appealing design.

You don't *have* to use master pages, but doing so is the most efficient and consistent way to achieve your layout goals. PageMaker 6.0 introduced multiple master pages, enabling you to use more than one kind of page layout within the publication. If you are designing a book, for instance, you could use a more complex master page layout for the first pages of the chapters, and a simple one to flow the rest of the text into.

Your master pages will contain several different kinds of items. First, you set up the margins and create a grid of guidelines to help you position text and graphics. Then, you add any other repeated elements, such as the page numbers, column rules, a header or footer, and anything else that remains the same on every page.

GUIDING THE GRID

Guides are the basic building blocks that make up the structure of your layout grid, as you saw from the layout grid and its resulting newsletter pages shown in Figure 3.1. The guides are the dotted lines arranged in (oddly enough) a grid. The lines don't print, but you can see them onscreen.

You can set three kinds of guides in PageMaker: margin guides, column guides, and ruler guides. These guides are only for onscreen display. They do not print out.

- **Margin guides** delineate the margins you set for master pages. Margin guides are both horizontal and vertical, and they are pink.

- **Column guides** are vertical lines. They have special powers to guide text when you flow it onto a page with the Place command. Column guides are blue.

- **Ruler guides** can be either horizontal or vertical. They get their name from the way you create them—by dragging them out from the rulers. Ruler guides are turquoise.

Setting Margin Guides

You can apply margin guides in either of two different places. For document master pages, set the margins in the Document Setup dialog box when you first create a document. After that initial step, adjust margins using the same dialog box, which can be accessed from the File menu.

To set margins for a new document:

1. Choose New from the File menu or type (Command-N) [Control-N] to open the Document Setup dialog box.

2. Enter the appropriate page dimensions and margin widths in the boxes. After you close the dialog box, you'll see your page(s), with the margins indicated.

If PageMaker's default margin settings (³/₄-inch outside, top, and bottom, and 1-inch inside) are too wide, you can reduce them by entering new numbers in the boxes. Select the number to be changed and type in a new value. Figure 3.2 shows the Document Setup box with the appropriate numbers inserted.

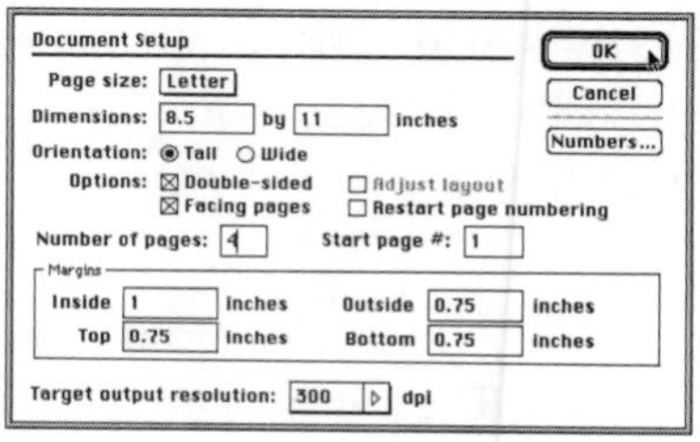

Figure 3.2

To change the margin widths, enter new numbers.

While you're here, open the Numbers box (see Figure 3.3) to make sure that PageMaker is using the appropriate style of page numbers. Your choices include Arabic or Roman numerals, or alphabeticals (AA, and so on.)

Figure 3.3

The Page Numbering dialog box determines the type of numbers, but not the starting page number.

For all other master pages, set and adjust margins in a similar Setup dialog box reached through the Master Pages palette (see Figure 3.4).

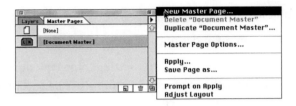

Figure 3.4

To add new master pages, use the pop-up menu on the Master Pages palette.

Margin guides are the most basic kind of guide. If you only have one column on your page, the margin guides are, in effect, the column guides. The margin guides run completely around the page, following the settings for the top, bottom, inside (left), and outside (right) margins. Many people believe that vertical margin guides are actually blue, not pink. That's because it actually looks that way when you first setup a page in PageMaker. The program naturally puts a column guide on the left and right margins of the page. And the column guides, which are blue (or dotted on a grayscale monitor), coincide with and obscure the location of the left and right margin guides. If you drag the column guides into a new position, as in Figure 3.5, leaving the margin guides in place, you see the difference. Notice that as you drag, the pointer tool becomes a double arrow.

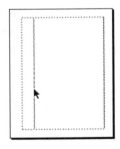

Figure 3.5

The left column guide was moved to show the margin guide beneath.

Setting Column Guides

Column guides possess power; like benevolent control freaks, they tell text where to go. If you create a page with three columns and autoflow text into it, the text automatically jumps from the foot of one column to the head of the next, and so on. To create these magic column guides, use the Column Guides command on the Layout menu (see Figure 3.6).

To set columns

1. Open Column Guides in the Layout menu.

2. If you're changing the default setting, type new numbers into the box. Enter the number of columns per page. Enter the amount of space between columns.

3. Use the checkbox to define left and right pages differently.

4. Click OK when finished, and you'll see your guidelines in place.

You can define the left and right pages differently, if you choose. The default setting is a single column, or the full page.

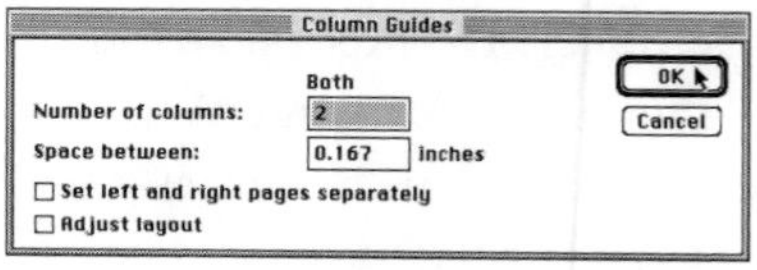

Figure 3.6

The Column Guides dialog box is located in the Layout menu.

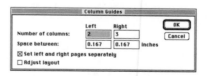

If you have opened facing pages, the Column guides box has a checkbox at the bottom enabling you to choose to set left and right pages separately. Click it and two sets of boxes appear, one for each page, as shown in Figure 3.7. You can leave a single column on the left, and change the right page to three columns. You also can change the default spacing between columns to give a little more room. When you're through making changes, click OK. After the dialog box closes, the changes are made on the page. If your publication is open to a single page, you can only set the columns for that page. The Set...separately checkbox is absent.

Figure 3.7

Setting left and right pages separately in the Column Guides dialog box.

Figure 3.7 also shows the result when you implement the Column Guides command with those settings. Notice the one-pica (.167-inch) space between columns. If you grab those spaced column guides and drag them to one side or the other, they move together as a pair, maintaining the spacing. You can adjust column widths visually by dragging the guides, as well as by entering new numbers in the dialog box. Moving the guides, however, has no effect on text you have already placed on a page, only on text you place after the guides are repositioned.

Setting Ruler Guides

In addition to establishing your page geometry (jargon for "the shape of the page") using margin and column guides, you can set up a third form of guides on an as needed basis. These guides are called ruler guides; you establish them, as shown in Figure 3.8, by clicking the ruler and dragging the guideline down or across into the page area. As you drag, the Pointer tool becomes a double arrow. (You aren't allowed to have ruler guides on the Pasteboard.)

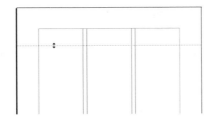

Figure   3.8

Placing a ruler guide.

Put horizontal or vertical ruler guides wherever you like and use them to help line up and position objects on the page. Ruler guides are particularly useful for precise positioning when used in conjunction with the Snap to Guides command, which is discussed later in this chapter.

Manually Managing Guides

The Grid Manager plug-in can automate the whole business of placing and repositioning guides, but in order to understand how to use it, you need to understand what it's doing. First you need to review some basic rules for working with guides.

Moving Guides

Adjust guides to a new position by clicking the guide and then dragging it. When you click the guide, you see a double arrow, and then you can slide the guide to its new position, as you did in Figure 3.5. You can adjust column and ruler guides, but you can't use a click and drag to move the (pink) margin guides.

Align to Grid

When you are working with more than one column of text on your page, it's important visually to have the lines of text in one column line up with the lines of text in the other(s). This is done automatically in PageMaker with two very powerful tools: *Baseline Grid* and *Align to Grid*. Use them to draw an invisible grid of text baselines, and to add space automatically between paragraphs to align the baselines of columns in multicolumn text, so that paragraph rules also align vertically. Baseline Grid can be found in the Grid Manager Plug-In, in the Utilities menu. Align Next Paragraph to Grid is reached through the Paragraph Specifications/Paragraph Rules/Paragraph Rule Options dialog box. For rules above a paragraph, PageMaker measures from the baseline of the first line in the paragraph to the top of the rule, adding extra space before the paragraph as necessary. For rules below the paragraph, PageMaker measures from the baseline of the last line in the paragraph to the bottom of the rule below, adding space as necessary.

Tip

It is easy to accidentally snag a guide and slide it to the wrong spot on the page instead of moving the object you intended to adjust. Immediately after making an accidental guide move, use the Edit menu to Undo the mistake. Also, if you haven't created any local guides for that particular page, you can use the Copy Master Guides command on the Layout menu to reset the guides from your assigned master page. On the other hand, if you have created local guides, copying the master guides will remove them and replace them with the master guides.

Locking Guides

Set the toggle command Lock Guides in the View menu, or press (Option-Command-;)[Alt-Control-;]. When the check mark has been toggled on for the Lock Guides command, you won't be able to adjust their positions. They are locked. This guide-locking move is the ultimate protection against accidentally disturbing your guide setup.

Hiding or Displaying Guides

If you want an uncluttered view of your publication design but don't want to delete your guides, use the Show Guides command in the View menu. If Show Guides is turned on, a check mark appears next to the command; the check mark is gone if you turn off the guides. Toggling off the Guides command makes all three kinds of guides disappear from view throughout your publication. The keyboard shortcut for toggling guides display on and off, (Command-;)[Control-;] is handy for forcing a screen redraw as well.

Note

Whenever you change something on the screen, PageMaker redraws the screen so you can see your changes; however, you don't have to sit and wait for it to finish. To interrupt the redraw, just go right on working. It will catch up. If, for any reason, it doesn't, or if you want to force the screen to redraw, use the Toggle Guides command. You might need to do this to temporarily see a graphic at a higher resolution. (If you press the [Control] key before a graphic redraws, it will do so at its best resolution.)

Deleting Ruler Guides

You can remove ruler guides individually by clicking them and then dragging them up into their ruler. Or, you can delete all your ruler guides at once on your current single-sided page or double-sided, facing pages by using the handy menu command, Clear Ruler Guides, in the View menu. If you haven't placed any ruler guides, the command is grayed out.

Imposing Master Page Guides

To delete the guides you set for the current page or pages and replace them with the guides from the assigned master page, select the Copy Master Guides command from the Layout menu. When you do this, the "local" guides for that page are replaced by whatever guides (margin, column, and ruler type) you assigned to your master page. This is really handy after a complex session of fine-tuning a page, in which you used a lot of ruler guides to help position items. It instantly resets your standard grid of guides.

Prioritizing the Guides Display

You can have the guides run in front of or in back of the elements on your page. PageMaker comes set up to have the guides in front. That's great for visibility and maybe that's the way you want the guides most of the time, but on a crowded page it's easy to grab a guide by mistake and move it. If you set the guides to the back you are a little less likely to accidentally disturb them. You can use the Set Guides to Back command in the View menu to get them out of the way, without actually locking them. When the guides are sent to the back, the menu item changes to Bring Guides to Front, so you can toggle them back and forth as needed.

GRID MANAGER PLUG-IN

PageMaker 6.0 introduced the guide manager plug-in, but PageMaker 6.5 has improved it and made it much more powerful. It's now called the Grid Manager and is located in the Utilities menu.

Use the Grid Manager to set up evenly spaced sets of ruler guide grids, custom ruler guides, and column guides. Instead of dragging out guides from the ruler, type your settings in one dialog box. The magical box that does all your work is shown in Figure 3.9. As you can see, there are lots of options and lots of choices to be made.

Figure 3.9

The Grid Manager plug-in dialog box.

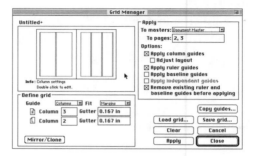

Creating a Grid

Creating a grid with the Grid Manager is similar to creating one manually in the layout window. The only difference is that you can use the Grid Manager dialog box to enter the numbers of guides and dimensions of columns, gutters, and so on, taking care of all of these at once in one single dialog box. You also can use the Grid Manager to save your grids for future use. Keeping a library of layout grids for projects such as monthly newsletters or pages of business cards can save you a great deal of time.

To create a grid "from scratch," follow these steps:

1. Open the Grid Manager from the plug-ins listed in the Utilities menu. In the Define Grid area, choose Columns and enter the numbers of columns per page. Enter a different gutter width, too, if you want. (The gutter is the space between columns.) Choose whether to fit the columns to the margins, or within the dimensions of the full page. Grid Manager subtracts the gutter width from the space available, and sets up as many equal columns as you've asked for. You can see the effect in the Preview area.

2. Next, place rulers. Choose Rulers from the pop-up menu in the Define Grid area, as shown in Figure 3.10, and enter the number of rulers to insert. Keep in mind that the vertical and horizontal rows and columns are ruler guide settings. They might look like column settings, especially if you set up a gutter, but they are simply ruler guides.

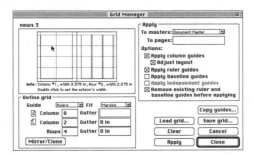

Figure   3.10

Using the Grid Manager to place rulers.

3. The Preview area shows your grid as you've defined it. To move a ruler, select it and double-click. Enter a new position in the resulting dialog box, as shown in Figure 3.11. Similarly, to move a column, choose Columns from the pop-up menu, and double-click the column to adjust it. Enter a new width in the dialog box.

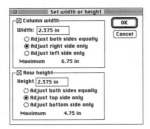

Figure   3.11

Moving rulers.

4. To apply your grid definition to the active publication, use the Apply area. You can apply the definition to master pages or to a specific page or range of pages in your publication. Enter the page numbers in the box. The options listed enable you to further define how guides are to be applied to particular pages of your publication. You can choose to add all of the guides

71

you've designed, or just the ruler guides or column guides. (You also can apply baseline guides and independent guides, which are discussed later in this chapter.) Apply the grid decisions you have made by clicking the Apply button, or the Close button, if you've finished working on the grid. Apply will make the changes without closing the dialog box. The Cancel button closes the Grid Manager without applying your grid.

5. After you have finished designing your grid, you can save it by clicking the Save Grid button. Enter a name for the grid, specify a location in which to store it, and click OK.

Selecting and Applying Grids

The Grid Manager is "sticky." If you are reopening a document you've worked on previously, the Grid Manager remembers and opens the appropriate grid. You can also recycle saved grids for new pages. To open a grid that you have used previously, open the Grid Manager and click the Load grid… button.

Tip

It is much easier to locate your grids if you keep them in one place, such as in a folder within the PageMaker folder.

Mirroring Your Grid

Grid Manager handles the intricacies of adjusting a grid for left- and right- facing pages with the Mirror and clone setting. You can select any of these options:

 ◆ Clone left to right

 ◆ Clone right to left

 ◆ Clone left to right with mirroring

 ◆ Clone right to left with mirroring

Mirroring flips the page as it copies. If you clone left to right with mirroring, and you have placed a page number at the outer (left) corner of the page, the mirrored page will have the number on the outer (right) corner. Cloning copies a page from left to right or right to left without mirroring it. The Mirror and clone dialog box opens when you click the Mirror and clone button (see Figure 3.12). As you can see, it helps you visualize the effects of cloning or mirroring.

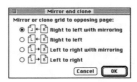

Figure   3.12

Cloning copies the page grid as it is. Mirroring flips it.

Determining a Grid Reference Point

Grid Manager's calculations of size and gutter width must be based on some reference point. You can base your guide and column settings on the edges of the page or the margin guides. Choose Margin or Page in the Grid Manager's Define Grid section. Figure 3.13 shows how this reference point concept works, with two views of the Preview and Define grid sections of Grid Manager. On the left, the column guides are set to fit within the page. On the right, they're set to fit within the margins.

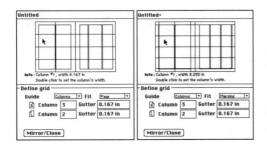

Figure   3.13

Notice the difference in column widths.

Copying and Deleting Guides

The Copy Guides command might better be called import guides. The whole concept of the Grid Manager is to enable you to replicate guides.

Use the Copy Guides command when you want to translate your layout grid to other pages. Copy, or import, the guides into Grid Manager, and then you can use the Apply command to send those guide settings out to as many pages—even master pages—as you like.

This import or copying process is accomplished by clicking the Copy guides button, which opens the dialog box you see in Figure 3.14. It copies the column, vertical, and horizontal guides from the current pages. You can even choose whether to bring in the guides from the left or the right page.

Figure 3.14

Choose whether to copy the guides from both pages or just one.

Setting Custom Guides

The Grid Manager settings produce evenly spaced grids. If you need a ruler guide or column guide that doesn't match the evenly spaced rows and columns—an independent guide—it's easiest to set it on the working page.

To put the guide in the same place on other pages, open the Grid Manager, make sure the Apply independent guides checkbox is checked, and click the Copy guides button. You then can apply the independent guide to additional pages or to your master in the usual manner, by choosing the master pages or page range on which to apply it.

Creating Baseline Grids

This specialized part of the Define Grid section of the Grid Manager has been created to help you set up a fine grid of rows—horizontal guides that match the baselines of a text block. Of course, you aren't limited to that purpose. It's suitable for any situation where you need a fine grid of horizontal guides.

The baseline setting has a Fill function not possessed by any of the other grid settings in Grid Manager. Baseline enables you to fill an area with fine horizontal grid lines. It will fill your chosen reference area—page, margin, or selected object—with evenly spaced rows of guides. You can adjust the distance between the guides by typing in an amount in the size box. When you select baseline from the pop-up list in the Define Grids section of the dialog box, the box will change to display a window where you can enter the spacing for the baselines. Figure 3.15 shows the Grid Manager with baseline grid selected. A baseline was placed at 1 pica. This will draw lines 1 pica apart all the way down the page. (Remember—there are 6 picas to a vertical inch.) To draw lines an inch apart, you would have to enter 6p in the box.

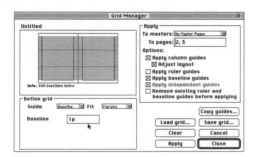

Figure 3.15

Adding a baseline grid.

Forms of Pages, Pages of Forms

Most people probably use PageMaker for newsletters, annual reports, book design, and other interesting projects. I often use the program to create the forms for my business. Invoices, labels, purchase orders, and business forms of all kinds don't make for very exciting work, but they're the "bread-and-butter" jobs for many graphic artists. If you're looking for a way to get started as a freelance desktop publisher, think about offering your services to local businesses as a custom designer of business forms. Accountants who divide their time among several small businesses use programs like Peachtree Accounting or M.Y.O.B. If you familiarize yourself with these, you'll see that the forms they print out could stand some improvement. You'll also get a feel for the information that must be included, and the general layout accountants prefer. Customizing forms to work with the software can help you pay the rent, and gives you a foot in the door when the business owner needs a catalog or other graphic design work.

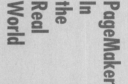

SETTING SNAP CONSTRAINTS AND MEASURING A LAYOUT GRID

Guides and rulers aren't just there to help you see where your text and graphics should go. They can actually help you place items precisely. When you turn on the Snap to Guides and Snap to Rulers settings in the View menu, you turn these items into magnets. (See Figure 3.16.) The guides and rulers grab your objects as you move them around the page and pull them into place. You can always tell when these options are on because an object jerks and jumps around as you move it, trying to lock itself into place.

Figure 3.16

How to make it "snappy."

With Snap to Guides, when an object comes within three pixels of one of the guides (all three kinds), the magnet takes hold. Guides snap in one dimension, depending on whether they are vertical or horizontal. An intersection of two guides works together to snap in both dimensions.

If Snap to Rulers is turned on, the tick marks on the rulers set up invisible criss-crossing lines on the page. This invisible grid of lines (not to be confused with the layout grid you create) sets up hundreds of magnet intersections that grab the corners of objects (or in the case of Align to Grid, the baselines of text). For ruler snap moves, you get two-dimensional snaps to this invisible myriad of intersections.

Measuring a Layout Grid

A grid would be meaningless unless you could measure your moves. For this purpose, you have a zero point and horizontal and vertical rulers.

Moving and Locking the Zero Point

A ruler measurement must start from a zero data point. In PageMaker, the zero point usually rests in the upper-left corner of a page (the default setting when you open a new document). If you are working with facing pages, the zero point rests by default on the top edge of the two pages, where they meet, at the upper-left corner of the right page in the spread. You can move this zero point anywhere you like, including the Pasteboard. Simply click the zero point marker and then drag it (two crossed lines) in the upper-left corner of the window. If you want to revert to the standard zero point position at the upper-left corner of odd-numbered pages, double-click the zero point marker. In Figure 3.17, the zero point was moved to the intersection of the upper-left corner margins.

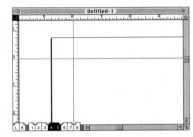

Figure 3.17

The zero point marker is black because it's "active."

Keep in mind that the Control palette measures everything from the zero point. Also, if you are using Snap to Ruler to help align page elements, the zero point determines the location and intersections of the grid. To lock the zero point, use the Zero Lock command in the View menu.

Setting Up Rulers

You can eliminate page clutter by turning off your rulers with the Rulers command in the View menu. You can also use (Command-R) [Control-R] as a shortcut. When the rulers are turned off, although you can't see them, they are still in effect. That means the Snap to Ruler command remains operative even when the rulers aren't visible.

To set the measurement system for your rulers (inches, picas, millimeters, and so on), use the Preferences command. When you set the measurement system, tick marks appear on the rulers. These marks are the visible manifestation of the invisible grid PageMaker creates when you set the Snap To Rulers constraint, using that submenu in the Guides and Rulers command, under the Layout menu.

UNDERSTANDING MASTER PAGES

For years PageMaker users have begged, cajoled, demanded, and otherwise importuned Aldus and then Adobe to include a master page feature in the program. Finally, you have not only master pages but multiple master pages and document masters. If you have only one set of master pages, those are, by default, the document masters. PageMaker now enables you to create and apply as many different master pages as you want to use within a single publication. There's no limit. If you have more than one kind of master page, obviously you're dealing with multiple masters. But, regardless of how many master pages you have, the fundamental nature of a master page has not changed one bit.

With master pages, PageMaker has provided a mechanism to set the layout grid and other common page elements just once for many pages. Whatever you put on a master page shows up on all the other pages that have been assigned that master page (unless you command PageMaker to do otherwise by turning off the Display Master Items command).

The discussion in this section emphasizes the use of master pages to carry grids of ruler guides, column settings, and margins, but also spends time discussing headers, footers, page numbers, graphic elements, and so on.

The Document Master

One master page dominates your entire publication. Unless you choose otherwise, all new pages are formatted with this one master page, the Document Master. If you add more pages to your publication using the Document Setup command, the new pages automatically are assigned the Document Master page. If you use the Insert Pages command from the Layout menu, however, you are given the opportunity to choose the master pages to be applied to the new pages. The Insert Pages dialog box includes a pop-up menu that lists all of the master page formats you've created. Choosing one of them applies it to the page(s) you are adding. You can also choose "none" to have your new pages come up with only the default (Document Master) format.

Applying Master Pages

The multiple master page feature means that you can have a whole list of page designs ready to accommodate all the various kinds of pages in your publication—ready to be applied to your pages with the click of a mouse in the Master Pages palette (see Figure 3.18). To open the Master Pages palette, select it from the Window menu.

You access the pull-out menu shown in Figure 3.18 by clicking the arrowhead in the upper-right corner of the palette.

Figure 3.18

Think of the Master Pages palette as a command center for assigning master pages.

If you want to apply the master page layout to one page or spread, move to the page(s) and click the master page of your choice in the Master Pages palette.

Tip

If you want to apply two different master pages on a single two-page spread, press the Option key and click the icons next to the master page listing in the Master Pages palette. The side of the icon you click, left or right, designates which page of the spread should get that master page. In Figure 3.19, you can see from the icons in the Master Pages palette that the left and right pages have different masters assigned. The Table of Contents master page was applied to the right-hand page by pressing the Option key and clicking the right-hand side of the icon next to the Table of Contents master page listing in the palette.

Figure 3.19

Assigning different master pages.

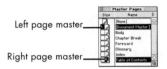

Left page master

Right page master

To quickly spread a master page across many pages, use the Apply command in the Master Pages palette pull-out menu, which enables you to build a list of pages to receive a master page assignment. Figure 3.20 shows the Apply Master dialog box. As you can see from this particular view, you also can choose here to apply different master pages to left and right pages. You can list as many pages as you like in the Page Range box, and it works just like the similar function in the Print dialog box. Compose a list using commas and hyphens. For example:

2,4-6,11,20-

would apply the master to page 2, pages 4 through 6, page 11, and page 20 and all remaining pages in the document.

Figure 3.20

This is much faster than assigning a grid to one page at a time.

You might want to turn on the Prompt On Apply setting in the palette menu as a safety measure, so that PageMaker will confirm your decision to apply a new master before making it final.

The Adjust layout option, also included in this dialog box, tells PageMaker to make items such as text or graphics that you have already placed on the page automatically move to follow the new master page format. If you apply a master page format with three columns for text to a page that currently has two columns of text, for example, the text will reflow automatically to fill the three columns. It can even scale graphics and adjust type sizes to make the contents fit the page.

Setting Up a New Master

To create a new master page, select the New option from the pull-out menu in the Master Pages palette. The New Master Page dialog box, shown in Figure 3.21, helps you perform basic setup operations. It combines several of the functions you find in the Document Setup and Column Guides dialog boxes, including page margins and the number and size of columns.

Each time you set up a master page, you need to specify its margins and number of columns. You also need to specify whether the master applies to single pages or to double page spreads. If, for example, the master is for the first pages of chapters in a book, you'd specify single page. The rest of the chapter would use a double page master because the text will be set on facing pages. Click the appropriate radio button for single or double pages and enter the margin dimensions and number of columns in the boxes provided. When you click Create, the page(s) will be created and added to the list on the Master Page palette.

Figure 3.21

Use the radio button to determine whether the master is a single or double page.

Navigating Between Master Pages

Your master pages are represented by the special page icons you see in the lower-left corner of the PageMaker window, just to the left of the icons for the numbered pages (see Figure 3.22). Click and hold on the master page icons to get a list of all the master pages in your publication. Navigate to any of them by making a selection from this list.

Figure 3.22

Click and then hold the document master icons to open the master page list.

Editing a Master

You have a couple of approaches to choose from when editing one of your master pages. You can, of course, navigate to the master page and do your work right on the page, just like the old master page setup in previous versions of PageMaker. This approach enables you to change anything on the page, from column guides to page numbering and graphic elements. Or, you can use Options in the Master Pages palette. When you use the Master Page Options command, except for the title, you get the same dialog box as the one shown in Figure 3.21. (You can also open this dialog box by double-clicking the name of the Master Page to edit.) To change the margins or number of columns on the page, just change the numbers in the boxes. Master Page Options gives you access only to grid elements. It does not allow you to edit objects that have been placed on the master page. The Master Pages Options dialog box is the only place you can change the name of a master page.

The effects of editing a master page are instantaneous. Any items displayed on any of your pages based on an edited master page show the changes immediately. Unlike most word processors, however, keep in mind that in PageMaker adjustments to margins and columns only affect newly placed text and objects—not items that have already been put on pages.

Basing a Master Page on Existing Pages

To make a new master page but base it on an existing master page, select the Duplicate menu item from the Master Pages palette's pop-up menu, and then do your work on the duplicate. This is the easiest method when you need to work a quick variation on a master page, as when you need to tune a text page for a chart layout, or add an advertising hole to a magazine page.

You can also duplicate an existing regular page in the same manner by choosing the Save Page As command. This is a great option when you've doodled a new layout into shape and want to capture the look for application to other pages.

Making a Master of None

To remove master page elements at your current page location, you can use the Layout menu commands for displaying master items or copying master guides.

Alternatively, you can use the [None] listing in the master page. It has various effects, depending on how you combine it with various keyboard shortcuts:

◆ Click-[None] removes objects, leaving column and ruler guides.

◆ Shift-click-[None] deletes everything including objects, column guides, and ruler guides.

◆ (Option) [Alt]-Shift-Click-[None] keeps ruler guides but deletes everything else.

◆ (Command)[Control]-Shift-click-[None] retains column guides but removes everything else.

◆ To apply any of the preceding moves to only one page of a spread, press the (Option)[Alt] key and click the icon next to [None] instead of on the [None] item itself. The side you click—left or right—determines the side that is affected by your move.

Putting Master Page Grids to Work

Everything discussed so far about guides and layout grids can—and should—be applied to your master pages. Put your layout grid on a master page whether you set your grid using the plug-in Grid Manager, or by using the old manual methods of the Column Guides command and hand-pulled ruler guides.

Your layout grid should not be a barrier to your design sense either. In the layout grid and sample page shown in Figure 3.23, the graphics spill across column guide boundaries, but the column guides on the grid are still used to line up the edges. The layout grid still lends the necessary structure by providing a starting point and a set of reference points for the reader's eye.

Figure 3.23

The structure remains, but you can be creative within it.

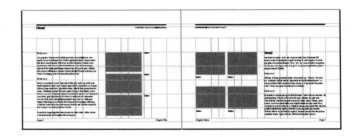

Usually, the more grid cubbyholes you design into your layout grid (with moderation), the better off you are. You have structure, backed by a lot of flexibility. Take the mail-order catalog grid shown in Figure 3.24. The designer uses a wide variety of graphics on the page, but averts the danger of a scattered, cluttered, hard-to-read look by setting four rather narrow columns across the master page.

Figure 3.24

Remember, the grid is there to help you, not imprison you.

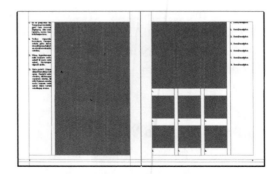

Adding Standard Master Page Elements

After you have arranged your columns, place standard elements onto your master pages. Footers, headers, page numbering, and a top-of-page rule are examples of the kind of elements you might want to design on your master page layout grid. Figures 3.25 and 3.26 show the page elements of a typical book and newsletter, labeled with proper terminology.

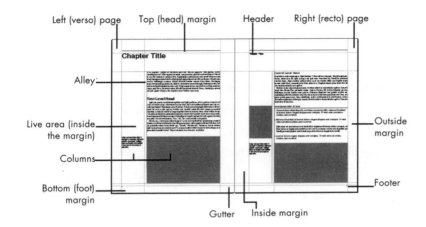

Figure 3.25

The page elements of a book.

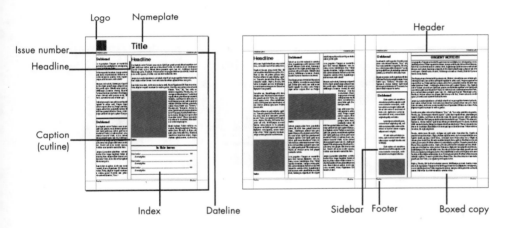

Figure 3.26

The page elements of a newsletter.

Drawing Page Rules

In Figure 3.25, you can see how the top-of-page rules on the master page translate onto a regular page, mixed with copy. These 8-point rules with the book title and major part headers automatically appear at the top of every page—a big work saver and a major aid to consistency.

Draw the rules where you want them on the appropriate master page. Use the Line tool on the Tool palette. The lines you place on the master page automatically appear on every page. You also can place column rules in the column guide alleys on your master page. Now that you have multiple master pages you can make adjustments for all sorts of layout situations that arise in various sections of a publication—one master page with rules and headers for two-column interior pages, another master page with an entirely different set of rules but a single column for the table of contents pages, and so forth.

Setting Automatic Page Numbers

Master page headers and footers in PageMaker are simply stories (text blocks).

1. Drag out a text block with the Text tool on the master page.

2. With the insertion point blinking, type the key combination (Command-Option-P)[Control-Option-P] to get the page-number symbol you see in Figure 3.27. (Because this one's from a double-sided publication, it shows up as RM—for "right master page.")

You can put this page number on any PageMaker page, but a master page is where you usually use it the most, perhaps preceded by the word *Page* or the same prefix (section number or chapter number) you entered in Numbers dialog box when you were in Page Setup.

Figure 3.27

When the pages are done, the number place holder will turn into the correct page number.

FITTING COPY

One of the reasons you spend so much time designing and fine-tuning your layout grid and master pages is that doing so makes pouring in the text a very easy job. The tools PageMaker gives you for working with text enable you to make your pages look better and communicate better. Text handling is discussed in greater detail in Chapters 6 and 7, but meanwhile, here are some things to think about when you're setting up the pages.

The idea is to link the layout grid concept with your PageMaker text tools. Choosing the right fonts and type sizes is easier if you understand the basis for column and page layout.

Establish Horizontal Copy-Fitting Controls

These checklist items help determine how much copy fits on each line of text in a column, and, therefore, how much text fits in a given column-inch measure.

◆ Coordinate type and column width. Select type size and font with an eye for fitting all the text into your standard column. The type shouldn't be so big that it justifies or rags into ugly open spaces because you've chosen a narrow column width. You might need to experiment some to get the best results. Decide whether body copy will be justified or ragged.

◆ Balance spacing and hyphenation with column width. After you've chosen the type and column width, experiment with the letter and word spacing and hyphenation controls until you're satisfied with the "color" of your type. It should be even, with no rivers of space running through the columns caused by justification spacing and with no ladders of hyphens down the right edge of the column.

Note

Justified type lines up with both margins. It's so called because the spaces are adjusted to make the line extend all the way to the end. Ragged type, as its name suggests, doesn't line up with the margin. It has a "ragged" appearance, but since the spacing isn't forced, many typographers claim that it's easier to read.

Work Out the Automatic Vertical Copy Fit Parameters

After you've resolved the line-width issues, you can establish vertical spacing settings—the ones locked into your body-copy styles.

◆ Design a leading grid. This is less complicated than it sounds. It simply means choosing a character size for the body text in the publication and an appropriate amount of leading space between the lines, thus establishing the basic vertical spacing color of your text. Vertically-measured type and page design elements such as paragraph spacing, graphics, and margins, should be based on multiples of the leading size. If, for instance your body text is in 10 point type, the leading will be 12 points. Subheads might have 18 point leading, with 6 points of space before the paragraph to total 24 points, or twice the leading. These elements would easily snap to a 12 point leading grid. Adjust the Align To Grid settings to eliminate holes and gaps in the vertical flow of your text.

◆ Control widows and orphans. Decide how sensitive you want to be about widows and orphans, and, thus, how paragraphs will break to the adjacent column or page. Will you tolerate a single line at the bottom or the top of a column? Set the controls for your body-copy style in the Paragraph Specifications dialog box.

Tune Each Page Manually

After PageMaker fits the copy into your columns, it's time to put the rest of your tools to work to individually tune each page.

◆ **Apply Balance Columns Plug-in.** Use the Balance Columns Plug-in from the Utilities menu to tune column alignment across the top and bottom of the page. Select the columns to balance and then select Balance Columns from the list of Plug-ins.

◆ **Slide windowshades.** If you aren't happy with the Balance Column Addition results, try tweaking the column length by dragging the windowshade handle down or up to see how the paragraphs are breaking with your previously designed automatic settings. On a case-by-case basis, you might want to turn off some of these controls or adjust them slightly.

◆ **Tweak graphics.** It's often possible to adjust a column length by cropping or slightly resizing a graphic in the column. Be careful not to throw your graphics out of whack when resizing them.

◆ **Edit copy.** If it's permitted, light copy editing can help you fit copy (in the most literal sense) into your columns.

TEMPLATES

A template is a document containing all of the master pages for a publication. It can be as simple as a ruled grid for positioning labels, or as complicated as the entire set up for a newsletter or magazine, with several dozen different kinds of master pages, and repeated text blocks and graphics already in place. Using a template saves you lots of time, as you don't have to re-create the grids and styles you have already developed. It also helps you maintain a consistent "look" to your publications.

You can use two kinds of templates: those included with PageMaker and original templates you create. PageMaker ships with a library of useful templates for different kinds of publications. You can also save any document you create in PageMaker as a template, simply by clicking the Template button in the Save As dialog box.

Opening a PageMaker Template

Adobe saves disk space by shipping PageMaker templates as scripts instead of sending them out as standard template files. Scripts are small programs written in the PageMaker scripting language. The scripts describe what the templates look like down to the finest detail, but take up less space than the actual publication files that they generate. To open one of these scripted templates, double-click it in the Scripts palette, as shown in Figure 3.28. Some of these templates offer you choices and options for such things as page size or language.

Figure 3.28

The Scripts palette shows which template scripts are available.

Making a New Template

When you set up a document just the way you like it, you don't need to repeat that process again. Just create a template to recycle your creative labors. Use the **Save As** command from the File menu and click the Template radio button to save a publication as a template.(You can also use this method to save the results of a template-editing session.) Many designers find it helpful to strip out the "old" text and graphics from a document before saving it as a template. Keep such things as the banner and masthead of a newsletter, but delete the text. Your file will be smaller and you won't have to clean it out when you open the template to reuse it.

Using a Previously Saved Template

You open a previously saved template the same way you open any other PageMaker publication. The difference is that you'll see an untitled document with the master page elements in place. You can double-click on the template or access it through the **File/Open** command. If you want to edit a Template, click on the **Open Original** button.

STARTING A NEW PUBLICATION

You can start a new publication from scratch, or you can open a template. The New command, in the File menu, begins a new publication, with nothing in it except PageMaker's default settings for margins and type. After you select New, you'll first see the Document Setup dialog box. Use it to adjust the page size and orientation, margins, and other document parameters. When you close the box, you'll see your blank page(s), ready to fill.

Using the Document Setup and Numbers Dialog Boxes

The Document Setup dialog box enables you to define the specifics of your publication (see Figure 3.29). When you begin a new document, or when you need to make changes in an existing document or template, this is the place to start.

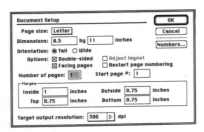

Figure 3.29

Here is a view of the Document Setup dialog box.

Page Size and Orientation

To set page size, choose between an automatic menu of standard sizes or manually enter your dimensions. Use the Page drop-down list to choose one of the standard page sizes (for example, letter or legal) on the list.

For nonstandard page size:

1. Enter page measurements in the fields you see in the Dimensions portion of the dialog box.

2. The reference in the Page size drop-down list automatically shifts from one of the standards (such as Letter) to Custom.

3. For page orientation, instead of portrait or landscape, PageMaker gives you much more descriptive terms. Tall orientation is obviously tall (portrait), whereas Wide is used for horizontal-format pages (landscape).

Number of Pages and First Page Number Options

Use Document Setup's Start Page # and Number of pages boxes to tell PageMaker how many pages your publication is to have and what number to use for the first page.

Many users choose *not* to set the number of pages, particularly for big publications. If you use Autoflow to place the text from your word processor, PageMaker automatically adds pages as needed when it pushes the text into your columns. The Document Setup dialog box changes, based on the measurement system you choose in Preferences. Page sizes will be expressed in picas, if that's your preference, rather than in inches.

Page Numbers

The Numbers button takes you to the page Numbers dialog box. Click the page-number style you need (Arabic is the most common). If you are using the Book command from the File menu to assemble a multiple-file publication, you can combine the use of more than one numbering system in different sections of your document by setting this option differently for each file. You might want to use lower Roman for the front and back matter, for example, and Arabic for the body of the book. You also can create chapter-level numbering by making an entry in the TOC and Index Prefix text box and clicking Restart Numbering in the Options section of the main Document Setup dialog box.

Printing on Both Sides of the Page

In the Options section of the Document Setup dialog box, click Double-sided if you want to print on both sides of each page of your publication. Clicking on Facing pages shows you the spread—the way the two pages look together in a double-sided publication.

Quick Add or Delete Pages

As a rule, you use the Insert Pages command on the Layout menu to add pages to your publication. If you need to add a bunch of pages to the end of a publication, however, open the Document Setup dialog box and increase the number in the Number of pages box. You will have added the pages (added only to the end of the document). You can also cut pages from a document quickly by putting a smaller number of pages in the Number of pages box. It's important to remember, however, that this method of adding and deleting pages works only on the pages at the end of the document. You must use Insert Pages to perform such surgery in the middle of the publication.

Margins and Gutters

Margins are the distance from an edge of the paper to the live layout area of the page. Just enter the measurements in the Top, Bottom, Left, and Right boxes. If you decide to display facing pages, you have Inside and Outside margins instead of Left and Right margins. Inside and outside margins provide a gutter to allow for binding. Allow 6 picas (1 inch), for example, on the inside and 3 picas ($^1/_2$ inch) on the outside.

Starting From a Template

Starting from a template, if you have one available, is simpler, although you might need to customize the template to the specifics of your new publication. It can be one of the templates that came with PageMaker or one you developed from a previous page layout job. PageMaker's templates can be found as scripts in the Script Library, which is a Plug-In palette in the Windows menu.

Note

When you work with an existing template, it opens fully formed. That's one of the major advantages, in fact, of templates, not having to go through the steps of setting up a publication from scratch. Whether you design your layout from a template or from a fresh start, after you establish the basic parameters in Document Setup, you need to name the document and save it. You'll probably find it helpful to start a new folder for your publication, too, and to store elements such as text and graphics files in the publication folder.

Setting Your Measurement System and Other Working Preferences

Everyone has his or her own working style, including such issues as whether you like to do layout by working in inches or picas, or how you like ruler guides to behave on the page. It is essential for efficiency that you spend some time setting up your working preferences before you start a new publication. You begin by setting your working preferences in the General Preferences dialog box in the File menu. Choose the measurement system you prefer, and use the buttons and checkboxes shown to determine how PageMaker displays graphics, warns you of violations, displays guides, and so on. Setting defaults when no publication is open makes them *program level* defaults. Your settings will be used whenever you open a new document. Setting defaults with a publication open applied them to only that publication. Thus, they're called *publication level* defaults.

Changing Document Setup (Beware!)

After you open a publication, organize it, and place some objects on the pages, some unwanted things can sneak up on you if you change the document.

If you must change any of the Document Setup dialog box settings, make a backup copy of the file first. Then, check the results of your changes throughout the document before you work any further. You don't want to invest a lot of time in a document that has been inadvertently mangled by a Document Setup change. The way you rescue yourself from the situation is to dump the file and go back to a previous version of it, your backup file. Another way to go back to a previous version would be to use the Revert command in the File menu. Save the document just before changing the Document Setup settings and then use the Revert command if you don't like the results.

TABLE 3.1

RESULTS OF CHANGING DOCUMENT SETUP OPTIONS

If You Change This	You Get This (Possibly Evil) Result
Page size	PageMaker attempts to center the objects in relation to the edges of the page. Your objects, both text and graphics, hold their position in relation to one another. If you shrink to a smaller page, your stuff may end up leaking off the edge of the page.
Tall/Wide	Objects hold their positions in relation to the edges of the Pasteboard; that means some objects probably end up off the page.

If You Change This	You Get This (Possibly Evil) Result
Number of pages	You can add or subtract pages using this box, but keep in mind that it works at the end of the document. As with all page deletions, you could have the evil effect of inadvertently and forever destroying pages that contain vital information if you subtract live pages from the end of the document.
Broken Spread Graphic (Odd pages to Even) (Even pages to Odd) (Start Page Number) (Double-sided to Single)	There are several changes you can make in the Document Setup dialog box that make a mess of a graphic placed to cross over between two facing (a spread graphic). Be alert for any change that swaps odd pages to even pages or vice versa. Whenever this happens, PageMaker tries to keep the spread graphic with its original left (even-numbered) page. That means it ends up as a right (odd-numbered) page with much of the graphic sticking out to the right onto the Pasteboard.
Start Page Number	In a double-sided publication, PageMaker uses the starting number information to decide which pages are left or right pages. If you change this starting number from even to odd or vice versa, you cause all the pages in a double-sided publication to trade between left and right position.
Single-Sided to Double-Sided	In a single-sided publication, with Double-Sided turned off, all the pages are considered to be right pages. Turning on Double-Sided converts every even-numbered single-sided page into a new left page with the old right margin converted to the new inside margin. That move may shift the position of graphics and text in relation to the new inside margin.
Double-Sided to Single-Sided	This move converts all even-numbered, double-sided pages from left pages to right pages. The inside margin of the even-numbered pages turns into the new right margin. You may see graphics and text shift on the page to adjust to the new margins.

continues

TABLE 3.1, CONTINUED

RESULTS OF CHANGING DOCUMENT SETUP OPTIONS

If You Change This	You Get This (Possibly Evil) Result
Margin Size	Changing margin size doesn't affect the layouts of any pages already set (this change is not retroactive). On the other hand, if you want to change the margins on existing pages, you must go to each page and readjust graphics and text to the new margins.
Numbering Style	Changing the numbering style produces a different page number display. The same thing happens in the TOC and Index Prefix dialog box. Unlike margin changes and single-sided or double-sided pages, this function is dynamic. The change isn't irrevocable, and you can simply change it back.
Target Printer Resolution	As with margins, changing the target resolution doesn't affect any black-and-white graphics you have already placed, but it does affect any future graphics resizing. For this reason, you may want to go back and redo any previously placed graphics.

PageMaker In the Real World

Inline Graphics Protect You During Major Page Structure Changes

Placing illustrations as inline graphics gives you some margin of protection from the unexpected results caused by Document Setup changes. Inline graphics, placed directly in the text instead of on the page, lock themselves in position in relation to text. As the text moves as a result of adjustments to the page structure, the inline graphics move right with the text.

SUMMARY

◆ You get most of your power from the layout grid when you are positioning your page elements—which is why you should check out Chapters 8 "PageMaker's Drawing Tools" and Chapter 9 "Graphics—Magic Tricks and Plug-Ins."

◆ When you are putting together a long document format (reports, books, and so on), you will really appreciate the layout grid automation, especially the Guide Manager and multiple master pages, described in this chapter. For many more details on all aspects of multipage documents, look at Chapter 12 "Endgame Issues."

◆ You will have a hard time implementing a fine-grained layout grid unless you have a solid understanding of leading and styles. For those concepts, see Chapter 6, "Working with Text."

Chapter 4

LAYERS

In keeping with its troika approach to computer art and desktop publishing, Adobe adds full layering capability to PageMaker 6.5. This brings the general feel of the interface close to that of the other two Adobe applications in the trio, Illustrator and Photoshop. Readers familiar with the layering capabilities of either of those applications can take their skills and experience and apply them directly to PageMaker's layering options. For users not experienced with the concept of layers, a short definition might be in order. Layers are similar to transparent sheets, sandwiched together to make up each page in a document. Each layer can contain any number of unique page elements. The topmost layer's elements automatically appear "in front" of any elements placed on a layer beneath it.

A new publication, or one converted from an earlier version of PageMaker uses only one layer, called the *Default layer*, and it cannot be removed or renamed; however, you can add one or more layers to the document at any time. To add a layer, select New Layer from the pull-down menu in the Layers palette. You can select the layer color to distinguish it from other layers. An alternative way to add a layer is to click the small layer icon at the bottom of the Layers palette (next to the Trash Can icon).

If you create new layers with no publication open, all subsequent new PageMaker publications have that multiple layer setting. The number of total layers a document can have is limited only by your computer's memory (RAM). Of course there's degree, extent, and common sense involved, too. Though layers enable you to separate elements on a page so that editing can proceed more clearly, too many layers can do the opposite. Six or seven layers is usually enough to do the job; more tend to make things confusing. The final decision, however, must be made by the designer, motivated by the way he or she works best.

Note

Layers apply throughout a publication, so all pages in a document share the same number of layers, including master pages. If you hide the default layer while editing any page of your document, for example, the default layer is hidden on all pages until you decide to make it visible again.

By using multiple layers, you can create and edit specific areas or types of content in your publication without affecting other content. If you placed your type on a specific layer and your images on another, for example, you could temporarily hide the image layer to make fine-tuning typography and proofreading easier. You can also freely experiment with different image backgrounds for your foreground text, replacing image elements with little fear of disturbing the text objects.

Creating a New Layer and Setting its Options

To create a new layer, follow these steps:

1. Select New Layer from the Layers palette menu.

2. Choose any of the following options:

   ◆ Type a name for the layer in the Name text box. By default, layers are named according to the order in which they were created, with the default being the backmost layer.

   ◆ Select a color from the Selection Color pop-up menu to indicate selected objects in that layer.

   ◆ Select or deselect the Show option to display or hide the layer.

   ◆ Select or deselect the Lock option to lock or unlock objects on the layer.

3. Click OK.

Choosing a Selection Color for Layers

Selecting a different color for each layer makes it easy to distinguish each layer in your publication. Selecting an object displays the object handles in the color specified for that particular layer. You can tell the selection color for a layer by the color of the box to the left of the layer name in the Layers palette.

1. Double-click the layer you want in the Layers palette.

2. Select the color that you want to use to indicate all selections on that layer.

3. Click OK.

Object Ordering on Layers

Two rules affect objects and their order on layers: Within each layer, all objects are stacked according to their determined stacking order (see Figure 4.1) and grouped objects are always on the same layer. If you group objects on different layers, all objects are placed on the frontmost layer of the grouping, directly behind the frontmost object in the group. You use the Layers palette to create, edit, lock, and delete layers (see Figure 4.2). The Layers palette also enables you to hide and show individual layers, as well as to determine the order in which layers appear (see Figure 4.3).

Figure 4.1

The Layers palette pull-down menu is accessed by pressing the small arrow to the right.

Figure 4.2

To display the Layers palette, select Show Layers from the Windows menu.

Figure 4.3

The New Layer dialog box enables you to select the layer's color, and whether it will be shown or locked.

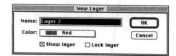

Choosing colors for layers can be very important as far as getting a quick visual cue that will help you navigate through your document. Choose colors for added layers that are different enough from each other to facilitate recognition. Some designers always place certain page elements (body copy, for example) on a layer colored in the same fashion. Over time, these habits enable you to work faster. Layers can be colorized within the standard Layers dialog box, or with the Layer Options dialog box (see Figure 4.4).

The elements on a layer are stacked according to the way the layers are stacked, and colors are assigned to the layer they are associated with. Selecting any element on a page jumps you to the layer the element is on (see Figure 4.5).

Figure 4.4

The Layer Options dialog box has the same data as the New Layer dialog box.

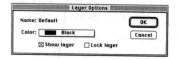

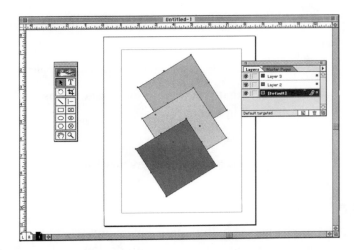

Figure 4.5

Stacked layers.

Moving Objects from One Layer to Another

When an object is selected, a colored box appears to the right of the layer name on the palette to indicate the layer to which the object is assigned. If a layer has an object (text or graphics) on it, the Layers palette will display a small Pencil icon to the right of the layer (see Figure 4.6). To move an object, first click the object to select it. By pressing the mouse and clicking the associated icon in the Layers palette, you can move the selected object to any other layer in the stack.

Figure 4.6

Selecting the object icon in the Layers palette and moving it to another layer in the stack moves the selected object to the new layer.

You also can move objects from one layer to another by cutting objects from one layer and pasting them into another. If you use the Paste command to move objects from one page to another, remember that pasting works differently depending on whether the Paste Remembers Layering option in the Layers palette menu is checked or unchecked. If the Paste Remembers Layering option in the Layers palette menu is checked, then objects cut or copied from different layers retain their layer assignments when pasted to the new page or position. Otherwise, objects cut or copied from different layers are pasted together onto the selected layer.

To paste objects to a different page or position and retain layering information:

1. Select Paste Remembers Layering from the Layers palette menu.

2. Select the object that you want to move, and choose Cut or Copy from the Edit menu.

3. Turn to the new page if necessary.

4. Paste the objects onto the same layers they had been on originally.

Moving Layers

By pressing the mouse button and clicking any selected layer in the Layers palette, you can move a layer up or down. All of the layers objects move in accordance, placing them in a new order relative to objects on other layers. (Press Shift to select multiple layers. When you drag two or more layers to a new position, they maintain their layer order relative to one another.)

Locking Layers

Locking a layer has an effect similar to that of choosing the Lock Position command from the Arrange menu—objects on locked layers cannot be selected or edited.

1. Click the Pencil icon to the left of the layer name.

2. Drag up or down to lock other layers above or below the first layer you clicked. This turns on the Lock option in the Layer Options dialog box for the selected layers.

3. Click again to turn off the option and unlock a layer.

Locking All Layers but Those Selected in the palette

1. Select the layer or layers you want to edit.

2. Choose Lock Others from the Layers palette menu.

Unlocking All Layers

Choose Unlock All from the Layers palette pop-up menu.

Locking Objects within Layers

In addition to locking layers, you can lock individual objects in place to help preserve the design of your pages through all stages of production, and to prevent accidental movement. You can change the attributes of any locked object, provided the change does not affect the object's size or position. You can change a color or fill applied to a locked object, for example, but not its degree of rotation or its skewing angle. You cannot cut or delete a locked object without unlocking it first, but you can copy a locked object; it will be pasted as an unlocked object. Select Layout Adjustment from the Preferences dialog box in the File menu. Select Ignore Object and Layer Locks if you want layout framework changes to effect objects you've locked either with the Element/Lock Position command or by locking layers.

Hiding and Showing Layers

To hiding a layer controls not just whether a layer displays, but whether it prints, and whether it can be edited.

Click the Eye icon to the left of the layer name. Drag up or down to affect other layers above or below the layer you first clicked. This turns off the Show option in the Layer Options dialog box for the selected layers. Click again to turn the option back on and redisplay a layer.

Hiding All Layers but Those Selected in the palette

To hide all layers but those selected, follow these steps:

1. Select the layer or layers you want to view.

2. Choose Hide Others from the Layers palette menu.

Displaying All Layers

Choose Show All from the Layers palette pop-up menu.

Deleting and Merging Layers

You can remove a layer from your document by deleting it from the Layers palette. The objects assigned to that layer on every page of the publication are either deleted or added to another specified layer depending on the option you choose.

Note

Remember that each layer appears on every page of a publication, not just on a specific page. Before deleting a layer, you might want to hide all the other layers first, and then turn to each page of the publication to check what objects are on the layer you are about to delete so that you can save them out or move them as necessary. If you merge layers, remember that this can also change the way objects overlap in your publication. Always double-check your pages after merging layers.

Deleting Layers

To delete a layer, follow these steps:

1. Select the layer name in the Layers palette.

2. Choose Delete Layer from the Layers palette menu, or click the Trash icon in the palette. (You can also drag the layer to the Trash icon located on the Layers palette.)

3. In the Delete Layer dialog box, select an option:

    ◆   Click Assign Items From Deleted Layer To, and choose the name of the layer to which you want the objects moved.

    ◆   Click Delete Items on All Pages From Layer to remove all objects throughout the publication assigned to that layer.

    To delete the selected layer and prevent the Delete Layer dialog box from appearing, press the (Option) [Alt] key as you complete step 2.

Deleting All Layers without Objects

To delete layers without objects, follow these steps:

1. Choose Delete Unused Layers from the Layers palette pop-up menu.

2. In the dialog box that opens, you are prompted to delete the first unused layer (click Yes), or to preserve it (click No). Click

Yes To All if you want to automatically delete the unused layers without being further prompted, or click No To All to cancel the action.

Object Groups and Layers

The following rules apply to groups (a group is a collection of objects on a page that have been grouped by the Group command):

◆ Frames cannot be grouped with other objects.

◆ A newly created group moves to the front of the stacking order. Objects in a group retain their stacking order in relation to each other until you change their stacking order with commands from the Arrange menu.

If the objects were grouped from different layers, the group is assigned to the layer of the topmost object in the grouped selection. Using layers to composite diverse elements of a design can help you when it comes time to position the elements for the best look. Figures 4.7 and 4.8 illustrate some of the possibilities.

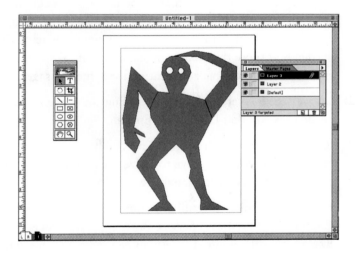

Figure 4.7

You can build a figure whose elements are positioned on different layers.

Figure 4.8

Elements can be repositioned without affecting the other elements on different layers.

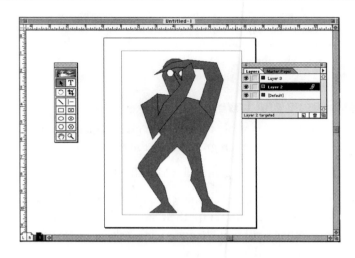

A Layers Project

There are as many uses for utilizing layers as there are designers. One that might interest you is to use layers to create a multilingual document. The process is straightforward:

1. Organize all of the nontextual elements of your pages on one layer, usually the bottom layer, of your document. Design the composition so that there is adequate room for placing the needed text (note that some languages might take a larger or smaller amount of space for stating the same message).

2. Create a new layer, and name it US English. Place all the needed text on that layer in US English.

3. Repeat Step 2 for each language needed by the document, realizing that you may have to resize the text a bit so that it fits the requirements of that language.

4. Explain the project carefully to your service bureau (see Chapter 15, "Prepress, Service Bureaus, and Printers"). Explain that the nontext layer will be used for each separate language document, and the other layers are to be used in turn for the text.

Layers Transported to Earlier Versions of PageMaker

PageMaker versions prior to 6.5 do not recognize some of the features added to PageMaker 6.5, especially layers. Attempting to open a PageMaker 6.5 document with layers in a prior version will cause all of the layers to be merged into a single visible layer. The stack (what is in front of or behind other elements) might or might not be preserved so tweaking might be necessary.

PAGEMAKER AS ANIMATOR

At first glance, the term "PageMaker Animator" seems confusing. After all, desktop publishing seems far afield from animation. But professional animators have been using DTP software for a long time, printing individual animation "cels" or frames to get camera-ready copy.

PageMaker 6.5's new layering capabilities enhance its potential as an animator's utility. A multilayered page can hold diverse elements of an animated figure, so that as the parts are moved to different positions, sequenced frames can be generated and printed. To use PageMaker 6.5 as an animation utility, proceed as follows:

1. Use the Layers palette and create a minimum of three layers to work on.

2. Draw a separate part of a figure on each layer using the Open Polygon tool. Shade each shape according to your desire.

3. When the figure is complete, choose Select All from the Edit menu, and copy the figure to the Clipboard.

4. Select Paste Special from the Edit menu, and select PICT (Mac) or WMF (Windows) to paste a graphic of the figure to the screen.

5. Select the graphic and go to the File menu. Select Export as Graphic and choose a TIFF export. Save the graphic as MyAnim_001.

6. Delete the PICT/WMF graphic from the page. Go back to the layered graphic, and move (rotate or resize) one of the elements in a layer. Go back to Step 3 and use the same process to save out MyAnim_002, and so on. When you have about 30 separate frames, you can combine them into a QuickTime or AVI animation, or print them for camera-ready animation art. You can create very complex graphics, and explore the possibilities using this method. It's all made possible with PageMaker 6.5's new layering capabilities. (See Figures 4.9 and 4.10.)

Figure 4.9

The Paste Special command is used to paste a non-PageMaker graphic back to the screen (the figure on the left).

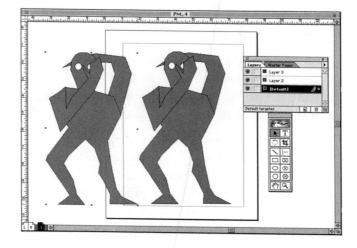

Figure 4.10

The graphic is exported from PageMaker as a TIFF graphic, and is named as one frame in the animation sequence. Combining a number of frames saved out in this manner, an animation can be produced.

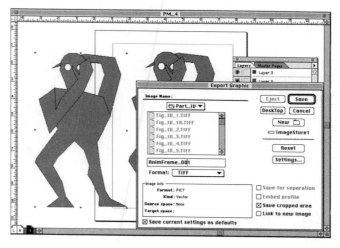

110

Frames to Movies

To combine the separate frame files into a movie file (QuickTime or AVI), you need a separate utility. Literally dozens of options are available for this purpose (commercial, shareware, and freeware products), but it is recommended that you investigate DeBabelizer from Equilibrium Software if you're really serious about doing this. DeBabelizer comes in both Mac and Windows flavors, and enables you to collect all the single frames you've generated into one batch file, and then translates them into a QuickTime (Mac) or AVI (Windows) compressed movie file. Some Browser utilities enable you to play QuickTime and AVI movies online, but most Web animators prefer GIF animations instead. DeBabelizer automates the process of creating a GIF animation from your selected single frames as easily as it creates QuickTime and AVI movies. This includes the ability to assign one color in the animation to transparent, a feature of GIF animations applauded by Web page designers.

SUMMARY

The new layers feature in PageMaker 6.5 offers users greater and more varied control of their page layouts. It is a substantial addition to this already powerful application.

FRAMES

PageMaker 6.5's frames option is brand new, and it gives the professional user an expanded list of page composition possibilities. To begin with, it's important to understand the difference between frames and strokes, because the two are often confused. A stroke is a border around a surrounded text block or selected graphic. PageMaker's strokes are configured in the Stroke and Fill and the Stroke dialog boxes. A stroked area is sometimes called a "framed" area in common parlance, and this is exactly where the confusion comes in. A frame in PageMaker 6.5 means something quite different. A frame is an area that acts as a receptacle for text or a graphic. It may or may not have a stroked border. The most common use for a frame where graphics are concerned is to allow the page designer to adjust the cropping of a selected graphic as it is placed in a frame.

PageMaker enables you to configure three types of frames:

◆ Rectangular

◆ Oval

◆ Polygonal

These frames can have stroked borders, just like any text block or graphic, but they have one attribute not found in a stroked area. Their contents are attached in a special way so that reconfiguring the frame instantly reconfigures the contents.

The three frame icons in PageMaker's Toolbox (Rectangle, Oval, and Polygon) have an "X" drawn through them to distinguish them from their non-frame shape counterparts. When a frame is placed on a page, it continues to have an X drawn through it (blue by default) so that frame shapes can be distinguished from similar non-frame shapes. See Figure 5.1.

Figure 5.1

The three frame icons in PageMaker's Toolbox (Rectangle, Oval, and Polygon) have an "X" drawn through them to distinguish them from their non-frame shape counterparts.

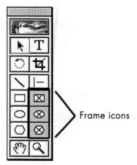

Frame icons

CREATING FRAMES

Polygons (whether standard polygons or polygonal frames) can be created by a click-and-move method. Instead of clicking a point and then dragging out a polygonal shape at the start, simply click from point to point. When you return to the first point, a clear rectangular box appears around the point of the cursor. Clicking at that point finishes the shape. Either method (click then drag then edit or click then move) can produce very complex polygonal shapes. If this is a polygonal frame, the resulting shape can be used as a shaped environment for attached text or graphics. (See Figure 5.2.)

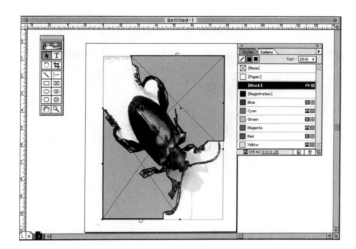

Figure 5.2

The click-and-move method can be used to create very complex polygonal frames.

Editing Frames

The Rectangular and Oval frames maintain their general shape proportions no matter how they are resized. The Polygon frame is the only one of the three that is adjustable. By double-clicking any side of the polygon frame at any time during an editing session, you can activate its reshaping mode. While it is in the reshaping mode, clicking any place on the polygon's perimeter adds a new control point. This new control point can be moved anywhere on the page, stretching the polygon's shape as it is moved. Using this method, any shape imaginable can be created, and any image can be used as an underlying form for a new polygonal frame. After a polygonal frame has been created, attaching the text is easy (see Figure 5.3). The text remains active and can be resized and manipulated even after it is attached to a frame, as long as it doesn't become so big that it breaks the bounds of the frame (see Figure 5.4).

The Frame Options Dialog Box

The Frame Options dialog box is opened by selecting Frame Options from the Frame submenu in the Element menu. If you alter the settings here before any frame is drawn onscreen, the settings will apply initially to all frames. If a frame is selected first, the settings will apply to only that frame. Frame settings can be altered at any time.

Figure 5.3

It's easy to attach text to a polygonal frame.

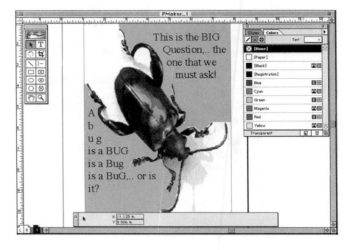

Figure 5.4

After the type has been attached, it can still be resized and manipulated.

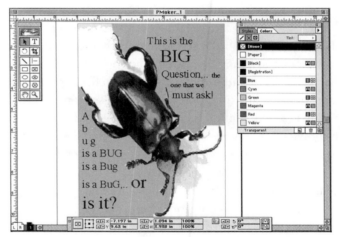

The Clip, Sizing, and Scaling options found in this dialog box have little or no effect on attached text, and refer to attached graphics.

◆ The Clip Content to Fit Frame option clips the graphic to the frame size. See the illustration of the Frame Options dialog box in Figure 5.5. If you resize the frame after the graphic is attached, the attached graphic displays a larger part of itself. Conversely, if you shrink the frame, a smaller portion of the graphic is visible. Even after the graphics are in the frame, you can use the Cropping tool to move them around to achieve the best composition.

- The Size Frame to Fit Content option expands the frame to fit the exact size of the graphic. Resizing the frame afterward displays either the blank space around the graphic or cuts off part of the graphic display.

- Scale Content to Fit Frame reduces or enlarges the graphic to the frame size. If Maintain Aspect Ratio is checked, the frame is resized to the graphic's aspect ratio as well. If it is not checked, the graphic is stretched to fit the frame.

The inset distances and the alignment for Vertical (Top, Bottom, Center) and Horizontal (Left, Center, Right) also can be adjusted. This has no effect on attached text, but is targeted to attached graphics. The Fill and Stroke options can be applied to any selected frame.

Referring to Figure 5.6, the illustrated examples started out with the same size frames and graphics, before frame options were applied. On the left, the Clip content to fit frame option was applied. The center figure was created with the Size frame to fit content option, whereas the framed graphic on the right shows the effect of Scale Content to Fit Frame.

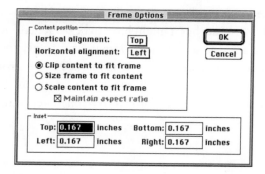

Figure 5.5

The Frame Options dialog box.

Figure 5.6

These examples started out with the same size frames and graphics, before Frame options were applied.

FRAMES AND TEXT BLOCKS: FREEFORM VERSUS STRUCTURED LAYOUTS

If you place the text cursor inside a framed area and start typing, the text automatically is connected to the frame. Conversely, the only way to connect text to a non-frame shape is to attach it after the fact. This makes a big difference when it comes to saving time, and also having the capacity for moving a text block to another area on a page to create a more freeform composition. Placing the cursor inside the frame and then typing is a faster alternative.

Frames are almost essential when it comes to designing freeform pages, although non-framed text can be flowed into column guides for a more structured look. A freeform page is one in which the symmetry between elements is not apparently rigidly structured, but structured more upon the perceived "weights" of the elements involved. Weights refers to their apparent density (blackness). Because the text attached to a frame is part of that frame, just as if it were a screen or a texture, any alterations performed on the frame alters the internal text.

There are some cautions, however. If you alter the frame so that the text is prevented from having enough space, strange results are guaranteed. The attached text inside a frame will attempt to reflow to the altered confines of the frame, but it might have to be detached and reformatted to a smaller size (or sometimes a larger size) to get the right result. Attached text will not automatically resize when its surrounding frame is manipulated, though it will reposition itself on different lines, including separating longer words into hyphenated equivalents.

Note

One option you can explore when attempting to fit a text block into a framed area is to include invisible characters in the text block. This can be done by using spaces, or by using letters that are modified to be the color of the paper.

Text Frames

Although you can use any of the frame shapes to enclose attached text, the most common choice is the rectangle. This imposes the least surprises on the text when you reconfigure the shape of the frame. The least common is the oval, because this frame shape imposes unexpected changes on the incorporated text. The polygon frame is a special case. By attaching text to a polygonal frame, the text can be altered in ways that make this a possible substitute for wrapping text around an image. If the polygonal frame's border is changed to the paper color (rendering it invisible), the reconfigured text inside takes on the altered shape of the polygon without you or your audience being able to see the frame. In this way, the polygon frame can be used to control text without it being obvious. Reconfiguring a polygonal frame is a little simpler than using the PageMaker text wrap process to do the same thing. Here's how to proceed:

1. Go to the Polygon tool in the Toolbox (not the Polygon Frame), and double-click it. This opens the Polygon Settings dialog box.

2. In the Polygon Settings dialog box, set the sides to four, and the Star Inset to 0%. Click OK.

3. Select the Polygon Frame tool from the Toolbox, and draw a shape on the page. Notice that it looks like a simple rectangle, which is the best frame to start with when working with text. Select both the frame shape and your text block, and Attach the text to the frame (Attach Content command found in the Frame submenu in the Element menu).

4. Adjust the frame as needed, which moves words in your text to alternate lines.

5. Double-click the frame, activating the Polygon Reshaping operation. Click once on any side of the polygon frame, which places a new control point at that spot. Adjust the polygon shape and watch how the text responds. Explore this method until you master it, and apply it to any needed text wrap situation.

Frames with Tighter Text Fits

Here is a tip if you need to have a tighter text fit in a frame:

1. Attach your text to a rectangular frame, and adjust the frame to get the right general alignment. Set the stroke (border of the frame) to "Paper Color" so that it becomes invisible.

2. Copy the frame with the text to the Clipboard.

3. Choose Paste Special from the Edit menu, and paste the frame and text back to the screen as a PICT (or WMF for Windows users) graphic.

As a side note, you can export selected graphics to the GIF89 format for use on the Web. You cannot, however, export to any format if the graphic is attached to a frame.

4. Draw a new frame, and attach the PICT (WMF) graphic to it. Now when you adjust the frame, you will be able to get the frame borders much closer to the text.

Text placed in a frame can always be restyled or resized with the Text tool. Just select the text area by dragging the text cursor over it, and apply the necessary changes.

Combining Frames in Text Blocks

PageMaker requires a little maneuvering to place frames as inline graphics in a text block, because all that are accepted for inline use are true graphics formats. There is a way around this taboo, however, using the tools that PageMaker offers. Here's how:

1. Bring your text block to a page. Use one of the frame tools to draw a frame, and set it aside. Place (import) the appropriate graphic, and set it aside (see Figure 5.7).

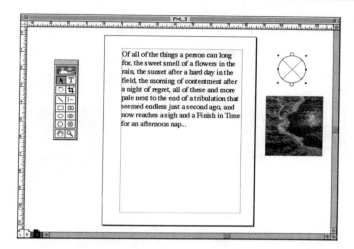

Figure 5.7

Begin by importing the text, and place your imported graphic in a frame.

2. Double-click the placed frame, opening the Frame Options dialog box. Make sure that Clip content to fit frame is selected, and click OK (see Figure 5.8).

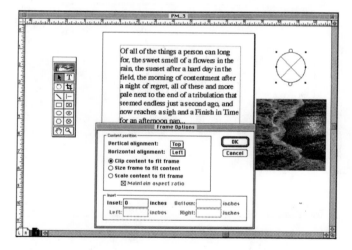

Figure 5.8

Select Clip Content to fit frame in the Frames Options dialog box.

3. Select the frame and then press Shift while selecting the graphic. Choose Attach Content. The graphic becomes part of the frame (see Figure 5.9).

Figure 5.9

Attaching the content makes the graphic a part of the frame.

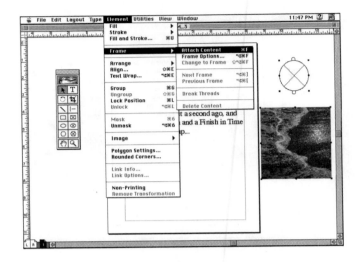

4. Copy the framed graphic to the Clipboard (see Figure 5.10).

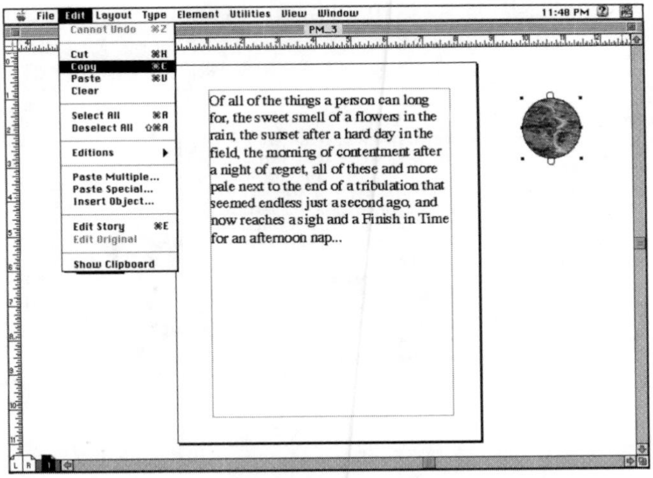

Figure 5.10

Copy the frame to the Clipboard.

5. Notice that the graphic fits the frame proportionately (see Figure 5.11).

Figure 5.11

*The graphic fits the frame
proportionately.*

6. Choose Paste Special from the Edit menu. In the dialog box
    that appears, select PICT (Mac) or WMF (Windows), and click
    OK (see Figure 5.12).

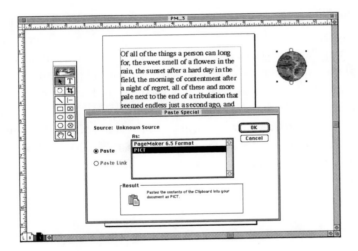

Figure 5.12

*Go to Paste Special in the
Edit menu.*

7. The pasted graphic now appears on the screen. Select it and
    copy it to the Clipboard. Place the text cursor at any place in
    your text that you would like the inline graphic to appear, and
    select the Paste command. The graphics that are placed in the
    text are inline graphics, and are now a permanent part of the
    text block (see Figure 5.13).

Figure 5.13

Place the framed inline graphic in the text block.

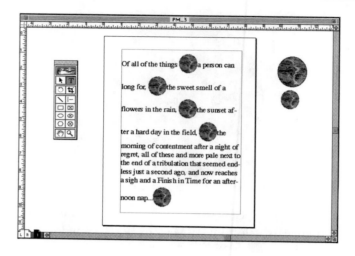

SUMMARY

Although this chapter has endeavored to cover all of the basic ways that the new PageMaker frames can be used to enhance a publication, the topic has not been exhausted creatively. You might want to refer to Chapter 9, "Graphics—Magic Tricks and Plug-Ins" for more creative inspiration. The real discoveries concerning the creative uses that frames may provide however will be up to each individual designer. An attribute with as many design implications as PageMaker frames has a near infinite amount of explorations to offer.

Chapter 6

WORKING WITH TEXT

Text is the "meat" of your publication. A picture might be worth a thousand words, but the words do the real communicating. There are two ways to work with text. The first is mechanics: bringing the text into PageMaker, keeping stories together and working with links, editing the text, checking spelling, and so on. The second is typography: choosing the faces and type sizes to make your words not only legible but beautiful.

Some of the best PageMaker desktop publishers began working with type years ago, long before computers. They were typesetters, punching out slugs of molten metal type for the press in a print shop. Today, they have adopted new technology, but it's really just a change of tools and media. The fundamentals of typographic design, whether set on the computer, cast in lead, or carved in stone, remain the same.

IMPORTING TEXT

You can do anything with the content or appearance of your text. Although you can use the Text tool in PageMaker to type into your publication, you'll find it's easier to use a word processing program for any story more than a few words long. A story, in PageMaker terms, is any block of text that's a single unit. A story can be many pages long, or just one or two words. Headlines are often handled as separate stories, as are picture captions and pull quotes.

Using the Text Tool

Use the Text tool to do anything related to type. In the upper-right corner of the Toolbox, you see the Text tool icon—the letter T. If you click the icon, you get the I-beam text pointer.

You can toggle between the Text tool and the Pointer tool by pressing (Command-Spacebar) [Control-Spacebar]. Notice that this is the same key combination you use to get the Magnifying Glass pointer. To get the Magnifying Glass, use the same two keys (Command-Spacebar) [Control-Spacebar] except press them for a few beats and continue to press them while you make your magnification adjustment.

CREATING TEXT FROM SCRATCH

As with most PageMaker operations, there are a couple of different ways to create text. If you know exactly what you want to say and where you want to put it on the page, the easiest way is to use the Text tool to drag a text box onto the page at the right spot and type your text into it. The box seems to disappear after you draw it, but as you type, your text wraps as each line reaches the right edge of the text block. This is by far the quickest and easiest way to put headlines, bylines, or other short bits of text on the page.

You can choose the font and type size for your text by selecting the appropriate attributes from the Type menu or the Control palette. Select the block of text by highlighting it, and then select the attributes. Or, conversely, select the attributes first and then type or paste from the insertion point.

See the section on "Typography" later in this chapter for more detail on fonts, sizes, styles, and other text attributes.

PLACING TEXT

Placing a story in a PageMaker publication can be accomplished in several ways. You can open a word processor or other program that created the text, copy the text to the Clipboard or Scrapbook, and paste it in.

New to PageMaker 6.5 is drag-and-drop editing. With both PageMaker and your word processing program visible onscreen, you can drag and drop selected pieces of text from one document to the other. Figure 6.1 shows a piece of text being dragged from Word 6.0 into PageMaker. You can drag and drop text or graphics from any other program that supports it, including ClarisWorks, Photoshop, Illustrator, and even Stickies.

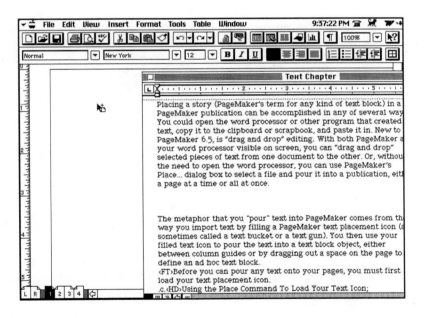

Figure 6.1

Notice how the icon changes when you drag text from Word to PageMaker.

Without even opening the word processor, you can use PageMaker's Place dialog box to select a file and pour it into a publication, either a page at a time or all at once. The metaphor of *pouring* text into PageMaker comes from filling a PageMaker text placement icon (also sometimes called a text bucket or a text gun). You then use your filled text icon to pour the text into a text block, either between column guides or by dragging out a space on the page to define a text block.

Using the Place Command

First, prepare the page(s) on which you'll place the text (refer to Chapter 3). Decide how many columns per page and how many pages you want to fill. Choose Place from the File menu and the Place document dialog box opens (see Figure 6.2). It resembles the standard File open dialog box. Select the file you want to import. When you select your file and double-click it or click OK, PageMaker brings the file into memory, conducts whatever file translation is needed, and loads the text from the file into a text placement icon.

Figure 6.2

Select the file you want to place and click OK.

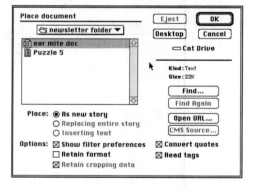

Other interesting choices in the Place dialog box include something new to PageMaker 6.5—the capability to open a URL address and place text from an Internet source. This, and how to use other options such as retaining format, converting quotes, and so on, are discussed later in this chapter.

Understanding the Three Text Placement Icon Types

Figure 6.3 shows the three different text placement icons. Think of them as three speeds of text placement.

Manual   Semiautomatic   Autoflow

Figure 6.3

The three text icons: Manual, Semiautomatic, and Autoflow.

The Manual Text Icon

Manual text flow is the slowest method. The icon looks like a tiny page of text. It places only as much text as the column can hold; then it stops. A red arrow at the bottom of the text block indicates there's more text to place. To place more text, you must position the icon in the next column or text block to fill, and click again.

The Manual text icon is best for placing text in one column or page at a time, or for drag-placing text—clicking the text icon and dragging out a box to size the text block to hold your poured text. Use drag-placing for intricate work where you are fitting text around graphics (captions, drawings placed across columns) or placing text across columns (a page headline).

If you click anywhere between two column guides without dragging out a text block, the Manual icon fills that column from the click point to the lower margin or another text block. To use Manual text flow, turn off Autoflow in the Layout menu or press the (Command) [Control] key to temporarily convert the Autoflow icon to a Manual icon.

Note

Using the Manual icon, text stops flowing when it reaches the bottom of a column or if it hits another text block lower in the column. The bottom windowshade displays a down-arrow tab, indicating that you must reload your Manual text icon by single-clicking the tab to place the next text block in the thread.

The Semiautomatic Text Icon

Semiautomatic text flow fills a column of text and stops. If there's more text to place, the icon reappears, enabling you to fill columns at your discretion. In speed terms, it's medium-fast. To use Semiautomatic, select Autoflow from the Layout menu. When you begin to place text, press the Shift key. This changes the Autoflow text icon to the Semiautomatic text icon shown in Figure 6.3.

Use this text placement method if you need to place text into defined spaces that don't fall one right after the other, as they do when you autoflow text. This icon is terrific for rapid-fire placement of text—spotting bits of text on a single page; placing text into multiple columns on double facing pages; clicking text onto a page and then jumping to the next spot where you continue the story thread; and alternating column placement with drag placement.

Semiautomatic text flow is a temporary state. It doesn't "lock in" as Autoflow does. You must press the Shift key each time you select a story to place. This feature actually makes Semiautomatic the most flexible of the three text placement modes. Using keyboard commands, you can easily switch between Manual or Autoflow as needed while laying text onto the page.

Note

The Semiautomatic icon acts like the Manual icon, stopping text flow at the bottom of a column; however, the icon automatically reloads itself and can place additional text blocks without clicking the down-arrow tab of the windowshade.

The Autoflow Text Icon

Automatic text flow, or Autoflow, is the fastest way to place text on a page. The curvy line of the Autoflow text placement icon suggests the way text blocks thread together on a page to create a story. This is an apt association because this is how the Autoflow icon functions—by placing an entire story at a time, automatically jumping from column to column and from page to page, placing text between empty column guides as it goes. If the Autoflow text icon reaches the last page of your publication and needs more room to finish placing a story, it adds pages to finish the job.

To use the Autoflow text placement icon, turn on Autoflow in the Layout menu. You can use Autoflow on a temporary basis by pressing the (Command) [Control] key when the Manual icon is showing. Autoflow works best for the initial placement of a large story that takes many pages, such as all the pages of a book chapter or a technical report.

Note

If you use Autoflow, the text placement doesn't stop. PageMaker lays text into place up to the lower margin or the Text Wrap graphic, and skips to the next available open spot in the current column or the next column.

You can slow down the autoflow process so that you can see each page as it fills with text. Open the Preferences dialog box in the File menu and click the Other button. Then click the button for Display All Pages.

If you decide to stop text placement for a while, but you still have some unplaced text, you have two options. If you already have at least one block on the page, click on any tool in the Toolbox to switch off the text placement icon. If you have not yet placed any text, drag-place a text block on the Pasteboard to give yourself a temporary placeholder. In either case, the last text block you placed displays a down arrow, as shown in Figure 6.4. To resume text placement, click the down arrow to reload your text placement icon with the rest of the story.

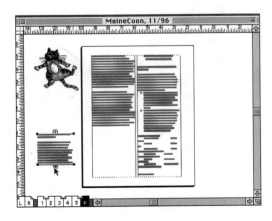

Figure 6.4

The arrow tells you there's more text in this story.

Warning

If you have not yet created any sort of text block, and this is a fresh load of text, you completely cancel the Place operation if you click on a different tool in the Toolbox. You lose all your text and need to use the Place command again to restart.

Importing Text From the Internet

New in PageMaker 6.5 is the capability to open and copy text files and JPEG or GIF images from the World Wide Web. You can also import HTML files from a disk complete with embedded images, hyperlinks, and HTML formatting. To import an HTML document from a disk, use the Place command, and it will import like any other text file, with its formatting intact.

To import information from the Web, you must have a supported Web Browser, such as Netscape or Internet Explorer. You must also set up PageMaker to communicate with the Internet. This is done in the Online Preferences dialog box in the File menu. First, open your browser and copy the port and HTTP Proxy information. Enter these settings in PageMaker's preferences dialog box, and specify the location (on your hard drive) of the browser. Also, designate a folder to receive downloads from the browser.

To place information from the Web using the Place dialog box, click Open URL and type the URL for the information you want to place. (It must be an HTTP, FTP, or Gopher source.) Click OK. PageMaker opens the URL and imports the information.

This procedure might be slow, especially during periods of heavy Internet use. It will tie up your computer and PageMaker for the time it takes to open the page. You might find it faster to open the Browser directly and use it to open the URL. Then, do something else while the page loads and either save it as an HTML document, which you can import into PageMaker, or drag and drop it into the publication.

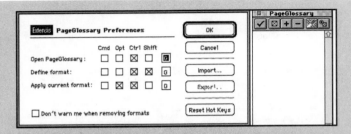

PageGlossary is one of the plug-ins from the Extensis PageTools set. This plug-in provides you with the capability to auto-enter frequently used text with a keystroke or mouse click. Glossary text can contain style attributes as well.

TEXT BLOCKS

Think of a block of PageMaker text as an object instead of a string of words. Although text blocks contain text, you can move and size them as you would move and size graphic objects. The text block acts as a container for your text. Fix this concept firmly in your mind—you'll use it many times a day when working with text blocks and stories.

When text block objects are combined, they make up a complete PageMaker story. They are threaded together from top to bottom, beginning to end. As blocks are expanded or reduced, the text thread flows freely between them, filling each block with text.

A story can have one text block, or it can have hundreds. The thread of text blocks in a book will probably be pretty straightforward, running from page one to the final page in serial order, but the thread in a newsletter, newspaper, or magazine might be a little more complicated. A story on page 1, for example, might continue on page 23, with a dozen other stories located on the intervening pages. Even though the story is separated by those pages, the page 1 story's text blocks are threaded together and text flows between them as the page 1 block is expanded and contracted during layout. Together, the text blocks constitute a thread that makes up a complete story. Unless you do something that breaks the thread, they always stay linked automatically.

Figure 6.5 shows three text blocks, placed into three adjacent columns.

Figure 6.5

The anatomy of a PageMaker story with three text blocks in three adjacent columns.

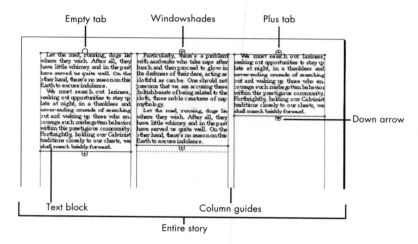

Empty tab · Windowshades · Plus tab

Down arrow

Text block · Column guides

Entire story

The horizontal lines across the top and bottom of each text block are called windowshades. Pull the tabs attached to each windowshade up or down so that they roll and unroll portions of the story's text like an old-fashioned, roller-type windowshade. As the text block expands and contracts in this manner, the text inside the block squeezes in and out of the other blocks in the thread.

Some windowshade tabs contain a symbol. A plain, empty windowshade tab at the top or bottom of a text block indicates that no text is left to be rolled out. A plus sign tab in the top or bottom windowshade shows that there's more text, but it's located in an adjacent text block in the thread—either before or after the selected one. A red down arrow indicates there's more text, but it hasn't been placed.

In Figure 6.6, notice what happens when the bottom windowshade of the second text block is moved upward. The move leaves less room in that text block for the text (less room in the container). As a result, the excess text in that block spills down the story thread into the next text block in the thread.

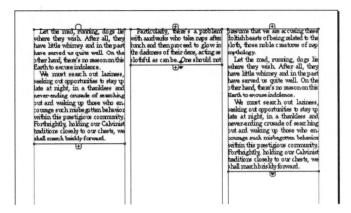

Figure 6.6

Text sliding up and down the thread among the three text blocks.

Drawing a Text Block

Sometimes you need to place text freehand fashion instead of within formal column guides. Use the drag-place move to pour text in this customized way. Draw the confines of the text block onto the page using a click-and-drag movement, which gives you a text block container shaped to your specifications. It looks like a rectangular box. Of course, you can click and drag on the text box any time to adjust the shape of the text block.

To drag-place, you can use any of the three text placement icons. Click and drag down and to the right from the upper-left corner of your text location (see Figure 6.7). Drag-place ignores column guides.

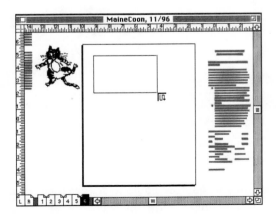

Figure 6.7

You can drag a custom text block using any of the text flow icons.

135

If you press the Shift key while you drag out your custom text block—giving you the Semiautomatic text placement icon—your cursor remains loaded and ready to lay down the next text block when your custom block is filled. Manual and Autoflow leave you with a pointer tool that needs to be reloaded with text if you want to keep going.

Sizing and Positioning Text Blocks

Because text blocks are objects, they can be sized and positioned just like graphic objects. To adjust the size of a text block, use the Pointer tool to grab one of the four handles at each end of the upper and the lower windowshades. The Pointer tool turns into a double-headed arrow resizing pointer, like the one in Figure 6.8. Click a handle and then drag it. The text block changes to a box (the handles disappear), and you can pull the text block into the desired shape and size.

Figure 6.8

Resizing a text block.

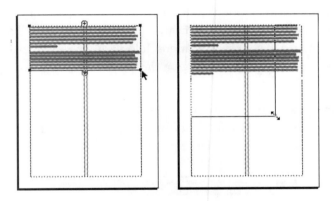

Note

You don't need to worry about distorting the horizontal or vertical shape of the type inside the text block, as you would in some paint or draw programs. Type specifications are assigned internally; all you are doing is changing the shape of the container.

You also can use the windowshades to change the vertical size of a text block without changing its width. By unrolling (or rolling up) text using the windowshades, you can fine-tune the way paragraphs break between columns and pages. To pull a windowshade up or down, click a handle and then drag it and adjust the text break.

Sometimes you might see a dotted line marker just below the end of the text block if PageMaker can't quite place all the text it thinks it ought to. This line is PageMaker's way of telling you how much farther to drag the handle down on the windowshade to place what it thinks would be the ideal amount of text. The dotted line indicates where the text could break, based on the widow and orphan controls you set in the Paragraph Specifications dialog box. Widows and orphans are "left-over" lines or words at the top or bottom of a column. Chapter 7 explains how to use paragraph attributes to automatically avoid them.

Place Centered Text Blocks Across Columns or Pages

You might be tempted to try centering text by eye, just by sliding the text block around on the page. Instead, size the text block completely across the area on which you are centering (a column or page, for example). Then center-align the text using the Control palette (see Figure 6.9) or the Paragraph Specifications or Alignment commands. This enables PageMaker to do the work for you, far more precisely than your eye could do it, by automatically centering your text in your target area.

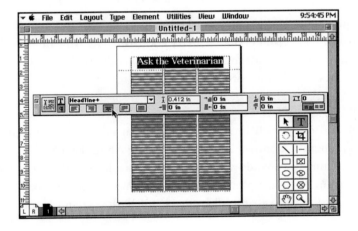

Figure 6.9

PageMaker is better at math than most artists.

PageMaker Filters

When you use the Place command to import text into PageMaker, you are bringing it in through a filter. A filter is software that interprets the text from a word processor or other source, converting it into a form that PageMaker can understand, while (usually) retaining your formatting.

PageMaker 6.5 has more text import filters than previous versions. This should make the process of importing most kinds of text nearly painless. The only problem will be the next round of word processor upgrades with new versions that don't work with the existing filters, but there's a way to handle that as well. Read on.

In almost every case, PageMaker gives you a sturdy and practical translation. Most common text and paragraph formatting attributes (bold, italic, indents, line spacing, paragraph spacing, and so on) are translated successfully. Other features, such as indexing, tables of contents, paragraph borders, and rules vary, depending on the feature set of the word processor. Of course, any word processor that doesn't use style sheets (and there might still be a few in use) won't have styles assigned to its paragraphs when it comes into PageMaker (unless you use style tags—see "Using Style Tags" later in this chapter).

You might wonder, "How do I know which filter to pick?" No problem. PageMaker does a pretty good job of figuring out which filter it should use. It reads the type and creator codes built into the files, and chooses the filter accordingly.

Installed Filter List

To find out which filters you have, open PageMaker and press the (Command) [Control] key while selecting About PageMaker from the Apple menu. A window opens that shows a list of installed filters (see Figure 6.10). It lists plug-ins first, and if you scroll down past those, you see a list of all your installed filters (for both text and graphics files).

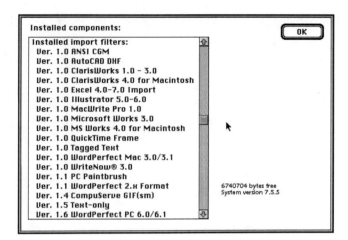

Figure 6.10

Scroll past all the plug-ins to see the filters.

All the obvious word processing options come with PageMaker 6.5, including a complete set of filters for all the Microsoft Word and WordPerfect varieties, a plain text filter (Smart ASCII), filters for various multipurpose integrated Works-type programs, DOS/Windows word processors such as XyWrite, several interchange formats, such as RTF (Rich Text Format) and DCA, and so on. PageMaker 6.5 has strong capabilities for importing database files and spreadsheets. If you do much of this kind of work, especially if you compose tables of information, you should install filters for the spreadsheet and database applications you are most likely to use.

PageMaker 6.0 introduced Tagging import and Export filters, similar to those used by QuarkXPress. In fact, the filter for the tagging language can digest QuarkXPress tags as well as the enhanced tagging codes that PageMaker includes.

Accessing Special Import Features

Some import filters have several options for enhancing the text as it is being imported. To see if there's a special Preferences dialog for any particular filter, press the Shift key as you double-click a document in the Place dialog box, or as you click Open in the Place dialog box. For a few text formats—such as PageMaker stories and plain ASCII text—the Preferences dialog box always comes up whether you press the Shift key or not.

The online help system lists what options are available for which formats under the topic of "Importing format-specific text options."

Note

It's not easy to stay ahead of the software publishers. Just as new versions of PageMaker are released every year or so, new versions of your favorite word processor, graphics, and other programs are almost constantly appearing. Each new "improved" version is slightly incompatible with the previous ones. As new filters are released, you can find them on the Adobe Web site (www.adobe.com) or in the libraries of online services such as CompuServe and America Online. If you can't find the filter you need, consult Adobe Customer Service.

Using Macintosh Easy Open

The Macintosh Easy Open Control panel has expanded the filter universe even more. The Control panel works in the background to pull in special Easy Open filters if you are bringing in text for which you haven't installed a PageMaker filter. The system works transparently, except that you see a second progress indicator sometimes as Easy Open runs a translation.

Exporting Text

Just as you can import text into PageMaker, you can export text back out of it. If you create a story in Story Editor, or do a lot of editing on something you have imported, it's a good idea to save a copy of it as a text file, just in case something unexpected happens. To export text, click the Text tool anywhere in the story that you want to export (or select the specific text you want to export) and choose Export from the File menu. The Export dialog box opens (see Figure 6.11).

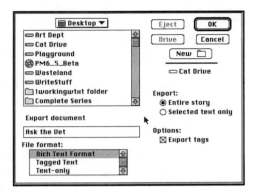

Figure 6.11

You can export your text in whatever format you need.

Choose the format you want to use for exporting the file (Tagging, Rich Text Format, ASCII plain text, Microsoft Word, and so on) by using the scrolling list at the bottom of the dialog box. Depending on your choice, you have various options to consider, such as whether to export with style tags. Many programs can interpret each other's style tags, saving you the trouble of reformatting the text you import. Check the documentation for the program into which you are exporting text. If style tags are supported, the manual or online help should say so. As of this writing, current versions of Microsoft Word and WordPerfect can read style tags.

As you might have noticed when you chose Export from the menu, the Export command gives you other options as well as text or graphics export. PageMaker 6.5 enables you to export your publications as Adobe Acrobat PDF's or as HTML documents for the Web. These are covered in Chapter 16.

EDITING AND MANIPULATING TEXT

Even if you always do your text work in your favorite high-end word processor before going to layout, you inevitably end up editing copy during the page makeup stage.

Fortunately, PageMaker has a built-in text editor (as opposed to a word processor) that's fast and capable called Story Editor.

Story Editor Basics

The Story Editor is a different, more utilitarian view of your publication. All you see are the words, not the layout or graphics.

When you see the Story Editor for the first time, you know right away that you're no longer in Layout view. The Story Editor might seem a bit ugly if you're used to seeing pretty pages (see Figure 6.12).

Figure 6.12

A document in Story Editor view.

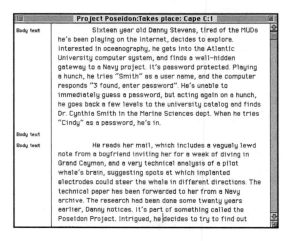

Forget line wrap. Don't even think about seeing your graphics. You don't even get to see your text in the correct font. The Story Editor's job is to let you read, change, and edit the story. Remember, the Story Editor is not a word processor—it's not that fancy. It serves as one if you're in a hurry and need to add some text to a publication. You can use Story Editor to check your spelling, but not your grammar.

Opening a Story and Changing Views

To open the Story Editor view of your text (working from the Layout view) you have several choices, which are discussed in the following sections.

Starting at a Particular Spot in a Story

If you are in Layout view and want to edit a specific point in a story, click an insertion point or select some text in that area. Use the Edit

Story command in the Edit menu and the Story Editor opens at that point in the story.

One of the easiest ways to switch to the Story Editor is to use your Pointer tool and triple-click on any text block belonging to the story you want to edit. The Story Editor pops up with the edit cursor at the top of that text block. Only the Pointer tool can open a story with a triple-click. If you triple-click with the Text tool, you will select a paragraph rather than opening the Story Editor.

You get the same result by using the Pointer tool to select the text block and then choosing Edit Story from Edit menu. The Story Editor opens with the insertion point at the top of that text block.

Returning to Layout View from Story Editor

You can return to Layout view by three different routes, depending on where you want to end up.

The easiest way back to Layout view is to click the Layout window. You will return to where you were before you opened the Story Editor, with all your Story Editor windows remaining open in the background.

You can return to Layout view at the same page you left. Close your story by using the Close story command in the Story menu, pressing (Command-W) [Control-W], or by clicking in the close box in the upper-left corner of the Story Editor. If you left an insertion point blinking in the Layout view and chose the Text tool, that's where you are when you return. Even if you roamed all over your story in the Editor, when you close the Editor window you return to your Layout view starting point.

Returning to an Open Story Window

If you have a story already open, you can reach it regardless of what tool you have chosen and whether you have clicked somewhere in the story. Pull down the Window menu in Layout view and select your story from the list, as shown in Figure 6.13. Only stories that are open in Story Editor are listed on this submenu.

Figure 6.13

If there's a story open, it's listed here.

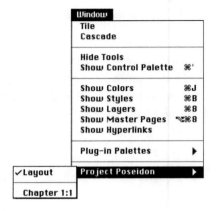

Creating and Editing Text in Story Editor

With no text selected, you can start a new story by using the Edit Story menu. This command gives you a blank Story Editor window. Instead of the title bar indicating the first few words of the story, its label reads *Untitled*.

To import a new story for editing, open Story Editor to a blank page, and then use the Place command to import a file. The resulting dialog box, shown in Figure 6.14, looks and acts like it does in Layout view, except that it's titled Import to Story Editor.

Figure 6.14

If you bring a story into Story Editor first, you can spell check and assign styles before you place it.

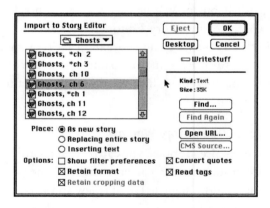

Tip

If you maintain the Link between PageMaker and your original word processor file, you can have instant access to the original. Just use the Edit Original command in the Edit menu. If you need to do a lot of editing, or if you need a Find/Replace function, this is preferable. It's much easier to edit in a word processor, and search capabilities in a program such as Microsoft Word are much more powerful.

Returning to Layout View with Unplaced Text

What happens when you want to return to Layout view, but you have unplaced text in the Story Editor? If you use the (Command-E) [Control-L] method to return to Layout view, you return with a loaded text icon, all set to place your new text. The story window remains open in the background. You can return to your unplaced story in the Story Editor if you get rid of the text icon (by clicking a tool in the Toolbar for example).

You do not get a loaded text icon in the following situations:

◆ If you click the Layout view, leaving the Story Editor without closing it, your new Story remains open in the background as unplaced text, but you come back to Layout without a loaded text placement icon.

◆ If you Quit in Story Editor view, your new text is left unplaced in the Story Editor. When you reopen a PageMaker document with unplaced text in the Story Editor, that story is the first thing you see when you begin your next work session.

◆ If you close the story window using (Command-W) [Control-W] or the upper-left corner close box, you get the dialog box shown in Figure 6.15, and you have to select one of the choices before you can return to Layout view. If you select the Place option, the story window closes, and you have a loaded text icon. You can discard the story, or you can click Cancel and remain in Story Editor.

Figure 6.15

You must place a story or discard it.

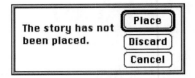

Getting PageMaker to Load with an Open Story

When you quit PageMaker, all the story windows shut down; therefore, when you open PageMaker you need to reopen any stories you want to work on using Story Editor—with one exception. As mentioned earlier, the exception to this rule is any story that has not yet been placed on a page. You might have used Story Editor to create a new story, for example, and you didn't use the Place command, or you might have imported a story that you had not yet placed because you wanted to edit it first. In either case, PageMaker will reopen with the unplaced story right up front.

Note

If you think you have an unplaced story, which you can't seem to locate, quit PageMaker and reopen it. Any unplaced story comes up in Story Editor. If you try to close it, you are given the options of discarding the vagrant story or placing it. This procedure works only for entire stories that have not been placed, not for left over text blocks.

Managing Story Editor Windows

The PageMaker desktop can get pretty crowded, especially if you have several stories open. Figure 6.16 shows one way you can manage all those windows (four are open in the illustration) by using the Cascade command in the Window menu.

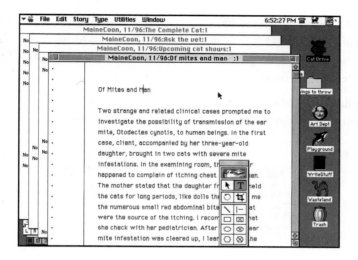

Figure 6.16

Cascade stacks the title bars of open stories so that you can read titles but not full stories.

Instead of viewing a cascade of title bars, you might want to see what's in all those windows simultaneously. In that case, you want a Tile view. Choose Tile from the Window menu to see everything laid out in neat squares like a mosaic. Tile view might be harder to read if you have many windows open.

When you have all those story windows where you can glimpse but not really see into them, the maneuvering can be challenging; however, your Option and Command keys can help.

Press the Option key and click the title bar of any window (including the Layout view) to send that window to the back. This maneuver is particularly useful when you want to get a view of what's behind the front window of a cascade. Using this technique, you can cycle through all your open PageMaker windows.

If you press the (Command) [Control] key and click a title bar, you can drag it around in the background for a better view without selecting it (which brings it to the front).

Story Editor Preferences

As plain as Story Editor seems, you can dress it up a bit and make it more useful at the same time. In the File menu, buried deep within the Preferences command, are three options you can set for Story Editor.

Figure 6.17 shows the dialog box you get when you click the More button in the main Preferences dialog box. Notice the Story Editor section.

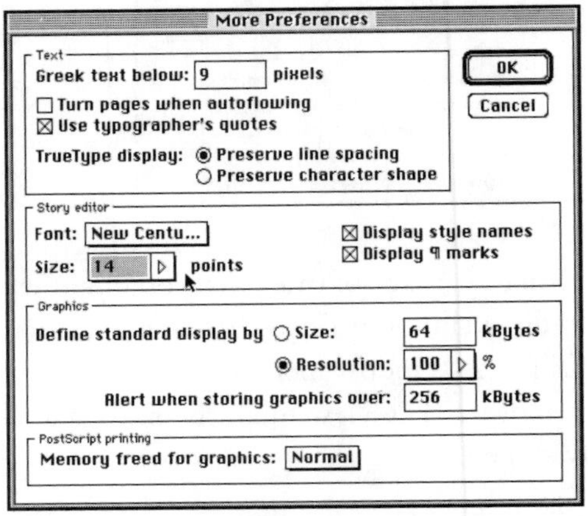

Figure 6.17

Choose a font that's easy to read.

You probably want to select your own favorite, most readable font for use in the Story Editor text display. Many people use their body text font for whatever project they happen to be working on. That way, the Story view looks a bit more like the Layout view. On the other hand, some PageMaker users prefer to view stories in a font that's distinctly different from their body copy, as a sort of visual reminder that they are in Story Editor, not Layout view.

While you are at it, consider setting your Story view display font to a larger size—say, 14 points. It's easier to read, and that's important if you are spending hours in front of the screen.

Assuming you are using the style sheet techniques discussed in this chapter, "Designing a System of Paragraph Styles," turn on the display of styles along the left edge of the Story view window.

Finally, you may find it easier to edit your text if you can see it—all of it. Turn on the Display Paragraphs option, and you can see more than your carriage returns. You also see all the symbols for new line characters, tabs, and spaces (see Figure 6.18).

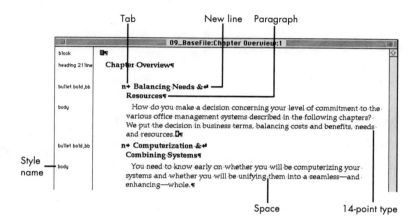

Figure 6.18

The Story Editor set up for optimum usefulness.

Navigating Through Text

Navigating in Story Editor is similar to navigating in your word processing program. You point and click with the mouse and use your arrow keys, and in Story Editor you can use the numeric keypad.

Using the Numeric Keypad

Most of PageMaker's non-mouse text editing power has been concentrated in the keypad—assuming you have the Caps Lock key turned off. You can use the arrow keys, but the keypad does pretty much everything.

Table 6.1 shows the text navigation options for the numeric keypad and the corresponding arrow keys on the keyboard.

TABLE 6.1

KEYBOARD SHORTCUTS FOR NAVIGATING AND EDITING TEXT

Insertion Point Movement	Action To Perform
Up one line	Up arrow or Keypad 8
Down one line	Down arrow or Keypad 2
To beginning of line	(Command) [Control] Option-Left arrow or Keypad 7
To end of line	(Command) [Control] Option-Right arrow or Keypad 1
To beginning of sentence	(Command) [Control]-Keypad 7
To end of sentence	(Command) [Control]-Keypad 1
Left one character	Left arrow or Keypad 4
Right one character	Right arrow or Keypad 6
Left one word	Option-Left arrow or (Command) [Control]-Keypad 4
Right one word	Option-Right arrow or (Command) [Control]-Keypad 6

Scrolling Movement	Action To Perform
Up one paragraph	(Command) [Control]-Up arrow or (Command) [Control]-Keypad 8
Down one paragraph	(Command) [Control]-Down arrow or (Command) [Control]-Keypad 2
Up one screen	Page Up or Keypad 9
Down one screen	Page Down or Keypad 3
To beginning of story	Home or (Command) [Control]-Keypad 9
To end of story	End or (Command) [Control]-Keypad 3

Making Basic Arrow Key Moves

The simplest of the arrow key moves are available both from the numeric keypad's diamond directional orientation or from the regular arrow keys.

The arrows move you a character at a time (right and left arrows) or a line at a time (up and down arrows). And you get the same action from the diamond pattern formed by the 4, 6, 8, and 2 on the numeric keypad. Your keypad arrow keys are in a diamond pattern of 4 and 6 for left and right, 8 and 2 for up and down.

Moving by Lines and Sentences

The corners of the keypad provide you with Home (7), End (1), Page Up (9), and Page Down keys (3). As with a regular word processor, Home takes you to the right end of a line, and End takes you to the left end of a line. To move to the beginning or ending of a sentence, hold down the (Command) [Control] key while pressing Home and End. (Keep in mind these are the Home and End keys on the numeric keypad.)

Scrolling through Stories

Page Up and Page Down on the numeric keypad work as scroll keys that move the display, but not the cursor, up and down a page (a window-full of text) at a time.

If you want to move the cursor to the beginning or end of a story in Story Editor view, hold down the Option key while pressing the Home or End key (as opposed to the keypad numbers 7 and 1).

Selecting Text

PageMaker follows the common word processor convention of selecting text using the Shift key. To select text instead of moving your cursor, hold down the Shift key while performing any of the keystroke maneuvers in this section.

Move to Story End or Beginning with Two Strokes

PageMaker scrolls to the beginning or end of a story with the shortcuts listed in the table, but that's scroll, not navigate. You could look but not edit, you might say.

Just use the scroll commands and arrow keys in combination. To move the cursor to the top of the story, press (Command) [Control]-Keypad 9 or Home, and then left arrow. For the end of the story, it's (Command) [Control]-Keypad 3 or End, plus right arrow.

TABLE 6.2

KEYBOARD SHORTCUTS FOR SELECTING TEXT

Type of Text Selected	Action To Perform
Word	Double-click with Text tool
Paragraph	Triple-click with Text tool
Range	Click insertion point in text, hold Shift, and press a keyboard cursor-movement shortcut

Selecting Large Amounts of Text

You can select the entire story, even unplaced text, by choosing the Select All command from the Edit menu, or use the keyboard shortcut (Command-A) [Control-A].

To select a paragraph, triple-click it. Or click the paragraph's style name in the left margin of Story Editor if that feature is turned on. Double-click a word to select it. Your double-click highlights the word plus its trailing space, and you can type over it or delete it.

Warning

Watch for trailing spaces when overwriting a selected word. PageMaker, unlike many word processors, overwrites the trailing space when you type over a word selected with a double-click. You could easily end up with two words jammed together.

Cutting, Copying, Deleting, and Pasting

The Cut (Command-X) [Control-X], Paste (Command-V) [Control-V], Copy (Command-C) [Control-C], and Clear commands work from the Edit menu in addition to the standard keyboard shortcuts. The Ins (0) and Del (.[decimal]) keys on the numeric keypad are even quicker shortcuts for Cut and Paste.

Your Delete (or Backspace) key can delete in both directions. Hold down the Option key while pressing the Delete key to delete the next character to the right. Press Delete to delete to the left.

Like most word processors, PageMaker works in typeover mode. If you select some text and then insert the Clipboard or just start typing, the new material replaces the old.

CHECKING YOUR SPELLING

Spell check only works in Story Editor. To access spell check, use the Spelling command in the Utilities menu (see Figure 6.19).

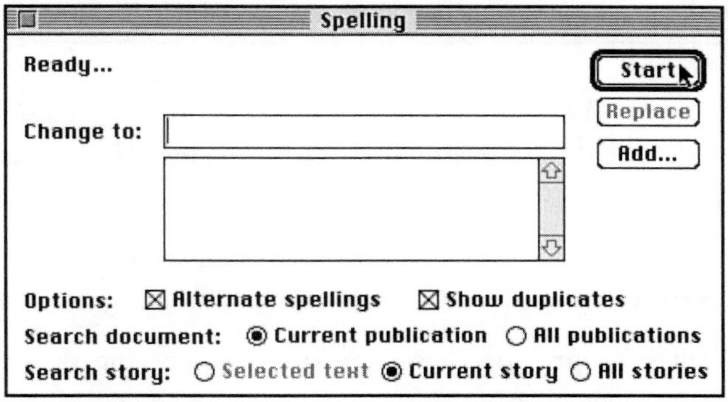

Figure 6.19

You must be in Story Editor mode to use spell check.

First, specify the text that you want to spell check. If you highlighted some text before giving the Spelling command, the Selected Text button is automatically turned on when the dialog box opens. You also can check an entire story, every story in a single publication, and every story in every open publication. You can even check every chapter in your book at the same time. It might take a while, but you can do it.

You can turn off the option for Alternate spellings. PageMaker then locates words that it doesn't recognize, but doesn't take the time to suggest alternates. This option is faster—if you need to be alerted to problems but don't need actual spelling help.

Spell check can find duplicate words, *like like this this*. Just check the option for Show Duplicates. This option, however, does not detect duplicated phrases *like this like this*.

Click the Start button or press Return and the spell check begins. When the spell check finds a problem word, it appears in the dialog box (see Figure 6.20).

Figure 6.20

Choose the correct word from the list of suggestions.

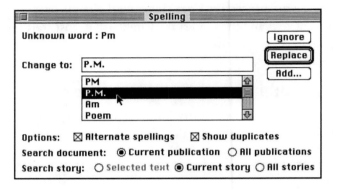

You can move the Spelling dialog box to expose as much of the story as possible. PageMaker highlights each wrong word it finds as it moves through the story, so you can check the word in context.

Click the Replace button to slip the suggested spelling into the text in place of the misspelled word, or double-click the suggested word.

If you click Ignore (or press Return to accept the default Ignore response), PageMaker moves on and ignores the detected word for the rest of that particular PageMaker work session.

Editing the Dictionary

From the spell check, you can add a word to your Spelling/Hyphenation dictionary. Using the Dictionary Editor utility, you can perform large-scale surgery and even create and import dictionaries.

Understanding PageMaker's Dictionary Setup

The dictionary you edit is not the big, mainstream dictionary that comes with PageMaker. Instead, you edit your own personal dictionary that augments the big one. PageMaker doesn't permit you to edit the standard Proximity dictionary at all.

Your personal dictionaries are stored in the language-specific folder (US English, probably), located inside the Proximity folder, inside the Linguists folder, inside your RSRC folder, which is located in the main PageMaker folder. If you want to take a look, your personal dictionary is the one that ends with .udc (which presumably stands for User Dictionary).

Adding or Editing a Single Word

You're only a button away from easy editing of your personal dictionary. The Add button in the Spelling dialog box takes you to the Add Word dialog box (see Figure 6.21).

If you are using more than one dictionary, be sure to check that the proper one is chosen in the list box in the center of the dialog box.

If there's a capitalization issue for the word you are adding, check the Exactly As Typed option. The other option, As All Lowercase, enables PageMaker to take into account all the likely capitalization variations (such as for the first word of a sentence) for spell checking and is the option you most often use when you add a word to the dictionary.

Control hyphenation by inserting tilde symbols (~) before or inside the word. A tilde before the word prevents hyphenation (for a company name, for example) and tilde symbols inserted in mid-word tell PageMaker where to break the word. One tilde marks your optimum break point, two tildes for the next best spot for hyphenation, and three for the least preferable option.

Checking Spelling in Layout View

Although the Spelling command isn't available in Layout view, you can still get to it quickly to check the spelling of a specified word or a short passage of text. Select your text and go into Story Editor (Command-E) [Control-E]. Don't wait for the screen to redraw. Press (Command-L) [Control-L] to open spell check. This technique works well for checking a single word or a couple of paragraphs.

Make sure you have Selected text turned on in the spell check dialog box, not All Publications; otherwise you will be off on a wild chase and lose your spot in Layout view. Press Return to put spell check in motion. You have a single-word spell check in no time. This spell-check-from-Layout tip works even faster if you open Story Editor and open the spell check at the beginning of every PageMaker session. Go back to Layout view without closing the spell check and Story Editor, and you have faster access because they are already loaded into memory. The spell check remembers its setting from use to use. You can set it up for Current Publication and Selected Text in advance for rapid spell checking when flipping back and forth between Layout and Story Editor view.

If you misspell a word when you add it to the dictionary, you can remove it by misspelling it again in exactly the same way, or, you can use the Dictionary Editor utility and pick the word you want to delete from the list.

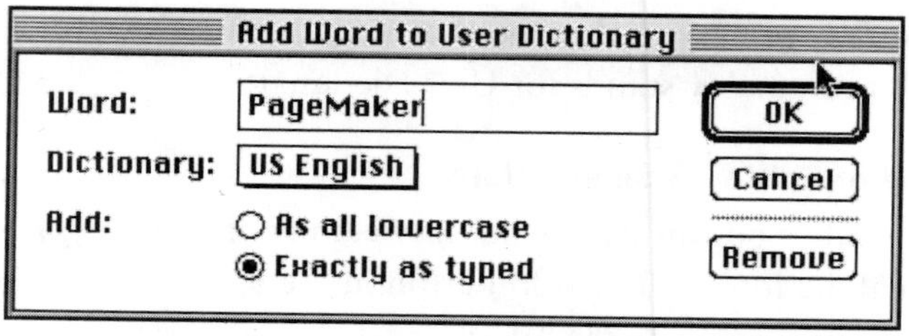

Figure 6.21

Enter the word(s) to add to the dictionary.

Add Word to User Dictionary

Word:	PageMaker	**OK**
Dictionary:	US English	**Cancel**
Add:	○ As all lowercase ⦿ Exactly as typed	**Remove**

Adding, Fixing, and Removing Words with the Dictionary Editor

Inside the Extras folder is an application called Dictionary Editor. Use the Dictionary Editor's File menu to access all the usual commands, such as New, Open, Close, Save, Save As, and Print.

You can use the Print command to print a copy of your personal dictionary for editing and proofing, with the name of the dictionary stamped on every page.

To edit your dictionary, use the File, Open command and look in the language-specific folder inside the Proximity folder for the file with .udc on the end and double-click it. (If you're using the US English dictionary, the .udc file would be in that folder.) When you open the file, you'll get a list of all the words in the dictionary, ready for editing and hyphenation.

To put a word in the edit box, double-click it. Now, you can correct a misspelling, or insert a tilde character [~] to indicate hyphenation. If you are doing a lot of hyphenation, you may get tired of pressing Shift-' all the time. In this Edit Word box, you can press Option and click to get a tilde. Finish all your editing, then click Replace.

If you are adding a word, enter it in the edit box and then click Add. You can remove misspelled words by selecting them (single click) and clicking the Remove button.

Sharing Dictionaries

If you're working with a group on a project, create a standard user dictionary that you all use (and warn users against any individual customizing). You can put special project-oriented words in it so that they are all spelled, hyphenated, and capitalized consistently, then copy this customized and shared user dictionary into the US English folder (or whatever language you are using) on everyone's hard disk.

Importing Dictionaries

You can use the Import command to bring in a text-only (ASCII) file of words and make them into a personal dictionary. This is convenient if you need to add a list of employee names, products, or other frequently-used words. Use the Import command for converting a dictionary from your word processor or to expand one that you already have loaded in the Dictionary Editor.

Choose whether to keep duplicate words or whether you want the inbound dictionary list to overwrite any duplicated words it finds.

When importing a dictionary, you can choose to let PageMaker attempt to hyphenate the incoming words using an algorithm (as opposed to actual dictionary syllable breaks).

Warning

Algorithm hyphenation has some pitfalls. At the very least, it's best to hand check the results for words that you have subjected to the algorithm process. The PageMaker software engine (algorithm) for creating hyphenation is a good one, but if you are a strict "hyphenarian" or work for one, the results might not match your expectations.

Installing Dictionaries

When you finish using the Import command, combining the imported word list with your existing personal dictionary and performing any fine editing, you are ready to install the new word list. Use the Install command so that PageMaker can see your new dictionary. Tell the Dictionary Editor which language folder is to be the storage place for your new personal dictionary.

Exporting Dictionaries

The Dictionary Editor's Export command saves the open dictionary into a text file. This is especially useful if your user dictionary contains a list of product names or terms that you need to verify, or if you need to create a glossary of words that you have used in a publication. Select Export from the file menu and tell the program where to save the file.

Managing Multiple User Dictionaries with a Disable Dictionary Folder

If you already have a user dictionary installed (chances are you do), the Editor asks where to store the old user dictionary when it puts the new one in place. Create a new folder in the Proximity folder to store your disabled dictionaries. This makes it easier to find a dictionary if you want to re-install it.

Converting Non-PageMaker Dictionaries

Before you can import a word processor (or other non-PageMaker source) dictionary, you must find a way to convert it to text (ASCII) format. The easiest way is to open the dictionary in your word processor and use the Save As command to save the file under a new name as ASCII or Text Only. You might need to consult the manual for your word processor to discover where it stores your personal dictionary files.

Many outboard dictionaries don't use tildes to signify hyphenation. If your dictionary uses a regular hyphen or some other symbol, search and replace it in the file to convert it.

FINDING AND CHANGING TEXT

When you need to make a repeated change in your text, use the Find and Change commands. These work exactly as they do in a word processing program. It's the best and fastest way to find and change all instances of a particular word. Suppose you're designing a brochure about your company's new product, WonderCream. Suddenly, the company law-yer calls, and tells you they changed the name of the product to MarvelCream. No problem. Type it once, and all 50 product mentions are changed.

Find and Change can do some other handy tricks too.

Accessing and Starting Find and Change

To use Find or Change, open Story Editor. The commands are grayed out in Layout view. Then, select Change from the Utilities menu (see Figure 6.22) or use the keyboard shortcut (Command-H) [Control-H].

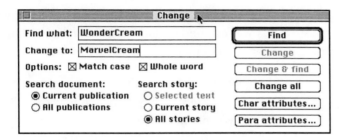

Figure 6.22

Enter the word(s) you want to change.

Find works the same way as Change, except you only see the find part. You can search the same territory with the same options, except you can't replace what you found. The Find dialog box is shown in Figure 6.23.

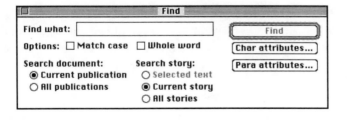

Figure 6.23

Enter the word(s) you want to find.

Select either Find or Change from the Utilities menu, or use (Command-F) [Control-F] (Find) or (Command-H) [Control-H] (Change). If the menu commands are grayed or the keyboard shortcuts have no effect, you probably already have one or the other of the two commands open. They can't both be operative at the same time, so you need to close one before opening the other.

Defining Your Search-and-Replace Parameters

Think of the search process as an exercise in narrowing things down. The process starts with all your text available. Then you limit the nature of your search, say, to the current story as opposed to the entire publication. With the Match Case or Whole Word options, you further define (or limit) your search. Then you get really specific by typing whatever text you want to find in the Find What text box—or by the formatting attributes you set with the Attribute button.

Pre-Load the Find or Change Commands for Faster Access

Like the Spelling command, you get faster response if you have the Story Editor and either the Find or Change command open in the background. (Because you can't have both Find and Change running simultaneously, it makes more sense to open Change. If you don't enter anything in the Change to box, Change will function exactly like Find.) This way, you don't need to wait for them to load into memory when you need them. Just open them up at the beginning of a session and return to Layout view without closing them.

Searching for Text

Computer science majors from Stanford or MIT refer to the text you put in the Find What and Change To boxes as "strings" or "literals." The text represents strings of characters to be taken literally. That's why searching for text is one of those times you face the cosmic truth about telling computers what to do. They do it exactly, nothing more and nothing less. Everything you say, the computer takes literally.

So, if you want to find cat and you enter cats in the Find What box, you won't find cat. You might get cats and catsup, but you won't get cat.

Locating Special Characters

You can use the Find and Change commands to access several other characters in addition to the alphabet and numbers. These characters are listed in Appendix C. A tab, for example, is ^t and a paragraph ending (carriage return) is ^p.

If you need to find a character that is not on the chart, you can search for its ASCII number, a three digit code that's assigned to every key on the keyboard. Search for any ASCII number you want by typing the carat sign (^) followed by the three digits for your search (or replace) character.

You can find the ASCII character for any character in any font by using many of the key cap type aids, such as PopChar.

Note

If you need to add a word—every occurrence of it—to the index, search for the word with the Change command. In the Change to box, type the index entry marker search character, which is ^; (a carat and a semi-colon), followed by the word you want to mark for the index. Press Change all, and that exact word is indexed every time PageMaker finds it in your search area.

Limiting the Search to Whole Words

If you select the Whole word option, you are telling PageMaker you want to find only text that exactly matches what you entered in the Find box—nothing else. To follow on with the cat example, if you enter cat in the Find box and check the Whole word option, cat is the only word PageMaker finds. If you don't check the Whole word option, PageMaker also finds occurrences of catch, catapult, cats, catsup or any other words with 'cat' in them.

Searching for Formatting Attributes

PageMaker can find many of the text attributes you set with the Character dialog box, in addition to any of the paragraph styles you have defined. More importantly, when PageMaker finds them, it can change them.

Revert or Mini-Revert When the Change Command Goes Wrong

Unlike many word processing programs, the Undo command in PageMaker doesn't work after you make a Change move. Keep a mistaken Change operation from ruining your day by always saving before you use the Change command; then you can Revert to the last saved version. Check your results after your search and before performing any other actions, or you might lose your opportunity to make a rescue.

If you forgot to save before using the Change command, you can do a Mini-Revert, which returns your publication to its appearance at the last time the program did an automatic mini-save. To do a Mini-Revert, hold down the Shift key while issuing the Revert command. (PageMaker does a mini-save every time you change the page, insert or delete a page, print, switch between Layout and Story view, use the Clipboard, click the active page icon, or change anything in Page Setup.)

Click one of the two attributes buttons—Char attributes or Para attributes—and you open the dialog boxes in Figures 6.24 and 6.25.

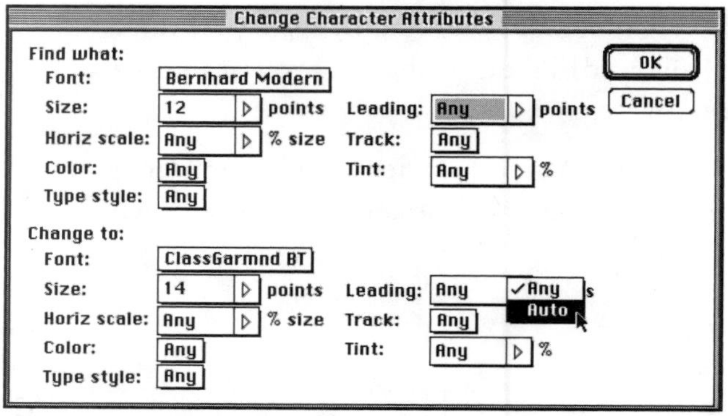

Figure 6.24

The Change Character Attributes dialog box.

Use the Change Button to Test Your Move Before Change All

If you press Change All, you don't have anything further to say about it—no checking to see if you're sure you want to take this drastic step. Instead, you might feel more secure if you use the Find button first. When you find a Change target, use the Change command. Unlike Change & Find, Change stays right there so that you can see if you have done the right thing. Try the Find and Change cycle a couple more times, and when you feel confident that you have programmed your search and replace correctly, then you can select Change All.

You can search for and change globally or instance by instance such character attributes as a specific font, the size of that font, a type style, leading amount, track, color, or tints. You also have the capability to search for and change these paragraph attributes: leading method, paragraph styles, or alignment.

If you want to change all the occurrences of boldface type to italic type, for example, you can set those attributes in the Find what and Change To boxes and then use the Change command to implement the change.

After you set attributes for your search definition, click OK and you return to a slightly modified Change dialog box. The dialog box labels "Change to" or "Find what" are underlined. The underlining is your visual clue that attribute settings are in place.

You don't need to use the Attributes button to get rid of these underlines and their underlying Find or Change attributes settings. Instead, pressing the Option key and clicking on the Attribute button clears the attributes setting.

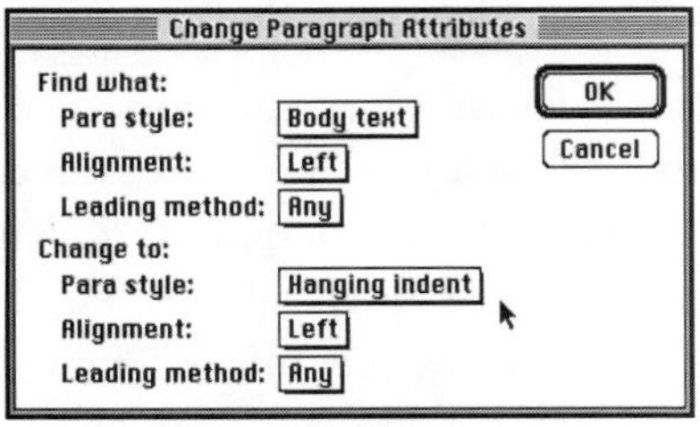

Figure 6.25

The Change Paragraph Attributes dialog box.

Making Changes Happen

When PageMaker finds the word you want to change, it is highlighted. Click Change to make the change, or Change & Find to fix the word and continue to the next. You also have the option of choosing Change all, which immediately implements your change operation for the entire area you have chosen, perhaps your entire publication or selection. Use Change all with caution, or you might make changes you didn't intend. If you change his to her, for example, unless you've made sure to check the Whole word option, you will also change *this* to *ther*. If you goof, the only way back to your original text is by doing a Revert or Mini-Revert.

The Find and Change boxes are like the Spelling command's dialog box in that you can move the dialog box around on the page. Moving the box enables you to see the target text in context when it's found.

Also, you can click the Story Editor box and leave the Find or Change box open in the background. Software engineers call this dialog box behavior non-modal. With the Find or Change box open, you can do a Find Next command using a keyboard shortcut, (Command-G) [Control-G].

SUMMARY

In this chapter, you learned the basics of working with text. You learned how to work with the Text tool to type words directly into a PageMaker publication. You learned how to import text from other sources, and the different ways to place it into a column. You learned all about text blocks—how they function as "containers" for text, how to create and resize them, and how text is threaded from one block to another. You learned about using filters when you import text, to maintain formatting. Next, you learned about the Story Editor, and how to use it to edit your text and check spelling, You learned how to work with PageMaker's spelling and hyphenation dictionary. Finally, you learned about using the Find and Change dialog boxes to change, not only the words themselves, but their appearance on the page.

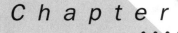

FORMATTING TYPE AND PARAGRAPHS

In this chapter, you learn how to work with type and paragraph formatting tools. You learn about leading and tracking, and how they can make type more readable. You'll discover the differences between manual and automatic kerning, and when to use them. You also learn about working with styles and how to use the style sheet to give your publication a consistent look.

FUNDAMENTALS OF TYPOGRAPHY

Writers *use* words. Typographers *design* with them. Up to this point, you have dealt mostly with the content of your text. Now, you should consider its appearance.

Choosing the right typefaces for a project is more than a matter of readability, although that's an important (and too often ignored) function. Type has a lot to say, even when it says nothing. Consider the following examples (see Figure 7.1).

Figure 7.1

The many faces of type…

Different fonts have different moods and weights. They can be playful or serious, heavy or light. Some suggest a place or a time. Some are unusual, others elegant. Make sure the font you choose is appropriate for the message and for the context. Display faces, such as Stagecoach and Circus are great for posters, but not for newsletters and corporate letterhead, unless your last name is Ringling.

Selecting Type Attributes

You want to design type that has snap; that means picking various type attributes to fit the needs of your publication. Maybe you want to use Bauhaus demi for a special headline. Perhaps the letters should be twice as big as the body copy or the keywords in a quote should be in bold for emphasis. These are type *attributes*.

PageMaker gives you three ways you can set type attributes. The hierarchy runs like this:

- You can use a dialog box (in this case the Character Specifications dialog box).

- You can select from a main menu item or one of its submenus (the Type menu for text).

- You can make many decisions from the Control palette.

The Character Specifications Dialog Box

The Character Specifications dialog box (previous versions of PageMaker called it the Type Specifications dialog box) is the most comprehensive of the three methods PageMaker provides for assigning character attributes. The Character Specifications dialog box contains or connects to all the possible text attributes. It might not be the most direct way to accomplish something in PageMaker, but it's a reliable common denominator.

If you want to make complex type attribute decisions, access the Character Specifications dialog box (see Figure 7.2) from the Type menu, or use the keyboard shortcut (Command-T) [Control-T]. This option has the advantage of permitting you to select more than one attribute in a single move. You can also access text attributes that aren't available through any other methods, such as assigning colors and tints to type, and setting the percentage levels for superscripting and subscripting.

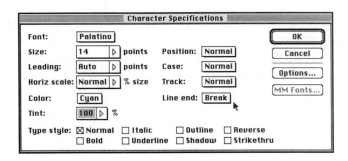

Figure 7.2

You can set all kinds of type attributes here.

Simple Formatting Using the Type Menu

The most direct and least complicated way to make formatting choices is from the Type menu. The submenus provide direct access to the most common formatting choices, without having to get into the complicated Character Specifications dialog box. As you can see in Figure 7.3, many type attributes on the Type menu and its submenus are also available from the keyboard by using various shortcut keys.

Figure 7.3

Use the Type menu to change a single type attribute.

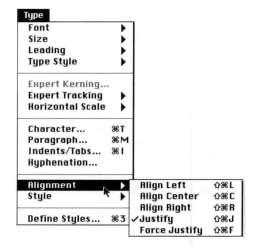

Experimenting with Type Effects Using the Control Palette

Virtually all of PageMaker's typesetting power is available from the Control palette. It's the most direct way to make type attribute decisions.

The Control palette works in Story Editor in both Character and Paragraph views, as do all the commands on the Type menu, except for Hyphenation, Expert Kerning, and the Indents/Tabs commands. (*All* of the Control palette tools and commands are available in layout view.)

Note

Perform text formatting with caution because, for the most part, you work blind in the Story Editor view and can't gauge the effects of your moves. Story Editor view also indicates paragraph indentations by bumping the first line of a paragraph in from the left edge of the Story Editor, but the indents aren't displayed with any accuracy.

Selecting a Typeface

The Type menu lists all the fonts in your system. If you attempt to open a PageMaker document that uses fonts that aren't currently installed, you'll get a dialog box telling you which fonts PageMaker is substituting for the missing ones. In the Type menu, the missing fonts are listed followed by the name of the substituted fonts enclosed in brackets.

Selecting a particular typeface for your text is easy, regardless of which of the three text formatting methods you choose: the Character Specifications dialog box, the Type menu, or the Control palette. Choose fonts from the pop-up list in the dialog box or the Control palette, or from the list on the Font sub-menu.

Seeing Your Typefaces in Real Time

Deciding which typeface you want is easy if you have one of the Macintosh tools, such as WYSIWYG Menus by Now Utilities, that displays type on the menu as it will appear on the page. Some lists even group various font families. You also can use a KeyCaps type program, like the one included with the Macintosh System, to get a global view of what the characters in a typeface look like.

Windows users can achieve a similar result by opening the Font Control Panel and using it to preview fonts, or by installing a font viewing utility such as TrueView, FontShow, or Typecast. These are all shareware programs, available from typical shareware sources such as America Online or the Internet.

Choosing a Type Size

In PageMaker, type sizes can be from 4 to 650 points, in increments of a tenth of a point. You choose type sizes with the same three methods you use to select a typeface.

Putting on a Good Face

Trying out wild typefaces can be so much fun that you might lose sight of the goal—to communicate. Before committing to a design, print a sample page and hold it up at arm's length. If you can't read it easily, maybe even with your reading glasses removed, try to figure out why and consider tweaking the design. It might be a simple matter of making the type larger or giving the lines of type more space (leading). Don't use display type for body copy. The more complex letter forms don't work in small sizes.

Sizing Type

In the Character Specifications dialog box shown in Figure 7.4, you can either type in a type size, specified within a tenth of a point or you can select from a list of type sizes in whole numbers by clicking the arrow to the right of the type Size field. Remember, you can also open this box by pressing (Command-T) [Control-T].

Figure 7.4

Selecting the type size from the Character Specifications dialog box.

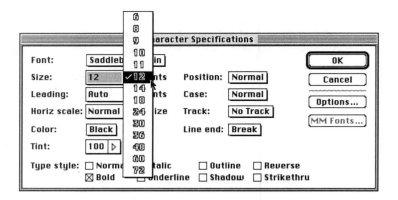

You can select a whole number type size from the Type menu by using the Size submenu. Use the Other option to type in a fractional point size.

Utilizing the Control Palette

Personally, if I need an "other" size of type or need to change a font's appearance, instead of using the Type menu's Size submenu, I either use the Control palette or the Character dialog box—it's much faster.

In general, the Control palette is the quickest way to accomplish most PageMaker actions; you might find, however, that it takes up a lot of screen room. The solution is to rest your right thumb and a finger on the (Command) key or [Control] key and apostrophe combination that toggles on and off the Control palette. If the Control palette comes up in Paragraph view, you can toggle to Character view by using (Command-Shift-') [Control-Shift-'] and use the same command to toggle back to Paragraph view.

PageMaker In the Real World

Adjusting Type Size with Keystrokes

Experiment with your type size choices directly from the keyboard by using the (Command-Shift->) [Control-Shift->] or the (Command-Shift-<) [Control-Shift-<] shortcut. The (Command-Shift->) [Control-Shift->] combination increases type size and the (Command-Shift-<) [Control-Shift-<] combination shrinks the type, toggling among the type sizes you find listed in the Type menu—a limited range of sizes. If you want to adjust type size in smaller increments, add the (Option) [Alt] key to the chord. Use (Command-Shift-Option->) [Control-Shift-Alt->] for bigger sizes in one-point jumps and (Command-Shift-Option-<) [Control-Shift-Alt-<] for smaller.

Setting Type Defaults

If you select the Text tool but don't click anywhere in the publication, you can make text attribute decisions before you actually put the Text tool to work. This creates one of the mini-defaults described in the section on "PageMaker Preferences" in Chapter 1.

To set a mini-default for the Text tool, make text-formatting decisions with the Text tool chosen but with no text selected. When you set a mini-default, it overrides any previous defaults you've set for that publication or for PageMaker in general.

Measuring Type Size—Picas, Points, and Ems

Traditionally, typography has been measured in picas and points. In the Preferences dialog box, you can set PageMaker's measuring system to picas, inches, millimeters, or even Ciceros, a measurement system used in Europe. Ciceros are slightly larger than picas; the name derived from a 1458 edition of the works of Cicero, in which the measurement was first used.

Type is traditionally measured in points. There are 72 points in an inch. Check out the PageMaker ruler in Figure 7.5 to see what a pica looks like compared to an inch. Six picas are in an inch; twelve points are in a pica. Picas, being much larger than points, are usually used to delineate page-sized specifications such as margins.

Figure 7.5

PageMaker rulers set side by side to compare picas and inches.

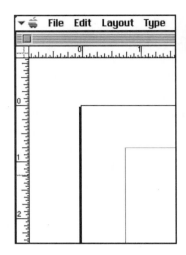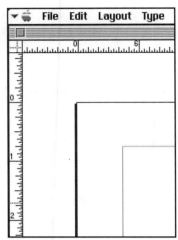

Varying Point Sizes

For any given size of type expressed in points, the apparent visual size of the characters varies—sometimes by a lot. This means 24-point Bauhaus is different from 24-point Avant Garde, which is different from 24-point Lubalin Graph (see Figure 7.6). This happens because the type has been designed to look good on a certain height of line, taking into account all the parameters of the type such as the relative height of the round tummy of the lowercase letter "b," (properly called the bowl) compared to the ascender, or height of the vertical stem.

PageMaker In the Real World

Figure 7.6

Typefaces vary in apparent height, even though they are the same point size.

Hi, I'm in 24 point Bauhaus

Hi, I'm in 24 point Palatino

Hi, I'm in 24 point Palatino Bold

Hi, I'm in 24 point Avant Garde

Hi, I'm in 24 point Lubalin Graph

Hi, I'm in 24 point Times

This traditional measuring system of picas and points helps communication with designers and others in the publishing and printing trade who use this method. Picas and points also make it easier to understand the size relationships between type and other page elements, such as margins. Knowing, for instance, that a half inch margin at the top of a page is 36 points high provides a reference point for choosing headline type. A font larger than 36 points will be more than a half inch high. Similarly, a half inch square inline graphic (a picture or symbol placed in a line of type) will disrupt the leading unless the type is 36 points tall or more.

Em spaces are the width of an em dash as opposed to an en dash. The names come from the widths occupied by the letter M, as opposed to the letter N. Each font has a slightly different sized character M, depending on its size and what the designer had in mind when creating the letter. Em dashes and en dashes are, incidentally, the most misused punctuation marks. Em dashes are used—in informal writing—to set off a phrase or thought. En dashes are used only with numbers. Typists used to use two hyphens to indicate an em dash and used one hyphen to replace an en dash. In most fonts, hyphens are a little smaller than a true en dash. There's also a "thin" space, which is a quarter of an em wide.

Em spaces are used for measuring kerning to improve the appearance of the type by adjusting the space between individual letters. It is important to make the adjustment in context—in proportion to the size of that particular font. Making the adjustment in the em width means the tiny kerning adjustment increments are automatically in proportion to that font's characters.

An em for any given typeface is almost always equal to the point size of the typeface. So 10-point type has a 10-point wide em.

For trivia freaks, PageMaker's internal software code can handle a measurement of one twip, which is 1/1440th of an inch. A twip? It stands for TWentieth of a Point.

Leading

The term *leading* comes from the old days when type was set by hand. The line spacing was achieved with strips of metal (lead or brass) that fit between the lines of type (called slugs). In those days, a typesetter might have added two points of leading to a section of type, meaning that a two-point thick shim of metal had been inserted to space out the slugs of type on the page.

In desktop publishing, leading has generally come to mean something different from the traditional definition. The Leading command in PageMaker sets the total space occupied by the line of type. That's the point size of the type, plus the amount of leading as it would have been expressed in the old days. A typographer, using PageMaker, might say that type has been set "11 on 13", or "11 over 13", meaning 11-point type in 13-point leading (11 points of type plus two points of old-fashioned leading).

Figure 7.7 shows a series of PageMaker slugs with different amounts of leading. In each case, some type has been highlighted by using the Text tool to reveal the height of the slug.

Figure 7.7

PageMaker slugs with different amounts of leading.

When the typesetter punched out this slug, he was slugged by the editor. This was no surprise, since the typesetter had made this type 14 points on 14 points leading.

When the typesetter punched out this slug, he was slugged by the editor. This was no surprise, since the typesetter had made this type 14 points on 16 points leading.

When the typesetter punched out this slug, he was slugged by the editor. This was no surprise, since the typesetter had made this type 14 points on 20 points leading.

When the typesetter punched out this slug, he was slugged by the editor. This was no surprise, since the typesetter had made this type 14 points on 24 points leading.

Unfortunately, PageMaker's leading scheme spreads the leading functions between two locations in the menu system. You set the amount of leading in the Character Specifications dialog box (13 points, 14 points, autoleading); however, you set the method for calculating that amount of leading (proportional, baseline, top of caps) in the Paragraph Specifications dialog box. Even more confusing, if you select autoleading in the Character Specifications dialog box, you must go to the Paragraph Spacing dialog box (reached from within the Paragraph Specifications dialog box) to adjust the percentage used to compute the autoleading amount. The solution is to select a leading scheme and stick with it. The leading method is a fundamental decision, but as long as you apply any one method consistently, your pages come out fine.

Choosing Your Leading Method

PageMaker must have a reference point for measuring out and calculating the effects of leading. PageMaker offers you three leading methods, which are essentially three choices of reference points:

◆ Proportional

◆ Baseline

◆ Top of caps

Before we discuss these, let's stop and define some terms. Study the example in Figure 7.7. These are slugs of type set in PageMaker, with the height of the slug revealed by selecting a chunk of text with the Text tool. The height of a slug, in PageMaker terms, is the total vertical space taken up by a line, including the type and its leading. If you specify 14-point leading, you get a slug 14 points tall. The baseline is quite simply an imaginary line drawn at the base of the characters.

In proportional leading, the standard method in PageMaker, the baseline serves as the reference point to divide the slug. One third of the slug falls below the baseline and two thirds above it, the 1/3:2/3 proportion giving the method its name.

In baseline leading, the leading slug is measured up as many points as you define from the baseline. This is more like the traditional method of leading, where the typesetter added a narrow strip of lead above the strip of type, adding the point size of the type and the leading.

With the Top of Caps leading method, the baseline is determined by the height of the tallest capital letter in the line. The baseline floats inside the slug, its precise location depending on the characteristics of that font. (If you intend to place a "dropped cap," you cannot use this leading method. If you tried, the leading would follow the line of the dropped capital letter and would interfere with the rest of the line of type.)

If you are a long-time PageMaker user, you might want to stick to proportional leading, which has been PageMaker's default since version 1.0. Otherwise, use baseline leading. It lets you know exactly where the type will appear and gives you an easy reference point for placing a second block of type below the first.

Note

Much of the PageMaker measuring system (rules for one example, baseline shift for another) depends on knowing where the baseline falls in a slug. With baseline leading and proportional leading, you assign the baseline to a specific position—either at the bottom of the slug, or a third of the way up. With top of caps leading, however, you can't be sure how far down into the slug the baseline will land. It varies with the font. Big problem unless you are striving for some sort of special effect, ignore top of caps leading.

Setting the Leading

As you can see in Figure 7.8, the Character dialog box enables you to type in your leading setting or choose from a pop-up list. As with the type size function, you can enter a leading amount in increments of a tenth of a point or choose from a pop-up list of PageMaker's "best guesses" for leading amounts based on the point size of the type you select. If, for instance, you're using 24-point type, PageMaker includes leading amounts in the pop-up list from 23 points to 26 points in half point increments, plus larger amounts of 36, 48, and 72 points, which would be the equivalents of a 1 1/2 spaces, double space, or triple space on a typewriter.

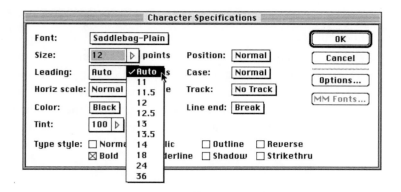

Figure 7.8

Leading two points larger than the type is generally correct.

Likewise, with the same degree of precision, you can set leading from the Control palette by typing in the amount you want or by using the arrow located to the right of the leading box to get a list of best guess choices.

In the Type menu there is a direct-access submenu for Leading that enables you to choose from among PageMaker's best guesses for leading settings. Also, like the Type Size submenu, you have a choice for Other that enables you to type in a more precise amount of leading. If you know you need a custom leading setting, it's quicker to use the Control palette or the Character Specifications dialog box.

Automating with Autoleading

Notice each leading list includes an option for Autoleading. Autoleading is the PageMaker factory-set default, so that's what you get unless you specifically tell the program to use fixed leading.

Autoleading multiplies the point size of your text by 120% and uses that leading. PageMaker makes this autoleading calculation based on the largest type in a line of text. You can autolead a single line (applying your own leading amounts to the rest of the document) or use autoleading for the entire publication. Unless you're trying for special effects, or need to adjust the number of lines within a block of text, you might as well go with autoleading and let PageMaker do the work.

You can adjust the autoleading calculation to something other than 120% by clicking the Option button in the Paragraph Specifications dialog box.

Using Baseline Shift

Baseline shift is a typographic "trick" that enables you to create some interesting effects, making a chosen letter, word or phrase rise above, or sink below the rest of the line of type. You can apply it from the Character Specifications Options dialog box or from the Control palette. Decide how many points above or below the baseline to position the selected text and whether the text is going to jump up or sink down.

Figure 7.9

Baseline shift can raise or lower letters relative to the baseline.

A hair raising experience may be demoralizing

Superscript and Subscript

Superscript and subscript are those tiny little numbers that ride above (super) or below (sub) the baseline. They're used for numbering footnotes, in mathematical notation, and occasionally for special effects. Superscript and subscript make use of baseline shift, as well as changing the point size of the type. Selecting superscript or subscript does the dual task of resizing and relocating the type.

The most direct way to create the scripts is to use the Control palette. Use the position buttons right below the font selection field—the buttons with the letter S and a choice between an up- or down-arrow for superscript or subscript.

You also can set the scripts from the Character Specifications dialog box by using the Position function. Click the box and a pull-down menu gives you a choice of Normal, Subscript, or Superscript. The sub- and superscript options are not available from the Type submenus. Use the Options dialog box in the Character Specifications menu to set a custom point size and position for subscript or superscript type, and to determine the amount of baseline shift.

Giving Your Type Weight and Style

In Table 7.1, you can see that PageMaker has many options for weighting and styling your type—bold, italic, underline, outline, shadow, and strikethrough. There's also a reverse style, used to etch out the shape of your type against a contrasting background, letting the underlying paper show through.

When typographers talk about the weight of type, they mean whether it is bold or italic. Italic is generally considered lighter than normal type and bold is heavier. Some faces are called *black* because they use thicker characters and require more black ink. They are the heaviest.

TABLE 7.1

PAGEMAKER TYPE AND STYLING OPTIONS

Type Styling	Keyboard Shortcut	
	Macintosh	Windows
Bold	Command-Shift-B	Control-Shift-B
Italic	Command-Shift-I	Control-Shift-I
Underline	Command-Shift-U	Control-Shift-U
Outline	Command-Shift-D	Control-Shift-D
Shadow	Command-Shift-W	Control-Shift-W
Strikethru	Command-Shift-/	Control-Shift-/
Reverse	Command-Shift-V	Control-Shift-V

The three standard techniques for accessing PageMaker commands hold true for applying all the type style keyboard shortcuts you see here. In the Character Specifications dialog box, you have a series of checkboxes to select or deselect each option. In the Type menu, the Type Style submenu lists the same options, which you can select by clicking them. In the Control palette, use the buttons below the typeface name field. You can remember which button does what from the first initial on the buttons and the appearance of the labeling letters. B stands for Bold and is a thicker letter than N, or Normal. I is Italic and is set at a slant. Outline shows the letter O outlined, and so on. Use the arrow keys to move between the options and turn them on and off by using the Spacebar.

The easiest way to use the options is with the keyboard shortcuts. The shortcuts are displayed beside their matching commands in the Type menu and submenus. They are also listed beside their respective text styles in Table 7.1

Note

The reverse attribute technically isn't a type style or weight. Reverse styling doesn't change the shape or thickness of a letter's strokes; it sets the type to the color of paper. This means that if you put a black box behind it, the reversed type cuts through the black to the paper behind it. Why not assign the color white to the type? That won't work if one of the printing plates has white ink. It also avoids confusion if you are working on non-white paper.

Outline and Shadow Type

Try to restrain your urge to use Outline and Shadow type attributes for anything but extremely limited circumstances. In the early days of the Macintosh, these styles were included for fun. Today, they only brand your publication as done on a Macintosh by a nonprofessional. Even worse, they're hard to read.

The pros don't use underlining often, either. The underline habit comes from the old manual typewriter days, when no other typographical tool was available to give emphasis. Use bold and italic type styles instead.

Italic type slants to the right. In some typefaces, italic styling can make it look as if you left out the space after an italicized word as your text switches back to normal (Roman) type. Try formatting the space following the italicized word (the word space, as a typographer would say) in normal type. That generally is more suitable spacing than the italic word space provides.

In headlines, try kerning the space between the italicized and roman typeset words. (Kerning is covered in this chapter's section on "Spacing Pairs of Letters with Kerning.") As a last resort, try using an em space or an en space, after the italic text. These special spaces tend to be wider than regular spaces. Type an em space with (Command-Shift-M) [Control-Shift-M]. An en space is (Command-Shift-N) [Control-Shift-N]. You can even try a thin space, which is (Command-Shift-T) [Control-Shift-T].

Small Caps

Small Caps set a title in capital letters, with smaller capital letters replacing the lowercase (see Figure 7.10).

THIS IS A HEADLINE
IN SMALL CAPS!
THIS IS A
HEADLINE
IN ALL CAPS!

Figure 7.10

Small Caps look better and take up less space than all caps.

If you want to adjust the relative height of the small caps and big caps in the small caps case styling option, click the Options button in the Character Specifications dialog box. The Type Options dialog box appears and you can adjust PageMaker's default figures. This is the same dialog box used for baseline shift and for customizing settings for subscript and superscript.

PageMaker sets the default for lowercase small caps at 70%. Many type designers feel it should be bigger—maybe 80%—to be more like traditional small caps styling. Some people also like to set small caps a little wider to aid legibility.

ADJUSTING HORIZONTAL SPACE

Three PageMaker type attributes—kerning, width, and tracking—have a lot to do with the space a line of type occupies on the page. It's important not to confuse width or tracking with kerning, although they have similarities.

◆ **Kerning** sets the space between specific pairs of letters.

◆ **Tracking** is an automated way to adjust the amount of space between characters over a range of text and to make that adjustment in proportion to the size of the type.

◆ **Width** adjusts the horizontal width of letters without changing the space between them and without changing their height.

Kerning Pairs of Letters

PageMaker makes it possible for you to make extremely fine adjustments to the space between letters, called *kerning*. You can adjust spacing by a little as 1/1000 of an em, or a bit more than a single dot on a 1,200 dpi imagesetter.

Why would you want to kern a pair of letters? Deciding whether to kern is pretty subjective, but aside from special effects you use kerning to make spacing adjustments that make your type more readable and more attractive. Manual kerning is generally only applied to type in headlines, or type over 18 points, but you can auto-kern type of any size.

You almost always adjust letter kerning by pairs. Because of the differences in letter shapes, sometimes more space appears between specific pairs of letters than between others in the surrounding text. Making some adjustment on the letters T and O, for example, is common (see Figure 7.11). In unadjusted type, the crossbar of the T ends before the circle of the O begins on the line. You can adjust a pair of letters so that they nestle together without encroaching on one another.

Figure 7.11

Kern letters so that they don't touch each other.

TO

TO

TO

It's possible to select many letters and kern the whole range of them, but that's like performing surgery with an ax. When you must adjust the overall space occupied by a group of letters, assign tracking—not kerning (see following section on tracking).

Manual Kerning

When you are kerning manually, you need to see what's happening to your letter pairs as you work. For that reason, it's best to use PageMaker's keyboard commands to perform fine kerning work. (That is, it is better to use keyboard commands unless you need 1/1000 em kerning, which you must do in the Control palette.)

To remove space between letters, use (Control-left arrow) [Alt-left arrow] (4/100 em). Subtract extremely fine kerning amounts with (Control-Shift-left arrow) [Control-Alt-left arrow] (1/100 em).

To add space between letters, use (Command-right arrow) [Alt-right arrow] (4/100 em). Add extremely fine kerning with (Command-Shift-right arrow) [Control-Alt-right arrow] (1/100 em).

You also can kern with the Control palette, using your mouse and the nudge buttons in the same way you would do keyboard kerning. These nudge button moves take effect instantly, giving you real-time visual feedback on the effect of your changes.

You can enter a kerning amount in the kerning box of the Control palette; your changes won't be visible, however, until you apply them by using the Apply button, pressing the Tab key, or pressing Return. The Control palette comes in handy if you know the precise amount of kerning you want to apply. This direct entry method is the only way to access 1/1000 em kerning. Type in a number with three digits to the right of the decimal point in the kerning text box.

Remove all your manual kerning by selecting the text and pressing (Command-Option-K) ([Shift-Control-0] (not on numeric keypad)). If you use the Control palette, highlight the text and enter a zero in the kern box.

Expert Kerning

Expert Kerning uses a special set of rules to examine every pair of letters in your selected text and tune them to optimum spacing. To use Expert Kerning, select the text that must be formatted in a PostScript Type 1 font and turn off tracking and automatic kerning in the paragraph where the text is located. Access Expert Kerning by selecting the command from the Type menu (see Figure 7.12).

Figure 7.12

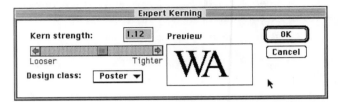

The Expert Kerning dialog box.

The pull-down Design class list enables you to give the plug-in's expert rules more information about the kind of type you are kerning. The rules try to take into account the basic design of the type in several different classifications. You can also click the Other button and enter a type size. Keep in mind that a font designer builds a font with a certain range of sizes in mind. That's where you should start working with Expert Kerning, using the designer's intent as a guideline.

PageMaker recommends that you use Expert Kerning only for very small blocks of type, such as headlines, because it can be extremely time consuming. In smaller fonts, the adjustments will generally be so subtle that the difference between Expert Kerning and Autokerning is imperceptible.

Automatic Kerning

PageMaker typesetting shines at automatic kerning. Most fonts are designed so that several hundred pairs of letters (and sometimes many more) are predefined for kerning whenever they appear together in a line of type. That's assuming the software is programmed to take advantage of these built-in *kern pairs*, as they're called. Generally, word processors are unable to take advantage of these built-in kerning pairs. PageMaker, however, puts the type designers' specifications to work when you turn on the Pair Kerning option. Because pair kerning obviously deals with characters, it ought to be included in the Character Specifications dialog box; it's not. For reasons known only to the creators of PageMaker, you turn on automatic kerning in the Paragraph Specifications Spacing dialog box.

The question is, at which type size should this automatic kerning trigger into operation? The smaller the type, the more difficult it is for the eye to discern any kerning effect. There's a point of diminishing returns. PageMaker is set so that automatic kerning takes effect on all justified type of sizes above four points. You might as well leave it there. You won't really see the effects until you're working with much larger type, but it makes the adjustments as the designer intended.

Tuning Overall Letter Spacing with Tracking

People sometimes refer to tracking as track kerning. This tends to annoy typographers because—for most of them—kerning is something you do on a letter-by-letter basis. Tracking adjusts the spacing of large expanses of text and does it with no regard to the individual pairs of letters. Tracking doesn't care if it's squeezing together a combination of T and O or the space between an O and an A.

Tracking choices range from no tracking at all, to very loose, to very tight. Apply tracking from the Type menu, the Character dialog box, or the Control palette. The tracks are individually tuned for each font, with many standard Adobe font settings included with PageMaker. If a font isn't in the PageMaker tracking database, a generic tracking setting kicks in.

Figure 7.13 shows how tracking adjusts the space between letters. In that way, it's sort of like simultaneously kerning a bunch of letters. You can also see that the tracking setting makes a big change in the width a given selection of type takes up on the line.

Tracking set very loose on 12 point type

Tracking set normal on 12 point type

Tracking set tight on 12 point type

Tracking set very loose on 9 point type

Tracking set normal on 9 point type

Tracking set tight on 9 point type

Figure 7.13

The effect of various Track settings.

PageMaker's tracking table system makes spacing adjustments on the basis of the point size of the selected type. The tracking table tries to keep the adjustment in proportion to the type. So a given tracking scheme applied to six-point type might actually spread it out a bit to make it more readable. On the other hand, that same tracking setting might tighten up 18-point type quite a bit because large type can tolerate space squeezing better while maintaining its readability.

Adjusting the Width of a Type Selection

The Horizontal Scale option expands or reduces the width of every letter in your text selection, which is a lot like the condensed and expanded effect you find in many word processors. In other words, Horizontal Scale, like tracking, changes the total line space taken up by a group of words, but it does so by changing the character width, instead of the spacing. (It does change the width of the space character, and therefore effects word spacing.) Except for some special effects, fine typographers generally don't use the Width command because it distorts the type shape.

Adjust the width of your text selection by giving it a percentage, with 100% being normal. To do this, access Horizontal Scale in the Type menu, the Character Specifications dialog box, or the Control palette.

Using Line End To Prevent Line Breaks

People make these typographical adjustments (width, tracking, kerning) to fit text on a line or page. The Line End function helps with this copyfitting task. You also can use it for special text, such as numbers or names that should be kept together on one line, with no break.

Highlight the characters that you need to glue together. In the Character Specifications dialog box, find the Line End function and choose No Break. This prevents breaks at the end of a line. You can see the effect and how to choose it in Figure 7.13.

A width setting of 80%

A width setting of 90%

A width setting of 100%

A width setting of 110%

A width setting of 120%

Figure 7.14

The effect of various width settings.

COPYFITTING

There's not much that a writer or editor is willing to tell a designer or graphic artist about copyfitting, other than "keep your grubby paws off." Writers are extremely jealous of their words. Of course, if you're the writer on the project as well as the layout person, the words you change are your own and you can do whatever you want to them.

Most of the time, you can make words fit by adjusting the tracking or leading. You can use a slightly smaller type size, but sometimes you have to change the copy to fit. If you're not the writer, ask the writer to work with you to make them fit. Often, it's just a question of substituting a shorter word for a longer one. You might be able to abbreviate or use a symbol such as a dollar sign. Using figures instead of spelling out numbers (33 instead of thirty-three) can save a lot of space. (It's generally taboo in headlines, though.) Removing repetitive, redundant adjectives saves space and improves the quality of the writing, in most cases.

In the advertising business, copywriters are given a space to fill and told approximately how many characters per inch the type font permits. They write to fit, knowing that if they don't, the art director might chop off the excess. If you're working with a writer on any kind of project, giving him or her a word count saves time and aggravation for all concerned. To do this most efficiently, decide first what font(s) you want to use. Allow six letters per word and determine how many six letter words fit across a column and how many lines per vertical inch. A little math, and you know that your 12-point Bookman permits between three and four words per line in a two inch wide column, and between five and six lines per column inch. So a block an inch high by two inches wide holds 25 words or less. Figure out how much space you have to fill, if space is critical, and let the writer write to fit.

FORMATTING PARAGRAPHS

After type, the paragraph comes next in the hierarchy of PageMaker pages. There's a common misconception about PageMaker paragraphs. In PageMaker, any text that ends with a carriage return symbol (¶)is a paragraph, even if it's just one word; therefore, each time you press the Return key, you mark a paragraph.

You can't see paragraph markers in the Layout view of PageMaker, but you can see them in Story Editor view (see Figure 7.15). Notice each paragraph has a ¶ symbol at the end of it.

Figure 7.15

Be sure to select Display ¶ from Story Editor's Type menu.

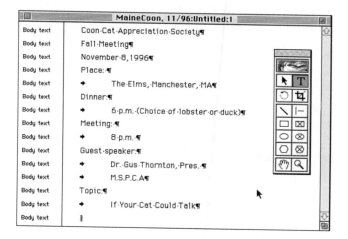

Indents, centering, justification, tabs, leading scheme, paragraph rules, control for widows and orphans, hyphenation schemes—these are paragraph-based attributes. You cannot apply tabs or indents or any of the other paragraph level attributes to just a few characters or words within a paragraph. PageMaker won't let you. These typesetting options apply to the entire paragraph.

You can apply a paragraph-based formatting attribute by clicking anywhere in the paragraph, knowing it will apply to the whole thing. Instead of selecting all the text in the paragraph—just click anywhere inside the paragraph text.

Also, the paragraph-based formatting attributes move with the paragraph marker. You can copy and paste a paragraph marker from one paragraph to another, and all the attributes in the first paragraph are transferred to the second paragraph. Think of the paragraph symbol as a sort of storage bin for the formatting for any particular paragraph.

Text Alignment Options

The following list describes the text alignment options and also lists their keyboard shortcuts. You can find these in the Alignment submenu of the Type menu. You can also set alignment on the Paragraph Control palette, reached by clicking the paragraph symbol on the Type Control palette.

- **Align Left** text is flush against the left side of the column, making a straight line of text along the left side. Sometimes you hear flush left alignment called ragged right, referring to the ragged edge you get along the right side because you are only aligning the left side of the column.

- **Align** or ragged left is the opposite of flush right—aligned along the right side of the column.

- **Align Center** is centered on the line(s). PageMaker automatically calculates the space occupied by the letters on the centered line, divides that distance in half, and places the center point of each line of text precisely on the horizontal midpoint of the column of type.

- **Justify** aligns text both ways, presenting a straight line down both the left and the right side of the column. PageMaker offers real typographic sophistication compared to any of the word processors (adjustable everything, from hyphenation to word and letter spacing).

♦ **Force Justify** stretches text across a column, even if that means putting a half-inch of space between two words on the line. It is used only for special effects, such as evenly spacing the letters of a single word across a column.

Flush Text versus Justified Text

Because English speaking users read the language from left to right, most agree that body copy should be set either flush left or justified. That way, your eye always knows where to go when it moves down the page because everything is lined up on the left side of the column. The controversy concerns what to do with the right side of the column—should you line it up (justified type) or rag it (flush left/ragged right)?

Because it has a ragged edge along the right side, flush left alignment gives your text an informal feel. The bumps of white space along the non-aligned edge have the effect of opening up the copy. Justified text fills all the space in a column; therefore it looks darker and because both ends of each line are even along the column edges, there's a formal feel to justified type.

Instead of always using justified or left aligned type, experiment with both on every project to see what's best for that particular situation. It's the only way to account for all the variables.

Note

What about flush right? It's harder to read, but it is useful in certain cases, such as setting up a catalog page, or achieving a particular effect. Use it sparingly.

Justification

You can use PageMaker's factory settings for justification by choosing Justify, or you can take advantage of PageMaker's capacity for fine adjustments. The factors that go into calculating justification, including word and letter spacing, have been set for basic everyday layout work. On the other hand, typesetting power is one of the

Justified Type

Which is easier to read? Some designers argue that the ragged space bumps down the right side of the column provide the reader with "landmarks" as the eyes scan down the page. Others contend that justified type is easier for people to read because the strict edges provide a better guide for the eye, so every line is the same length and the reader always knows what to expect. Justified type requires more hyphenation, and if poorly set may have uneven word and letter spacing, which can reduce readability. You can help improve readability by making adjustments as needed.

primary reasons to use PageMaker. So, to get the most out of it, you need to delve deeply into its settings for word and letter spacing.

Setting justified text requires that you give special consideration to PageMaker's word and letter spacing power. Not only does PageMaker enable you to adjust these settings to compensate for the requirements of your publication, it also has a potent set of internal algorithms working in the background putting your adjustments to work.

Word spacing, letter spacing, kerning, hyphenation, width, and tracking all affect each other and must be changed with care. You can really screw up typesetting quality if you don't carefully monitor the collective, interacting effects of these settings as you work. When you punch up one factor, you generally need to shave down another related one. The best way to learn it is to practice and study the effects.

Setting Paragraph Spacing Attributes

Word and letter spacing, along with hyphenation, are PageMaker's primary justification tools. You control them through the Paragraph Spacing Attributes dialog box. Open the Paragraph Specifications dialog box and click the Spacing button.

When you first install PageMaker, the program comes with values already entered in each field of the Spacing Attributes dialog box. You can change these settings as needed (see Figure 7.16).

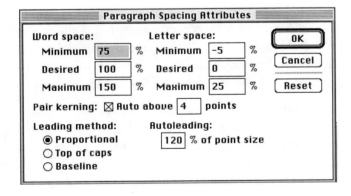

Figure 7.16

Type new values in the boxes to change the default settings shown.

Word Spacing

There are three Word space settings: Minimum, Desired, and Maximum. Every font comes with a built-in standard allowance for the *space band*, which is a typographer's term for the amount of space allotted to the space character that is inserted when you press the Spacebar. In justified text, PageMaker narrows or widens the space based on these Word space percentage settings. The result, along with the other spacing attributes, is a line that completely fills the column.

Set Desired at 100% so that PageMaker attempts to provide exactly what the font designer intended for space between words. When you are working in a justified text paragraph, the Minimum and Maximum settings specify a range on either side of your desired setting. PageMaker uses this range as it makes line lengths work out correctly.

PageMaker comes with factory defaults for a Minimum setting of 75% and a Maximum setting of 150%. This means that PageMaker, when creating justified lines, is allowed to reduce spacing between the words on a line to as little as 75 percent of what the designer felt was optimum and increase space to a maximum of 150 percent.

Letter Spacing

PageMaker also can adjust letter spacing to justify a line. As with word spacing, the designer of a font builds into the design an optimum space between letters, called the *side bearings*—the spaces on either side of the actual character.

The defaults for the Letter space settings are Minimum at 5%, Desired at zero%, and Maximum at 25%. That means PageMaker tries to make zero changes to letter spacing, but if it must, it will try to remove no more than 5% of the letter spacing in a line and add no more than 25%.

Of course, you can type in values that better suit your needs. You might even want to put 0% in each box. Many highly respected typography experts feel strongly that anything else would be wrong because letter spacing is usually created by a typographer, who intended the type to look a particular way with a particular amount of space—the side bearings designed into each letter.

Hyphenating Words

Justified text almost always requires that some words be hyphenated. In PageMaker, hyphenation is simple. The software handles the job for you. As a matter of fact, you could do a lot worse than letting PageMaker run the way it comes from the factory. You can fine-tune it, too, for even better performance.

Using the Hyphenation Dialog Box Options

Use the dialog box in Figure 7.17 to control hyphenation in your publication. Access the dialog box by choosing Hyphenation from the Type menu.

The Hyphenation dialog box provides the following options:

◆ **Hyphenation: On/Off**. You can turn off hyphenation so that it doesn't work, even if you attempt to manually hyphenate the text with soft hyphens.

◆ **Manual only**. PageMaker does not actively perform any hyphenation but permits you to insert manual hyphenation (soft hyphens).

◆ **Manual plus dictionary**. Stepping up in hyphenation assistance, PageMaker can use the spelling dictionary to hyphenate words at syllable breaks.

◆ **Manual plus algorithm**. PageMaker can calculate where to break words by using an algorithm in addition to its spelling dictionary.

◆ **Hyphenation zone**. You can set up a hyphenation zone, the strip of territory at the right side of your column where PageMaker makes its hyphenation decisions. If a word starts within this zone and can't fit on the line, it moves to the next line. For this reason, it's sometimes more helpful to think of it as the no-hyphenation zone. This function does not work in justified text.

◆ **Limit consecutive hyphens to**. You can tell PageMaker how many lines in a row can have hyphens.

Hyphenation is all about line length. Whatever alignment you have chosen—ragged right or left, centered, or justified—you are striving to get the lines as near as possible to the same length, unless you are trying for some special effect.

Figure 7.17

Use the Hyphenation dialog box to set Hyphenation parameters.

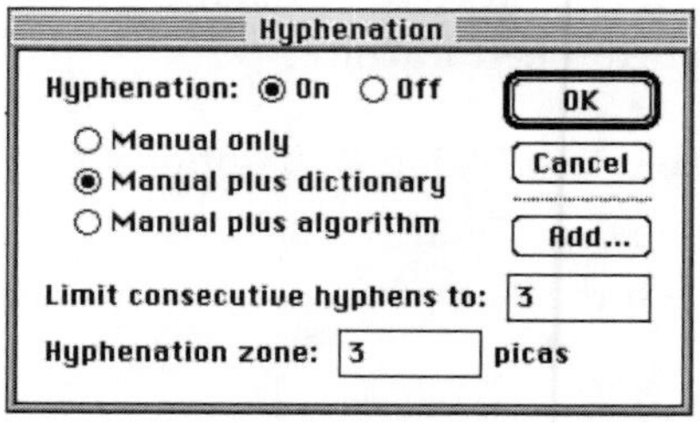

```
┌─────────────────────────────────────────┐
│            Hyphenation                   │
│ Hyphenation: ◉ On  ○ Off    ┌──────────┐ │
│         ○ Manual only       │    OK    │ │
│         ◉ Manual plus dictionary └────┘ │
│         ○ Manual plus algorithm ┌──────┐ │
│                             │  Cancel  │ │
│ Limit consecutive hyphens to: 3 ┌────┐  │
│                             │  Add...  │ │
│ Hyphenation zone:  3    picas           │
└─────────────────────────────────────────┘
```

Manually Hyphenating Your Text

Turn on manual hyphenation in the Hyphenation dialog box. Do *not* turn off hyphenation. This might seem a bit confusing, but if you turn off PageMaker's hyphenation, you turn it completely off. PageMaker then loses its capability to read the special soft hyphens you insert for manual tuning of hyphenation breaks.

The primary tool of manual hyphenation is the *discretionary hyphen* or *soft hyphen* that you enter with the "+" - (hyphen) key combination. If a line falls so that your hyphenated word is in the hyphenation zone, as defined in the Hyphenation dialog box, the line breaks at your soft hyphen mark. Soft hyphens have priority over PageMaker's hyphenation dictionary or algorithms when the program is making hyphenation decisions.

If the column width changes, or if you change the hyphenation zone, or the line is edited, the soft hyphen disappears from view when it is shifted up into the line. The soft hyphen comes back into effect if further editing slides it back into the hyphenation zone.

Adding, Editing, or Removing Hyphenated Words in the Dictionary

Notice the Add button in the Hyphenation dialog box. You use the Add button to add words to your custom User dictionary. Fortunately, PageMaker uses the same dictionary for spelling and hyphenation, so adding a word in hyphenation also expands your spelling dictionary.

Preventing Hyphenation of Specific Words

To prevent hyphenation, you can still use the traditional PageMaker move of inserting a discretionary hyphen "+" - (hyphen) directly in front of the non-hyphenated word, so PageMaker will choose to break in front of rather than in the middle of the word.

You also can permanently lock specific words by unhyphenating them in your dictionary, following the same general principle but using the Add Word dialog box. Type the word you want to lock in the Add Word dialog box. Or highlight the word in text and open the dialog. Then place one tilde directly in front of the word and remove any other tildes.

Force Justifying

The term *force justification* qualifies as justification only in the most literal sense. Force justification does make the first and the last letters in a line sit flush against their respective column edges—but it does so even if only two letters are on the line! That's the only resemblance to justification. The concept of force has much more to do with what happens. This method divides the line length by the number of characters and then applies brute force to space everything out evenly, putting most space between words, spreading all the characters over the entire line.

You'll probably use force justification only for special effects, as shown in Figure 7.18. In this example, en spaces, which have a fixed length, have been inserted between each character and several more have been placed between the words and bullet points.

The · Honor · Of · Your · Presence · Is · Requested
At · The · Retirement · Party · For
The · Right · Honorable · Henry · Slugbinder

Figure 7.18

Special effects with force justification.

TAB STOPS AND INDENTS

Indents and tab stops shape your PageMaker paragraphs into columns and other structures, shaping the container of your words. Instead of trying to remember to press the Tab key to indent the first line of a paragraph, you can use the first line indent function, setting it so that every paragraph you type has the same indent. In tables of information, you can set your tabs once for the first row of information and make those tab settings line up all the rest of the data columns beneath it.

Using the Indents/Tabs Ruler

The ruler-style dialog box you see in Figure 7.19 is the basic PageMaker tool for setting indents and tabs. Select Indents/Tabs from the Type menu or use the keyboard shortcut (Command-I) [Control-I].

Figure 7.19

The Indents/tabs dialog box.

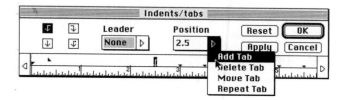

PageMaker stretches the ruler across the entire screen, even if you have a super-wide monitor. This wide view gives you access without scrolling the ruler back and forth. In addition, you get a better perspective on your entire column of text, even at super-high magnification and with extremely wide columns of data.

The ruler attempts to line up its zero point with the left of your column—assuming the left column edge shows in your page view—making it easy to visually estimate your tab locations. PageMaker adjusts the scale of the ruler to whatever view magnification you were using when you called up the Indents/tabs dialog box.

Setting a Tab and Choosing Tab Alignment

To set a tab, select some text and then open the Indents/tabs dialog box. Click one of the tab icons on the left side of the dialog box. You have a choice of four tab alignments: left aligned, right aligned, centered, and decimal. In Figure 7.20, you see examples of all four alignments.

After you choose a tab style, click anywhere on the ruler. The tab symbol is placed where you click. You can slide the tab to a different position, or you can type an exact position in the Position box.

Leftie	Centered	99.99	Rightedge
Left	Center	1,000.1	Right
Leftwise	Center Tab	1,000,000	Rightmost
Leftmost	Center Central	100.222	Right!
Leftie	Centered	99.99	Rightedge
Left	Center	1,000.1	Right
Leftwise	Center Tab	1,000,000	Rightmost
Leftmost	Center Central	100.222	Right!
Leftie	Centered	99.99	Rightedge
Left	Center	1,000.1	Right
Leftwise	Center Tab	1,000,000	Rightmost
Leftmost	Center Central	100.222	Right!

Figure 7.20

A sample table showing all four types of tab alignment.

Tabs are applied to any PageMaker paragraphs that you selected (even partially, or even by clicking an insertion point) when you opened the Indents/tabs dialog box.

Tabs take effect when you click the Apply button or OK. The Apply button helps when you try to set up a complicated table, because you can view your changes without repeatedly opening and closing the Ruler dialog box.

Tab Characters

Tab settings are different from tab characters. *Tab characters* are inserted as invisible markers when you use the Tab key. If you open Story Editor, you can see them, just as you can see the paragraph markers (provided Show ¶ is enabled). When you type tab characters into your text, they force your words to line up on the tab settings. If you haven't created any tab settings, your words line up on the default tab settings built into PageMaker.

Setting Tabs for Multiple Rows of Data

When you create a table like the one in Figure 7.19, you can use your first-row tab settings in several ways throughout the rest of the table.

The most intuitive way to format tabs for a table-style list is to enter all your data, highlight all of it, and experiment with your tab settings. Use the Apply button to evaluate the effects of your moves as you proceed. After you have all the columns set at the right width to accommodate the data, click OK.

Note

A better way to set tabs for multiple rows of data is to set up a paragraph style for your table and tweak it as needed. You learn more about styles later in this chapter.

You can use PageMaker's tab adoption technique to set all the tabs in a group of rows, using the first row as a model. To adopt tabs, set the tabs for the first line. Then close the Indents/tabs dialog box, highlight the entire table of data, and open and close the ruler again. The settings in the first row are adopted by all the rows you highlighted.

Keep in mind that PageMaker passes paragraph formatting on to following paragraphs. If you are typing columnar information directly into PageMaker, arrange the first row of data with tabs and press the Return key at the end of it, carrying all those paragraph attributes, including the tabs, to the new paragraph below. Each ensuing (newly typed) paragraph also assumes the formatting.

This method has one drawback. It doesn't take into account that the paragraphs following the first one may have wider columns of data. You might need to go back through the table and tune the tab settings. If you use style definitions for the table, however, it is easy to perform this tuning operation.

Using the Position Box for Precision Tabbing

Sometimes it's tough to place a tab exactly where you want it by using the click-and-drag methods. The Indent/tabs dialog box offers the most precise way to add or move a tab. To add a new tab in an exact spot, type the location information into the box. Choose Add from the arrow list (see Figure 7.18). To move an existing tab, select it by clicking its "tail," type your location point into the Position box, and then pick the Move option.

Dotting a Leader Tab

Leader tabs add legibility to lists like the tables of contents, where the eye needs to follow from one entry over to the next.

To set a leader, select a tab by clicking its tail and pull down the arrow list from the Leader box in the Indents/tabs dialog box. Choose from dots, dashes, a solid line, or a custom job. The solid line leader works really well for drawing precise lines for an order form. You can also type in any two characters and create your own custom leader.

Setting Precision Multiple Tabs with the Repeat Command

PageMaker can set up to 40 different tabs in any given paragraph. To set precision multiple tabs, use the Position box and the Repeat function to set a series of regular spaced tabs. Type a number into the Position box to tell PageMaker how far apart you want each new tab. Click Add tab and then click Repeat tab for a series of tabs across the ruler at the specified interval.

Setting Paragraph Indents with the Indents/Tabs Ruler

If you understand how the Indents/tabs ruler dialog box works, you have paragraph indents mastered. The ruler has left and right indent markers. The left marker even has a split in it like the indent markers in Microsoft Word and MacWrite. The upper-left indent marker corresponds to the first line of a paragraph, and the lower one to the rest of the paragraph, enabling you to set the first line indented.

Suppose you want to indent the first line of a paragraph. When you have selected the paragraph, or as many consecutive paragraphs as you want to apply the indent to, open the Indents/tabs dialog box.

In Figure 7.21, notice the black sideways triangles at each side of the ruler, where the column edges sit. These (if you've never seen them in a word processor) are the indent markers. Vertical dotted lines also act as place markers for the column edges. When these two indent markers sit right on the column edges (where the dotted lines are), that indicates there's no indent at all. You can click and drag the markers wherever you like on the ruler, as long as you stay inside the column margins. Set the indent by dragging the upper marker to the right, to the point where the indent should begin.

To indent an entire paragraph, as for a quote you want to stand out, move both left markers. To indent the right side of the column, move the right marker. It's that simple.

Figure 7.21

Dragging the top-left indent marker to indent the text.

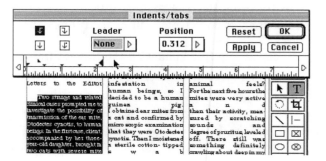

Indenting Paragraphs by Menu and Control Palette

As intuitive as it is to work with the Indents/tabs ruler, sometimes it makes more sense to use a menu or the Control palette to set indents. (You can only set tabs with the ruler.)

You can set left and right indents and first-line indents right from the keyboard by using the Paragraph Specifications dialog box or the Control palette. Just enter the amount, in hundredths of an inch, or in picas or whatever measurement system you are using. You don't get the visual feedback of lining up margin markers in the ruler, but if you know exactly what you want to do the keyboard entry method is much more precise and possibly faster.

Controlling the Flow of Lines and Paragraphs

PageMaker can help you control the way your paragraphs and lines fit together and even where they appear on the page. From the keyboard or by using the Options section of the Paragraph Specifications dialog box, you can force lines to break at a given point, keep paragraphs together or force one to the next page or column, and avoid unsightly widowed or orphaned type.

Forcing a New Line with Shift-Return

The simplest control you have over where a line breaks is a brute force technique—the new line character. Insert this character in text by clicking an insertion point and pressing Shift-Return. (This is also known as a hard return. The "normal" kind is a soft return.) Instead of creating a new paragraph, you force the line to break and start over again on the next line. Like the tab character and the carriage return character, this new line character is visible in the Story Editor but not in Layout view.

Controlling Paragraph Flow Using the Paragraph Specifications Dialog Box

Each checkbox in the Options section of the Paragraph Specifications dialog box works directly on the way a paragraph relates to the page. They enable you to control the location of page breaks and the way paragraphs break between pages. Use the Keep Lines Together option whenever you want all the lines of that paragraph to stay together on one page. You might use this option to prevent a multiline headline or a multiline row in a table of data from breaking across to a new page.

To force a paragraph to snap to the top of the next page or the next column, choose Column Break Before or Page Break Before in the Paragraph Specifications dialog box. This option is used a lot with first and second level headlines in books, where a chapter or major new section should begin on a new page. It's especially useful when you pour new text into a PageMaker publication, because your most vital page breaks are automatically set up for you, saving considerable time when you do your page-break tuning.

Tell a paragraph to stick on the same page with its following paragraph by choosing Keep with Next. This option is great for headlines; if you use it, you will never see a lonely headline sitting at the bottom of a page or column, apart from the text it is supposed to introduce.

Preventing Widows and Orphans

Academics have actually written weighty monographs on the definition and origin of the terms *widow* and *orphan*. Nobody seems to know for sure when typesetters and art directors first began using these terms, but they've been talking about widows and orphans since sometime back in the late 1600s. You'd think by now somebody would have worked out a definition that everybody could agree upon. Because this is a book about PageMaker, what really counts here is what PageMaker thinks about widows and orphans. PageMaker looks at widows and orphans like this:

◆ A widow is the first line of a paragraph that has been isolated from the rest of its paragraph by being stuck all alone at the bottom of a page or column.

◆ An orphan is the last line of a paragraph stuck at the top of a page or column, with the rest of the paragraph left behind on the previous page or column.

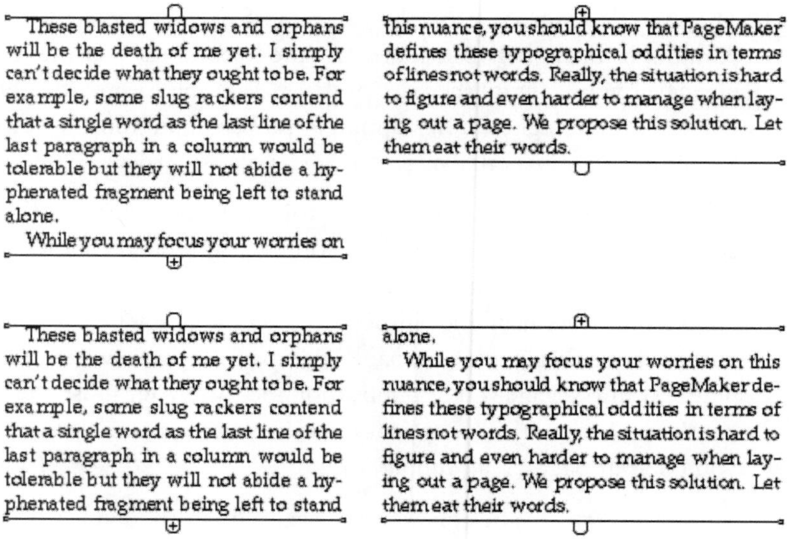

Figure 7.22

A widow and an orphan.

These blasted widows and orphans will be the death of me yet. I simply can't decide what they ought to be. For example, some slug rackers contend that a single word as the last line of the last paragraph in a column would be tolerable but they will not abide a hyphenated fragment being left to stand alone.

While you may focus your worries on

this nuance, you should know that PageMaker defines these typographical oddities in terms of lines not words. Really, the situation is hard to figure and even harder to manage when laying out a page. We propose this solution. Let them eat their words.

These blasted widows and orphans will be the death of me yet. I simply can't decide what they ought to be. For example, some slug rackers contend that a single word as the last line of the last paragraph in a column would be tolerable but they will not abide a hyphenated fragment being left to stand

alone.

While you may focus your worries on this nuance, you should know that PageMaker defines these typographical oddities in terms of lines not words. Really, the situation is hard to figure and even harder to manage when laying out a page. We propose this solution. Let them eat their words.

The best cure for widows and orphans is to edit the copy until it fits, but that's not always an option. If you want PageMaker to assist you by exerting widow or orphan control, type a number from zero to three in the Widow Control or Orphan Control boxes in the Paragraph Specifications dialog box.

If you enter a two in the Widow Control field, you give PageMaker a definition to follow as it paginates your text into columns. If PageMaker finds a paragraph breaking across two pages, it checks your Widow Control definition. If you have at least two lines in a portion of the paragraph at the bottom of the page, PageMaker knows to allow the page break to go ahead. Otherwise, it tries to adjust the paragraph break to conform to your definition.

When PageMaker finds itself about to break a paragraph between pages, it checks the orphan control definition. It adds the number you entered in the Orphan Control option field to the lines at the top of the page. If the number of lines falling at the top of the page equal your definition, it knows it must take action and it adds a line from the previous page to avoid the problem.

Setting Off Paragraphs with Spacing and Rules

PageMaker provides two major tools for framing your paragraphs. You can allow extra space above and below them or you can set a line (a rule) either above or below a paragraph.

Remember that in PageMaker, not all paragraphs are prose text. Paragraphs are any text followed by a carriage return character. Headlines are paragraphs and so are captions.

Primarily, rules visually set aside your headlines or other special paragraphs by emphasizing and separating them from your body copy. You can also use the paragraph spacing attribute for setting off headlines, but spacing has much broader purposes.

Spacing Before and After Paragraphs

You might wonder why not just press the Return or Enter key a couple of times to space out paragraphs? That works, but it locks you into paragraph spacing that exactly equals your leading or multiples of it. No finesse. No flexibility. Instead, it's much more elegant to precisely define the space you'd like to see between paragraphs.

The Paragraph Space settings are found in the upper-right corner of the Paragraph Specifications dialog box. You can also enter an amount to space on the right end of the Paragraph Control palette. Figure 7.23 shows some examples of different amounts of paragraph spacing.

Figure 7.23

Experiments in paragraph spacing.

No Space After This Headline
The backbone of great design will often be experimentation and flexibility. Without the ability to quickly try out your ideas and to try them out with precision, your cause may be lost.

2 Points After This Headline
The backbone of great design will often be experimentation and flexibility. Without the ability to quickly try out your ideas and to try them out with precision, your cause may be lost.

5.5 Points After This Headline
The backbone of great design will often be experimentation and flexibility. Without the ability to quickly try out your ideas and to try them out with precision, your cause may be lost.

9 Points After This Headline
The backbone of great design will often be experimentation and flexibility. Without the ability to quickly try out your ideas and to try them out with precision, your cause may be lost.

Adding Rules to Paragraphs

You add rules (lines) to paragraphs for one reason: to make them stand out. To place a line between two paragraphs, first open the Paragraph Specifications dialog box. You can reach the basic Rules dialog box by clicking the Rules button. Here you can set up the thickness of the ruled line, its color or tint, width, and position. This box has its own supporting dialog box with further options for defining the rule's position in relation to the baseline. You can reach these options by clicking the Paragraph Rules Options button (see Figure 7.24).

The rule lines available to you here are nearly identical to those offered for drawing purposes in the PageMaker Elements menu. You have several thousand variations of spacing, thickness, style, and color that you can put together by using these checkboxes, text-entry boxes, and drop-down lists.

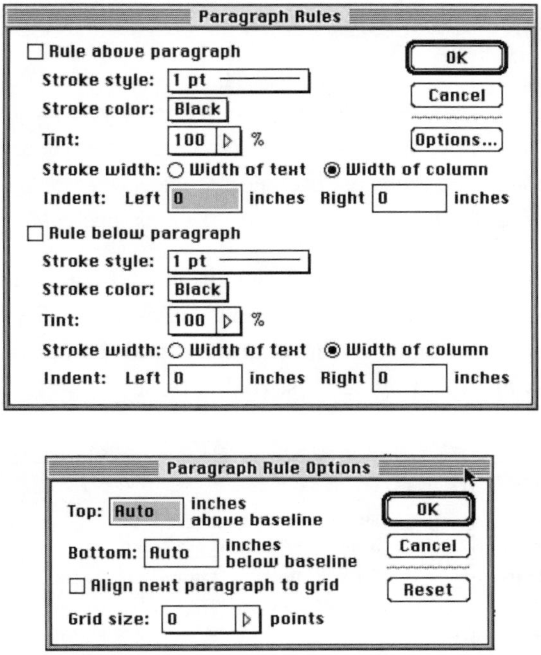

Figure 7.24

Rules and rules options.

You can color your rules or even assign them a tint. Select colors other than black by using the Line Color list in the Paragraph Rules dialog box. Top and bottom rules are independent from one another meaning you could choose a hot-pink top rule and a lime-green bottom rule.

USING STYLES

Think of a style as a collection of formatting commands, conveniently gathered up into a set of instructions that you can apply in a single keyboard or menu move.

The entire collection of styles for a publication is sometimes called a *style sheet*.

Note

Style sheets is a term left over from years ago when word processors first came out with styles, which were maintained outside the document in a separate file called the style sheet. PageMaker, like modern day word processors, keeps style information inside the main publication file.

To understand the power of styles, look at Figure 7.25. One style definition, applied with a single mouse click in the Style palette, can implement every one of the character and paragraph formatting attributes controlled by all these dialog boxes.

Figure 7.25

A graphic demonstration of all the formatting you can apply with a single style.

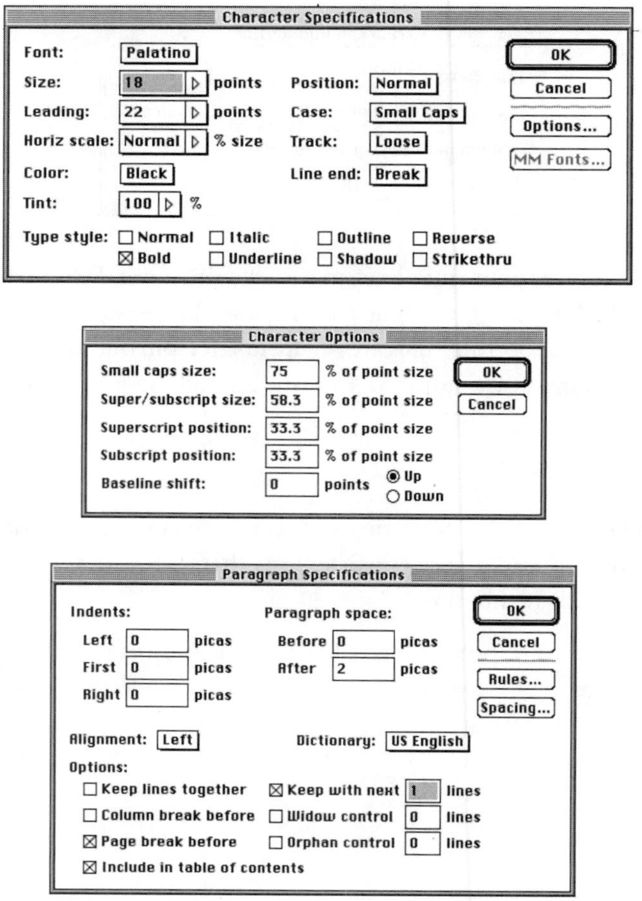

Paragraph Rules

☒ Rule above paragraph

Stroke style: `8 pt ▐▬▬`

Stroke color: `Black`

Tint: `100` ▷ %

Stroke width: ○ Width of text   ● Width of column

Indent: Left `30` picas   Right `0` picas

☒ Rule below paragraph

Stroke style: `1 pt ───`

Stroke color: `Black`

Tint: `100` ▷ %

Stroke width: ○ Width of text   ● Width of column

Indent: Left `0` picas   Right `0` picas

[OK]   [Cancel]   [Options...]

Paragraph Spacing Attributes

Word space:		Letter space:	
Minimum	`75` %	Minimum	`-5` %
Desired	`100` %	Desired	`0` %
Maximum	`150` %	Maximum	`25` %

Pair kerning: ☒ Auto above `4` points

Leading method: Autoleading:
○ Proportional   `120` % of point size
○ Top of caps
● Baseline

[OK]   [Cancel]   [Reset]

Hyphenation

Hyphenation: ○ On   ● Off

○ Manual only
● Manual plus dictionary
○ Manual plus algorithm

Limit consecutive hyphens to: `3`

Hyphenation zone: `1` picas

[OK]   [Cancel]   [Add...]

Indents/tabs

Leader   Position   [Reset] [OK]

`None` ▷   ▷   [Apply] [Cancel]

A VERY STYLISH HEADLINE   ▬▬▬▬

Taking the time to set up a style for even a short passage of text is worthwhile. Defining the style requires you to do the formatting once. From then on, you can apply this collection of formatting commands with one click of the mouse on the Styles palette (or you can choose the style from the Styles menu or the Control palette or a keyboard shortcut).

Consistency and flexibility are other reasons for using styles. Making sure headings and captions match from one book chapter to the next is much easier when you can assign styles.

Applying Styles

Styles apply to entire PageMaker paragraphs. That's a critical point. You can use a style to create a headline with bold type, but you can't use a style to selectively format just a few words within the headline. You can apply the style and override it to put a single word or phrase in bold or italic.

There are four methods of applying styles:

- Style palette

- Text mode of the Control palette

- Style submenu in the Type menu

- Keyboard shortcuts

In each case, you must use the Text tool and click an insertion point in the paragraph you want to format, or select as many consecutive paragraphs as you like. Be careful, though. Undo can't undo style changes. The only way to undo a changed style is to use Revert or to apply a different style to it.

Styling with the Styles Palette

The Styles palette is the easiest way to apply PageMaker styles. When you open the Styles palette (press (Command-B) [Control-B] or select Show Styles from the Window menu), you see a list of available styles, as in Figure 7.26. You can add new ones, too. Select the paragraph to style, move the Text tool to the Styles palette, where it changes to a pointer, and click the style you want to apply.

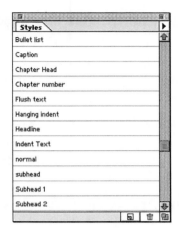

Figure 7.26

The Styles palette lists styles you can apply.

Styling with the Control Palette

With the Control palette in Paragraph mode, as shown in Figure 7.27 you can select a style from the menu list at the left of the palette. You can also have the Control palette look up your style for you by typing the first few letters of its name. The list jumps to the style that most closely matches what you type, and as you keep typing, it keeps guessing at where you are headed (the same way you can look up a font in Character view). After the style has been selected, tab to the next field or press Return, and the style is assigned to whatever text you selected for formatting.

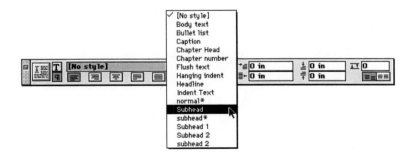

Figure 7.27

Choosing a style from the Control palette's pop-up menu.

Styling with the Style Submenu

You may use the Style submenu, located in the Type menu. (Don't confuse it with the Type Style submenu.) Choose your style from the list.

Automatic Styling by Inheritance and Cascading

When you are typing new text into PageMaker, you can automatically assign styles to new paragraphs and you can do it in two ways. Both of the following methods work by passing on a style assignment from one paragraph to the next as you are typing:

◆ **Inherited Style Assignment.** When you press Return at the end of a paragraph, the previous paragraph's formatting carries on to the new paragraph. Think of it as the new paragraph inheriting its style assignment from the preceding one.

◆ **Cascading Style Application.** If you defined a Next Style attribute within the original paragraph's Style Options dialog box, your new paragraph does not inherit the previous style, instead it is formatted with your Next Style designation. Use this when you know which style will always follow the current one. For instance, make next style Flush Text after a Subhead.

Local Formatting: Augmenting and Overriding Styles

The style process does not need to limit you. Any time you like, you can override a style by imposing what PageMaker calls local formatting. In fact, that's an example of local formatting. The bold styling on the words local formatting has been applied on top of the body copy style definition for this paragraph. (This entire book was composed in PageMaker.)

Type styles are not the same as paragraph style definitions. The term type styles refers only to typographic attributes:

◆ normal

◆ **bold**

◆ *italic*

◆ underline

◆ ~~strikethru~~

◆ outline

◆ shadow

Paragraph styles are the collections of text and paragraph attributes that you define and then apply to paragraphs through the Type menu's Style command, the Control palette's list of styles, or the Styles palette. Type styles and paragraph styles do interact with one another, however, and you need to understand how that interaction works.

Hard Formatting and Paragraph Styles

Applying a new paragraph style, or reapplying a paragraph's current style, *doesn't* completely reformat a paragraph to comply with the new style definition. It depends on whether there's local formatting involved. Some kinds of local formatting are permanent. (You occasionally hear the term *hard formatting* used instead of local formatting.) Type styling attributes, such as bold or italic, stay put when you apply a new paragraph style. So does case formatting (all caps or small caps) and position formatting (super- and subscripts). But, beware... If you're using a font that's designated bold or italic, such as Adobe Garamond Italic or Helvetica Demibold, applying a new style or reapplying an existing one will change the type back to normal Garamond or Helvetica.

To help you remember which type attributes are permanent, you have a list in the Control palette—the buttons beneath the typeface name control the attributes that are retained even when you apply a new paragraph style.

There's a twist to this interaction of paragraph styles and type styles. If you apply a paragraph style to some text that has local formatting and the paragraph style contains the same kind of type styling, your move has the same effect as assigning the type style twice. It reverses your old type styling, toggling it off.

You can control the interplay between local formatting and paragraph styles with some keyboard shortcuts. To preserve all local formatting (for any text or paragraph attribute) as you apply a new style, press the Shift key as you click in the Styles palette. Remove type styling (returning it to what PageMaker calls normal style) by selecting the text you want to normalize and pressing (Shift-Command-Spacebar)

[Shift-Control-Spacebar]. PageMaker considers "normal" to be a style just like bold, italic, or underlining, and that's why it is listed on the Type Style submenu.

You might see a plus sign (+) or an asterisk (*) next to a style name. The plus sign means that the style has some local or hard formatting assigned somewhere in that paragraph. The plus sign indicates that you have overridden the style. An asterisk means the style has been brought in from outside and, strictly speaking, isn't yet a PageMaker style. This often happens when you edit a document in a word processor. PageMaker lists the word processor style but doesn't fully adopt it until you edit it for the first time in PageMaker.

Note

Case (all caps and small caps), superscript, and subscript aren't listed on the Type Style submenu; therefore, you can only reverse these by reapplying the type style, which toggles it off. Case, as well as sub- and superscripts, do not respond to the normal type style key shortcut.

Generate a Style Reference List

Applying styles in a complex document is much more manageable if you keep a printed reference list of all your styles and how they relate to one another. The overview you get from this master list of styles helps you use the styles more effectively and consistently. The Pub Info plug-in can do this style reference list job for you. Find it on the plug-ins submenu under the Utilities menu.

Identifying Styles and their Status

With PageMaker, you have several ways to determine what style you assigned to a particular paragraph and you can determine if the style has been given any special additional formatting.

You can see what style is applied to a paragraph by glancing at the Styles palette, the Style submenu, or the Control palette. The style name is highlighted in the Styles palette and in the Control palette the style is the one showing in the selection box. On the Style submenu, the style in effect is checked.

If you are working in the Story Editor, you can tell Preferences to display style names alongside each paragraph down the left edge of your editor window.

Defining or Redefining Styles

The real power of PageMaker styles comes from defining your own. Figure 7.28 and 7.29 show the Define Styles and Style Options (previously called Edit Styles) dialog boxes.

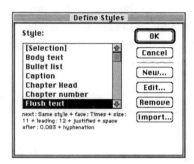

Figure 7.28

The Define Styles dialog box.

Open the main Define Styles. To edit an existing style, scroll through the list of styles in this dialog box and choose the style you want to edit, clicking Edit button to modify it.

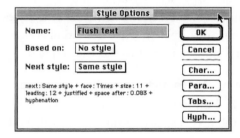

Figure 7.29

The Style Options dialog box.

From the Define Styles dialog box, you can also create a completely new style. Click New to get the Style Options dialog box with no name entered into the Name field. Name the new style and change the default entries as needed to define its text and paragraph formatting.

PageMaker bases the initial entries in the New Style dialog box on an existing style if you happened to choose one before clicking on the New button. Or, if you click the **Selection** option at the head of the scrolling list, the new style is based on whatever text was selected prior to opening the Define Styles dialog box. If no text was selected, the new style is based on the current mini-defaults for character and paragraph formatting. Click OK to adopt your finished style.

The Remove button does just what it sounds like—it removes a style. This option cannot be undone. If you remove a style by mistake and catch your error in time, you can click the Cancel button and back out of the situation. If you do a Save before removing a style and then realize you made a mistake and need to undo it, use the Revert command in the File menu.

Create Instant Styles with the Control Palette

To use the Control palette to create an instant style, format some text, and then highlight the text. Open the Control palette and tab to the style list section. Enter the name of your new style and press Return. Presto, instant new style. Note that if you duplicate an existing style name, PageMaker offers to assign the existing style to the highlighted text. This Control palette technique performs a two-step procedure in a single powerful move. When you use the Style menu command, you need to first define the new style and then use the Styles palette to apply the style. The Control palette style definition routine simultaneously defines the style and applies it to the selected text.

Editing Existing Styles and Formatting New Ones

If you click the Edit button in the Define Styles dialog box, you gain access to all the text formatting functions of PageMaker in the Style Options dialog box. Notice the four buttons that appear on the lower-right side of the dialog box (refer to Figure 7.29).

These four buttons—Character, Paragraph, Tabs, and Hyphenation—take you directly to the corresponding dialog boxes you open through the Type menu.

Each dialog box, when opened in Edit Styles, works almost exactly the same way it does when opened through the Type menu, with one major difference: The actions that you perform when you access the dialog boxes through these buttons are recorded as style definition information, whereas when you access them through the Type menu they apply to the type you've selected, or to the type you're about to place. Unfortunately, there's one minor exception to this behavior. The Apply button doesn't work in the Indents/tabs dialog box when you are defining a style.

Notice the space directly below the Based On and Next Style functions. All your style decisions are reflected here in the form of a style definition that spells out the character and paragraph attributes in the definition.

When you open the Style Options dialog box, the Name field is filled out differently, depending on what you selected from the scrolling list of styles before you clicked the Edit button. If you highlighted the [Selection] item, the Name area is empty because you are creating a new style. If you choose a style name from the list, the existing style name is automatically entered in the Name field. Your style definition actions modify the existing style.

Cascading Styles by Using Next Style

When you use the Next style pull-down list shown in Figure 7.30, you are telling PageMaker which style to assign to a following paragraph as you are typing text into your publication.

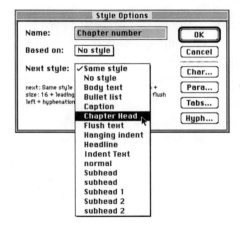

Figure 7.30

The next paragraph will have this style.

The Next style applies when you press Return to start a new paragraph (starting it with the next style). In Figure 7.30, the Chapter Head style follows the Chapter Number style. The Next Style attribute won't change any paragraphs that already exist in your document, only new ones that you type. Also, it won't assign the next style to paragraphs as they are imported. It only operates when you are working in text and press Return.

Mimicking Styles with Based On

The Based On style definition attribute, unlike Next style, forms a parent/child link between two styles. When a style has been subordinated to another style through the Based On pull-down list, any change to the parent style (the style the child is "based on") ripples down through all its subordinate paragraphs. The ripple can go many layers deep if you make a number of paragraphs dependent on one another.

This Based On attribute is powerful, but use caution or you could get some pretty wild and unexpected effects. If you have a subhead style subordinate to a major headline and change the typeface, for example, you change the typeface of the subhead as well. About the only text attribute that doesn't change when you make one of the Based on moves is the size of the type. Practically everything else changes though—bold, italic, typeface, superscript, and so on.

Merging Two Styles

This usually comes up when you've created two similar styles and want to combine them. You might be tempted to use the search-and-replace function of the Story Editor to accomplish a style merger, but merging through the Define Styles dialog box is usually easier and faster.

To merge two styles, you must first decide which style contains the formatting information you want to keep. When you merge, you replace one style with the other. Think of the style you want to keep as the survivor style. Next, press the (Command) [Control] key and click the survivor style's name in the Style palette to select it. The Style Options dialog box opens, with the name of your survivor style showing in the name field.

Edit the name of the survivor style to exactly match the name of the style being replaced, and then click OK. You get a dialog box such as the one in Figure 7.31, asking whether you want to replace the old style with the new style. This is your last chance to cancel because you cannot undo the move. If you aren't sure about your decision, click Cancel. Assuming that you're ready to go ahead, click OK.

Figure 7.31

Don't click OK unless you're sure. This action can't be undone.

Throughout your publication every instance of the old style is replaced with the survivor style formatting. The merged style has the name of the old style, but you can rename the new merged style to anything you like.

Importing Styles from Another Publication

You can use the Import button in the Define Styles dialog box to "borrow" style sheets from other publications.

Clicking the Import button opens a dialog box, similar to a standard Open file dialog box. Select the source publication that contains the style sheet of definitions you want to copy and click OK.

This style-copying operation behaves a lot like the style merge discussed in the preceding section, except that it operates on a large scale. It takes in the entire style sheet from the source publication. If a style name on the inbound style sheet already exists in your current publication, you get a dialog box asking whether you want to copy over existing styles.

◆ If you reply yes, all the inbound styles named exactly the same as styles in the current publication merge over the top of those existing styles. In other words, the inbound duplicate styles are the survivor styles.

◆ If you say no, PageMaker preserves your old styles as the survivor styles and does not copy any inbound styles that have duplicate names. In either case, all the non-duplicated styles from the inbound style sheet are added to the style sheet of the current publication.

Use the Import Button for Style Consistency Across All Chapters of a Book

The text throughout a book should have consistent formatting. It would look strange, for example, to set Palatino body text in one chapter and specify Times New Roman body text in another chapter. Use the Import Style command to achieve consistency in a multi-chapter book. Select one chapter to set the styles for the publication. It's called the style leader because, just like the models in the fashion magazine, it determines the style everyone else will follow. Whenever you make a style adjustment, make the adjustment in the chapter that's the style leader. Then copy the styles from the style leader chapter into each of the other chapters.

Planning Your Basic Style Needs

Start by outlining your document. The outline of this chapter, for example, starts with the chapter head and includes four levels of subheads, plus body text, sidebars, and notes. This shows how your styles should relate to one another. The outline

Importing Styles with Inbound Text

Anytime you bring styled text into PageMaker, you can make the styles part of your PageMaker style sheet. For PageMaker to incorporate the inbound styles, the source must be coming into PageMaker through one of three possible ways:

- Paste, following cut or copy

- Drag and drop from another PageMaker publication or the Library palette

- Text imported through PageMaker's Place command

PageMaker first checks the inbound text for style information. If any new styles come in, PageMaker adds those styles to your existing style sheet, putting an asterisk (*) next to the name to indicate that it is an imported style.

If any inbound styles have the same names as those in the destination document, PageMaker gives the destination document styles the leading role so the existing style attributes always come out on top over the inbound styles. The style import operation works exactly the opposite of the Copy command in Edit styles.

Naming Your Styles

Name your styles by function, not appearance. Instead of calling a style by its dominant type attribute, use its function in the name. "Bold Helvetica," for example, should be named "Headline One," signifying that it's a level-one headline style. When possible, name your styles the way your word processor does. If you use Microsoft Word and use the outline function, name your headlines for the built-in outline heading styles of Word. This way you can import your heads with styles already assigned from your Word document. These heads can easily be set up for your table of contents and for page breaks.

PageMaker always lists styles in alphabetical order. For this reason, try to name special purpose or little-used styles so that they are out of the way down at the bottom of the list. If you want a style to go to the top of the list, use a punctuation mark at the beginning of its name—*!Style* appears on the list ahead of *AStyle*.

Defining Styles with the Cascade Approach

By using the Based On attribute in the Style Options dialog box, you can link your styles into a typographic design system. Create a few fundamental character styles and base all your other styles on them. Headlines share a common base style. Body copy is based on another common style. This enables you to make massive changes in a complex style sheet by adjusting a single base definition.

makes clear your style requirements. You could start by creating a headline style for each level of the headline. When you know how many headline styles you need, you also have a handle on how your body text styles need to fit into the holes beneath each style of headline. Then you can decide what special purpose styles you need for captions, illustration callouts, bulleted lists, and so on.

To do this, establish a *base head* style for your headlines, including typeface and paragraph alignment and any other attributes that are going to be common to all your headlines. Use this base head style as the beginning point for all your headline styles. If you decide your headlines look better in Helvetica than Franklin Gothic, make the change in the base head style, and the change is automatically incorporated in all the headline styles based on it.

Do the same thing for body copy, perhaps sharing the base body style among the main text and bulleted text styles. You can set up a special text base style if your captions, callouts, page numbers, and other special page elements share a common typeface.

Be conservative about linking too many styles together. It's easy to completely twist your style sheet system by making a small tweak in a base style. For that reason, the *base body* and base head styles ought to be reserved for simple character formatting. Make changes to table of contents, page break, column break, and indent attributes in the individual styles rather than the base styles.

Building a Library of Styles

After you have created a particularly useful style sheet you should save it for future use in other publications. Your options for building style libraries include the following:

- Individual styled paragraphs stored in the Library palette, ready to be drag and dropped into your publication. The individual style is automatically incorporated into your style sheet.

- PageMaker templates with sets of styles that are common to certain kinds of publications (books, advertisements, brochures, newsletters).

- Scripts written to add styles to your publication, available at the click of a button from the Scripts palette.

- Tagging language files that you can place into your publication, bringing their style definitions in with them.

Selecting a technique is up to you. The important thing is to build a style library. Any time investment in doing so is more than compensated by the time you save pulling a ready-made style into a publication with a mouse click or two.

The easiest way to collect and save your styles for reuse is to add them to the Library palette. The Library palette can be easily searched so that you could have 50 or 100 styles in it and be able to find them when you need them. If you want to use the Library palette method, here's a rundown:

1. After creating a great style, copy and paste a paragraph of the style into a text block.

2. In the text for the paragraph, include the name of the style and a brief description so that you can remember it in the future when you call on it.

3. Switch to the Pointer tool and select the text as a block.

4. Open the Library palette in the Window menu if it isn't already open and click the plus sign in the lower-right corner of the palette. Your item is added to the list of objects in the Library palette.

5. Name your library entry for easy searching. Double-click the untitled item and fill in the dialog box blanks with the name of your entry, your notes, and with keywords so that you can search it out in the future by using the palette's search feature.

6. When you want to pull one of these styles out of your library, drag and drop it into your publication from the Library palette. The style name appears like magic in your Style palette. You can then delete the little text block because it has served its purpose.

7. Note that the Library drag-and-drop method follows the same style dominance rules as cut and paste or inter-publication drag and drop. The style is adopted only if it is new. PageMaker's own styles dominate whenever there are duplicate style names.

SUMMARY

This chapter continued the job begun in the previous chapter—to teach you how to work with text. You learned how to use PageMaker's character and paragraph formatting tools. You learned how to apply leading and tracking, and you learned several ways to kern pairs of letters. Then, you learned about paragraph spacing and paragraph rules. You learned all about styles, from how to apply existing ones to how to create your own and use them to maintain a consistent "look" in your PageMaker publications.

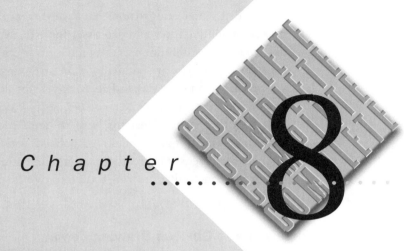

Chapter 8

PAGEMAKER'S DRAWING TOOLS

THE BASICS

Why draw in PageMaker when the results of many great drawing applications on the market can be exported to PageMaker? You could choose to do so for several reasons.

The first is that it's always easier to remain in one application, rather than moving around in alternate software packages. The second is tool-dependent. If PageMaker's tools offer you capabilities not found in the drawing program you're used to, and they fit your needs for a specific project, remaining in PageMaker is the best choice. Third, the term "drawing" in a layout application has to be interpreted differently from when you're using vector drawing software. Ninety-nine percent of the time, you "draw" in a layout program to produce larger elements for page design, usually elements that act as frameworks or mortises to hold text. The framing and embellishment of text is the number one priority of a layout program. If the design of a page makes the text clearer to understand (visually and aesthetically), then the drawing that occurs has a purpose. Drawing that is accomplished in a page layout program is meant to accentuate the text.

That said, it's interesting to note that PageMaker offers the professional user some unique tools and processes for creativity when it comes to drawing. If your definition of drawing tools is limited to the expected pens and pencils you are familiar with in a drawing program, you limit your creativity in PageMaker. PageMaker is not a drawing application and this is further emphasized if you define drawing tools too narrowly. On the other hand, learning how to repurpose and manipulate PageMaker tools not normally associated with standard drawing implements widens your creative pursuits immeasurably. In that regard, let's group PageMaker drawing tools into two categories: obvious and hidden.

PageMaker's Obvious Drawing Tools

These tools are limited in number and include Line, Restricted Line, Oval, Rectangle, and Polygon. This also applies to the frames that address these same general shapes. The Polygon tool in version 6.5 is a special case tool because it can be reshaped by control points, making it the most useful shape composition tool of the lot. The new Polygon's drawing potential is examined later in this chapter, including its capability to act as a DTP Rotoscoping tool.

PageMaker's Hidden Drawing Tools

Perhaps it is better to call these composition tools rather than drawing tools, although their results contribute to a PageMaker drawing all the same. These tools and processes include layering, masking, the application of patterning without stokes, and the repurposing of other options not normally considered part of the drawing toolkit.

Drawing Projects to Target within PageMaker

As already mentioned, if your aim is to devote yourself to digital illustration, than you should get the tools meant for such tasks, including the best drawing and painting applications your budget allows. If, however, your main focus centers upon PageMaker layout composition, you can expand both your creative options and your client base by thoroughly exploring what PageMaker has to offer in these areas. There is no limit to the project categories that a knowledge of these tools can open up, but a few general examples might serve as a motivation for further thought:

- **"Message" concentrated posters.** These are posters whose central headlines dominate the composition. Usually this type of poster consists of nothing more than a short headline and a few lines of text, perhaps just an address and phone number (see Figure 8.1). Examples of these posters are those that call attention to health issues such as AIDS, substance abuse, or other dominant social issues. A well-placed graphic or symbol is often required as a backdrop or text mortise for this type of work. A silhouetted face might be used to "say" the main message element inside a voice balloon. The drawing tools within PageMaker, especially the Polygon Reshaping tool, can help you do everything that's needed without leaving the program.

Figure 8.1

A message poster has one headline that dominates the composition, with little else.

◆ **Logo-centered publications.** One of the best uses of
PageMaker's drawing tools is to trace over an imported logo so
that a representation of it can be used as a background element
(usually grayed out) for text (see Figure 8.2). Combined with
the placement of a photographic or illustrative import of the
logo, this can accentuate logo identification and image recognition. The same process can add interesting shadow effects
behind an illustration or photographic logo image. The Polygon Reshaping tool, combined with an effective use of screened
shading, can serve as a creative choice in this category. When
you trace over lettering to create this publication type, zoom in
very close before using the FreeHand Polygon tool. This will
minimize jagged curves, because there is no Bézier curve
adjustment possible in PageMaker 6.5.

Figure 8.2

*A logo-centered piece uses
a logo or a part of it as a
background for body text
placement.*

◆ **Certificates and awards.** The correct use of proper text styles,
embellishment, and framing are all that's needed here (see
Figure 8.3). PageMaker's new framing option covers the text
handling and an effective use of graphic embellishment options
can complete the project (also see the section on the ShadeTree
Fraemz PageMaker plug-ins covered later in this chapter).

Figure 8.3

PageMaker's frames act as natural borders for certificates and awards.

◆ **Customized bulleted lists.** It is often desirable to use a customized graphic shape for a bullet in a data list. Though imported drawings or photo elements are used in this situation, a simpler graphic or image silhouette can suffice. Using the polygon reshaping process in PageMaker, and then copying, pasting, and aligning the results makes this task almost automatic. This works especially well when creating overhead transparency output (see Figure 8.4).

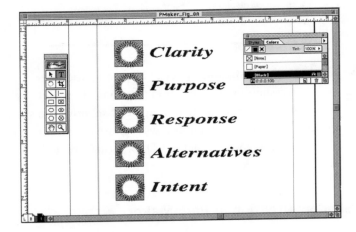

Figure 8.4

Using customized bullets offsets the copy.

◆ **Die-cut work.** Die-cuts are created from exacting keylined shapes, and can be simple or complex. PageMaker has always been capable of basic die-cut keyline design, and with the new polygon reshaping capabilities and layering components of PageMaker 6.5, making more complex die-cut keylines is a much simpler task. You might want to clone the die-cut shape, resize it, and place it on the underlying page so that there's a match between the shapes (see Figure 8.5). There, it can act as the masking outline for a photo, as a frame for a text block, or as yet another die-cut to another page. All of this can be accomplished within PageMaker with the Polygon tool, making the importing of die-cut shapes no longer necessary in many cases.

Figure 8.5

Die-cuts act as frames for the content on the following page.

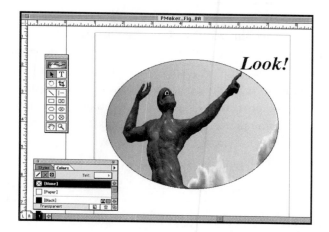

◆ **Shadowing and shading effects.** Combining the layering, polygon reshaping, and screening options offered in PageMaker helps you craft an unlimited number of shadow and shade effects. Three dimensional is always more eye-stopping than 2-D, and a simple way to get a 3-D look is to add a drop shadow to the text block.

Text Shadow Creation in PageMaker

There are dozens of plug-ins on the market that perform one simple task by adding shadows to selected text blocks (see Figure 8.6). You can perform this operation from within PageMaker without the necessity of using a plug-in. Here's how:

1. Select the Text icon in the Toolbox, adjust the type size and style in the Type menus, and write your text message.

2. Select the text with the Text tool (pass over it while holding down the mouse button on the Macintosh, or the left mouse button for Windows users), and use the Copy and Paste commands in the Edit menu to clone the text block.

3. Displace the cloned image with the selected color (you can experiment with different colors and tints here). Color selection is accomplished by selecting tints and colors from the Color Palette.

4. Group the two text blocks and move them as a single unit wherever you want them in the composition (see Figures 8.7 through 8.10).

Figure 8.6

Text shadows add interest to headlines.

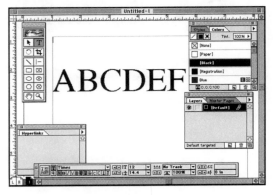

Figure 8.7

Shadow creation for a selected text block starts by using the Text tool to write the text on the page.

229

Figure 8.8

Next, copy and paste the text block at a determined distance from the original.

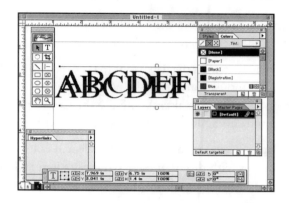

Figure 8.9

Colorize the "shadow" lighter than the block casting the shadow.

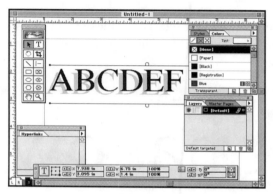

Figure 8.10

Group the two text blocks together, and move them to their final position on the page.

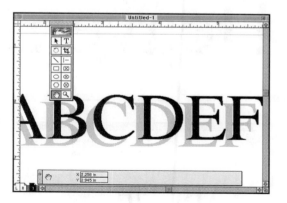

Note

You also can add shadows with the two text blocks positioned on different layers (see Chapter 4, "Layers"). This makes it easier to select elements that are close together for colorizing and image manipulation. You could also sandwich more clones together, colorizing them differently to produce more unique effects, and perhaps even rotate them at different angles. This is definitely a place where layers make work easier.

PAGEMAKER'S DRAWING TOOLS AND THEIR SPECIFIC USE

Each of the drawing tools in PageMaker has a specific range of uses, and each adds creative options for page design. Though PageMaker is not a drawing program as such, its tools offer a wealth of creative possibilities.

The Polygon Tool

The Polygon tool is the single most effective new drawing tool in PageMaker, and users will discover a variety of unique uses as they explore its possibilities. We have mentioned some of those possibilities but haven't come anywhere near exhausting the options.

Activating the tool is simple enough. Just click the Hexagon above the Hand icon on the left side of the PageMaker Toolbox. Doing this enables you to generate the specific polygon configuration to which the tool is set. To customize the settings, double-click the icon. This opens the Polygon Specifications dialog box (see Figure 8.11).

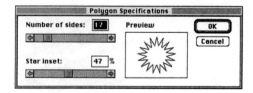

Figure 8.11

The Polygon Specifications dialog box.

The Polygon tool enables you to set both the number of sides of the polygon, and the dimension and sides of the possible Star Inset. You can create everything from basic polygons to explosive starbursts by exploring these settings (see Figure 8.12). The real magic begins after you have used the tool to create a polygon on your page. After the polygon is created, double-clicking it while the Selection Arrow is highlighted reveals its control points. The control points can be moved to create new polygon shapes (see Figure 8.13) not available in the Polygon Settings dialog box. When the control points are activated, clicking any line that connects the control points adds a new control point. Clicking a control point deletes it. Using all of these options, it's possible to use a basic polygon to create a shape with any number of control points. Moving these points to new positions can be a way to achieve a graphic with any shape (see Figure 8.14).

Figure 8.12

Using a polygon's control points enables you to create new shapes.

Figure 8.13

Any number of control points can be added to a polygonal shape in PageMaker, allowing you to create whatever new shapes are desired.

Figure 8.14

After it is reconfigured, the new shape can receive a stroke and fill just like a standard polygon.

The complex symbol in Figure 8.15 was created from a circular polygon with 100 sides and no star points. Points were then moved into place, and stroke and fill added. By using the maximum number of points (100), line segments can emulate curves. The graphic could even be exported as an EPS for further manipulation and refinement in a drawing program if needed. After the image is set, you can add apparent 3-D extruded depth by cloning the image and setting it on top of itself with a new fill (in the example in Figure 8.16, the fill was set to zero).

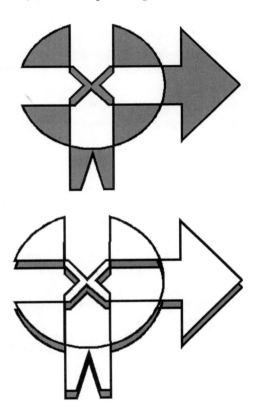

Figure 8.15

The Polygon tool can be used to create complex imagery.

Figure 8.16

Adding apparent 3-D extruded depth to a reconfigured polygon graphic is simple.

The Polygon Frame Tool

The Polygon Frame tool works the same way as its non-frame counterpart. In fact, whatever settings are used in one automatically transfer to the other. The difference is that a polygon frame is meant to be filled with text. The only way to get text into a standard polygon is to shape text as you create it by using spaces and returns, and then manually place it in a polygon (perhaps grouping it with the polygon). If you place text in a polygon frame and then reshape the frame, the text attempts to conform to the new frame. There is no guarantee that the result will meet your expectations, or that it will be aesthetically desirable. Stick with non-headline type sizes if you're going to use a customized polygon shape as a frame. It's much easier and more controllable to place headlines in a graphic by masking rather than using the Frame tools. This is because both the graphic and the headline text can be maneuvered freely until you achieve what you want.

Polygon Masking

When thinking about drawing tools and operations in PageMaker 6.5, a graphic shape's capability to act as an integrated mask for another shape has to stand out in importance. This is because the masking action presents us with limitless ways to achieve visual effects without leaving the PageMaker environment. Masks can be used in two ways to create unique graphics:

◆ They can be used to erase areas of the receiving graphic, the graphic targeted to receive the mask.

◆ The mask cutter can be text or a photo, and can be added internally to the receiving shape.

Note

The graphic that is created first always becomes the active mask, no matter what order the elements are selected in. If you use text blocks in a mixed composition of graphics and text blocks, however, they become the active mask. If you select more than two elements for a masking operation, the last one chosen becomes the element to be acted on (the element that "receives" the others). No matter what order a text block is chosen in, it always disappears until parts of it are made visible by the one "receiving" graphic. At least one graphic must always be involved in a masking operation. You cannot get two text blocks to act as masking partners. The only way to achieve that would be to transform a text block into a graphic (into a path object) in an external application, and then to import it into PageMaker as a graphic. As of version 6.5, PageMaker offers no transformation options for changing a text block into a graphic, which is one of PageMaker's biggest shortcomings at the moment.

If you want to erase a part of one polygon with another, create the eraser (the cutting form) first. Next, create the object that will be acted upon. No matter in what order the two polygons are selected, the first one created always becomes the active element. The other receives the action. The active element, the first polygon, has to be moved to the top of the stack, or in the case of separate layers, to the topmost layer. The receiving and action polygons must be colorized differently, or you won't see any results. To make the action polygon an eraser, make sure that its color and fill are set to "Paper" in the action graphic (the "cutter"). Another option is to set both color and fill to 0% black. No Stroke should be set for the receiving graphic, or the cut will show the edge. Make sure that the action graphic (the "cutter") is moved to the top of the stack, or if layers are in use, that it resides on the topmost layer. Then just move it over the receiving graphic until you have achieved the desired object.

Composite Graphics and Masking

Use the Oval tool in PageMaker to create two circles of approximately equal size. Color the first Paper and no Stroke, and the second as a 40% Cyan with no Stroke. The first one disappears from view except for its control points. Select both graphics (see Figure 8.17).

Figure 8.17

Use the Oval tool to create circles.

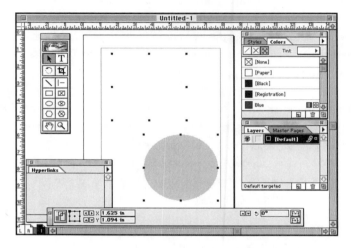

1. Go to the Element menu and select Mask. The first graphic is now the "cutter" for the second. Deselect both graphics and reselect the first one. Go to the Element/Arrange menu and select Bring to Front. The cutter is now positioned correctly in the stack to do its work (see Figure 8.18).

Figure 8.18

Go to the Element Arrange menu and select Bring to Front.

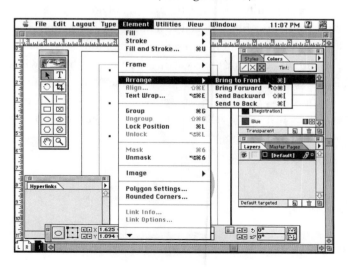

2. Move the cutter over the second graphic, and notice that a bite is missing, creating a crescent moon shape. If you want, you can select both graphics and group them, and move the shape to another part of a PageMaker document (see Figure 8.19).

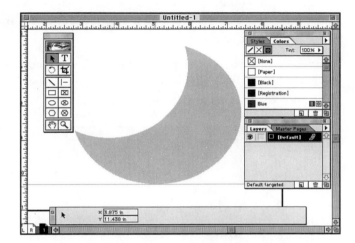

Figure 8.19

Move the cutter over the second graphic.

3. Very complex shapes can be created by using the mask function to enable one polygon to cut away another (see Figure 8.20).

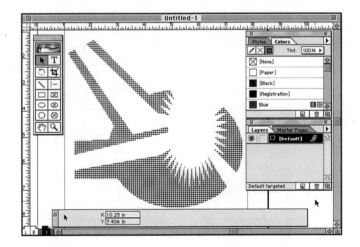

Figure 8.20

Complex shape creation is a snap by using this method.

An Alternate Way to Use the Masking Operation

Now you want to focus on the second way that masks can be used to create unique graphics in PageMaker. This time, instead of cutting away parts of a graphic, you'll add content to the receiving form. The first graphic is always the actor, and the second is the shape acted upon. Choose an imported photo as your first graphic, and a customized polygon shape as your receiving form.

1. You begin the second mask process the same way you began the first example, only this time you are going to use a CMYK TIFF photo as the first graphic (see Figure 8.21).

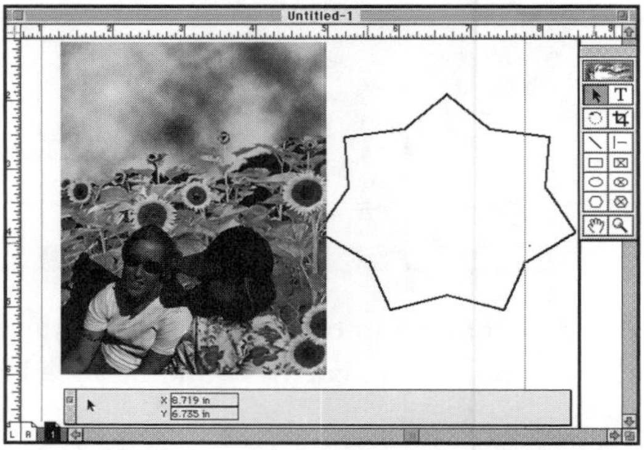

Figure 8.21

Use a CMYK TIFF photo.

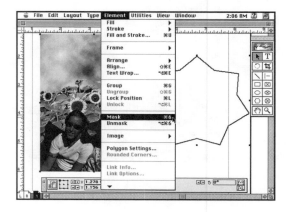

2. The Photo and the selected shape are selected simultaneously and Mask is chosen from the Element menu (see Figure 8.22).

Figure 8.22

The Mask command is chosen after the elements are selected.

3. After making sure that the photo is brought to the top of the image stack (or placed on the topmost layer), it is moved into place. The polygon shape has now become its graphic frame (see Figure 8.23).

Figure 8.23

The polygon shape is now a graphic frame.

4. Using the command Element/Frame/Attach Content allows for the automatic filling of a frame with either a graphic or a text block. When using a frame instead of a mask operation on a non-frame polygonal shape and photo selection, you have much less control over how the image is placed. By using the Mask method, you can reposition the photo in the outlined shape (see Figure 8.24).

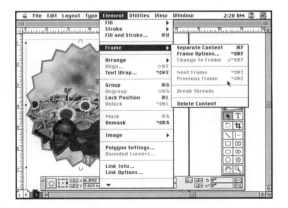

Figure 8.24

The graphic frame is automatically filled.

Using Open Polygons

Open Polygons represent PageMaker's closest approximation to a real drawing tool. The tool is accessed from the same icon as the Closed Polygon is in the Toolbar. Instead of clicking and then dragging to form a closed polygon, however, you just click and release the mouse button to place connected points onscreen. When you're finished with a line, a double-click ends it. Although basically simple to operate, the Open Polygon process can be used to create complex vector drawings. The nicest feature it has is that by drawing short line segments, you are able to approximate gentle curves. True, this is not a Bézier pen or a Freehand pencil or brush, but it does represent a tremendous leap in the right direction for users who want to incorporate more illustrations in their layouts without leaving PageMaker.

One of the main shortcomings of PageMaker is its inability to change text to a path (or to a graphic). Were it able to do so, you could use text as a mask for fills, and also reshape text blocks much more intuitively with freer flowing lines. This is especially important to PageMaker users who need to craft a drop cap on a page. With the Open Polygon tool, you can manually trace around a letter to get a graphic that can be filled with patterns or used as a mask. You could also do this to a headline, though the process would be far more labor intensive (see Figures 8.25 and 8.26).

Figure 8.25

You can use the Open Polygon tool as an illustrator's pen to create your own graphics.

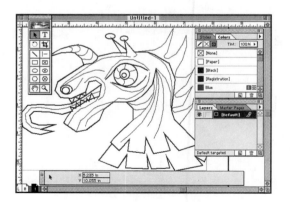

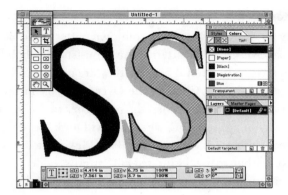

Figure 8.26

Using the Open Polygon tool over a letter results in a graphic that can be manipulated further.

Strokes and Fills

A stroke is the perimeter of a selected graphic and a fill is what is contained inside it. Strokes and fills can be considered basic creative ingredients in PageMaker, though limited as far as creative options go. Strokes are consigned to a limited number of patterns, from solids to multilinear and dashed in various thicknesses. Fills can be patterned or screened solids in a limited palette of colors. Artists are always challenged to work within limited boundaries and to come up with uses and solutions that take advantage of what is available. With this in mind, you might want to experiment with the multilinear strokes as a design ingredient when using open polygons to craft an illustration. If you transform the strokes in the illustration to multilinear strokes, it abstracts the image, although at the same time maintaining most of its recognizable features (see Figure 8.27).

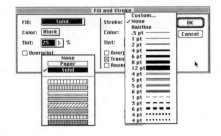

Figure 8.27

The Fill and Stroke dialog box is accessed through the Elements menu. Stroke options can be selected from a list of choices.

Fill Patterns

Presently no way exists to create your own patterns for the PageMaker library. PageMaker's Fill Pattern library consists of eight basic patterns. You also have to be careful because they are not WYSIWYG as far as printing is concerned. Clicking the Overprint box in the dialog box enables them to overprint when the piece goes to the printer, but you have no way of appreciating what that will look like onscreen. If you are adamant about using patterns for PageMaker art, it's wiser to make other choices than to use the limited Fill Patterns resident in PageMaker. Perhaps importing EPS art from an external illustration program is a strong alternative.

The artwork pictured in Figure 8.28 was pattern-filled in Illustrator and saved as a 1-bit EPS file. It was imported into PageMaker and cloned, with the copy placed over the original. The result was a pattern made up of the two interlaced patterns involved. A framed border was placed on top of the pattern to separate it from the excess graphics. You could cut the excess away by using a masking operation. If you need to create your own patterns for use in PageMaker, consider this method. You cannot achieve pattern buildups as a native PageMaker option.

Figure 8.28

With a little invested time, you can customize pattern-fills.

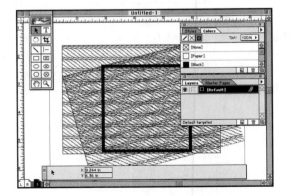

ShadeTree "Patternz" for PageMaker

"Patternz," from ShadeTree Software, is a collection of 100 PageMaker patterns. Patternz is a PageMaker plug-in that must be installed separately from the PageMaker application. Of the 100 patterns, 20 are editable so that you can create customized patterns to fit your current

PageMaker projects. Unlike PageMaker's native patterns, you can place Patternz on top of each other to create a pattern sandwich and the results can be viewed onscreen. Patternz shapes can be masked with other PageMaker elements and can be rotated to create angular results, which is not possible with PageMaker patterns.

The Patternz plug-in has 20 patterns that can be customized. Each can be applied as a rectangle, oval, or round-cornered rectangle (see Figure 8.29).

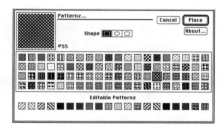

Figure 8.29

ShadeTree offers 100 patterns to choose from.

Look at figure 8.30 and you see that the oval on the left contains a Patternz selection. On the right, the same pattern has been cloned and rotated over itself for a mix. Any number of Patternz can be sandwiched together in PageMaker to create a new pattern. PageMaker patterns, on the other hand, offer no such options or variations (see Figure 8.30).

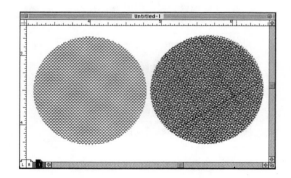

Figure 8.30

You can overlay and mix the ShadeTree Patternz.

The top row displays four of the Patternz graphics. In the bottom row, the rectangles are masks that show the effect of placing combinations of Patternz in a sandwich with each other, and then masking them into another shape (see Figure 8.31).

Figure 8.31

ShadeTree patterns can also be sandwiched.

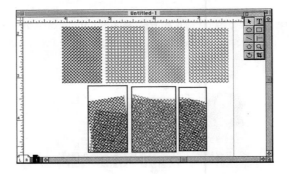

Making Your Own Patterns with Patternz

The last 20 boxes in the ShadeTree Patternz dialog box contain patterns you can customize and save in the library. By selecting one and clicking the Edit button, a separate Patternz Edit dialog box appears. From there, it's an easy and fun process to craft your own patterns. By using a pencil tool, you can select to fill the pixel boxes or erase them. Finished customized patterns can then be written to the document, and manipulated as desired (see Figures 8.32 and 8.33).

Figure 8.32

The ShadeTree Patternz Editing dialog box.

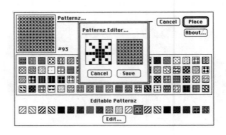

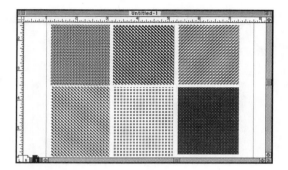

Figure 8.33

A collection of customized patterns ready for use in PageMaker.

ShadeTree Arrowz

A PageMaker document requires the addition of arrows at times, whether as pointers or as stand-alone graphic elements. You can use the Open Polygon tool to craft arrows when this need arises, or you can create them in a simple point-and-click fashion with the Arrowz plug-in, also from ShadeTree Software. With Arrowz, draw a straight line on the page, and leaving it selected, open the Arrowz plug-in dialog box (see Figure 8.34). Here, the tail and head of the arrow can be chosen from a list of possibilities, and the thickness adjusted. Tails and heads can be placed on either one or both ends of the arrow. Remembering that the original shape the arrow is being written to is a line, there are no possibilities for internal fills. There is, however, the capacity for colorizing the arrow from within the dialog box. As you can see from Figure 8.35, the possibilities for meeting all of your arrow graphics needs are present.

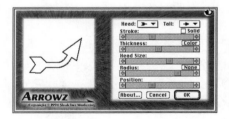

Figure 8.34

The ShadeTree Arrowz dialog box enables you to set all of the necessary variables for creating straight or curved arrow graphics.

Figure 8.35

The variety of arrow shapes possible with the Arrowz plug-in includes the capability to choose from a variety of points and ends.

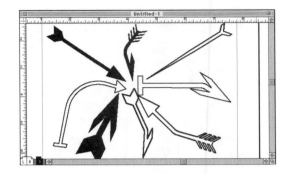

ShadeTree Starz

If you like the way that PageMaker's Polygon tool enables you to configure polygons and star shapes, you will love the PageMaker Starz plug-in from ShadeTree Software. The ShadeTree Starz dialog box (see Figure 8.36) enables you to craft star graphics with two shapes at time, with color for each as well. The thickness and distance parameters of each separate pattern can be altered independently. The result is a near limitless variety of star shapes, medallions, flowers, and other symbolic graphics useful to the PageMaker user (see Figure 8.37).

Figure 8.36

The ShadeTree Starz dialog box enables you much more freedom to create star-like shapes than PageMaker's Polygon dialog box.

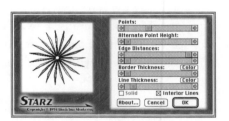

Figure 8.37

The variety of different star-shapes that can be created with ShadeTree's Starz plug-in is almost limitless.

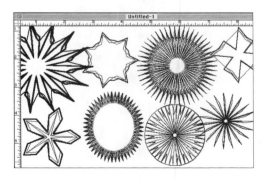

ShadeTree Fraemz

With ShadeTree Software's Fraemz plug-in (see Figure 8.38), the PageMaker user can add certificates or fancy borders to any selection. Fraemz come in a collection of separate libraries and install easily into PageMaker as a plug-in. The process for using one of the Fraemz designs is as follows:

1. Select the graphic.

2. Open the Fraemz plug-in in PageMaker's Utility/Plug-ins list.

3. Choose a Fraemz style.

4. Apply (place) the Fraemz border .

Fraemz attach themselves to PageMaker frame graphics permanently, but may not be resized. Fraemz can be moved away from non-frame graphics selections, and then can be resized.

Figure 8.38

Opening the Fraemz plug-in presents you with a scrollable listing of available styles.

Creating Special Effects with Frames

PageMaker's new Framing tool gives you many opportunities for graphics and layout creativity. When it comes to placing text in a frame, it is strongly suggested that you keep the frame shape somewhat rectangular, especially for headlines. This is because large type gets randomly displaced if placed in a curvy frame. If the text size is small (relative to the frame graphic), you can explore more curve-oriented frames. Nothing is "poured" into a frame as some other layout applications allow, but text must be placed there with the command Element/Frame/Attach Content. After text is placed in a frame, it can be resized and restyled according to your needs. This is often necessary when working with larger type sizes. You cannot attach frames inside other frames as content, but you can manually drag them into, or over, the targeted central frame graphic. Once inside, set the inserted graphics Stroke to None in the Stroke dialog box. You could, of course, add borders and fills to an internal framed element if you want to set it off from the larger frame's background.

The Frame Options dialog box must be mastered if you want to make the most out of framed graphics and text. It enables you to justify and resize frame content to best fit graphics; all that a frame can address when the content is a PageMaker or an imported text block is justification. Frames can be resized to the graphic content's configurations and graphic content can be resized to a frames dimensions and shape. This becomes all the more necessary if you plan to use curved or reconfigured Polygon Frames for graphic content, to avoid unpleasant surprises (see Figure 8.39).

Figure 8.39

The Frame Options dialog box offers some vital tools for PageMaker frame operations.

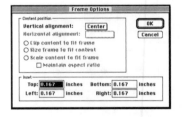

You can place imported graphics or photos inside a frame, but frames do not address other frames as components, nor are they able to digest PageMaker rectangles, ovals, or polygons. You cannot incorporate grouped elements or multiple elements in a frame. You can, however, place any or all of these elements in a framed area manually, taking care to adjust their Strokes and Fills as needed.

Tip

If you need to move text or graphics inside a border, and don't care about cropping some of the content, use masking instead of frames. If, however, you want the targeted content displayed in its entirety inside a border, and that the content remain stable within that border, use frames. The choice between using a masking or a framing technique depends on each PageMaker user and how he or she likes to work.

The pictured exploration of PageMaker's Frame option shown in Figure 8.40 incorporates more than just framing. The "face" object is a frame polygon. The large text is a part of the frame, so it no longer behaves like separated text (it does not react to a text wrap, for instance). The smaller text beneath it sits in its own frame, which is invisible because it has None selected for the Stroke. The words DO IT! are not a part of a frame but are simply placed over the frame graphic in an outline type style. Everything is then grouped so that it can be placed anywhere on the page.

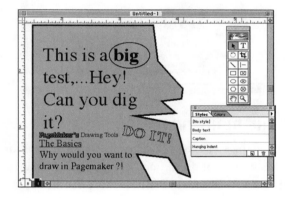

Figure 8.40

An example of the creative use of the framing option.

The Grammar of Ornament CD-ROM

Hundreds of CD-ROMs contain photographic and clip-art graphics that the PageMaker user can accumulate, and this number grows each year. If one such collection could be singled out as an absolute must-have for PageMaker, it would be the *Grammar of Ornament*, created and distributed by Direct Imagination. This CD-ROM displays 112 of the 600 full-color lithographs of Owen Jones, one of the most influential collectors and lithographers of world ornament of the nineteenth century. These works influenced such notable artists and architects as Frank Lloyd, Louis Sullivan, and William Morris. The CD-ROM comes with one of the most extensive and beautiful PDF manuals you will ever come across, detailing all the history and browsing information you need to make use of these exquisite images in your PageMaker designs. All of the images are included as EPS files. They load into PageMaker easily and can be resized and manipulated to suit your needs. They work as mask components and can also be incorporated into frames (see Figure 8.41).

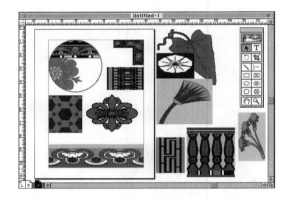

Figure 8.41

The Grammar of Ornament CD-ROM is one of the most treasured collections of EPS images you can hope to find for PageMaker ornamental uses.

CHOOSING THE RIGHT GRAPHICS FORMAT

PageMaker enables you to import graphics in a number of formats for both the Macintosh and PC, including: WMF (Windows Metafile), EMF (Enhanced Metafile), BMP (Windows Bitmap), PICT, TIFF (Tagged Image File Format), and EPS (Encapsulated PostScript). EPS and TIFF are the most common and your best choices for both the Macintosh and PC, although you should avoid EPS graphics if you're printing to a non-PostScript printer. EPS is a vector graphics format and TIFF is a bitmap format. If you intend to do image processing in PageMaker, your best graphics format to import is a CMYK (Cyan-Magenta-Yellow-Black color separated) TIFF. TIFFs were designed to incorporate more image information than other formats, though the files can be large. You can compress them at the image-creation end with what is called "LZW compression," as long as the software that is used to save them allows this. For more information on Web specific file formats, see Chapter 16, "HTML and the World Wide Web."

You also can import single frames from AVI and QuickTime movies, aided by an onscreen dialog box that enables you to select any movie frame from a VCR-like dialog.

In all cases, output determines format. The type of printer you're outputting to (PostScript capable or not) is one determining factor, and whether the graphics are meant for Web publishing or another purpose. PageMaker documents targeted to the print-to-paper medium have to take advantage of the type of printer being used. Unless you are printing to a device that sits next to you in your studio, it is important that you learn everything about the printing device you'll use. This enables you to design your PageMaker documents accordingly. The printing facility or service bureau that you plan to use will be more than willing to tell you what they prefer in terms of image formats, because they want your return business. Find out these facts as early in the design process as possible. In most cases, you will find that EPS vector graphics and TIFF CMYK bitmaps are the best choice for printing to paper. (See Chapter 14, "The World of Print Publishing" and Chapter 15 "Prepress, Service Bureaus, and Printers.")

Web publishing is another story altogether. Though the future may allow more variety in Web graphics publishing, at present the choices are very limited. Two graphics format options are still dominating Web publishing, with a third choice coming up fast. The two dominant choices are GIF (Graphics Interchange Format) and JPEG (Joint Photographic Experts Group). GIF graphics have 256 (and sometimes 216) color palettes, whereas JPEGs can incorporate 24-bit (16,000,000) color palettes. GIF graphics are used when sharp line elements are important and JPEG is used for larger images (usually background and photographic) when the color palette demands a wider choice. Growing quickly as a favorite among Web publishers in-the-know is the PNG (pronounced "PING") format. PNG was developed to replace GIF, because CompuServe, the owners of the GIF format, want to add a fee for any developers who utilize the GIF format, and PNG is free (and intends to remain so) to all present and future developers and users.

One reason that you might choose GIF over JPEG is that GIF backgrounds can be made transparent for Web use. This can be accomplished with one of the appropriate image translators listed on the following pages. JPEG graphics for the Web come in two associated formats, JPEG and Progressive JPEG. The option offered by Progressive JPEG files is that they are downloaded from the Web in a way that makes them progressively visible, from a blur to full clarity. This helps the viewer recognize the image faster so that he or she can either stick with it or go to another Web page if it doesn't meet his or her needs.

Do not work with LZW-compressed TIFF images if you are working on a Web-page graphic. Always store TIFFs as non-compressed, as you can store a separate compressed TIFF for print purposes later. If a TIFF is to be targeted to a Web page, you will want to translate it as a JPEG for the Web. JPEGs are compressed images and you never want to re-compress an already compressed image for any medium because it can degrade the image content. Web pages have a dpi setting of 72. Working at larger print dpi settings is a waste of time as far as Web output is concerned. The only reason to work at print dpi settings is if the image is going to be reproduced in print, and later repurposed for the Web, in which case it should be transformed to a 72 dpi size. Work with a palette that represents what you want your images to be, not what the Web or a Web browser demands. You can translate the images to alternate palette and resolution settings later.

A third option to consider is to publish and distribute your documents as PDF files, in which case the graphics format you use will have no bearing at all. Adobe Acrobat's PDF format files are viewed with everything, text and graphics, in the same way as the original. It doesn't matter that the recipient lacks the fonts for the text and the graphics elements are represented without file format concerns. PDF files can be sent peer to peer on removable media, or they can be displayed on the Internet with special plug-ins added to your Web browser application.

Useful Image Translators

You may occasionally need to translate image files from one format to another before importing them into PageMaker. If so, you will find that most paint and image processing applications have a variety of formats they read and write, and using these applications to do format conversion works quite nicely. If, on the other hand, you either lack an application that does this or want a more enhanced application that can handle more formats, a number of format conversion applications are on the market, including the applications listed in the following sections.

DeBabelizer 1.6.5 (Mac)/DeBabelizer Pro (Win)

DeBabelizer converts over 70 graphics file formats and includes a Web utility called "ProScripts" for translating Web site graphics. This includes GIF with a transparency option, JPEG, Progressive JPEG, and the previously mentioned PNG format. It automatically creates the best Web palette configurations. It displays optimized Web graphics on a Mac or Windows system with no palette shifting. It also adjusts the image resolution automatically. DeBabelizer also has the capability of applying Photoshop filter effects over a series of images. DeBabelizer Lite offers about 60 file translators in comparison with the professional version.

Conversions Plus

Conversions Plus from DataViz enables you to read, write, and format Mac disks in a Windows environment. It translates word processing, spreadsheet, database, graphics, and binary formats (including PageMaker) and can read/write out the translations to Mac disks (including removable media). Conversions Plus can read BMP, GIF, JPEG, PCX, TIFF, WMF, and WPG and can write GIF, TIFF, JPEG, and PICT.

Graphic Converter (Mac)

Lemke Software in Germany offers this application as shareware. Graphic Converter can load over 80 file formats, both bitmap and vector graphics. It can save the following formats: BMP, Color Table,

EPS, GIF, HPGL, TIFF, IMG, JPG, MacPaint, QuickTime Movie, PBM, PCX, PIC, PIX, PICT, PICT in Resource, PNG, PPAT, PSD, RAW, SGI, Softimage, Startup Screen, SUN, TGA, and TIFF. Graphics Converter also comes with its own basic paint and image processing program. Graphics Converter is listed on many graphics Web sites for free downloading, with a request from the author for a $35 appreciation fee.

Hijaak Pro (Windows 95)

HiJaak Pro for Windows 95 translates 33 bitmap formats and 18 vector formats, including JPEG, GIF, and PNG. It also translates 3-D object files (3DS, DWG, DXF, IGES, and VRML). HiJaak Pro supports multiple platform graphics: Windows, RGB, Sun Raster, Amiga IFF, IBM IOCA and GOCA, and Mac PICT.

HVS PhotoGIF and PhotoJPEG for Photoshop (Boxtop Software)

Each of these Photoshop plug-ins has a preview inset in their dialog box so that any changes you make while exploring the options (like JPEG compression percentages) can be seen in the image before you save it. HVS PhotoGIF creates small high-quality GIF files and provides capabilities for creating Web GIF animations. It contains a preview with advanced GIF transparency tools, including an Eyedropper, Color Picker, Touch-up Brush, and Automatic "Halo" Removing Edge tool. HVS PhotoGIF also enables you to batch process selected image files.

HVS ProJPEG creates high-quality JPEG files, with advanced control over compression settings. HVS ProJPEG can produce image files two to five times smaller than other JPEG translators. It gives you direct control of the image output quality, progression options, and more. HVS ProJPEG can also batch process groups of selected files at one time.

MacLink Plus/Translators Pro (from DataViz for the Mac)

This application installs on a Mac and enables you to write out translated PC files to a DOS disk. Translators Pro can read and write PC word-processing, graphics, and spreadsheet/database programs. Translators Pro can read DXF, CGM, PIC, CGM, PCX, GEM, IMG, BMP, WMF, and WPG. It can write PICT, PCX, TIFF, BMP, WMF, and WPG. Version 8.1 and above of MacLinkPlus has special features for Web graphics users. Full HTML translators are included, so you can reshape any necessary HTML code. The application addresses GIFs, JPEGs, and PNGs.

Transverter Pro (Mac/Windows)

Transverter Pro takes EPS vector drawings and exports them as either Illustrator, PICT Vector, TIFF, or JPEG. This makes it a perfect translation utility for PageMaker users wanting to develop Web output. Because EPS images normally cannot be edited, this opens the whole world of EPS graphics editing and translation to the PageMaker user. Now, EPS color can be modified and shapes customized. Results can then be translated to appropriate file formats for use on PageMaker pages destined for the Web.

You have to take care when compressing images using the JPEG format. This is a lossy format, meaning that lower JPEG settings deteriorate the image more. The top picture in Figure 8.42 was saved using a 95% JPEG quality ratio, whereas the bottom image was saved using a 20% JPEG quality setting.

Figure 8.42

JPEG is a lossy format.

IMPORTING GRAPHICS

Starting with PageMaker 6.5, you now have the capability to import native Illustrator files directly into PageMaker. Because FreeHand and other vector drawing applications also have the capability to save out graphics in the Illustrator format, this capability also includes all other vector graphics applications by default. This is both a time-saver and a more intuitive way to work for users who own and use both Illustrator and PageMaker on a daily basis. Care must be taken as far as colors are concerned when importing graphics. Whether the imported graphic is an EPS file or an Illustrator 5.x or 6.x file, the colors that were saved out with it are imported, sometimes resulting in a limited arrangement of spot or process colors. Time and money can be reduced by editing the spot colors in an Illustrator or EPS graphic, and merging them with the colors already in the publication. This reduces the number of color separations involved.

Both Mac and Windows PageMaker users can import necessary graphics file formats for use on either platform. As far as applying Photoshop effects within PageMaker, it is still required that the image be a TIFF CMYK.

The New QuickTime Import Filter

The world of publishing is influenced as much by video as it is by what's happening on the Web. Video means pictures and one method for storing video pictures on the computer is through QuickTime movies. Each frame of a QuickTime movie can be a picture by itself and PageMaker takes advantage of this situation by enabling you to view QuickTime movies in its own VCR-like viewer screen. Pausing a picture in the playback window enables it to be selected for placement in PageMaker as a graphic. One important fact about QuickTime movies is that they are often too low in resolution to make for acceptable printed frames. A way to get around this is to treat the separate frame(s) with an image processing filter, changing it from a photographic to a more "painterly" graphic. (See Figures 8.43 and 8.44.)

Figure 8.43

The QuickTime dialog box that appears when you place a QuickTime movie in PageMaker enables you to select any frame for placement on the page as a graphic.

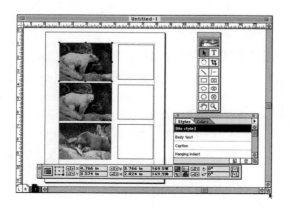

Figure 8.44

PageMaker and the new QuickTime import facility can be utilized to create a professional storyboard for film or video.

Your QuickTime frames and other placed graphics may look a bit fuzzy when placed in PageMaker. To sharpen them, go to the File menu and select Preferences/General. Click the High resolution radio button to sharpen your view of the images on the page (see Figure 8.45).

Figure 8.45

Adjust the Graphics display in the Preferences dialog box.

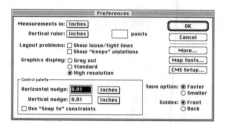

Tip

You can use a video camera to take a sequence of images of a subject (a sporting event, for example) that you are referencing in a PageMaker document, and transform them into a QuickTime movie. Grabbing separate stills from the sequence enables you to add dynamic variations to a PageMaker graphic not available through stills alone. You could, for instance, take several frames from the QuickTime video and place them over each other on different PageMaker layers, creating a dynamic composite from the frames in the sequence. For users doing procedural documentation, perhaps a PageMaker reference manual, PageMaker's capability to display separate frames as a QuickTime movie can add just the clarity you're searching for. The final step might be to add callout text over the images to call attention to the mechanics of the process involved.

A PAGEMAKER STORYBOARD

The new QuickTime facility in PageMaker enables you to create a storyboard, an overview of images that make up a movie, in a fraction of the time normally associated with this task, and at a more reasonable cost than the fees to hire an illustrator. Here's how:

1. Script out a rough outline of your sequence.

2. Using a video camera, walk through the script, blocking out (setting) the main focus points (keyframes), and duplicating the walkthrough with different camera angles. When you use alternate camera angles at the keyframe points, you get a better sense of what the best camera angle is for developing a more dynamic final result that fits your story.

3. Using the video translation software of your choice and the hardware necessary to import the video into the computer for storage (a frame grabber), import the video and save it to disk as a QuickTime movie.

4. Use PageMaker to open the movie, and selecting the frames that represent the best way to tell the story in as few steps as possible, place those frames in a PageMaker document. Place basic descriptions from your story script next to each frame, and indicate the audio that is used when that frame appears. Show the results to your clients as a comprehensive storyboard of your ideas, in preparation for the final filming.

THE IMPORTANCE OF A UNIFIED INTERFACE STRATEGY

Starting with PageMaker 6.5 and Photoshop 4.0, and incorporating Illustrator in the near future, the user who decides to master all three of these applications as a set of unified tools is going to have an easier time of it than one who decides that mastery of only one or two is vital. The PageMaker/Illustrator/Photoshop troika has always been seen by Adobe as a three-part solution for page layout, vector graphics creation, and image processing, and as an integrated approach for the DTP user and the professional print shop. Each one of these tools is complex in its own right, so to keep users from having to constantly keep the documentation on their lap, all three are merging as far as the look of their tools and interfaces go. This is evident in PageMaker's layering dialog box and processes in version 6.5, and is now comparable to the layering dialog box in Photoshop. More movement toward similar interfaces in all three applications can be guaranteed for future releases as well. Learning to master any one of the three gives new users a head start when it comes time to add the others.

THE PLACE COMMAND

Place (found in the File menu) is the central command for bringing anything into PageMaker. A useful option in the Place dialog box enables you to search all of the drives on your system for files whose named elements you can configure, all JPEG files for instance, or perhaps all files with the word "cloud" embedded in them. You can also place URL (Uniform Resource Locator) strings (see Chapter 16). Text can be placed as a New Story, or as a replacement block for a selected existing story (see Chapter 6, "Working with Text").

Note

As far as graphics are concerned, click the High Resolution checkbox in the General Preferences dialog box to see sharper versions of your graphics. This takes some RAM but is worth it if you want to see what the graphics really look like, or at least a close approximation of them. To save a little time in redraws and RAM as the page is being composed, you can leave High Resolution off until all of the elements are in place.

Using the Place Command with Templates

The Place command has a special purpose when working with PageMaker templates. In a template, all or most of the represented elements (text, graphics, logos, and so on) are called placeholders. This means that they are represented for position only to keep content restricted to the template's structure. Activating an element in a template (clicking it), and then using the Place command, enables you to place your text and your graphics at the same location as the placeholder material. You can Replace an Entire Graphic or Replace an Entire Story. (For more information on using the Place command in a text context, see Chapter 6.)

Placing an Inline Graphic

If you need to incorporate a graphic inside a text block, PageMaker makes it simple. This type of graphic is called an *inline graphic*, and once placed inside a text block, it responds to whatever adjustments are made to the text block.

Use the Text tool to place the cursor in the text where you would like the graphic to appear. Next, go to the Place command in the File menu, find the appropriate graphic, and import it. The graphic appears where you placed the cursor. Move the text block and the inline graphic moves along with it. The graphic can still be manipulated on its own as far as sizing and other parameters are concerned, but it is no longer a stand-alone item. It is now considered as part of the text block. Delete the text block and you delete the graphic along with it.

Using Inline Graphics as Internal Drop Caps

A special project might arise in which you need to place a drop cap in the center of a line of text. Perhaps you've created the drop cap as a customized character in Photoshop, or another image processing application, and saved it as a separate TIFF bitmap or as a vector graphics object from Illustrator. Drop caps are usually thought of as large, fancy letters that start a paragraph, but PageMaker enables you to use them in a whole new way by placing them within a text block as an inline graphic. Drop caps are used to call attention to important sections of a story, usually the start of a major section. They can also be used to break up the rather boring visual that too much running text presents to the eye. The most ornamental drop caps are found in sacred texts throughout the world, from the medieval scriptures enhanced by numerous scribes to the manuscripts of the ancient Celts. Here's how to create your own drop cap elements (see Figures 8.46 and 8.47):

1. Design the drop cap in either a bitmap or vector application, and save it to your hard disk.

2. Open PageMaker and load the project that contains the text block you're targeting for the inline drop cap. Place the text cursor in the text where the graphic will appear. Place the graphic from its storage path.

3. Adjust the inline drop cap as needed and save the project.

Figure 8.46

Accessing the Place command in the File menu opens a file dialog box that enables you to locate the element to be placed on the page.

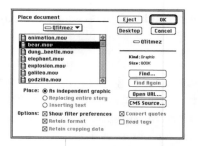

Figure 8.47

Although it can be resized and adjusted as needed, the inline graphic remains a part of the text block to which it was targeted.

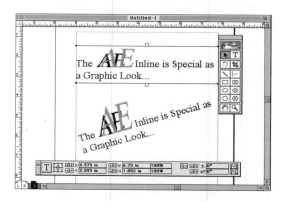

PAGEMAKER DRAG AND DROP

PageMaker drag and drop uses the Drag-Drop Manager on the Mac and OLE 2 on the PC. With PageMaker 6.5, you can drag and drop elements between PageMaker and other applications, and among any open PageMaker 6.5 publications. You can, for instance, drag graphics from a PageMaker document into Photoshop and rasterize them for Web publishing purposes. This does not work with PageMaker native graphics, such as rectangles, ovals, and polygons created in PageMaker itself, although this could be a possibility in a future version. Grouped graphics can be drag-dropped as well, but not multiple choices. If you must drag and drop multiple elements at the same time, temporarily group them first.

Drag and drop enables you to either move the original or a copy. Dragging and dropping a QuickTime movie

Scanning Images into PageMaker with TWAIN

Some of your best opportunities to control the look of an image will come as you scan the item. Because PageMaker includes TWAIN technology, you can scan photographs and other art directly into a publication. You access this capability through the Acquire command in the File menu.

continues

works differently than placing it. Drag and drop writes only the first frame of the sequence and doesn't allow you the luxury of selecting any frame. The biggest caution with drag and drop operations is that RAM is of the essence. You must have enough RAM to be able to open the required multiple applications at the same time.

Tip

Remember that the source and target applications must be open at the same time to use the drag and drop feature. Times may occur, however, when drag and drop is not the perfect choice, especially when the applications to be opened need total memory that strains the system. At such moments, Clipboard copy and paste operations are just as useful. Clipboard operations, however, allow only limited file transfers, in that you have to switch to the other application to paste the results. The best advice is that you should load your system with as much RAM as you can afford so that drag and drop operations can be used when necessary.

Drag and drop is also the mainstay of PageMaker Library functions. A PageMaker Library can be set up

Your scanner manufacturer must provide a TWAIN module so that you can put this feature to work. Depending on the approach used by your scanner maker, it's possible that you can have full-image controls when you import the scanned image (including control of contrast, cropping, dodging, and so on). What you see when you call the TWAIN driver for your scanner is entirely up to the scanner manufacturer. PageMaker has nothing to do with the interface, because it merely provides the "slot" to enable your scanner's innate TWAIN talents.

After the scan has been completed and saved in whatever file format you choose (probably TIFF), you are shifted into the standard PageMaker Place command mode and given a loaded graphic icon so that you can pour the graphic onto the page.

Keep in mind that it might be a better strategy to scan the graphic outside PageMaker and edit it with a full-fledged photo-retouching program (such as Photoshop) that may have more powerful capabilities than your scanner's TWAIN module.

from the Window/Plug-in Palettes/Show Library command. You can either open a stored library or create a new one. Items placed in the library can be drag-dropped to the page or to other applications.

PLACING GRAPHICS FROM THE WEB

You can use the drag and drop method to grab and place a graphic from a Netscape or Explorer browser window. The only consideration here is that you should be aware of the emerging copyright issues involved with using graphics, or any elements, lifted from the Net.

One way artists can mark their work has been initiated in Photoshop 4.0. Watermarks, or personalized artist signatures, can be embedded and remain within a graphics file. These graphics, when posted to the Web, contain the artist's signature identification so that original works remain tagged as such. The best advice is that you should always check to be sure that the elements you're using on your page are either copyright free (public domain), or get permission from the creator before publishing them yourself. If you contact the originator of an element you need, you can probably get permission to use it for little or nothing. In this world of artistic litigation, it's far better to be safe than embarrassingly sorry.

PLUG-IN IMPORTANCE

PageMaker's move to an extensible plug-in architecture is a great benefit to everyone who imports graphics into PageMaker because of the customization fostered. Extensibility means that the application is open to plug-ins from other developers. New plug-ins down the line promise to let you add new features and capabilities to PageMaker. Four Photoshop special effects plug-ins that can be accessed from within PageMaker are covered later in this chapter, giving you a good idea of the creative power accessible to the PageMaker user. The whole topic and range of importing graphics into PageMaker is affected by plug-in use, because it's often vital to tweak or manipulate the graphic in some way after it's placed on the page.

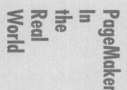

Extensis: Intellihance

Intellihance is a Photoshop-compatible plug-in that either applies "intelligent" changes to your image itself (meaning that the plug-in will grind away and produce a result without your direct intervention), or enables you to manually control the changes. It addresses an image's Contrast, Brightness, Saturation, Sharpness, and Despeckling (getting rid of dust marks found after an image is scanned). A preview screen, showing the image before and after transformations are applied, is always visible in the automatic mode and it can be toggled on in the manual mode. If you plan to use Intellihance as a preparatory step in Photoshop before porting the image to PageMaker, you can use the included Pixelcraft separation table to change an RGB image to a PageMaker-necessary CMYK. The separation table included with Intellihance emulates a sheet-fed offset press using a commercial ink set on coated stock.

IMAGE CONTROL

Color graphics do not dominate the publishing market. The cost of working in color, especially for shorter run jobs, remains high. Because PageMaker can incorporate 1-bit (black-and-white) as well as grayscale (usually 256-color) images, and because designers still use a wealth of black-and-white and grayscale images, PageMaker has some options located in the Image Control selection, accessible by Element/Image/Image Control in the menu bar. This PageMaker command enables you modify black-and-white and grayscale bitmap images.

MetaTools: KPT Convolver

Convolver allows more user interaction than Intellihance, so if you have to choose between the two, the way you work as a designer will determine which one to choose. An incremental "reward" is even given to the user who spends time accessing all of Convolver's options (one to five stars).

A convolution, in computer jargon, refers to a convolution matrix, a grid of numbers that tells the system how neighboring pixels should be transformed. Operations such as sharpens, blurs, hue, saturation, brightness, tints, fades, and similar image changes fall within the boundaries of a convolution matrix change. Convolver is a visually-oriented plug-in that hides the numerical components of the convolution grid in exchange for interactive buttons and space-age controls. If you

Image Control does not work with color images, so the choice is grayed out. Image Control enables you to increase or decrease the lightness or contrast of an image by applying a line or dot halftone screen and a halftone screen ruling value for the image. A tighter screening value (more dots to the inch) creates a darker image, whereas an image with more space in between the halftone elements creates a lighter image. There are complications, however, because the fewer halftone elements an image has the less information the graphic has, and a much more contrasted image can result. You have to experiment with the setting and get good comparative printouts (proofs) to understand what the implications of changes in these settings mean in terms of select images.

With Image Control you can alter the following:

◆ **Image Brightness:** Alter brightness by percentage. On the Mac only, you can also vary the brightness for one or more levels of grayscale.

◆ **Image Contrast:** Separate objects in the image can have their contrast against the background heightened or dampened. On the Mac only, you can also vary the contrast for one or more levels of grayscale.

◆ **Image Screen Angle:** You can enter an alternate screen angle to override the printer's default angle (typically set at 45 degrees).

◆ **The Image's Screen Pattern:** You can specify a line screen for special effects if desired.

want to explore the convolution matrix itself, it can be brought up with a simple menu command. Convolver addresses image Blur, Sharpen, Edges, Relief, Hue, Saturation, Brightness, Tint, Fade to Gray, and Color Contrast. Refer to Figure 8.48.

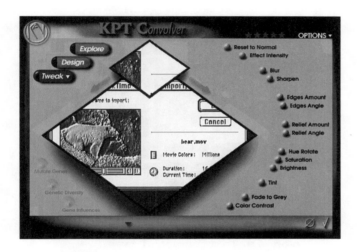

Figure 8.48

MetaTool's KPT Convolver enables you to target image fine-tuning from within PageMaker through the use of a space-age interface.

MODIFYING POSTSCRIPT PRINTER OUTPUTS

You can enter a screen-ruling value to override the PostScript printer's default (usually 53 lpi for 300-dpi LaserWriters, and 90 or 150 lpi for imagesetters).

Macintosh users also have the following options:

◆ **Black-and-white control:** This control is selected automatically if the system detects a black-and-white 1-bit image. (See Figures 8.49 to 8.51.)

Figure 8.49

The Image Control dialog box
is located in the Element
Menu/Image/Image Control.

Figure 8.50

As you tweak the settings in
the Image Control dialog box,
the targeted image displays a
preview of the changes.

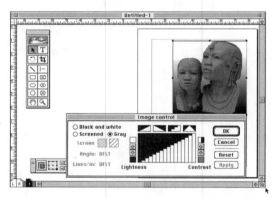

Figure 8.51

The downward Ramp using the
Image Control setting on
a grayscale image.

◆ **Screened control:** Changes the screen value for a black-and-white image.

◆ **Gray control:** If gray is selected when a grayscale TIFF image is displayed, the screen ruling selected in the Color printing dialog box prints the image. Customized settings for the screen ruling can be achieved by entering a value in the Lines/in text box. (See Figures 8.52 and 8.53.)

Figure 8.52

The staircase ramp setting using Image Control on a grayscale image.

Figure 8.53

The pyramid ramp setting using Image Control on a grayscale image.

◆ **Gray-level patterns control:** Click an icon to change the pattern. Here you can modify lightness, contrast, and halftone screen settings of the image. On the Mac, drag individual slider bars to create custom effects or use the Up or Down arrows to adjust the image globally. You can also click one of the four listed effects. Windows users can adjust the values in the Lightness and Contrast text boxes from -100 to +100 percent. Images can be reversed by negative settings.

Windows and Mac users have the following options:

◆ Click the rightmost icon in the Screen option (called Screen Patterns in Windows) to specify a line-screen pattern. (See Figure 8.54.)

Figure 8.54

Applying a screen with Image Control to a grayscale image with a pyramid ramp.

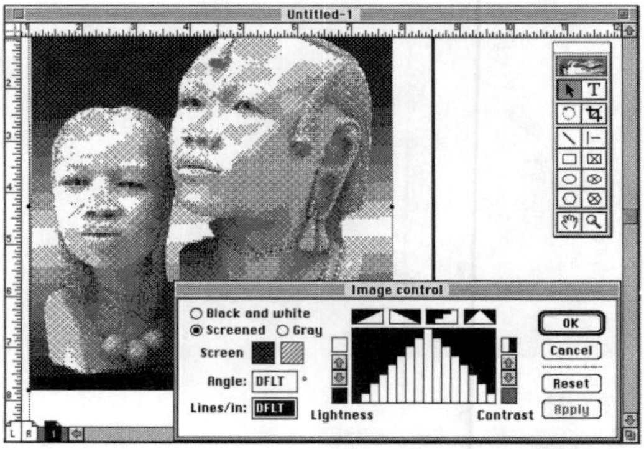

◆ To override the PostScript printer defaults for lpi (or screen frequency) and the screen angle, type new values for those options in the boxes provided. The screen angle can range from -360 to 360 degrees and the lpi setting can range from 10 to 300 lpi. To restore the printer's defaults, type "DFLT." On the Mac, click Screened in the Control provided.

LINKING METHODS

Each time you import a text or graphic file into PageMaker, you form a *link*. A link is a software connection or relationship between the original source file and your publication. That link can save you disk space, and also enables you to update the linked material easily using the word processor or graphics program that created it. But which linking method should you use? The answer depends on the specifics of the project you are producing and who is producing it with you. By the end of this section, you'll be able to assess those variables and answer these questions for yourself.

Three Basic Link Strategies

You can forge three different kinds of links between your original word processing or graphics file and PageMaker:

◆ You can use the original PageMaker proprietary linking method (generally the best approach).

◆ Publish/Subscribe, on the Macintosh side. Obviously, you can't use Publish/Subscribe if you are using PageMaker 6.5 for Windows 95.

◆ Object Linking and Embedding (OLE), created originally for the Windows side but also available on the Mac.

Why Link in the First Place?

You may be wondering why all this linking business is so important. When you get right down to it, there are really just three reasons to link:

◆ To economize on disk space

◆ To update the contents of a publication frequently

◆ To share your work with someone else

Linking to Save Disk Space

You actually store a file twice when you simultaneously include it in your publication file and keep the original for future use and editing—once internally and once externally. But when you link a file, depending on your choice of a linking method, you may have the option to maintain only one complete form of the imported file. Its complete form exists only outside the publication, and it has been merely represented visually in a much more economical form in your publication for the purposes of WYSIWYG layout editing.

Think about it. If you make a habit of storing 20MB to 60MB graphics files twice instead of just once, how much hard disk space will that chew up? And if you use a small graphic file repeatedly, doesn't it make sense to store it just once outside the publication and then apply it many times using a link? When you import a 250K graphic 200 times, for example, you could waste 50MB of expensive hard disk space.

Updating Work

Publications exist in a world of change. What do you do, for example, if you are publishing the documentation for a manufacturing process? The documentation might be changed often as worker time and motion studies and new technology offer ways to improve speed and economy. You need an easy way to update the contents of such documentation. Linking enables you to set up your publication using easily updatable modules, and then to do a good part of your editing in the originating applications (programs for drawing illustrations, drafting, spreadsheet charts, and so on).

Sharing with a Group

To take the documentation publication example a step farther, imagine that this is a very large document and there's an entire team of people producing the publication (illustrators, writers, designers, engineers, and management). All of these people have contributions to make, but they aren't all going to take turns sitting at one Mac or PC located at a single spot in the building. That would be inconvenient for most of them. Nor would it be efficient for them to pass around a single copy of the publication. They want to collaborate, and the only way that can happen is by being able to work simultaneously, feeding their efforts (editing comments, illustrations, charts, and so on) into the main publication document. Such collaboration is much easier because linking enables the entire work group to easily feed their updated material into the shared publication.

Linking Is Mostly for Graphics

Although you can link text, linking is used mostly for graphics. It's just as easy to link a passage of text as it is to link a graphic, but when you think about the three reasons why you would want to link, they don't come down conclusively on the side of linking text.

◆ For collaborative projects—workgroup situations—linking text does seem to make sense on the surface. But there's one mammoth drawback to any sort of text updating using linking in this circumstance. Updating text through a link writes over the old text. It wipes out all your fine typography, indexing, and inline graphics, the very reasons you are using PageMaker in the first place.

◆ Aside from the issues of preserving typography and other PageMaker work, text does need updating, and links would help to do that, but PageMaker has excellent internal text editing capabilities, whereas its graphics editing capabilities are limited, even considering the advances included in version 6.5.

◆ Text files aren't that big compared to graphics files, so saving disk space isn't the priority it is when dealing with graphics.

LINKING YOUR GRAPHICS INTO PAGEMAKER

When you import a graphic into a PageMaker document your method determines the kind of link you will form. There are three main choices. You can use the regular PageMaker Place command (generally the best approach), you can use one of a couple of flavors of OLE, or you can use Publish/Subscribe (if you are working on a Mac).

> ### Don't Copy and Paste Graphics, Use Links
>
> A common mistake is to Copy and Paste a graphic into PageMaker from a drawing or painting program such as Photoshop, Illustrator, or FreeHand. That will give you, at best, low resolution images. Your operating system, with a few minor exceptions, will take the graphic down to a lowest common denominator format (such as a PICT on the Mac, or a WMF in Windows) in order to move between the two programs. You will have better results if you export your graphic and then use the Place command to bring it into PageMaker. As a rule, you'll want to export vector graphics as EPS and bitmapped graphics as TIFFs.

In the next few sections we describe each of the PageMaker graphic import methods in terms of their linking approach, spelling out each one's pluses and minuses so that you can make the best choice for a particular graphics importing situation.

PageMaker Place and Link

You create a PageMaker link (as opposed to an OLE or Publish/Subscribe link) by using the Place command. You don't need to think much about it. It just happens. No exceptions, the link is forged every time you import a file through the File/Place command (see Figure 8.55).

Figure 8.55

Forging a link with the Place command.

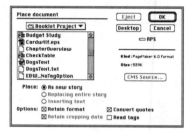

Of the three linking alternatives, the PageMaker Place/Links technique gives you the most power and flexibility. That's why it is so heavily favored in our advice in this section.

♦ When you create PageMaker links using the Place command, you get all the benefits of PageMaker's import filters, generally a robust means for retaining the formatting of inbound graphics and text, and you maintain your ability to edit the material.

♦ On the other hand, if there's no filter for whatever you want to import, or if the originating program cannot export in a format that PageMaker can read, you can't have a link. That's a rare problem these days, but if you can't make a filter match you can't use Place and must instead resort to other linking methods to get the material into your publication.

◆ Working with a PageMaker link, you can make on-the-fly choices between storing a graphic entirely within your PageMaker document, or saving disk space by storing it outside and updating it with the link.

◆ You can have cross-platform connections by using a link, connecting a Macintosh graphic to a Windows PageMaker file and vice versa. This would also be possible by using the Windows linking technology, OLE. It isn't possible using Publish/Subscribe.

◆ It's not well-known but PageMaker's Edit Original command (in the Edit menu) works just fine through Place command links. No need to envy the instant access capability of the other linking technologies. As with OLE and Publish/Subscribe, you can open and edit your imported graphic in its original application, right from inside PageMaker.

Apple Publish/Subscribe

This Mac-only linking method has its own set of commands in the Edit menu (see Figure 8.56). With this technique, you first Publish an Edition file from the originating application program (the actual command depends on the originating program's menu structure), and then use Edit/Editions/Subscribe to incorporate that Edition file into your PageMaker document. The Edition file acts as an intermediary, and PageMaker and the original software program are linked through the Edition file.

Figure 8.56

Use the Edit menu's Editions command to subscribe to an item that you have Published from its originating application.

Following are some of the key characteristics of an Apple Publish/ Subscribe link, compared to the PageMaker Place command link:

◆ If you want to snatch a small chunk of a larger file, most Publish/Subscribe-capable programs can help you do that. Small chunk importing isn't possible using PageMaker's Link facility. This could be your method of choice if, for example, you want to pull out just the figures for the first quarter from an entire year's worth of spreadsheet data. You can publish just that chunk and subscribe to it from PageMaker.

In addition, you get a great little thumbnail preview in the Subscribe dialog box when you are selecting the Edition item for importation.

◆ If your originating application isn't supported by a PageMaker filter, but it does have Publish/Subscribe capability, you've got at least one way to get the information into your publication. On the other hand, it's a rare application these days that isn't supported at some level by a filter. You might want to explore file conversion options or the application's alternative file export formats to see if you can establish a filter match.

◆ Publish/Subscribe works strictly with Macintosh System 7 and above, and it cannot connect you to a Windows program.

Microsoft OLE

With OLE (Object Linking and Embedding), you can either link or embed. You decide between the two based on your starting point. (Don't confuse OLE linking with PageMaker's own Place/Link process. They're not the same.)

So you have two ways to use OLE in PageMaker.

◆ You can OLE link an object, meaning there is an intermediate file that is the source of a link between PageMaker and the application that originated the object. The OLE linking process begins inside the originating application.

◆ You can OLE embed an object, meaning it has no intermediate file and exists only in PageMaker, although there is a software connection established between PageMaker and the application that originated the object. Unlike OLE linking, OLE embedding begins inside PageMaker.

In deciding whether to use one of the two forms of OLE you want to consider the following factors:

◆ As with Publish/Subscribe, OLE might be an option if your originating application supports it, but isn't supported in any way by the PageMaker Place command filter collection.

◆ OLE brings objects into PageMaker as graphic objects that can only be edited in their originating programs, even when they are nongraphic source material such as text (like a data layout created in Adobe Table) or a spreadsheet.

◆ Because OLE works with a graphic representation of the object, your importation will be limited to one page of text. No page breaks will be allowed in the middle of a table.

◆ OLE embedding only works by way of the Clipboard, so it's RAM intensive, requiring you to have both PageMaker and the originating application open at the same time. You might run into difficulties, for example, if you attempt to bring a large graphic file into PageMaker by this method.

◆ Because OLE linking works with an intermediary file, that file can be edited, and with a single update move, the file can be used to simultaneously update all occurrences of that

Make Sure Adobe Table Has Been OLE Registered

This advice goes both for you and your service bureau. If you decide to use OLE embedding or linking for Adobe Table material, you risk major problems at output time if you do not make sure that PageMaker and Adobe Table have been properly registered. It's possible, and even likely, that your service bureau won't feel it has any particular reason to install Adobe Table. After all, they expect you publications to come to them in final form with no table editing needed. However, to output your job they must install Adobe Table at least once. Adobe reccomends opening and quitting Adobe Table once and then opening and quitting PageMaker once. This registers both applications in a special OLE registration file. (Note that this is not the same as sending in your PageMaker registration card— but you should do that too!)

object within a PageMaker document. In this sense, it works just like the other two linking options (PageMaker's Place command and Publish/Subscribe). An embedded object does not have this intermediate file; therefore, it can only update one location in your PageMaker publication.

OLE Linking

To OLE link an item into PageMaker, you can choose from two approaches. Either one establishes the OLE connection through a file saved out of the originating application.

To use the Paste Special approach, follow these steps:

1. Within the originating application copy the material you want to bring into PageMaker.

2. Go to PageMaker and use the Paste Special command in the Edit menu.

3. The Paste Special command might offer you a choice of formats, depending on the capabilities of the application that created the object that you are OLE linking. PageMaker lists the formats in descending order, with the richest one first—the one that has the most robust formatting capabilities and will be most likely to retain the characteristics of your original imported file.

   Using this technique, if you wanted to use OLE to link an Excel chart into PageMaker, for example, you would start in Excel by constructing the chart and saving it, and then copying the chart to the Clipboard. Then open PageMaker and use the Paste Special command.

To use the Insert Object approach, follow these steps:

1. Create the object you want to bring into PageMaker as an individual file.

2. Go to PageMaker's Edit/Insert Object command. Choose the From File option in the dialog box and select the file you are linking (see Figure 8.57).

3. Click the Link checkbox so that you will have an OLE link.

4. The Result box in the Insert Object dialog box will give you a description of your link.

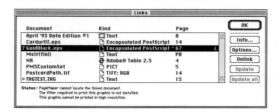

Figure 8.57

The Insert Object dialog box has been set up here for an OLE linked file.

5. To use this method to bring an Excel chart into PageMaker, you would first create the chart and save it. Then you would use the Insert Object command, click From File and Link, and select the Excel chart file.

OLE Embedding

As with OLE linking, you can use two methods to create an OLE embedded object, but you work exclusively through the Insert Object command. Paste Special cannot embed OLE objects.

The most important thing to understand about OLE embedded objects is that they don't exist outside PageMaker. You are not linking to an external file. You are embedding the file completely within PageMaker. Even if you base the embedded object on an existing file, all you have in PageMaker is a picture of the material in the file. That picture, not the file, is the sole basis for the link between PageMaker and the originating application. You don't have a master linked file that can be changed and updated. You can, however, use Edit Original to update embedded objects, and you can double-click to open the object in the originating application.

New Object Approach

Probably the most common way to create an embedded OLE object is to do the following:

1. Select Insert Object from the Edit Menu and choose New from the Insert Object dialog box.

2. Choose your application from the resulting list and you will be taken to it so you can create the item you will OLE embed.

3. When you are done in the originating application, quit out of it and you will be bounced back to PageMaker where you can position the new item in your layout.

This literally creates a new object that exists only within PageMaker.

Existing File Approach

Alternatively, you can embed an OLE object based on an existing file.

1. Choose From File in the Insert Object dialog box, but do not click the Link checkbox.

2. After you have selected the file you will be bounced back to PageMaker, where you can position your OLE embedded object on the page. If you do a Link Info command on the resulting object, you see that it isn't linked to a file location.

Remember, even though you have embedded an object from an existing file, once you have completed the OLE link, the file doesn't count anymore. Unlike the Place/Link method, changing the file won't update the embedded OLE object inside PageMaker.

MANAGING LINKS

After deciding which linking method to use and importing a graphic into PageMaker, you will need to manage the link between PageMaker and the imported graphic. Mostly that boils down to getting information on the current status of a link and controlling when and how the graphic will be updated if the original is changed in some way.

Your Overall Links Manager

PageMaker has a central location for managing links, reached through the Links Manager command in the File menu. This single dialog box (see Figure 8.58), with its related sub-dialog boxes and commands, enables you to control the way that items get updated using PageMaker Links, OLE, and Publish/Subscribe.

Use the Links Manager command in the File menu, (Command-Shift-D) [Control-Shift-D] to reach this link management master tool. From this one central location, this tool tells you the status of any link in your publication, enables you to update or break the link, and enables you to decide how the link should be managed from this point forward. A variety of codes indicate the status and location of each link. Refer to Table 8.1 for more detail on the meaning of these codes.

Figure 8.58

The Links Manager dialog box.

TABLE 8.1
SYMBOLS USED IN THE LINKS DIALOG BOX

Links Symbol	Definition
Link Status Codes	
NA	No link to an external file. Item either pasted in using the Clipboard or embedded using OLE.
ø (circle with slash)	Link broken to an EPS graphic that would be linked to an Open Prepress Interface image, except the OPI images can't be located.
?	The link has been broken. PageMaker cannot locate the linked file.
+	External file has been modified since last update. It will be updated the next time you click the Update or Update All button or the next time you open the publication.
- (hyphen)	External file has been modified, and you have in-structed against automatic updating.
!	You have edited an external file in two locations—both inside and outside PageMaker. If you trigger an update, the external file changes overwrite the internal changes.

continues

TABLE 8.1, CONTINUED

SYMBOLS USED IN THE LINKS DIALOG BOX

Links Symbol	Definition
¿	An image will be printed but might not be at high resolution (missing linked file, filter or OLE file not available, cross-platform translation).
	A Placed object.
	A Publish/Subscribe object.
	OLE linked or embedded object.
Page Location Codes	
Page #?	Some or all of the linked material is in a story that has not been placed, so its page location is ambiguous.
LM, RM	The linked object is on one of the Master pages.
PB	The linked item is on the Pasteboard.
OV	The linked item has been stranded in some text that hasn't been poured onto a page yet. OV means overset.

Getting Link Info

If you select one of the linked objects in the dialog box list and then click the Info button in the lower-left corner of the Links Manager dialog box, the Link Info dialog box opens (See Figure 8.59). The Info button is grayed unless you select something. This dialog box provides you with a complete description of the file's location and enables you to relink or completely replace the item with a new or updated file. To do so, select the new file and click the Link button or press Return.

Retain Cropping Feature

The Retain Cropping Data checkbox that you see in Figure 8.55 can save your life. Use this feature if you have cropped the file in PageMaker and are now going to relink (replace) it. If you don't turn on Retain Cropping Data, PageMaker will try to smoosh the updated graphic into the smaller cropped space—distorting it sort of like it would look in a funhouse mirror. You have a fighting chance to get a good-looking image if you click it on. It won't, however, help much if you have changed the proportions or the size of the incoming file.

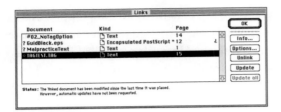

Figure 8.59

The Link Info dialog box.

Setting Automatic Updating

If you select an object in the Links dialog box and then click on Options, you will get a dialog box (see Figure 8.60) that you can use to control when your imported object will be updated if it has been edited—automatically or only after giving you an alert.

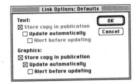

Figure 8.60

Click the Options button to open the Link Options: Defaults dialog box.

You can choose to have PageMaker update the linked object automatically each time you open the publication. If you are nervous about this kind of automatic modification of your internal linked material, check the Alert Before Updating checkbox to have PageMaker provide a failsafe dialog box for update control.

There are several versions of the Link Options: Defaults dialog box. If you select an object before clicking on the Options button you will only get half of this dialog box, depending on whether you chose a text or graphic item. This feature is terrific because it enables you to establish your own standard way of handling text and graphics link updates. It's especially useful if you are working on a project where you'll be working quickly as you import a lot of objects. Setting the default here means you won't have to worry about the setting each time you bring in a new item.

You can also access the Link Info and Link Option dialog boxes for an individual imported object, instead of going to the Master Tool dialog box, the Links Manager. Just select a linked item in Layout view and then choose Link Info or Link Options from the Element menu see Figure. 8.61).

Figure 8.61

Use the Element menu to set options or get info on an individual graphic link.

Breaking Links

In the Links Manager dialog box, the Unlink button breaks an existing link. This can be a great advantage if you want to be absolutely sure that someone in your workgroup doesn't inadvertently update a file that you want to preserve in its present stage. As a standard practice we generally unlink text files to make sure that they don't get accidentally overwritten by a relink. Relinking text writes over the old text and you could lose lots of the fine tuning that you can do only in PageMaker, not within your word processor.

Forcing A Links Update

At the far right of the Links Manager dialog box are two buttons for updating links—Update and Update All. You can update an individual item by selecting it and then clicking the Update button. Or, if you have multiple items that have been modified or you have selected multiple items, you can click Update All and conduct a sweep of all the linked objects shown.

Helping PageMaker Find (or Not Find) Linked Files

It's easy to accidentally break links when you reorganize the way your files reside in folders on your hard disk, or take in a file from someone else who (naturally) had organized her disk differently. The next time you open your publication, you might be told that PageMaker cannot find files that have been rearranged.

PageMaker helps you relink everything if you give it a few hints. When you relink a single file in a group of files, PageMaker adds that folder to its search list for links and relinks all the other items in that folder automatically. If you want to prevent this automatic relinking to the items contained in the new folder, press the Option key as you click OK or press Return. (PageMaker can find linked graphics if you put them in the same folder as the PageMaker document.)

Express Access: Editing Originals

No matter what linking method you choose, the resulting link gives you express access for editing your imported items. The Edit Original command is the secret.

This feature might be the best reason for using links. It will easily and quickly open a linked object for editing in its originating application.

1. To do it, select a linked item and use the Edit Original command located in the Edit menu.

    Note that the menu reads a bit differently if you select an OLE object. The command works exactly the same but instead of Edit Original it says Edit followed by the type of file you selected for editing (Edit Excel Chart Object, for example).

2. When you finish editing, save the original file.

3. Exit the application and you end up back in PageMaker with the linked object updated by your editing session. (It takes longer to describe it than to do it.)

There's an alternative way of accessing the express editing power of Edit Original. Press the (Option) [Alt] key and double-click on the linked object. Again, in the case of an OLE embedded object there's a slight nuance. You don't need a helper key and you can simply double-click on the object.

These steps allow you express access to edit an item in the application used to create it originally. However, you may want to do your editing in another application. If you are working with a Place/Linked objected (not OLE or Publish/Subscribe) you can have your choice. Just hold down the Shift key as you select Edit Original from the menu or double-click on the object. You will get a dialog box that allows you to choose FreeHand, for example, to edit an Illustrator graphic. The Choose Editor dialog box also contains a status panel that tells you, among other things, whether you can edit the chosen document using the program you have highlighted in the list box.

If you plan to make a lot of use of Edit Original try this trick. Make aliases (Mac) or shortcuts (Win95) for the programs that you frequently use for editing material in PageMaker. Put the aliases or shortcuts in a folder location that will be easy to find when you are using the Choose Editor dialog box, perhaps in the PageMaker folder. This will save you a lot of searching through multiple levels of folders to find the application you want.

MANIPULATING PAGEMAKER GRAPHICS

PageMaker enables you to manipulate graphics in a number of ways, some of which, such as masking and placing in a frame, have already been covered. The graphic manipulations still to be covered include: Moving, Resizing, Rotating, Cropping, Cutting, and Pasting. Refer to Figures 8.62 and 8.63 for a visual description of PageMaker's Control palette options.

Figure 8.62

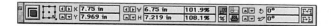

The Control palette.

The most important helper in manipulating PageMaker graphics is the Control palette, accessed from the PageMaker Windows menu. Mastering this palette gives you control over all of the facets of image manipulation. The items in the Control palette act as a supplement to many of the functions in the Toolbox and give you better numerical and percentage control over images.

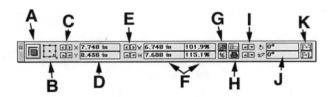

Figure 8.63

Each of the icons in the Control palette has a special image manipulation purpose.

Refer to the callouts in Figure 8.63 with the items listed below:

A. The Apply button.

B. This control is used to place the image control point at any of nine specific parts of the image.

C. This control is used to adjust the placement of any of the selected control points.

D. The numerical input boxes for readjustment of control point placement.

E. The dimensioning controls for the image (regardless of where the control point is located).

F. The numerical input for adjusting image dimensions by both direct measurements or percentage.

G. Top of this switch = resizing control, bottom switch = cropping.

H. Top of this toggle switch = free or constrained resizing, bottom toggle switch for resolution reconfiguring (On or Off).

I. These are controls for adjusting rotation (Top) and image skewing (Bottom).

J. The numerical input boxes for rotation (Top) and skewing (Bottom).

K. These controls flip the selected image horizontally (Top) or vertically (Bottom).

It's a good idea to have both the Tool palette and the Control palette onscreen at the same time so that you have options regarding what tools to use when manipulating an image. (See Figure 8.64.)

Figure 8.64

You can have both Tool and Control palettes onscreen at the same time.

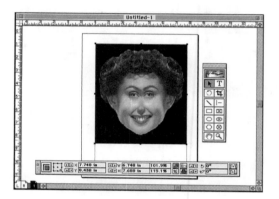

MOVING A GRAPHIC

Moving a graphic from one part of a PageMaker page to another is accomplished by using the Selection Arrow in the Toolbox. Click to select the image and then drag it to move it somewhere else. If you have Snap to Guides turned on the placement of the object to the new position can be fine-tuned. Manual control, however, isn't always exacting enough when you want to reposition just one side, or perhaps the top or bottom of an image so that it lines up with other page elements. In this case, you may need to access the Control palette to make the necessary adjustments by either numerical or percentage input. Of course, PageMaker's Snap to capabilities for page guides can automate much of the placement of graphics to a new location or page. Sometimes however, you may want to turn Snap to Guides off, because it can interfere with a freer, less restricted placement of the selected element. It depends upon what the page design is like, and also upon the designer's work preference.

When you want to use the Control palette to move a graphic, click the central control point in the Control Point Grid on the left side of the Control palette. This enables you to move the graphic with the directional arrows on the left of the Control palette, or by entering the exact number of inches, or fractions of an inch, in the appropriate X or Y box (the leftmost numerical input boxes).

Note

If you move a graphic by using the Control palette with any other point on the grid activated, only that side of the graphic will move, stretching the graphic in that direction.

Any graphic in PageMaker can be moved by using the Selection Arrow in the Toolbox or by entering measurements in the space provided in the Control palette. Graphics also can be moved by using the movement control keys in the Control palette. (See Figure 8.65.)

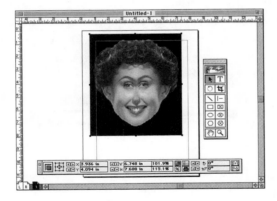

Figure 8.65

Graphics can be moved with the Selection Arrow or by adjusting the Control palette listings.

If you select any other control point on the Control Grid (in Figure 8.66 the top midpoint was chosen), the image will be stretched in the direction your new dimensions indicate.

Figure 8.66

Images can be stretched through the Control palette adjustments.

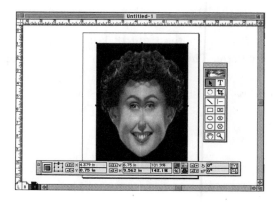

PageMaker In the Real World

Extensis PageMover

A way to move PageMaker graphics off the present page is to use the plug-in from Extensis PageTools called PageMover. PageMover enables you to move any selected items to any place on the pasteboard, the area surrounding the active page. It also moves any selected elements to any other page in your document, either by cutting and pasting, or by copying and pasting. This is especially useful when you want to move an item, such as a logo, to exactly the same position on more than one page.

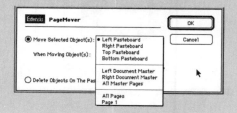

RESIZING A GRAPHIC

By using the Selection Arrow in the toolbox and clicking and dragging over any of the control points on the image itself, you can resize the image to a new size or proportion. If you want to resize the image and maintain its present proportion, hold down the Shift key while performing this action. Using the Control palette to perform a resizing operation is more complex but a lot more exacting:

1. Select the image by clicking it.

2. Go to the Control palette and activate the Resizing Control (above the Cropping Control on the right of the Control palette).

3. Click the icon to the right of the Resizing Control and toggle it to the shape that shows a dark square sitting in the lower left of a dotted square. This constrains the resizing to a proportional result. Alternatively, if you want to resize the graphic to a non-proportional manner, select the alternate icon represented.

4. To the left are four input areas, each pair representing horizontal and vertical adjustments, one pair by measurement numbers (inches) and the other pair by percentage. Use either dimensions or percentages to indicate the resized parameters.

5. Click the Activate button on the far left of the Control palette.

Extensis PageScaler

An alternative method for scaling your graphics is to use the PageScaler plug-in in the Extensis PageTools collection. The plug-in brings up its own action palette to the PageMaker interface, making all scaling operations instantly accessible. Because it offers both customized resizing and resizing by set percentages (25, 50, 75, 200, and 400, as well as repeat last resize), it is an excellent partner to the resizing operations found in PageMaker's Control palette. The PageMover palette is small enough not to obstruct the PageMaker editing screen. Using its customizing feature, you can scale Line Weights, Graphics, and Text separately. As a Scaling tool, I prefer it over the Control palette except when it comes to small incremental movements.

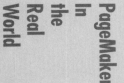

PageMaker In the Real World

ROTATING A GRAPHIC

Rotating a selected object in PageMaker can be accomplished in two ways, from the Toolbox and from the Control palette. If activated from the toolbox with the Rotation tool (the icon of an arrow in a dotted circle), rotations are real-time interactive. This is good for most uses, but when you need accurate results and the degrees of rotation have to be numerically exact, use the Control palette. The Rotation icon is easy to find in the Control palette because it has the same design as the icon in the toolbox. On the left of the icon are two control arrows, facing up and down (left and right rotations). Clicking either rotates the selection by a tenth of a degree. If you need to rotate the selection by a hundredth of a degree, use the numerical input areas to the right of the Rotation icon in the Control palette.

CROPPING A GRAPHIC

Cropping a graphic is another operation that can be accessed from either the Toolbox or the Control palette, using the same icon. In the Toolbox, click the Cropping tool to activate it. After placing it over one of the control points on your selected graphic, click and hold as you move the mouse into the selection. You can see the cropping operation taking place. The first part of this cropping operation sets the new size of the cropped area. Now, with the cropping tool still activated, click and hold in the center of the new selected area. As you move the mouse, notice that the graphic inside the new area is also moving, enabling you to get the exact composition desired. When finished, release the mouse button.

If cropping is activated through the Control palette, you start by clicking the Cropping icon to activate the process, and then place it over one of the control points in the image to activate it. Next, use the fine-tuning controls in the Control palette to move the graphic inside of the cropped area by numeric input.

DELETING A GRAPHIC

Graphics and any other elements in your PageMaker document can be deleted by selecting them and pressing Delete, or by selecting Cut or Clear from the Edit menu. If you find that you have acted mistakenly, you can always recover the deletion by using the Undo command.

PASTING A GRAPHIC BACK TO PAGEMAKER

Cutting and pasting operations are familiar to anyone who has used a word processing application and using the same processes in PageMaker with graphics produces similar results. Normal Paste operations write data copied or cut to the Clipboard back to the PageMaker edit screen. PageMaker also includes some variations on this theme that must be considered: Paste Special, Paste Multiple, and Insert Object.

Paste Special

Paste Special has different options for graphics as opposed to text objects. With graphics selections, Paste Special can paste copied or cut graphics back to the screen as either PageMaker elements or as PICT graphics (Mac) or TIFF (PC). PageMaker vector shapes are thus transformed into PICT/TIFF vector graphics. If the original selection is a Text block, Paste Special allows it to be written back to the screen as a PageMaker 6 format, Rich Text Format, Vector PICT, as Text (Mac), or as PageMaker. This allows any selected graphics or text blocks in a PageMaker document to be transformed and exported (File/Export) as a TIFF, JPEG, GIF, or a DCS color separation.

Note

If you plan to use Masking on a Text block that has been turned into a graphic, realize that the masking process treats Text-as-Text and Text-as-Graphics very differently. Text-as-Graphics, once masked, always maintains whatever line configuration was present at the start. Text-as-Text, once masked, may show up as words written to alternate lines, depending upon the Mask shape and how much space is involved. Text-as-Text can be resized and recolored after masking. Text-as-Graphics cannot!

Tip

Transforming an entire PageMaker page by copying all the elements, writing them back as PICT Vectors, and then exporting it as a GIF or JPEG enables you to import the page as a JPG or a GIF Web backdrop image.

When saved as a TIFF image, a PICT vector can be re-imported into PageMaker. As a TIFF, it is now able to be transformed through PageMaker's Photoshop Effects filters. This means that a Text block can be transformed so that PageMaker's internal Photoshop effects can be used on it, as well as on other TIFF graphics. Just follow this procedure:

1. Create a text block in PageMaker, typing in your message.

2. Copy the Text block to the buffer by using the Copy command from the Edit menu.

3. Use Paste Special to paste the text block back in as a graphic.

4. Select the new text block graphic and select Export from the File menu.

5. Export and save the new text block out as a TIFF file.

6. Re-import the TIFF and place it on the page.

7. Go to Element/Image/Photoshop Effects. Select an effect to apply to the TIFF.

The Export dialog for graphics can be accessed when you select to save a Vector PICT image as a graphic. This enables you to transform the Vector PICT into a TIFF for image processing, or into a JPEG or GIF for Web specific incorporation. (See Figure 8.67.)

Paste Multiple

If you are interested in creating cloned compositions within PageMaker, this pasting operation is your cup of java. By using Paste Multiple and an interesting basic shape, you can create limitless graphics expressions without ever opening up a Vector Drawing or Bitmap Image Processing application. Paste Multiple, in Edit menu, takes whatever information has been written to the Clipboard (by Cut, Copy, or Clear operations) and deposits multiple cones of that selection back on the PageMaker screen. You can control both the number of clones and their horizontal and vertical separation from each other. With a little creative ingenuity, you can create complex backdrops by using the Paste Multiple operation in conjunction with other tools.

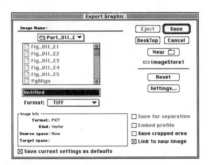

Figure 8.67

The Export Graphic dialog box.

Using the Paste Multiple operation in the Edit menu, shapes can be cloned from graphics or text, whether singly or grouped. The figure on the left was created using the Polygon tool and was cloned, flipped horizontally, and then rejoined with itself. It was then used in a Paste Multiple operation, resulting in a chain of clones. (See Figure 8.68.)

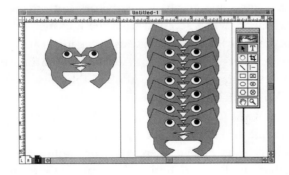

Figure 8.68

The Paste Multiple command in the Edit menu.

Taking the actions performed in the previous figure in another direction, the original figure was copied four times and joined to itself with various elements flipped, creating an optical illusion of faces and a butterfly. Paste Multiple was then used to create the final composition. (See Figure 8.69.)

Figure 8.69

The final Paste Multiple composition.

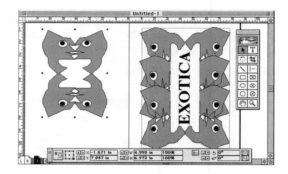

ALIGNING GRAPHICS

The PageMaker alignment function moves two or more graphics (or type elements) into a chosen alignment with each other. The Alignment function must be accessed from the menu bar. It offers numerous alignment options and lets you choose how the selected graphics are separated on the page, either evenly or by a set dimension in inches.

THE INSERT COMMAND

Though not seen as part of a graphics operation, the Insert Object command opens some graphics possibilities not otherwise possible from PageMaker. When accessed from the Edit menu, Insert Object brings up a menu of choices. The items in the menu are dependent on the applications resident in your system. You can insert an Adobe Acrobat Document, Adobe Chart, Adobe Table (including 2.5), and a variety of Microsoft Word utilities and documents. Just make sure you have enough RAM to cover the overhead. As just one example of what this can provide the PageMaker designer who also has Microsoft Word resident on the same system, there is a Word utility called Microsoft WordArt that has all sorts of options for wrapping a text block around or on shape chosen from a library of graphics options. Nothing like this exists in PageMaker, but using the Insert Object command makes WordArt a creative utility of PageMaker. This is only one of dozens of possibilities, depending upon what other options might be resident on your system. Remember that you must have enough RAM available to run both the selected utility and PageMaker at the same time, and this amount can vary depending upon which utility you try to access. An extra 2MB or 4MB over PageMaker needs is probably a minimum safe bet. Refer to Figure 8.70.

Extensis PageAlign

As another of the plug-ins in the Extensis PageTools collection, PageAlign offers you an easier and more visual way to align two or more selected elements on a page. The icons and actions of PageAlign emulate those found in the PageMaker alignment option. The difference is that PageAlign is contained in a small, onscreen palette, whereas the PageMaker alignment operation is accessed from the menu bar. It is much quicker to perform alignments from the PageAlign palette.

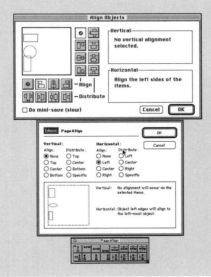

Figure 8.70

The Insert Object command in the Edit menu brings up a menu of choices.

SUMMARY

In this chapter, you visited some of the drawing tools native to PageMaker. In the next chapter, you will learn advanced tricks that take full advantage of PageMaker's drawing tools.

Chapter

GRAPHICS—MAGIC TRICKS AND PLUG-INS

19 MAGIC PAGEMAKER TUTORIALS

A technician always follows the rules when it comes to learning how to work with software, memorizing how to use just the right tool for a specific purpose. One PageMaker technician's output looks like the next technician's output, with little variance and no discernible signature to the composition. This may be exactly what's needed for standard industrial tasks, but PageMaker has more to offer under the surface. To become a PageMaker artist as opposed to just a technician, you have to pry under the hood, poke around, and explore doing what you were never told. After you have established an exploratory mindset in PageMaker or any other application, your original signature will start to peek through your work. Establishing that personal signature takes time and hard work, but once established, it sets you apart from the crowd. To provide some motivation for using PageMaker in new undocumented ways, here are 19 short tutorials.

Tutorial 1: Using Oversized Stroke Clones with the Line Tool

Oversized Stroke Clones sounds like the title of a grade-B horror film, but the results of mastering this process can be beautiful as far as PageMaker layouts are concerned. Figure 9.1 is a collection of page designs created using the methods described. The "Yes-No graphic" and "Industrial Strength" were exported to Photoshop where a gradient was applied.

Figure 9.1

Some examples of Stroke Cloned graphics.

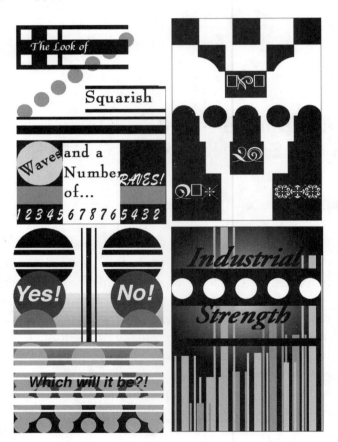

Here's what to do:

1. Double-click the Line or Constrained Line tool in PageMaker (constrained lines are written either vertically, at 45 degree angles, or horizontally). The Custom Stroke dialog box opens.

In it you will see a pop-out list for Stroke style, a Stroke weight box (in Points), a Transparent background and Reverse stroke checkboxes. Leaving the Transparent background box checked as a default for all cases is OK, as your interest centers upon the other three items (see Figure 9.2).

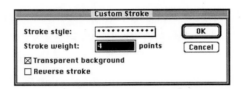

Figure 9.2

Clicking twice on the Line or the Constrained Line Tool in PageMaker opens Custom Stroke dialog box.

2. Select a stroke style from the list (press the mouse over the list name for the Mac, and click then release the list for the PC).

3. Enter a large point size in the Stroke weight input box, from 72 to 120.

4. Go to the page and draw a line. Notice that it is very large, rather like drawing with a rectangular block.

5. Draw a pattern of oversized lines on the page to get used to the tool and the process. You can open the Stroke and Fill dialog box in the Element menu (Command-U) [Control-U] to change the color of the line to another hue or a screened tint.

6. Select another stroke style and repeat the process. Notice that the lines now contain even repetitions of the pattern, a designer's layout dream. Each of the patterns can become an element in a page design and the more you get used to the process, the more your design ideas will flow. Any of the stroke styles can be used as interesting frames for placing text or graphics. At large sizes, the dotted line Style generates large circles. The layout results of this design look very contemporary, many of which are reminders of Bauhaus designs of the 1930s and 1940s. Keep a record of your exploration for later use or save appealing pages as PageMaker documents.

Why is this method of oversized stroke clones valuable for page design? The shapes are always in sync, both in style and measurement. When you use one of the broken styles to draw with, the elements are automatically adjusted internally to the length of the line. Reversing the styles allows them to overprint in interesting symmetries. Reversed shapes also can be used as cutters for shapes they're placed over—masks without masking! Finally, very exacting compositions can be generated and the shapes can act as mortises for text blocks (text can be reversed out of the solid colored lines).

As you can see in Figure 9.3, custom strokes can be solid, multiple line (four options), or broken (rectangles, squares, and circles). All of the patterns can be colorized or percentage screened by opening the Element/Stroke and Fill dialog box. All patterns are perfect clones without ever having to resize them to match.

Figure 9.3

Custom strokes create varied graphic elements.

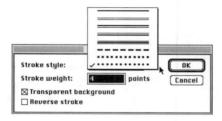

Tutorial 2: Creating Primitives with Primitives

In the computer arts, basic shapes (whether 2-D or 3-D) are called *primitives*. Primitives are the literal building blocks of more complex scenes and compositions. In 2-D applications, primitives are commonly consigned to circles/ovals and squares/rectangles. In 3-D applications, these same primitives are given volume and appear as spheres and cubes. Primitives can include more shapes than these, but these remain the basics. It also can lead to graphics that are unique in their simplicity and strength. You are going to add a triangle as another primitive in this PageMaker exercise.

The most common way to use primitives to form a 2-D shape is to focus on the human form. Stick figures are the first human forms that children learn to draw and using primitive basic shapes to construct graphics grows out of that same stick figure basis. Circles are always the primary building block of the human form, so we will definitely use circles in our constructs. Squares are used less often, usually for the torso areas. Triangles, apex down, can be used effectively for heads. All of the basic shapes we start with should have a 2 point Stroke and a 50% fill. It's best to group the primitives into larger elements as you go. Heads can be completed with all of their elements grouped and so can other larger body parts. The reason is that by utilizing a handful of grouped elements, you can alter the forms quickly by using rotation on grouped objects. This enables you to develop characters that you can copy and choreograph. Some of you may want to copy the grouped elements to the Clipboard and Special Paste them back in as PICT graphics. Here's an exercise that should allow you to develop needed experience with this process:

1. Create a triangular shape in the Polygon Specifications dialog box (see Figure 9.4) by double-clicking the Polygon tool and setting Number of Sides to 3, and Star Inset to 12 (you are free to change these settings to your own liking, especially the Star setting). Draw the shape in PageMaker and rotate the shape 180 degrees.

2. Use other basic shape tools to add facial elements as needed (see Figure 9.5 as one alternative). Group all of the facial elements together and either save the graphic to a file or to the PageMaker Library.

3. Build figures from the saved and grouped elements. You can even build groups of figures as an illustration, or use them as ornaments to point to certain text blocks. Besides being useful, building primitives with primitives is a lot of fun (see Figure 9.5).

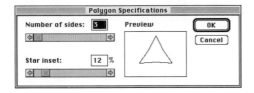

Figure 9.4

The Polygon Specifications dialog box enables you to configure a Triangular shape, suitable for a basic "head" shape.

Figure 9.5

You can create basic shapes in PageMaker and group them for ease of use. Here's one example of a finished "head."

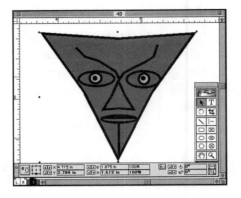

Figure 9.6 illustrates an example of what your grouped figure elements might look like. Except for a few straight lines, the elements used to make these groups relied strictly on PageMaker ovals, rectangles, and polygons. All of the elements are now ready to act as building blocks in a larger page composition. When you find composite figures you like, save them to a file. These can then be imported and recombined into a larger work. Finished figures that utilize this method take on a cubist look (see Figure 9.7) and can act as powerful graphic elements in your PageMaker projects.

Figure 9.6

An example of grouped figure elements.

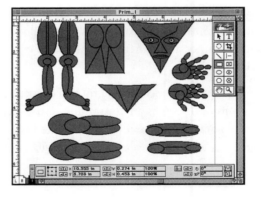

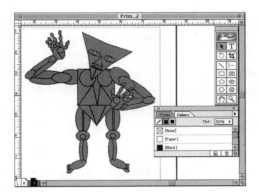

Figure 9.7

A finished graphic with a cubist look.

Tutorial 3: PageMaker Gradient Depth Stacks Revealed

Gradients are commonly created in PageMaker by cloning a shape several times, and with Strokes set to None, placing the cloned shapes either in a straight line or concentricly, with each one smaller than the next. Then, each clone adjacent to the next is selected and a progressively lighter (or progressively darker) screen tint is applied as a fill. The result is what appears to be a smooth gradient in the overall shape, as long as care is taken to make each adjacent screen tint no more than 5% different from its neighbor. That's all well and good, but it doesn't explore any variations on this theme. For that reason, here's a project that enables you to appreciate PageMaker's gradient capabilities:

1. First, click the Oval tool and go to the Fill and Stroke dialog box. Set the Fill to None and the Stroke to Custom, which opens the Customizing dialog box. Select the dotted line as the Stroke Style and select a size of 40, with a color of 100% Black.

2. Test an oval out on the page. Notice that what you get is a round string of large Black Ovals. All are evenly spaced from each other. Now select Copy from the Edit menu.

3. Select Paste Multiple from the Edit menu and set both the horizontal and vertical numbers to zero. This pastes a clone of the oval shape exactly over itself.

4. After selecting the center Control in the Controls palette, change the size of the selected clone of ovals to about 5% less than the original it came from (this can be done in the Control palette by number or percentage). Activate the settings. Notice that the cloned ovals are now smaller and that they rest within the center of the original ovals. Go to the Fill and Stroke menu, and make the cloned ovals Strokes 5% lighter than they are.

5. Repeat these steps until you have a series of oval rings more or less centered upon each other, whose tints get progressively lighter as they reach the center. Select all of the rings and group them as one. See Figure 9.8 for an example of what your graphic should resemble.

6. Copy the new graphic to the Clipboard. Use an image application such as Photoshop to import the Clipboard image. Save it to disk as a 256 grayscale TIFF.

7. Go back to PageMaker and import the TIFF file just saved. Make a copy of the image and put it aside (name this copy Image C). Open the Image Control window in the Element/ Image/Image Control menu.

8. Use the image controls to alter the look of the image, making it a negative of itself, or perhaps a customized halftone screen. Then apply the changes. Now take Image C and alter it in some way under Image Controls. You should now have three different variations of the same image: the original, the first altered Grayscale TIFF, and the second altered Grayscale TIFF (see Figures 9.8 and 9.9).

9. Create a composition made up of the three images, placing the original graphic above the rest. Refer to Figure 9.10 for a view of the possibilities. Notice that when you place an image above a negative clone of itself, it seems to fly off the page. This is what is called a Gradient Depth Stack (see Figure 9.10).

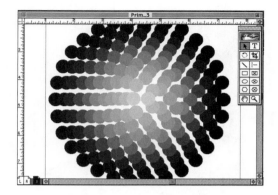

Figure 9.8

An example of the initial Gradient object, made up of large dotted Strokes in an oval shape.

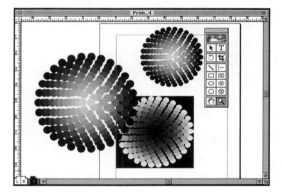

Figure 9.9

The original Gradient object is on the left. The other two objects are the TIFF grayscale clones transformed with PageMaker's Image Controls.

You can also use a variant of this effect for developing speed lines for a graphic. Speed lines is a cartoonist's term for what you perceive as an object that moves past you quickly. You see transparent frames of the object fading into the distance away from the direction it's heading. To appreciate speed lines on your own, move your forearm while holding it in front of you from a vertical position to a position parallel to the ground. If you move it at just the right speed, you should see transparent clones of your arm following along behind it. (If you can't see them, not to worry; this PageMaker speed-line example will work anyway.)

Figure 9.10

This is one possible layout that is the result of this exercise. Notice how the original graphic seems to jump off the page when placed against its negative clone in the background.

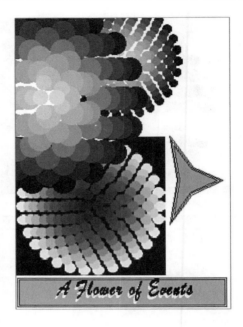

Tutorial 4: Creating 3-D Text Cubes

If you want a text block to be noticed more than the text that surrounds it, here's a guaranteed method that will do the trick.

1. Place a rectangular frame on the page, using the Frame tool in the PageMaker toolbox. Create a line of text, appropriate in size to the Rectangular Frame. Select both the frame and the text. Go to the Element/Frame/Attach Content (Command-F) [Control-F] command and watch as the text is placed inside of the frame.

2. Go to the Fill and Stroke dialog box in the Element menu and make the Stroke around the frame equal to a 100% Black border. Leave the Fill set to None.

3. With the Rectangle tool, create a rectangle about the same size as the frame and butt it up against the bottom of the frame.

4. Using the Control palette, with the rectangle selected, set the Skew function to 40% by inputting that number into the box provided (on the right of the Control palette) (see Figure 9.11).

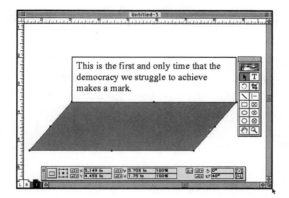

Figure 9.11

With the Control palette, set the rectangle so that it has a Skew of 40%.

5. Place a 1-point stroke on the rectangle and tint it a 40% Black, using the Fill and Stroke dialog box.

6. Using the Polygon tool, create the third side of your box. Click the points necessary to make this third side look as if it's connected to both the frame and the rectangle on the left (see Figure 9.12). Remember, you can always tweak it if the sides need adjusting. There you have it! Group all of the elements so you can move it if needed and save the results to disk so that you have a reminder of how it was accomplished. (See Figure 9.12.)

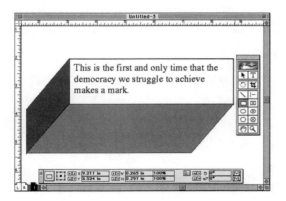

Figure 9.12

The finished 3-D text block described in the tutorial.

Tutorial 5: Creating Unique PageMaker Drop Shadows

Drop shadows are an extension of the 3-D topic covered in the last tutorial—making flat, 2-D objects appear to be 3-D. With PageMaker, you can use several options to generate drop-shadowed art. Let's investigate three cases: Text Drop Shadows, special Photo Drop Shadows, and Rotated Zoom Shadows.

Text Drop Shadows

Text Drop Shadows are the highest in demand and the basic process couldn't be simpler. Users commonly just clone (copy and paste) the text and place the duplicate lighter version underneath the darker original one. That works, but it's also boring (been there, done that!). Shadows in the real world are not the same size as the objects that cast them and they're often more or less condensed than the object. To get a better drop shadow, create your text and clone a copy of it. Make the clones' filled area light by using a 40% or lighter tint in the Color palette. Copy the text and get rid of the text object you just copied again. Use the Paste Special command to write another copy back to the screen as a PICT image. Now you should have the original text block and a PICT copy of it. The PICT version is light, so make the original a dark color. The nice thing about PageMaker PICT text blocks is they can be resized, so make the lighter "shadow" text larger and more condensed. Now place the original dark colored text over it. The shadow seems to be enlarged compared to the text, which makes it look more realistic, like a large shadow cast on a wall in the background (see Figure 9.13).

Figure 9.13

A customized text shadow.

Photo Drop Shadows

Instead of using a rectangle to emulate a shadow cast by a photo, you are going to explore another option. You will want to use either a color or high-definition grayscale image as the original and a muted image as the shadow (see Figure 9.14). You can create the muted shadow image by using PageMaker's Image Controls. Just open the Image Controls dialog box, and use the mouse to move each of the bars in the ramp Window up a little. You may have to do this a few times, by quitting the dialog box and previewing the results, to lighten the image enough for your liking. You can also mute the image using Photoshop Effects in PageMaker. You could also do the work outside of PageMaker in an image processing application. In the end, you will need to place both the high definition and the muted image on the PageMaker screen, and place the original over the muted clone. This has much more character than using a screened tint to act as the shadow, and printing it out on glossy stock really brings out the effect (see Figure 9.14).

Figure 9.14

The muted Photo shadow as described in the accompanying tutorial.

Rotated Zoom Shadows

This effect utilizes the basic shadow technique at the start, making clones of selected text. Select some text and copy then paste about six clones of it on a PageMaker screen. Select each clone and vary its tint by about 10% by using the Color palette to edit the Fill color. The lightest clone should be rotated 70% with the next lightest rotated at less of an angle. Continue this process until all of the clones, except the original text, are rotated. You could rotate the original as well, but we'll leave this to your explorations. Place the lightest clone at the bottom of a stack and place the rest on top of it in a linear increase of the tints, with the darkest text block on top. You should end up with an interesting stack of text blocks, similar to those shown in Figure 9.15.

Figure 9.15

Rotated Zoom Shadowed text adds a lot of dynamics and movement to a page.

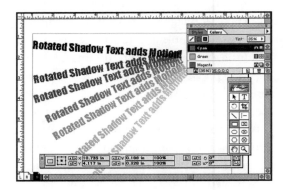

DTP Rotoscoping Possibilities

When computer artists use the word Rotoscoping, they are referring to video or film, not to desktop publishing. Rotoscoping as a process, however, is not directly connected to any medium per se. To *Rotoscope* means to take a photograph or a photographic movie frame and trace over the elements in order to achieve the look of a hand-drawn illustration. In today's digital world, this can be done with software such as Adobe's Streamline and other Bitmap-to-Vector applications, but the automated process is only one way to generate a Rotoscoped graphic. The Polygon tool is the most useful Freeform Graphics alternative in PageMaker. Developing a Rotoscoped drawing demands its use, so if you haven't spent time with it by this point, now is the time. Whether the polygon that is developed with this tool remains open or is closed by returning to the first point again, the operation of the tool is the same. Clicking from point-to-point is the way it's done and you can double-click when you're finished. For open polygons, set the Fill to None in the Stroke and Fill dialog box.

Here's how to Rotoscope a Photo for DTP use:

1. Select a photo that has a recognizable silhouette and large blocks of color. You can use a photo with hundreds of smaller blocks of color, but because this is a hand-crafted technique, it will take a lot longer to get results.

2. After placing the photo on the Pasteboard, zoom in until some of the shape elements in the photo are large enough to work on.

3. With the Polygon tool, use the click point-to-point method to outline all of the important shapes in the photo, colorizing them to match the approximate colors in the photo as you finish each polygonal shape. It's a good idea to make your background shape a little larger, allowing them to overlap the sizes represented on the photo. This way, you will create an illustration with no blank spots.

4. When finished, Group the shapes together. Place the new Poly-shaped, Rotoscoped illustration alongside the photo. Compare them to see if additions or revisions are needed. (See Figure 9.16.)

Figure 9.16

The Rotoscoping process enables you to stylize an illustration based upon a photo.

As Figures 9.17 and 9.18 illustrate, a Rotoscoped PageMaker illustration can be an effective way to utilize a photographic cover, duplicating it as an illustration on the inside of a publication, connecting everything together while giving the piece some artistic variance. The chances are, your illustration will look more like a caricature of the photo.

Figure 9.17

A Rotoscoped PageMaker graphic.

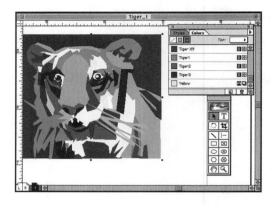

Figure 9.18

Rotoscoped images make wonderful cover designs, especially when cloned into a group.

Tip

Always save a copy of the illustration in your PageMaker Library for other possible uses. It's also a good idea to copy the illustration to the Clipboard and Paste it back in as a PICT file (Paste Special). That way, it can never be ungrouped while you're working with it.

Tutorial 6: Spirals

The Spiral is one of the oldest world-class symbols in existence and it still attracts attention when used in a publication. The eye is always drawn to the center of a spiral, so spirals make great frames for important text. You can, however, create a selection of spiral shapes and effects without too much trouble.

1. Start by drawing four circles, each about 2/3 the size of its largest neighbor, and call them A, B, C, and D. A is the largest and D is the smallest. Place them on the page so that B touches A at the top of A, C touches B at the bottom of B, and D touches C at the top of D (see Figure 9.19).

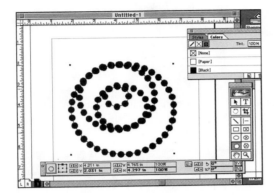

Figure 9.19

Following the directions in the tutorial, construct four circles of dots in this arrangement. Then, with the Open Polygon tool, use the dot centers to draw a spiral path.

2. Select all the circles and open the Stroke and Fill dialog. Select None for Fill and Custom for Stroke. When the Custom dialog box appears, choose the dotted line as the Stroke Style, with a Size of 22. Now apply the settings.

3. The four circles now transform into a series of dots. This will be your form for constructing the Spiral graphic.

4. Select the Polygon tool. You want to use an Open Polygon to construct the Spiral. Starting at the smallest circle of dots, click the mouse button in the center of each of the circles of dots. Move to the next circle when two circles become tangent.

5. When you have completed a spiral line with the Open Polygon shape, double-click to close the operation. Cut the four circles out of the page.

6. After removing the four dotted circles, smooth out the Spiral, using PageMaker's capability to allow for the adding and deletion of points in an open polygon. You can spend as much

time as you need on smoothing out the spiral shape. Everywhere a control point appears, a broken line Style element is written. (See Figure 9.20.)

Figure 9.20

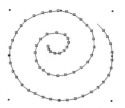

Your final Spiral should look something like this after you're done smoothing it out a bit. The more time you spend adding and moving control points, the smoother you can get it.

7. You can now use the Spiral as an element in your page design. (See Figure 9.21.)

Figure 9.21

By using different Stroke settings, your spiral can take on alternate appearances.

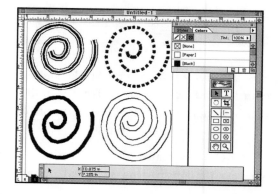

Tutorial 7: PowerPaste Background Page Effects

Using the Paste Multiple command in the Edit menu, you can create complex backgrounds for Web pages. Paste Multiple takes the contents of the Clipboard and enables you to clone the contents as many times as necessary, with control over the horizontal and vertical separations. Here's how:

1. Create a shape with the Oval, Rectangle, or Polygon tool, or use a frame with attached text or graphic data as your root graphic.

Note

Yes Virginia, you can use PageMaker Frames in a Multiple Paste operation! This means that all sorts of backgrounds can be created with the Paste Multiple operation, utilizing your graphic and texture data as content.

2. After making sure your original graphic element is selected, go to the Edit menu and copy it to the Clipboard. Now select the Paste Multiple command from the Edit menu.

3. In the Paste Multiple dialog box, set the Vertical offset to zero and the Horizontal offset to 1 inch (you can play with these settings depending upon the dimension of the original image). Determine how many copies of the image are to be generated and enter that number in the area provided. This writes out a horizontal string of images in PageMaker. Apply the commands from the dialog box. (See Figure 9.22.)

Figure 9.22

In the upper-left is a PageMaker Frame with a placed graphic content. The Paste Multiple dialog box is the first step in a multiple paste operation.

4. Select the Pasted graphics and the original, and group them. Copy this group to the Clipboard and use Paste Multiple to add a Vertical arrangement of the group to the page (Horizontal offset should be set to zero and Vertical offset adjusted to whatever is right for fitting rows of the graphic to your page). You can redo whatever steps are necessary in order to achieve a pleasing arrangement of the pasted graphics. (See Figure 9.23.)

Figure 9.23

The finished Paste Multiple background, ready for use as it is or as a text frame overlay.

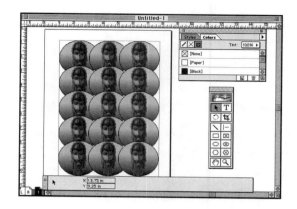

Tutorial 8: The PageMaker Graphics Library

PageMaker Libraries are not only time-savers, but act as your available reservoir of personal images. A PageMaker Library can be accessed from any PageMaker document and the contents can be drag-dropped onto a page. You should create a new Library for every document you create; just leave it sitting on the page. When you come across an element, text or graphic, that you have customized, drop it in the Library. You do this by clicking the Plus item after selecting the page element you want to store. Another use for the Library is to store graphics in development, so you can retrace the steps used to develop a specific graphic style you're involved with. Doing this at several points along the way enables you to generate and store your own tutorials, and enables you to share your discoveries with others in a visual manner. Use the PageMaker Library option in every document you do.

Tutorial 9: The Panning Camera Effect

This effect works best if the image is a fairly high contrast graphic in a landscape picture ratio (longer than taller). This allows the masked panning camera to focus upon different areas. With the right photo, the panning Camera Effect is a great way to develop a cover for a brochure.

Here's how to proceed:

1. Select a photo to bring into PageMaker. The type of photo that works best is a close-up of a face (human or otherwise) in

portrait orientation. Portrait orientation is better for this effect than landscape because our Panning effect should include sections of the previous image, and a landscape picture used for this effect will look like a series of strung-together shots. A printed page is usually in portrait orientation anyway, except for a Web page. Even for a Web page, however, this effect works best on a portrait oriented photo.

2. When you have the right Photo, clone it at least four times. Set each of the clones off to the side on the Pasteboard for the moment but keep one on the page. Go to the toolbox and select the Cropping tool. Crop each image to the same rectangular size, to encompass the total height of the image, but only about half of its width.

3. Remember that when using the Cropping tool, placing the tool inside the image while pressing the mouse button enables you to move the image within the new frame. This is the secret of creating a panning effect. In each case, you are going to move the image by a slightly different amount, but in the same direction of movement (like a panning camera). For the first cropped image, move the image so that only its right side is showing. In the second image, move the pan a little left. Continue this so that in the last image you are showing the maximum pan to the left side. For variations on this theme, you could also reverse this whole process and start from the left and move right, or even move from up to down or down to up, depending on the project and the contents of the photo.

4. When the images are complete, paste them next to each other with equal spacing, or for a more dynamic effect, resize the rectangular areas with the cropping tool so that the width of the images shortens as they move in the direction of the pan. The effect is comparable to seeing frames of an animated sequence and can be quite captivating. It also emulates the images displayed on an animation storyboard (see Figure 9.24).

Figure 9.24

The final results of a panning camera effect in PageMaker.

Tutorial 10: Smokin' Stroke Screens

Most PageMaker users are aware of the effect that linear screens have on an image. They not only break it up but also add a certain illustrative quality. Did you know that you can emulate line screens in PageMaker? To accomplish some interesting results, do the following:

1. Create a second Layer and draw a Horizontal Line at the top of the page, select it, and go to the Strokes and Fills dialog box.

2. Set the line as a one point Stroke in 100% Black.

3. Select the line again and access the Paste Multiple dialog box. Clone 20 copies of the line 2/10 of an inch apart, with zero for the Horizontal shift, so that you have 21 evenly spaced lines.

4. Select the 21 evenly spaced lines one at a time from the bottom up. Use the Stroke command to make the bottom one 12 points, the next up 11 points, the next 10, and so on until you reach the middle that will be one point in thickness. Then reverse the process, so that the very top line will be 11 points thick. Then group the lines. (See Figure 9.25.)

5. Bring in a photo on Layer 1 and place it under the newly created Stroke group.

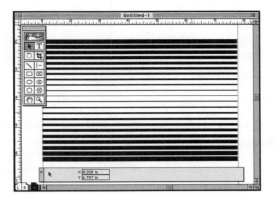

Figure 9.25

This is the initial arrangement of lines you should have on your page.

6. Go to the second layer and set the Stroke color to paper, making the lines knock out the color in the photo beneath. We are creating a line screen for the photo. To explore the possibilities further, use dots and dashes for the solid lines or vary their thickness, number, and spacing. If you're brave enough to devote some time to explore this process, you can create concentric circles and other screens to apply to an image in the same fashion. (See Figure 9.26.)

Figure 9.26

The result of applying PageMaker line screen over a photo.

Tutorial 11: Radial and Other Gradient Fills

Creating gradients, subtle changes in tone in an image, is a simple process in PageMaker. Combined with other possibilities, however, some of which you already investigated, a range of interesting results can be achieved. PageMaker's internal gradients are limited to jumps of 5% increments in screen percentages, but this is usually enough for page layout purposes. For graphics however, it forces you to work in less subtle gradient washes.

To construct a concentric gradient, follow these steps:

1. Draw a series of circles, starting with the outermost first and proceeding to the smaller one at the center.

2. Select them all and choose Align from the Element menu (Shift-Command-E) [Shift-Control-E] to center all of the selections.

3. Select the outermost circle only and using the Stoke and Fill dialog box, set it to Stroke None and Fill 80% Black. Move toward the next one inward and decrease the Fill by 5%. Repeat this action until you have reached the central circle. Select all of the objects and Group them. The result will be a gradient object that seems to have a central glow. If you reverse the order of percentage Fills, you will end up with a dark central circle that seems to be glowing (see Figures 9.27 through 9.29).

Figure 9.27

PageMaker gradients can be configured from a series of shapes.

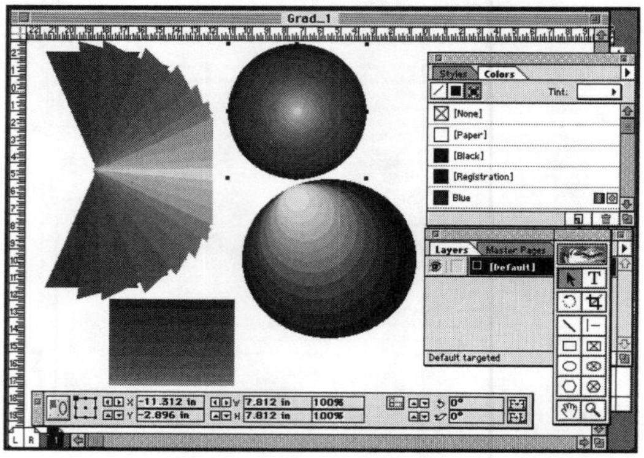

Figure 9.28

Simple but effective PageMaker illustrations can be built using the gradient procedure. Gradients add depth and warmth to PageMaker illustrations.

Figure 9.29

Gradient enhanced illustrations can be just the right touch for a publication. Gradients also can be used effectively as a backdrop for text.

Tutorial 12: Mastering the Open Polygon Mask for a Photo Montage

PageMaker is a world-class layout application, but many users prepare their graphic elements elsewhere, preferring to import them to Page-Maker and place them in a ready-to-print layout. PageMaker, however, especially 6.5, has some very deep creative tools that enable you to create content and place it in a page design. As a result, PageMaker users can make complex Montages without opening up another piece of software. The key ingredient in constructing a Photo Montage in PageMaker is the mastery of the Open Polygon tool. Open polygon shapes are created with the same tool as are polygons. The difference is that instead of click-hold and drag, which produces a polygon, you just click the screen from point to point.

To explore a simple Montage operation, you'll first need to select three interesting photos from your database. You could use illustrations and text as well, but save that exploration until later. Photos enable you to get a quicker grip on the process, which will be applied the same for each photo. Only the content of the individual images, and therefore the shapes you create with the Open Polygon tool, will differ. Your purpose is to outline everything in an image that you want to use as a part of the Photo Montage, disposing of the rest (making it invisible). After you do this with one image from each of the photos you have selected, you can create the final Montage composition.

1. Select a photo. Go to the Polygon tool in the toolbox and place your first point on the photo where you want to start making a mask. Click and release as many times as needed to outline the area of interest. When you reach the first point again, you'll see a rectangular point-box saying you've come full circle. Click and release, and you should see your finished polygon. (See Figures 9.30 and 9.31.)

Figure 9.30

The first step is to create a masking polygon with the Open Polygon tool that outlines the subject matter of interest.

Figure 9.31

Making the open polygon shape a mask for the photo enables you to see only the portion you want.

2. Select the photo and place it at the top of the image stack by using the Element/Arrange/Bring To Front menu. Now select both the photo and the masking polygon and select Mask from the Element menu. The photo should disappear.

3. Move the masking polygon until it matches the area of the photo outlines. Remember that the mask can now be treated as any other graphic element. It can be copied to the Clipboard, pasted, or duplicated.

4. Go through this same series of steps with parts of other photos. When you're done, you'll have your photo montage pieces and all that remains is to place them in an interesting arrangement. (See Figure 9.32.)

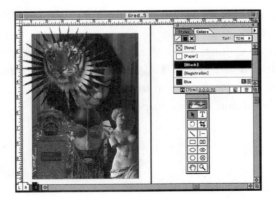

Figure 9.32

In this finished Montage, the three figures at the bottom were all masked with copies of the same Polygon Mask. The Tiger was masked by the Polygon burst at the top-left.

325

Tutorial 13: Reflected Text Options

Although most PageMaker users realize how easy it is to create text with a drop shadow, few explore the topic any deeper. All sorts of text shadows and reflections can be created without leaving the PageMaker environment. This section investigates how to create text with a reflective shadow and also how to manipulate the shadow for more dynamic effects.

1. Create a block of text in any font at a size of 48 points. Zoom in so the text block can be seen clearly. Copy the text and paste it in again.

2. Select the text and use the Flip Vertical button in the Control palette. Butt the cloned and flipped version up against the original text line. Color the original whatever hue you desire and color the new reflection a 60% Black. This serves as a straight reflection, as if the text were sitting on a sheet of ice, but it has little character.

3. To give it more pizzazz, clone the reflective text block and resize it to 130% taller than the original by first making the typeface larger, and then using the Horizontal Scale command in the Type menu to shrink its width. You'll have to play around with this to get it exact. Place this new block in the back layer (Element/Arrange/Send to Back) and get rid of the original reflection.

4. Now take the reflection and turn it into a cast 3-D shadow by Skewing it at 50% (use the Skew input in the Command palette). Color the new shadow dark and the original text lighter (or vice versa). This same operation can be used to make the text cast a shadow in front or in back of itself, just by moving it and altering its position in the stack. (See Figure 9.33.)

Figure 9.33

The top text block shows a standard reflection scheme. The bottom two text blocks use a variation of the same technique to create cast forward and backward shadows.

Tutorial 14: Inline Graphics Options

In PageMaker, you can create an inline graphic within any text block, but that's not the only way to take advantage of the inline technique. You don't need text to use the inline method. Inline graphics offer many of the advantages of Grouping, without ever having to select the Group command. Here's how:

1. In the Type menu, set Text Size to 72 points and click the text tool.

2. Click the Text tool on the Pasteboard, but instead of writing any text, press the Spacebar 30 times. You have just created a text block with no visible text. This is one of the best secret alignment options to use for special case graphics.

3. Click the text cursor at the beginning of the empty text block. Go to the Place selection in the File menu, which brings up a Path dialog box. Inline should be automatically selected because the program is aware that you are asking to have a graphic placed within the text block. Choose an item from your saved graphics files. It appears in the text block (you may have to resize it to fit). Note that you cannot move it independently and that the whole text block moves with it. Place about three or four inline graphics in the text block in the same manner.

Why is this a great option to use when the situation warrants it? All of the inline graphics placed in the text block, illustrations or photos, are connected (see Figure 9.34). They all share a common baseline, so they line up automatically. Whatever you do to the text block (flip it, resize it, or skew it), everything inside is affected in the same manner.

Tip

This method of graphics placement can be used to generate a pseudo-filmstrip. You can place frames from a movie as inline graphics, rotate the whole block, and emulate a film strip showing a selection of separate frames—all of this without ever going to the Align command.

Figure 9.34

Using the inline graphic procedure on an empty text block enables you to select whatever number of photos and artwork fit in the block for automatic alignment and manipulation.

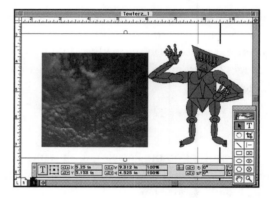

Tutorial 15: Comics and Voice Balloons

PageMaker is the perfect tool for creating comic books and comic strips. Using any of the drawing methods described so far in this section you can generate many of the graphics needed for a comic strip, a comic book, or a comic book look in your Photos. The new Polygon tool's restructuring options make the creation of accompanying voice balloons a snap as well. You don't have to be creating an actual comic book to give an illustration or a photograph a comic book style when you create voice balloons. Comics attract readership because they remind people of their childhood and they present a story in an easy-to-digest fashion. Instructional material, particularly that aimed at the primary and secondary schools, is a prime target for the comic book look. PageMaker's Library is a central focus if you're interested in creating comic book characters.

Illustrated characters can be put together from saved parts, as you saw in the tutorial on creating graphic elements with Primitives. For comic book art in PageMaker, however, the elements need not be limited to only PageMaker's Primitives. You can, for instance, import video stills of a character's head in several orientations (frontal, 3/4, profile, or back) and use a Polygon Mask to outline each head. The photographic heads can then be transformed into illustrations by using the Roto-scoping methods described earlier. Each of the heads would then be saved to your PageMaker comic book library for later use.

The graphics also could be illustrations imported from a bitmap or Vector drawing application and stored in a PageMaker Library for placement in panels and frames. One finished illustration could suffice for many panels by cropping it and zeroing in on an area of interest (as described in the section on panning with the Cropping tool).

Using voice balloons as a frame for your text is not only the way to treat comic book text, but also a way to add interest to a PageMaker Photograph. Voice balloons add viewer interest. Where appropriate, they add more warmth than a cold caption.

Here's how to generate simple voice balloons:

1. Load in a suitable photo. The obvious choice would be a face, but there are other options. A Voice Balloon coming from a building causes the viewer to perceive that someone inside the build is talking. This is something the comics have trained you to understand.

2. Go to the Polygon tool and double-click it to activate the Polygon dialog box. In the dialog box, set the Number of Sides to 20 and the Star Inset to zero. (See Figure 9.35.)

Figure **9.35**

The Polygon Specifications dialog box, showing the setting for creating a voice balloon.

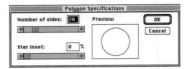

3. Use a blank area of the Pasteboard to generate your text block. Use a loose typeface, perhaps a brush script. Center the lines on each other if there are multiple lines. You can resize everything as you go, so don't worry about the type size at this point.

4. Draw a polygon with the settings just detailed on your photo in an oval, large enough to accommodate the text that will be placed in it. Select it and open the Stroke and Fill dialog box in the Element menu to set the Stroke at 4 points and the Fill at Black/Zero% (these settings can be customized to your needs). Now apply the settings.

5. Make sure the Polygon is sitting on the top layer, above the Photo (Element/Arrange/Bring to Front). Double-click the polygon. This shows all of the polygon control points. You want to drag out a spike in the direction that the voice is coming from on the photo.

6. Resize your text to fit the balloon and place it in the top layer of the stack over the blank area in the balloon. Group everything together. (See Figure 9.36.)

Figure **9.36**

Voice balloons add reader interest to any photo and can be reshaped by altering the polygon control points.

Note

You can use the Framing capability in PageMaker to create a voice balloon, but the text may be a bit more difficult to manipulate and adjust. This is, however, an option. For more information on frames, see Chapter 5.

Tutorial 16: Developing a TextPun Library

A TextPun is a visual play on words, such as the word fire with flames rising from the letters. All sorts of TextPuns can be created in PageMaker and their easy use is dependent upon how well you know the ins and outs of creating a Library. So start at that point, refreshing your memory on how a Library is added to a project. To access the PageMaker Library, go to Window/Plug-In Palettes/Show Library. The Library palette opens (see Figure 9.37). You can either create a new Library or access one already on file by clicking the arrow at the upper-right corner of the Library. This brings out a pop-up menu that lists commands for Adding a Library (see Figure 9.38), Loading a Library, Searching a Library, Removing an Item from a Library, and Displaying the images in a Library by graphic, name, or both.

Figure 9.37

The Library palette is shown on the left. Click the small plus sign at the bottom-right of the Library palette to add selected screen elements to the Library.

Figure 9.38

Using the commands in the Library pop-up menu, you can add, load, and delete Libraries and change the attributes of the listed Library contents.

Now for TextPun graphics. The best tool to use in their creation is the Polygon tool. Different from other Library graphics discussed, DO NOT transform TextPun graphics by using the Paste Special command, but keep them as native PageMaker polygons when you add them to the Library. This is because you can edit PageMaker polygons, resizing and reshaping them. This is an absolute necessity for TextPuns because that way you need only a few graphics to get an infinite amount of variants when they are applied to a page. TextPuns need to be variable because pasting the same TextPun graphic on text characters looks much too even and you lose the impact that the process can provide.

What elements would be worth considering as TextPun graphics? Try these for a start: Fire, Ice, Tear Drops, Smoke, Balloons, Clouds, and Snowflakes. There are innumerable choices to add from there, but this gives you a basic TextPun Library of elements. You can even name the Library "My_TextPuns." All of these graphics can be created within PageMaker using the Polygon tool, the Color palette, and a little imagination. (See Figure 9.39.)

Note

For a more in-depth discussion of type effects, please consult Photoshop Type Magic, Volume I or II, *published by Hayden Books.*

Figure 9.39

Using the saved graphics of a TextPun sequence to the PageMaker Library enables you to drag and drop them into place whenever needed.

Tutorial 17: Is PageMaker Animation Possible?

Here's how:

1. Develop a graphic in PageMaker using the Polygon tool. This can be a freeform shape or a Polygon configured from the Polygon Specifications dialog box.

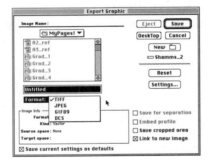

Figure 9.40

In PageMaker, you can export a Place Special graphic as a TIFF, JPEG, GIF89, or DCS file.

3. When these files are called up in your Web page design application (which might even be PageMaker), the GIF files will load as an animation. This is a special property of GIF files. Special software is on the market for Macs and PCs that will read in same-named sequences of GIFs and output a GIF animation file. Check with your computer vendor for information on these utility applications. (See Figure 9.41.)

Figure 9.41

This simple eight frame sequence (read left to right, top to bottom) was produced in PageMaker. Following the procedure outlined in the text, it could be written out as GIF89 animation frames.

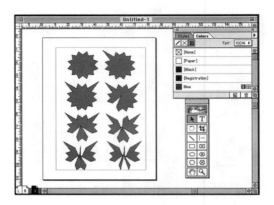

Tutorial 18: Basic Graphing in PageMaker

If you have to generate complex charts and graphs, PageMaker is not the place to do it. For those times, however, when a simple bar graph or pie chart is needed, there are ways to craft them within PageMaker.

A Simple Bar Chart

PageMaker offers its own chart making facility. In order to understand how to use it to develop a basic Bar Chart, work through the following steps:

1. Open the Layout/Column Guides dialog box (see Figure 9.42). Enter 8 for the number of columns (or whatever number of columns your bar graph demands up to 20), and .25 for the Space Between Columns.

2. Select the Rectangle tool and use the ruled measurements on the side of the PageMaker Pasteboard to determine the relative height of your bars to each other. Make sure Snap to Guides (Shift-Command-;) [Shift-Control-;] is turned on in the View menu.

3. Draw in your bars, each in a representative color or screen tint.

4. Create a Bar Key, a box that shows what data each of the bars represent, and save the Bar Chart to disk (see Figure 9.43).

Figure 9.42

This is the place to start a simple Bar Graph operation in PageMaker, by accessing the Column Guides dialog box in the Layout menu.

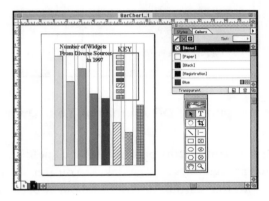

Figure 9.43

Your finished Bar Chart might look something like this.

A Simple Pie Chart

Pie Charts are commonly used to show how something is divided up. The best way to generate a Pie Chart in PageMaker is to use the Polygon tool with a high setting in the Polygon Specifications dialog box for the Number of Sides and NO STAR DATA. A high number of sides creates a smoother circular shape. For each section of the Pie, create another clone of the first circular shape. Use a full circular shape as a background for the Pie Chart and overlay each of the Slices.

To create the Slices, use the Polygon Control Points. Remove all but those necessary to produce the correct section of the circumference and then stretch out one point to generate the straight sides. Color or tint each of the sections differently to distinguish one from another. Refer to Figure 9.44 for a visual example of a finished Pie Chart.

Generating a Pie Chart in PageMaker requires knowledge of the Polygon tool. The section percentages can be estimated and text data entered after the graphics are complete. You can even use the sections (slices) as masks to hold pictorial data. When you pull the slices away, it's called an Exploded Pie Chart.

335

Figure 9.44

A PageMaker Pie Chart.

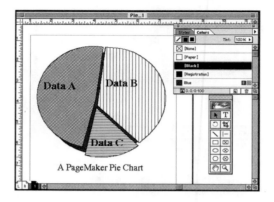

A PageMaker Pie Chart

Tutorial 19: Keeping a PDF Journal of Your Own Magic Tricks

Who is the most trustworthy person when it comes to exploring all of the tools and passageways in PageMaker? You are! Most professional artists are aware that startling discoveries about media and tools are not half as important as repeating the process again if needed. It's easy to get great graphics in PageMaker, but can you get the same look again? Most creative discoveries in computer graphics proceed and develop in the same way they have for centuries in the traditional artistic realms. You start with a simple and well-known process that attracts your attention, and become drawn into the "what if" syndrome—what if I don't follow these rules exactly, what if I stretch this line further than what is expected, what if I place this under the circle instead of over it— ad infinitum.

In the days before computers, artists and scientists kept journals of their explorations. Then along came the computer, and most folks carried on with the same process, just using a word processor instead of paper to enumerate the steps in their discoveries. But now, thanks to Adobe, there's PDF, the Page Description File Format. PageMaker writes out PDF files, which couldn't be better as far as your journal efforts are concerned. PDF saves text and graphics without any need for the viewer having to own or use the same software or fonts that created the PDF file in the first place.

PageMaker file saves are twice the size of a PDF file with the same data and PDF is also a great way to transmit files over the Web. With PDF files, you can share your PageMaker exploratory notes with peers and friends. How can you use the PDF capabilities in PageMaker to your best advantage when detailing your paths to discovery? Here's a suggested way to go about it:

1. Choose a PageMaker tool, say the Polygon tool, and start to explore its possibilities. When you discover something new and exciting, create a graphic that acts as a visual reminder of your explorations and ideas. Alongside the graphic, create a text block and spell out the steps it took you to reach your discovery, detailing as much of the data in a step-by-step fashion as you can.

2. After the PageMaker session is complete, and you've finished with a train of thought, save the page as a PDF file. To do this, select File/Export/Adobe PDF. Select the options you need from the PDF dialog boxes that present themselves and save the file. Repeat this for every exploratory session and in no time you'll have amassed your own teaching journal.

The dialog box shown in Figure 9.45 is the first PDF Export dialog box to greet you. If the View PDF using box is checked, Adobe Acrobat Reader (in whatever version you have installed) runs immediately after the save, showing you what the saved PDF file looks like. The Control option (see Figure 9.46) can be accessed from the initial Export Adobe PDF dialog box. It gives you several other options, including the capability to adjust the output color to either RGB or CMYK in the PDF file. The PDF Options dialog box also lists HyperLink and Bookmark options for the PDF file (see Figure 9.47). The Distiller PDF Job Options dialog box (see Figure 9.48) enables you to fine tune how the associated PDF file will be configured and how the incorporated images will be addressed in the translation.

Figure 9.45

The Export Adobe PDF dialog box.

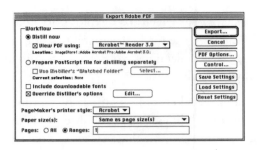

Figure 9.46

The Control option in the Export Adobe PDF dialog box.

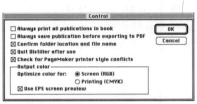

Figure 9.47

The HyperLink and Bookmark options.

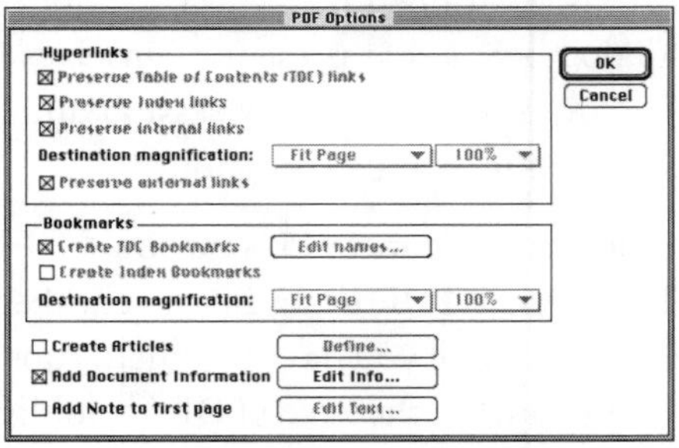

Figure 9.48

The Distiller PDF Job Options dialog box.

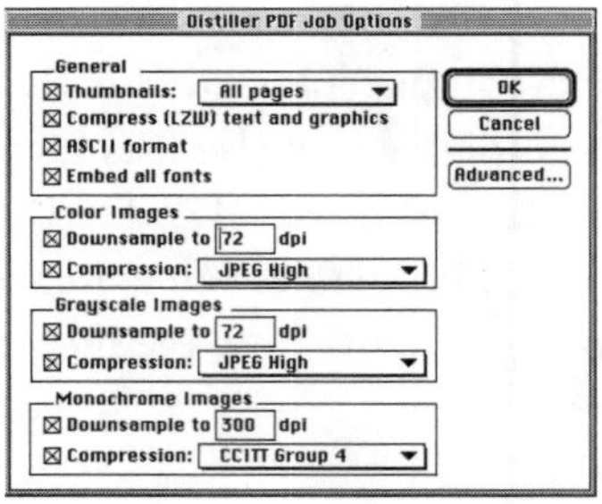

SUMMARY

This chapter gave you 19 tutorials to help you become a PageMaker artist instead of just a technician. Chapter 10, "Using PageMaker's Basic Color Tools," will give you the basics you need to work with color.

Chapter

10

USING PAGEMAKER'S
BASIC COLOR TOOLS

Whether you're using a single spot color for emphasis in a logo or creating a glossy, full-color piece, you need to know some basic about color printing technology and the tools available to you in PageMaker. This chapter covers the necessary background to make sense of working in color, and you also learn how to make the most of PageMaker's color features. Chapter 11, "Taking Color from Computer to Paper," covers more advanced issues, such as trapping and color management. Read this chapter for information about:

◆ Working around the fact that the color on your computer screen never perfectly matches the color you get on the printed page—even with PageMaker's new color management capabilities.

◆ Understanding the nature of the two kinds of color used in printing a page: spot color and process color.

◆ Planning the color system for your projects, choosing between a color-matching system (spot color) and process color, or perhaps using both.

- Using PageMaker's redesigned Color palette to define and apply colors in your publications.

- Selecting colors from PageMaker's built-in color libraries, and creating color libraries to meet your needs.

UNDERSTANDING THE BASICS OF COLOR

Your screen doesn't match the printing press. It's sad but true. No matter how carefully controlled your production process, WYSIWYG does not exist when you arrive in the world of digital color. Sure, the type is shaped correctly, and the line breaks are accurate—the problem is the color. Open an image of a dewy pink rose on any dozen computers, and you are apt to get a dozen subtly different shades of pink and the color you get on paper from a printing press won't match any of them.

What about the standard color-matching systems, such as PANTONE? Those colors are the same every time aren't they? Well, sure, unless someone screws up when mixing the ink—not too likely. But even though you get consistent colors on the printing press, your printed PMS color still won't match your computer screen.

Well, you say, I will be okay if I use a calibrated color management system, right? Yes—up to a point. Color management helps, and PageMaker's implementation of color management has many professionals feeling as confident and excited about color accuracy as they have been for a long time. But these color-management systems still aren't perfect.

No matter how much color management systems improve, no calibration system will ever resolve one central difficulty: the way your computer produces color onscreen and the way a printing press produces color on a page simply do not compare. In Figure 10.1, the computer screen shoots light at you by making phosphor glow inside a glass tube—projected light. A printing press puts ink on paper so you only see it from light that bounces off the paper—reflected light.

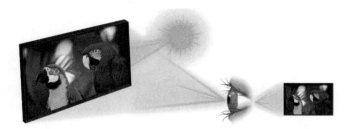

Figure 10.1

Your eye receives reflected or printed (top) and projected light (bottom) in entirely different ways, so the "same" color looks subtly different depending on how it is viewed.

Aside from the core technological differences between computers and printing presses, a few other variables get in the way of seeing accurate color onscreen:

◆ Computer monitors build colors from red, blue, and green (RGB), whereas printing presses build colors with inks (some premixed, some blends of process color ink dots).

◆ The printing press and the computer can use any one of a dozen or so methods of describing colors—called color spaces. The translations between those systems generally result in surprises and compromises.

◆ Printing press results can be inconsistent due to batch variations in the "same" ink colors and variations in the way plates are burned by different press operators.

◆ Phosphor varies from one computer screen to the other, resulting in inconsistent color representations—even if they are plugged into the same computer and even if they are made at the same factory using the same batch of phosphor.

- As it ages, a computer monitor screen sprays a varying number of electrons at the phosphor, resulting in brightness and contrast inconsistencies over time.

- Paper makes a major difference in the color of your final printed product, absorbing more or less ink (depending on the weather and storage conditions) and adding its own underlying tint to the color mix.

- The systems that provide color proofs—as good as they are— aren't perfect. So when the service bureau pulls a proof, you can't rely on it to perfectly match the final printed page.

- You may not even be publishing on paper. If you are using PageMaker to create a slide or overhead presentation, other factors can create variations in color. Fundamental differences are triggered when you shine light through transparent material. For slides, many other variables are introduced by the operator of the film recorder and the slide developing process. And for overheads, the range of color printer options—from an inexpensive inkjet to a dye sublimation printer that costs as much as a new car—introduces yet more variables.

- And to top it all off, your brain constantly makes judgments, so you see colors differently depending on all sorts of environmental factors, such as the amount and type of overhead lights and the color of the walls.

The point of all this? Don't trust the color you see on your monitor because it only resembles the colors on those standard ink swatches or the photograph of your dewy pink rose.

How can you work around this problem? Simply keep in mind that you can't pick or edit colors based purely on what you see on the computer screen. Be constantly aware of the challenge you face in translating color from the computer screen to some other medium.

Actually, the one partial solution to the challenge of getting the color you want in your final printed product is experience—either yours or the experience of your service bureau or print shop manager.

If you have an in-house, million-dollar imagesetter system and a six-tower litho press (another bunch of commas and zeros in the budget) and can do experimental color runs to your heart's content, you can learn pretty quickly what works and what doesn't—especially if you have an experienced hand to be your mentor.

Unfortunately, those tools aren't part of the average desktop publishing setup. And throwing out 10,000 muddy-looking four-color brochures is fiercely expensive—especially if you have to eat the cost yourself because your client rejected the job. If you don't have color experience and an unlimited budget for experimentation, you can make your life a little easier by calling on the expertise of others who have that kind of experience. Remember, printing color is as much as a craft as it is a science, and variables as subtle as the humidity at print time can have a big impact on the outcome of your job. That's why this chapter makes such a big deal at the beginning and at other points in this book about the need to take into account the full publishing process.

Collaborate early and often with the other people on your color production team—the print shop, the service bureau that provides your prepress services, and the photographer who shoots the photographs for your publication. Those folks' eyes have already been trained by years of expensive mistakes, and they're usually willing to help you learn to avoid the problems they've encountered on other jobs.

> ### Color Spaces
>
> The idea of color spaces takes a bit of getting used to. The spectrum of visible light includes millions and millions of colors, but the devices which we use to represent and reproduce color—color monitors, proofing devices, and printing presses, among others—can only reproduce a subset of the full spectrum reliably. The colors each device can reproduce are known as that device's gamut. Working with color is tricky because each device you use has a different gamut. In 1934, and international group of color scientists (the Commission Internationale d'Eclairage, often shortened to CIE) defined a universal color space in an attempt to create common color ground; the standards developed then are still in use today.

WORKING WITH SPOT COLOR

When you use a rubber stamp or pick up a brush to paint the trim of your house, you are using spot color. In printing, spot color means you are smearing a solid swatch of ink onto the printed page. In a sense, when you print an all black-ink publication you are printing with spot color—the color of black ink in that case.

Usually, though, when someone says, "I just did a spot color job," they mean they ran a job on a printing press using black ink and one or more additional spot colors. The spot colors are premixed ink, concocted by the printer or by the print shop's supplier, almost always using one of the standardized color-matching systems. In addition to printed swatch books, the major color-matching systems usually have electronic color libraries (where the colors are defined using the RGB color model) so you can choose the colors directly in PageMaker. That's how you pick your color—by selecting from standard color swatches, either the printed or onscreen versions.

Spot Color Means Accurate Color

Because you are working with premixed inks, spot color, within its limitations, pretty much solves the challenge of achieving accurate color.

You still can't necessarily see the color accurately on your computer, but you can see what you will get by using the pre-printed swatch books that are designed to be used with the standard color matching systems. These books of color swatches—which are just like the paint chips you get at the paint store except that you pay dearly for them—enable you to see the printed colors that you're specifying. PANTONE's color matching systems are the most widely used in the United States. To create PMS swatch book, the folks at PANTONE mixed up all those standard colors of ink under scientifically controlled circumstances and laid them down on paper using specially designed presses.

The printed colors in swatch books correspond to electronic color libraries that come with PageMaker. When you pick your color from the swatch book, you can select the same color from the libraries that come with PageMaker and work with the confidence that your printer can reproduce the color exactly—regardless of how it looks onscreen.

You could create a spot color in PageMaker without using one of the standard color matching systems, but it's not a good idea. You have no guarantee that any print shop in the country could come up with whatever color you design. Besides, your monitor probably wouldn't represent the color accurately.

Even when you use pre-defined colors, there are still some variables. Your paper choice will influence the results from the press and your perception of the color depends in large part on the ambient light under which you examine the color swatch (fluorescent, sunshine, incandescent, rose-colored glasses, and so forth). Spot color, however, by and large, means accurate color.

Spot Color Overlays and Press Plates

When you work with spot color you generally use two or three inks (although you could have many more). The printer makes up a plate for black ink, a plate for your second color, and another for your third, then prints your pages by running the paper over all those plates. You can have as many inks as your printer can handle on the press during a single run, and the print shop can even run the paper through more than once to add still more colors. (At some point, however, it makes more sense to use process color or even hi-fi color, because you get a wider range of color possibilities for the same expense—more on this in the next section.)

In order to create these plates—one for each color you are specifying for the job (including black)—you need to make paper or film overlays. As you can see in Figure 10.2, each overlay isolates all of its particular assigned color onto a single sheet of paper or film, which the printer uses to photographically expose a plate to use on press.

Overlays

Why are these spot color mechanicals called overlays? Because that was the term traditionally used when a graphic artist pasted up a project for the printer. The type was pasted down on a stiff board and each spot color was represented by an acetate overlay mounted in layers over the top—overlays, in other words.

Pages are now pasted up electronically, in the computer, instead of using an Xacto knife, T-square, Rubylith, acetate, and poster board or foam-core. When you print color separations, PageMaker automatically creates an overlay for each spot color you've defined.

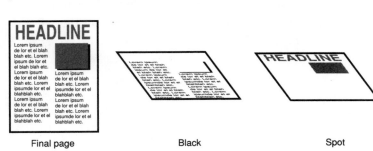

Final page   **Black**   **Spot**

Figure 10.2

Each overlay isolates all elements of that particular color, and is used by the printer to create a printing plate.

Halftone Screening

Halftone screens were invented as a way to reproduce continuous tone images, such as photographs, on commercial printing presses. The same principle applies to both black-and-white and color images, but it's a little easier to explain in black and white.

To get around the fact that a printing press can only print solid colors, printers developed halftoning as a way to render the shades of gray that make an image convincing. Halftone screens turn a continuous tone image into a series of tiny cells—between 85 and 200 cells per inch—each of which represent the lightness or darkness of that cell's area by a variable-sized dot. When printed together, these tiny dots give blend together to give the appearance of a continuous tone image.

The halftone screen ruling, or frequency, determines how many dots per inch you get, and is determined by the type of paper and press you'll be printing your job on.

WORKING WITH PROCESS COLOR

Think of process color printing as a major eyeball scam job. It might seem that the four CMYK colors—cyan, magenta, yellow, and black—are mixing on the page to create new colors. But that's not quite so. Each color is getting its set of dots on the paper, and those sets of dots are generated by the halftone screening process. It's your eye that is mixing the color, or rather it's your brain that mixes all those tiny dots when they arrive from the optic nerve from your eye.

You get the dots by turning your publication into four halftones, one for each color. Understanding halftones is important, and you can get more detail on the concept and how it relates to resolution and line screens by checking Chapter 15, "Prepress, Service Bureaus, and Printers."

Understanding Traditional Process Color

At some point, if your full-color publication job is heading for a printing press, you must convert it to CMYK four-color process color.

In desktop publishing you separate your color work electronically by using software such as PageMaker that breaks a page down into four separations—four layers of color that together compose a full-color image. Before the advent of computers, this separation of color into four component parts was done photographically in a print shop darkroom. You can see how they all add up in Figure 10.3.

Figure 10.3

From left to right you see the original picture, the four negative films, the impressions from each in the CMYK colors, and how they combine to produce a final image.

Separating the image into the four CMYK colors of cyan, magenta, yellow, and black is just one part of the job PageMaker does when you print color separations. Those layers of color must also be turned into halftones called screens, and the screens turned at an angle to one another so they don't just stack up, one dot on top of the other. Why? Because that's how the four-color process scam is pulled off. The famous four process colors aren't mixed on the press; they're mixed in your brain. At some level your brain conveniently ignores the fact that the page is as dotty as measles, and it blends the adjacent dots into a continuous perceived color. Look at Figure 10.4 to see how the dots mingle.

Newspapers, for example, print with coarse screens of 85 to 100 dots per inch (dpi) because newsprint is very absorbent and smaller dots tend to blob together; a fancy full-color brochure on high-quality paper is more likely to use a fine screen of 175 or 200 cells per inch so the details in the image are easier to see.

Everything about black-and-white halftones and line screens and resolution applies to process color, except it's all four times more important because four screens make up your process color publication. For more information about halftone screens, see Chapter 15.

Figure 10.4

The eye blends the cyan, magenta, yellow, and black process-color dots into a continuous image—rather than perceiving them as separate colors.

Keep in mind that cyan, magenta, and yellow can be combined to create almost any color, but they aren't actually mixed together except in your brain. Ideally, these dots all cluster together in a sort of rosette pattern so distracting moiré patterns are avoided. The percentage (size and number of dots) of each of the four determines the apparent color on your printed page.

K—Black

Black is used in addition to the CMY, because it allows purer blacks (the cyan, magenta, and yellow pigments are never pure, and therefore make a muddy brown rather than a strong black. Often, designers specify a "rich black," one that has been heightened by the addition of cyan (to create a cool black), magenta, or yellow (to create warmer blacks).

Another reason cyan, magenta, and yellow aren't combined to create black is a potential problem called over-inking. It may have occurred to you that 100 percent of CMY adds up to 300 percent. That's a lot of ink to be in one spot on a piece of paper. Commercial printers generally try to avoid ink coverage of more than 250 percent to 320 percent; the amount of acceptable coverage for any job depends on the paper and the press. To compensate for the technical problem of ink buildup caused by the artificial CMYK color system, prepress experts use something called GCR, for gray component replacement. This and many other technical issues relating to color and the printing press—including color management systems and trapping to compensate for misregistration of colors on the printing press—are summed in Chapter 11, "Taking Color from Computer to Paper."

DECIDING BETWEEN SPOT AND PROCESS COLOR

Up to a point, you choose between spot color and process color because of money. Basically, you want to use the minimum number of color plates on the press because the price goes up with every additional ink color (which requires adding expensive printing press plates). That means that if you have any more than three colors, then you probably want to use process color. Why? Because when you're already paying for four colors, you might as well use process color and have the freedom to design with as many colors as you like. That's over-simplified, of course, because in some circumstances you need the accuracy of spot color's premixed inks. But the basic premise holds true: when you're using more than three spot colors in a job, you should consider printing with process colors.

Introducing High-Fidelity Color

High-fidelity color extends the range of traditional four-color process color systems by adding extra color plates to the printing process. There are multiple approaches to producing high fidelity color, but PANTONE's Hexachrome system is well on the way to becoming the standard. The fact that PANTONE—the de facto standard for color matching systems—is behind it sure doesn't hurt. But aside from a strong name brand and a powerful marketing apparatus, the Hexachrome solution has two major advantages: it's backed up by a complete set of support materials (printed swatchbooks, custom inks, and electronic color libraries), and it can be printed on any six-colorpress.

Even with all the well-deserved enthusiasm this new technology is receiving, the most important thing to know about high-fidelity color is that it's still relatively new. Although a growing number of vendors are familiar with it and have experience producing hi-fi color jobs, it's still far less common than standard process color printing. For more information about Hexachrome support in PageMaker, see the section "The Brave New World of Hi-Fi Color" in Chapter 11.

Sometimes, expense issues aside, you have to use process color in order to reproduce a color photograph or because spot color simply can't do the job. Conversely, for some jobs you absolutely must use spot colors. You might, for example, require a particular shade of green to reproduce a company's logo. For those jobs, you use standard inks from one of the color-matching systems, as discussed in the section on spot color. The PANTONE Matching System (PMS) has become ubiquitous since its introduction back in the early 1960s, but other systems such as Dainippon (often referred to as DIC) and Toyo do exist for achieving standard color.

Often it's necessary to combine both spot and process inks for a single job. You might, for example, need inks from one of the color-matching systems to create certain unusual ink effects, such as fluorescent yellow, pearlescent blue, or metal-flake tangerine. Or, more commonly, you need to reproduce a color photograph (using CMYK) and you need to match a signature color in a logo exactly using a premixed spot ink. In these cases you can (and sometimes must) run a spot color and process color on the same job. Eight-color jobs, where four-color process photos are combined on a page with several spot colors aren't common because they're so expensive—but they do happen (and they're excellent candidates for considering hi-fi color as an alternative—see the section "The Brave New World of Hi-Fi Color" in Chapter 11 for details). A job like that might even require multiple passes through the printing presses, which in turn means considerable amounts of expensive labor, press time, and wasted stock and ink to get the paper in registration during the second pass through the press.

In general, six colors (including any varnish coating) is the break point of combining process and spot colors. Many large commercial printers have six-tower presses that can run that many colors in a single pass. Of course, you won't find that kind of expensive press at your local quick printer, but most of them can handle spot color jobs. The point is the more colors, the more money.

Converting Between Color Systems

In PageMaker, converting colors between various color libraries and methods of describing color is deceptively easy. Click a radio button in the color editing dialog box and PageMaker seems to easily make the switch. The catch is that converting colors from one color system to another can cause problems down the line when you're printing your job, so this chapter is going to digress a bit here and explain why you should think twice about converting an RGB color to CMYK or vice versa.

Additive and Subtractive Color Models

Your color monitor paints images onscreen using three colors—red, green, and blue (RGB). If you add equal proportions of all three primary colors, you get white. But rather than using actual colors, the additive model uses beams of light at the particular wavelengths of red, green, and blue, which when combined, create the wavelength for white light. Notice the word "add." For that reason, scientists call the RGB color model an additive color model. The trick is that there's also a subtractive color model, and that's used to print color on paper. Unlike the additive model, the subtractive model starts with white light being reflected off of the surface of paper; the other colors in the spectrum are created by using inks to block the light which reflects back from the white. Cyan, magenta, and yellow are opposites to RGB colors. Cyan is a mix of green and blue. It absorbs (subtracts) red and reflects the remaining RGB colors from the original light source.

Colors defined using the RGB color model are usually either spot colors or are designed for use onscreen, as is the case with designs created for use on the World Wide Web, where the images will be viewed on a computer monitor. Colors defined using the CMYK model, in contrast, are used almost exclusively for projects that will be printed using the standard process colors.

Look at Figure 10.5 to see how you get white on the press. At the top, there's the old familiar prism experiment from school days, the primary colors of red, green, and blue adding up to white. Below the prism, you can see the RGB color definition dialog box from PageMaker, adding up 100 percent of each color to get white. At the bottom, you see the process method of getting white, by subtracting colors until there is zero percent of each of the four inks (assuming you are printing to white paper, of course).

Figure 10.5

A prism and RGB monitor add projected light to get a color. A printing press puts CYMK colors on paper to reflect a color.

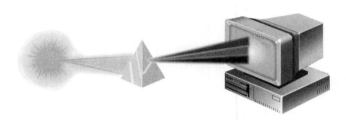

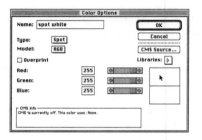

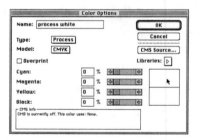

Bringing this back to the topic at hand, these two PageMaker dialog boxes for editing colors make it very clear that RGB and CMYK color systems arrive at "white" through two different routes.

When you define a color using the RGB model, increasing the component colors brings you closer to white. When you use the CMYK model, increasing the component colors makes the color you're defining darker. It's not a perfect world. Although cyan, magenta, and yellow are the opposites of red, green, and blue, the way these ideal colors are translated into inks and phosphors means that the color spaces—or gamuts—each defines aren't the same. This is a problem, because it means that colors defined in one space might not have an exact equivalent in the other space (see Figure 10.6). The rub really comes when you try to convert colors at the outer limits of a color system's capability, many of which can't be translated with any degree of color fidelity. And because getting predictable, reliable color results is the name of the game, it's a good idea to play it safe and avoid converting colors from one color model to another.

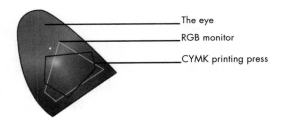

The eye
RGB monitor
CYMK printing press

Figure 10.6

Your eye can discern colors that your computer monitor can't project, and the printing press can reproduce colors that your computer monitor can't create.

There are a couple of caveats. Color management—which is discussed in Chapter 11—is designed to mitigate this fundamental problem by translating all colors though a neutral, device-independent color space. You'll have more control and get more consistent results if you use color management, but the basic problem remains: colors defined in one color space may be out of another space's gamut, and therefore they won't translate well.

The other caveat is that in some cases, color fidelity may not really matter. If you're designing publications for distribution online, where everything is displayed in RGB, all that really matters is how things look onscreen. In that case, converting CMYK colors to RGB isn't a problem, as long as you like what you see onscreen. (It's worth pointing out that what you see on your screen might not match what someone else will see on a different monitor, but that gets back to some basic color management principles.) In some production situations, there are some color-matching systems that make this whole color system conversion a lot easier. These systems specify spot color inks to be mixed out of the four standard process colors of cyan, magenta, yellow, and black. TRUMATCH, Focoltone, or the PANTONE Process matching systems all work this way, and if your commercial printer supports them, you can work in process colors and somewhat more accurately specify spot colors.

PAGEMAKER'S COLOR TOOLS

This section covers all of the tools PageMaker provides for working with color on your pages:

◆ Getting the most from the new Color palette, which is command central for working with color.

◆ Defining colors in PageMaker, either by making them up yourself, choosing them from a color-matching system library, or importing them with EPS graphics.

◆ Editing colors after you've defined them.

◆ Applying colors to text, PageMaker-drawn shapes, and imported graphics.

PageMaker's New Color Palette

Part of the facelift PageMaker received in this release is a newly designed and vastly improved Color palette. Although the basics are unchanged, it now lists all colors you've defined, and enables you to apply them to objects on your pages—there are at least a dozen new refinements that make working with color faster and easier than ever.

Let's start with a quick tour of the palette (see Figure 10.7). This first point may be obvious, but it probably bears repeating: You can drag the Color palette out on its own, or combine it with other palettes to create a new palette window. By default, the Color palette is in the same window as the Style palette, but you don't have to keep it there unless it's convenient for you.

The new Color palette has loads more information available at a glance. You can see whether a color was defined as spot or process, whether the color model used was RGB, CMYK, or hi-fi, and you can even see what the numeric definition of the selected color is.

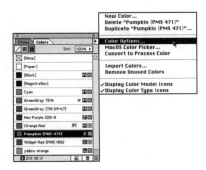

Figure10.7

The Color palette.

At the far right edge of the palette window is a triangle indicating a drop-down menu. As with all of the other new palettes in PageMaker, you can access color-specific menu options here. If you're an old PageMaker hand, notice that many options that used to be buried on the main menus are here instead—making them much quicker to locate. The New, Delete, and Duplicate commands are pretty straightforward: they create a new color, delete the selected color, or duplicate the selected color, respectively. Color Options opens a dialog box for editing the selected color (or defining a new color if you had one of the default colors selected).

Choosing the MacOS Color Picker (available on the Macintosh only) option opens up the standard Mac window that enables you to define colors visually using hue, lightness, and saturation as variables. This isn't new exactly, as PageMaker always had a secret shortcut for opening this. The good news is that for those of you who can't always remember hidden shortcuts, getting here is now as plain as day.

Convert to Spot Color redefines a selected Process color as a Spot color; if you have a Spot color selected, this option reads Convert to Process Color. This can be a real time-saver, but be sure you understand the implications of converting colors between color spaces (see the "Converting Between Color Systems" section earlier in this chapter for more information).

Import Colors sucks the colors from the Color palette of an existing publication, which is handy if you're working on a large project where color consistency is key. This option can also save you the trouble of redefining your favorite colors if they already exist in another publication. Remove Unused Colors will appeal to the neat freak in you. It's easy to get carried away when you're setting up the Color palette for a new job, and it's easier still to lose track of which colors you've used after you're in the flow of a project. This simple command cleans up your palette by deleting the colors that are unused. (If you still have duplicate colors, you can always merge them—details on that can be in the section "Merging Colors" later in this chapter.)

Display Color Model Icons and Display Color Type Icons control whether those groovy little icons to the right of each color name appear or not. The Color Model icons are the more colorful options: the striped one indicates an RGB color, the X with the cyan, magenta, yellow, and black quadrants indicates a CMYK model, and the swirly rainbow one indicates a hi-fi color. The Color Type icons at the far right edge of the palette are even easier to identify: the gray dot in a white box indicates a spot color, all the others (those plain gray boxes) are process colors.

Just below the palette name, you'll see the Line, Fill, and Both buttons at the top left of the palette window. This is where you decide which portions of the selected object you want to apply a given color to. (To apply a color, select an object, click on the Line, Fill, or Both icon, then click on the color swatch of the color you want to apply.)

To the right of these buttons is the Tint pull-down menu, which enables you to apply a tint of the selected color to the selected object on-the-fly.

Default Colors in the Colors Palette

The first four colors in the list—None, Paper, Black, and Registration—are default colors that are built into PageMaker. Try as you might, you'll never be able to delete them. Here's how to use them:

◆ **None** removes any color added in PageMaker, and is a quick way to make any PageMaker-drawn object transparent. For imported graphics to which you have applied a PageMaker color, it is also a handy way to return the object to what you might call its natural color. It works the same way as the setting in the Print command to preserve EPS colors (for PostScript printers only), except it applies to any imported file to which PageMaker colors have been assigned, including TIFFs.

◆ **Paper** means no ink or knockout (knockouts are discussed in more detail later in this chapter). PageMaker applies no ink to any area or object to which you assign the color Paper, including any point where a Paper-colored object overlaps an object of another color. One way to think of it is as electronic white-out: any object covered with a paper-colored object essentially disappears, without so much as a trace of that chalky white stuff. If you are printing to colored paper, you may want to edit the definition of the Paper color in that publication so you get a monitor display that more closely resembles your actual finished page. Just be sure to remember that paper means no ink.

◆ The color **Black** is defined as a process black set to overprint, and, like the color Registration, cannot be edited. If you want to create a Black that knocks out, duplicate the default black and edit it accordingly, being sure that the new color's name indicates it is set to knockout.

◆ The color **Registration** has been specially defined as 100% each of CMYK as well as every spot color you've specified, so any object assigned this color will be separated to every overlay or plate. Use the color Registration for anything—such as put production notes or custom-trim cross hairs—that you want to print on every spot-color overlay or process-color separation. You cannot edit the Registration color.

The other colors in the palette by default are Red, Blue, Green, Cyan, Magenta, and Yellow. Any colors you have defined or selected from a color library also appear in this alphabetically ordered list. Any colors defined as a tint of another color display a % symbol to the right of the color name. If Display Color Model Icon and Display Color Type Icon are checked, these icons are visible to the right of any tint symbols.

Colors riding in with an imported EPS file from an outside source have the PostScript logo to the right of the color name.

For more about the nuances of how this works, see the "Adopting Colors from Imported or Clipboard Objects" section later in this chapter.

The precise numerical definition of each color is displayed at the very bottom of the palette when that color is selected. Say, for example, you've selected a shade of process green on the palette. The left-hand space at the bottom of the palette will display the Process Color Model icon (the X with four colors) followed by the numeric values for each of the four inks, in this case 40:0:75:10, indicating that the color is made up of 40% of the cyan ink, 0% of the magenta, 75% of the yellow, and 10% of the black.

Creating and Deleting Colors

To the right of the color definition area are two icons: a page icon for creating new colors and a trash can for deleting existing colors. To delete any color, select it on the palette and then click the trash icon. You'll be prompted with a message asking you if you're really sure you want to delete the color; if you do, say yes and it's gone. If the color has been used anywhere in the publication, even as the base color of a tint, PageMaker gives you a warning dialog box asking for confirmation and letting you know that it will turn all the occurrences of that color (including the related tints) to black.

Note

It's common to build up a clutter of unused colors if you are experimenting with color families or importing EPS graphics. PageMaker's Remove Unused Colors command (on the pop-up menu to the right of the palette name) gets rid of them.

Adding colors to the Colors palette is equally straightforward, but it requires making a lot of decisions along the way. This section guides you through the process.

In order to add any new colors to your palette, you need to get to the Color Options dialog box. The fastest and easiest way is to click the new page icon (next to the trash icon). Here's a complete list of the ways you can get to the Color Options dialog box when you want to create a new color:

◆ Click the page icon at the bottom of the Color palette.

◆ Double-click the default "Black" or "Registration" colors on the palette.

◆ Choose New from the menu on the left of the palette. You also can go to the Define Colors command in the Element menu and select New, but why bother when there's a faster way? After you open the Color Options dialog box, it's time to make some choices.

Editing Colors

Editing a color's name is easy: simply double-click the color's name on the palette. The Color Options dialog box opens, and you can highlight the existing name and type in a new one. Click OK, and you're done.

Changing a color's definition is pretty much the same. After you've double-clicked the color name on the palette to open the Color Options dialog box, you can modify the values used to create it, change the color model, or replace it with a different color from one of the color libraries. After you click OK, the new definition is there to stay. Here's a quick recap of some things you might want to avoid when editing colors:

♦ Unless you're designing for onscreen viewing, it's probably not a good idea to change the color model in order to convert colors between RGB and CYMK. The two color spaces don't match exactly, and you could end up with unacceptable printed output.

♦ It's fine to change the definition of a spot color so what you see onscreen matches a printed swatch, but only if you aren't ever going to convert it to a process color.

Selecting the Type of Color

Before you even think about naming your new color, your first to-do item is to select your type of color: spot, process, or a tint percentage of one or the other. For more on the difference between spot and process colors, look at "Working with Spot Color" and "Working with Process Color" sections earlier in this chapter. Keep the following information in mind when selecting a type of color:

♦ Remember that using a spot color means you will be isolating everything assigned that color to a single color overlay so the printer can burn a plate to apply a premixed ink. The color you see in PageMaker is really there as a color reminder, but it doesn't actually have a whole lot to do with how the color appears on the final printed page.

♦ Using process color means that you will be creating color separations in CMYK. In this case, the color definitions in PageMaker have everything to do with how the color looks when it's printed, because the CMYK percentages determine how much of each ink is applied during the printing process.

♦ You can only create a tint after you have defined a base color. The tint will be a percentage of that base color. The "Defining Tints" section later in this chapter gives more detail on this operation.

Make your color type selection with a clear idea of where you are heading in the design process. Use spot color if you are working with one of the spot color-matching systems, for example. If you know you will be working with a process color-based matching system and not with standard premixed inks, click the Process Color radio button.

Editing Spot Colors to Match Your Swatches

Given the limitations of working with color on a computer, the color as it appears on your monitor may not match the appearance of your printed color swatch. If you are absolutely positive that you won't ever need to convert your spot color to a process color at some point, feel free to adjust your color to match the swatch. If you keep the color as a spot color, you won't affect the finished color of your printed piece because that color is determined by the printer's premixed ink, not by its representation on your screen. It might aid your design work to have a good match between the swatch and its onscreen representation. Remember: If you ever make a conversion to CMYK color from spot color, the percentages will be all screwed up, and you are guaranteed poor results from your separations.

Selecting the Color Model

Select a color model next, keeping in mind the pitfalls discussed earlier in this chapter. Theoretically, each system can describe a color accurately, but uses a different technique to do so. In practice, you need to carefully match your color model to the end result. If, for example, you have chosen process for your type of color, right from the beginning you should define your colors using the CMYK color model. The Color Options dialog box offers the following Model options:

- ◆ **RGB** gives you three slider bars for red, green, and blue, each one running from 0 to 100%. The RGB color model is an additive one and is based on the fact that red, green, and blue light added together create white light. The RGB model is generally used for defining colors intended to be viewed on computer screens or for spot colors.

The HSL Color Model

HLS tends to be most widely used by professional digital artists. Many of these people like HLS because it more closely resembles the way they work when they draw or paint something. Printers must continue to work in CMYK, however, because they can't very well get accurate color on the press otherwise.

In the HLS color model the H stands for hue, L for lightness, and S for saturation. Hue is measured in degrees as a radial on a circle of color. A color's hue is the position of a particular HLS color on the visible color spectrum which evolves from red through orange, yellow, green, blue, and peaks out at violet. Saturation refers to the amount of pigment in an HLS color, the intensity or purity of the color. Sometimes people think of lightness as the gray value of an HLS color or a way of describing how much white there is in a color. In fact, lightness is the amount of light reflected or projected from the colored object.

HLS, HSB, and HSV color systems are all close cousins to one another. They share the H for hue and S for saturation component, and the L, B, and V all refer to the same component of lightness, brightness, or value.

- ◆ **CMYK** has four slider bars for each of the process colors, cyan, magenta, yellow, and black. The CMYK model is used when you're defining standard process color to use when printing full-color jobs.

- ◆ **HLS** stands for hue, lightness, and saturation, and each has an associated slider bar. Hue is the color itself—red, orange, purple, and so forth. L is the lightness or luminance of the color. And S is the saturation of the color; another way to think of saturation is as a tint value of the hue. HLS colors are often used by artists used to working with more traditional media, because the color model more closely approximates the way you might mix colors on a palette.

Set Color Management Preferences Early

Color managing the colors you define in PageMaker means that if you do have to translate them between RGB and CMYK, you'll get more consistent results. While that's clearly an advantage in some circumstances, there are some drawbacks worth considering. Using color management requires you to consistently follow a rigorous workflow. It is also memory-intensive, and unless you're using a really high-end computer with tons of RAM, it can slow things down.

You can specify your CMS Source from the Color Options dialog box (see Figure 10.8), but your best bet for consistency is to set your CMS in the Preferences command so that all your colors will be defined using the same color management parameters.

Figure 10.8

The CMS Source button in the Color Options dialog box enables you to set the color management source profile for each new color you define.

One of the new features added in PageMaker 6.5 is the capability to see whether color management is on or off and what CMS parameters have been defined for each individual color—from within the Color Options dialog box. This can be a real time-saver, because it makes it easier for you to see what settings individual colors use without having to go into another level of dialog boxes.

Selecting a Color from a Library

PageMaker includes a number of color libraries full of thousands of pre-defined colors, including a complete selection of the PANTONE systems, the leading color-matching standard in the United States. These libraries are by far the easiest and most accurate way to define a new color onto the PageMaker Colors palette. Table 10.1 shows the list of libraries you can choose from in PageMaker.

Notice that the PANTONE Hexachrome libraries are included. New in PageMaker 6.5 is the capability to edit high-fidelity colors, even the ones in the Hexachrome library. As other high-fidelity color systems become available, you'll be able to add them to PageMaker and edit those colors as well. You can even define your own hi-fi color libraries (which are covered in the section "Installing and Making Your Own Color Libraries").

In addition to proprietary color specification systems, PageMaker offers you custom libraries of crayon colors and grays. (The Crayon library, by the way, was based on the 64-pack Crayola color system. You know, the one you used when you were five years old and had trouble staying in the lines?)

There are five commercial ink standard color-matching systems ready for your use in PageMaker, not counting the foreign variations on the basic system from PANTONE. Table 10.1 lists these systems and tells how each one is built on the press.

363

TABLE 10.1

THE PROPRIETARY COLOR-MATCHING LIBRARIES THAT ARE BUILT INTO PAGEMAKER

System	Colors	Method	Notes
DIC (Dainippon)	1,280	Spot	Classified by category (gay and brilliant, quiet and dark, plus basics, grays, and metallics).
FOCOLTONE	763	Process	Classified by quantity of one of the four process colors.
MUNSELL	Depends on system	Spot	Matching system based on the hue, value, and chroma (saturation) model.
PANTONE	Depends on system	Spot or Process	The predominant color system in the United States, available in swatches to match various paper coatings. Also available in EURO form to match the European variations on the system and a Process color version, so you can compose standard swatch colors from CMYK inks.
TOYOpc	1,050	Spot	Colors classified by the HSV color model, hue, and saturation.
TRUMATCH	2,093	Process	Technically, process color because it requires four-color printing, but it can be called a color match.

When you select a library from the Libraries menu in the Color Options dialog box, you get a scrollable window of color swatches like the one in Figure 10.9. Click to select the color swatch you want and click OK to bring the color into the Color Options dialog box. Another click on OK makes the decision final and inserts the color into your Colors palette.

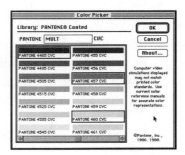

Figure 10.9

Press Shift and click to select multiple colors at once in the Library window, and all of them will be added to your Colors palette.

Selecting Multiple Colors

You can make multiple swatch selections and define many new PageMaker palette colors at the same time by pressing the Shift key or clicking and then dragging to select multiple swatches. If you select more than one color, the Name field in Color Options will read "Multiple," and all of the colors you selected will be added to the palette when you click OK to close the dialog box.

If you accessed Color Options through the Define Colors command, all of those nested dialog boxes get pretty cumbersome. Don't forget that (Option-click) [Alt-click] is a quick way to close nested dialog boxes, and that it works here as it does elsewhere in PageMaker.

Installing and Making Your Own Color Libraries

Want an elegant solution for making color consistent? For workgroups or for your most common color situations you can set up your very own color library.

Use the Color Options Dialog Box as a Color Picker

If you're bewildered by the thousands of colors in the PageMaker color-matching system libraries, you can narrow down the choices pretty quickly. Tune the slider bars in the Color Options box to approximate the color you want. Then select a color-matching system. PageMaker does its best to automatically take you to a swatch that matches the values you set with the slider bars with one of the predefined colors within that color system.

1. Define the colors you want in your library by adding them to the Colors palette. You can select colors from PageMaker's Library dialog box or by creating your own spot colors. (You can't store a tint in a library.)

2. After you have all the colors you want to appear in your library available on your Colors palette, choose the Create Color Library Plug-in from the Plug-ins menu in the Utilities menu. The dialog box is shown in Figure 10.10.

Figure 10.10

Use this cool plug-in to create your own color library that appears on the menu in the Color Options dialog box.

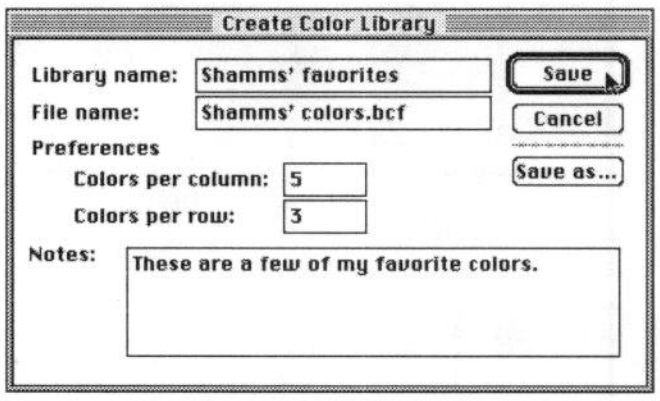

3. In the dialog box that appears when you run the plug-in, name your custom library with the name you want to see in the Library pull-down list in the Color Options dialog box. Specify how many rows and columns you need (although it can't be bigger than 10×10) and add any notes you want to keep about the library. These notes are displayed when you click the About button in the Library dialog box when you select your custom library.

4. Finally, click Save or Save As and save your library with a name of your choice, ending it with a period and the three letters BCF. (If you forget about the .BCF extension, the Plug-in will add it for you, but it's nice to know ahead of time.)

5. To access your new library from the list in the Color Options dialog box, you must store the library file in the Color folder, which you'll find in the RSRC folder located in your main PageMaker folder.

Using the Slider Bars and Color Evaluator Square

Using the slider bars in the Color Options dialog box, you can create a nearly infinite number of colors, which you can evaluate by observing the changes in the large, colored square in the lower right-hand corner of the dialog box (keep in mind the limitations of the computer's attempts to show you what you get from the printing press). If you are editing an existing color or creating a new one, this square splits in half so you can evaluate your changes compared to the old color.

Defining a Non-PageMaker Color-Matching Swatch

What if your favorite color-matching system isn't available? If you're working in spot color, there's an easy solution. Do the best you can to approximate the color onscreen, defining it as a Spot color. Then use the name and number from your printed color system matching swatch book when you name the newly defined color in PageMaker. When you print separations, the correct ink name is printed on that color's overlay (assuming of course that you've selected to print Printer's Marks). Naming the overlay the actual ink color will help prevent a mistake on press.

Naming Colors

When you chose a color from one of the libraries, that color's name is automatically entered into the text box in Color Options dialog box. When you or your service bureau prints out overlays for spot color, the color name is listed along with other printer's marks on the appropriate piece of film output. As a rule, if you have selected a color from one of the color-matching systems (such as PANTONE, Toyo, TRUMATCH, and so on), leave that name as it is to get the benefit of this built-in mistake prevention.

You also can name a color to remind you of the color's purpose. You might name some particular red you use for a corporate logo, for example, with the name of the company—"Widget Red" or something like that. If the logo is a PMS color, you can retain that as part of the name as a way to avoid confusion at the printer. Call it "Widget Red (PMS 186)."

Design Color Names as Memory Aids

When you define colors to include in your Color palette, use some of these naming tricks. In the palette in Figure 10.11, for example, it's easy to see at a glance that the process color GreenGray color was based on a

TRUMATCH color matching swatch from the PageMaker library, because the name includes the original TRUMATCH reference. And you wouldn't need to go to the Color Options dialog to find out the amount of the tint defined for GreenGray, because the name has been defined to include the percentage. You can tell at a glance that it is a 75% tint.

Figure 10.11

Name your colors so they provide as much information at a glance as possible.

Use Braces in Color Names

If you attempt to include parenthetical information in the name of a color, as a memory aid, you get a message from PageMaker that says, "Invalid character(s) in color name," and the parentheses are not permitted. The same goes for square brackets. PostScript makes extensive use of parentheses and square brackets, so PageMaker reserves their use to avoid inadvertent errors. However, curly brackets (braces, as they're properly called) are legal.

Defining Tints

You must define a color before you can define a tint, because a tint can only exist as a percentage of a base color. But why would you bother defining a separate tint color if you can apply tints on-the-fly using that nifty pull-down menu at the top of the palette? If you use the same tints over and over, having the tint on the palette can save you time—it's one click instead of multiple ones. It also helps ensure consistency by making it easy to apply the same tint every time. When you're in production mode, it's easy to forget whether you're using a 40% or 45% tint, because the screen appearance is so similar. Finally, you can define tints in 1% increments, whereas you're limited to 5% increments if you use the pull-down menu. In practical terms, this isn't a huge issue because most printing presses aren't capable of reproducing tints in gradations that subtle.

To define a tint, first select your already defined base color on the palette, then click the New color icon (the one that looks like a page) at the bottom of the palette. In Color Options, change the Type to a Tint, then adjust the slider bar or type in the tint percentage that you want. The color evaluation square in the lower right corner splits in half, and the upper half shows you the effect of your adjustments. Click OK, and the color appears in your Colors palette with a percentage sign to the right of it to indicate that it's a tint. Figure 10.12 shows what the Color Options dialog box looks like when you're defining a tint.

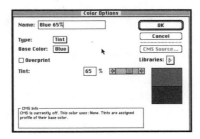

Figure 10.12

Defining a tint using Color Options means it is always on your palette, making it easier to apply than using the Tints pull-down menu.

When naming tints, include the percentage and the base color in the name. That will make it easier to know at a glance what the base color is and how much lighter the tint is from the base. This technique also helps when you need to sort out the possible effects of deleting a base color. If you remove a base color, its dependent tint is converted to black.

Avoid Very Light Tints or Small Tint Variations

Consult with your printer beforehand so that you get good reproduction in these situations.

- Anything less than a 20% tint might be difficult to reproduce on a printing press, no matter how good the tint looks on your imagesetter film.

- It's generally not a good idea to use a tint on a thin line. In either case, you might end up with faint color that looks more like dirt or a blemish than what you intended.

◆ Also, keep in mind that few printing presses can reproduce a difference of only 1% between tints. About 5% is the practical limit, which is why the pop-up tint menus in PageMaker are constructed in 5% increments.

Tints Are Cumulative

Tints are always expressed as percentages of a base color—a screening back of a color. If you apply a defined tint color to a filled object and then apply an object level tint from the Fill menu or the Color palette, you subtract color twice. A 60% tint color with a 50% shade applied actually ends up as a 30% tint.

Specifying Overprint and Knockout

When different colored objects on your pages overlap, you need to decide what you want to happen when you print separations for those colors. You have two options: the topmost object can knock out the ones below it, or each color can print on top of, or overprint, the ones underneath. Knockouts prevent two colors from mixing on the page to create some unexpected or unwanted third color. What you see on-screen approximates what you'll get if you specify knockouts; there's no way to display the cumulative effects of overlapping color areas so overprinting can't really be simulated onscreen in PageMaker. All colors (and all objects) in PageMaker are set to be knockouts unless you take specific action to make them overprint.

Note

Unless you change PageMaker's default trapping settings, black text below 24 points always overprints in order to avoid trapping problems caused by mis-registration on press.

Sometimes, however, you want to overprint. A common example of such a situation is using black type over a lighter color background. Rather than have the type knockout the lighter background (which can lead to press registration problems that leave unprofessional-looking white lines around the type), you simply have it print over the underlying color. You don't have to worry about an unwanted third color, because black can overcome most color mixing problems.

PageMaker gives you two levels of overprint and knockout control: object level and color level. *Color level* overprinting sets the default behavior for an entire color, and is what is covered here. *Object level* overprinting enables you to make an exceptional object—either a line or a fill—do the opposite of what the color is set to do.

Note

These concepts of knockout and overprinting—especially object level overprinting—are critical to the process of manually trapping objects on PageMaker pages, a subject that's covered in considerable detail in the Chapter 11. For more information on layers, see Chapter 4.

Setting a color to Overprint is so easy, it's bound to be anticlimactic after all of this background information: in the Color Options dialog box, check the Overprint box, and the color will overprint in every instance (unless you set a manual override).

Using 100% Tint to Get Overprint Colors

If you need to overprint some objects but knockout others that use the same color, you can designate individual items to overprint in the Fill and Line dialog box. Or, if you want to have an overprint version of the color available with a click in the Colors palette, you can define two versions of the same color—one to knockout and the other to overprint.

The solution is to take advantage of an important fact about tints and their base colors: they print on the same overlay. If you define a tint that is 100% of the base color and set it to overprint (leaving the base color to knockout), objects with either color applied will print on the same overlay. Very tricky! Remember, though, that this trick won't work if you follow your first impulse and create two different color names. The dual definitions will generate two overlays (plates on the press) instead of one, causing extra expense and complication.

Making Color Definitions Consistent Within and Between Publications

Almost any service bureau operator can tell you horror stories of projects that came in with, for example, 20 different definitions on the Color palette for the same color of deep violet. Naturally, the client wants all the violets to look the same, even though each had a slightly different value on the slider bar, and the variations in their names cause PageMaker to look at each of the colors as a different ink and therefore trigger the production of 20 different spot color overlays.

This sort of thing happens mainly for two reasons: Imported objects come in with colors defined in other programs, and different people working on different aspects of the same publication used different color definitions.

Copying Colors Between Publications

You can import Color palettes from another publication, just like you can copy paragraph style sheets. Simply go to the menu in the Color palette and choose Import. You get a standard Open File dialog box. Select the publication you want and click OK or double-click the publication title. Unfortunately, you can't pick and choose which individual colors you copy from the publication. The Define Colors Copy button is an all-or-nothing proposition.

Using Color Templates and Mini-Defaults

Sometimes you develop colors that you use every time you open a new publication, maybe a set of gray percentages. For those colors, consider setting up a mini-default for your Color palette (described in Chapter 2, "Personalizing PageMaker"). Set up the Colors palette with no publication open, defining your standard set of colors, and those colors will be there every time you open a new document. You also can create templates for each of your common color publication situations and define the colors you use in each one. You might have a set of templates for each of your major clients (or in-house corporate departments).

Merging Colors

In PageMaker, you can permanently remove a color from the Color palette and at the same time globally replace every occurrence of that color with a new color definition. The concept is similar to the way you replace or merge paragraph styles.

1. In Define Colors, define the color that will survive the merger of the color definitions, then select the color you want to replace and click Edit.

2. In that color's name box, type the name of the new color, the one you want to end up as the surviving color in the merger.

Make sure that both the new and old color names are spelled exactly the same and click OK.

3. When you click OK, you get a warning dialog box, asking to confirm that you indeed want to replace the old color with the new one. Click OK, and you're done.

Adopting Colors from Imported or Clipboard Objects

You can copy colors between PageMaker publications and other software applications in another way—by adopting them. Many graphics objects come into your current PageMaker publication with their own colors attached. After these adopted colors arrive in the Colors palette, you can use them just like a color defined right in your current PageMaker publication. This technique can help a lot in your efforts to achieve consistency between your drawing program and PageMaker. (The evil flip side of this feature is the one already discussed—this is the way a lot of those artifact colors get into your publication.)

Spot colors come into PageMaker from EPS graphics files very cleanly, and you can even edit them after importation. Named process colors can also be imported. Color of either type appears with an EPS icon next to their name on the palette. You can control how these imported EPS colors come into your publication. When placing an EPS, click the Options button. You'll get an EPS import filter dialog box similar to the Smart ASCII filter or the enhanced dialog for the Microsoft Word filter. In this dialog box (see Figure 10.13) you can control how process and spot colors are added to your palette and whether spot colors are converted to process colors when imported.

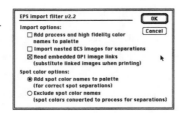

Figure 10.13

When importing EPS files, access this dialog box by checking Show Filter Preferences in the Place Document dialog box so you can control how the colors defined in those files will import.

PageMaker objects pasted or dragged-and-dropped through the Clipboard bring their colors with them as well. You can use this technique to copy individual colors between publications. Assign the color to some quickly drawn box or circle as a temporary holder for the adopted color. Cut and Paste it into your target publication, and the color is adopted by the target publications Colors palette. Then delete your "carrier" graphic.

APPLYING COLORS

PageMaker's Colors palette makes it easy to apply colors—much easier than understanding all the theory and technology of color printing presses. Of course, it's so incredibly easy that you must use some care and moderation because you could color your way into a mess of muddy ink and garish colors. For more information about color theory and the potential pitfalls of color production, refer to the "Understanding the Basics of Color" section earlier in this chapter.

Coloring Text

Applying a color to your text is easy. You have three alternatives:

- **Direct Selection.** Select the text with the Text tool and click the desired color in the Colors palette. You can use the pop-up menu on the palette to assign an object level tint in 5% increments.

- **Type Specifications**. You can also choose color from the Type Specifications dialog box. You can use the pull-down Tint menu to select an object level tint in 5% increments, or you can type in your own number in the provided box in increments of 1%.

- **Paragraph Styles**. Color entire paragraphs of type automatically by defining color as part of a paragraph style. You can access the Type Specifications dialog box through the Define Styles command. Styles are the fastest way to assign the same color to all your headlines.

Readability Issues When Coloring Text

Certain combinations and circumstances of color are not good ideas for type. Problems arise primarily when you put colored text on a colored background, but even coloring type for placement on white paper has its considerations.

Here are some guidelines for you to keep in mind when you design colored type.

- **Seek contrasting letters and background.** Be sure that you work with high contrast colors, not colors that are similarly dark or light. To the eye, for example, red and green "read" as having about the same darkness, so avoid using them together.

- **Test colors in grayscale.** To test the contrast of two colors, switch your video display over to grayscale for a quick look. This technique won't work absolutely every time, but it helps to evaluate readability. If the combination of letter color and background color looks okay in grayscale, chances are that this combination will work fine in color.

- **Stroke letters.** If your design really requires you to run text against background using a low contrast combination of colors, consider stroking letters with a contrasting color to improve their readability. For display type, you might want to set the letters in a drawing program such as Illustrator or FreeHand, which enables you to convert to paths and assign separate stroke and fill colors. Another option would be to set the type in a paint program such as Photoshop where you could use edge filters and anti-aliasing—meaning you don't need to worry about the trapping problems that might be caused by color strokes.

- **Avoid vibrating color juxtapositions.** To the eye, yellow and red are irritating together. Other color combinations also "ring" on you; sometimes these combinations are so bad that they're the visual equivalent of fingernails on a blackboard.

- **Be Cautious about Trapping Effects.** Be careful about putting colored letters on a colored background if they must be trapped by choking them or spreading them. Eyes are very sensitive to distortions of type; both these trapping techniques cause the type to fatten and block up (spread) or to get too thin to read (choked serif or cursive type). More information on choking, spreading, and other trapping issues appears in Chapter 11.

◆ **Consider the Effects of Size and Serifs.** If you need to spread the type for trapping (making it generally fatter), serifs or other cursive aspects of the type hold up better if the type is a larger size. Larger type won't block up as badly, meaning the open spaces in the type won't fill up with ink (for instance, the center of the letter "O" or the holes in the letter "B"). As a general rule of thumb, serif type blocks up worse than sans serif type.

Coloring PageMaker-Drawn Objects

You have two main ways to assign color to a PageMaker-drawn object: the Colors palette and the Fill and Stroke dialog box, and a few related tweaks you can manage with the Fill menu and the Stroke menu.

Using the Stroke, Fill, and Both Icons on the Colors Palette

Applying color to a PageMaker drawn object—lines, ovals, rectangles, or polygons—is just a touch more complex than assigning color to text. You can color the object's perimeter line or stroke, the fill area inside that line, or both.

You have fast access to most of the functions contained in the dialog boxes for the Fill, Stroke, and Fill and Stroke commands right from the Colors palette. When working with PageMaker-drawn objects, specify whether your color application will be applied as a fill for the object or only to the stroke portion of the object or to both, by clicking one of the three buttons in the upper-left corner of the palette (see Figure 10.14).

Figure 10.14

The icons at the top left of the palette enable you to specify whether the color you choose applies to the fill, stroke, or both of the selected object.

Applying Colors using the Fill and Line Dialog Box

The Fill and Stroke dialog box gives you more power over the fill and line attributes of a PageMaker object than you get by using the Colors palette (see Figure 10.15) You can open it from the Element menu or through the keyboard shortcut (Command-U) [Control-U].

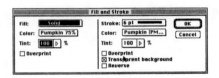

Figure 10.15

The Fill and Stroke dialog box.

The Fill and Stroke dialog box gives you more control over how colors are applied to PageMaker objects. Although it lacks many of the visual cues of the Colors palette—color swatches and color type indicators—the Fill and Stroke dialog box gives you simultaneous and independent color lists on both the fill and line halves of the dialog box, and you can make a more precise specification of Tints by typing in the amount in 1% increments.

Warning

Don't use PageMaker Fill Patterns for high-resolution output. The fill patterns available from the Fill drop-down list in the Fill and Fill and Stroke menus are actually resolution-dependent graphics elements—not PostScript elements that look the same regardless of the resolution at which they're printed. If you plan to go to high-resolution imagesetter output, consult with your service bureau and consider having them test a couple of typical pages. When output on an imagesetter, PageMaker fills—imaged at high-resolution—tighten up into very fine screens that will not convey the effect you see when you choose them from the menu.

Assigning Object-Level Overprinting

In both sides of the Fill and Stroke dialog box, you can click the Overprint checkbox. Overprint means two overlapping objects both print in entirety, thus mixing their inks on the paper. This option is extremely valuable—especially when it comes to trapping—but you'll want to use it with some care because of the problems of inks mixing to create an unwanted color and the difficulty that arise from building up too much ink on the page. By default, PageMaker objects and colors knock out all layers beneath them. Setting an object to overprint or defining a color to overprint overrides this default. A consultation with the print shop that will run your job may help evaluate the particular circumstances of your project.

Make Colored Strokes Transparent

Unless you are trying for some special effect, always make colored strokes transparent. The reason? If you don't, you might inadvertently introduce a third color into your design—the underlying paper.

Coloring Imported Objects

There are only two kinds of imported graphic objects in the PageMaker color world: those that you can color and those that come in with permanent and untouchable color. The difference? It's a moving experience.

Moving an Imported Object to an Overlay or Separation

PageMaker colors an imported graphic by moving it to the proper printing plate or plates. It doesn't modify anything in the guts of the colored object's file (or the guts of a monochrome file, for that matter). Keep in mind that a color assigned to an imported graphic applies to the entire object. You can't selectively color portions of a graphic.

At print time, PageMaker merely substitutes its own directions for the color plate location, ignoring the ones built into the file. A monochrome graphic could be sent to a spot color overlay, for example, rather than being put on the black layer. Likewise, all the process colors built into an EPS graphic might instead be sent to the black overlay and portrayed in their intrinsic levels of gray.

Some objects, however, simply can't be switched around like this at all, notably color TIFF graphics and DCS files. When considering color and an imported object you have four issues to consider:

◆ What type of graphic is it?

◆ Does it have color already built into it?

◆ Will any color changes be visible onscreen?

◆ Can the object be colored in PageMaker?

Table 10.2 can help you sort out these questions. Look down the left column for the graphic format you are importing. Then select the row, depending on whether the graphic has color built into it. From there, you can answer the two questions concerning whether you can override any color in PageMaker and whether that coloring will be visible onscreen.

TABLE 10.2

A DECISION TABLE FOR COLORING IMPORTED GRAPHICS

Type of Graphic	Can You Apply Color?	Applied Color Shows Onscreen?	Applied Color Prints?
Bitmap (B/W)	Yes	Yes	Yes
Bitmap (Grayscale)	Yes	Yes	Yes
Bitmap (Color)	No	No	No
EPS (Vector, B/W, Grayscale Bitmap)	Yes	No	Yes
EPS (RGB or CMYK, DCS, Composite Bitmap, Duotone)	No	No	Yes
PICT (B/W Bitmap)	Yes	No	Yes
PICT (Grayscale Bitmap)	Yes	No	No
PICT (Color Bitmap)	Yes	No	No
PICT (Vector)	Yes	No	Yes

Restoring a Graphic's Original Color

When you need to annul an accidental assignment of color (say you accidentally applied black to a fancy multi-color EPS graphic), just select the object then apply the color [None] from the Colors palette. This removes PageMaker's color assignments from the object, letting its true colors shine through.

SUMMARY

This chapter has covered the basic of working in color using PageMaker. The key thing to keep in mind is that you should know where your project is heading before you start designing, because you'll make different choices concerning color if you're designing for a fancy color brochure than you will if you're designing for online or for output on a color copier. Planning may not be the glamorous part of a project, but it's bound to make the process of getting what you want on paper go much more smoothly, which leads to Chapter 11 , "Taking Color from Computer to Paper," where some of the more printing related topics, such as trapping, hi-fi color, and color management, are covered.

Chapter

11

TAKING COLOR FROM COMPUTER TO PAPER

Sometimes we all are so swept up in the excitement of using our newfound computer horsepower that it's easy to lose sight of the fact that the basic principles of putting ink on paper haven't changed for more than 100 years. No matter how computerized the prepress process, at some point a job still comes down to a mechanical process of smearing ink onto paper in a printing press. This chapter is designed to give you a head start on some of the issues you'll need to be savvy about, like the fact that computer screens don't display accurate color without a lot of effort, and the fact that printing presses are imperfect mechanical devices. More specifically, we'll cover the essential tactics and techniques for transforming an electronic page of color into a paper page:

◆ Items that require special attention (and collaboration with your printer and service bureau) when you design a color publication.

◆ Using PageMaker's color management for optimal color accuracy.

◆ Understanding why trapping is necessary.

- Deciding whether to assume responsibility for trapping.

- Designing your publication to avoid trapping.

- Using PageMaker's built-in trapping.

- Understanding Hexachrome and hi-fi (or high fidelity) color.

- Using PageMaker's built-in support for Hexachrome color.

PageMaker In the Real World

Collaboration

Collaboration is a fundamental skill when you want to create color jobs on a printing press. You need to work with a printer who knows how to get the most out of that printing press. You also need the skilled service bureau operator who runs dozens of jobs every day through a sophisticated high-resolution imagesetter. Always keep in mind that after you've performed your computerized design magic, a person in a pressroom still ties on an ink-smeared apron and loads your job onto a printing press—and remember that their involvement in the planning process is crucial to the end results you see.

COLLABORATING WITH YOUR PRINTER AND SERVICE BUREAU

At the earliest possible stages of creating a color publication, bundle together your preliminary sketches and comps and set out for a talk with your printer and your service bureau. Don't consider doing a color publication unless you and your collaborators have given thought to the following:

- **Choosing a printing method.** Most jobs go on an offset lithography press, but will it be sheet fed or a web press? If you are doing point-of-purchase retail product displays or packaging, you may be designing a job that needs to go on a special press that can do flexography. Perhaps you are working on something that can be done best with the silk screening process. You might need to take into account the printing method when creating your design. These experts can point out those special considerations and save you time and money.

◆ **Deciding how many colors will be on-press.** Work out a color strategy. Should you specify color in CMYK so you can work with the four process colors? Or will you use black ink and a couple of spot colors? How many colors can the press your job is likely to be printed on handle? You may need to work out design (and cost) issues if the printing press requires multiple runs to achieve all the colors needed for your job.

◆ **Selecting a color matching system.** If you and your printer decide on spot color over process color, find out which color-matching systems the print shop supports. You will have wasted a lot of time and effort if you specify Hexachrome colors because you think Hexachrome high fidelity color is really hot and en vogue, and then find out the printer doesn't have the press to handle the job. Alternatively, the printer may recommend a particular color system as being best suited for your project. If you will be running both spot color and process color, a process color-based matching system might make sense, and perhaps even save you a fifth plate on the press.

◆ **Choosing paper.** The absorbency and stability of the paper you print on determines some color printing parameters, such as how fine-grained a line screen you can use. Ask your printer if any alternative papers can get you the same effect but with improved quality (and, possibly, for less money).

◆ **Determining screen frequency for halftones.** You can't do process color without a line screen, and you can't do any prepress photo scanning (or have anyone do it for you) without knowing the line screen frequency in advance. You also may need to confirm that standard screen angles will be okay so you can avoid moiré problems. Or maybe the service bureau and printer can print stochastic screens.

Your paper choice and the specific characteristics of the press (such as the equipment's age) have a major influence on your line screen frequency. These issues are the domain of the print shop. Are you printing on newsprint or coated stock? How much ink will your job be putting down on the paper, and does the press have a heat set oven to help dry ink as it goes through the press? All these issues help your printer decide how fine a line screen can hold on the press for your project.

- **Discussing ink issues.** Ask your printer if your project has any design considerations that may cause problems with dot gain or ink building. Dot gain is the spread of a halftone dot when ink soaks into the paper. Software can be used to provide dot gain compensation. Ink buildup happens when overlapping inks (usually in a process color situation) accumulate on the surface of the paper to such an extent that they can't dry fast enough. Based on your printer's advice, work with your service bureau on these issues. They have software that can compensate for ink build-up problems.

- **Specifying mechanicals.** Your printer knows what's needed to get plates on the press. Will film or paper be best? If you ask the printer to use traditional methods to trap your publication's color elements, the printer probably will use paper. If you have halftones in your job, you should stick with film if possible. Specifying mechanicals is a point of collaboration, and an important one. You need to pass these specifications on to your service bureau when you hand off your files.

- **Agreeing on responsibility for color proofs.** Whoever has responsibility for color accuracy probably should do the proofing on their own proofing system. If the service bureau has separated your job and trapped it for you, you need a proof at that point. On the other hand, the printer may not want to work without proofing on the print shop's own system as a point of reference.

- **Managing color image files.** High-end color photo scans are huge. Photo scans with a file size of 20MB are normal and high-resolution scans can climb up to 60MB or more. Work with your service bureau on the best way to deal with this issue. Usually you'll use a low-resolution reference scan that can be linked back to your job after you finish your design and the publication is ready to be run on the imagesetter. The tactics for this linking vary a great deal, depending on the prepress system (OPI- or APR-based) used by your service bureau, so you need to work with them up front.

Color correction and accuracy comes up in a big way when scanning photos. You need color proofs for any scanned photos. You also need to talk with the service bureau about who takes responsibility for the accuracy of color photos, the procedures used to keep them accurate during the production process, and the role of color management in your workflow.

◆ **Agreeing on responsibility for trapping.** If your design has two or more colors touching, trapping will almost certainly be required unless your printer can guarantee perfect registration on the press (not likely, and potentially quite expensive). Until the last few years, trapping was the responsibility of the printer, not the designer. These days, the issue isn't so clear, and PageMaker now offers built-in trapping that can handle situations you encounter. Even so, you'll need specifications from the printer so you know how to set up the trapping job.

UNDERSTANDING COLOR MANAGEMENT

Your computer screen lies about color. Some systems tell smaller lies than others, but to one degree or another, this basic premise holds true no matter how good your hardware and no matter how good your color management system. However, you can optimize your system to get the most accurate color possible.

We don't make this point to discourage you from using color management. It's an important thing to do and a big leap forward for PageMaker. However, it's critical that you remain aware of the limitations and that you don't automatically accept what you see onscreen as 100 percent accurate color.

With the release of version 6.5, PageMaker has the best color management tools available in any publishing software. PageMaker's approach to color management is extensible, so you can choose which color management system to work with. Kodak's highly acclaimed Precision Color Management System (CMS) is what we'll focus on here, but PageMaker also supports Apple's ColorSync2 tools (available on the Macintosh only); as other CMS solutions become available, it's likely that PageMaker will support them too. The advantage of this approach is that it gives you more control over the tools you use, so you can configure a highly specialized CMS workflow without having to customize PageMaker otherwise. Each system will have its own idiosyncrasies of installation and use, but the basic principles of operation should be similar from system to system.

Note

For some fundamental background on this subject of color accuracy, check out the first few pages of Chapter 10. The short story is this: A printing press and your computer monitor are fundamentally different and couldn't possibly represent the "same" color in the same way. Your monitor combines three colors (red, green, blue) whereas a process color printing job uses four (cyan, magenta, yellow, black). And the press uses ink on a surface that reflects light to your eye, where a computer monitor uses a spray of electrons that shines directly into your eye.

Color Management and the Problem of Device Dependent Color

The main reason color management is so important is this: Color publishing is device dependent. Assume that you took a picture of a brick wall, and your camera got the color pretty accurately. But now imagine the flow of your color work from that point forward and all the way out to the printing press and a final product:

◆ Your scanner may want to describe that red as a bluish-red.

◆ Your computer monitor may think red should be a deep red color with some orange in it.

◆ Your composite proofing device, say a Tektronix Phaser, may see the red as having a more brownish tone to it.

◆ This string of color imperfection deteriorates even further if, at any time during this process, you try to "correct" the color based on what you are seeing on your computer monitor or your composite proof printer.

With all of these differences, who knows how the picture of the brick wall will actually turn out when you separate it and run it on the printing press? Color management tries to smooth out these differences by electronically adjusting color as you move from scanner, to computer screen, to printing press. In each case the color management system translates the color for the appropriate device, "I know you tend to look at brick red and see bluish-red or brownish-red or whatever. Add a pinch of this and take away a pinch of that to compensate for your color error factors."

The CMS does not make these translations by going directly from one device to the other. It constantly refers all color information back through a sort of touchstone, a method of describing the color that is device independent: the CIE color model (Commission Internationale de l'Eclairage or, in English, the International Committee on Illumination).

Note

This business about CIE color is important to remember because at various times in the process of saving color files you have opportunities to cut yourself loose from device dependent color descriptions and save your file as a "CIE Lab TIFF." One example would be when you import a Photo CD image directly into PageMaker.

The Role of Device Profiles

One of the most important things you will do in working with color management is to specify for PageMaker the devices that are being used in the electronic publishing process. This information is necessary so that the CMS can make the color translations between different devices.

The color management system must know:

- The source for the digitized color image files being used in the publication, usually a scanner.

- The video monitor you are using to view the color images as you work.

- The printing device you will be using for composite proofing of your color, often a desktop color printer.

- The color characteristics of the printing press, the device that will use the process color separations you will be generating.

When you make all these choices you are selecting *device profiles*. These are files that electronically describe for the color management system the characteristics of the chosen device. Dozens of these profiles come with PageMaker. If one of your devices isn't listed, you need to get a profile from the manufacturer or you need to get the manufacturer's advice on which of the generic profiles would be best suited to emulate your device.

One of the big improvements in PageMaker 6.5 is that PageMaker now supports the Inter-Color Consortium (ICC) standard for color management profiles, so multiple color management systems can theoretically share the same device profiles. Although PageMaker 6.0 also supported an extensible CMS architecture, this new support for a common device profile standard—instead of the proprietary standards previously supported—makes it much more feasible to use different systems. As mentioned earlier, Kodak's CMS is well-respected in the industry—but other vendors well acquainted with color science (such as AGFA) are also developing color management systems.

What You Can Color Manage

You can only color manage certain elements in your PageMaker publications, and knowing which up front is key to making your color management workflow go smoothly. PageMaker can color manage:

- Any color you define in PageMaker.

- Bitmap images, such as TIFFs.

- Spot colors contained within EPS files, because they're added to PageMaker's Color palette and can be edited.

The list of things you can't color manage in PageMaker is a little longer:

- EPS files of any description.

- TIFFs contained within EPS files, because they are "protected" inside the EPS shell.

- DCS files, because they have already been separated for commercial printing purposes and are actually EPS files in disguise.

- WMF and PICT files, because their color is determined at print time by the system's printer driver.

Setting Up Color Management

The first color management task on your list is to settle what you expect from your color management system. Maybe there's no such thing as being too thin, too rich, or too color accurate, but there are some practical limits. Here are some questions you can ask yourself, save some time and money.

- Are you working primarily in spot colors, perhaps specifying colors with a color matching system? Are you using color swatches, like PANTONE books to obtain color accuracy? Will you ask your computer monitor to give you some idea of what your decisions look like?

  There's no such things as being too color accurate. But if this more results-based approach fits your needs for color accuracy, you can ease off on spending top dollar for your equipment and perhaps even save computer memory by turning off color management most of the time.

♦ Are you working in process colors, CMYK or High Fidelity? Are you making major color decisions based on what you see on the screen, as opposed to standard color swatches? Will you be color correcting photographs? Will you perhaps even be mixing custom colors?

If your work falls into this category you will need to be ultra methodical about your color management, get the best possible equipment, and set up your system in a distortion free viewing environment. Nothing less will do.

There's a viewing environment discussion in the section of this chapter titled, "Optimizing Your Color Viewing Environment." Also, you want to get high quality color proofs before committing to press. There's information on this in Appendix C, "Proofing Your Publication."

Color Management System Preference Dialog Box

Regardlessof the CMS you plan to use, the process for working with it is the same. In our examples, we'll use the Kodak CMS—but the same process applies to other systems as well.

The dialog box at the heart of PageMaker's approach to color management is shown in Figure 11.1.

Figure 11.1

Use the Color Management System Preferences dialog box to set up your color management preferences.

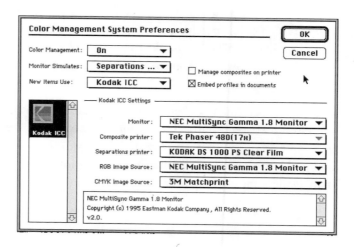

All the sophisticated color theory aside, little could be simpler than using this dialog box. Simply click through the pop-up lists in this dialog box to describe your system. Here's a run down on the items in the dialog box and how they work together:

- ◆ **Color Management.** If you don't actually need color management, turn it completely off using the pop-up menu in the upper left corner of the dialog box. It will save memory, and your publications will open faster because they won't need to take time to initialize CMS. If you see a dialog box that says PageMaker is initializing CMS, you'll know what we mean. It's better than it was in PageMaker 6.0, but it still takes a while.

- ◆ **Monitor Simulates.** If you plan to make color management decisions based on what you see on your monitor, you can use this option to have your monitor simulate either your final output device (the Separations Printer option) or the device you'll proof the publication to (the Composite Printer option). Previewing the color management changes onscreen takes additional processing power and therefore more time, so it's best to use this option periodically to check your results, instead of leaving it on all the time.

- ◆ **New Items Use.** If Color Management is on, then the CMS you specify here is applied to any new color you define or any image you import. If you leave this option set to None, then you can choose a device profile for each item you want to color manage as you import it or as you define a new color.

  Setting a default CMS for new items can be a time-saver, but it can also cause trouble by applying the default profile to items from different sources. Say, for example, you almost always have your scans done on a particular device, and you have a device profile specially calibrated for that scanner. If your CMS preferences have set the RGB Image Source option to use that scanner's profile, you automatically have the right device profile applied to imported scans—which is good. However, if you define any new process colors—that should use a different source profile—you have to remember to change the CMS source they use. If you don't, the results could be worse than not using color management at all.

◆ **Manage composites at printer.** This option enables you to take advantage of the built-in support for color separations offered on PostScript Level 2 imagesetters. Although it theoretically saves you time by offloading work to the computer in your printer, there are so few of these devices available at the moment that this option is of limited practical value.

◆ **Embed profiles in documents.** Because the whole point of having a color management system is to try to standardize your system's color view of the world, you generally want to turn on this option so that when you take files to another system, all your color management systems will be brought along with them. This is particularly crucial when you're handing off files to a service provider.

◆ **Settings for the Selected Color Management System.** Because this is where you choose the device profiles to use with each color management system, think of this as the heart and soul of your color management settings. Each CMS you have installed will display an icon to the left of the Color Management Settings area. When you select a system's icon, its name appears in the divider bar and the profiles you've selected for that system's defaults appear in the Color Management Settings list boxes.

You have options to specify different default profiles for the key devices in your workflow—your monitor, your composite printer, your separations printer, a source (such as a scanner) for RGB images, and a source for CMYK images. Think through your usual production process before you specify devices for these settings. Suppose you make color corrections in Photoshop, for example, and output your files as CMYK TIFFs. You might want to select some CMYK profile for the CMYK Image Source. But you would be wrong. Because you made the color correction decisions based on an RGB computer monitor, you should set your CMYK source for the RGB monitor you use with Photoshop.

Ad Hoc Color Management Settings

One of the really convenient things about PageMaker's implementation of color management is its flexibility. For any object or color that can be managed, you can set a different source device and even a different color management system. Sometimes PageMaker handles this for you automatically; other times you need to make the settings yourself.

Say you are importing a scanned graphic. Here's how PageMaker looks at that file and decides how to apply your preferences:

◆ **Kodak CMS Source.** If the Kodak ICC Color Management System was used in producing the graphic, maybe by the program used to scan it, and that information is embedded in the file, PageMaker will read that information and automatically apply the CMS information.

◆ **Source Not Installed.** If the device profile for the source used to create the scanned graphic is not installed on your machine, PageMaker will revert to whatever CMS you have designated in Preferences and will take its best shot at a profile that will work with the identification embedded in the file.

◆ **No Source Listed.** If the file doesn't have any embedded CMS identification, PageMaker will use the default CMS and the source you designated in Preferences (your RGB source preference if it is an RGB graphic, or CMYK if it is a CMYK graphic).

But what if you want to take control instead of letting PageMaker go to these default decisions? Well, you can. When you are importing the image look, click the CMS Source button in the Place dialog box. There's also a CMS Source button in the Define Colors dialog box and in the Photo CD Place dialog box, and you can access it anytime in the production process by selecting the image you want to color manage and choosing CMS Source from the Image submenu in the Element menu. You can designate your own source Precision Transforms for each individual graphic object you import and for each new color you define. When you click the CMS Source button you get the dialog box in Figure 11.2, where you can customize CMS images on an image or color basis.

Figure 11.2

You can override the default device profile for any image or color by opening the CMS Source dialog box from the Image menu (for images) or from within the Color Options dialog box (for colors).

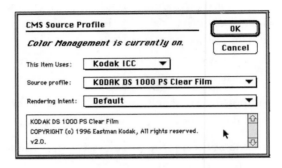

You can also make ad hoc color management settings from the Print dialog box, where you get the same dialog box as the one accessed through the Preferences command.

Warning

Be extremely cautious about changing the separations device setting at print time. Color management calculations during the design process are sometimes based on the destination device, and changing the device just before press time might throw off the accuracy of those calculations.

Calibrate Your Monitor

If you're using the Monitor Simulates option to preview color management changes onscreen, you want to make sure your monitor is calibrated for use by the color management system.

PageMaker comes with a nifty procedure to do basic monitor calibration, but there are far more sophisticated tools you should consider using if you're serious about integrating color management into your workflow. These devices will help you perform precise monitor calibration, but they're expensive. If you're looking for basic calibra-tion—and basic calibration is better than no calibration at all—check out the Getting Started manual for instructions on using the Knoll Gamma control panel. To use it you place some targets in a PageMaker file and look at them from a distance of several feet to determine whether you have the correct black-and-white points set on your monitor—it should be fairly obvious if they are off. You also set up gamma, usually for 1.8. After you have done this, you are better informed for picking a monitor from the CMS list (see Figure 11.3).

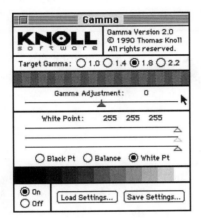

Figure 11.3

Use the Gamma control panel that's included with PageMaker for basic monitor calibration.

If your monitor isn't covered by one of the device profiles that come with PageMaker, you can use your new calibration settings to make an educated selection about which profile to use. Better yet, use the Kodak Monitor Installer (located in the Extras folder in the Adobe PageMaker 6.5 folder) to create a custom profile that matches the calibration settings you just worked up (see Figure 11.4).

You need to recalibrate your monitor periodically, though, because your monitor's display changes over time. In some high-end production environments, monitors are calibrated daily—and sometimes even more often than that.

Figure 11.4

The Kodak Monitor Installer enables you to modify existing monitor profiles or create new ones from scratch based on your monitor calibration settings.

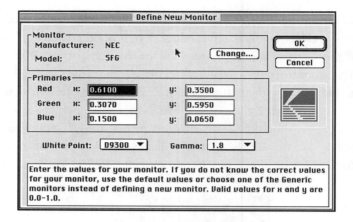

Figure 11.4

The Kodak Monitor Installer enables you to modify existing monitor profiles or create new ones from scratch based on your monitor calibration settings.

Optimizing Your Color Viewing Environment

This might surprise you, but the weakest part of your color management system may be the room you are sitting in right now. If you are in front of your computer, examine your environment, including your computer monitor, and see if your viewing environment helps you or distorts the accuracy of your color view:

◆ Work with a plain gray screen desktop, none of those fancy bozo backgrounds. They practically vibrate with distracting color that will zap any chance that your brain will properly read colors for the page you are setting up.

◆ The same goes for your work room. No distracting wallpaper. No wild colors. No extremes. Go for gray, and let the color happen on your monitor.

◆ Have the room lighting set to a moderate level. It ought not be much darker—or brighter—than the amount of light coming from your monitor.

◆ Windows and bright, sunny days are great, but they wreak havoc with color accuracy. Again, no wild extremes for your room lighting, and sunlight in particular is a problem. It constantly changes color from sunrise to high noon to sunset.

TRAPPING

What a pain. This is progress? Science advances the art of desktop publishing, and you get stuck worrying about trapping. Or do you? Is it really true that you ought to assume the responsibility? Perhaps it's less risky if you let the prepress service bureau or the print shop handle your trapping.

This section contains background information and decision-making tools to help you make a solid business decision about who should do your trapping. Because determining who does the trapping is just that, a business decision. You need to weigh any of your perceived savings in time and money and increased control over the final product against the risks of having to swallow hard and pick up the tab for an unacceptable job off the press.

What Is Trapping and Why Do I Need It?

Basically, trapping exists because the perfect printing press doesn't. As the paper screams past the plates at high speed (or even at low speed) it shifts around. It slips from side to side. It stretches. The paper changes dimensions as it soaks up wetting solution and ink. After all, a press is a mechanical device, and you can't expect anything made out of iron to roll all day without a little slop.

Well, a little slop might be okay when you are working with only one color. But slop is absolutely not okay if you are laying down multiple colors. The colors ought to align properly (register with one another). The chances are pretty strong, however, that anywhere two colors meet on the page a little sliver of white paper will show through between them—unless you trap the point where those colors meet. Figure 11.5 shows two non-trapped abutting colors, their misregistration exaggerated just to make the point.

You can see there are two problems caused by this misregistration. First, there's that sliver of pristine white paper showing through between the two brilliant cyan and magenta plates.

The sliver of white visible here is the reason trapping is so important when you want to create professional-quality color.

To trap the triangle and its background color together, one or the other of them must expand or shrink so they have a very slight overlap. That's what trapping is, overlapping two ink colors. It's a cover up. Trapping doesn't make the press register correctly, it merely covers up the misregistration with a slap of ink.

PageMaker In the Real World

Trapping—Who is responsible?

More and more of late, trapping has somehow become the responsibility of the designer, not the printer. It wasn't always like this, that the designer had to fret about press registration problems. In times past, the printer and the stripping crew did the fretting. You generated your mechanicals, delivered them to the printer, and they came back looking great. The folks who worked on the light table with Xacto knives and masks and Rubylith worried about registration problems. You may have learned to avoid certain design elements in order to make your printer's job easier, but you never had to seriously concern yourself about trapping.

Now we have the power to produce pages all stripped together electronically, ready to go to final film and be burned to plates. That means we can skip the expensive and time-consuming step of hand-stripping at the light table. When you put it like that—saving time on deadline and saving money on the budget—it really sounds great, doesn't it?

PageMaker
In
the
Real
World

But as deadline approaches, reality sets in and maybe it doesn't sound so great any more. Now it's you who pops the aspirin, and when it all looks like a mess on press, the client gives you one of those death stares. When you take on trapping responsibility, you have only yourself to blame if the job looks a mess. And it will be your bill to pay.

Fundamental Trap Construction: Choking and Spreading

The easiest of all the trapping concepts to understand are choking and spreading. You choke an object to make its knockout smaller, and that's why chokes are sometimes called shrinks or thinnies. Spreads, also called grips or fatties, are the reverse. To create a spread, you make the object itself slightly larger. Figure 11.6 illustrates the basic idea of a spread and a choke. Whether you trap with a spread or a choke is determined by whether the foreground is lighter or darker than the background: you always want to adjust the shape of the lighter object, as its perimeter has less visual weight than that of the darker object.

Figure 11.6

The spread is on the top and the choke on the bottom.

Note

When you print separations of two overlapping objects in PageMaker using the default settings, the object in front "knocks out" its exact shape from the object behind it. Knockouts prevent two colors from mixing on the printed page, but because they are so precise—and printing presses aren't—they introduce the need for trapping.

In order to make traps less visible, you will always trap using the lighter color. Neutral density value is an indication of the intensity or relative lightness or darkness of a color, and it is the value that PageMaker uses when making decisions about which color to use for a trap.

Trapping creates its own problems because you get a line that adds the two colors where the inks overlap. The resulting artifact can be an unsightly dark line that looks worse than the dreaded sliver of white it covers up. However, by creating traps only with the lighter of two intersecting colors, you minimize the visual impact of any trap artifacts.

Three Trapping Methods

How do we actually accomplish this spreading and choking? Well, you have three techniques to choose from: the way it used to be done, mechanically on a light table; the object trapping method; and the high-end pixel edge trapping method sometimes called *raster trapping*.

The Way It Used to Be: Mechanical Trapping

To understand how all this trapping works, it may help to have a look at the traditional, non-computer techniques used to create traps.

Traps used to be created using what you might call a sandwich of light to make a contact print from a film of the original image. Printers placed a thin filling of clear material, such as plastic, between the original film and the contact film (see Figure 11.7). This sandwich filling of clear plastic allowed the light to spread out so it created an overlap on the receiving negative film. The amount of the trap could be varied by using different thicknesses of clear material and by altering the amount of light used for the exposure.

Some areas of a complex design might need different traps. To create varying traps on a page, the stripper photographically (not literally) carved up your mechanical into different zones with masks made of Rubylith and opaque material. Each zone was then exposed as needed, and the final trapped flat was then used to expose the lithographic plate. This dependable technique has worked well for a long time. However, the technique is time-consuming and requires a high degree of skill, and that means money that you or your client must pay. Also, it does go against the grain to carefully paste up your pages electronically and then have a stripper use old-fashioned trapping techniques on them.

Figure 11.7

Mecahnical traps are created photographically, using a thin layer of clear film. This layer diffuses the light as it passes through the negative, causing it to scatter and create an object slightly larger than the original.

Object Trapping

PageMaker's built-in automatic trapping uses electronic object level trapping methods. As you can see in Figure 11.8, object trapping involves setting an overprinting line on the object that needs to be trapped. If you want, you can perform this operation manually on simple objects by applying overprinting strokes to the perimeter of objects drawn in PageMaker using PageMaker's Fill and Line dialog box.

Figure 11.8

Object-level trapping involves stroking the perimeter of the object to be trapped with an overprinting line the color of the trap color.

Notice that the object knocks out the background, the normal behavior for a graphic object in any PostScript-based program, including PageMaker. The stroke line, however, has been set to overprint so it overlaps the background.

When the colors you're using are close in value, the choice of the trapping color can be pretty mind-boggling. Fortunately PageMaker automates this choice. If you are working with spot colors, simply use the lighter of the two abutting colors. Process colors, however, can combine to make some really weird and garish third colors, called trapping artifacts. If you design yourself into a corner like that, get advice from your printer. Better yet, have someone else do the trapping.

PageMaker's Automatic Object Trapping to Work

If you decide that PageMaker's built-in trapping can handle your design, it's time for the simplest part of the process. After all, it's automatic!

As a first order of business, it's collaboration time. You need to get some technical specifications in order to create your traps, and you'll need to get the information from your printer. You need, in fact, a fair amount of technical information so you can set the trapping parameters in PageMaker—things such as the neutral density values for inks, the black limit, when black should be over-printed, and so on.

You may see standard guidelines for these technical specifications, but it's silly to trap without asking the printer what trap settings you should use. Trapping is, after all, something you are doing to compensate for misregistration on the press, and it varies a great deal from press operation to press operation.

The most important item on your technical information list is the width of the traps you'll want PageMaker to set for you. Your printer knows how loose or tight the press is, the line frequency of your screens, the paper you're using, the position of your piece in the flat, and how much dot gain to expect. From that information your printer determines the trapping amount. The amount of ink overlap will probably range from 0.18 to 2.2 points (0.0025 to 0.0308 inches), and there will be a different amount for black ink and all the other color inks.

Dot gain, by the way, is the way ink spreads on paper when printing a halftone. It soaks in and makes a bigger halftone dot (and widens the trap overlap).

Raster Trapping

Raster or edge trapping beats one of the big problems with object trapping. Object trapping requires that you be able to access the object from within PageMaker. If it's an imported graphic, no desktop layout program—including PageMaker—can do any trapping on the areas inside that image. For trapping imported graphics, you need to go back to the drawing or photo-retouching program used to create the graphic.

What to do? Well, there's no better trapping available than raster edge trapping. If you've designed a job that PageMaker can't handle, or if you're apprehensive about taking the trapping risk, you may need to send your job to a service bureau or printer that offers raster trapping. Several trapping systems are out there, and most of them have one thing in common—a price tag of thousands of dollars. In the hands of a skilled operator, these systems can do excellent trapping work, but they aren't the kind of thing most of us are likely to install in our own studios.

A high-end trapping system goes into your completed PageMaker file, rasterizes (a fancy word for translating the code that describes your page into an actual image) the entire page right down to the pixel level, and automatically works out traps for everything on the page. That includes imported EPS graphics and, depending on the system, virtually all the other avoid-these-situations trapping problems discussed in the next section. Raster trapping does a good trapping job quickly, no matter how convoluted those abutting color objects may be.

The two big names in raster trapping are Luminous' TrapWise (formerly owned by Adobe) and Scitex FAF, for Full Auto Frame. You needn't care very much about what system is used, as long as your service bureau delivers a good-looking job on time.

DECIDING WHETHER TO DO YOUR OWN TRAPPING

Trapping isn't a mountain, and you don't need to climb it just because it's there. You may want to, but you don't necessarily need to. Ask yourself these questions before you decide whether to do it yourself:

♦ **Money versus time.** How much is your time worth, and how much will it cost to pay someone else to do the trapping? Although times are changing, trapping traditionally has been part of the printer's job.

♦ **Risk versus benefit.** Are you willing to risk it? When deciding, remember that a success has many proud parents, but a failure is an orphan. If you take responsibility for the trapping and it comes out badly, you might be reaching into your bank account for some not-so-petty cash to pay for those 10,000 color catalogue sheets the client rejected.

♦ **Stripper or designer.** Do you really want to sit in front of the computer making trapping decisions? Or, would you rather be designing another job?

♦ **Quality.** How good will the job be when you get done? Is the piece important or complex enough that it deserves high-end raster trapping? Do you have all the skills and experience needed to handle it?

♦ **Design to avoid trapping.** Is it possible to design around the need for trapping? If no colors touch one another, there's no need to trap. Or try overprinting, using one of the overprint techniques in the "Performing Simple Object Trapping" section.

◆ **Job complexity.** Is doing the job yourself with object trapping techniques reasonable or even technically possible? PageMaker and your drawing program simply can't handle some things; the following section lists and discusses trapping situations you need to avoid.

Consider Running with No Trapping: Kiss Fit

Kiss fit means to run the job without trapping, allowing the abutting colors to "kiss" each other without overlapping. If you know your printer really well, you might run the job just fine without trapping. If you don't know your printer really well, and ask to print your color job kiss fit with no traps, the printer will give you a big belly laugh for a few minutes, then ask you to sign a waiver stating that any flaws in the job are your fault. Still, it's an option.

If you've ever seen the 16-page *Before&After* newsletter, you would never guess that it's run kiss fit. It's full of tricky color, because that's the point. *Before&After* is a newsletter all about pulling off PageMaker design, primarily in color. The newsletter's publishers run plenty of blends against blends, for example, which are tough to do.

How do they do it, and why? The publisher, John McWade, prefers an occasional white line over bad traps, and thinks that a publication looks cleaner if it can be run without traps. How does he get the printer to make the commitment? For one thing, *Before&After* is the most important job on his printer's client list so that helps a lot. They do a very long make-ready run to get everything in good register, which wastes a lot of time and paper. But the printer regards the newsletter as a showpiece for his shop and believes it's worth the time and effort. What's even more amazing is the fact that the print shop isn't a high-end shop. The shop does mostly one- and two-color work on uncoated stock. Their old press, built in 1968, has so much wear that it literally rattles during a run. (That's a manually adjusted press, by the way, not one of those laser-registered, computerized fountain jobs.)

One other thing. All the color in the newsletter gets specified as process color. Therefore, plenty of abutting colors share a common CMYK color component, which tends to minimize any misregistration. If two plates are not spot on, the other two plates will—by the law of averages—naturally tend to cover for the errant pair (that just happens to be one of the trapping techniques covered in this chapter).

So some people do publish without trapping. It may not be something you want to insist on, but if you collaborate well with the printer, you can get good results.

Design Away the Need for Trapping

If your communications challenge permits, develop a design that doesn't require trapping or at least avoids the worst of the trapping risks.

Overprinting Black

If you have black type to run over a colored background, just overprint it, assuming the type is large enough to read well. In PageMaker, black type automatically overprints the background by default if it has been set at any size larger than 24 points. Before you take this approach, though, make sure you check with your print shop about the amount of ink being applied to the page, or you might end up with problems caused by overinking.

Try to avoid such obvious legibility and design problems as putting black type on a midnight blue background. Check contrast by looking at the page design with your monitor set to grayscale mode.

Sharing CMYK Colors

As long as abutting process colors share a common process color, you don't need to trap them. Perhaps, for example, the adjacent objects contain at least 10% or 20% of cyan. (Check with your printer on the minimum amount of common color, but 10% is a typical figure.) If the other colors slip on the page, the cyan ink fills in the gap, and you see no dreaded white sliver of paper showing through due to the misregistration. The sliver is cyan blue instead, but many designers and printers believe that's less noticeable than white.

This trick doesn't work with spot color mixed inks. However, process color-based spot color inks work just fine. Check with your printer.

Taken to its extreme, you could even overprint two process colors as you might overprint black. You need a swatch book for sure if you want to try that one. The mixture of all those process colors could result in too much ink and an unsightly color to boot. Figure 11.9 shows how you can stack the two process colors to create a third color.

Figure 11.9

The purple color here is created by overprinting cyan on magenta; if the cyan plate shifts during printing, there's no risk you'll see through to the paper because the magenta is common to both colors.

Frame the Untrappables

Consider running a stroke around the edge of an item that might otherwise be untrappable, such as a color photo. Simply put the element in a frame, and then overprint the frame (see Figure 11.10). You need to decide whether you like the idea of doing this to your design, but it does (literally) cover any misregistration.

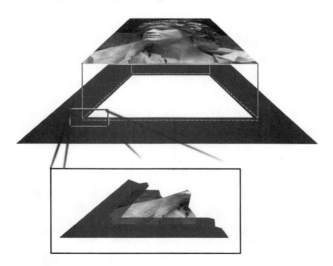

Figure 11.10

If it will work within the context of your design, putting an overprinting frame around imported graphics can eliminate the need to trap them.

Using Raster-Based Trapping

PageMaker's object trapping simply can't handle some things, and knowing its limitations can help you make better decisions about when to use it and when to find an alternative trapping solution.

PageMaker can't trap imported graphic objects. This may be the most common trapping dilemma of them all, because page layout programs, such as PageMaker, were invented so they could do assemble text and graphics. For now, you have to trap imported graphics in their originating programs or use a raster-based trapping application to trap the entire page after you're done with production.

Also, keep in mind that even after you have figured out a way to trap your imported graphic, you can't resize it unless you are willing to redo the trapping. Resizing a trapped graphic changes the thickness of all the stroked lines, which usually ruins your traps.

Note

Some graphics are used over and over again. Logos are just one example. So, you can do the trapping once and save the items in a sort of electronic stat sheet. Compose a sheet of logos (or other frequently used graphic elements) in every size you might need. Trap them all, and then you easily can place these pre-trapped and pre-sized graphics in PageMaker without worrying about trapping.

PageMaker also doesn't have a good solution for trapping objects that overlap halftones. Figure 11.11 shows one of the toughest trapping challenges—an object or type superimposed over a photograph. You simply have no way to stroke your object against the picture, because the colors change underneath the object, creating problems similar to those you encounter when trapping gradated fills in drawing programs.

Figure 11.11

Colored type over a color halftone is one of the toughest things to trap unless you use a raster-based trapping program.

Finally, type sitting on top of other type won't trap, even though type will trap to any PageMaker drawn objects below it in the stacking order. Strange but true.Take the Dialog to the Printer, Literally

Take the Dialog to the Printer, Literally

One really good way to collect all this technical information is to take screen shots of the Trapping Options dialog box and the Ink Setup dialog box to a meeting with your printer. Also, take proofs of your project. Ask the printer what values to type into the dialog box, and if there are any areas of your design that will be trapping problems.

Don't Do a Half Trap Job

Don't run PageMaker trapping if you have any of the trapping nightmare situations. Handing the printer films that have been trapped in some areas but not in others will make it impossible for the printer to complete the job. Trapping software like TrapWise, and traditional printing darkroom techniques for trapping, usually work over the entire area of a page. That creates a sort of all-or-nothing situation. Running trapping software over your existing PageMaker generated traps would give you double traps in some spots. That's not good. Don't do it.

Understanding How PageMaker Traps

Your publication will not actually be trapped until you output your separations, which means that you can change any of the trapping settings at any time before you run your film.

One drawback of this flexibility is the fact that PageMaker can't preview traps for you because there's nothing to see in the actual PageMaker file or on any composite proofs. By contrast, high-end trapping systems enable the operator to examine each trap and make adjustments as needed. The only way to proof your traps is to create a separations-based laminate color as discussed in Appendix C, "Proofing Your Publication."

Here's how PageMaker tackles its automated object level trapping chores. First, it looks for all edges where two colors meet. It then decides which of the two adjacent colors is lighter (based on the neutral density values of the inks). When colors have similar neutral densities, PageMaker runs a centerline trap so the trap is shared equally between the two objects. What makes PageMaker's trapping so much better than that found in other desktop publishing programs is the fact that it only traps those parts of an object that really need it. If you've designed a logo where a yellow triangle partially overlaps a blue rectangle, only the part of the triangle that touches the rectangle will be trapped. Other programs spread the entire perimeter of the triangle, which looks terrible.

As a general rule of thumb, the lighter colored object will be spread over the darker value to make the trap. However, PageMaker sometimes mixes up a new color to construct a trap if two adjacent process colors must be trapped (neither one is a spot color). PageMaker starts by selecting the lighter of the two colors. It then pulls a new color out of that lighter color, using the CMYK ink values that are more intense than the CMYK values found in the darker color.

Trapping Preferences Dialog Box

After you have the technical specifications and have a basic grasp of how PageMaker trapping works, the rest is really simple. Open the Trapping Preferences dialog box by selecting it from the Preferences submenu in the File menu (see Figure 11.12), check the Enable trapping for publication option, make any other adjustments to the settings there, and print your separations.

Figure 11.12

PageMaker's Trapping Preferences dialog box, where you set trapping parameters for an entire publication.

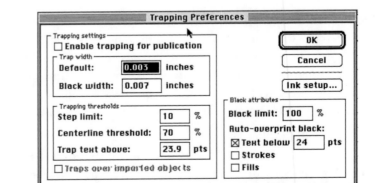

Here's a run down of what's in the dialog box. Your printer will tell you what values to use in most cases. PageMaker actually provides some insane levels of control here, so there's a pretty good likelihood that you won't need to adjust all (or even most) of these settings. Nice to know what you have control over, though.

◆ **Enable trapping for publication** turns trapping on. Don't forget to check this box before you run your separations.

◆ **Trap widths.** PageMaker mimics high-end trapping programs by offering two trap width settings: one for black, and one for everything else. Conventional wisdom on the topic has it that it's a good idea to use extra-wide traps for black objects, because any gaps next to black are even more noticeable than those next to other colors. Generally, the default width for black traps should be twice that used for other colors.

◆ **Step limit threshold.** The Step limit defines when PageMaker should make a trap. If the colors vary by more than the amount entered in this box, the program will go to work and create a trap. If you want everything to trap, lower this percentage. If you only want traps between extreme color variations, increase it. This is one of those cases where you can change the default, but you probably shouldn't.

◆ **Centerline threshold.** This setting determines when PageMaker creates a centerline trap instead of a full spread or choke. A 100% setting tells PageMaker not to do any centerline trapping, whereas a 0% setting would request that all traps be centerlines. If the Centerline Threshold is set at 70%, then PageMaker will try to build a centerline trap for any abutting colors that are 30% or less apart in neutral density values. Another excellent setting to leave alone.

◆ **Trap text above.** PageMaker automatically overprints text that is smaller than the value you enter here, and text larger than the cutoff point is trapped. Why? Text larger than the default of 24 points starts to have real presence on a page, and if it's overprinted, you can usually make out the colors under it. On a solid field of color with black text, this is no big deal, but when you're putting type over a background with color variations, it can be pretty distracting. On the flip side, trapping text smaller than the default will often cause the text to start losing its shape, which is probably even worse. The control this handy option offers is nifty, but it's another one that you shouldn't muck with unless you have a really compelling reason to do so.

◆ **Traps over imported objects.** This is a strange one. Generally speaking, if you have a PageMaker-drawn object on top of an imported graphic, there's no good way to trap it unless you use a raster-based trapping program. This option gives you an alternative. If the text or PageMaker-drawn shape happens to be sitting on a solid area of color in an imported graphic, you can trick PageMaker into trapping it. Here's how: define a spot color that approximates the background color in the graphic. Draw a box or other shape that covers the elements you want to trap, then send the object to the back of the stacking order to hide it. Check this option when you turn trapping on, and be sure to deselect the spot color when you print separations. PageMaker will trap the top object to the PageMaker element hidden behind the graphic. Sneaky, and only useful in limited circumstances—but worth a try in a pinch!

◆ **Defining Black.** The Black limit setting defines what is considered to be black for trapping purposes. Sometimes blacks are screened back a bit, or designers use an enriched black with a little bit of CMY thrown in, and a slight reduction in K. Under those circumstances, you can tell PageMaker trapping to consider black any color that has, say, 95% black or more. You can also automatically set all black lines and fills and text below a certain size to overprint, so they won't need to be trapped at all.

◆ **The Ink setup dialog box.** In general, don't mess with the ink neutral density settings you see in this dialog box. The values here reflect industry standards; in the United States, the values used have been set by the Graphic Arts Technical Foundation, the same group that established the SWOP standards (Specifications for Web Offset Publications). The only reason you should even consider messing with these values is if you're using a specialty ink that you want everything else in the publication to trap to (say an opaque or metallic ink). Because PageMaker uses these values to determine what traps to what, you can artificially increase the neutral density of a color and therefore force all other colors to trap to it.

THE BRAVE NEW WORLD OF HI-FI COLOR

Hi-fi color is one of the single biggest advancements in color printing technology since the advent of desktop publishing, and it has the potential to revolutionize color printing by changing the ink set that has been standard for almost 50 years. It's had the industry abuzz with excitement for the past three years or so, but it's only since the introduction of PANTONE's Hexachrome System and PageMaker 6.0 that there's been any reasonably practical way for non-specialists to produce hi-fi color jobs. In this section, we'll cover the basics of hi-fi color as well as how to produce hi-fi jobs in PageMaker.

Why would you want to use hi-fi color? Aside from the novelty of using the latest cool technology, the range of color you're able to print far surpasses that of traditional four-color printing. That means that it's a way for your printed materials to stand out, which is increasingly important as more people are using color to get their message across. For certain applications, such as clothing catalogs, inaccurate color directly affects the bottom line when merchandise is returned because the color of the item didn't match the catalog. Hi-fi color is a great solution in these cases, as it's an economical way to increase the range of printable color. Another practical advantage is the fact that with Hexachrome, it's possible to reproduce about 90 percent of the PANTONE spot color libraries with just six inks—so you can get almost the entire spot library for the cost of printing just six inks!

DuPont's Hypercolor System

Although Hexachrome is currently the most practical and widely available hi-fi system, there are other solutions for producing hi-fi color. DuPont's Hypercolor system uses the standard CMYK colors as bump plates, essentially systematizing an approach printers have used for some time. However, Hypercolor requires the use of a seven- or eight-head press, and they're relatively rare. There's also the Krüppers system, which adds orange, green, and violet to the standard CMYK ink set. In addition to not being very widely used or promoted, this approach also requires the use of a seven- or eight-head press.

Hi-Fi Systems: Hexachrome and the Rest

PANTONE's Hexachrome system adds orange and green to the traditional CMYK ink set to expand the printable color gamut; the cyan, magenta, and yellow inks have also been enhanced to be richer and brighter. In addition to supplying the inks, PANTONE provides color swatch books, digital libraries for use in software such as PageMaker, and additional software tools that make producing Hexachrome a reality. As a result, Hexachrome is accessible to a wide range of customers and printers.

Producing Hexachrome with PageMaker 6.5

Practically speaking, we're going to assume that if you're producing hi-fi color, you're using the Hexachrome system. As we've already discussed, it's far more widely available than any other approach—and it's also very well integrated into PageMaker, which makes it really pretty easy to produce great stuff without many hassles.

In this section, we'll go through all of the different elements you might include in a color job, and provide information about how to integrate them into a hi-fi color workflow. The workflow is pretty much the same as producing regular color, but there are a few extra things you need to be aware of.

Probably the biggest difference between Hexachrome and traditional four-color work is the role that color management plays. For other color jobs, using a color management system is a great way to make the production process more predictable—but it's still entirely possible to create good-quality color separations without using a CMS. Not so with hi-fi color. The only way you can create hi-fi separations of images is to use Kodak's Color Management System and to specify a Hexachrome profile for the Separations printer.

Another aspect of hi-fi color to keep in mind is that it is still relatively new. Although some printers have been experimenting with it for years now, others may balk at the idea of working with something they consider relatively untested—especially if the job you're proposing using it on is a mission critical one to begin with. An even more common problem is lack of familiarity with the details of the production process on the part of prepress professionals, especially when it comes to scanning and proofing. If you can, run some tests on smaller, less critical jobs before you take the plunge on, say, an annual report. And as always, involve the prepress and printing professionals you work with at every step along the way, so you can work together to resolve any issues that may crop up.

Setting up a Hexachrome Job

The first step when you decide to produce Hexachrome separations is to set your color management preferences. In the Color Management System Preferences dialog box, choose the Kodak CMS, and set the device profiles as you normally would—except for the Separations printer. For that, choose one of the Hexachrome profiles. Use Figure 11.13 as a guideline.

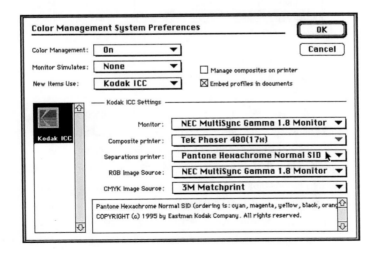

Figure 11.13

When you choose your CMS preferences, specify one of the Hexachrome profiles for the Separations printer option.

Specify your Hexachrome colors next. In the Color Options dialog box, choose one of the Hexachrome libraries form the pop-up menu. After you're in the Hexachrome color picker (see Figure 11.14) go nuts: you can select as many colors as you like by pressing shift and clicking to select each one. It's a good idea to invest in the printed swatch books for Hexachrome so you can choose your colors based on the way they look in print. Finally, you need to discuss your paper choice with the printer before you decide whether to select colors from the coated or uncoated library.

Figure 11.14

Select Hexachrome colors from one of the libraries included with PageMaker so you can apply them to objects in your publication.

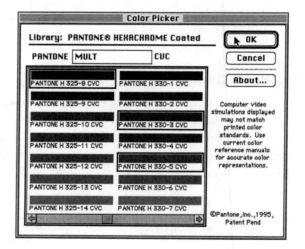

Note

One of the new features in PageMaker 6.5 is the capability to edit hi-fi colors, including the colors in the Hexachrome library. Don't do it, for the same reasons you shouldn't tinker with the values for colors in any of the other color libraries that come with PageMaker. If you do tweak the values in the Color Options dialog box, those values are what you'll get when you print separations—and there's no telling how the colors will look when printed. The only time you might want to consider doing this is if you and your printer have enough experience to know that the values in the color library aren't delivering the results you want: a pretty unlikely scenario.

After you've got these basics covered, producing the PageMaker part of the job is a snap. As you add text and draw lines and other shapes in PageMaker, you simply apply the Hexachrome colors as you would normally.

Where the process gets a little more complicated is when it comes to imported graphics. Both scanned images and EPS files have different issues associated with them, so these are covered separately in the following sections.

EPS Files and Hexachrome Color

At the time of this writing, neither FreeHand nor Illustrator support the Hexachrome color libraries, so specifying Hexachrome colors as you create the illustration you plan to use isn't an option. However, you want the colors in the EPS file to separate into the Hexachrome space. What to do?

You have two options, and both involve taking advantage of the fact that PageMaker enables you to import colors from EPS files and manipulate them in PageMaker. Hold on to your hats, because these workarounds get a little hairy.

Approach A involves pre-naming your FreeHand or Illustrator colors to match the Hexachrome names you'll use in PageMaker. When you import the EPS file, you'll be asked whether to import the colors with conflicting names. Clicking no means the color definitions in the EPS file will automatically be superseded by the definitions of the same name in PageMaker, which are the actual Hexachrome colors as specified by PANTONE. This works well, and is great if you're a well-organized sort who manages the production process pretty tightly.

Approach B involves using spot color definitions in Illustrator or either spot or process colors in FreeHand. When you import the EPS file, click the checkbox to Show Filter Preferences in the Place dialog box. In the EPS filter options, check the option to Add process and high fidelity color names to palette, and select the Add spot color names to palette radio button. After you've imported the color names, edit each one to be a 100% tint of the Hexacrome color you want to map it to. Although this approach involves a little more work on your part, it's a life saver if you're working with EPS files created for another use or by someone who hasn't worked with Hexacrome before.

In either case, after the colors in the EPS file are mapped to the Hexacrome colors you've added to the palette in PageMaker, you're all set. When both Illustrator and FreeHand support the Hexachrome color libraries, this process will be more straightforward—but it's likely that these workarounds will continue to be useful as old process-color EPS files make the transition to the world of hi-fi color.

Bitmap Images and Hexachrome Color

Working with images is easier than dealing with EPS files in some ways, and harder in others. After you import the files, all you need to do is make sure that they're being color-managed, and that the Hexachrome output profile is selected in the CMS Preferences. When you print separations, PageMaker automatically separates the images into six colors, and everything is okay.

If only it were that simple. The problems that arise with images all stem from the fact that the prepress world thinks in CMYK, and that images scanned as or saved in CMYK format don't look especially good when translated into the larger Hexachrome color space. The obvious answer is to just save the scans in that wonderful, device-independent color space, CIE Lab TIFF. For some types of images, such as Photo CD files, that's a snap. When you're working with high-end scans, though, it's often not as straightforward.

Many high-end scanners automatically convert scanned image data from RGB (what the scanner uses) to CMYK, and most of them do a great job doing it (if they didn't, you'd be less inclined to pay the premium for high-quality scans). With Hexachrome, that's a real disadvantage, because one of the primary reasons you'd use Hexachrome is to get beyond the gamut limitations inherent in CMYK.

The only real solution to this particular dilemma is to check with your prepress folks ahead of time. They may look at you like you're crazy when you ask at what point your scans are converted to CMYK, and if there's any way to receive them in either RGB or CIE Lab TIFF format—but that's what you need to do to get decent quality output.

In any event, after you've placed your RGB or CIE Lab TIFF file into PageMaker, all you need to do is color-manage it. When you print separations, the image will be separated into the Hexachrome color space.

Editing Hexachrome Images in Photoshop

In PageMaker 6.0, the biggest weakness with the whole hi-fi workflow was the fact that Hexachrome was pretty much a one-way street. You couldn't edit the Hexachrome color definitions even if you had wanted to. An even bigger problem was the fact that images you converted to Hexachrome separations couldn't be edited at all, because there was no way for Photoshop to read the images. If you liked what you got, great. Otherwise, too bad.

With PageMaker 6.5, that's been changed. By pre-separating your images using the Image Separation command off of the Image submenu (on the Element menu), you can create a multi-channel DCS file. Although Photoshop can't yet edit this file format directly, an Amsterdam-based company called VISU Technologies makes a Photoshop plug-in that can. The plug-in, called Channell 24, doesn't come with PageMaker, but if you're planning to do a lot of Hexachrome work, it's an invaluable tool to have. For more information about it, contact VISU by sending email to visu@euronet.nl, or by calling them at 31-20-669-12659.

Trapping Hexachrome Publications

There's good news and bad news on this topic. The good news is that you can trap elements created in PageMaker that have had Hexachrome colors applied, just like any other color. The bad news is that that's your only option. None of the raster-based trapping programs currently support hi-fi color of any description. The best approach is to design your job so that the worst trapping nightmares are avoided altogether.

Hi-Fi Color and Stochastic Screening

Most often, instead of traditional angle screens with regular patterns, your service bureau and print shop will use stochastic screening. That means random dots instead of a woof and warp weave of dots.

Stochastic screening probably shouldn't be described as a screen at all, even though everybody does use the term that way. It is correct, however, to describe it as a halftone. The traditional screening methods, going all the way back to when printers sandwiched a finely engraved glass "screen" with a film to screen a photograph, produce a very regular pattern of dots in a grid pattern. That's the major difference; stochastic halftones have random dots. They aren't at any particular angle or in any particular pattern. The stochastic approach helps simplify things when you have more than four inks going on the paper. It gets nearly impossible to calculate all the angles so that many ink colors can fit together without creating a puddle of muddy ink on the sheet of paper.

Although stochastic screening is great for images, its very randomness can create distracting noisy patterns in large areas of solid colors. As with everything else, you want to make sure that you choose the screening method that'll give the best results for the particular job you plan to print. If your budget is large enough, you may want to consider running two sets of separations and having them manually stripped together to take advantage of the benefits each approach offers.

Proofing Hexachrome Separations

You have three options for proofing your Hexachrome jobs—you can preview, or soft proof, onscreen using PageMaker's CMS; you can have separations-based color proofs created, or you can wait to do an on-press proof.

Obviously, an on-press proof will give you the best idea of what your final piece will look like—but it's also a fabulously expensive proposition. Conversely, don't expect much from a soft proof on your monitor. You might be able to see the most glaring deficiencies, but the subtleties that make the difference between an acceptable and an unacceptable color job certainly won't be visible.

Separations-based proofs are the most practical, and anyone who has worked on four color jobs should be familiar with the process. The biggest difference between standard CMYK proofs and Hexachrome proofs is the fact that PANTONE licenses only two Hexachrome-based proofing systems: the AgfaProof 2 system and DuPont's Chromalin system. Finding vendors who can actually provide Hexachrome proofs has been an issue in some areas, and you should be sure to check into this issue before you decide to go the Hexachrome route.

SUMMARY

This chapter, along with Chapter 10, gave you some insight on how to use color effectively and helped you understand how to get the colors you see onscreen to match those in your printed document. Chapter 12 "Endgame Issues" switches gears and shows you how to use the Control palette to perfect your pages. It also explains how to create book length documents and publications.

Chapter

12

ENDGAME ISSUES

PageMaker gives you a great deal of flexibility in the layout
of text and graphics. This chapter looks at how PageMaker
is used to paste-up and repurpose pages, and how it is used
to construct long book-length documents and publications.

ELECTRONIC "PASTE-UP"

The term *paste-up* derives from the "old days" of page assembly, where strips of output type were actually pasted into position on a stiff mechanical board. The term survives because that is what is essentially happening—even though digitally—when you assemble pages in PageMaker.

PageMaker enables you to position page elements with an accuracy of 1/1440th of an inch. This is much smaller than the smallest printer spot generated by the highest-resolution output device. Old paste-up artists using T-squares and waxing machines could only dream of such accuracy!

The first half of this chapter focuses on PageMaker's Control palette and its power in positioning, grouping, aligning, and locking page elements.

Magnification

All the positioning tools in the world won't help if you can't actually see what it is you are positioning. So, before jumping into the Control palette, have a quick look at the ways in which PageMaker enables you to magnify—or reduce—the display size of a page. PageMaker has several preset display sizes—25, 50, 75, 100 (actual size), 200, and 400% (but you can magnify up to 800%). There are several ways to adjust the magnification:

◆ **View Menu.** The View menu contains several commands to adjust the size. The Zoom In command increases the magnification to the next preset increment (such as from 100 to 200%, or from 200 to 400%) whereas the Zoom Out command decreases the magnification by one increment (such as from 400 to 200%, or from, 200 to 100%). The Actual Size command sets the display to 100% and the Fit In Window command shrinks the page down so that the entire page fits on the screen. The Entire Pasteboard command reduces the image so that the entire pasteboard—including the page and any marginal material or, in other words, all that is PageMaker—fits onscreen.

◆ **Zoom Menu.** The Zoom pop-up menu in the View menu
enables you to directly select the degree of magnification—25,
50, 75, 100, 200, and 400%.

◆ **Magnification Tool:** On the Tool palette, you can click the
Magnification Tool and the pointer changes to a magnifying
glass with a "+" in the center of it (see Figure 12.1). Clicking
the page increases the magnification by one increment (100 to
200 to 400%). Whatever object you click the Magnification
Tool on will appear in the center of the magnified display. If
you hold down the (Option) [Alt] key, the "+" in the center of
the Magnification Tool changes to a "-" and clicking reduces
the page by one increment. Double-clicking the Magnification
Tool in the Tool palette automatically sets the display to
100%.

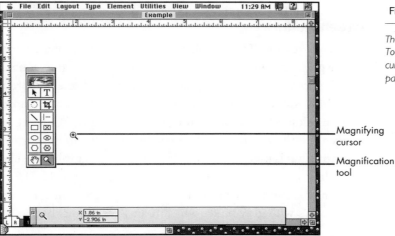

Magnifying
cursor

Magnification
tool

Figure 12.1

*The Magnification tool on the
Tool palette, and the Magnifying
cursor. Clicking anywhere on the
page increases the magnification.*

◆ **Keyboard Shortcuts.** You can Zoom In on a page by pressing
(Command-+) [Control-+], and Zoom Out by pressing
(Command--) [Control--]. You can get to 100% by pressing
(Command-1)[Control-1]; to 200% by pressing (Command-2)
[Control-2]; and 400% by pressing (Command-4) [Control-4]
You can get to 50% by pressing (Command-5) [Control-5],

and to 75% by pressing (Command-7) [Control-7]. You can get to Fit In Window by pressing (Command-0) [Control-0]. There is no keyboard shortcut to take you to 25%.

- ◆ **Custom Views.** Although PageMaker doesn't allow you to numerically enter a magnification percentage, you can, when the Magnification Tool is selected and, while pressing the (Command and Option) [Control and Alt] keys, drag a selection marquee around a page element. When you release the mouse button, the selected region will fill the screen.

Confused yet? There is no need to even try to remember all of that. Some people hate keyboard shortcuts, and other people love them. Pick the system that works for you and stick with it. Or, better yet, get even more of your money's worth with this book and keep it open to this page as you work with PageMaker.

Screen Redraws

If you are using TIFF graphics on your page, you might want to reduce the graphics resolution if screen redraws are bogging you down. (EPS graphics always display using their embedded screen representations, so this section does not apply to them.) There are three graphics resolution settings that you can select using the General Preferences menu in the File menu. High resolution is the most redraw-intensive setting but is useful if you need to have screen graphics displayed at the highest quality. The Standard setting (see Figure 12.2) is useful for regular editing, placing, and navigation, whereas Gray out replaces the graphics with gray boxes which redraw very quickly.

You can force a redraw of a graphic if, for example, you are in the Standard mode and need to view the graphic at the highest resolution. Select the object, and hold down the Control key while forcing a screen redraw. To force a screen redraw, press (Command-Shift-F12).

Pressing the Control key while forcing a redraw gives you a high-resolution view of the graphic only if you are in the Standard mode. In Gray out mode, you still get gray boxes.

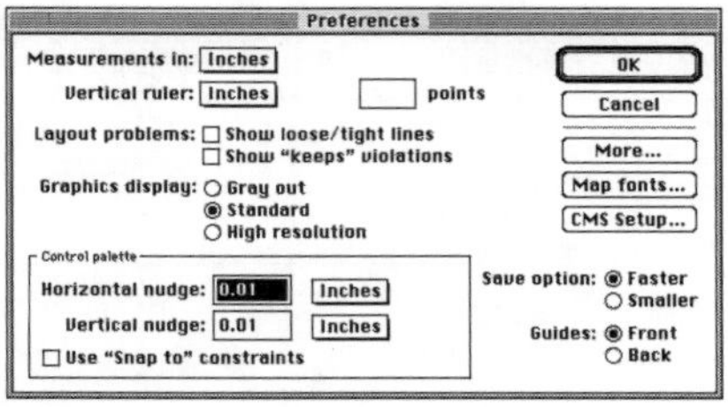

Figure 12.2

The General Preferences dialog box with Standard graphics resolution selected.

Note

If you don't need to see specific colors, you can set your monitor to grayscale, rather than color (in the Monitors control panel). You can also reduce the color depth from millions or thousands to 256 or less (also in the Monitors control panel). This will save you some screen redraw time.

The Basics of Positioning

Although many users place page elements wherever they look good, often you need to know the specific, objectively-measured location of an object. There are several ways of determining exactly where you are in PageMaker.

Rulers

The first and most obvious is by looking at the rulers located along the top and left of PageMaker's window. Notice as you move the pointer around the screen that a set of short dotted lines moves along the vertical ruler and along the horizontal ruler with it. If you click on a picture box, for example, and begin to move it, notice that four dotted lines, or tracking marks—one for the left, right, top, and bottom borders—appear on the rulers (see Figure 12.3). These tracking marks enable you to position the borders of the graphic with extreme accuracy. Increasing the magnification also increases the size of the rulers correspondingly, thus giving you even greater accuracy in positioning. Text boxes, lines, and any other selected page element all have their on-page coordinates indicated on the rulers.

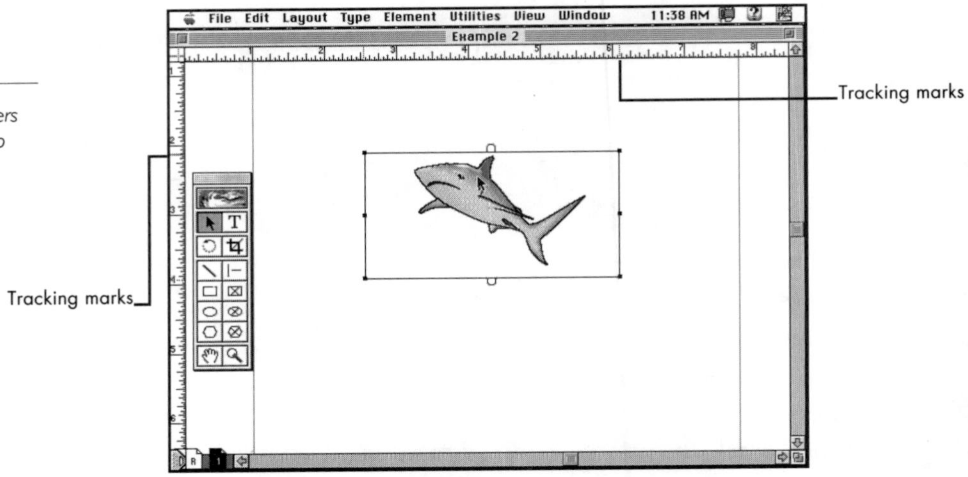

Figure 12.3

Horizontal and vertical rulers show the tracking marks to indicate the position of a placed graphic.

Tracking marks

Tracking marks

If the rulers interfere with your view, turn them off by selecting Hide Rulers from the View menu. To put them back, select Show Rulers from the View menu. Or, for you keyboard shortcut fans, (Command-R) [Control-R] toggles the rulers on and off.

Clicking the crosshairs where the two rulers intersect allows you to change the zero point of one or the other (or both) of the rulers. Simply drag in the direction you would like, and this sets a new zero point where you release the mouse. This is useful for measuring specific distances. To prevent accidental movement of a new zero point, you can turn on the Zero Lock (in the View menu), which, as its name indicates, locks the zero point in place. The default zero point is at the top-left-hand corner of a page. If you've moved the zero point, and would like to set it back to the default, double-click the crosshairs (with Zero Lock turned off).

In the General Preferences menu (which is located in the Preferences submenu of the File menu), you can set the rulers to display metric measurements. Select Millimeters from the pull-down menus for both the Measurements in and Vertical ruler boxes. The rulers display centimeters, but the Control palette readouts are in millimeters. You can also specify measurements in Inches, Decimal, Picas, or Ciceros.

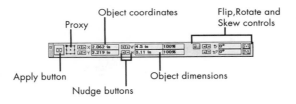

PageRuler is one of the plug-ins from the Extensis PageTools set. Horizontal and vertical moveable rulers enable you to measure distance between any PageMaker document objects.

Control Palette

The Control palette provides extremely precise coordinates for selected objects (see Figure 12.4).

Proxy — Object coordinates — Flip, Rotate and Skew controls

Apply button — Nudge buttons — Object dimensions

Figure 12.4

The Control palette.

You can display the Control palette by selecting Show Control palette (in the Window menu) or hide it by selecting Hide Control palette.

The Apply Button

The large icon on the far left of the Control palette is the Apply button. It is used to apply a change made to coordinates. It also tells you what specifically the selected object is. Table 12.1 lists most of the Apply button icons.

TABLE 12.1

APPLY BUTTON ICONS

Picture Box	⊠
Text Block	T
Rectangle	▭

continues

TABLE 12.1, CONTINUED
APPLY BUTTON ICONS

Oval	
Polygon	
Line	
Multiple Objects	
EPS Graphic	
TIFF Graphic	

Proxy

The second symbol, which looks like a kind of square bracelet, is called the Proxy (see Figure 12.4), and it enables you to select your reference point. You can get a total of nine different coordinates using the Proxy. Each of the small boxes on the square (or oval if an oval is selected) corresponds to one of the reference points—or "handles"—on the actual graphic. By clicking one of these boxes in the Proxy, you can get the X (horizontal) and Y (vertical) coordinates for it. The largest box is the reference point currently displayed; in the case of Figure 12.4, the point in the upper-left-hand corner of the image is selected.

The first set of figures indicate the X and Y coordinates of the selected object. The arrow buttons let you "nudge" an object along one or both of the axes. (Alternately, you can enter your own coordinates directly in the boxes.)

The second set of figures tells you the width of the object, which you can also nudge larger or smaller.

The last set of buttons enables you to rotate and skew the object.

The Control palette functions essentially the same regardless of whether the selected object is a line, picture box, shape, or a text column, and so on.

There are two ways of making precision positioning adjustments in the Control palette: using the nudge buttons or by directly entering coordinates.

Nudge Buttons

As you might remember from high school geometry class, the X-axis is the horizontal direction, while the Y-axis is the vertical direction. The nudge buttons (see Figure 12.5) can be used to move a selected object in either of those directions.

Nudge buttons

The two horizontal nudge buttons—the two arrow-bearing buttons next to the X—move a selected object to the left or the right by a preset amount. The two vertical nudge buttons—the ones next to the Y— move the selected object up or down by a preset amount. You can set the nudge amount in Control palette section of the General Preferences dialog box (see Figure 12.6). You can set any nudge amount you want, as long as it is not less than zero nor greater than the total width or height of the pasteboard. The default nudge amounts (0.01 inch) are good to begin with, but your own specific needs may require a larger or smaller nudge.

You can set the horizontal nudge differently than the vertical nudge. Also, if you hold down the (Command) [Control] key while making a nudge, the nudge amount is magnified ten times. Nudges can be undone either using Undo or by clicking the opposite button.

The second set of nudge buttons controls the size of the picture or text box. These nudge buttons also adjust the size of the object by the preset nudge amount. Changing the percent numbers alters the size of the image within the box by whatever number you enter.

Figure 12.6

*The nudge amount setting
in the General Preferences
dialog box.*

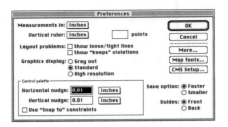

The final set of nudge buttons adjusts the amount of skew or rotation of a selected object.

Direct Coordinate Entry

If you know the exact position at which you would like to place an image, you can click in either of the coordinate text boxes and enter a specific number.

After entering a number, press Return and the change goes into effect. The cursor also disappears from the Control palette box (and the pointer disappears from the screen). To save time having to go back into a particular coordinate box, however, you can press Shift-Return, or click the Apply button, and the change goes into effect, leaving the cursor in the coordinate box, should you want to make further adjustments. (Simply moving the mouse will return the pointer to its last-known position.)

Note

You can also use the Control palette as a calculator by entering mathematical symbols. If your X coordinate is already at 5 inches and you want to try a 4.25-inch move, type **+4.25** *after the 5. Use the hyphen for subtraction, the asterisk for multiplication, and the slash for division.*

Constraining Dimensions

If you have ever tried to line up a graphic or column of text along both dimensions simultaneously, you know what a pain it can be. PageMaker, however, enables you to constrain one dimension while you move in the other.

1. Align the object along one dimension (for example, the horizontal).

2. Hold down the Shift key. At this point, your next move will decide to which axis the object is "locked."

3. Move the object up or down (but not side-to-side). Notice that the pointer changes to a double-arrow aligned parallel to the vertical. Also notice that you will not be able to move the object from side-to-side.

4. Now, move the object to the desired position on the vertical axis.

Although this can be useful when aligning two objects with each other, the Align Objects command is a simpler means of accomplishing this.

Snap to Guides

If you have column guides selected (in the Column Guides dialog box under the Layout menu), you can turn on what are known as Snap to Guides. From the View menu, you can select Snap to Guides. They can also be toggled on or off using (Shift-Command-;) [Shift-Control-;].

Essentially, Snap to Guides help align objects by acting as "magnetic" strips. Drag an object toward them and you "feel" a kind of tug on the object, and the object "snaps" to the guide. The distance from the guide at which the magnetic pull can be felt can be set in Layout Adjustment preferences (under Preferences in the File menu).

Snap to Guides are a wonderful feature to help align objects very precisely. If you are laying out a newsletter page, for example, and you have several text boxes you need aligned to the left margin, turning on Snap to Guides can help align them all with each other as you create them. Also, by keeping the Snap to Guide settings the same on each page, you can ensure that all text boxes are precisely positioned from page to page.

Multiple Objects

On those occasions when you need to move, skew, rotate, or otherwise manipulate two or more objects as a single unit (so as to maintain their relation to each other), you can, as in most programs, click each object while holding down the Shift key. With more than one object selected, most of the Control palette is unavailable (the Proxy and the coordinate buttons). The reference points on the Proxy correspond to points on a rectangle encompassing both selected objects.

Cropping and Scaling

In PageMaker 6.5, the cropping function is primarily the job of the Cropping Tool, which is located on the Tool palette. With the Cropping Tool selected, you can click within a picture box. The cursor changes to a hand (a Move tool) and you can move the graphic about within the box. (Actually, the term "Cropping tool" is a bit of a misnomer, as it simply moves a graphic within a picture box without changing the size of the box itself. Adjusting the size of the picture box, either by dragging its handles or clicking the nudge buttons, affects what is normally thought of as "cropping.")

Scaling, in contrast to cropping, changes the size of the image or picture box itself.

You can adjust the scaling using the H and W buttons and coordinates (in the center of the Control palette). These adjust the height (H) and width (W) of the image. The Proportional Sizing Button (see Figure 12.7) enables you to toggle between two different scaling modes. With proportional sizing turned on, the height and the width always remain in the same proportion; therefore, the shape of the object always remains the same. Turning off proportional sizing enables you to stretch the vertical dimension independently of the horizontal dimension, and vice versa.

Figure 12.7

Proportional Sizing button

The Control palette's Proportional Sizing button.

Manipulating Graphics and Text

Although the manipulation of graphic objects has been explored in other chapters, there is only one place in PageMaker to flip, rotate, and skew graphics and text, and that—as you might have already guessed—is in the Control palette.

Flipping

Flipping—or, in more technical terms, *flopping* (derived in the late 16th century as a phonetic variant of "flapping," meaning "folding like a door, hinge, or book flap," which in turn is derived from the Middle English and Dutch *flappen*, meaning "to strike a blow")—graphics and text blocks about an axis can be done in one (or both) of two directions—horizontally and vertically. The two buttons at the far right of the Control palette control the flips.

The top button flips the selected object about a horizontal axis, thus reversing the image. The selected reference point in the Proxy decides which axis is chosen. (See Figures 12.8 and 12.9.)

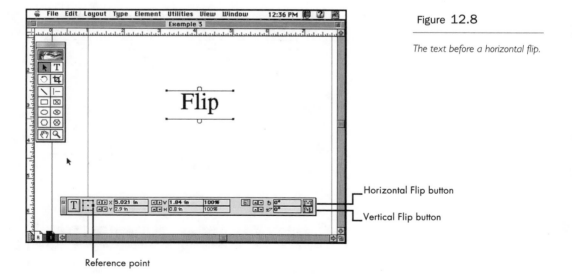

Figure 12.8

The text before a horizontal flip.

Figure 12.9

The result of a horizontal flip. Note that after the flip, the selected reference point in the Proxy is in a new position.

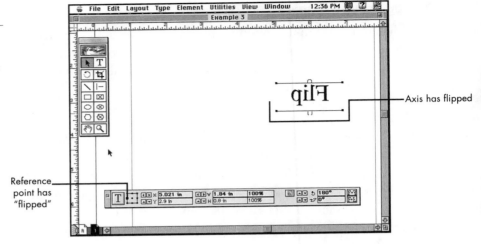

Axis has flipped

Reference point has "flipped"

Notice that the flipped image is not in the same position as it was before the flip. This is because the flip essentially "swung" the image about an axis drawn through the selected reference point. To keep the image in the original position, select the center point as the reference point. A vertical flip works on the same principle (see Figure 12.10).

Figure 12.10

The result of a vertical flip.

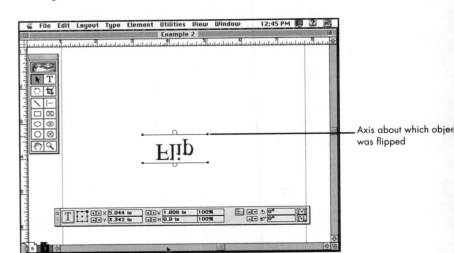

Axis about which obje was flipped

Rotating

Flipping is considered a type of rotation, but PageMaker also enables you to rotate at finer increments. In the Control palette, you can rotate using the buttons adjacent to the rotate symbol, (which increase or decrease the angle of rotation by an amount equivalent to the preset nudge amount), or by entering a number in the rotation angle box (see Figure 12.11). (You can also use the Rotation tool on the Tool palette.) Negative numbers indicate movement in a clockwise direction. All angles are relative to the horizontal.

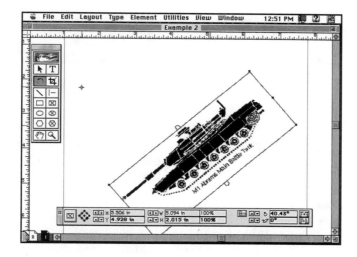

Figure 12.11

The effect of Rotation.

When rotating, it is important to pay attention to whether the Proxy is in the Sliding or Locked mode. In Locked mode, the image rotates around the selected reference point, whereas in Sliding mode, it rotates about the center. (You can also select the center point in the Proxy, as it has the same effect in both Sliding and Locked mode. If you use the Rotation Tool, hold down (Command) [Control] while performing the rotation, and you also rotate around the center point.)

Skewing

Selected images are skewed by using the nudge buttons adjacent to the skew symbol in the Control palette, or by entering a skew amount in the box. You can tell from Figure 12.12 that the skew amount is -18.4 degrees.

437

Figure 12.12

The effect of Skew.

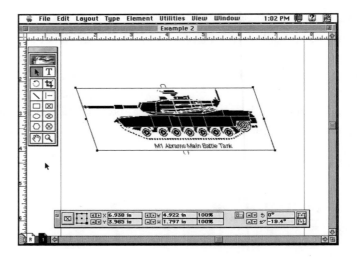

Again, the Proxy mode—Locked or Sliding—affects the skew. If in the Locked mode, the reference point does not move, but rather anchors the image down and the skew is performed relative to that point. In Sliding mode, the reference point does move, the skew is distributed among all reference points equally.

Flipped, Rotated, and Skewed Text

Text blocks can be manipulated just like graphics. They also can be edited and added to even after these actions have been performed. Simply select the Text tool from the Tool palette and edit just as you would unrotated, unflipped, and unskewed text. (If you are moving from line to line with the arrow keys, however, you may get a little confused about up and down versus left and right, though!)

Maintaining Positions

In page layout, it is often convenient to group separate elements together, especially if they need to be moved as a whole to new positions yet keep their same positions with respect to each other. Many programs—most

A Caveat About Manipulating Graphics

PageMaker enables you to manipulate graphics in wonderfully flexible ways. But you might want to think twice about whether or not you want to do it in PageMaker. This is covered in more detail in Chapter 14, but suffice it to say here that heavily manipulated graphics in PageMaker might not output. The reason involves the way PageMaker makes changes to a "piped in" version of the original, untouched graphic, then provides instructions to the output device (through the PostScript page description language) as to how to re-make those changes. Too many instructions can snarl output traffic severely. Any rotations, skews, and flips—especially of TIFF images—are best handled prior to Placing them in PageMaker, if possible.

drawing programs, such as Adobe Illustrator, CorelDRAW!, FreeHand, or other page layout programs such as QuarkXPress—have this feature. PageMaker is no exception. PageMaker also enables you to lock a page element to the page, to keep it from being moved accidentally.

Grouping

If you had the little drama unfolding in Figure 12.13—comprising four separate page elements—and needed to move them together, at one time you would have had to move each element independently of each other and reposition them all in the correct relation.

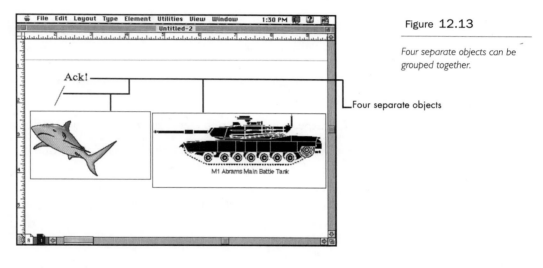

Figure 12.13

Four separate objects can be grouped together.

Select all the elements (hold down Shift while clicking each one), and then select Group from the Element menu. Notice that the individual handles are replaced by one set of handles for the group, which can now be moved or manipulated together (see Figure 12.14).

Figure 12.14

The objects can be grouped and rotated as a whole.

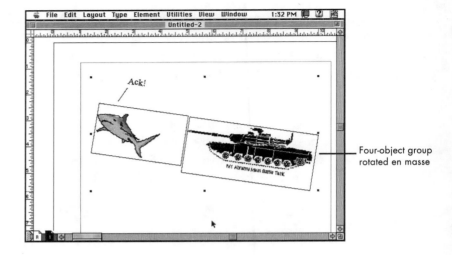

Four-object group
rotated en masse

To separate them back into individual elements, go to the Element menu and select Ungroup.

A few aspects of the Group command should be pointed out:

◆ Text can be formatted and edited as part of a group by selecting the Text tool and clicking in the text block you want to change. You can also change the formatting (such as font, type size, and so on) when text is grouped, unlike in other programs where grouped text "locks" to its characteristics at the time of grouping.

◆ Individual elements can be temporarily taken out of a group for editing without ungrouping the lot. Simply press the (Command) [Control] key and click the element you would like to work on. It becomes individually selected. When you deselect it, it is still part of the group.

◆ You can group objects in stages (called, in other programs, *nesting*). You can have the shark and the tank as a group, for example, then add the line and "Ack!" to the group. In PageMaker, however, everything ungroups at once, regardless of how the group was put together.

◆ You can make a group consisting of only one element. Why would you want to do this? Well, groups are treated as graphic objects. If you wanted to wrap text around another text block (as in the case of a pull-quote), the only way to do it would be to group the text block to be wrapped around, then set Text Wrap boundaries around it. You can't, however, group the wrapping text block with the wrapped text block, or you'll lose the text wrap.

◆ If you need to save your document to a version of PageMaker earlier than 6.0, your groups will become ungrouped, as version 6.0 was the first version to support grouping.

◆ If you create a group over other objects, that group moves to the top of the stacking order. When you ungroup, all the elements will be on top of ungrouped objects in the stack.

◆ If you scale a group, which you can do using the nudge buttons, hold down the Shift key while doing so (or select the Proportional Size button in the Control palette) and all the elements within the group retain their shape. If you scale and distort a group, however, the individual objects retain their distortion after ungrouping.

Aligning and Distributing

PageMaker makes it easy to line up objects with respect to other objects (aligning) and to scatter them at certain predetermined intervals about the page (distributing), through the Align Objects dialog box, located in the Element menu (see Figure 12.15). Two or more objects must be selected, otherwise the command is grayed and unavailable.

Using this box and the combinations of options within it, you can align and distribute objects in a variety of ways. You're not limited to only certain types of objects: You can align and distribute text boxes, TIFFs, EPS graphics, and so on.

Figure 12.15

The Align Objects dialog box.

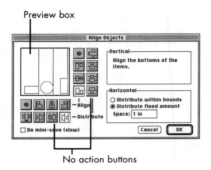

Preview box

No action buttons

You can combine Alignment and Distribution in one action. You can, for example, align along one axis and distribute on the other.

1. Referring to Figure 12.15, notice that you want to align the bottoms of three objects. Click the appropriate button on the Vertical alignment menu.

2. You then want to distribute them such that the right sides of the objects are a fixed distance apart. Click the appropriate button along the Horizontal distribution menu.

3. To distribute the objects at fixed intervals, click the "distribute fixed amount" radio button on the right side of the dialog box, and enter the amount by which each will be offset (say, 1 inch) in the space.

4. The text boxes on the right side of the dialog box tell you exactly what it is you are going to be doing. If it is correct, click OK.

You can also select the No Alignment option for either axis, if you only want to align or distribute along the other axis.

One thing to worry about before selecting this command is that the alignment is performed according to the farthest edge. That means, if you are aligning objects along their top boundaries, PageMaker aligns all the objects with the edge that is the closest to the top of the page. Similarly, if you select Align Bottoms, PageMaker aligns all the objects along the edge that is closest to the bottom of the page. It is the same deal with right and left edges, and centers. This is something to keep in mind when situating objects on the page that will ultimately be aligned. If you spend a great deal of time positioning one object to which all the others align, this object's position will be lost if another object is closer to the edge of the page corresponding to the edge you want to align.

In the distribution options, notice that you can distribute within bounds. This means that objects can be spaced evenly between two outermost objects (which will remain stationary). This option is useless if you only have two objects. Alternately, you can specify an amount of space between distributed objects. To make objects overlap, enter negative numbers in the Distribute Fixed Amount of Space box.

Before going ahead and doing an alignment, you can click the Do Mini-Save checkbox, which enables you to undo the command if you are unsatisfied with the result (press Shift-Revert). Keep in mind that unlike most other commands in PageMaker, the Align Objects command cannot be undone by the regular Undo command.

Pasting

Pasting—what could be simpler, right? Actually, PageMaker offers some variations on this basic theme, thus expanding the precision possible by traditional pasting.

Say you want to paste several copies of the same object, aligned either vertically or horizontally with each other. Sure, you could paste each one individually and use the Align function. A quicker way is to use the Paste Multiple dialog box (see Figure 12.16). Cut or copy the desired object (it can be text or a graphic), and select Paste Multiple from the Edit menu.

Select the number of copies you need and how far apart you want them (be sure this exceeds the size of the object itself, or your copies will overlap). If you want them to align horizontally, enter zero in the Vertical offset box. If you want them to align vertically, enter zero in the Horizontal offset box. (See Figure 12.17.)

Figure 12.16

The Paste Multiple dialog box.

Figure 12.17

Objects aligned using the Paste Multiple dialog box.

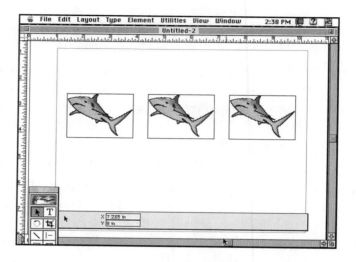

Locking Graphics to the Page

When you have a graphic or other object exactly where you want it, you can lock it to the page by selecting the Lock Position command from the Element menu. If you then try to move the image, the cursor changes to a padlock, indicating that it cannot be moved or resized. To unlock it, select Unlock from the Element menu.

Remember that the object is locked to the page position, not to another object, group, or position in text. Although you can't change the object's position, size, skew, or rotation angle, you can change its color and its fill. The Lock Position locks the object's position.

Objects can be locked on a Master page, which helps maintain the positions of objects already added to the Master page while new objects are added.

You can select a group of objects and lock them all into position. These locked objects, however, are not a true group in the Group-command sense.

You can put a Text Wrap around a locked object, and text that has been locked can be edited. Although you cannot adjust the length of a locked text block, if you delete or add text the size of the block changes automatically.

Masking

Often, you only want to see part of a text block or an image, depending on the design you have devised for a page. This is called "masking," and it means, essentially, to use a graphic object as a "window" to another graphic object beneath it, the shape of the object on top determining the portion of the bottom image that is visible.

1. To mask a graphic in PageMaker 6.0, first Place a graphic (such as a TIFF or EPS) on the page in the desired location.

2. Draw the shape of the mask over the desired object and position it in such a way as to have the desired portion of the bottom image visible within the bounds of the drawn shape.

3. Hold down the Shift key and select both objects.

4. In the Element menu, select Mask.

5. Now, only that portion of the bottom image that was visible through the top image appears on the page. It is also movable as a single selected object. To break the masked image into two separate images again, simply select Unmask from the Element menu.

PageMaker 6.5, however, has eliminated the previously mentioned steps and made this simple for graphics (but not text). Each shape that can be drawn in PageMaker has a corresponding picture box. Create the picture box in the shape you want—rectangle, oval, circle, polygon (which can also be used to create star shapes)—and select Place from the File menu (see Figure 12.18). You have an instant mask (see Figure 12.19). There is no longer any monkeying around with the Mask command.

Figure 12.18

A picture box drawn in a desired shape.

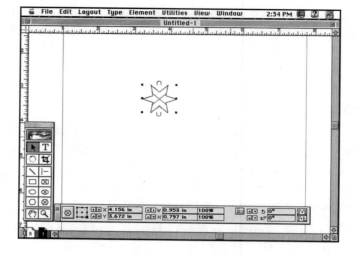

Figure 12.19

A graphic placed within picture box.

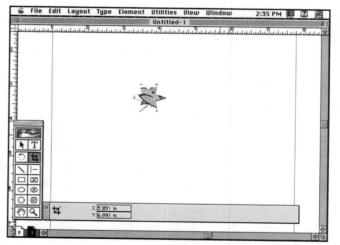

You still have to use the Mask command and the steps outlined previously, however, to mask text.

1. To create masked text, enter your text and then adjust the size of the text block.

2. Choose the Circle, Rectangle, or Polygon tool and draw the shape and size you would like.

3. Position the text under the object, allowing as much text to show through as you want.

4. With both objects selected, go to the Element menu and select Mask. The text is then masked within the shape.

Figures 12.20 and 12.21 show the before and after of this process. You also can use fills and other effects to create special masking effects.

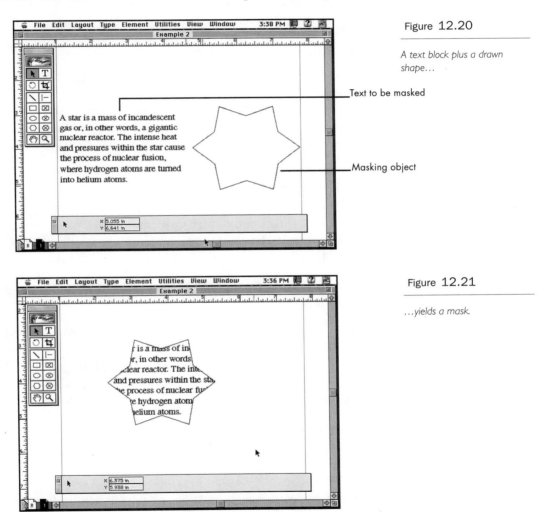

Figure 12.20

A text block plus a drawn shape...

Text to be masked

Masking object

Figure 12.21

...yields a mask.

Reusing Pages and Page Elements

Very often, you'll want to reuse the same page layout(s) or page element(s) in another publication. If you're designing a newsletter, magazine, book, or other publication that will remain fundamentally similar from issue to issue, you will of course want to save a template of your default layout and simply place new content on it.

Templates

You can create a template by saving a duplicate of a publication and stripping out all the old material and replacing it with new content, or you can automatically save a page or pages as a template in PageMaker. When you have created a document you want to reuse, select Save As from the Edit menu and check the radio button marked Template.

The next time you open the file, notice that the checked radio button on the Open File dialog box moves from Original to Copy. Click OK, and the file opens like any other PageMaker document, except that it is labeled Untitled, and you can save it under a new name corresponding to the new material you are adding. If it's a newsletter or magazine, it might be the issue number or publication month of the issue.

To edit a Template, click the Original radio button in the Open File dialog box.

If you want to check out the templates that Adobe provides with PageMaker 6.5, go to the Window menu and select Show Scripts. (To save disk space, Adobe's templates exist as scripts, not files.) A menu will come up and you scroll down to the Templates folder and see if there is anything you can use.

There is now, however, a much more elegant way of reusing your material—layers.

Layers

One of the best additions to Adobe's Photoshop (introduced in version 3.0) was the concept of layers, which function essentially as transparent overlays. The advantage of this is that you can add elements to an image without affecting other elements. If you dislike something, and it is on a separate layer, you can expunge the undesirable elements (or delete the layer entirely), and everything else remains untouched.

This concept has been applied to PageMaker in version 6.5 and it is a terrific way of trying out different aspects of a layout, or even reusing basic elements of a layout from job to job. To use this feature, put the variable elements on a new layer, and they can be stripped off and replaced by new elements.

The Layers palette is located in the Window menu in Show Layers. (See Figure 12.22.)

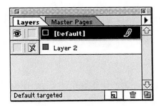

Figure 12.22

The Layers palette.

A default layer is produced when a new document is opened, and clicking the arrow at the top of the Layers palette enables you to manipulate the layers.

If you select New Layer, you will be asked to name it. Notice that the new layer has been assigned a color. What this means is that the handles of graphics and text blocks are in a different color for each layer, which enables you to determine at a glance what layer a page element is on. (Using the Color pop-up menu in the New Layer or Layer Options dialog box, you can change the color if you want.) Layers are added to the palette from the top down, which means that a layer at the top of the palette is the topmost layer on the page. Clicking and dragging the layer in the palette enables you to move it to a new location.

Objects on layers block or mask the objects on the layers beneath them. (In other words, just as transparent overlays would do.) You can rearrange the layers, for example, so that text is on top of a background. You can also create masks this way.

You can render a layer—and the page elements contained on it—visible or non-visible by clicking in the leftmost checkbox next to the layer name. If an eye appears, the layer is visible, and when you look at the page on the pasteboard the layer and layer elements are visible (and will block out layers beneath it). Clicking the eye renders the layer invisible. If the layer is rendered invisible, it will not print.

The layer that is currently selected, and which can be worked with, is indicated on the palette by highlighting. A line of text at the bottom of the palette also tells you which layer is active. All new page elements are added to the targeted (or active) layer.

Adding Layers

New layers can be added by clicking the icon at the bottom of the palette that resembles a dog-eared sheet of paper. The active layer can be deleted by clicking on the trash can icon. You can't accidentally delete a layer; you'll be asked to which other layer you want to move items on the trashed layer, or you can press Cancel.

Locking Layers

You can lock a layer, or render it completely unalterable, either by checking Lock Layer in the Layer Options dialog box, or by clicking in the right checkbox next to the layer name (next to the eye icon) until a pencil with a red line through it appears. The layer can be unlocked by clicking in either of those boxes again.

Selecting Layers

Selecting two or more layers simultaneously (they must be adjacent layers, however) enables you to merge them using the Merge Layers command. Many layers tend to suck up a lot of RAM, so if you don't need that many layers consider some merges.

Pasting Layers

With the Paste Remembers Layering function activated, if you cut or copy an object on one layer, selecting Paste will place it on the layer it originated from, regardless of what target layer is selected. Turning this off lets you cut, copy, and paste objects from layer to layer.

The uses of the Layers feature of PageMaker are limitless. It can be used as a template function, or to house your Master page grids (simply suppress them on printout). You can use layers to create a background for a page (either a screen tint or other image) and yet keep it perfectly editable and removable. If you are including spot color artwork, you can place each separate color in a different layer and, by selectively suppressing layers at printout time, ensure that they are in the proper register beforehand *and* print each separate color. (Just make sure that if you send your file to a service bureau for output that they know that you've put your separate colors in different layers.) You can also use layers to try out different type styles for portions of your page. If, for example, your text style has been predetermined, you can create the same head in different fonts on different layers, especially useful when someone else's approval needs to be obtained. This saves the time of repeatedly selecting the text and cycling through a set of fonts in the Style menu. Simply delete all the unwanted layers when you have made a selection.

Library

PageMaker's Library palette (located in the Plug-In palettes command under the Window menu; see Figure 12.23) enables you to store elements—graphics, text, and so on—that can be used in other jobs or documents, as well as throughout a current document (such as a book with many recurring icons). The advantage to the Library is that the same library is available regardless of what file is open. When you open the Library palette, the last Library you used will be the one displayed. However, by selecting Open Library, you can open any other Libraries you have created.

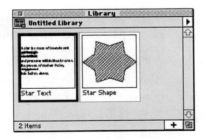

Figure 12.23

The Library palette.

The pop-up menu at the top of the Library enables you to create a new library. With the palette open, you can add objects to the library by selecting the object and clicking the plus sign at the bottom of the palette. You can view objects in the library by name or icon, and you can assign keywords to an object, enabling you to use the Search Library function to find objects by name or keyword(s).

The advantage to the Library palette is that you can save and easily access often- (or even not-often-) used objects and text. Objects in the library can be clicked and dragged onto a page and manipulated just like any other object placed into PageMaker.

Master Pages

Master pages (see Figure 12.24) have been covered in Chapter 3 but suffice it to say here that your work can be preserved by saving specific page formats as master pages. Master pages are now located with the Layers palette (accessed in the Window menu) and the Master Pages palette is similar in appearance to the Layers palette.

Figure 12.24

The Master Pages palette.

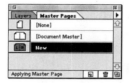

You can create new Master pages, assigning each one a set of specific attributes. You can also use the Apply command (see Figure 12.25) to apply a new Master page to the document you are currently working on, or to one or a range of pages. Say you have a one-column page of text, for example, and you suddenly realize you'd like to have the text on a two-column page. Here is how you can create and apply a new Master page:

1. Open the Master Pages palette in the Window menu. Click the arrow at the top of the palette and select New Master Page....

2. In the New Master Page dialog box, give the new Master page a distinctive name (such as "2-column" or something similar) and enter the margin settings, number of pages ("1" if it's a single page or "2" if it is designed to be a two-page spread), the number of columns and space between columns in the appropriate fields. Click Create when finished.

3. The new Master page is now selectable in the palette. Click on the arrow at the top of the palette again and select Apply....

4. In the Apply...dialog box, enter the page range (or "all") of the pages to which you would like the new Master page to apply, and select—from the pop-up menu in the center of the dialog box—the name of the Master page you just created.

5. Click Apply.

You can watch your text reflow into two columns. If you decide you do not like the two-column look, simply click your original master page in the Master Pages palette, and you'll be asked if you want to apply that Master page to the current page. (By simply clicking on a different Master page in the palette while a page is active, you can change Master pages at will.)

Figure 12.25

The Apply Master pages dialog box.

You also can toggle back and forth between or among your Master pages in the Master Pages palette.

Bailing Yourself Out

A lot of page design and layout is a case of trial and error. This was admittedly easy in the old days of paste-up; the adhesive wax used to fasten page elements to the board allowed things to be pulled off and repositioned easily enough. Somewhat similarly, PageMaker has two commands that can bail you out of a bad move.

Undo

As in many other applications, (Command-Z) [Control-Z] in PageMaker is an often-repeated formula, activating the Undo command (for mouse-oriented users, Undo is located in the Edit menu). This command, true to its word, "undoes" whatever action you just performed. If you moved something, selecting Undo returns the document to the state it was in before the action. Usually, the command tells you what it is you are undoing. If you typed something, for example, it will say, Undo Typing; if you moved a page element, it will say Undo Move, and so on. Although keyboard shortcuts save time and effort, it is helpful to use the pull-down menu, just to make sure you're undoing the right thing.

Unlike some programs, PageMaker has only one level of Undo; thus it only allows you to cancel the last action you made. Be careful about deselecting things because sometimes an action can only be undone as long as the page element or object involved is still selected. If an operation cannot be undone, the Edit menu item says Cannot Undo, and the command is grayed. This means you have deselected something and might be stuck with it.

After you Undo something and before you do something else, the Edit menu item enables you to Redo something you undid. If you Redo something, you can then Undo it again. You can use this Redo/Undo combination to toggle between two different approaches.

The Undo command is remarkably useful despite its seeming limitations. There is a way of subverting the one layer of Undo, but this approach is based on how often you save your documents.

Revert

The Revert command is located in the File menu. By selecting Revert, you can close your document and reopen the last saved version from the disk. This is a shortcut for closing a document without saving it and opening the original. Keep in mind that you can't Undo a Revert. Before you use Revert, you need make sure you have saved the document recently. You should always save frequently, and some find it handy to quick-save a document before doing anything, or at least anything drastic.

Mystery Reverts

PageMaker does several automatic saves of documents every so often, primarily for its own purposes. Specifically, every time you move to another page, PageMaker saves a temporary copy of the document, so that it remembers what is on the page you left so that it is there when you return to it. This is called a mini-save. So, if you don't remember if you saved recently, but you know you're on a new page, you can press Shift-Revert and you return to the document as it existed before the last mini-save (there is no menu location for this "Mini-Revert" command, however; the command exists only in the netherworld of PageMaker tips and tricks books.)

Save versus Save As...

When you select Save, PageMaker—like every other program—doesn't save a completely new version of the document. Instead it saves the changes you have made to the file and adds directions to the changes to the already-saved file. Depending on your hard disk, the new saved bits might exist in a different place than the original file. (This is why it helps to run Norton's Speed Disk occasionally to "defragment" files.) Although most programs do a good job of hiding the fact that your file is in pieces, all the fragments can take up more space than a new version of the file would; therefore, it is a good idea to use the Save As command occasionally (but be sure to save your file with a different name, otherwise it functions just like the general Save command). Using the Save As command enables PageMaker to collate all the fragments together and construct an entire file that is slightly more compact than the original. Depending on the complexity of the file, and how many fragments there are, any size differential might not always be perceptible in the File Size window of the Finder.

You can also use Save As as a safety net when trying moves and approaches that you are unsure of. Then, you can close the poorly-modified file and go back to whatever earlier version you liked best. This approach is slightly more labor-intensive (and keeping many different versions of the same file can get confusing), but it is a more flexible approach than the Revert or Undo commands.

Those are the basics of electronic paste-up in PageMaker. The next section covers ways of creating very long documents, such as books.

BUILDING MANY PAGES

A report, book, or catalog—any of the long form document types that might contain dozens or even hundreds of pages—require special organizational tools: table of contents, index, illustration list, page cross-references, chapter breaks, and specialized page numbering methods. PageMaker can help you quickly and efficiently accomplish all of these tasks—if not painlessly at least with a minimum of tedium.

Building a Book List

Here is some important advice for managing almost any long form document. Break long form documents into a series of smaller "chapter" publication files. By doing this you:

◆ Gain the advantages of PageMaker's automated book building command.

◆ Enable specialized page numbering using chapter prefixes or different numbering styles for front matter, tables of contents, appendixes, and indexes.

◆ Minimize the risk if you run into computer problems, because your job is broken down into more manageable pieces.

Using the Book Command

In order to glue together the sections of a long form publication, use PageMaker's book list feature—the Book...command in the Utilities menu. This command opens a dialog box like the one in Figure 12.26.

Figure 12.26

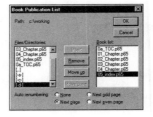

Assemble multiple files into one big publication with the Book Publication List dialog box.

In this dialog box you use the side-by-side scrolling lists of files, and the Insert, Remove, Move Up and Move Down buttons, to build a list of the files or chapters that you want to include in your publication.

Numbering Multiple-File Book Pages

The order of the book list you build on the right side of the Book command dialog box determines the order of your table of contents and the page numbering of your index items.

Your settings in the Auto Renumbering section of the Book command dialog box tell PageMaker how to adjust pages at the glue point between sections. PageMaker even automatically adds pages to your document so each chapter section begins on the correct left- or right-hand page. Here's how the Auto Renumbering section settings work:

- **None.** This button turns off Auto Renumbering. PageMaker uses the page numbers as they exist in the individual publication files in your book list. No new pages are added to your book.

- **Next page.** This setting gives consecutive numbers to all the pages in all the files in your book list. If the first chapter ends on page 29, the second chapter is automatically numbered beginning with page 30. No new pages are added to your book.

- **Next odd page.** With this button, PageMaker forces the first page in each new file to be an odd-numbered page (the usual setting for a book, with each chapter beginning on a right-hand, odd-numbered page). If the first chapter ends on page 29, for example, PageMaker inserts a new page 30 at the end of the chapter one file and moves on to begin chapter two with page 31. The new page 30 is blank except for the Master page material.

- **Next even page.** This button works just like the Next Odd Page button, except it makes the first page of the next file in a book list an even numbered page (a left-hand page), adding a fresh page at the end of the previous file if necessary.

Note

Auto Renumbering only affects pages that have the PageMaker page number symbol on them (either directly or on the Master pages). For basic page numbering information, see Chapter 3.

Organizing Chapters with Prefix Style Numbering

Technical documentation and other highly structured long form documents often use prefix style chapter numbering. The pages in the third chapter, for example, might be numbered 3.1, 3.2, 3.3, 3.4, and so on, and an appendix might be numbered with a letter prefix—A.1, A.2, A.3.

Prefix style page numbers can save you major grief if you must revise a long form document (which happens all too often, as any tech writer will tell you). If you number the book pages continuously from 1 to 200 and then cut page number 19 late in the production process, for example, PageMaker can easily renumber the pages; you might be forced to re-output more than 180 pages just because their page numbers shifted—even though the text on those pages had not changed in any other way. With prefix numbering the page numbers start over again with each chapter. This approach confines the "damage" to a single chapter.

In order to implement prefix numbering you must visit several PageMaker locations, and you must do so in each of the files in your book list.

1. Select Document Setup...from the File menu to open the Document Setup dialog box, (Command-Shift-P) [Control-Shift-P]. Check the Restart page numbering box.

2. In the Document Setup dialog box, click the Numbers...button to open the Page Numbering dialog box (see Figure 12.27). Type in your prefix and select the style of numbering you want to use.

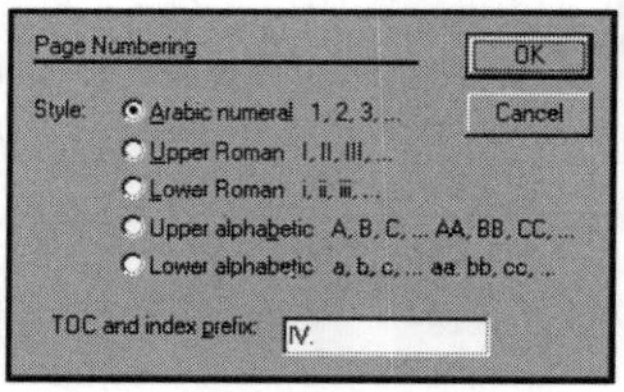

Figure 12.27

Creating chapter level prefix style numbering.

3. Edit the page numbering on the actual pages of the chapter file. (The Page Numbering dialog box only sets up prefix numbering for generating the table of contents and index.) Generally, you need to type the prefix before the page number in the header or footer story block on the Master page.

Table of Contents and Indexes

The basic PageMaker process of creating a table of contents and an index is basically the same, although you use different commands to do the work.

The steps are book, mark, compile, place, format.

1. **Book:** Assuming you are making a long form document by combining multiple-files, compose your book list as described at the beginning of this section.

2. **Mark:** Within the body text, mark your table of contents and index entries. The two marking methods are the biggest difference between PageMaker's indexing and table of contents facility.

3. **Compile:** Generate the actual table of contents and index lists using the appropriate commands in the Utilities menu, Create TOC...or Create Index....

   The Create TOC and Create Index commands only take a snapshot of your document. If you change the pagination of your document during editing, or change the order of the files in the book list, or modify the TOC or index marks, you must run the command again to update your table of contents.

4. **Place:** The compilation process creates a PageMaker story that you must then Place in the appropriate location in your document.

5. **Format:** The compiled TOC and index stories are formatted with standard paragraph styles. Among other fine tuning steps, you want to redefine those styles to conform with your publication design. (See the section on paragraph styles in Chapter 6 "Working With Text."

Constructing a Table of Contents

Although the basic principle of marking and compiling a list is quite similar for an index and a table of contents, here are important specific notes you need to actually put together a table of contents.

Put TOCs and Indexes In Their Own File

In a booked publication you probably want to place the TOC or index in their own separate publication files so you can give them their own numbering scheme, such as lowercase roman numerals or a special page number prefix. PageMaker won't allow you to change numbering schemes in mid-publication but you can easily accomplish this task by using the Book command to combine files with varying page numbering formats.

Marking Table of Contents Entries

It is easy to mark your table of contents entries. The mark is a paragraph level attribute; therefore, you can click anywhere in the paragraph you want to mark (you don't need to select the entire paragraph). Select Paragraph...from the Type menu to open the Paragraph Specifications dialog box. Check the Include in table of contents box.

Without a doubt, the very best way to mark your table of contents entries is by using paragraph styles. Instead of tediously marking paragraphs one-by-one, build the table of contents attribute right it into the structure of your document. You should already be using styles to format chapter titles, heads and subheads, which are the natural entries in a table of contents. You can easily make the Include in table of contents attribute a part of your paragraph style definitions for these elements.

Compiling a Table Of Contents

To create a table of contents, open the Create Table of Contents dialog box by selecting Create TOC...from the Utilities menu (see Figure 12.28).

Figure 12.28

The Create Table of Contents dialog box.

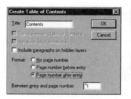

By using the options in the Create Table Of Contents dialog box you can automatically insert a title in your table of contents story, update the existing table of contents story by replacing it, and create a book-level table of contents by including all the files listed in the book list for the current publication file.

An important set of options enables you to set up the format of your TOC entries. You can specify the location of the page number in relation to the text of the entry.

You can also insert special characters to specially format your entries. Normally you want the default, a tab character (^t) to be inserted between the table of contents entry and the page number. However, the Create Table of Contents dialog box has a space where you can customize the entry layout. For example, you can insert a new line character (^n) to drop the page number to the next line. If you have a tab leader in your TOC entries, you might insert a thin space (^<) prior to the tab character so you can fine tune the format of the leader by applying formatting to the thin space.

Formatting TOC Entries

PageMaker's TOC feature attempts to automatically format your contents page by assigning some standard paragraph styles to the entries in the contents list. If you use styles to mark your TOC entries, your new TOC styles will adopt that style formatting. In doing so, PageMaker makes two style definition changes. It adds the initials "TOC" in front of the base style name, and it adds a right alignment tab at the right margin of the TOC story.

It is rare these TOC styles are suitable for your table of contents, because they are usually based on your book headlines that the TOC styles when first generated and they contain all sorts of styling not appropriate to your TOC—paragraph rules, all caps styling, tab settings, and so on. Go through each TOC style and edit it to your liking.

However, even though you can edit the TOC style definitions to your heart's content, you must not change their names. If you rename one of these standard TOC styles, PageMaker generates a new TOC style to replace the old one if you run the Create TOC command again, and you will lose all of your TOC style tuning work.

Use Find/Change to Fine Tune the TOC

The Create TOC command sucks up everything—and I mean everything—that's in your marked body text headline paragraph. This might

---

Dotting a Leader Tab

Leader tabs can improve the legibility of lists like a table of contents, where the eye needs to follow from one entry to the next.

To set a leader for a table of contents entry, open the TOC style and go to the Indents/Tabs dialog box. Select the tab that should get the leader by clicking the pull down arrow list from the Leader box in the dialog. Choose from dots, dashes, a solid line, or a custom job. You can also type in two characters and create your own custom leader.

include inline graphics, section numbering, dingbats, or any other material that you wouldn't want to include in the TOC. Open the TOC story in Story Editor and use the Find/Change dialog box to remove these extraneous items.

Use Book/Change Features for Special Book Lists

Nothing says that you must limit yourself to one table of contents—the one at the front of your book. Run detailed TOCs including the first three or four levels of headlines for each individual chapter by eliminating the other book chapters from that publication's book list. Then, when you create the TOC story for the entire book, use the Change feature to find and strip out all the lower-level heads. You can also create a special paragraph style for captions and use this same technique to create illustration lists.

Use Layers to Create Special Book Lists

Another option for special book lists is PageMaker 6.5's new capability to exclude or include table of contents entries based on their layer assignments. The Create Table of Contents dialog box now includes a new option and checkbox that makes this possible. The checkbox is labeled Include Paragraphs on Hidden Layers.

One way this might work to compile illustration lists is to isolate all your illustrations and captions on a single layer, apart from the other page elements such as the body text. This is especially easy to do if you are using frames to assemble illustrations and captions.

To establish a new layer for this purpose, open the Layers palette, and use the New Layer command on the palette's pop-up menu. You might name this special layer something that suggests its content, such as "Illustrations."

Don't forget that each layer has a color associated with it and you can designate that color when you create the new layer. This is an easy way to make sure your objects are in the proper layer because the sizing handles on the object will take on the color of the object's assigned layer.

Then, as you layout your document, make sure all the illustrations (or other special content such as maps or tables) are placed on your pages in this special layer. Just select the layer as the target layer (showing the pencil icon next to its name) prior to placing the item. Or, you can move an item from one layer to another without changing its position on the page by selecting the item and then clicking and dragging the tiny colored square next to the layer name in the palette to the target layer.

When you are ready to run your special book list, turn off all the layers except the one with your special items (illustrations or whatever). Make a layer invisible by clicking on the eye next to its name in the Layers palette.

Then, turn off the Include Paragraphs on Hidden Layers checkbox in the Create Table of Contents dialog box before completing the TOC creation operation. The resulting TOC story will only include the entries on the visible layer, the one containing your special content.

One caution is in order. Beware of page number inaccuracies and other bad consequences from editing your main body copy. By isolating your special content on a different layer from your main body text you cut yourself off from being able to include the content right in the text stream, perhaps as inline graphics. Therefore, the content won't automatically reposition when you edit the text and will require manual readjustment.

Indexing Basics

If you are constructing an index, chances are you've also compiled a table of contents. Many of the concepts already covered in the table of contents section apply to indexes. You should create a separate publication file to hold your index file, and you need to tweak the standard index paragraph styles to suit your own book design.

This section on constructing an index focuses in on some basic strategic advice about indexing in general, the special index coding power built into PageMaker, and the rich formatting power of the Create Index command.

Index versus Word List

A lot of the index construction process depends on whether you want a simple word list index, or a real index that includes multiple levels and cross-references between entries.

A simple word list—a *concordance*—is an alphabetical index of the principle words of a book. That's fairly easy to produce using a utility such as SonarBookends, but it's usually not what a reader really needs to find something in your book.

A truly useful index is more than a list of words. It's a list of themes, concepts, and topics. The rigorous indexer thinks hard about how the reader might be looking at the subject of the book when attempting to find some bit of data. An index also includes cross-references for items that might be referred to in more than one way.

A book on mammals that offers only a concordance, for example, might include references in its index for every species named in the text. But a mere concordance might omit useful references to endangered species or habitats or even quotes from poems that mention the animals. And that means the reader relying on the concordance for help might miss all that information.

Your choice—concordance or true index—determines the amount of work you must do. The computer can help you get started, but not even the powerful indexing features of PageMaker can do the thinking for you.

SonarBookends: Index/ TOC Generator Plug-in

SonarBookends from Virginia Systems is a stand-alone application that can be launched from within PageMaker by an accompanying plug-in. The plug-in is titled "Export to Sonar," and when it is accessed, it switches SonarBookends on and ports any selected text over for processing.

Master Topic Lists

Whether you are making a concordance or a real index, you should begin by creating a master topic list. This is true whether you are going to try to mark the index in your word processor during the writing process, or you are marking an index for a complete manuscript. There are two basic reasons for using a master topic list, and they both can save you hours of work—automation and consistency.

◆ **Automation:** Creating a master topic list in advance of marking your index entries in the text enables you to quickly assign those topics to your entry locations. You won't have to type a topic.

◆ **Consistency:** If you use inconsistent headings you waste a lot of time editing your final compiled index to bring these inconsistent headings together. A master topic list helps you avoid inconsistencies such as variations in spelling and multiple ways of referring to the same subject.

As mentioned in the previous section, if you are indexing a completed manuscript, consider using the SonarBookends Plug-in to make a strong start on creating your master topic list. This Plug-in can quickly compile a concordance of the words in your document based on their frequency of appearance. You can then massage this text file in your word processor to create a master topic list for importation into PageMaker.

One good way to compile a master topics list is to take notes as you work your way through the text. This approach works really well if you are not only the layout person on the project but are also writing the text in the first place.

Also, you may want to compile the table of contents before you do the indexing. Table of contents entries, especially ones that compile multiple levels of headlines, are great sources for index topics.

SonarBookends works in a very different way from the more powerful PageMaker tools for this purpose. It basically is a search engine that looks for occurrences of words or phrases. Instead of marking index or TOC entries directly in PageMaker by inserting index entries or by turning on the attribute to include a paragraph in the table of contents, SonarBookends compiles page number locations by finding matches for words or phrases in reference lists that you provide.

SonarBookends can format the resulting compilations of entries and page numbers into a variety of formats, from a basic list to a multilevel style index. It can compile entries from a single file or an entire folder. There is a mechanism for compiling cross-reference data.

SonarBookends can be used in three different ways to compile a list of entries, though all three can be mixed and matched to produce the final index:

◆ **Word Frequency:** This is based on how often words appear in the documents being indexed, with more common words automatically eliminated.

continues

◆ **Word/Phrase List:** This is based on a user-supplied list of words and phrases stored in a Text-only file, incorporating advanced indexing techniques such as Boolean operations and wild cards.

◆ **Proper Noun:** Using capitalization and punctuation rules, words that make up a proper noun can be identified, with more common items automatically eliminated.

The indexing capabilities of PageMaker are more powerful and interactive than those found in SonarBookends, but some people also feel they are more complex to master. SonarBookends, on the other hand, allows you to easily automate the process of creating a simple index if such will suffice for your publication. If you can get by with a concordance or word list type of index, then SonarBookends would probably be a great way to go. On the other hand, it can sometimes be more tedious and time consuming to tune the SonarBookends search results than to simply mark the index entries in PageMaker. You'll need to experiment to see what's best for you.

Importing a Master Topic List

After you have created your master topic list you must still find a way to get all those topics listed in PageMaker's index topics dialog box. That's the only way they'll be available to you as you mark your index entries. If you don't import your master topic list into PageMaker, you need to type each index entry topic as you enter it and that takes a lot of time. It will also inevitably lead to inconsistent entries due to spelling mistakes.

PageMaker doesn't have an index topic importation feature. The fastest way to get a master topic list into PageMaker is to set up the topic list in your word processor. You might use the concordance list you compiled using SonarBookends for this purpose. Mark each item in the list as an index entry in your word processor using its particular method for doing so. In Microsoft Word 7 for Windows 95, for example, you would highlight each topic in the list and press [Alt-Shift-X] and then press Enter to accept the entry.

Place the word processor text into PageMaker. The topics are automatically entered in your publication's index, ready for quick and consistent use as you mark your entries. As soon as you've Placed the file of index entries, you can turn right around and immediately delete the word processor text. The index entries will remain as topics in the Show Index dialog box.

As mentioned earlier, you can use SonarBookends as a starting point for building the list from an existing manuscript. Also, some word processors, such as Word 7, have a built in feature for generating concordance lists.

Although it won't be a problem if you are simply importing a list of topics, there is one general drawback with importing index entries from a word processor. Any page range index coding in the word processor—Microsoft Word for example—will appear as two separate entries in PageMaker, one each for the first and last page in the range. You should avoid making page range entries in your word processor, because they cause work rather than save it. All the markers for the last page in the range have to be searched out and removed, recoding the first markers with PageMaker's page range information.

Coding Index Entries

Think of your index entries as additions to a list—a database—of locations and keywords. Basically, coding your entries involves clicking at the location in your text and entering that spot in the index database along with an index topic.

It's possible to select a word or phrase and have the selection automatically added to the index entries. However, it is generally smarter to work with a master topic list for reasons already explained—consistency and efficiency.

Do your indexing in Story Editor view. The indexing tools work in Layout view, but there's no advantage to working on the page during indexing. On the other hand, in Story Editor you can see the diamond shaped index markers as you add them to the text (see Figure 12.29). Also, you can work on the text in a continuous

One thing is for sure. You can use both together to save a lot of time. SonarBookends combined with PageMaker's own indexing features makes for extremely efficient and powerful indexing. SonarBookends is the fastest possible way for you to create an initial word list (using the word frequency type of search). You can then quickly massage that word list into the master topics list mentioned in the next section and import it into PageMaker using the techniques described later on in this chapter. With all those topics already set up you can then easily work your way through the text making your index entries.

SonarBookends also bills itself as a TOC generator. But it is hard to see why you would use it for that in PageMaker. The fastest way to compile a TOC in PageMaker is still by using styles to format your major headlines, and including the Include in TOC attribute in your style definitions.

stream without turning pages. Furthermore, you don't need to wait for Layout view to redraw the screen, a special problem if there are a lot of graphics on a page.

Figure 12.29

Using Story Editor view for indexing.

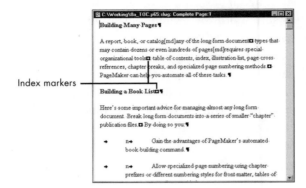

Index markers

Take the time to learn the keyboard shortcuts for indexing. Indexing requires a series of repetitive moves as you work your way through a large volume of text. You'll work faster if you keep your hands on the keyboard instead of being forced to reach for the mouse all the time. Table 12.2 provides a quick reference chart of the shortcuts you will need most often.

TABLE 12.2

INDEXING KEYBOARD SHORTCUTS

Function	Keyboard shortcut	Notes
Add entry	(Command-Y)[Control-Y]	The Add Index Entry dialog box appears.
Instant entry	(Command-Shift-Y) [Control-Shift-Y]	The selected text becomes an index entry; the Add Index Entry dialog box does not appear.

Function	Keyboard shortcut	Notes
Name entry	(Command-Option-Y) [Control-Alt-Y]	Enters the selected text—a person's name—so that it is listed last name first. Insert non-breaking spaces to lock middle names and titles into correct positions.
Copy to empty boxes	(Command-OK) [Control-OK]	After you've filled in your main topics, use this shortcut in the Select Topic dialog box. Any remaining empty boxes in the Add Entry box will be filled with the corresponding topics from the Select Topic dialog box.
Inspect entry	(Command-Y) [Control-Y]	Select the entry marker in Story view; then use this shortcut to view it. It's the same shortcut you use to add an entry.
Search	^;	When using Find to check a series of index entries, enter these characters in the Find box to search out index entry locations in Story view.

QuicKeys

One of the best products for creating macros is QuicKeys by CE Software (Mac only). QuicKeys enables you to record complex actions and assign to them a single keystroke.

You might, for example, record opening the Index dialog box and scrolling down in the "Next use of style" box. This saves time, and because the creation of an index is usually the last part of a document, time is of the essence.

Making an Index Entry

Click an insertion point in the text where you want to make a page reference. Use the keyboard shortcut (Command-Y) [Control-Y] or select the Index Entry command from the Utilities menu to open the Add Index Entry dialog box (see Figure 12.30).

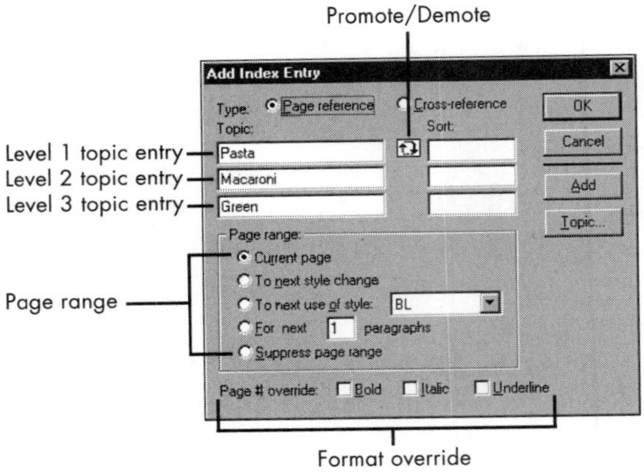

Figure 12.30

Adding an entry in the Add Index Entry dialog box.

Notice in Figure 12.30 the Page reference button (as opposed to a Cross-reference entry) has been selected automatically.

At this point, PageMaker knows where you want to locate the new index marker but still needs a topic to reference. You can type in a topic of your own here, or you can work from your existing topic list as much as possible (for the sake of consistency). Click the Topic...button to open the Select Topic dialog box (see Figure 12.31).

Figure 12.31

Selecting a topic from your master topic list.

Topic Dialog Box

The Topic dialog box does not list any page numbers; it provides a selection list of topics. You can now choose topics from your previously entered master list in this dialog box or from previous entries. The listings are grouped alphabetically into sections. You can move to a new section by using the Topic Section pull-down list or the Next Section button.

After selecting your topic, click OK. You return to the Add Index Entry dialog box.

Referencing Page Ranges

Sometimes an index needs to refer to a stretch of text—not just a single page but a range of pages. To create a page range reference, follow the basic index entry scenario and use some special buttons in the Index Entry dialog box (see Figure 12.30).

You can enlist PageMaker's help in compiling and calculating multipage index references. The Page Range options are smart enough to kick in only when needed. You can set a multiple page range option and let PageMaker automatically figure out whether the reference covers more than one page. Multiple page references are compiled only if the parameters extend over one or more page breaks.

Better Indexing Across Multiple Chapter Files

If you are working on a publication composed of several files, synchronize your index entries. This increases consistency by making the entire book's topics available for easy selection. The book list is a list of all the publication files being compiled by PageMaker Book feature, which is available in the Utilities menu.

Copy the book list to each file in the book by pressing the (Command) [Control] key (as you select the Book command in the file where you've created your book list. PageMaker immediately copies that book list to every listed file. Next, use the Import button in the Topic Selection dialog box. This button tells PageMaker to pull in all the index entries from all the files in the current publication's book list.

To set the page range reference for an index entry topic, use one of these Page Range options:

- **Current Page.** This is the standard, basic, single page reference mode. As you might expect, you get a single page number reference, tied to the insertion point you clicked in the text before using the Index Entry command.

- **To Next Style Change.** This option extends the index reference from your current page to the next change in paragraph styles. This button helps in situations that naturally breed style changes—for example, if you are referencing a sidebar that's formatted in a special style, which then returns to body text style. Likewise, use this button if you are coding a topic that has been styled for body text and continues to the next subhead.

- **To Next Use of Style.** This button specifies the end of a reference that is based on the next occurrence of a particular style. If you are making a reference at the beginning of a major headline section and the reference should carry the topic through that entire section, use this option and select the next major headline break paragraph style from the pull-down list.

- **For Next [x] Paragraphs.** If you know that the index topic runs for a certain number of paragraphs, this button enables you to enter a number, such as 16. PageMaker uses this entry to spike the ending page reference for the index entry 16 paragraphs later.

- **Suppress Page Range.** In some cases, you might want to insert an index entry without a page number reference. Use this button when you are first marking up a publication and you are not yet sure about your eventual page range reference.

Special Index Page Formatting

You can assign special text formatting to the page number of a particular entry by selecting one of the Page # Override options shown in Figure 12.32. How would you use this feature? You might italicize the page number for all entries that contain illustrations, or you could use bold face formatting to emphasize the principle index entries for a topic.

Now here's the tricky part—the Page # Override checkboxes are toggles, and they interact with any existing formatting, including paragraph styles. If you used italic styling for any of your index paragraph styles, checking italic for Page # Override will toggle off the already existing italic formatting for that entry's page number, giving you regular roman type instead of italic.

Think of it this way—these checkboxes have the same effect as if you applied the italic command (or bold or underline) to selected text using the Text tool. If the text is already italicized, then the command turns italic off.

One last thing about the Page # Override checkboxes. They are smart and they remember your override decisions. When you click one of these checkboxes, it stays clicked until you click it back off. In the meantime, until you turn off the checkbox, all your entries get that Page # Override formatting. You could end up with dozens of unintended italic (or bold or underline) page numbers if you forget to turn off a checkbox. On the other hand, if you want to italicize a bunch of consecutive entries, you don't have to bother about constantly clicking the override checkbox, because it stays clicked from entry to entry.

Setting Index Entry Sort Order

PageMaker uses strict ASCII sorting when compiling your index, sorting from left to right through each letter or digit of an entry. Spaces, symbols, and punctuation come first, followed by the alphabet.

When it comes to numbers, PageMaker sorts from left to right, one digit at a time, ignoring the overall magnitude of a multi-digit number. This means that when sorting numbers, PageMaker lists 1, 100, and 1,000 together before proceeding to 2, 20, and 2,000,000.

Also, the name St. James, for example, appears in the index closer to entries for street, store and state than to an entry for Saint Joseph (where you might like it to be).

You can deal with this sorting order challenge by using the Sort boxes located to the right of the Topic boxes in the Index Entry dialog box (see Figure 12.32). Your Sort box entry tells PageMaker to ignore the spelling of the actual topic entry and to sort the entry as if it was actually spelled a different way—as if it was the word you have entered in the Sort box.

Keep in mind that there's no global override for index sorting order, and you can't set the sorting order for a topic. It must be done at the individual entry level, so you must make one of these Sort box adjustments for every entry you want to be specially sorted in your index.

The illustration in Figure 12.32 shows an entry for the number 20, but tells PageMaker to sort it in the index so that it falls into proper order with three digit numbers. In other words, this entry sorts with the other two digit numbers, because it has a leading zero in the Sort box. Without the Sort box special instructions, this topic entry is sorted to the same location as 2, 200, and 2,000 because PageMaker uses left to right ASCII sorting.

As for the St. James and Saint James sorting problem, as you see in the illustration, you type out the full sort name—**Saint James**—in the Sort box next to the entry for *St. James*. This entry then sorts properly next to Saint James in the compiled index.

Setting Multiple Entries at One Location

The best indexes often help the reader find a book topic by referring to it in several different ways in the index—overlapping topics. These overlapping topic entries provide many different index gateways to a specific concept.

Use the Add...button in the Index Entry dialog box to place more than one entry at a single location, without returning to your text to click a new insertion point. When you click the Add button, you get a fresh Add Index Entry dialog box in which you can set a new index entry by going through all the normal topic selection steps. A new index marker appears in Story view for each click of the Add button.

When you use the Add...button the previous entry information carries over so that you can reuse part of it if you want. To prevent you from accidentally making duplicate entries, the Add button is grayed and unavailable until you make a change to the previous entry.

You can have PageMaker automatically help you fill out your Topic boxes. Add topic information at one of the three index entry levels. Then press the (Command) [Control] key as you click OK. The topic boxes you left empty are automatically filled in when you select your topic, without wiping out the topic information you've already provided.

The Promote/Demote button, the one with the curvy arrow symbol between the Topic and Sort boxes (refer back to Figure 12.30), makes quick work of helping you compose overlapping entries.

If you were indexing your cookbook, *Pasta for a Colorful Life*, for example, you would naturally end up with a lot of interlinking entries for the different kinds of pasta. Say you've just completed an entry for Pasta: Macaroni: Green, for example, and given the title of the book, you know somebody will want to access kinds of pasta by color. Click the Promote/Demote button. Each time you click it, this button rotates the topics on all three index levels like a carousel. The third level topic moves to the top and the top level topic slides down one. Your entry for

Pasta: Macaroni: Green, rotates to Green: Pasta: Macaroni. You now have a new index entry for the reader who might think to look under Green instead of Pasta or Macaroni.

Embedding Indexing Notes for Speed and Accuracy

This is a tip for the advanced indexer. To increase the speed at which you index, as well as increase consistency, place notes to yourself at the sub-levels in the Index dialog box. If you have a first level of *Internet,* for example, you might make a single entry for *World Wide Web* with a note to yourself on the third level to get all of the entries for *World Wide Web* from its first level heading. This saves time and ensures consistent entries.

One caution, PageMaker only supports three levels in the index. So, when you move the entries from the first level World Wide Web to Internet, you have to combine all of the third levels with the second levels. See the following example.

World Wide Web

> navigating, 100-101

>> links, 102

... might translate to:

Internet

> World Wide Web

>> navigating, 100-102

The indexer has judiciously combined the third level entry for links into the page range for navigating.

When used conscientiously, this technique can increase speed and consistency.

Don't forget, however, that notes you make in the indexing entry boxes must be edited out at some point in your indexing process or they will end up in the printed version of your book.

Adding a New Topic from Text

There are situations where you don't need to use the master topic list to select a topic. To make one of these ad hoc index entries, highlight some text and choose the Index entry command. You get an Add Index Entry dialog box that's already filled. You can fine tune the entry if you like, or you can click the Add button at this point to simultaneously make a new topic for the index and create a page reference entry at the location of the highlighted text.

If you know you won't need to tune an ad hoc entry, there's an even faster way to do this, bypassing the dialog box step. Highlight your text and press (Command-Shift-Y) [Control-Shift-Y] or and the Index Entry dialog box doesn't even appear. The index entry is made immediately using the defaults that are in place when you hit the key chord.

Making a Cross-Reference Entry

Cross-reference index entries don't have page numbers; instead, they link two related topics with *See* and *See also*. Under the index topic pasta, for example, you might find cross-references suggesting that you also see the entries for durham, semolina flour, sauce, and linguini.

When you click the Cross-reference button, the Add Index Entry dialog box looks slightly different than it does when you click the Page Reference button (see Figure 12.33).

Many of the important dialog box features remain the same regardless of which type of entry you are creating—page or cross-reference. The cross-reference version of the Index Entry dialog box, however, has one major difference when compared to the Page Reference dialog box. Look right in the center of the dialog box at the buttons that set up your *See also* language.

Figure 12.33

Adding a Cross-reference entry.

Here's what each of the cross-reference options does:

◆ **See [also]** This button—the smart version of the feature—puts PageMaker in charge of choosing between *See* and *See also*, making it the best choice for most occasions. It's so good, in fact, that most people use this option exclusively and don't bother with the other options.

You get a *See also* cross-reference when the reference topic matches one or more index reference that contain page numbers. This tells PageMaker that there's more than one place to find the information.

Instead of *See also*, you get a *See* reference when the cross-reference stands alone at its topic level and does not share the index location with any page number type entries. There's only one location to find the information.

◆ **See.** Use this button if, for some reason, you want to bypass PageMaker smarts for cross referencing and lock in an order for a simple, one-way style *See* cross-reference.

◆ **See also.** Use this button if you are sure that the current topic will have some page number references and therefore want to lock in this type of two-way cross-reference.

◆ **See herein and See also herein.** These two options work exactly like the *See* and *See also* cross-references, except you use them to refer to another location within a single level-one index entry topic. Use these cross-reference types to make sure the reader doesn't miss important information in a lengthy topic area.

Indexing Every Occurrence of a Word

When you want to be sure that every occurrence of a word has been indexed, PageMaker makes the job easy using the Change command. Enter the word or phrase to be indexed in the Find What box in the Find dialog box. Enter ^; (a carat and a semicolon) in the Change box. That's the metacharacter or special character code for an index marker in PageMaker.

Now you might be thinking, "what if my weird word appears in clusters, maybe five times close together. Aren't I likely to get five index entries referring to the same page?" You don't need to worry. PageMaker eliminates duplicate references on the same page when it compiles the index.

As with any mass search and replace operation, do be cautious about unleashing this technique. You might clutter up your index with a lot of spurious index entries if you don't build your search correctly.

Indexing Names

PageMaker makes it easy to properly sort indexed names. If you highlight *John Doe* and use a special keyboard combination, your entry appears in the index as *Doe, John* so that it can be sorted in last name order.

There is, however, one caveat to keep in mind when indexing names. PageMaker, without your help, has trouble making a last name sort out of any name that has more than two words in it. If you want to index a name such as *John Edwin Doe* so it lists under *Doe*, for example, you must insert a non-breaking space between *John* and *Edwin* so that PageMaker treats the first and middle names as a single word.

Keep in mind, if you insert non-breaking spaces in names, this technique affects line and page breaks. Although you should almost always index in Story Editor view, here's the one time where that advice breaks down. In this situation, you must check your line breaks as you index. You can work in Layout view so you can get instant feedback on the effects of your work, or you can work in Story Editor view and switch to Layout view (Command-E) [Control-E] to check line break effects whenever you make a complicated name entry.

Editing Your Index Electronically

The Show Index command can save you hours of drudgery. Instead of scanning through all your text, you can open a single dialog box to edit your index references. It's still a good idea to perform a final edit on a hard copy of your index, but an initial pass using this electronic edit technique makes it easy to clean up duplications and inconsistent spellings, and show where you should add overlapping cross-references.

Showing the Index

Select Show Index from the Utilities menu to open the Show Index dialog box (see Figure 12.34).

Figure 12.34

Using Show Index to edit your index.

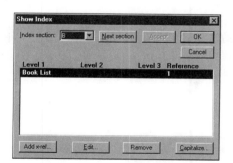

It looks a bit like the bottom of the Select Topic dialog box, doesn't it? Except here you are not merely looking at topics. You are able to edit the actual page references and cross-references for each of the topics.

When you use the Show Index command, PageMaker performs nearly the same work as when you use the Create Index command. It stops short, however, of loading a text placement icon with an index story for you to place in your publication. Instead of the text placement icon, you get an electronic list of your index entries.

It helps to think of this as a database screen, because that's essentially what it is. It's a list—a database—of all the entries associated with each of the diamond-shaped index markers embedded in your publication's text, including the page number where that specific marker is located.

In almost every other respect, the Show Index dialog box works just like the dialog boxes you use to initially create an index entry or cross-reference. To work on an entry, click the Edit button or double-click the entry. Depending on the type of entry you choose (page reference or cross-reference) you get a dialog box that has the word Edit instead of Add in the upper-left-hand corner. Everything else looks and works the same—page ranges, various reference options, and type style override checkboxes.

Saving or Discarding Index Entries

Use the Accept button regularly as you perform your electronic edit. Your edits are saved when you click OK at the end of an editing session; however, a single editing session can involve dozens or hundreds of edits. If you don't "Accept" them as you go and there's a power failure or similar problem before you click the final OK to end the editing session, you could lose all that work. The Accept button consolidates your work as you go.

You can remove an individual entry by clicking the Remove button. If you want to remove all index entries of any kind, press Command-Option-Shift-Remove) [Control-Alt-Shift-Remove]. Remove all page references with (Command-Option-Remove) [Control-Alt-Remove], and remove cross-references with (Command-Shift-Remove) [Control-Shift-Remove].

If you want to remove only the entries you have made since you last clicked OK or Accept, press the (Option) [Alt] key while clicking the Add X-ref button. You can reverse your decision (as long as you do it before you click Accept or OK again) by using (Option-Remove) [Alt-Remove].

Understanding Entry Location Codes

You might see some odd-looking two-letter codes next to or instead of the page numbers in the Show Index dialog box. Here's what they mean:

- **PB** tells you that the reference is in text that appears on the Pasteboard rather than a page.

- **LM** or **RM** means that the index marker somehow got onto one of the master pages, left or right.

- **OV** indicates that an index entry has been orphaned in some unset text (or overset text, as the typographers sometimes say), in a text block with a solid triangle at the bottom window-shade.

- **UN** tells you that the index marker is in some unplaced text in the Story Editor.

- **?** means that the page reference might have changed since the Show Index box was compiled.

- **HI** indicates that the entry is on a hidden layer.

Capitalizing Index Entries

PageMaker can handle the capitalization of all your index entries for you automatically. Click the Capitalize...button in the Show Index... dialog box to open the Capitalize dialog box (see Figure 12.35). You can then choose to capitalize only the current topic, all your level one entries (the usual form), or all entries.

Figure 12.35

The Capitalize dialog box.

Beware of one major catch when using automatic capitalization. The Capitalize button only works for the current publication; it is turned off automatically when you have a book list in place. You don't need to change your book list; instead, press the (Command) [Control] key when you select the Show Index command. Doing so temporarily opens just the index entries for your current publication so that you can make use of PageMaker's capitalization magic without messing about with your book list. After you've set your capitalization preferences, you can close and re-open the Show Index dialog box to conduct further editing on the entire book list.

Contextual Index Editing

Unfortunately, as terrific as the Show Index feature is for getting a lot of indexing work done in a hurry, you get no sense of context when you use the Show Index database to edit your index electronically. The Show Index dialog box does not show you the text that surrounds an entry location. That index entry referring to page 98 might or might not be perfectly appropriate and accurate for the text that appears on that page and this is especially true if you are working with text that was indexed by the writer at the word processor stage and imported into PageMaker, or when you have a team of people working on an index and making a final editing pass. For top-flight index editing the only way to be absolutely sure is to go to page 98 and read your body copy, opening up the index marker to see what it says in context.

To quickly work you way through your text, checking existing entries in context, use the Search Again command. In Story Editor, at the top of a story, open up the Find box. In the Find What box enter ^; (carat-semicolon). Click Find and PageMaker highlights the first index marker. Click the Story Editor text to switch it forward without closing the Find dialog box. With the marker highlighted, you can use the (Command-;) [Control-;] semicolon keyboard shortcut to quickly open up the marker so that you can see the entry and simultaneously read the text where it's located. To find the next index marker location, use Find Next by pressing (Command-G) [Control-G]. Use this technique repeatedly to move through your text and you are able to conduct a fine-grained, contextual edit of your index.

Creating, Placing, and Styling Your Index

Now for the easiest part of making an index in PageMaker—actually turning all these index markers into a story you can place in your book. You can accomplish this step with the Create Index command in the Utilities menu; it works much like the Create TOC command. Create Index searches through your text, including all your book publications if you like, and compiles the topics and page locations into a list.

Keep in mind—just like the corresponding table of contents operation—the Create Index command isn't updated in real time. In other words, if you edit your index markers after compiling your index story, the index story will not be updated. You need to run the Create Index command again.

Creating Your Index

The Create Index dialog box is simple to use (see Figure 12.36). Make a few obvious choices and then click OK, unless you want to spend some time tinkering with the formatting of your index. More on the Format button in a moment.

Figure 12.36

The Create Index dialog box.

You can automatically include a title in your index story by typing one into the Title entry box. Logically enough, it is formatted with the Index Title style. Again, this works just like the Create TOC command.

If you have previously run the Create Index command, and have an index placed in your publication, you probably would like to replace the old one. If so, check the Replace Existing Index box.

You almost certainly want to check the Include Book Publications checkbox.

Removing Unreferenced Topics

There's a dangerous but powerful option in the Create Index dialog box. It's the Remove Unreferenced Topics checkbox. Don't turn that option on unless you are irrevocably and unequivocally certain that you are at the final stage of making your index. It's a great way to weed out orphaned topics but compiling an index with this option checked deletes empty topics forever.

Formatting Your Index

Click the Format button to open the Index Format dialog box (see Figure 12.37).

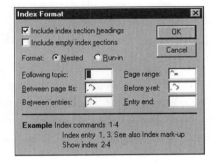

This fairly complex dialog box has been set up by default to handle most situations but you can harness the power of this dialog box to apply many special formatting options to your index:

◆ The Example section at the bottom of the dialog box gives you a visual representation of the effects of your formatting option choices.

◆ In most cases, section headings are left out for any letters of the alphabet that have no index entries. You can override the default and include these headings by checking the Include Empty Index Sections checkbox.

- Nested index entries are indented and allocate a separate paragraph to each entry. The Run-in style is also indented but runs together the entries for each level in a single paragraph.

- The remaining six entry boxes cause the insertion of characters in various positions in an index entry (generally one of the metacharacters used to represent special characters in the Change and Find dialog boxes):

  - **Following Topic.** Whatever you enter in this box is inserted between each topic and its first page number reference at all three possible topic levels.

  - **Page Range.** Some users place a hyphen between page numbers to indicate a page range. But because you're a typesetting pro, you want to use an en dash. The ^= metacharacter does just that.

  - **Between Page #s.** In most indexes, the page numbers relevant to a topic appear in a list. You probably want commas but you might also use colons, semicolons, or a regular space with no punctuation at all.

  - **Before Cross-references.** Cross-reference entries (See, See also, and so on) generally ought to ride on their own line and shouldn't be mixed in with page numbers. The default for this box is a new line character (^n), which drops whatever follows down to the next line.

  - **Between Entries.** This formatting option is determined by your choice between a run-in or nested style index although you can add your own formatting choices to the basic setup.

  - **Entry End.** An entry is any item that has a cross-reference or a page number after it. The default is to leave this box empty, because PageMaker inserts a paragraph return automatically after each entry in the index.

Placing and Styling the Index

After you have finally finished all the preparatory steps it's almost anticlimactic to click OK in the Create Index dialog box. When you perform this step PageMaker goes through the same sort of compilation work as when you use the Create TOC command. When it is finished, you get a loaded text pointer with which to place your index story. If you had previously generated an index and chose the Replace Existing Index option, the index is updated automatically.

As with a table of contents, it's usually best to build the index as a separate document that can be included in the book list for a large book.

PageMaker creates some automatic and standard styles for the index. Each style begins with the word *Index*; one is created for the title, the sections, and each topic level (Level 1, Level 2, and Level 3). As long as you don't change the names of these styles, you can edit the style definitions into any format you want, just as you can work with the TOC paragraph styles. You probably want the entries, for example, to appear in a small point size (such as 9 or 10) of the same font as your body copy.

Finishing Touches for the Book

This section offers some finishing touch tweaks that can help you make your book-length document look more professional. You can add running headers and footers, create page cross-references, set up footnotes, and establish bleeder tabs.

Making Running Headers and Footers

Running headers and footers are the entries at the top or bottom of pages that tell the reader at a glance the specific contents of the page. Dictionaries, encyclopedias, catalogs, phone directories, classified ads— these types of publications have traditionally been bone-wearying, tedious endeavors. The running heads had to be constructed by hand, and any change in the text triggered a whole new editing cycle.

You must select a text block within the target story with the Pointer tool before running this Plug-in. Figure 12.38 shows the Running Headers & Footers dialog box.

Figure 12.38

The Running Headers & Footers dialog box.

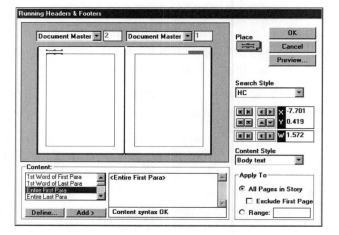

Follow these steps to set up your running headers and footers.

1. Open the Running Headers & Footers Plug-in and begin by selecting the grid you want to use to position the running header or footer text blocks. Choose a master page or specific regular page from the pop-up menus at the top of the preview box area.

2. Use the Place button to drag a running header or footer text block out onto the page preview area of the Plug-in.

3. Use the X, Y, and W Position & Width boxes and the nudge buttons to position the running header/footer text blocks. The row of buttons on the left can be used to snap the text blocks to guides or the edges of the page.

4. If you need more than one header/footer, repeat the process until you have text blocks to meet your needs.

   Keep in mind, as powerful as this Running Headers & Footers Plug-in is, it does not move other page elements. It merely adds the header or footer to the page. This means you must design your page to leave space for the insertion of the header or footer text block.

5. Next, tell PageMaker what paragraph styles should be used for the running header/footer operation. Select a Search Style. Often this is a headline style. It might also be the style used for the listings in a directory. Or you can select Any Style to get the broadest possible search.

6. Select a Content Style. Generally you want to set up special paragraph styles for this purpose, perhaps using different styles for left and right pages.

7. Tell PageMaker which pages should get each of your headers and footers in the Apply To section. You can exclude the first page, as you would want to do if you were composing headers and footer for a chapter with a major chapter break. You can also list a page range in the provided text box.

8. Select a target text block by clicking it.

9. In the Content section, select one of the predefined items, you might want the running header on the left page of a text book, for example, to contain the "Entire First Para" of your chosen Search Style (which in this case would be one of your headline styles).

10. When you click the Add button (or double-click the chosen item) the selection is copied into the right-hand scrolling list.

11. Add any static text you want to go with the extracted content—a chapter number or title, for example.

12. You might want to create your own specialized content definition, or to prevent the standard content items from picking up certain words. Click the Define button to open the custom selector dialog box (see Figure 12.39).

Figure 12.39

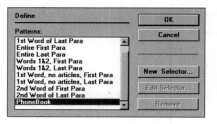

The Custom Selector dialog box for the Running Header & Footer Plug-in

13. Choose a Selector from the list. You can base your custom content definition on one of PageMaker's pre-built definitions, or you can edit a Selector you had previously defined. You are only allowed to edit a Selector that you have created, so you can't wreck the built-in Selector definitions.

Usually it's easiest to choose an existing Selector and click the New Selector button. This opens the Edit Selector dialog box (see Figure 12.40).

Figure 12.40

The Edit Selector dialog box, based on the pre-built Selector "1st Word of First Para."

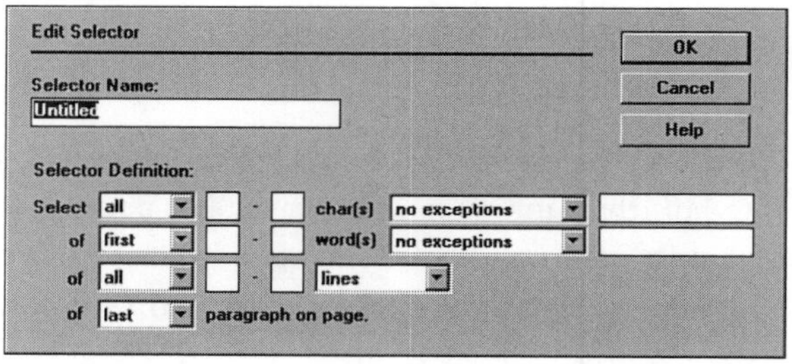

14. Name your new selector.

15. Choose your defining terms. You can extract characters, words, lines (or sentences in a pull-down list), and paragraphs—all from items in your chosen story that match the Search Style you chose in the main Running Header & Footer dialog box.

Take special note that the character and word definitions enable you to exclude or limit content to certain letters or words that you can type into the available text entry box. You could exclude numbers, or foreign language items, or titles, or almost anything you want.

After you've performed these steps, you can check your results by clicking the Preview button.

16. After you finally click OK in the main Running Headers & Footers dialog box you get a thermometer progress bar and you are taken back to the location where you originally selected a text block for the target story.

Remember, this Plug-in processes your document and must be re-run to pick up changes if you edit the document after it has been run. However, you can run the Plug-in again at any time to update the entries. You can remove headers or footers by opening up the Plug-in after clicking the target story. Then click and drag the header/footer text blocks from the preview box pages.

Setting Up Page Cross-References

A page cross-reference is where the text covering a subject on one page refers to some additional information on another page. Books tend to use a lot of these references; it would have been nice to have such a feature in producing this book, in fact.

PageMaker doesn't support dynamic cross-referencing. You must do it by hand, which is not fun. That is to say, unlike most professional level word processors, PageMaker won't automatically track your page cross-references and you will need to perform the task manually. The procedure outline here helps you automate it about as much as that is possible in this stage of PageMaker's development.

You can use PageMaker's indexing tools to automatically compile lists of your cross-references. Using these lists you can easily flip through your publication and type in the page numbers for the references. This technique uses the index as an easily updateable database to manage the locations of all your page references.

Beware that you'll be generating a number of temporary index items, and at the end of the process you need to be absolutely certain you remove those items from the index. It would be horribly embarrassing if your book went to press with all those strange entries accidentally left in the index.

Here are the steps to partially automate the page cross-referencing process:

1. Insert cross-references in the text. When you want to make a cross-reference, refer to it in text in a standard way. In text at the source locations, for example, always use a format such as (see page [*?*]). You need some pattern you can search out when you want to insert the actual page numbers.

2. Code references in the index. When the text is layed out, insert index markers at each of your cross-referenced locations, source and target. Use the Find command to locate the text references and number each reference consecutively in its index entry. Begin all your index entries with the same set of characters so the references will all be collected in one location when you compile your index story. You could use *so for your source entries, for example, and *ta for your target entries. Number the entries.

3. Compile your master cross-reference list. After all the references are marked, compile the index story and print it. Cut out the lists of marked source and target locations, side by side. Line them up so that each entry in one list corresponds to the entry in the other list.

4. Back up your document. Before inserting reference page numbers in text, make a copy of your publication in case you need to do this job over again for some reason. After you replace your searchable page reference placeholders with the real page locations you will have a hard time finding them again.

5. Use Story Editor and Find Again to locate references. In Story Editor, search your test for your page number reference points (for example, you might have used [*?*] as a placeholder for the page number.

6. Insert cross-reference page numbers. At each found location, use the list from your index to find the page number and type it in, replacing the placeholder.

7. Be sure to remove the lists from the index. When you're finished, don't forget to delete the Seek and Locate lists from your real index.

Setting Footnotes

PageMaker does not provide a footnoting feature, despite its impressive indexing and table of contents power. The best way to generate your footnotes is to compile them in a word processor. The PageMaker import filter for certain word processors, notably Microsoft Word, leaves all the footnote numbers (in superscript) in place and collects all your page level footnotes into endnotes at the end of the story. If you bring your Word text into PageMaker in chapter-size bites, you can create chapter-level endnotes with little discomfort.

If you want page-level footnotes rather than endnotes, here's a recipe you can try:

◆ **Use a Master Page frame to create a footnote preserve.** Before you place your main body copy, establish a frame placeholder at the bottom of the master pages that applies to your body copy where you want footnotes. Set a text wrap on the frame.

◆ **Place text.** Place your main body copy. Notice the footnote frame with the text wrap fends the body copy out of your intended footnote area.

◆ **Pasteboard the endnotes.** After the story has been placed, use the Text tool to cut and paste your endnotes onto the Pasteboard as a new story. You can pull your page notes out of this text.

◆ **Paste notes into frames.** Go to each page and Copy/Paste each note into the frame at the bottom of the appropriate page.

Creating Bleeder Tabs

Bleeder tabs are an excellent visual tool for getting a grip on a complex book. Bleeder tabs are the bars of ink that step down along the edges of pages from one section or chapter to the next. The first chapter gets the top bleeder tab, the second chapter gets one slightly lower, and so on down the line.

Why are they called bleeder tabs? Because they are a poor person's version of those die cut tabs you find in loose-leaf binders and some bound books. They are created by bleeding the block of ink off the edge of the page, past the crop marks. The printer then trims the page, leaving ink right to the edge of the paper. The final result is a series of strips along the page edges that show you exactly where each chapter begins and ends.

To make your own bleeder tabs, follow these steps:

◆ **Consult with your printer**. You must consult with your printer before doing bleeder tabs. The success of this process depends on how much the ink spreads on the edges of the paper you have chosen, in addition to many other factors. Describe what you plan to do and ask the printer how much bleed you need to allow outside the crop marks.

◆ **Set up your Master Page**. Design a master page template that contains all of the bleeder tabs. This helps you get the spacing just right between the tabs. You can use this template as a base to make a new master page for each tabbed section. Remember that you should put the bleeder tabs only on the right-hand pages if you are working with facing pages.

If you are going to place some type over the bleeder types, set that up on this template master page as well.

◆ **Create your tab index**. One page at the front of the book needs to contain all the tabs, so the reader can use it as a reference to go to the tabbed locations. You use your master page template to create this page. It's the only other page in addition to your master template that contains all the bleeder tabs. It's the visual guide to your tab system (see Figure 12.41).

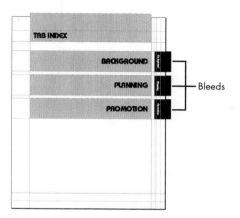

Figure 12.41

The bleeder tab index page.

◆ **Setup the rest of your chapter files.** For each of your publication files, copy the bleeder page master template elements to your body copy master, then delete all the tabs that don't apply to that chapter, being careful not to disturb the remaining tab. The tab will appear on all the body copy pages based on this Master Page.

SUMMARY

PageMaker is all about final products: documents, newsletters, books, and so on. This chapter provided some tips and techniques in this area. The following chapter discusses scripting techniques that can help you save time over the course of a long project.

Chapter 13

AUTOMATING PAGEMAKER

In this chapter, you are given a brief introduction to PageMaker's two main automation tools: scripting and tagging.

Scripting can be done in PageMaker to automate tasks, and tagging can be done in a word processor to format text you're going to import into PageMaker.

Both scripting and tagging can save hours of work; and, at the same time, they improve consistency and eliminate mistakes. If any of this sounds good to you, read on for an explanation.

SCRIPTING

A script is a computer program. If you have any knowledge or understanding of what computer programs can do, then you know what PageMaker scripts can do. If you don't, you're about to learn.

Note

PageMaker scripting has been around since version 4.2. It has been very significantly enhanced in version 6.5; but, if you're familiar with an earlier version of PageMaker scripting, you'll notice that much of what you already know hasn't changed—except for the better.

A PageMaker script can do anything you can do manually in PageMaker. A script can do something as basic as save your document, or change the font or size or color of selected text; or it can do something as complex as delete all unused styles.

The PageMaker scripting language is, for a programming language, easy to learn. There definitely is a learning curve, but on the other hand it's not quite rocket science either.

A script (or any computer program) is a series of instructions that execute themselves, based on data that is provided to the program. The program can execute simple instructions (change font to Helvetica). It can also make decisions (if font is Helvetica, change color to red) and loop back on itself (examine every style, one at a time; determine whether it is being used; delete it if it's not).

Why Script?

The reasons for using scripts are many. Depending on the task, a script can be faster, more accurate, or more consistent than doing the task by hand.

What you have to weigh, if you're writing or modifying your own script as opposed to using a ready-made one, is the trade-off between the time it takes you to get the script ready to run and the time you save by running it. There's obviously no generic answer to that question. It depends on your own circumstances. If you run some of the scripts that come with PageMaker, however, to give yourself an idea of the time a script can save, and invest a little time into looking at PageMaker's scripting language to learn how much time it takes to write or modify a script, then you are that much closer to being able to evaluate the advisability of scripting specific tasks.

The Scripts Palette

PageMaker scripts are found in the Scripts palette, which you access through the Plug-in palettes pop-up menu in the Window menu (see Figure 13.1).

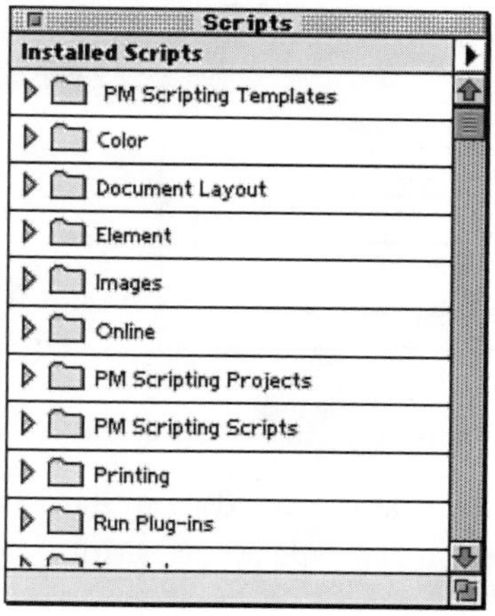

Figure 13.1

PageMaker's Scripts palette.

The things you see in the scrolling list in the Scripts palette, by the way, are sub-folders and text files that are physically located on your hard disk. On the Macintosh, they're inside your PageMaker folder, in RSRC/Plugins/Scripts.

On the PC, they're inside your PageMaker directory, in RSRC/ USENGLSH/PLUGINS/SCRIPTS. If you have a script that's a text file and you want it to show up in your palette (which you must do if you actually want to run it), put that text file in the location just mentioned.

Now, back to the palette itself: Toggle the little triangular arrows to the left to open the folders, until you find the script you want. To run a script, double-click it.

Notice the black triangle in the upper-right corner of the Scripts palette? Just like many other palettes, that's the pop-up button for the Scripts palette's own menu (see Figure 13.2).

Figure 13.2

The Scripts palette with its menu popped-up.

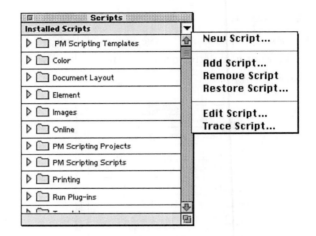

The items on the menu are fairly easy to explain:

◆ New Script opens a new window in the script editor (see Figure 13.3), where you can type a new script.

Figure 13.3

The script editor's window, with a portion of a script showing.

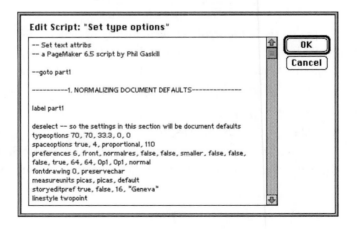

◆ Add Script enables you to find an existing text file, anywhere on your computer, and move it (through dialog boxes) to the same location as your other scripts, so that it displays in the palette. This might or might not be easier than manually moving the text file in the Finder; the final result is identical.

◆ Remove Script is a very handy tool—it enables you to remove a script from the display in the palette by putting the script's text file into a different folder. The script is not deleted from your computer: it's just removed from view. Because the list in the Scripts palette can quickly grow unwieldy in size, it's smart to use this for scripts you seldom use but don't want to trash.

◆ Restore Script reverses the "Remove Script" process, moving a script you've "hidden" back into view.

◆ Edit Script opens the selected script for editing, in the same window that the "New Script" command invokes (see Figure 13.3). The shortcut keystroke for this is (Command-Click) [Control-Click] (on the script's name in the scrolling list).

◆ Trace Script runs the selected script in "trace" mode, which means one step at a time. This is handy for troubleshooting: if an error occurs, you see a message telling you what (and where) the error is.

That's all you have to know in order to run an existing script. Just find the script in the palette and double-click it.

Writing a Script

PageMaker includes about 480 scripting commands, controls, functions, and operators. In other words, it includes the elements of scripting. That's way too many to mention in this chapter, let alone describe how they work. If you want to get into writing scripts, read the Adobe documentation; for that, you can begin with the online help file that comes with PageMaker.

Rather than describing all the possible scripting commands, here is a listing and explanation of one script, so you can get the general idea of what scripting is all about.

Note

Part of the Adobe scripting documentation is a separate book from Adobe Press titled Adobe PageMaker Scripting: A Guide to Desktop Automation, *by Hans Hansen. This book is the only complete reference to all the script elements.*

The online help file that ships with PageMaker lists many of the scripting elements, together with their descriptions, and provides helpful information about scripting in general. If you don't have the book, you won't know about all the elements—and, by direct implication, all PageMaker's scripting capabilities.

Grammar

The first thing you have to know about any programming language is its "grammar"—its particular rules of syntax and vocabulary.

Note

To draw a parallel between a programming language and the English language, in programming languages you can't say "ain't" (nonexistent word), nor can you say "It's been over fifty years between now and the end of World War II" if you mean "between the end of World War II and now" (wrong order).

The reason you have to be careful about syntax and vocabulary is that computers (and computer programs such as PageMaker) have no intelligence; your computer attempts to do *exactly* what you tell it to—no more, no less. If you run a script that tells PageMaker to delete all its colors or all its styles, for example, PageMaker doesn't know whether you meant it or not; it can only assume you *did* mean it. Similarly, if you use the wrong word in a script or program, the computer attempts to do exactly that. If the word doesn't exist in that programming language, the computer comes to a halt because you gave it an illegal instruction. If your computer does know that word, you could be in deep trouble (depending, obviously, on the effect of that wrong word or wrong instruction).

The bottom line here is that you can't write a program, including a PageMaker script, without having access to—and literally following—the documentation that lists the exact syntax for each command. You have to spell every word correctly and include the proper additional information (called *parameters,* or *arguments*) with each command; every open parenthesis has to have a close parenthesis, every loop has to have an end-loop command, and so on.

How a Script Works

A script works very simply—it starts at the beginning and executes each instruction sequentially until it reaches the end. Of course, there are many potential twists on the "sequential" concept, because there can be loops and subroutines and jumps, but when you get right down to it, these "twists" are still sequential executions of instructions.

This chapter only has enough space to list an illustrative example script, and to discuss it point by point.

Scripting Considerations

In preparation for looking at the sample script in the next section, a couple of things should be explained first.

The first thing is that two hyphens (regardless of where the two hyphens are on a line), together with everything on the same line *following* the two hyphens, are ignored when the script executes; double hyphens, in other words, introduce what's called a *comment.* Comments are very useful, as you can easily see below, for such things as: script titles; descriptive "informal labels" for features of the script; testing of commands (such as turning commands on and off without having to delete and re-type them); and reminders to yourself of what you were doing, in case you want to study or modify the script later.

And, obviously, as you'll see in the script, more than two hyphens is also all right.

Use comments and labels freely. They can do no harm and they can do a lot of good. Document what you've done and the reasoning behind it. This can be very important when re-examining or improving the logic later. Programming needs to be very structured: Use comments and labels to show the structure, in terms of labeling the parts of the overall structure and what they do.

Be as excessive and redundant as you want in your use of labels. You can see, and it is explained later, that there is an actual command called *label;* you can also use a comment as an "informal label." You can use the label command to label a section of your script, whether you intend to ever have the script actually *use* that label or not; regardless, it's there for you to see.

As you can see in the example, there are numerous strings of hyphens, sometimes with informal labels in the middle, as a sort of "super" blank lines. There's nothing there, as far as the program is concerned; but there's plenty of helpful stuff there for the user's own benefit. Again, anything that helps you see or remember what you're doing is a good thing, and you should do it.

Use white space freely. White space (spaces and tabs) at the beginning or end of a line (which includes at the end of the "real" part of a line, before a comment that follows) is ignored by the program or script, as are totally blank lines. Use this to your advantage, by indenting things so that you can see their structure. As you read the script, you can see that things were indented and blank lines were inserted to make the structure more obvious to the reader. The *programming language* doesn't need this kind of help; *you* do. Use your own scheme; particularly, most people don't use quite as many blank lines as this example does. But none of it hurts; and if it helps you, it's all worth it. Use your own scheme, but use *some* scheme.

The most obvious example of the use of indents is to show the structure of a loop, especially if there are other loops inside an outer loop. But there are plenty of other uses. Do whatever makes sense to you.

A Sample Script

The script you'll see listed in this section, and then discussed after that, is a script written for a very specific purpose: I have a customer for whom I update a tool catalog a couple of times a year. He makes some of the easy changes in PageMaker himself, and then turns over the files to me for the "hard" stuff. Unfortunately, he doesn't know PageMaker very well, and his files are often a mess. It was the worst the first time I worked on the project, because this catalog had been going for a few years before I got involved; and the worst thing was the fractions, which he didn't know how to construct. And there's a *ton* of fractions in this catalog.

I needed a quick way to edit about 100 PageMaker files, changing the type options (where the settings for super- and subscript size and position are) for every existing text block. So I wrote this script. (It actually was a bit different in its original form, because PageMaker 4.2's scripting capabilities were less robust than the new version's, but the basic idea of the script hasn't changed from the beginning.) It has grown a bit over time, as I've added more bells and whistles to it. It later occurred to me, for example, that I could fix up the preferences on all these files in the same script. I've fixed the type options in the paragraph styles, which I was unable to do in PageMaker 4.2, 5.0, and 6.0; and, although all these files are single-page documents, I added multi-page capabilities just so I could demonstrate that in this chapter.

This is a fairly long script. Don't worry about studying it or trying to understand it at this point, although you should be able to pick up the general gist from the embedded (double-hyphened) comments; I'll discuss it afterwards and explain everything I've done.

```
=============================================================
-- Set text attributes
-- a PageMaker 6.5 script by Phil Gaskill, ©1996


--goto part1


----------1. NORMALIZING DOCUMENT DEFAULTS--------------


label part1


deselect -- so the part1 settings will be document
➡defaults
typeoptions 70, 70, 33.3, 0, 0
spaceoptions true, 4, proportional, 110
preferences 6, front, normalres, false, false, smaller,
➡false, false, false, true, 64, 64, 0p1, 0p1,
normal fontdrawing 0, preservechar
measureunits picas, picas, default
storyeditpref true, false, 16, "Geneva"
linestyle twopoint
zeropointreset
rulers on
guides on
view fit
stylepalette on


--goto end


--------------2. MODIFYING STYLES---------------------


label part2


getstylenames >> numstyles,mystyles


label LOOP #1
loop s = 1, numstyles
```

```
        stylebegin (mystyles(s))
        typeoptions 70,70,33.3,0,0
        styleend
endloop
label ENDLOOP #1


--goto end


--------3. MODIFYING EXISTING TEXT BLOCKS--------------


label part3


-----------Compensating for facing pages--------------


getpagenumbers >> startpage,numpages,...
getpageoptions >> ...,facing


p = startpage
oddeven = startpage%2
lastpage = startpage + numpages - 1


-------------Here we go.---------------------------------


label LOOP #2
if facing = 1          -- i.e., if facing pages is ON
        i = 2          -- we'll always jump by 2 pages
        --------------------------------------------
        label LOOP #3 - which is inside LOOP #2
        if oddeven = 0              -- first no. is even
                j = 0
                -- message "First page number is
                ➡even."
             else               -- first no. is odd
                j = 1
                -- message "First page number is
                ➡odd."
```

```
                endif
                label ENDLOOP #3

          . . . . . . . . . . . . . . . . . . . . . . . . . . . . . . . . . . . . . . . .
        else                  -- i.e., if facing pages is OFF
              i = 1           -- we jump by one page
              j = 0           -- and don't need to worry
                              -- about all that other stuff.
    endif
    label ENDLOOP #2

    --goto end


    . . . . . . . . . . . . . . . . . . . . The Loops . . . . . . . . . . . . . . . . . . . .


    label LOOP #4
    repeat    -- this is the beginning of the page "loop"
         page p

         getobjectlist >> objects,...
                         -- gets list of objects on this page
                         -- or spread, including pasteboard;
                         -- the only reason we need this is
                         -- to get the number of objects

         label LOOP #5 -- which is inside LOOP #4
         loop n = 1,objects
                         -- this is the beginning of the
                         ➥object loop

             select 1 -- object #1 is simply the back-most
                         ➥object

             getselectlist >> ...,...,kind,...

             label LOOP #6 -- which is inside LOOP #5
                         ➥if kind = 1
```

```
                              -- the number after "if kind ="
                            ➥narrows the scope:
                              -- 1=text; 3=line; 4=box; 5=oval;
                            ➥6=TIFF or bitmap;
                              -- 8 or 9=PICT; 10=metafile; 11=EPS;
                            ➥12=multigon

            textedit
            selectall
            typeoptions 70, 70, 33.3, 0

            --font "Times"
            --color "Blue"

                              -- we're done with this
                            ➥object;
                              -- now let's get the next
                            ➥one:

            select 1          -- necessary, since we used
                            ➥the text tool
            bringtofront      -- what was object #2 now
                            ➥becomes object #1
                                  -- because what was
                                ➥formerly back-most
                                  -- is now, thanks to
                                ➥the bringtofront,
                                  -- front-most, so what
                                ➥was formerly next
                                  -- to the back now
                                ➥becomes back-most.

            --elseif kind = 5

                --color "Blue"
                --bringtofront
```

```
        else          -- referring to kind = 1 at top of
                      ➡LOOP #6
                      -- so if kind *isn't* "1" or "5,"
                      ➡then it wasn't
                      -- the kind of object we were looking
                      ➡for, so we
                      -- just skip it:

                bringtofront      -- it's not necessary to
                                  ➡select it
                                  -- again, since we never
                                  ➡used the
                                  -- text tool on this
                                  ➡object

          endif
          label ENDLOOP #6

      endloop
      label ENDLOOP #5

                -- and on to the next page:

    p = p + i - j      -- increment page number for next
                       ➡iteration
    j = 0              -- we only subtract 1 once
                       ➡(if ever)

until p > lastpage     -- loops back to the «repeat»
label ENDLOOP #4

--goto end

-----------4. CLEANING UP AFTERWARDS-----------

label part4
```

```
page startpage      -- using variable, in case
                    -- first page no. isn't "1"
save                -- (if desired)
close               -- (if desired)


label end


======================================================
```

Whew! Quite a mouthful, isn't it? But it's actually pretty simple, once you see what it's all about. Only two concepts in this script are difficult; and it's entirely possible that you won't even think *those* two are difficult. I'll mention them as we come to them.

In order to save a little space, I'm going to delete most of the embedded comments in the following explanation, because the explanations cover what's in the comments anyway.

The explanations of each point follow the appropriate line or lines of code. Sometimes it's obviously appropriate to explain more than one line of code at a time, as in the very first two lines:

```
-- Set text attributes
-- a PageMaker 6.5 script by Phil Gaskill, ©1996
```

It's always a good idea to have a title, and any other information you think might be useful, at the beginning of a script. In fact, you could— and often should—put complete operating instructions here (all in comment form, of course).

```
--goto part1
```

The effect of this, if it weren't "commented out" (that is, if it didn't have the two hyphens in front of it) would be to jump directly to the line in the script that contains the command `label part1`.

This and the other `goto` instructions throughout the script are here for testing purposes. As I was developing the script, I would often want to test only one section of it, to save time. So I would un-comment (that is, remove the two hyphens from) this *goto* instruction right here, change the *argument* (the stuff after the command) to the appropriate label name (part1, part2, whatever), and also un-comment the *goto end* command at the *end* of the section I wanted to test (at the end of part1, in this example). Just remember to re-comment everything after you're done testing.

```
----------1. NORMALIZING DOCUMENT DEFAULTS-------------
```

This is what I've referred to above as an "informal label." Remember, *everything* after (and including) two hyphens is ignored when the script executes.

```
label part1
```

The above is an example of the `label` command. This command takes one argument: the name you want to give it. To jump to this particular line, you would need a `goto part1` command somewhere in the script.

```
deselect
```

This is to ensure that the following settings become document defaults. If you didn't deselect, and if anything actually was selected before you ran the script, then you wouldn't be setting defaults at all. Remember that changing defaults affects all *new* objects of the appropriate kind ("new" meaning being created after the time the default is changed); it does not affect any existing objects.

```
typeoptions 70, 70, 33.3, 0, 0
```

This changes the Type/Character/Options... dialog box settings. In order (which is, typically and unsurprisingly, the same order as in the dialog box), these numbers mean 70% small-cap size, 70% super- and subscript size, 33.3% superscript position, 0% subscript position (on the baseline), and no baseline shift. These are the settings I need for my fractions.

```
spaceoptions true, 4, proportional, 110
```

This changes the settings found in the bottom half of the Type/ Paragraph/Spacing dialog box to pair kerning on above four-point, proportional leading, and 110% autoleading.

```
preferences 6, front, normalres, false, false, smaller,
false, false, false, true, 64, 64, 0p1, 0p1, normal
```

The above changes some of the settings found in the General Preferences Menu to greek below six pixels, guides in front, graphics displayed at normal resolution, don't display loose lines, don't display "keeps" violations, save "smaller," curly quotes off, don't constrain values in Control palette to ruler increments, autoflow off, display the PPD name in the Print dialog box, reserve 64K RAM for drawing graphic elements, a 64K limit for maximum size image to include, a one-point horizontal nudge, a one-point vertical nudge, and the "normal" amount (250K) of Virtual Memory to free up in a PostScript printer prior to downloading a graphic.

```
fontdrawing 0, preservechar
```

This sets TrueType fonts to retain their character shape instead of their line spacing onscreen.

```
measureunits picas, picas, default
```

This sets the rulers to picas in both dimensions.

```
storyeditpref true, false, 16, "Geneva"
```

This sets the Story Editor preferences to display invisibles, to not display style names, and to use 16-point Geneva for its font.

```
linestyle twopoint
```

This sets the default "line" (rule) style to a two-point rule.

```
zeropointreset
```

This resets the zero point to the upper left corner of the page.

```
rulers on
guides on
```

These make sure that rulers and guides are turned on.

```
view fit
```

This sets the view to "fit-in-window."

```
stylepalette on
```

This one should be pretty obvious.

```
--goto end
```

This is one of the "commented-out" commands I use for testing while developing a script, discussed previously.

```
--------------2. MODIFYING STYLES---------------------
label part2
```

You have finished setting our document defaults; now you start Part 2 of the script—modifying the type options of the paragraph styles. Again, you don't have to comment out the labels like this one; you just have to comment out the *goto* instructions.

```
getstylenames >> numstyles,mystyles
```

This one short line combines several interesting and powerful features of PageMaker's scripting language:

1. The `getstylenames` command is an example of a query. It actually interrogates PageMaker, and this document specifically, to get the complete list of—in this case—style names that exist in the document.

2. The >> indicates that the scripting language should store the data returned by the query into the *variables* that are listed, separated by commas, to the right of the >>.

A *variable* is a data-storage area. Variables, or more properly the data in them, after first being *defined,* can be accessed at any later time in the execution of the script.

You name your own variables. You can use any combination of letters and numbers that is not already reserved or used by the scripting language. You can name your variables "x," "y," and "z" if you want. For variables that are important to the script and whose meaning you'll need to be able to understand at a glance, however, it's better to give them some kind of meaningful, descriptive name. For variables that are only used for temporary "counting" purposes in a loop, for example, it's fine to use single letters, because you normally don't need to remember exactly what bit of data they hold. If you notice which variables in this script I give meaningful names to, and which ones I only give letters to, you'll see what I mean.

In the end, it's up to you, though. Name your variables anything you want. I'm only *suggesting* that you use a meaningful scheme.

I've named my two variables here *numstyles,* because into this variable goes a number that *is* the number of styles; and *mystyles,* because into this variable goes the list of style names themselves. (I could probably have named it *stylenames,* but decided not to for some reason. *Mystyles* is descriptive enough.)

Anyway, if the first piece of data returned by the *getstylenames* query is the number 5, for example, then it is followed by five style names. In this same example, my variable *numstyles* would contain the value 5, and my variable *mystyles* would consist of a list of five style names.

3. The data returned by the query is allocated to the list of variables to the right of the **>>** according to the following scheme: The first item (call it a "value") returned goes into the first variable, the second value goes into the second variable, the third into the third, and so on. But—and this is both an

important and a handy "but"—if there aren't enough variables on the right to hold all the values, all the "extra" values are put into the *last* variable listed. That's how this line in this script works for me—no matter how many styles there are in this document, the number of styles goes into the first variable *(numstyles)*, and then *all* the style names go into the only other variable that's there *(mystyles)*.

These variables, acting on their contents, are used very shortly.

```
label LOOP #1
```

Again, this is a documentary label, for the reader only. It *could* be used by the script, but this particular one isn't.

I've numbered my loops sequentially, which, looking back on it, was probably a dumb thing to do during the development of a script (because I might have added more loops and screwed up my numbering scheme); it might have been smarter to use descriptive names.

```
loop s = 1, numstyles
```

Here's the first example of the powerful programming feature called the *loop*. The syntax of PageMaker's scripting language means that the effect of this line is:

1. Execute all instructions until encountering the appropriate *endloop* statement. In this particular case, the first *endloop* encountered is the appropriate one; but if there were another loop inside this one, the first *endloop* would belong to the inside loop, not the outside loop. (In this regard, nested loops work like nested parentheses: the first close parenthesis belongs to the *last* open parenthesis preceding it, not necessarily the first one at all.)

2. When the *endloop* statement is encountered, return execution to this *loop* command again.

3. When the variable *s* is encountered inside this loop, assign it the value 1 throughout the first iteration of the loop.

4. Increment *s* by 1 every time execution is returned to the *loop* command again.

5. When the value of *s,* because of its being incremented, equals the value of `numstyles,` whatever that value might be, go ahead and execute the instructions in the loop one last time, and then exit the loop (by executing the next instruction in the script after the *endloop* statement and then, of course, continuing from there).

In other words, if `numstyles` is 5, for example, then the loop is executed five times. And if the loop instruction says `loop s = 2, numstyles,` for example, then it executes only four times, for values of *s* from 2 through 5; because of the first argument after the equal sign, *s* never equals 1.

```
stylebegin (mystyles(s))
```

This is how to edit a style. The command `stylebegin` is normally followed by the actual name of the style to be edited, in "quotes." But because, in this instance, you are plugging in the value of a variable for your style name, the scripting language makes you do it this way.

The *s* means to use the *s*th stylename from the `mystyles` variable. This is the same *s* that I talked about in the last few paragraphs. So, in going through the loop, in the first iteration, the value of *s* is 1, so you use the first name from `mystyles;` in the second iteration, the value of *s* is 2, so you use the second name from `mystyles,` and so on.

```
typeoptions 70,70,33.3,0,0
```

`Typeoptions` is the same as it was in Part 1 of this script, except that here you are editing a style instead of setting document defaults.

```
styleend
```

`Styleend` is the command that must be present so the script language knows when to stop editing a style and start doing something else. This is a good example of a required command that you *must* include, or your script won't work.

```
endloop
```

This is the `endloop` command that you *must* include so the script language knows where your loop ends. If this command is missing, your script goes exactly nowhere.

```
label ENDLOOP #1
```

This is another unused descriptive label that's just there for my own benefit. Again, it's a real label, so I *could* have actually used it for something in the script, but I didn't. `Label` is the only scripting command that you can use in this way: that you don't have to actually impart an effect to, in other words.

```
--goto end
```

And another commented-out `goto end` command. While I was testing part 2 of the script, I removed the two hyphens, and therefore parts 3 and 4 were skipped (because there's a `label end` at the very end of the script). When I forgot to put the two hyphens back in, the first time I tried to run the entire script after my testing of part 2, parts 3 and 4 *still* didn't execute.

```
--------3. MODIFYING EXISTING TEXT BLOCKS-------------
label part3
```

Part 3 is really the meat of the script; it also contains the two "advanced" or "difficult" concepts I mentioned earlier.

As I was testing the early implementations of the version of this script that allowed for multi-page documents, I made a discovery—when you turn to a page in a facing-page document and get the object list (explained later), you get a list of *all* objects on *both* pages. Then when you perform an action on all those objects, again it's to all objects on both pages.

When you turn to the *next* page, you're turning to the right-hand page of the two facing pages; and again, you're going to select and act on all objects on *both* pages.

While there's no harm done by this, at least under most circumstances (actually, if you were, deleting something on each pass, you might get in trouble), it does make the script take twice as long to run. So I decided to increment the page number to turn to by *two* instead of one, so I am only turning to each *spread* instead of each page.

Then I ran into this scenario—the first page is a right-hand page, and the last page is a left-hand page (for example, a four-page document beginning on page 1). What happens there? I can't turn to the last page, page 4, because prior to that I started on page 1, then turned to page 3, and now I try to turn to page 5 (3+2), but there isn't any page 5. So the loop ends and I haven't done the last page.

This can only happen if the first page is a right-hand (odd-numbered) page. So I came up with a way of compensating for this. If the first page is a right-hand page, only turn to *one* page number higher on the *first* iteration of the loop; *then* you turn two pages thereafter. This has the effect of getting you onto a left-hand page as soon as you leave the first page; then you are okay for the rest of the document, because turning to a left-hand page will always ultimately give you the last page (think about it—either the last page is a left page, in which case you just turned to it, or it's a right page, in which case you just turned to the left page of the same spread).

This is the first of the two difficult concepts I mentioned earlier. It took me a few hours of thought and re-thought before I had it fully worked out. (And, as is normally the case when you finally see the light on something like this, when I finally had it working, I smote my forehead with my palm and said to myself, "How could you *possibly* have been so dumb that it took so long to figure this out?")

You can see exactly how it works in the following step-by-step explanation.

```
-----------Compensating for facing pages-------------
getpagenumbers >> startpage,numpages,...
getpageoptions >> ...,facing
```

These two queries get data about the page numbering and whether facing pages is on. They also get other data that is not needed for this script. Here's how these two lines work:

1. `getpagenumbers` returns, among other stuff we don't need in this script, the starting page number as its first value, and the total number of pages in the document as its second value. Store those values in the variables `startpage` and `numpages`, respectively.

   The three periods at the end of the line constitute a "throw-away" variable. They enable you to avoid "wasting" a variable name. A value (or, if it's at the end of a line like here, all remaining values, as discussed earlier in relation to the `getstylenames` command) is stored in this variable, and is then immediately discarded by the scripting language.

2. `getpageoptions` returns two values: whether the document is double-sided, and whether it's facing-pages. For this script, I only need to know the latter, so I use the throw-away variable for the former.

   ```
   p = startpage
   ```

Here the value of one variable is assigned (`startpage`) to yet another variable (`p`). The reason for this is that I want to use p in a loop, where the value of p is going to be changed, but I also want to use the starting page number later in the script.

At this point in the execution of the script, if your starting page number is 1, the values of both p and `startpage` will be 1.

```
oddeven = startpage%2
```

Here I've created another variable called `oddeven`. This variable contains the value of the operation that follows the equals sign; this value tells me (and, more important, tells the script) whether the starting page number is even or odd.

The operation following the equals sign uses the % operator. This operator uses a misleading symbol, because what it does is *not* to extract a percentage of something; instead, it divides the number to its left by the number to its right, *and returns the remainder (if any)*. This operation, in most programming languages, is called *mod* or *modulo*:

the remainder left after a division. I don't have a clue as to why Adobe chose to call this the "percent" operator.

It's a very useful operation to determine whether a number is even or odd. Divide the number by 2: if there is a remainder, the number is odd; if there is no remainder, the number is even. Think about it. So my variable *oddeven* will contain either the value 1 or 0.

```
lastpage = startpage + numpages - 1
```

This is a variable I've put at the end of the loop to determine whether we're done or not. This is an *algorithm* that you can use anywhere, at any time, in any programming language (or in your head) to determine the last page of a document, book, or whatever, assuming all the pages are numbered consecutively, and assuming you know the starting page number and the total number of pages. Again, think about it: if you know there are nine pages, and the starting page number is 1, then the last page is 9+1-1, or 9. If there are nine pages and the starting page number is 2, the last page is 9+2-1, or 10.

```
- - - - - - - - - - - - - -Here we go.- - - - - - - - - - - - - - - - - - - - - - - - - - - - - -


label LOOP #2
if facing = 1
```

This is the beginning of another kind of loop, although it doesn't use the `loop` command. There are several other variations, all involving conditions, making them known as *conditional statements* or *commands*. Some are used later in this script.

Not all these loop variations actually loop back on themselves, by the way, which probably means I technically shouldn't call them loops, but there isn't a better term. Technically, they're called "control structures," but I didn't want to start labeling them "Control Structure Number 1."

521

This kind of loop is called an "if-then" loop. In its most basic form, it means that if the original "if" condition is true, the commands following it are executed; if it's not true, the commands following are not executed until, when the required `endif` statement is reached, execution of the script continues, whether the statement was true or not. (Again, an if-then "loop" does not loop back on itself.)

In its less basic forms, the if-then loop can contain other provisions, such as something specific to do if the *if* is simply not true (the *else* statement), or something that allows for more than two possibilities (the *elseif* statement: if x = 3, do this; elseif x = 2, do this; elseif x = 1, do this; else [in other words, if x is neither 3, 2, nor 1] do this; endif).

Here, you only need to allow for two possibilities: the variable *facing* is always going to be either 1 or 0, because it was retrieved from `getpageoptions`, and, from reading the documentation, we know its value can be only 1 or 0.

```
i = 2
```

This is what happens if `facing` = 1 (in other words, if facing pages is turned on for this document). What I am going to use the new variable *i* for is the increment to add to the current page number when going to the next page to edit. If this is a facing-pages document, as already discussed, you want to jump pages by twos, so set the variable `i` to 2.

```
label LOOP #3
```

Here's another `if-then` inside the first `if-then`, which is still in progress (you haven't seen an `endif` yet).

```
if oddeven = 0
```

This variable, `oddeven`, was the result of the "percent" or *modulo* operation, where you divided the starting page number by 2 and paid attention only to the remainder. If the remainder is 0, the starting page number is an even number.

```
j = 0
```

This new variable, j, is going to be the "fudge factor" that will get us onto a left-hand page if the starting page is a right-hand page. But we are currently in the part of the if-then loop that has determined the starting page is a *left-hand* page, so we don't need the fudge factor here: it's set to zero. (As you can see in the following example, j will be subtracted from i the first time through the page loop.)

```
-- message "First page number is even."
```

This was something I stuck in for testing purposes, just to make sure my logic was correct and my coding was working. I left it in here for illustrative purposes only; it's been deleted from my final working copy of the script.

The message command is very simple. You see the format right here. You get a little dialog box containing the message and an "OK" button.

```
else
```

Here's your first else statement. What this means is that if the previous if statement is *not* true, then, instead of executing the commands between that if statement and this else statement, the script executes the commands *following* this else statement.

This particular one means that if oddeven is not 0, then the starting page number is necessarily odd, and so you want to set j to 1:

```
j = 1
-- message "First page number is odd."
```

j is set to 1. Again, it comes into play at the end of Loop #4. Here is another commented-out message command, to again demonstrate my testing procedures.

```
        endif
```

This is the required endif statement for the if-then loop labeled Loop #3. Remember you are still inside the if-then loop labeled Loop #2. The label that follows this paragraph is another unused label statement.

```
        label ENDLOOP #3
```

```
    else
```

This is another *else* statement. Remember that now you are back in Loop #2, the one that began with the statement *"if facing = 1;"* therefore, this `else` statement means: "if facing is NOT 1."

```
i = 1
j = 0
```

If it's not a facing-page document, you want to jump by one page at a time, and you don't need to worry about variable j and what it's compensating for.

This is followed by the required `endif` statement, ending Loop #2; the unused label below it; and the commented-out `goto end` command that we would un-comment, along with a couple of other things, as discussed earlier, if you wanted to test this section only.

```
endif
label ENDLOOP #2

--goto end

--------------------The Loops--------------------

label LOOP #4
repeat
```

This is another variation of a loop and this one is a "real" loop. It's known as a *repeat-until* loop and the conditions are in the *until* statement, which appears at the end of the loop. If you'll look down to the *until* statement at the end of the loop, you'll see that this one repeats until the variable p is greater than the variable `lastpage`, whose value you assigned earlier with the algorithm discussed.

`Repeat-until` does not automatically increment a variable (remember that `loop-endloop` does), which you need so the loop knows how many times to loop, so you have to do your own incrementing. In this script, that happens right before the `until` command.

```
page p
```

One of the simplest PageMaker scripting commands, this turns to page *p*. Whatever the value of the variable p is, that's the number of the page PageMaker turns to.

At this stage in the execution of the script, the value of p is the same as the starting page number. p is what is incremented right before the end of the loop we're in right now.

```
getobjectlist >> objects,...
```

This query gets a list of all objects (the potential kinds of objects are all listed a little lower in a comment in this script) on the current page (or spread) plus all objects on the pasteboard. If you were going to run this script on a multi-page file, you'd probably want to move everything off the pasteboard; if you don't, everything on the pasteboard will be edited once for each spread your file contains.

The only reason you need this query in this script is to get the number of objects, which you put into the variable *objects;* you can throw away all other data, as it's not needed here.

```
label LOOP #5
loop n = 1,objects
```

Here's another loop, inside the other one you just started. The nested-loop effect is simple and this script is a good example:

1. First, turn to a page

2. Next, do something to all objects on the page, which requires its own loop;

3. Then control is returned to the first (outside) loop, which then takes you to the next page.

In a nutshell, control passes from the first loop to the second, until the second is done, at which time control reverts to the first loop. Of course, you can theoretically have many loops inside each other.

Just don't get confused about which one you're "in"; and don't forget your end-of-loop statements (these are the two best arguments for indenting things, as I have in this script).

This loop introduces a new variable, n, which is initially assigned the value 1. The loop does what it does, then returns to the beginning where n is incremented by 1; it loops as many times as it takes for n to reach the number of objects on the spread-plus-pasteboard, which is represented by the variable objects.

Every time this loop is encountered (that is, from the line above it in the script), it will be a new iteration of the *outside* loop (Loop #4), which means you are on a new spread with a new object list, so you want n to begin at 1 again. This loop command does that.

```
select 1
```

The first thing you do inside Loop #5 is to select the back-most object. Every object on a spread-plus-pasteboard has a stacking order, which, if it's never been changed by Bring to Front commands, and so on, is that the first object that was put on that spread is Object #1 and is in the back; the second object put on that spread is Object #2 and is next to the back, and so on.

The best way to select a bunch of unknown or generic objects, do something to them, and leave them like they were is to select them one at a time, beginning with the back-most object, do whatever to it, and then bring it to the front, which then makes the old Object #2 into the new Object #1, so you again select Object #1 the next time through the loop. By the time you've done this to all the objects, they'll be back exactly the way they were.

```
getselectlist >> ...,...,kind,...
```

The getselectlist query again returns a bunch of data, of which you only need one thing for this script: the kind of object it is. (I've left the list of what kinds of objects there are in my comments a short distance below. It's the next set of comments after this paragraph.) Throw away the first two items of data returned by this query; retain the third one and put it into a variable named *kind;* and throw the rest away.

```
label LOOP #6
if kind = 1
```

Here is another loop inside a loop, although this one's an *if-then* quasi-loop.

This script is built to do something to text blocks, so you are searching for "kind" #1 from the following list. If you're modifying this script for your own use, of course you might need to change the number in the *"if kind = 1"* statement above.

```
                     -- 1=text; 3=line; 4=box; 5=oval;
  6=TIFF or bitmap;
                     -- 8 or 9=PICT; 10=metafile; 11=EPS;
  12=multigon
```

If the back-most object is a text block, you are going to perform the following actions on it.

```
        textedit
```

The `textedit` command puts an insertion point at the beginning of the selected text block.

```
        selectall
        typeoptions 70, 70, 33.3, 0
```

Selectall is self-explanatory and this is the same `typeoptions` command that you've already used twice in this script—but this time you use it for type that's already on a page.

This one command is the bottom line, the meat, or the crux of the original script. All the rest is simply getting here.

```
        --font "Times"
        --color "Blue"
```

These two commented-out lines are ones I was using (after un-commenting them, of course) for testing the script—and if the test was successful, then I would change the font and color to something different for the next go-round. I left them in here just to show that you could have *any* text-related commands in this section of the *if-then* loop.

```
        select 1          -- necessary, since we used
  the text tool
```

I left the comment here this time, because it's critical. If you used the text tool on the object selected with the *previous "select 1"* command, then you have to re-select it before you can bring it to the front.

If you *haven't* used the text tool, as in the commented-out *elseif kind=5* section, then you don't need to re-select the object. But it can't hurt to re-select it, so I think it's much safer to actually always leave this command right where it is.

```
bringtofront
```

This is the rest of the trick, bringing the object to the front so that, on the next loop, you can select the next object, which will now be rearmost.

```
--elseif kind = 5
--color "Blue"
--bringtofront
```

This is just an example of the fact that you could do something to *many* kinds of object with this one script. This one turns PageMaker-drawn ovals blue (because object type #5, in the list above, is ovals). I used it for testing the script, and I left it here so you can see how an `elseif` works.

```
else
```

If you only want to edit one kind of object, you only need the `if` statement (and all that follows it, up through the `bringtofront` command) and this *else* statement and all that follows it. If you want to edit more than one kind of object, you need an `elseif` statement, like the one we just talked about, for all kinds of object past the first one.

The `else` statement means "if none of the *if* or *elseif* statements was true, then do this." So pretend the *elseif* above was not commented-out: What this `else`would be saying is "If the selected object is neither a text block nor an oval, do the following." With the *elseif* commented-out as it is, this `else` means "If it's not a text block, do the following."

```
bringtofront
```

And it turns out, in this script, that "the following" is simply to skip it—after bringing it to the front, of course, so you can go on to the next object.

```
endif
label ENDLOOP #6
```

This is the required *endif* for Loop #6, the one that began with *"if kind = 1."*

```
endloop
label ENDLOOP #5
```

This is the required *endloop* for Loop #5, the one that began with *"loop n = 1, objects."*

```
p = p + i - j
```

This is the incrementing of p for the next iteration of the page loop, Loop #4. You add, to the previous value of p, the value of i (the increment that you determined earlier) minus the value of j (the right-page fudge factor that I also discussed earlier). If you just finished the first spread of the document, and the starting page number was 2 (so that the first spread contained pages 2 and 3), you now go to page 4; but if the starting page was page 3, you also go to page 4, because if the starting page is odd, j is initially set to 1.

```
j = 0
```

And this is where you make sure you don't subtract 1 again after you have done it once. The reason you want to do this is that you are now on a left-hand page, and you want to stay on left-hand pages for the rest of the document. To make this happen, set j to 0 before you go through the loop again, so you don't subtract anything from *i* again; and it won't hurt anything to continue to set j to 0 every further time through this loop.

```
until p > lastpage
```

This is the end of Loop #4. The way this structure *(repeat-until)* works is that when the condition in the *until* statement is attained, the loop does *not* loop again. You might have thought the line should read "*until p = lastpage,*" but that doesn't work, because then the script doesn't execute the last page. You have to say until it's *greater* than the last page. This is an example of the kind of thing that might work differently between one programming language and another; another language might have had it the other way.

```
label ENDLOOP #4
--goto end


------------4. CLEANING UP AFTERWARDS------------


label part4
```

This entire part4 is all optional stuff, but it's a very good idea to get used to cleaning up after yourself.

```
page startpage
```

I always like to save my documents while the first page is displayed at fit-in-window view. You already set fit-in-window view in your preferences in part 1 of the script; this is where you turn to the first page before saving. You use the variable startpage here rather than the number 1, of course, in case the starting page isn't page 1.

```
save
close
```

Self-explanatory. You might or might not want the close command; but when you're sure your script is functioning properly, you'll normally want the save command for obvious reasons.

```
label end
```

This is the label I jumped to, when testing the script, with the commented-out *goto* commands at various points in the script. You do *not* have to end your scripts with this, or any, label command.

TAGGING

PageMaker has what's called a *tagging* language. After scripting (or perhaps even before it, depending on the particulars of your workflow), this can be your biggest automation tool.

What are tags? Tags are formatting codes that you can—in your word processor—see, play with, act on, search for, replace, and so on. Tags cover both paragraph and character formatting and they also enable you to import inline graphics. In their paragraph-formatting mode, they simply call out paragraph styles; in their character-formatting mode, they can do anything to individual characters or strings of characters that you can do with your mouse and keyboard and dialog boxes.

There's not enough room to begin to list all the possible tags in this chapter—in fact, this section, like the previous Scripting section, is only going to be an introduction to tagging. To see, and learn about, all PageMaker's tags, read Appendix D, "PageMaker Tags," of the PageMaker 6.5 manual (that is, the manual that comes in your PageMaker box, not this book).

Why Use Tags?

Tags give you much more text-formatting flexibility than does a normal formatted word-processing file.

For one thing, you can search and replace tags in your word processor. And one reason for doing this, even for those instances where you could have done the same thing in PageMaker, is that it's much faster to do in a word processor.

There are a million potential uses for doing search-and-replace on tags, from changing all instances of one font to another (which you can do in PageMaker, but, again, more slowly), to applying a certain style to all paragraphs that begin with certain text (a bullet, maybe,

continues

PageMaker In the Real World

or certain words), to much more complex stuff that is mentioned later, including things you can't do at all in PageMaker or in a word processor.

I ran into a good example of this latter in a chemistry textbook I did the production work on. This book had several places where a subscript had to be kerned back under a superscript. Fortunately, there were only a few variations of the actual text involved; I was able to search and replace the tagged text file, searching for just a few different combinations of text-plus-tags and inserting the appropriate kerning command. I'll guarantee you can't do that in PageMaker, QuarkXPress, or Word.

It's also nice to have tags if you're dealing with a formatted word-processing file that you've converted to tags and you want to make sure the paragraph styles, for instance, have been used consistently, because you can see the names of the styles right there in front of you: you don't have to depend on whether something *looks* right, and you don't have to worry about the fact that some styles can look right at a glance but actually aren't right: they're just similar. With tags, either it's the right tag or it isn't.

I could spend many pages going over potential scenarios where tags are nice to have. The best thing I can suggest, though, is that you work with them for a while, and possibilities will occur to you, based on your own particular workflow and the problems you run into there.

For a purpose like the latter, by the way, I recommend a word processor like BBEdit (Mac-only, but there are equivalent programs on the PC, such as Boxer), which is really classified as a text editor and which shows each paragraph in one long line of text, extending off the right-hand side of your monitor. This makes it very difficult to read the entire paragraph (although BBEdit does have a text-wrap facility that you can turn on and off), but it makes it wonderfully easy to see what's going on at the *beginning* of each paragraph, which is,

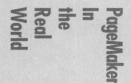

generally speaking, the most important part, because that's where the paragraph-style tag is. I estimate that at least 90 percent of the tags I'm interested in are at the beginnings of paragraphs.

And text editors are much faster programs than word processors, because they're not trying to do as much. (They don't show you any formatting; you typically get to choose one font and size for your entire document, and you don't get to see any bolds or italics or indents or anything else. On the other hand, you don't *need* to see any formatting, because there isn't any: This is a text-only document, remember.)

How To Use Tags

Tags are specially marked text you put into a text file that cause PageMaker, when it imports that text file, to format the text the way the tags specify.

You can type your tags into place, you can paste them after you've typed each one once (which is quicker and more accurate than typing them all) or you can get some of them there through search-and-replace in your word processor/text editor.

When you eventually import your text file (after all your tags are in place), PageMaker converts the tags into formatting commands that take effect on the appropriate paragraphs and characters. (And, of course, the tags themselves don't show up as text in PageMaker.)

Note

A very good way to see how PageMaker Tags work is to export some text from PageMaker. Format the text exactly the way you want it; export it as "File format: Tagged Text" with "Options: Export tags" un-checked (I know, you'd think you'd want it checked; but believe me, you don't); and look at the resulting text file in your word processor. You see exactly how PageMaker would have tagged that text.

Tagging Requirements

Every tagged text file has to start (at the very beginning of the file, before *anything* else) with the line (in other words, on a line by itself, followed only by a return):

◆ <PMTags1.0 Mac>

◆ <PMTags1.0 Win>

depending on which platform the text file was *created* on. (This has nothing to do with which platform the text file will be *imported* on.)

PageMaker's tagging language, just like its scripting language, has its own grammar, which you must follow. There's nothing to keep you from typing an illegal tag. Read Appendix D in the PageMaker 6.5 manual, and follow each command's syntax as given there.

How To Import a Tagged File

1. Issue the Place command, as you would for any other text file.

2. In the Place document dialog box (Figure 13.4), after selecting the filename in the scrolling list box, set your Options as illustrated.

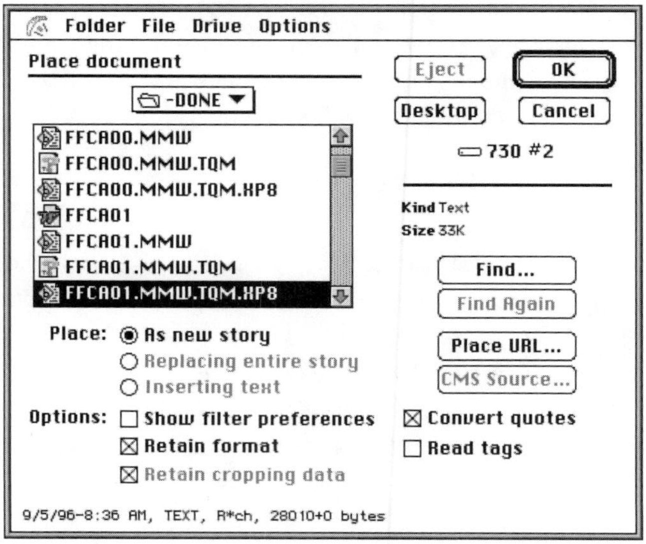

Figure 13.4

The PageMaker Place document dialog box.

```
   Folder  File  Drive  Options

Place document                    [ Eject ]   [  OK  ]

        [ -DONE ▼ ]               [Desktop] [ Cancel ]

  FFCA00.MMW                 ▲        ⬠ 730 #2
  FFCA00.MMW.TQM
  FFCA00.MMW.TQM.HP8
  FFCA01                           Kind Text
  FFCA01.MMW                       Size 33K
  FFCA01.MMW.TQM
  FFCA01.MMW.TQM.HP8         ▼      [  Find...  ]
                                    [ Find Again ]
Place: ◉ As new story
       ○ Replacing entire story    [ Place URL... ]
       ○ Inserting text            [ CMS Source... ]

Options: ☐ Show filter preferences  ☒ Convert quotes
         ☒ Retain format            ☐ Read tags
         ☒ Retain cropping data

9/5/96-8:36 AM, TEXT, R*ch, 28010+0 bytes
```

- Retain format checked.

- Convert quotes checked or unchecked, whichever makes sense, as normal.

- Read tags un-checked. Yes, that's right: do *not* check Read tags. It sounds like you'd want it, but believe me, you don't.

Tip

Of course, you normally don't check "Read tags" anyway. The only time you want it checked is if you have a text file that has only the old-fashioned [that is, pre-6.0] PageMaker paragraph-style tags in it, and you want those tags to be read. For PageMaker 6.0 and beyond, you don't want it.

3. Click the appropriate radio button for Place: As new story, Replacing entire story, or Inserting text. Click OK.

   In other words, you really don't do anything different from the way you normally place a formatted word processor file.

Importing QuarkXPress Tags

A great feature of PageMaker is its capability to import a file that has been tagged for QuarkXPress.

I am not going to go into how to use XPress Tags themselves, of course. Suffice it to say that XPress Tags do the same things PageMaker Tags do, only in a different language. If someone gives you an XPress-Tagged file, you can easily use it in PageMaker after taking these simple preparations:

1. Make sure the XPress Tag file begins with the proper XPress header, which is

   ```
   <v1.70>
   ```

on a line by itself (but see the next paragraph), rather than the PageMaker header that was listed previously.

2. If there's also an `<e0>` code after the `<v1.70>` in an XPress Tags file you've been given, you can leave it. This tag tells XPress which platform the character set is from (Mac or Windows). My Mac PageMaker 6.5 beta read the Mac character-set code just fine, but wouldn't read the code for the Windows character set (`<e1>`). Anyway, you don't need the tag for PageMaker (or for XPress, for that matter; it's optional there), so it's probably better to just delete it.

3. You'll have trouble importing files that contain some "double" or "ganged" tags, such as `<\f\f>`, which is two en-spaces inside one set of brackets. This ganged tag works in XPress but doesn't work in PageMaker (you get an error message while importing the file); but when changed to `<\f><\f>`, which is two en-spaces each in its own set of brackets, it works fine.

    On the other hand, `<BI>`, which is bold and italic inside one set of brackets, works. So be prepared to have to break some of your "ganged" tags out into individual sets of brackets. A bit of a hassle, but easily done with search-and-replace.

Converting Formatted Word-Processing Files to Tags

This section covers the true power of tags. Unfortunately, for folks on PCs, the software discussed is Mac-only. But, believe me, you gain so much text-processing power by using the little utilities that it would almost be worthwhile to go out and buy a Mac just so you can do all this. (You'd only need a cheap one.)

All the software about to be discussed is written, and sold, by Greg Swann. You can download demo or limited versions (this varies from one utility to another) of these utilities from `http://hyperarchive.lcs.mit.edu/HyperArchive.html` or you can purchase full commercial versions by calling Greg at 602-890-0355.

Mark My Words

The first utility, which you need in order to convert a formatted Macintosh Microsoft Word 3, 4, or 5 file to a text-only XPress Tagged file, is called "Mark My Words." (Greg's software always has punny names—and documentation too, by the way; don't let any of that bother you. It's great software.)

Don't have Macintosh Word 3, 4, or 5? Or the file you want to convert isn't in that format? This shouldn't be much problem. Word 6 can read almost any format and can save into many, including Word 5. Even Windows Word 6 can save in Mac Word 5 format.

You need to make sure the Word file is not "Fast-saved." (If it is, Mark My Words will tell you it can't read it, and you'll have to open it up in Word and un-Fast-save it.)

After you've gotten that far (in other words, an un-Fast-saved Mac Word 3, 4, or 5 file), drag and drop your file(s) on the Mark My Words icon.

Mark My Words gives you plenty of options as to what formatting to retain. Make these choices according to your own particular circumstances. It's a very easy program to run, almost a "no-brainer."

Regardless of what options you choose, the end product is a new file (none of Greg's utilities overwrite your original file; so if you've made a mistake or want to try again with different settings, you can always go right back to your original), in text-only format, with all the Microsoft Word formatting that you've specified translated into XPress Tags.

XP8

One of the two Swann utilities that you might want to use on the file produced by Mark My Words in the previous step is called XP8. This program performs clean-up operations on your file, most of which are user-selectable. Drag your text files and then drop them onto the XP8 icon.

How XP8 works is all very self-explanatory, or at least explained in the XP8 documentation; again, I am not going to go into the exact meanings of all the dialog box choices here, but I will mention some examples of the clean-up XP8 can do. It can strip multiple returns and tabs, convert three or more spaces to a tab, convert an asterisk or a lowercase "o" at the beginning of a paragraph to a bullet, and put a discretionary hyphen before the last word of a paragraph (thus preventing one kind of typographic "widow").

If you're still not convinced, how about the absolutely best quote conversion in the industry (that is, converting typewriter quotes to curly quotes)? It's not only much better than what I've observed in the past from either PageMaker or QuarkXPress, but I don't think I've ever seen it make a mistake at all.

And, if you're *still* not convinced, how about automatic conversion to expert-set ligatures and old-style figures? Actually, I shouldn't tell a lie. It's not a 100-percent total, 100-percent fully automatic conversion. You have to do one search-and-replace operation afterward, but I'll settle for something like that any day of the week.

Torquemada

As great as XP8 is, Torquemada (also known as "Torq" for short) is the king of them all, in my humble opinion. This Swann utility is a super search-and-replace engine for text-only files.

You don't even have to reserve it for tagged files. Use it to do any search-and-replace operation on *any* text-only file, anywhere, anytime, but it's on tagged files that Torq really shines.

You can create up to 20 search-and-replace *strings* (that is, 20 searches and 20 corresponding replacements; a string is simply computer talk for more than one character, strung together) per Torq *set* (a set is the file you get when you save a window-full of strings); and you can use as many as 32 sets at a time. This gives you 640 search-and-replaces at once, which you could call practically unlimited search-and-replace power, especially because you could then run another 32 sets and another and another. It's just that you can "only" run 32 sets *at once*.

(Again, you drag and drop your text file[s] on the Torquemada icon; but with Torq you also drop your sets at the same time, and they run in alphabetical order.)

You have a text-only file with XPress Tags that you got from Mark My Words and you've done some clean-up with XP8: now just what the heck are you supposed to *do* with it in Torquemada?

Well, one obvious thing is that you can translate all those XPress Tags into PageMaker Tags. Now, remember that PageMaker can read XPress Tags, so you might well not need to do this at all, but you might want to for some reason or another. And, like we discussed above, you'll at least probably need to split out some "ganged" tags, like, for instance, <\f\f> into <\f><\f>.

(By the way, Torq comes with a bunch of useful pre-built search-and-replace sets, one of which is a set to convert XPress Tags to pre-6.0 PageMaker Tags—which is not too useful with PageMaker 6.5, because this means paragraph style tags only; but if you look at this set, it gives you a couple of good ideas about how such things work. An XPress Tags-to-PageMaker 6.5 Tags set would have to be much more extensive than this one; but, still, once you get into using Torq, it would be quite easy to build.)

Whether you go the XPress Tags route or the PageMaker Tags route, there's still plenty more you can do in Torquemada. You can do all the literal searches (such as replace all occurrences of one word or string with another) you want; and, believe me, there's plenty of power in being able to do that, especially for multi-file or repeating jobs. Think about it: just set up your search-and-replace strings once, and then use them a kazillion times. Save yourself time and increase your accuracy and consistency.

Wildstrings

The *real* power in Torq comes in its capability to do *very* complex things with *wildcards* (and the logical extension of a wildcard, a *wildstring*).

A wildcard is something that can represent something else; the more you can *type* a wildcard (in other words, narrow the scope of what it can represent), the more powerful it is. And a wildstring is, conceptually, a bigger wildcard.

A *simple wildcard* can represent any one character—using one of Torq's wildcards, ^1, for example, if you searched for b^1n, we'd find all occurrences of ban, ben, bin, bon, bun, and byn, plus bbn, bcn, and so on.

A *simple wildstring* represents any text of any length until the full search pattern is matched: using the wildstring ^*, if we searched for b^*n, we'd be looking for all occurrences of "b" followed by *anything of any length* followed by the first "n" encountered; you find ban, ben, bin, bon, bun, byn, bbn, bcn, all the things you found in the previous paragraph using a wildcard; plus you find burn, burin, barn, bran, bragan, burstein, and a million other conceivable things, but you won't find bernstein, because the search ends when the full search pattern is matched by the "n" in the "bern" part of bernstein.

A *typed wildcard* narrows the search to, for example, any one upper-case character, or any one digit, or some such. I'll list here all the possibilities, because they're so ingeniously constructed that they allow searching for almost anything, especially in combination with each other: uppercase character, lowercase character, character of either case, alphanumeric character (not space or punctuation), tabular character (not alphabetical), printable character (not space), any character except a return, punctuation character, sentence punctuation character (don't worry, they're all fully defined in the documentation), digit, white-space character (space, return, tab, option-space), and another white-space character (space, tab, option-space, but not return).

There's a lot more to Torq's language than this. I hope I've whetted your appetite sufficiently to get you to try it.

Here's a fairly simple example of a Torquemada process that saves me hours of time in a typical week.

I have a client for whom I do the production work on a repeating job, a series of booklets. The client sends me formatted Word files. This client isn't really expert in how Word or PageMaker or QuarkXPress works (I actually use QuarkXPress for this client at their request, sorry; but all the same things would be true in PageMaker).

One of the paragraph styles in these booklets is a numbered-list style, where the number and the period after it are to be in a different typeface than the rest of the paragraph. It's a bold face (Futura Heavy), and the client just styles the number and period bold (Minion) in Word. It's up to me to change all those numbers and periods from Minion bolded to Futura Heavy unbolded.

I do not want to do this manually in QuarkXPress: it would take too long, and I would certainly miss some of them (some chapters have 200 or more of them).

So I first use Mark My Words to make a tagged text-only file. And I then use Torquemada to search for the end of a numbered-list paragraph style tag (there are several varieties, but they all end in "NL:" so that's what I search for), followed by a bold tag, followed by one or more digits, followed by a period, followed by a bold tag, followed by a tab. (This is what I have determined is sufficient to define the search to find all the occurrences I'm looking for, while narrowing it to find nothing else.)

And I replace that with the same "NL:" tag fragment, followed by a change to Futura Heavy (and deleting the bold tag), followed by the same digit or digits, followed by a period, followed by a change back to Minion (and deleting the other bold tag), followed by a tab.

This is a very simple use of a *typed wildstring* ("one or more digits"), yet illustrative of the power of Torquemada's search-and-replace capabilities. And it's obviously something you can't do in your word

continues

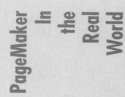

processor. (I didn't get into typed wildstrings above, did I? Just like I didn't get into lots more detail. Believe me, there's a lot I haven't mentioned at all.)

By the way, I have to include several variations on this whole procedure in my Torq set, because sometimes they don't bold the period, and sometimes the period is missing, and so on. Torq enables me to automatically catch and correct those variant scenarios.

Oh, and the benefits? I spent some time writing this Torq set. I don't recall how much time it was; probably just half an hour or so. But even if it had been *10* hours, believe me, I'm sure I saved myself at least 10 hours in the first *month* I used it, and I've been using it for more than a year as I write this.

Torquemada versus XP8

There are two mini-issues with these two utilities. First, Torquemada can do many of the things XP8 does, but it could conceivably fit your circumstances that you could do everything you wanted to do in Torq, which means you wouldn't need XP8 at all.

Think this through carefully, though, assuming you have acquired XP8. It does a lot of clean-up stuff. It can't hurt to run any text file through it, and it can nearly always help. Read its documentation thoroughly before you decide you don't need it.

In addition, a side issue of this mini-issue: be careful not to duplicate your effort if you do run them both. Doing so can both waste your time and create undesirable results in certain circumstances (for example, if you were going to search for something that isn't there any more because the other program already did something to it).

Second, which order do you run them in? Obviously, if you're starting with a formatted Word file, you have to run Mark My Words first; but you might wonder if it's important whether you run XP8 second and Torq third, or Torq second and XP8 third.

The bottom line is that it really doesn't matter intrinsically. The answer is to do it in whichever way makes sense to you. I've done it both ways. There's no "right" and "wrong"; rather, it depends on your preferences and, potentially, on exactly what you're trying to accomplish. XP8 might do some things you'd rather not have to run through Torq; or, conversely, you might *want* XP8 to do some things first before you run the file through Torq. It is up to you.

Note

Both text editors and search-and-replace utilities are available on the PC (shareware examples: Boxer and SNR, respectively), but there's nothing like Mark My Words or XP8 that I know of. If you're starting with tagged text-only files rather than formatted word-processor files, you could apply the principles discussed earlier on the PC platform—just not as easily as on the Mac. (If you have a friend who has a Mac, you could use Windows Word to convert your Word files to Mac Word 5 files, then get your friend to do the Mark My Words part of the process for you, and do the rest on your PC.)

SUMMARY

Refer to the documentation in the PageMaker 6.5 manual, if only simply for the list of tags and their syntax; but the actual use of tags is quite simple. You can increase your text-processing power tenfold by doing search-and-replace operations on your tags, especially if you use something powerful like Torquemada.

In this chapter, we also covered PageMaker scripting. If tagging isn't the best, most efficiency-enhancing PageMaker production tool, then scripting is. Especially for repetitive projects or tasks, you'll end up saving yourself an unbelievable amount of time in the long run if you get to know them both well.

In the next chapter, you will explore the world of print publishing, examining different presses, output devices, and other important print considerations.

Chapter **14**

THE WORLD OF PRINT PUBLISHING

This chapter, along with Chapter 15, deals with the subject of digital prepress and the ways in which PageMaker can be used not only to generate camera-ready output on the desktop, but also to create files that can be output to film ready for platemaking. Before dealing with the specific application of PageMaker to these tasks, it is first necessary to spell out what is meant by the term "prepress" and to address the issues the desktop publisher is likely to run into. This chapter discusses these basic issues as well as the specific output options from the desktop. PageMaker's many-faceted Print options are also covered in detail. Chapter 15 discusses the concept of the service bureau and how best to provide files for trouble-free imagesetter film output.

OVERVIEW OF PREPRESS PROCESSES

Before turning to the particular use of PageMaker to the prepress processes, this chapter must first spend some time outlining what the prepress processes and issues actually are.

A Brief Survey of the Major Printing Processes

For most of the history of printing (from circa 1450 to about 1900), there was only one commercially popular form of printing. In this century, there are about a half dozen common means of printing, with new technologies expanding that number rather quickly. Although the basics of prepress are the same for nearly all of them, there are certain considerations that need to be taken into account for each one. Almost all of the commercial printing the average PageMaker user is going to be involved with is *offset lithography*, the most common printing process today. (Generating distributed copies of a publication is also commonly performed on a photocopier or on a laser printer, as well.) It is not, however, inconceivable that at some point in the future one will come into contact with other processes, and it doesn't hurt to at least be familiar with them. This section provides a very brief overview of each of the major printing processes, and some of the specific prepress issues raised by each of them.

Letterpress

Letterpress is also known as *relief* printing, as it prints from a raised— or "relief"—image. Bits of raised metal type, initially hand-set characters, later cast lines and raised metal plates (called stereotypes), are locked into a frame, inked, and brought into contact with a sheet of paper. Letterpress—the original form of printing—has gradually been phased out over the course of the 20th century.

Offset Lithography

Offset lithography—the most common and economical form of printing today—prints from a flat surface. The principle of lithography is often summed up in the phrase "oil and water don't mix," which is somewhat misleading because they do need to mix to a very small extent in order for the process to work. Essentially, an oil-receptive image area is photographically transferred to a sheet of metal, plastic, or paper (a *plate*). The remainder of the plate is rendered oil-repellent (or water-receptive). Thus, the oil-based ink adheres to the image areas and a water-based solution keeps the non-image areas ink free. The "offset" part of the process uses a synthetic-rubber "blanket" to transfer the inked image from the plate to the paper. (The image is much clearer and sharper when transferred using a rubber blanket than the plate itself.)

Note

Offset Lithography is also called planography, which is actually a more correct term. The word "lithography" derives from the Greek word lithos, meaning "stone," the first image carrier used in the process; metal, polyester, or paper plates are now universally used as the "litho"graphic image carrier.

Offset lithography is used for everything including single-page flyers, pamphlets, brochures, books, and newspapers.

Correctly or no, the assumption is made throughout the remainder of this chapter and Chapter 15 that this is the intended printing process.

Gravure

Gravure—also called *intaglio*—printing uses as its image carrier a copperplated metal cylinder which has been etched—either chemically or mechanically—with thousands of tiny pits, or *cells*. As the cylinder rotates on the press, it passes through an ink fountain, where a thin, liquid ink collects in these cells. As the paper (or other substrate) is pressed against the inked cylinder, it is forced partially into these cells where a combination of physical contact with the ink and capillary action transfers the ink to the substrate.

Gravure is a very high-quality printing process and is used for packaging, advertising, magazines, and color newspaper supplements. One way of determining if something has been printed by gravure is by examining printed type (not photographs) through a magnifying glass or loupe. If it appears to comprise many small dots, it is gravure-printed. (As an example, examine the Sunday *New York Times Magazine* or *Parade* magazine through a magnifier.)

In terms of prepress issues, text that is to be gravure-printed typically needs to be at a size larger than six points, otherwise the etched cells do not reproduce it very well.

Flexography

The direct descendent of letterpress printing is flexography (often referred to as just "flexo"), the printing from raised, flexible rubber plates. Plates are made by making a metal or plaster mold and pouring melted rubber into it, producing a relief plate. More and more commonly, however, special photopolymer plates use acid-resist etching to engrave plates.

Flexography uses highly liquid ink (unlike the thick, viscous, oil-based ink of letterpress and lithography) and is primarily used in the printing of plastic packaging, with some paper and paperboard printing also being performed.

In terms of prepress, the issue at hand is the contraction of an image when a molded rubber plate is cooled, and the elongation of an image when a rubber or flexible photopolymer plate is stretched around a plate cylinder on press. Original art for flexography needs to be scaled up or down to compensate for these factors. There are general mathematical formulas that are used to calculate the amount of enlargement or reduction required, but if you are laying out to-be-flexo-printed material it is best to check with the production department or print shop to find out the exact requirements.

Screen Printing

Also known as "silk-screening" (but only if you want to tick off screen printers), the screen process uses a finely-woven mesh to which a stencil—either cut by hand or imaged photographically—is mounted. Ink is forced through the screen, where it passes through the stencil only in the image areas.

New Processes

These are the "traditional" printing methods. But advances in technology, chemistry, physics, materials science, and computers have resulted in a number of new processes, some of which are becoming entrenched in the printing industry, but often only for short print runs. Few new processes are able to generate the quality and economy at as large a scale as these older processes. Such newer processes include *electrophotography*, or *xerography*, the principle behind photocopiers and laser printers; and *ink-jet printing* (see the "Overview of Output Devices" section later in this chapter). There is also "waterless lithography," which uses silicone-based lithographic plates to eliminate the need for a water-based solution. Xerography and ink-jet printing are used primarily in computer printers, while waterless lithography (also known as *letterset* printing) is still trying to perfect itself.

The End of Prepress?

As its name indicates, *prepress* refers to all those activities that occur prior to printing. Technological innovations since the beginning of the twentieth century have constantly altered the meaning of prepress. It is likely that the definition will continue to change, especially as new "on-demand printing" technologies become increasingly practical. The ironic thing about prepress is that new technologies are working to eliminate it as much as possible, in much the same way as desktop publishing (invented by PageMaker) and high-end prepress systems rendered much of graphic arts photography obsolete. Even direct-to-plate systems may very well render conventional platemaking and the production of negative films obsolete.

An Historical Explanation of Prepress

Those of us old enough to remember a time prior to the personal computer (but, thankfully, not old enough to remember metal typecasting) recall that prepress involved setting type on a phototypesetting device, developing the exposed photo paper, cutting it into pieces, and literally pasting it to a mechanical board. The anachronistic term "paste-up," by the way, still survives in the digital age, although the process itself is now passé.

Today, however, prepress involves creating pages in a page layout program (such as PageMaker) and generating PostScript output either on an imagesetter or other output device. (A lot of prepress also takes place on high-end, proprietary color electronic publishing systems that use custom page layout software. Because PageMaker is rarely involved in these systems, they are not dealt with here.)

The future, which is descending upon us very quickly, is aiming to eliminate even *more* of the prepress aspects of printing and publishing. New *computer-to-plate* systems don't even bother with output at all (except for proofing purposes); the computer information drives lasers that image the printing plates directly, often while they're mounted on press. Even newer technologies—comprising what is known as "on-demand printing"—print directly from computer to paper at speeds that make the "instant book" economically feasible in many cases. (Books printed on-demand by devices such as the Xerox DocuTech have been published.) New color systems are making "process color" printing feasible on an on-demand basis, as well. None of these technologies, however, is close to supplanting the major "traditional" printing process of lithography, gravure, and flexography, so it will be some time before you ever have to worry about the death of prepress.

Explanation By Way of an Explanation

Prepress essentially comprises seven stages:

1. Creating type, either directly in PageMaker or by placing it in PageMaker from a word processing program or other source. This also involves the formatting of type according to the design specifications created for the document or publication in question.

2. Acquiring and Placing graphics—line art created in Illustrator, FreeHand, or other such drawing program, or photographic images captured with a scanner, PhotoCD, or digital camera and manipulated in a program such as Photoshop—in PageMaker.

3. Assembling all type, graphics, and other page elements in PageMaker according to a design created by the art director, designer, or other person.

4. Generating a mechanical, or camera-ready copy, directly from the desktop or from a service bureau.

5. Preparing photographic films of the proper pages, either from a service bureau's imagesetter or by utilizing a graphic arts camera. Preparing color separations is also performed at this time.

6. Stripping the photographic negatives into flats ready for platemaking.

7. Making plates from stripped negatives.

Other chapters of this book deal with the first three phases in detail, whereas the last two or three phases are rarely performed in-house. Consequently, this chapter discusses phase five—creating a mechanical ready for the camera or imagesetter. None of these stages, however, exists independently of the others. So you need to constantly look backward and forward when deciding how best to proceed.

Fonts

In PageMaker, you can set three variables with regard to type: "font," "style," and "size." (This is virtually the same for any word processing or page layout program.) Collectively, these three variables are known as the font, each variable corresponding to the type family, the typeface, and the font, respectively.

If you are using a PostScript printer, all you really need to worry about with regard to fonts is that you have both screen fonts and printer fonts. *Printer fonts* are the actual PostScript (or other) codes that mathematically describe how to draw the fonts. This is what the interpreter or RIP in the output device needs to render type smoothly. *Screen fonts* are bitmapped versions of printer fonts used to display the font onscreen. You more often than not need both types of fonts. Without screen fonts, the display defaults to Geneva (on the Macintosh), which might either offend your sensibilities or impede your ability to lay out and proof a page prior to print out. Remember, the advantage to desktop publishing is that you can see fairly accurately what you're going to output before you output it. Without printer fonts, however, you are in much worse shape, because the output device uses the bitmapped versions of a font, which result in aliasing and poor output.

Proper and Artificial

You should be careful about using "proper" bolds and italics and "artificial" bolds and italics. Computer programs can generate bold and italic variants of a font simply by slanting the type or thickening the stroke, in contrast to using specifically designed bolds and italics. The specially-designed bolds and italics tend to look better, especially as the computer simply thickens or slants strokes willy-nilly, without regard to aesthetics. Caution should be taken, however, in not inadvertently (or even advertently) clicking a bold or italic version of an already bold or italic typeface. In a pinch, however, artificial styles work fine.

The PostScript Page Description Language

Any understanding of digital prepress requires at least a rudimentary understanding of PostScript. PostScript is a *page description language (PDL)*, which is a means of expressing in words, numbers, and symbols where page elements are located and how to draw them. When you create a PostScript file of a page (or page element), all the information pertaining to that material is translated into a formula that an *interpreter* in the output device uses to tell the laser (or other imaging mechanism) where to place the dots that form objects.

If you want to see what a PostScript file looks like:

1. Create a small page in PageMaker, and select Print from the File menu (see Figure 14.1).

2. Click the Options button on the right-hand side of the dialog box.

3. In the Options dialog box, check the option marked Write PostScript to File and name it (see Figure 14.2). Notice that the Print button at the top of the box changed to Save.

4. Click Save.

Figure 14.1

The Print Document dialog box.

Figure 14.2

The Print Options dialog box.

Save the PostScript data to a text file. Opening it in a word processing program—or PageMaker— yields about 20 (or more) pages of commands. Experts in PostScript can in fact read through the code and edit it, which in fact is what many people used to have to do when early versions of PostScript introduced errors into files. (This dialog box is revisited later in this chapter.)

Why is PostScript (or any PDL) important? Several reasons. The first is the way PostScript describes all page elements in terms of *vectors*.

If you look at a computer monitor, you notice that all images are composed of small dots called *pixels*. Thus, anything that is displayed on the screen is made up of a series of dots. This becomes evident if you type a character at a large point size. Notice the stairstep pattern along diagonal lines and curves. This is called *aliasing*, and is the result of the dots forming images not being small enough to produce smooth lines and curves. Almost all computer output devices—such as laser printers and imagesetters—also use bitmaps, only those dots are much smaller, so lines and curves appear much smoother. The alternative to a bitmap is a vector, in which a computer describes lines, curves, and shapes as mathematical formulas. The advantages to vectors are that they take up less computer memory, require less processing power to manipulate, and they can be *scaled* easily. This latter advantage is important with respect to PostScript.

Say you have a bitmapped letter "A," for example, and you want to increase its point size. With a bitmapped font, the computer just increases the number of pixels, which has the effect of enlarging the pixels and accentuating the aliasing phenomenon (see Figure 14.3). When it is printed, what you see on-screen is *exactly* what you get, aliasing and all, regardless of the printer resolution. (In terms of typography, despite the advantages of WYSIWYG monitors, what you see is rarely what you *really* want!)

Figure 14.3

Notice how much more pronounced the aliasing ("jaggies") becomes when a bitmapped font is increased in size from 12 to 48 points.

In a system that uses vectors to describe fonts, however, enlarging that letter "A" instructs the computer to recalculate the formula describing it (see Figure 14.4). Consequently, it looks just as smooth when it is output at 48 point as it does at 12 point (despite the fact that on the monitor—which can only ever display as a bitmap—it will still look jaggy).

Figure 14.4

Notice that vector-based fonts are scaled much more smoothly.

This is the advantage of PostScript. Fonts can be scaled to any desired size and still retain their smoothness and legibility, the output quality only limited by the resolution of the output device.

The other advantage to PostScript is what is known as its *device independence*. This means that once a page is translated into the PostScript language, all the attributes that have been set into it are read in exactly the same way by any output device having a PostScript interpreter. Consequently, barring strictly mechanical limitations such as resolution, paper size, and so on, any PostScript file outputs exactly the same on any compatible output device. This becomes important when pages need to be output by service bureaus and other systems that might differ significantly from those on which the pages were created.

One somewhat recent development that casual users need to be aware of is the so-called "PostScript clone," or a raster image processor containing a PostScript interpreter not actually authorized by, nor with engineering assistance from, Adobe. These devices—commonly laser printers or imagesetters—are touted as having 100 percent PostScript compatibility, and most do generate output that is virtually identical to that obtained with a proper PostScript device. But if you're shopping for such devices...*caveat emptor*.

PostScript versus TrueType

Not surprisingly, challengers to the PostScript hegemony have appeared, and it is probably also not surprising that Microsoft was involved. TrueType, developed jointly by Microsoft and Apple, was designed as a rival font format to PostScript.

Although TrueType operates under the same principle and has many of the same advantages as PostScript—scaling fonts mathematically and producing device-independent files, to name two—there are a couple of disadvantages to TrueType that need to be mentioned.

◆ The first is that TrueType is limited to describing fonts; it is not a true PDL (although TrueImage, a successor, is designed to be a full-fledged PDL).

◆ The second, more important reason is that PostScript, by virtue of having been created first, is firmly entrenched as the "standard" page description language in the electronic publishing industry.

If you are outputting your own pages, it really makes no difference which PDL you use. You will run into trouble if you need to send your files out to a service bureau, however, if you use TrueType and your service bureau uses PostScript. Service bureaus have invested heavily over the years in font libraries that happen to consist of PostScript typefaces. Few see any advantage in having to pay for TrueType counterparts.

Warning

Keep in mind that although some users tend to take computer fonts for granted, providing service bureaus with your own fonts—be they TrueType or PostScript—is in violation of licensing agreements or, in other words, is illegal and unethical.

QuickDraw

PostScript is used almost exclusively to control the output of pages, and has little if anything to do with the way things are displayed on the computer screen. This aspect of desktop publishing is the purview of system extensions such as Apple's QuickDraw (and its successors QuickDraw GX and QuickDraw 3D). (On the Windows side of things, GDI—graphics device interface—handles the onscreen representation of fonts and graphics.) Often, Adobe Type Manager (ATM), another system extension, is also used to enhance screen fonts and graphics. Keep in mind that if you use ATM to handle your screen fonts *do not* attempt to add the TrueType system extension. They are not only incompatible but downright hostile. Having both extensions will crash you system hard. Some Macintosh printers, rather than being PostScript-based, are QuickDraw-based. When shopping for a printer, make sure you pick one that is compatible with whatever PDL you'll be using. QuickDraw also often needs to work in tandem with ATM for good results.

TrueType, however, has found a niche in office environments—especially those running Windows software—and they are less expensive than PostScript fonts. Although TrueType is becoming more and more prevalent, especially as more Windows users become involved in the traditionally Mac-dominated world of desktop publishing, if you plan on dealing with service bureaus, your best bet is to stick with PostScript.

Note

For more information on PostScript, see the section on PostScript in the PageMaker Print dialog box.

Resolving Resolution

The quality of the material you provide in the prepress phase of printing is, needless to say, crucial to the quality of the material that will eventually come back from the printer. As the saying goes, "A chain is only as strong as its weakest link." Although there are many factors involved in generating high-quality output, either at the desktop or from service bureaus and printers, let's look at one of the most basic: *resolution*.

Resolution is basically defined as how well the individual components of a particular image produce the illusion of a smooth, solid, complete image. In computer terminology, this tends to refer to the dots that make up an image. All computer-generated images are composed of hundreds or thousands of tiny dots. As mentioned earlier, if you look at your computer screen, you'll see that all the letters, graphics, and photographs are made up of dots (pixels). If you print out something from your laser printer and examine it with a magnifying glass or loupe, also notice that it is made up of dots. But to the naked eye, it doesn't appear as if it is. This is because the dots that make up laser-printed output are much smaller than the dots that make up a displayed image on a computer screen.

Most computer monitors have a maximum resolution of around 72 pixels per inch (ppi). (Some IBM-compatible monitors have slightly higher resolutions than Macintosh monitors.) This means that in one inch of space, only 72 pixels can fit which, on a monitor, is determined by the *dot pitch*, or the size of the grid through which the electron beam strikes the back of the screen. Resolution on screen is also often referred to by listing dimensions, such as 640×480. This means that a particular display is 640 pixels wide × 480 pixels deep.

The resolution of a computer monitor isn't of crucial importance in prepress, thanks in large part to PostScript. It's the resolution of the output device that matters. Desktop laser printers, as of this writing, have a maximum resolution of 600 ppi, which is fine for most text and line art. If you are going to be outputting halftones, this is a bit more problematic, which is discussed in further detail later in this chapter.

(The size and resolution of a computer monitor might be of importance to you only insofar as it is more convenient to display as much of a page on the screen as possible, without having to scroll up and down and back and forth.)

It might seem logical that the higher the resolution, the better, but that isn't always the case. Outputting straight text at 3,000 ppi would be overkill. In many cases, outputting text at 600 ppi is fine. Although it does no harm to deal with resolutions that are higher than is strictly necessary, keep in mind that when dealing with photographs or other scanned images the higher the resolution the greater the size of the file, and the more RAM (random-access memory) and processing power is required to manipulate—or even display—the image. Dealing with even moderately-high-resolution scanned images on a 680X0 Mac, for example, is a test of even the most patient of us.

A term you will often encounter to describe resolution is *dots per inch (dpi)*. This is synonymous with ppi, but ppi is the preferred term when discussing general resolution so as to distinguish screen pixels and printer pixels (technically called "spots") from halftone dots. You'll also occasionally see the term *lines per inch (lpi)*, often in connection with a monitor display. This is also synonymous with ppi, and refers to how many lines of dots fit vertically on a screen. A monitor with a vertical resolution of 480 can be described as 480 lpi. Lines per inch, however, is more often used to refer to the screen count of a halftone screen.

OUTPUT: PRODUCING MECHANICALS

Not only is the creation of pages and files an important part of the prepress process, but so is optimizing the output. Output can refer to "rough" copies used as page proofs to check the positioning of page elements and to send to any proofreaders to spot typos, as well as color proofs used to check and sign off on the color choices and reproduction characteristics of a job. Output also refers to the generation of mechanicals—camera-ready art from which negatives for platemaking will be made—or the negative film itself. Needless to say, the better the output device, the better the quality of the ultimate reproduction.

This section begins with an overview of output devices in general, then moves to how they can be used to generate mechanicals and films.

Overview of Output Devices

There are a variety of output devices available, both for proofing purposes or for generating camera-ready mechanicals. The following sections examine each device, and explain some of the advantages and disadvantages. This section provides an brief overview of output options. Afterward, it looks at PageMaker's printing options in more detail.

Ink-Jet Printers

The second most common type of desktop output device is the ink-jet printer. The ink-jet printer, as its name indicates, produces an image by directing droplets of colored liquid inks at the paper. As you would imagine, a drawback to ink-jet printers is a phenomenon called *wicking*, or an absorption of the ink by the paper, causing a blurred or fuzzy image. This is less of a problem on some models than others, and the use of special coated papers can reduce it significantly.

Although ink-jet printers have somewhat higher resolutions than laser printers (as of this writing, 720 ppi is the maximum), few are PostScript-compatible and glacially slow print speeds are still par for the course for many models. Ink-jet printers are widely used for generating color output (they still surpass laser printers in terms of quality and economy of color output) and are good for generating color proofs. Ink-jet output is rarely—if ever—used as camera-ready copy.

Laser Printers

The most common form of output device these days is the laser printer. A laser printer works on the principle of electrophotography, much like a photocopier. A laser exposes an electrically-charged plate in areas corresponding to the image areas of the material to be printed. This exposure imparts an opposite charge to those areas of this plate struck by the laser. Then, fine particles of pigment (called toner) are directed at the plate, where (because they possess a charge opposite that imparted by the laser) they adhere only to those areas exposed by the laser. Having the same charge as the non-image areas of the metal plate, they do not stick there. A sheet of paper is brought into contact with this plate, and the image is transferred to it. Heat is then used to fix the toner to the paper.

Most laser printers are PostScript-compatible, meaning that they have a PostScript interpreter built into them. Remember when we saved a document as a PostScript file previously in the chapter? That's essentially what happens during output. PageMaker converts the document to a PostScript file and sends it to the printer, where the interpreter then rasterizes it. (A PostScript interpreter on a larger scale is called a raster image processor.) The process of rasterizing converts the PostScript description of the page back into a bitmap. (A *raster* is simply another term for a bitmap, and to *rasterize* simply means to make into a bitmap.) This bitmap has a much finer grid than, say, the bitmap used by a computer monitor. The interpreter or RIP addresses every point on this grid and determines what should go there—a dot or no dot.

The relatively low cost of a laser printer these days has made it the output device of choice for casual and professional use. As of this writing, the maximum resolution of a desktop laser printer is 600 ppi, while much larger, high-end laser printers can exceed 1,000 ppi. Most popular brands of laser printer are PostScript-compatible.

There are two ways in which a laser printer is controlled by PageMaker. One is by means of the *PostScript Printer Description (PPD)* file. The PPD is essentially a reference manual used by the printer *driver* (the software—existing in your System Folder—that forms the link between the computer and the printer) that enables PageMaker to know what the idiosyncrasies of your specific printer are. The printer driver links the computer in general and the printer while the PPD links PageMaker and the printer.

The second way the laser printer is controlled by PageMaker is via a two-way communication link. Essentially, this is a memory-management function, keeping track of, among other things, which fonts have already been downloaded to the printer's memory, which eliminates the need to reload them from scratch every time you want to print a document.

For more information on PPDs, see the following section entitled, "PPDs and Drivers."

PPDs and Drivers

Your laser printer driver exists in the Extensions folder of your System Folder. If you already have been using a printer before you obtained PageMaker, you don't need to worry about installing it. It came with the diskette accompanying your printer and if you have been merrily printing all this time, you don't need to worry about it. Another system extension called LaserWriter 8 also exists in this folder, which came with the Mac system software to communicate with laser printers. You need both your driver and the LaserWriter 8 extension (or the PSPrinter extension—LaserWriter 8 is supplied by Apple, while PSPrinter is supplied by Adobe).

In addition to the printer driver, as mentioned previously, a PPD is needed to provide the program and the driver with information about your printer. Again, if you have been merrily printing all this time, you already have one selected. In a moment, this chapter covers to how to customize your PPD, but here is how you would go about selecting one:

With your printer on:

1. Open the Chooser (in the Apple Menu).

2. Click the driver that corresponds to the printer you use (either LaserWriter 8, PSPrinter, or another one). This activates the Setup button, as indicated in Figure 14.5. In all the corresponding figures, there might be variations in the dialog boxes depending upon your system.

Figure 14.5

Select your printer driver in the Chooser and click Setup.

3. Clicking Setup in the Chooser opens the Setup dialog box (see Figure 14.6).

Figure 14.6

The Printer Setup dialog box.

4. Clicking Auto Setup automatically checks with the printer (this is why you needed to turn it on before beginning this process), gleans all the pertinent information, and selects a PPD itself. Unless you want to select a special customized PPD (see following), this is the only route you'll need to take.

5. Clicking Select PPD brings up a box containing all the available PPDs (see Figure 14.7). Select the one that corresponds to your printer (which is the default), or you can select a customized PPD you have created.

Figure 14.7

The Select PPD...dialog box.

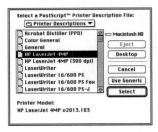

6. Clicking Printer Info calls up all the pertinent information about your printer, including what version of PostScript it is using. (See Figure 14.8.)

Figure 14.8

The Printer Info dialog box.

7. Clicking Configure enables you to take advantage of any special features your printer manufacture has included (such as multiple paper trays, color options, and so on). In most cases, however, you'll be told that there are no installable features available.

One of PageMaker's strengths is that it understands the power of the PPD. When you installed PageMaker, you were asked to select your default PPD. Whenever you print, you can change the PPD directly from the Print dialog box. Many people seem inclined to ignore the PPD file, simply setting it up when the printer is installed and then forgetting about it. In most cases, this is probably adequate; there's no real need to monkey around with the PPD file unless you really like fiddling with things. Keep in mind, however, that the more information that is contained in your PPD, the more information PageMaker has regarding your printer, and the more it can optimize your output. Assuming that the default PPD information tells everything about your printer and your system might be analogous to assuming that your driver's license tells everything about you as a person, which is probably not likely to be the case.

There are several levels of tweaking you can make to your PPD. Within PageMaker, in the Utilities menu, is a function called Update PPD..., which scans your printer and enables you to make several default adjustments to the PPD, such as maximum paper size, adding fonts to the printer's memory, and adjusting the amount of time the program takes trying to print a file.

Another option is to locate the PPD file (which is commonly found in the Extensions folder in a sub-folder called Printer Descriptions) and open it in a text editor such as SimpleText. There, you can read through it (to the extent that it's possible) and make any changes you'd like. As Figure 14.9 indicates, for example, the default font in one particular PPD is Courier.

This means that when the printer cannot find a PostScript font corresponding to one that has been used in a document, it substitutes Courier. This default font could be changed to something more distinctive (thus making it easier to locate on a printed page). If you do make any changes, be sure to give it a different name, in case you make a mistake. That way your original PPD file isn't damaged. Also be sure to use straight ASCII text format, not, say, PageMaker or Microsoft Word.

One reason you might want to create new PPDs is to create different default settings for different tasks, such as commonly-performed jobs that require different page sizes or default fonts.

Figure 14.9

A portion of a PPD file pertaining to fonts.

Imagesetters

Unlike laser and ink-jet printers, imagesetters are large, expensive, high-end devices, owned primarily by service bureaus, typesetting houses, and organizations that generate enough output to warrant the expense. Imagesetters, unlike laser printers, use a laser to record tiny dots making up an image on photographic paper or, more often, film. (Hence, imagesetters are often also known as "film recorders" and, on occasion, "film plotters.")

An imagesetter uses, in lieu of a PostScript interpreter, a device (either built in or standalone and either as software or hardware) called a *raster image processor (RIP)*. A RIP functions much like the PostScript interpreter we discussed previously. The RIP essentially translates the PostScript code into a fine grid of dots. The laser then exposes each of these dots on the film or photo paper.

Imagesetters are capable of much higher resolutions than laser printers or ink-jet printers (>3,000 ppi), because, among other reasons, the dot size is not limited by the size of a toner particle. (Another critically important reason is that an imagesetter has a much more powerful computer built in, which enables it to make the more complex geometric calculations needed for high-res imaging.) As a result, you often see the somewhat redundant phrase "high-res imagesetter." Imagesetters, by their very nature, are "high-res."

Imagesetters are the output device of choice for all serious prepress personnel. Using PostScript and a good RIP, halftones and screen tints can be output on the same film as text and line art as negatives that are nearly ready for platemaking. This can happen because neither PostScript nor the RIP really cares if an image is text or halftones; dots are dots, whether those dots are forming the lines and curves of letters or forming halftone dots. It's all the same to the hardware and software. Imagesetters are also used to generate color separation negatives for process color printing. (See Chapter 10 for more information on process colors.)

Note

In imagesetter output, halftone dots are made up of the much smaller printer "spots." A halftone dot made up of smaller spots is known as a "halftone cell."

Imagesetters are dealt with more in depth in Chapter 15 when the preparation of material for service bureaus is discussed. The remainder of this chapter deals primarily with the PageMaker "Print" command in general, and laser printer output in particular, as that is the most commonly used output device on the desktop. There are also tips for imagesetter output, as one can use a desktop laser printer to anticipate potential imagesetter output problems. Chapter 15 covers imagesetters and service bureaus in more detail.

Laser Printers versus Imagesetters

All resolutions are not created equal. There are high-end laser printers that have resolutions of 1,200 ppi. Would this not be a suitable alternative to a 1,200 ppi imagesetter?

Not really, no. The advantage of an imagesetter over a laser printer is not only in terms of resolution, but in how that resolution is arrived at. The electrophotographic process of transferring particles of pigmented toner to a sheet of paper does not generate output that looks as good as the direct laser imaging of dots on a photosensitive film, even at the same resolution.

The difference between the two types of devices is a case of "what you can get away with" and "what is desirable for high-end work." Laser printers, even at 600 ppi, work fine for generating camera-ready art. It's not going to win any awards for high quality, but it won't look cheesy either. (In fact, a successful newsletter on the desktop publishing industry is produced by outputting 600 ppi laser prints and shooting negatives of them. It looks fine, and no one is any the wiser for it.) However, slick, high-quality magazines (such as *Art Direction* or other such publications) are most likely not produced in this way.

Walk-Through of the Print Dialog Boxes

Selecting Print from the File menu brings up the Print dialog box. Unlike most other applications' Print dialog boxes, PageMaker's boxes are multi-faceted, possessing five different modes that provide a great deal of variability in output options.

Document Mode

The default dialog box that comes up when the Print command is first selected is the Document mode dialog box (see Figure 14.10).

Figure 14.10

The Document mode of the Print dialog box.

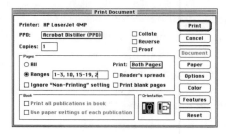

Notice along the right side of the dialog box a set of buttons (Paper, Options, Color, Features). These access the different modes. The commands in this dialog box enable to you specify the basics of the output: number of copies, pages, and so on, along with several other advanced capabilities that we will discuss in the following sections.

Printer and PPD

The first line tells you what printer is attached, which you cannot change through PageMaker. But remember how you could select a PPD through the Chooser or during the installation of PageMaker? Well, PageMaker's Print dialog box enables you to pick a PPD prior to printing, on-the-fly, saving you from having to wade through the layers of dialog boxes in the Chooser. Although you can't change the printer on-the-fly, you might have several custom PPDs that vary according to the job you'll be printing. Here you can select which one you need for the job you are about to print.

Copies

Fairly straightforward: the number of copies of the publication you would like (up to 32,000). When PageMaker prints out multiple copies of a multi-page document, you get all the copies of page one, followed by all the copies of page two, and so on.

By clicking the Collate checkbox, however, PageMaker will print the document in complete sets. Clicking the Reverse checkbox prints each set of pages of a document from the last page to the first (rather than from the first page to the last).

Note

Keep in mind that the collating mode takes as long as, perhaps even longer, than it would take to collate the sets by hand. This function is more useful for many copies of larger documents rather than one or two copies of a one- or two-page document.

Selecting the Proof checkbox is useful for the quick printing of pages containing Placed graphics; PageMaker doesn't try printing out the graphic, merely replacing it with a plain rectangle filled with an X. This saves time (and toner) when making prints of pages for text proofing purposes. It is also useful for locating output problems. Often, pages won't print due to the inclusion of complex graphics (see the "Ensuring That Your Pages Print At All" section later in this chapter). Selecting the Proof checkbox can help determine if the graphics are indeed causing any output problems.

Pages

In PageMaker, you can check the All radio button and, as the name indicates, print out all the pages of a document, or you can click the Ranges button and select a range of pages. As you can tell by looking at Figure 14.10, you can specify continuous ranges of pages (separating the first and last pages of a range with a hyphen), individual sets of ranges, or individual pages (separating them by commas). You can also enter a single page number or range more than once, if you want more than one copy of only certain pages. In the case of the Print job in Figure 14.10, you are printing pages 1–3, page 10, pages 15–19, and a second copy of page 2. Also, ranges and individual pages can be placed in any order, although when specifying a range, the lower page number needs to precede the higher one (for example, you can't specify "3–1").

Alternately, there is a Print pop-up menu in the center of the Pages section of the dialog box that enables you to specify whether you want to print Even pages only, Odd pages only, or Both Pages (such as, both even and odd). You also can select Reader's Spreads, which fit a two-page spread on a single sheet of paper, reducing the size of the pages to fit. This also automatically changes the orientation of the sheet to landscape.

If you are including any blank pages in your document (for layout and imposition purposes), PageMaker ignores them (as a paper and time-saving feature) unless you check the Print Blank Pages box. And you can override any non-printing designations you have applied to objects by checking the Ignore "Non-Printing" Setting box.

Orientation

As in any other application, you can specify whether your pages should print in the portrait orientation (such as the longer dimension running vertically) or landscape (the shorter dimension running vertically). Notice that this is based on the page dimensions you selected when you began the document. $8^{1}/_{2} \times 11$, for example, is portrait. $11 \times 8^{1}/_{2}$ is landscape. If you selected Reader's Spreads, landscape is automatically chosen for you.

Book

If you specified a book list prior to beginning the document, you can opt to print all the chapters on that list, as long as the document you are printing from contains the entire book list. One caveat is that the orientation you select in each publication is the one that is honored, regardless of whether you checked the Use Paper Settings of Each Publication box. By checking this box, you can select an individual paper size, paper tray, and so on, for each individual publication.

Paper Mode

By clicking the Paper button, you open the dialog box (see Figure 14.11) that enables you to specify the paper size desired for the publication.

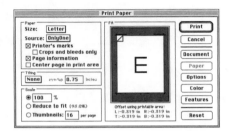

Figure 14.11

The Paper mode of the Print dialog box.

Paper Size and Source

The options available from the Paper Size and Source pop-up menus are gleaned from the PPD file. If your printer has only one paper tray, it is the only one available. If the PPD indicates that you can use custom paper sizes, you are able to select it, generating another dialog box that enables you to specify the parameters of the desired size.

Printer's Marks and Page Information

The Printer's Marks function generates a printout that includes registration marks, crop marks, and color and grayscale density bars. The Page Information function includes file information at the foot of the page (see Figure 14.12).

If you are using the printout as camera-ready copy, you need Printer's Marks selected, which the printer or binder uses as a guide for cropping and trimming the publication, as well as keeping track of the ink density and successive color registration during the print run. (Registration refers to the ability to print successive images or colors in the proper position on a page, used primarily in reference to multi-color printing jobs.) New to version 6.5 is the Crops and Bleeds Only marks, which is useful if you only want crop marks and don't need to worry about registration.

Figure 14.12

Example of output with Printer's Marks and Page Information selected.

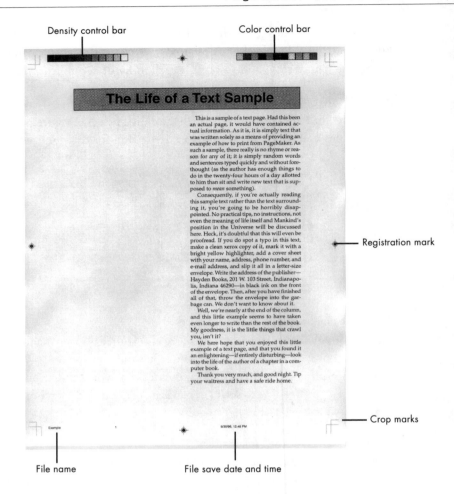

Density control bar

Color control bar

Registration mark

Crop marks

File name

File save date and time

When selecting Printer's Marks, the size of the page needs to be $^3/_4$ inch smaller than the paper size. If you are printing onto standard letter size paper ($8^1/_2 \times 11$), for example, your page size can be no larger than $7^3/_4 \times 9^1/_4$, otherwise the edges of the page are cropped. Selecting Page Information requires $^1/_2$-inch of space at the edges of the page. Using both together requires 0.875 inch.

Note

If you select the Center Page option, PageMaker will center the page on the paper.

Page Fit

PostScript-compatible printers use the Fit box to enable you to see in advance how your page fits on the paper, even with the Printer's Marks and Page Information selected (see Figure 14.13).

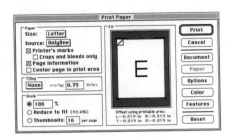

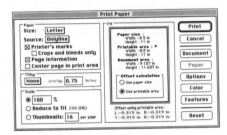

Figure 14.13

Two ways of checking page fit.

As you can tell, there are two means of checking the page fit, which you can toggle between by double-clicking in the center of the Fit box. The first view shows you graphically how the fit is, while the numbers at the bottom tell you by how much the page size is offset by additional marks and information. (If the numbers are in red it is a bad fit.) The second view is based on the information gleaned from the PPD.

Scale

Notice that in the Scale box, you can click the Reduce to Fit button to shrink (or enlarge) the page size to fit the paper (PageMaker automatically calculates the percent reduction or enlargement needed). Keep in mind, however, that if your ultimate page size is the original page size before you reduced it to fit, the service bureau or printer will need to enlarge it again. This effectively reduces the resolution of the page (see "Artificial" Resolution later in this chapter). You also can scale a page up and down by (from 5% to 1,600%) entering a number in the top box (100% is the default).

In the Scale box, you can also print a set of Thumbnail "sketches" of the pages in a publication on a single sheet of paper, which is useful for checking the overall design and layout of all the pages with respect to each other. By checking the radio button and entering a number in the Thumbnails box you can specify how many thumbnails you'd like on a single page, and PageMaker will scale the pages to fit.

Options Mode

If you click the Options button on the right side of the dialog box, you'll be in the Options mode (see Figure 14.14).

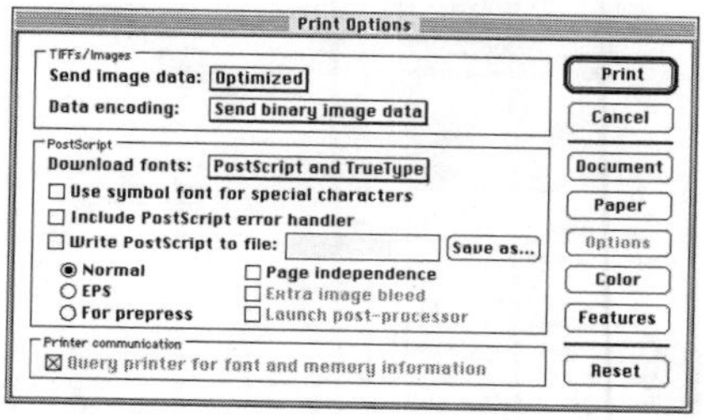

Figure 14.14

The Options mode of the Print dialog box.

The Options mode enables you to enhance the efficiency of your output, especially with regard to images.

Send Image Data

The first pop-up menu—Send Image Data— provides you with four options for sending TIFFs and other image data to the printer. The default setting, Normal, sends image data to the printer at the maximum available resolution.

The Optimized Subsampling option sends the printer whatever data is needed by the printer to render the image. When you generate a halftone, you impart to it a certain line screen. The resolution of most desktop laser printers, however, is often far less than that required to generate many digital halftones. This topic is discussed in greater detail in Chapter 15, but suffice it to say here that sending a maximum resolution halftone image to a laser printer incapable of reproducing it will take a great deal of time, and to no avail. Consequently, the Optimized option ignores all the unnecessary data and only sends the printer that data needed to render the best image the printer can. This can save time during output, because there is far less data for the printer to deal with.

The Low-Resolution option is geared for speed rather than quality, and is useful if your output is only including an image for FPO (for position only) purposes. There is also an Omit Images option, useful primarily when saving a publication as a PostScript file to send to a service bureau, which creates a placeholder in the file for the image. The image can then be inserted by the service bureau.

Data Encoding

The Data Encoding option sends image information as either ASCII or binary image data, which are two different means of encoding the information comprising the image. Binary tends to be faster, but some networks don't transmit binary data very well, if at all. Files sent by email, for example, often need to be encoded as an ASCII character set.

PostScript

The PostScript management box enables you to save the publication as a PostScript file (see the section in this chapter on PostScript). The Download Fonts option enables you to embed the fonts you have used in your document for later use by the service bureau who might or might not have them. You can embed TrueType or PostScript fonts. This option takes up a great deal of disk space, so check with your service bureau (and check your font licensing agreements) before you select it. Keep in mind that only the fonts that don't exist in the target printer will be embedded in the file (gleaned—you guessed it—from the PPD). This is another reason to check with the service bureau before selecting this option.

- The Use Symbol Font option is a bit of an anachronistic feature that dates back to the days when symbols, such as the copyright symbol, trademark symbol, daggers, and so on, were not included in Key Caps but were instead in a special font called *Symbol*. Generally, you will not ever need to check this option.

- You've seen the Write PostScript to File option already, but here is where we save it to disk rather than send it to the printer. If you select Normal from the list below this box,

PageMaker generates its own name for it (the file name plus the extension ".ps" to indicate that it is a PostScript file). Using the Normal option saves the document as a "pure" PostScript file.

♦ If you click EPS, you get each page of your document saved as an EPS (encapsulated PostScript) file. This function is useful if you are going to be importing the pages into a more advanced post-processing program such as TrapWise or if you want to take a picture of the pages and open them in a drawing program such as Illustrator or FreeHand. If you select this option, PageMaker assigns it the .eps extension.

♦ The For Prepress option is used for saving color separations to be output by a service bureau. If you select this option, PageMaker assigns it the .sep extension.

♦ You can create your own names for files of course, but the file extensions—anathema in the Mac world, admittedly, but useful on occasion—should be kept as is, as they are a handy reference for the service bureau or whoever else might need to know at a glance how a particular file has been saved.

♦ The Page Independence option is useful only if you are sending a PostScript file to a service bureau, the most important aspect about it being that it places font information on each page. Check with your service bureau before selecting this step, as it takes up additional disk space and might be all for naught.

♦ The Extra Image Bleed option is used in those cases where PageMaker's default 1/8-inch bleed for TIFF images is not enough. This option allows for up to a one-inch bleed, but is available only when saving the file as an EPS file or with the For Prepress option.

♦ The Launch Post-Processor option automatically launches a post-processing program, such as TrapWise or PrePrint, when the write-to-file has been completed. If you are going to do your own prepress work with any of these applications, check this option.

Color Mode

Clicking the Color button in the main Print dialog box opens the Color mode dialog box (see Figure 14.15), which is where you can set the screen angles, the line screen, and so on, for each of your color separations. Your service bureau will most likely be the ones who will use this dialog box, but it is also here that you indicate your settings for outputting composites for proofing purposes.

Figure 14.15

The Color mode of the Print dialog box.

If you send your publication to the service bureau as a PageMaker file, they can access this box directly. However, if you save a PostScript file of the publication to disk (see the section on the Options Mode above), you need to make the settings here.

Let's briefly run through each of the settings.

Composite

If you are printing your publication on a laser printer, you need to check Composite, which means that all your color separations are grouped into one document. When you click Grayscale, all the colors are reproduced as grays. This is the best setting for general proofing; green will come out as grayish, red will come out as blackish, and so on. If you are outputting a mechanical for a spot color, click Print Colors in Black. This prints out whatever spot color you have selected as black. If you have imposed a screen tint on any spot color, it outputs honoring the percentage you have set. (When outputting mechanicals to be shot as negatives and as plates, you need to select Print Colors in Black, or as black minus any screen tint. This is so it will photograph well. The actual color itself is imparted by the ink on press.)

Mirror/Negative

When an imagesetter outputs onto film, it can do so either as "right-reading" or as "wrong-reading." Also, it can do so as "emulsion-up," or as "emulsion-down." This refers to the orientation of the imaged film coming out of the imagesetter. Sometimes, to expedite platemaking, a film needs to have its image produced a certain way with respect to the film emulsion. Neither Mirror nor Negative should be checked without first consulting with your service bureau and printer. More often than not, the service bureau will handle this aspect of it, often bypassing the option here and orienting it correctly on the imagesetter. Film can be wasted if these are set incorrectly.

Preserve EPS Colors

Checking this box ensures that the colors contained in a placed EPS graphic print as originally specified, regardless of what changes you made to the colors in PageMaker.

Separations

The service bureau takes care of this set of specs, but you can click the Separations radio button if you want to output an individual sheet for each color separation, to see if the correct color has been applied to the right object.

The CMS Setup...button accesses PageMaker's Color Management System (covered in Chapter 11).

The Remove unused button keeps PageMaker from outputting blank sheets of paper or, more expensively, blank sheets of film when a color has been defined yet not actually used in a publication. Service bureaus really like this feature.

The Print all inks and Print no inks buttons are shortcuts to selecting all or no inks, often before selecting one or more individual colors.

The All to process button is a dangerous function, and really should not be used. Essentially, it converts colors contained in the publication to the CMYK color space. This is fine and needs to be done, but in doing it here you are at the mercy of PageMaker's color conversion algorithms, which might or might not generate accurate CMYK equivalents. You are better off setting colors as discussed in Chapter 11.

Frequency and Angle

This is where you can select your line screen. The Optimized screen pop-up menu enables you to know what the best setting is, using information gleaned from the PPD file. The subjects of screen frequency and screen angle are covered in greater detail in Chapter 15. Suffice it to say here, always consult with your print shop or service bureau before changing the default screen setting.

You should not change the default screen angle unless you *really* know what you are doing. Even changing a screen angle by as little as 0.001 of a degree can generate an undesirable and perceptible moiré pattern. If you are adding a spot color *in addition* to the process colors, check with the print shop to find out at what angle to set the spot color. If you are doing only spot color or black-and-white work, the default angle is 45 degrees which, as was mentioned, is the angle that best eliminates the perception of halftone dots.

PageMaker will only use these screen functions when a continuous-tone graphic has been placed in PageMaker, or a screen tint has been specified.

Despite the wide flexibility of this dialog box always check with your printer and service bureau before selecting anything other than the default settings, especially if you are going to be saving your publication as a PostScript file. Refer to the following sections ("Ensuring That Pages Print Well" and "Ensuring That Pages Print at All") on generating desktop laser proofs as a means of spotting egregious problems *before* sending your job to the service bureau. It can save time and expense.

The specific topics relating to the settings in the Color dialog box are covered in Chapter 15. Also, refer to Chapters 10 and 11 for more in-depth color reference.

Features Mode

The Features button accesses the Features dialog box. As you remember from setting up the PPD, some printers have additional features. This is where they can be accessed. If you don't have any special features available with your printer, you'll get a dialog box similar to the one in Figure 14.16.

Figure 14.16

*The Features mode of the
Print dialog box.*

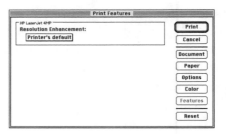

Most of the choices here are related to resolution or other variables indicated in your PPD.

Using Non-PostScript Printers

If you are using a non-PostScript-compatible printer, there are several differences to the previously mentioned Print dialog boxes:

◆ *Paper Mode*: If you are not using a PostScript printer, the Paper button found in the main Print dialog box (or the Document mode) changes to a Setup button. This "Setup mode" functions similarly to the Paper mode. But because a non-PostScript printer doesn't use a PPD (which stands, after all, for "PostScript Printer Description"), PageMaker needs to glean printer information from the Chooser and the System themselves. The Setup mode dialog box varies from printer to printer, and in some cases (especially for ink-jet printers) might look remarkably like the Color mode dialog box.

◆ *Features Mode*: If you click the Features button when using a non-PostScript printer, you'll probably be told to select the Setup mode.

After you have wended your way through all these dialog boxes and modes, click the Print button while in any mode, and the publication prints according to the chosen specifications.

Using Printer Styles

In addition to being able to switch from PPD to PPD on the fly, PageMaker now enables you to create preset "printer styles," which you can switch between or among. As you saw previously, the Print dialog boxes have many variables, and clicking through them all can take some time. Often, you'll have need for some characteristics that differ from the default settings. If you use these new parameters a lot, you might not want to click through all those dialog boxes every time you want to print something. You also might not remember what specific settings you used the last time you printed the same type of document. Printer Styles keeps you from having to worry about it.

If you look at Figures 14.17 and 14.18, you'll see the difference between the [Current] printer style (or the default) and a new one that can be created.

Figure 14.17

Printer Styles main dialog box showing the attributes for the [Current] (or default) printer style.

Figure 14.18

Printer Styles main dialog box showing the attributes of a second printer style.

Here's how you can create a new Printer Style.

1. Select Printer Styles from the File Menu, which opens the main Printer Styles dialog box we saw in Figures 14.16 and 14.17.

2. Click New.

3. Name your new style.

4. You can then access the main Print dialog box, where you can set all the parameters and attributes you like.

5. When you are finished, click Save, and all your parameters will be saved.

Alternately, you can open the main Print dialog box as you are going to print, enter a set of parameters, then click [CMD], which changes the Print Button to Style. Clicking Style opens up the dialog box in which you can name the new style. All the parameters you set for the job will then be saved as a new printer style.

Note

By the way, if you work with a number of other people all using PageMaker, the Printer Styles are stored in the RSRC folder in the main PageMaker folder. If you want to give any of your custom printer styles to coworkers, they can be copied from your own RSRC folder to another person's.

Styles can be edited by scrolling to File/Printer Styles/Define...and clicking the Edit button enables you to revise a style. You might notice that you are not able to edit the [Current] style. To make any changes to it you need to create a new style incorporating the alterations. The Remove button on the Define Printer Styles dialog box, as one would expect, deletes the selected printer style. Notice also that you cannot delete the [Current] style.

There are several attributes that you cannot preset in a printer style. These include the range of pages to be printed, the Query printer for font and memory information option (in the Options menu) the spot color ink Frequency, or an Angle setting (in the Colors menu).

Ensuring That Pages Print Well: Optimizing Laser-Printed Mechanicals

As you might have learned by now just from basic experience, there are a variety of ways of optimizing the quality of your laser printouts. These do not necessarily have to require an intimate understanding of how computers and printers work. In this digital age, we often look for "high-tech" solutions to problems, while neglecting such mundane aspects of desktop printing as toner and paper.

"Artificial" Resolution

The term "artificial" is used somewhat facetiously here, I admit. The concept of resolution—such as the using of small dots to form letters and images—is based on an optical illusion anyway (as is the concept of the halftone), so noodling with documents to produce the illusion of greater resolution is not somehow a "cheat."

As you might recall, in the Paper option of the Print dialog box (see Figure 14.19) you can scale the output up by as much as will fit on the paper size your printer can handle (most likely 8½×11). When it comes time to shoot it for reproduction, it can be scaled back down by the same percentage. By outputting at a greater size and then reducing it again, you essentially have increased the number of dots per inch. Of course, this only works on pages that are smaller than the maximum size paper of your printer. If you are dealing with 8½×11 pages, you won't be able to scale up the pages unless you have a larger paper-size printer.

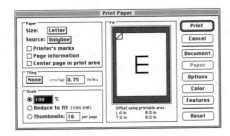

Figure 14.19

The output size can be scaled in the Paper options of the Print dialog box.

Toner

Another means of mechanically optimizing output is to adjust the toner controls on the printer (the toner density adjustment) and the toner cartridge itself. Most printers let you adjust the amount of toner the printer lays down on a page.

Look at a page of sample output and see if openings in small letters (such as the center of the lowercase "o" in small point sizes) are closed. If so, you might want to reduce the toner density. Conversely, if you notice some degree of lightness anywhere on a page, you might want to boost the toner density.

Keep in mind, however, that the toner density changes as you print more jobs. (This is because a laser printer—which functions on the process of electrostatic attraction between toner particles and an oppositely-charged metal drum— generates more of a static charge the more pages have been printed, resulting in greater amounts of toner adhering to the drum.)

Note

You should print several (such as 10) all-black pages just after turning the printer on. You'll not only get darker copy, you'll also get consistently darker copy. Notice the distribution of toner across an all-black page printed just after start-up. It will most likely look streaky. This streakiness will disappear as more pages are printed. (This might seem like a waste of toner—and, admittedly, toner doesn't come cheap—but anything that increases significantly the quality of your output cannot be considered a waste.)

Toner density can be adjusted—on many printers—by a wheel or knob located inside the printer, near the cartridge bay. On some printers, toner density can be adjusted through the control panel. Alter these various adjustments until you see sharp, crisp output.

If you are printing pages to be used as camera-ready copy, do not use a toner cartridge that is running on empty, especially if you have a number of pages to print. Although shaking and rocking a "dying" cartridge can resuscitate it to some degree, it might not last very long, resulting in a need to change toner cartridges halfway through a job. This will result in inconsistent densities throughout the pages. As the sheets printed with the dying cartridge become lighter, the sheets printed with the new cartridge become darker.

Also keep in mind that shaking and rocking a toner cartridge before a job helps evenly distribute the loose toner within as well as loosen any clumps of toner. You've probably noticed that you can run a "Toner Low" printer for several weeks simply by removing the cartridge and shaking it a bit. Similarly, even if a cartridge isn't on its last legs, shaking can help make it distribute more evenly on the drum and, consequently, the paper.

Warning

One caveat, however, that one invariably learns from bitter experience: if you purchase "cut-rate" cartridges don't shake them too hard. (Especially if you're wearing a white shirt.)

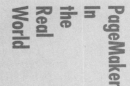

Toner Reclamation

One fact about toner cartridges that is worth mentioning, especially for those of us who are ecologically aware: many toner manufacturers now have reclamation policies, where you can send empty cartridges back to them for reconditioning and refilling. This is a worthwhile endeavor and should be supported. Often, new toner cartridges come with a return label, shipping being paid for by the manufacturer. Please do take advantage of this. The more people do, the more likely it is that other companies will begin doing so, which will go some distance toward reducing the amount of material poured into landfills.

Artists' Fixatives

Another trick occasionally used to improve laser output quality is to use what is known as artists' fixative, or fixative spray such as Krylon. These sprays are often used, as their name implies, by artists to keep original artwork and drawings from smudging. When sprayed on laser prints, it dissolves and fuses the plastic-based toner particles, making them less likely to be rubbed free of the printed areas of the sheet. (Hairspray will also work.) Use such sprays in small doses, both for the sake of the print quality and for the ozone layer.

LaserWriter Paper

If you have ever used an ink-jet printer, you know how well image quality can be improved by using special smooth, coated papers. The same is true with laser printers. Special LaserWriter paper is not just a marketing ploy as some people suspect; the coating and texture of the paper really can optimize the production of images. The high whiteness of this paper also improves contrast and allows mechanicals printed on it to photograph better. It can, of course, be a little more expensive than regular xerographic paper, but it can often be worth it.

Regardless of what paper you ultimately decide to use, be certain you have enough of it to make it through the job. This might seem like a blindingly obvious thing to mention, but running out of one stock and switching to a seemingly similar type of paper can result in inconsistent pages.

Larger Paper Sizes

If you want to output at a size larger than $8^{1}/_{2}\times11$, most laser printers enable you to output at $8^{1}/_{2}\times14$ (so-called "legal size"), but that only expands the page in one direction, which might not help a great deal. Some computer rental or copy shops (such as those that also lease time on computers) might have 11×17 laser printers, which might be desirable. Such are appearing more and more frequently, especially in larger cities. It might be worth a trip to check out their equipment and costs.

Ensuring That Pages Print at All: Optimizing Files for the Service Bureau

Although the following remarks could just as easily be placed in the next chapter, as they involve problems that cause more trouble (in time and expense) when a service bureau encounters them, they are placed here because the desktop laser printer can be used to determine if problems are likely to arise further down the line.

Nothing is more disheartening to everyone involved in a print job than designing a page or a document that looks terrific in theory and on screen but is completely unprintable, either from a laser printer, an imagesetter, or on a printing press. The combination of PageMaker and your imagination enables you to do a lot of things. Remember, though, that laser printers and imagesetters are mechanical devices, and your imagination needs to be constrained by what is physically possible.

A good way of avoiding that depressing moment when your service bureau calls to let you know that your job won't output is to output it first—graphics and all—on your own laser printer. Any serious snags *it* has will not be likely to disappear when sent to a service bureau.

Just as there are many colors that exist in nature that cannot be reproduced by a printing press, so too are there certain page designs and elements that do not print well—if at all. Modern desktop computers and the computers found in output devices are very powerful, but they're not perfect. Here are some common examples of output problems that can be anticipated in advance and planned for.

Manipulate Scans Before Placing Them in PageMaker

As was covered in previous chapters, you can manipulate photographs and other graphics directly in PageMaker, leaving your original image files untouched. PageMaker enables you to rotate, skew, crop, and resize images. Remember how long it took you to make all those changes? Well, a laser printer or imagesetter also takes quite a long time to deal with them.

Here's why: PageMaker pipes a copy of the graphic into your document, and all the changes you make are done not on the original but rather on the way PageMaker interprets this copy. When it sends the PostScript file of the page to be printed, it doesn't send the cropped and rotated image to the output device; it sends a copy of the untouched illustration along with the instructions for making your changes to it. Consequently, the printer needs to make all the changes again itself. (Think of it as analogous to showing up for dinner at a friend's house not with a fully-cooked pie, but rather with a recipe for making the pie.)

For the printer to re-make all these changes takes a good deal of time and computing power. If the manipulations you performed were excessive, it might even simply abort the job entirely and not print it. The same thing is likely to happen if you send the job out to a service bureau. Although an imagesetter has a much more powerful internal computer than your laser printer, it still might be more than even it can handle.

You can avoid these kinds of problems by doing as much manipulation as possible to original images *before* bringing them into PageMaker. If you want to keep an unretouched scan on hand, duplicate the image file, and make all manipulations in Photoshop to the copy. Then, Place this altered copy into PageMaker, keeping the untouched original safely stored elsewhere.

Image rotation is one operation that can *really* knock out an output device. PageMaker makes life *too* easy by enabling you to rotate images placed within it. Outputting PageMaker-rotated TIFFs is trouble waiting to happen.

Keep Resolutions Low

You can also avoid output problems by not using an excessively high resolution for scanned images. A halftone photograph should have a resolution that is no more than twice the screen frequency (covered in Chapter 15). If you are going to be printing a 150-line screen, for example, the highest resolution you need is 300 ppi. Anything higher than that is overkill. Reduce the resolution of the original file, if necessary, before bringing it into PageMaker.

Don't Cover Page Elements with Other Page Elements

Another trick is to avoid covering page elements. You can hide elements that you don't want to print by putting white boxes over them, or using the Send to Back command. This is sneaky and clever. However, PostScript is remarkably thorough and meticulous, and spends a great deal of time describing the hidden element before it describes the means of hiding it. This causes snarls in output traffic. Try to avoid hiding things—just because you can't see it doesn't mean it's not there.

Keep EPS Graphics Simple

Complex graphics created in Illustrator or FreeHand and placed in PageMaker can also cause output problems. Simplify curves and reduce the number of blends, if possible. The more calculations a computer has to make, the more trouble you're going to get into.

Also try to avoid nested EPS files, which can really tax the processor and memory of an output device, resulting in something as relatively benign as the file not printing, or something far more serious such as a system crash.

Also, try to avoid embedding text in EPS files. Granted, this might not always be possible. A way of avoiding problems than can arise from embedding text in EPS files (such as the output device not seeing the font and putting in a substitute, which is never a decent-looking font) is to convert all such text to graphic objects. (Different drawing programs call it different things, but it is usually a "create paths" function.) This is an especially good idea if you are using an unusual font that a service bureau is not likely to have. This, however, does tend to thicken the strokes of some typefaces, which is particularly egregious at small point sizes. In this case, it can sometimes help to import the graphic without the text, and simply type the text over it in PageMaker, sticking them together with the Group command.

Avoid Non-PostScript Fonts and Graphics

As was mentioned earlier, service bureaus tend not to use TrueType fonts. Most imagesetters are PostScript devices, and TrueType causes trouble when the RIP encounters them. Similarly, the PICT graphics file format is also not a PostScript-supported format (it is based on QuickDraw) and also causes big problems on imagesetters. Try to stick with the TIFF or EPS graphics file formats. Macintosh TIFF can differ somewhat from Windows TIFF, so be careful. Check with your service bureau beforehand to determine what the best file format option might be.

Avoid Hairline Rules

We all know the hairline rule, a line one pixel wide. These look fine onscreen and look great when output at 300 or 600 ppi. Why shouldn't they be used for imagesetter output? Well, look at that first sentence: "...a line one pixel wide." Think about the difference between high-resolution and low-resolution devices. Imagesetters can achieve such high resolutions because they are capable of generating much smaller printer spots (pixels) than laser printers and computer monitors. Onscreen and on a 300 or even 600 ppi laser printer, the pixels are kind of large. On a 2,000+ ppi imagesetter, the pixels are very small, and thus one pixel wide is nearly invisible. (PageMaker, however, does use a hairline rule that is a fixed 0.20 point wide, which can eliminate this problem.)

SUMMARY

Now that you have explored some of the basic prepress issues and desktop output options, the next chapter discusses how to deal with service bureaus and printers, and how best to format and lay out your pages so as to minimize problems and difficulties as much as possible.

PREPRESS, SERVICE BUREAUS, AND PRINTERS

You saw in Chapter 14 how PageMaker and the Print function can be used to produce laser-printed output from the desktop, which can be used either as camera-ready mechanicals or as proofs and tests for imagesetter output. This chapter begins with some advanced prepress issues (which can be handled either at the desktop or by the service bureau, then looks beyond PageMaker itself at the world of service bureaus and print shops and provides a guide to economically and effectively bridging the gap between the desktop and the print shop. The end of this chapter looks ahead to the rapidly growing world of the Portable Document Format (PDF), using Adobe's Acrobat, and its place in prepress. In addition to this chapter, consult Appendix D "Master Checklist," for a quick list of the considerations to keep in mind when preparing a job to send out to the service bureau and the printer.

ADVANCED DESKTOP PREPRESS ISSUES

The following sections cover some important prepress issues including imposition and color halftones.

Imposition

One important aspect of prepress is called *imposition*, a procedure that has traditionally been performed by print shops at the stripping stage of the process, or earlier at the service bureau when negatives are output. Imposition is the process of orienting pages on a negative film or plate so that several pages can be printed simultaneously on a single press sheet, the correct order and orientation being accomplished by folding and trimming the printed press sheets.

The Need for Imposition

If printers printed everything one page at a time, imposition wouldn't be an issue. Printing in such a manner, however, is hardly economical, so printers prefer to minimize the number of independent press runs as much as possible. They do this by printing multiple pages on a large press sheet, then folding and cutting these printed sheets down to the proper size. These folded groups of pages are called *signatures*, and they can comprise any size press sheet folded into any number of pages (well, an even number anyway), depending on the size of the press and the size of the job. How the final publication is going to be bound is also an issue.

Here's an example of how an eight-page, $8^1/_2\times11$ newsletter might be printed and bound. Assume that there will be no special cover; the paper used for the inside pages will be the same as that used for the cover (cleverly called, in binding, a *self-cover*). (Also, for the sake of this example, don't worry about trimming, or cutting the publication down to its specified size.) A printer not interested in time or money could simply run four sheets of $8^1/_2\times11$ paper through the press twice (to print the front and back), for a total of eight independent press runs. A printer slightly interested in time and money could run two sheets of 11×17 paper through the press twice, then fold each sheet in half. This cuts the number of total press runs down to four.

Most printers, however, are likely to run one sheet of 17×22 paper through the press twice, printing all eight pages in two press runs. But as you can imagine, pages cannot be laid out on these sheets in the same order as they would appear in the final newsletter. That's what the folding accomplishes. Figure 15.1 shows how these pages would be oriented on the top side of the sheet, and Figure 15.2 shows how the reverse would need to be printed.

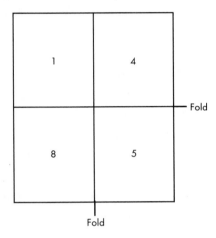

1	4
8	5

Fold

Fold

Figure 15.1

Side one of a 17×22 press sheet.

2	3
7	6

Fold

Fold

Figure 15.2

Side two of a 17×22 press sheet.

After printing, the sheet would be folded along the indicated fold lines and the top fold slit open after saddle-stitching (or, in other words, binding the pages by means of staples driven through the spine fold of the sheets).

The orientation of the pages in the correct position to accomplish the previous layout is the process of imposition. It was traditionally handled by the negative stripper, who would mount the negatives of each page in the correct position on a carrier sheet slightly larger than the press sheet. Increasingly, imagesetters are used to output large negatives with each page properly imposed.

Different size publications use different size press sheets and impositions to reduce the number of press runs as much as possible. These are known by specific names:

- A *broadside* is a sheet of paper printed as one leaf, or two pages, with no folding. (A leaf is one sheet of paper with two sides.)

- A *folio* is a press sheet that is folded once to produce two leaves comprising four pages.

- A *quarto* is a press sheet that is folded twice to produce four leaves comprising eight pages. The book size known as quarto is commonly $9^1/_2 \times 12$.

- An *octavo* is a press sheet that has been folded three times to produce eight leaves comprising 16. The book size known as octavo is commonly 6×9.

- A *16-mo* is a press sheet that has been folded four times to produce 16 leaves comprising 32 pages. The book size known as 16-mo is commonly 4×6.

- A *32-mo* is a press sheet that has been folded five times to produce 32 leaves comprising 64 pages. The book size known as 32-mo is commonly $3^1/_4 \times 5^1/_2$.

Binding the Publication

How a book or other publication is bound is dependent upon the length or thickness of the publication (which in turn is dependent upon the thickness of the paper). Most newsletters and many magazines are bound through *saddle-stitching*, or by staples driven through the spine. (Check out *Time*, *Newsweek*, or most of the other weekly news magazines for examples of saddle-stitching.) Thicker magazines, catalogs, phone books, and paperback books are bound through *perfect binding*, or the application of an adhesive along the spine that holds the pages together and holds the cover on the book. Hardcover books are bound by means of *thread sewing* (in which all the signatures are sewn together by thread) followed by *case binding* (where cloth-covered sheets of paperboard are bound to the pages by means of adhesive).

What does this have to do with prepress? In the case of perfect binding and case binding, not a great deal. Each page will essentially retain its integrity throughout the binding process. But if you are designing a publication that is going to be saddle-stitched, you have to worry about a phenomenon called *creep*. Here's what creep is: We speak of something as being "paper thin," but paper *does* have a thickness. When folded pages are gathered for saddle-stitching, one two-page sheet is inserted inside another one, and the spine increases in thickness. This results in the edges of an inner sheet protruding slightly beyond the sheet in which it has been inserted. The more pages that are inserted, the more the inner sheets will protrude. If the publication has enough pages and the paper used is thick enough, the inner sheets will stick out quite far indeed. Or, in other words, they "creep" out from beyond the outer pages. In terms of bindery operations, this is not a problem; when the publication is folded into a book, the right edge is simply trimmed off, resulting in pages that are even and square with each other. But think about what will happen to the margins of the inner pages when the sheets are trimmed. If you open a thick publication that has had its edge cut square, notice that the margin along the trimmed edge gets progressively narrower, as more paper was trimmed from the inner pages than the outer ones. It, too, will "creep" forward. (The binding edge will also creep, as well.)

The effects of creep are eliminated in prepress by a process known as *shingling*, or the slight increase in the outer margins of inner pages. You probably don't need to worry about shingling or creep if you are preparing a thin (less than 15–20 total pages) publication. If you are planning a thick publication, it pays to make up a dummy using the same paper you intend to print on to determine how much allowance should be made for creep.

Imposition with PageMaker's Build Booklet

In this section you learn how to use PageMaker to create booklets and correctly impose pages.

Build Booklet is based on PressWise, which is a high-end page imposition program published by Adobe. Build Booklet enables you to impose pages in the correct "order" and on sheets perhaps as large as those that would be used on press.

Warning

Build Booklet is a powerful utility, but with power comes the need to use it responsibly. In theory, you can impose a book-size publication (300+ pages), but do you really want to? As you recall from the simple eight-page newsletter example previously, it can get confusing determining which pages go where. For larger publications, it is probably advisable to let the printer worry about imposition, unless you're confident you know what you're doing. Doing it incorrectly might be more of a hindrance than a help, and waste a great deal of time and effort.

Build Booklet is really useful for small brochures and newsletters, but do check with your printer to determine their exact requirements. They will probably prefer to use a more powerful and professional imposition program—such as Adobe's PressWise—rather than the Build Booklet plug-in. A limitation of Build Booklet is that your imposition choices are not as great as you—or your printer—might want. It is, for example, not possible to set up the 17×22 sheets as mentioned in the previous example.

You would have to construct two 11×17 sets to accomplish the same thing.

Before beginning the build, be certain you have the disk space to handle it. Build Booklet creates an entire new publication from scratch, based on your laid-out pages. Also, make sure that you do the build last; it can be a real pain to proof and correct typos and other errors after the booklet has been built.

Building a Booklet

PageMaker's Build Booklet is found under the Utilities Menu, and under the Plug-Ins submenu. Selecting it brings up the main Build Booklet dialog box (see Figure 15.3).

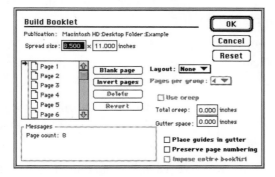

Figure 15.3

The main Build Booklet dialog box.

The Layout pop-up menu provides you with several options:

◆ **None.** Fairly self explanatory. It places each of your laid-out pages on its own page.

◆ **2-Up Saddle-Stitch.** This orients two of your pages side-by-side on a press sheet large enough to accommodate the spread.

◆ **2-Up Perfect Bound.** This option enables you to create sub-groups of two-page spreads (signatures), specifying how many pages should be grouped in each signature.

◆ **2-Up Consecutive, 3-Up Consecutive, 4-Up Consecutive.** These options create two-, three-, and four-page panels, as you would find in foldout booklets and brochures.

The Spread Size boxes indicate the default sizes of the sheets needed to accommodate your desired layout, based on the size of the pages you have created. You can adjust this number, but do heed the warnings that might appear in the Message window, especially if it indicates that the spread size is too small; you'll get a steady stream of error messages and an aborted build if you don't.

When the 2-Up Saddle-Stitch and the 2-Up Perfect Bound layouts are selected, you can specify how much space to allot for creep. There is no way to calculate this in advance, save to print out the spreads on the actual paper to be used, fold them, and insert the sheets inside one another, creating essentially a dummy of the publication. Then you can see how much you're going to need to allow for creep. If you have already accounted for creep in earlier stages of page layout, you don't need to worry about it here.

If you haven't already specified a gutter margin (in the Page Setup box, with the Facing Pages function), you can specify it here by entering a desired gutter amount.

Checking Place Guides in Gutter inserts a ruler in the gutter margin between two facing pages which Build Booklet has joined together on a single sheet.

You can check Preserve Page Numbering if you used the auto-pagination on your master pages. This function adds the proper page numbers to the pages when the booklet is constructed. If you have manually inserted page numbers on your pages, you don't need to check this.

Note

If you have created a booklist for your publication, you'll be able to check the Impose Entire Booklist function, which will impose all the items on the booklist. If you have not established one, this function will not be available.

The scrolling box toward the left center of this dialog box shows all the pages of the publication in order. The advantage of Build Booklet is that you don't need to put them in the proper imposition order. If you *do* want to change the order of the pages, you can do so at this point by pressing the (Option) [Alt] key. This changes the arrow cursor to a hand, and you can click and drag pages into the order you would like. If you want the page order to run in reverse order (say, from eight to one, rather than from one to eight), you can click Invert pages. If you change your mind and you really *do* want to keep them in ascending chronological order, click Invert pages again.

If you pick an imposition and a spread size that requires more pages than you have, the Message window lets you know how many blank pages you will need to fill out the signature(s). By moving the arrow up and down the scrolling box, you can indicate where to insert blank pages, and the pages themselves are inserted by clicking Blank Page. If you want to remove any page—be it blank or otherwise—simply highlight the page and press Delete. (If it was a text page, pressing Delete will not remove it from the original file; it simply won't be included in the booklet build.)

If you decide you don't like the settings you have selected, click Revert or Reset.

When you click OK, you'll be asked to save the original file you started with. (You always should, otherwise unsaved changes will be lost, because PageMaker closes the original file.) PageMaker will then make a copy of the original file and build a booklet out of it. You'll be able to view the new file, and make minor changes to it.

Understanding Halftones

An important aspect of prepress that needs to be taken into account is the concept of the *halftone*. Essentially, any continuous-tone image cannot be printed by a conventional printing press. In other words, a single continuous grayscale (or continuous shades of a color) cannot be printed. There really is no such thing as gray on a printing press; something is either black or white. (Printing could be said to be the first binary medium.) Consequently, any continuous-tone image (such as a photograph) needs to be "digitized" (in a matter of speaking), or converted to discrete dots. The densities of these dots provide the illusion of a continuous-tone image. Look at any printed photograph through a magnifier, and you can see the distinct dots. Because the dots are so small, they can't be distinguished by the naked eye. Thus, all printed photographs are essentially optical illusions.

Detail within a halftone image is a function of the concentration of dots in that particular area. A *highlight*, or the lightest part of an image, has very few, scattered dots, and prints lightly. A *shadow*, or the darkest part of an image, has many dots bunched together tightly, and thus prints very dark. (The tones falling in the region between the highlights and the shadows are known as the *middle tones*.)

Digital halftones—as well as any page elements—are a function of PostScript, and it is one of the functions of the PostScript language and the raster image processor. For a more detailed look at PostScript, see Chapter 14.

Essentially then, the printing process is a "binary" one: There is no gray on a printing press. There is either ink or no ink. All color and tone gradations are optical illusions produced by printing dots of ink with varying dot densities (see Figure 15.4). If you look at a photo-graphic print straight from the photolab, you'll notice that it is a true continuous-tone image: The photographic paper and emulsion can reproduce a wide range of gray shades and color gradations; however, in printing, you do not have that luxury. Consequently all continuous-tone artwork (this applies to paintings as well as photographs) needs to be converted to a *halftone* during the prepress stage. Originally, this was done photographically, but now is almost exclusively done using PostScript.

Figure 15.4

Any continuous-tone image destined for printing needs to be converted to a collection of halftone dots.

Line Screen

In the days of photographic halftones (which aren't gone entirely, by the way) the continuous-tone image was photographed through a fine grid, called a screen. This screen was classified according to its *resolution*, or how many lines of dots per unit length were created. This is known as the *line screen*, also known as *screen frequency*. This is important because obviously the finer the screen, the more dots the image will comprise, and the less easily the dots will be perceived by the viewer; however, printing presses can only reproduce so fine a screen. (Not only the press, but the paper and ink used also affect the line screen which can be used.)

As you can tell, it pays to check with your printer before selecting a line screen. (Another issue involving screen frequency is the problem of banding, which is related to the resolution of the output device. See the "Banding" section later in this chapter.)

Halftone Cells

As you remember from the discussion of PostScript in Chapter 14, all PostScript output comprises very small printer spots. This includes halftones. Halftone dots generated by a raster image processor (RIP) driven by PostScript data consist of much smaller printer spots (now you know why the use of the word "dot" is avoided to describe printer resolutions). The collection of printer spots that make up one halftone dot is called a *halftone cell*. As you can tell from Figure 15.5, each dot of a PostScript-generated halftone screen comprises a much smaller grid of printer spots bunched together.

Screens

The different printing processes (which you saw in Chapter 14) also determine how fine a screen can be used. Offset lithography is capable of 150–200 lines per inch (lpi) screens. Lithographic printing on uncoated papers can print 100–133-line screens, while newsprint is only capable of reproducing less than 100-line screens. Waterless lithographic plates have been known to effectively reproduce as high as 600-line screens. Flexographic printing can only manage up to 150-line screens. One of the advantages of gravure printing, on the other hand, is that because all images—text, line, or continuous-tone—that are printed are converted to very small cells anyway, halftoning is scarcely an issue. And because in most gravure cylinder-engraving processes the depth of each cell is (usually) variable, continuous-tone images can be reproduced with excellent tonal range without the need for a halftone screen.

Figure 15.5

Halftone dots, halftone cells, and printer spots.

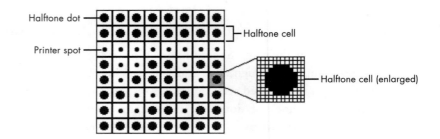

As you can probably surmise at this point, the size of the line screen, which can be obtained, is a function of the resolution of the output device. _Dot density_ was mentioned previously. Like printing presses, imagesetters and laser printers can't reproduce shades of gray either. They simulate shades of gray by turning on or off individual printer spots within a halftone cell. The number of shades of gray that can be simulated is directly proportional to the number of spots that can fit within that cell. A 300-pixel-per-inch (ppi) printer, for example, can generate a 5-spot × 5-spot matrix capable of only 60 cells per inch (300 divided by 5). (This also is equivalent to a 60-line screen.) Within this 5×5 cell grid, there are only 25 pixels that can be turned on or off, thus allowing only 26 shades of gray to be simulated within it (25 pixels on or off, and all white). However, the eye can detect over 100 shades of gray; thus halftone output on such a low-resolution printer will likely be poor.

In contrast, a 2,400-ppi printer (an imagesetter, for example) can generate a 16×16 cell grid, which contains 256 individual printer spots, and thus can generate 256 shades of gray, suitable for most halftone work. (This would also be equivalent to a 150-line screen.)

The number of individual printer spots that can be fit into a cell also affects the amount by which the size of the dots can be varied. This works on the same principle of turning spots on and off discussed previously in this chapter.

In essence, a low-resolution printer can be used to generate a high-enough line screen, but you would reduce the number of gray levels possible even further.

Dot Shape

Different types of images and different portions of images often require different halftone dot shapes, as well. Various optical illusions caused by traditional round dots can affect the perceived tonal range of a printed image. Often, elliptical, square, or other-shaped dots are used to compensate. PostScript, in later incarnations, allowed by this variation in dot shape. In fact, with a little programming skill, you could conceivably instruct PostScript to create any dot shape you wanted—bow-ties, rectangles, giraffes, whatever. There is no guarantee what the final image would look like with giraffe-shaped dots, but that really isn't PostScript's problem. Various special effects can be achieved by such dot-shape alterations.

Color Halftoning

When you are printing "full-color" (more properly called *process color*) the extra step of creating color separations needs to be made. In other words, a separate negative and plate needs to be made for each color to be printed. Process color works by using three primary colors—cyan (bluish-green), magenta (purplish-red), and yellow—with black added to improve contrast and darken shadow areas. (The process colors are collectively referred to as CMYK, "K" standing for "key"—or black—as black has traditionally been the key color laid down first and with which all the other colors were kept in register.) When these three colors are print on top of each other (or are *overprinted*) at various densities, they combine to produce a wide range of secondary colors. It is the combinations of these three primaries that produces the wide variety of reproducible colors.

Screen Angles

One important aspect of halftones that has caused many problems even in the days before digital halftoning was the concept of screen angles. This is more important in color printing than in black-and-white printing.

In order for the optical illusion that produces the appearance of a continuous-tone image to work, the rows of dots have to be oriented at a certain angle to the horizontal. In black-and-white halftoning, the screen is traditionally placed at a 45 degree angle to the horizontal (and thus also to the vertical). This is because the dots become more visible to the human eye when they are oriented along either the horizontal or the vertical axis. Keeping the dots aligned at an angle equidistant from either of these axes reduces the ability to perceive them.

This is more problematic in process color printing. Each of the four process color inks needs to be at a different angle to reduce the appearance of a *moiré* pattern, or another, undesirable, optical illusion caused by different screens interfering with each other and producing perceptible patterns in an image. In the days of photographic color separation, the best angles were determined to be zero degrees (or horizontal) for yellow (because it is the lightest color, the yellow dots are less perceptible when oriented horizontally than darker colors are), 15 degrees for magenta, 45 degrees for black, and 75 degrees for cyan. For trigonometric reasons however, PostScript computers could not calculate the cells for 15 degree and 75 degree angles (it's a complicated explanation, but suffice it to say here that the tangents of these angles are irrational numbers, or in other words numbers that repeat endlessly; an example of an irrational number is [pi], which works out to 3.14159 . . . and continues to infinity). After much noodling and experimentation, later versions of PostScript worked out optimal screen angles that could be used in lieu of the traditional angles, and which still reduce moiré patterns as much as possible. These optimal angles are programmed into a PostScript Printer Description (PPD) file (and you thought you were done with the PPD, didn't you?). Unless you are an expert, it is not recommended that you alter the preset screen angles.

Process Color versus Spot Color

What was just described—full-color printing by superimposing halftone dots of the different process colors on each other—differs from *spot color* in many important ways. When you are designing, a letterhead (to use a very basic example) and you want to have the name of the company print in a color (say, red) that is different from that of the rest of the text on the page, it is said to be "spot color," or color that is added to a page in "spots." (This is not to be confused with printer spots.) Spot color is specified differently from, and uses different types of inks than, process color. This is dealt with more later in this chapter, but suffice it to say here that although process color functions by overprinting each other, spot colors should only be overprinted with caution. Without delving into printing ink chemistry, process inks are what are known as "transparent inks," which means that they can be seen through, which is what produces the secondary colors. Spot inks, however, are often opaque, which means that if you try to create a secondary color by overprinting two spot inks, you're going to get something that is, quite frankly, pretty yucky (a technical term, by the way). When specifying spot inks, try not to overprint.

Note

For more information on process and spot colors, see Chapter 10.

Screen Tints

Before leaving the subject of color and halftones, the concept of the screen tint should be briefly mentioned. Using PageMaker's Define Color command, you can *screen back* any color. What this means is that you are reducing the density at which the color prints. In actual fact, what you are doing is essentially making a *halftone* of the image to which you are applying the color and the screen tint. By converting the image into dots and varying the density of those dots (in the same way as you adjusted the density of the dots making up an entire continuous-tone image) you are adjusting the density with which that color and image will ultimately print. This is what is meant by a screen tint, and it is also subject to the same vagaries of output resolution as other halftone images.

Banding

Banding is a problem that can occur in blends created in Illustrator (or other drawing programs) and in halftones. The goal of blends and halftones is to provide a seamless transition from gray (or color) value to gray (or color) value. Banding is thus defined as the visibility of the steps in the blend, which can vary from barely noticeable to horribly unsightly. Banding occurs when the output device does not have enough gray levels to effect a seamless transition (see Figure 15.6).

Figure 15.6

A series of blends showing the effects of banding.

Banding can also be caused by too low a screen frequency, or too low an output device resolution. Banding can become more egregious the higher the screen frequency, more noticeable on a low-resolution device than a high-resolution one. Consequently, if you notice a smallish degree of banding on your laser proofs, it will likely not be an issue when output from an imagesetter. If the problem is dreadfully severe, it might not disappear entirely. Needless to say if you are using your laser prints as mechanicals, the banding problem will carry through to the final print.

Improvements in drawing programs such as Illustrator and FreeHand have helped reduce the occurrence of banding, as they can calculate automatically the optimal number of steps to avoid it.

You can also do your own calculations to determine the optimal number of steps required to effect a seamless blend. The formula is:

$$\text{\# of steps} = (\text{ppi} \div \text{lpi})^2 \times \text{range of blend (\%)}$$

where *ppi* is the resolution of the output device, *lpi* is the line screen, and the range of the blend is expressed as the percent change over the range of the blend. So, if you are printing out at 600 dpi and have an 85-line screen, and the blend ranges from 85% to 65% (a change of 70%, or 0.7), you will need about 34 discrete steps ($600 \div 85 = ~ 7; 7^2 = 49; 49 \times 0.7 = 34.3$).

If math is not your forte, don't worry about it. At imagesetter-esque resolutions, a useful rule of thumb is to allow 26 steps for every 10 percent of change in your blend. And as a double-checking mechanism, you just need to ensure that the screen frequency is not higher than the resolution of the imagesetter (or other output device) divided by 16. Thus, if you are using a 2,450-ppi imagesetter, your line screen should not be higher than about 153 (actually 153.125) or banding will begin to occur. (There is a shareware program called Blender that can be used to determine your optimal number of steps, resolutions, and screen frequencies.)

FM Screening

Although there is no great need to mention it, you should be given some basic familiarity with what is known as *stochastic screening*, or *FM screening*. As you saw, tonal gradations in halftones are produced by varying the sizes of the dots, while the distribution of the dots remains fairly constant. Stochastic screening, in contrast, works on the opposite principle: All the dots remain the same size, while their distribution is changed, clusters of dots forming darker areas and scattered dots forming lighter areas. Stochastic screening has the potential to produce much higher-quality color reproductions than conventional AM screening. (As you know from radio, AM stands for amplitude modulation whereas FM stands for frequency modulation.) And because the dots are not distributed equally, moiré is not really an issue. However,

FM screening is still in its infancy and the dots required to make the process effective are much smaller than traditional halftone dots, which puts it out of the reach of many prepress and desktop systems. FM screening is starting to appear on desktop systems, however, and might become widespread.

SENDING THE JOB TO THE SERVICE BUREAU

Now that the basics of optimizing your output have been covered, you will see how to deal with a service bureau, and what else is required of the desktop publisher after the job is off the desktop.

What to Send the Service Bureau

The service that the bureau performs is the output of your pages directly to film (as negatives or positives) or, on occasion, to paper (called RC for resin-coated paper) from which negatives can be made. Additionally, the service bureau can also perform any other prepress work for which you do not have the equipment or the facilities. This most commonly involves high-resolution scans, which is covered at the end of this section.

PageMaker Files versus PostScript Files

One initial question that you need to ask yourself is: Do you send the publication as a native PageMaker file or do you send a PostScript file and not worry about the PageMaker file? There are several ways you can answer this question.

If you send it in native PageMaker format, you take much—but not all—of the responsibility off your own shoulders should problems arise during output. The bureau can go into your original file and perhaps spot any problems or potential difficulties you missed. Service bureau personnel have made it their business to deal with hundreds—if not thousands—of such files, and often can tell at a glance if an incorrect setting or other glitch exists. They can then correct the problem before wasting time and film (and you money) on flawed output. Although the designer is technically responsible for any problems, more often than not service bureaus are interested in solving the problem rather than assigning blame. (However, any significant time or labor required to fix a design-related problem will likely increase the amount you are charged. They won't fix files for free, but you might be on a deadline and having them fix a problem can end up being less expensive in the long run.)

Although native PageMaker format might on the surface appear to be the best way to send a file, there are other considerations you might have. You might not want anyone going into your original file, for example, and changing special settings, such as crop marks. You might have carefully and manually hyphenated or laid out text, a layout that might be very fragile. Any slight change to the file might very well alter that layout and positioning. Or you might want to ensure that the publication is completely font-independent. It is not inconceivable that a service bureau will assume that a setting you failed to adjust was an oversight and not intentional and so on.

If you want to make your publication completely tamper-resistant, you can save it as a PostScript file (in the Options mode of the Print dialog box; see Chapter 14). This locks down any and all settings you have made. This option was particularly useful some time ago, before service bureaus began to amass all the software they are likely to need to open application-specific files. The drawback is that you ultimately shoulder the responsibility (economically, that is) for any wasted film.

One good compromise is to send the service bureau both a PostScript file and a backup comprising your PageMaker file. This way, your file retains its tamper-resistance, yet if problems do occur, the original file is there and can be fixed.

Whichever way you decide to go, discuss it with the service bureau in advance. They might only want to deal with PostScript files. See also the section on PDF and Adobe Acrobat at the end of this chapter for a growing alternative to sending PageMaker or PostScript files.

Specifications

When submitting a job to the service bureau, you will need to fill out a disk submission form, which tells the bureau everything they need to know about what you're sending them. It is imperative that these forms be as complete, accurate, and thorough as possible.

Figure 15.7

Sample disk submission forms.

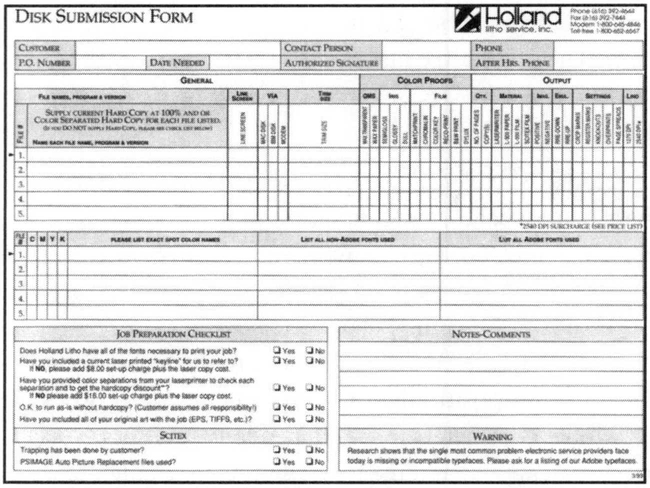

DISK SUBMISSION FORM

Holland litho service, inc.

CUSTOMER		CONTACT PERSON		PHONE	
P.O. NUMBER	DATE NEEDED	AUTHORIZED SIGNATURE		AFTER HRS. PHONE	

GENERAL · COLOR PROOFS · OUTPUT

SUPPLY CURRENT HARD COPY AT 100% AND OR COLOR SEPARATED HARD COPY FOR EACH FILE LISTED.

NAME EACH FILE NAME, PROGRAM & VERSION

FILE #	File names, program & version	Line Screen	Via	Trim size	Color Proofs	Output
1.						
2.						
3.						
4.						
5.						

*2540 DPI SURCHARGE (SEE PRICE LIST)

FILE #	C	M	Y	K	PLEASE LIST EXACT SPOT COLOR NAMES	LIST ALL NON-ADOBE FONTS USED	LIST ALL ADOBE FONTS USED
1.							
2.							
3.							
4.							
5.							

JOB PREPARATION CHECKLIST

Does Holland Litho have all of the fonts necessary to print your job? ❑ Yes ❑ No

Have you included a current laser printed "keyline" for us to refer to? ❑ Yes ❑ No
If NO, please add $8.00 set-up charge plus the laser copy cost.

Have you provided color separations from your laserprinter to check each separation and to get the hardcopy discount**? ❑ Yes ❑ No
If NO please add $18.00 set-up charge plus the laser copy cost.

O.K. to run as-is without hardcopy? (Customer assumes all responsibility!) ❑ Yes ❑ No

Have you included all of your original art with the job (EPS, TIFFS, etc.)? ❑ Yes ❑ No

SCITEX

Trapping has been done by customer? ❑ Yes ❑ No

PSIMAGE Auto Picture Replacement files used? ❑ Yes ❑ No

NOTES-COMMENTS

WARNING

Research shows that the single most common problem electronic service providers face today is missing or incompatible typefaces. Please ask for a listing of our Adobe typefaces.

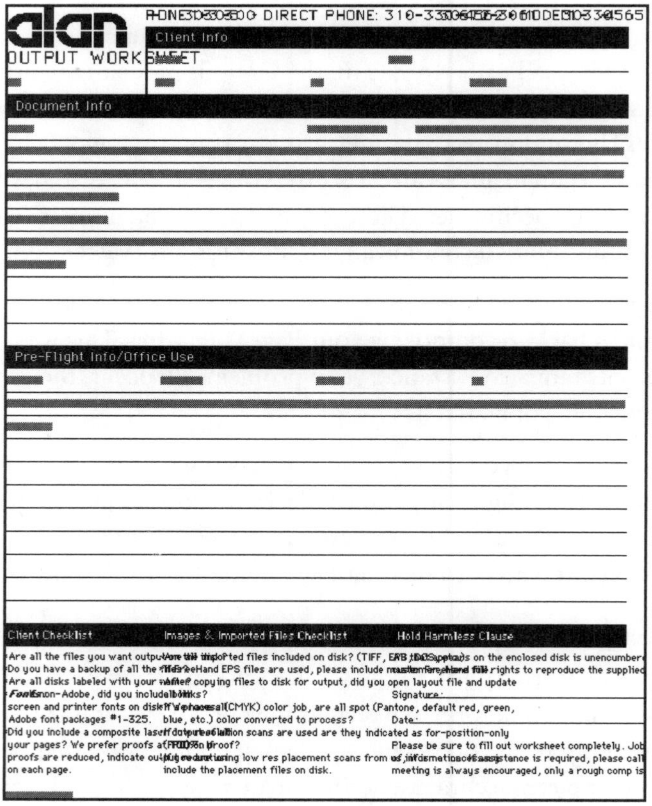

alan

PHONE: 310-330-3300 DIRECT PHONE: 310-330-6455-2061 MODEM: 310-330-4565

OUTPUT WORKSHEET

Client Info

Document Info

Pre-Flight Info/Office Use

Client Checklist · Images & Imported Files Checklist · Hold Harmless Clause

Are all the files you want output on this disk? Are all the imported files included on disk? (TIFF, EPS, DCS, etc.) ... on the enclosed disk is unencumbered ...
Do you have a backup of all the files? If FreeHand EPS files are used, please include ... rights to reproduce the supplied ...
Are all disks labeled with your name? When copying files to disk for output, did you open layout file and update links?
Fonts: If non-Adobe, did you include both screen and printer fonts on disk? If a process (CMYK) color job, are all spot (Pantone, default red, green, blue, etc.) color converted to process?
Adobe font packages #1-325.
Did you include a composite laser output of all your pages? We prefer proofs at 100%. If proofs are reduced, indicate output reduction on each page. If low resolution scans are used are they indicated as for-position-only (FPO) on proof? If you are using low res placement scans from us, include the placement files on disk.
Signature:
Date:
Please be sure to fill out worksheet completely. ... of information or assistance is required, please call ... meeting is always encouraged, only a rough comp is ...

All service bureaus have their own forms, but there are common elements to them all, which it helps to be aware of in advance.

◆ **Contact Information** This seems self-explanatory, but you should include more than just the company name and the main company phone number, unless the receptionist who answers is an expert on the publication in question (which might be the case). Include the name(s) and number(s) of whoever is in charge of making decisions on the project and who the service bureau should call if problems arise. Include after-hours numbers, as well (many seemingly straightforward yet time-consuming output runs are done in the middle of the night).

Remember that the longer it takes a service bureau to get in touch with someone concerning problems, the longer the job takes, and the nearer to your deadline you will come.

◆ **Deadline**   Generally speaking, the tighter the deadline the more you'll have to pay. Remember that a service bureau probably has many other jobs coming in at the same time as yours, the designers of which all considering their own to be the most important. In many cases, a service bureau might not even take the job if an unreasonable rush is involved.

◆ **Lists of Publication Files and All Links**   This includes not only your PageMaker file(s) (or PostScript file), but also any graphics (or other) files you have placed in your publication. Remember to not only document the links, but be sure that you have included *all* linked files. PageMaker makes this easy through the Files for Remote Printing option in the Save As command. This saves a great deal of aggravation by automatically copying all linked files into the same folder (or a special folder you've designated) as the main publication. If you do not choose this option, be sure that all links are present and accounted for. If PageMaker can't find the original file, the service bureau might have to guess, and you can end up with the wrong graphic in a particular location. Even if you did use the Files for Remote Printing option, you still need to thoroughly document all the files you are including.

If you have a lot of files to include and get writer's cramp easily, ask the service bureau if you can simply include a Print Window of the folder(s) or directories containing the files, and if so staple it to the disk submission form. This might even be a preferable alternative, as then there is no sloppy handwriting to contend with.

Speaking of sloppy handwriting, do write legibly on these forms. Some people need to supply a secret decoder ring with any handwritten material. Or, if you still actually have a typewriter, use it.

◆ **Applications**   Be sure to indicate what program(s) (and version numbers) you have used to create your files (not just the PageMaker files). Unless otherwise instructed, there is no need to include a copy of the application itself on the disk. (Which would be illegal, by the way.)

◆ **Resolution**   Indicate the optimal resolution at which a job is to be printed. This should be coordinated with your print shop, especially with regard to halftone screen frequency.

◆ **Imagesetter Type**   It might not surprise you that there are many types of imagesetters available, many of which have very different performance characteristics and resolution capabilities. Often, service bureaus have more than one type, which affords them a certain degree of flexibility. There are two basic configurations you should be aware of: A capstan imagesetter feeds a continuous sheet of film or paper from a cartridge through a set of rollers, whereas a drum imagesetter mounts a fixed length of film or paper on a rotating drum. The latter device tends not to stretch the paper or film, and is widely believed to produce the higher quality of the two types of imagesetters. If you are outputting halftones with a greater than 155-line screen, specify a drum imagesetter.

◆ **Film and Paper Specs**   Another thing to check with your printer about: Will he or she require right- or wrong-reading film, and emulsion-up or -down? (Emulsion-down, wrong-reading is the most common orientation but is by no means universal.) Also, does the printer require negative or positive film? (Some plates, known as *positive-working*, are imaged from positive film rather than negative film.) And, finally, does the printer require film or paper?

◆ **Crop Marks**   Did you add your own custom crop marks, or do you need PageMaker's Printer's Marks function turned on? If you generated your own crop marks, make sure that PageMaker's automatic printer's marks are turned off and specify that no one subsequently turn them on.

◆ **Mode of Transmission**   Or, in other words, how specifically is your job being sent to the service bureau? By modem? By email through an ISP? By external media cartridge? If the latter, what kind?

On the subject of external media, there are so many different types of external media drives and cartridges on the market that is necessary to ensure that the device you are using is compatible with the device your service bureau is using. If you are using a diskette, you're probably safe, but if you have a lot of graphics files, you might not be able to fit everything on a diskette. (Try to minimize the number of diskettes you send.) If you are using SyQuest cartridges, are you using the 5.25-inch cartridges or the 3.5-inch cartridges? If the former, are you using the 44MB, the 88MB, or the 200MB cartridges? If the latter, are you using the 105MB, the 135MB or the 270MB cartridges? (As you might know, some devices can read and write to some sizes, only read some sizes, or not read at all other sizes.) Are you using Iomega's Zip or Jaz cartridges? Are you using magnetic optical discs? Are you using Bernoulli disks? Or have you archived everything on a CD-ROM? Always check with the service bureau to be certain that they can actually read your disk. Many service bureaus now have more than one type of drive. SyQuests—usually either of the 5.25-inch sizes—are most widely used, but Zip and Jaz cartridges are gaining ground.

You might want to include back-ups of your files elsewhere on the disk or cartridge (labeled "Backup" or "Spare" to avoid confusion) if there is room, in the event that a disk error renders one (or more) of your original files unreadable (270 MB SyQuest cartridges spring immediately to mind).

On a similar note, be sure that if you are using a Windows machine that the service bureau also has a Windows machine. More and more often, service bureaus have both Windows and Macintosh capabilities. Don't assume true cross-platform capability, however.

Also let the service bureau know if you have compressed any of your files, using StuffIt or other compression program. If possible, try to make such files self-extracting. If sending the files by email or over the Internet, does your ISP impose any encoding algorithms on attached files, such as BinHex, AppleDouble or AppleSingle? If so, trying to decode them can be horribly bewildering and frustrating.

◆ **Project Size**   Specify the total number of pages in the project. Also specify how many scans the service bureau is going to have to make.

◆ **Colors**   Specify if the job has any process color, and if color separations are needed. If using spot color, specify the colors you have defined in your publication. (The PANTONE system is covered later.)

◆ **Fonts**   The font issue was mentioned in Chapter 14. Check with your service bureau to see which fonts they support. (If you are simply sending them a PostScript file you don't have to worry about this; all font information is automatically embedded in the file.) Be sure to find out the manufacturer of the fonts; a simple type family name doesn't really help. (Adobe Helvetica might be different from another type foundry's Helvetica. They might look superficially quite similar, but subtle differences can accrue and spoil a layout.) If you provide your service bureau with your fonts, keep in mind that you might be indulging in software piracy. Be sure to check your font-licensing agreement to see what their policy is. It might be illegal to send your fonts. Oh, sure, you might say, "everyone does it." True, but still...you might decide to run for president some day, and would you really want an ethics committee investigating a possible "Font-gate"?

◆ **PostScript Error Checking**   In the Options mode of PageMaker's Print dialog box, there is a checkbox corresponding to the Include PostScript Error Handler function, a way of finding any PostScript errors that might creep into a publication saved as a PostScript file. Most service bureaus are likely to use a more advanced diagnostic tool, but check with them to see if you should turn this function on when saving your PostScript file.

♦ **Include Proofs**   It is always a good idea to send the service bureau copies of any laser-printed (or other) proofs you have generated of the job. Not only does it reassure them that the job at least printed on a laser printer, but it also acts as a kind of rudimentary guide so they know what the publication is supposed to look like. If you are submitting a job with color separations, submit separation proofs as well.

♦ **Specify Proofs**   Indicate to the service bureau what types of proofs you would like to see back from them. (See the section on Proofing later in this chapter.)

And, as mentioned before, always check your own output before sending a file to a service bureau.

The foregoing might seem like a lot to worry about. And you're right. It *is* a lot to worry about. But if you don't worry about it, no one else will, and you'll end up with files that don't print (or don't print well), missed deadlines, inferior publications, and one heck of a bill from the service bureau.

Other Service Bureau Functions

In addition to simply outputting your job, the service bureau can do a lot more for you. But be sure to coordinate this with your printer in advance.

Scanning

You might need high-quality, high-resolution scans that are beyond the capability of your desktop scanner. A service bureau most likely has a high-end drum scanner at their disposal, which can capture images with a much greater dynamic range than a flatbed scanner. Drum scanners can also enlarge images, and can usually scan and enlarge slides and transparencies, something that flatbed scanners are not often able to do. And transmission copy such as transparencies tends to yield better scanned images than a reflection copy such as prints.

There is also more to scanning than...well, scanning. There is also color correction. Scans rarely capture every color accurately, and a scanned image might require more or less color correction. Color correction, however, is a skill that requires a great deal of experience to get it right. Service bureaus usually have personnel who are pros at fixing unhealthy scans. If you are doing a fashion or decorating publication such as a catalog, for example, you don't want an unpleasant color cast to render your images aesthetically unappealing.

These services can cost more than you'd like to spend, of course. If you already have a flatbed scanner, be sure that you absolutely need the increased quality of a drum scanner. If you do a lot of scanning, it might be more cost-effective to buy a flatbed scanner. If you do few scans, it might be more cost-effective to have the bureau do it.

There are also those who predict that scanning is on its way to obsolescence, as PhotoCDs and digital cameras become more prevalent and affordable. If you deal with many photographic images, consider either of those routes. Perhaps your service bureau has a PhotoCD service.

Trapping

Trapping is a means of ensuring that colors or images that are to be printed on top of each other line up correctly. In many cases, trapping is simply a question of manipulating the sizes of successive images to that there is some degree of overlap, preventing the occurrence of gaps. On more complex jobs, however, it is best to leave it to a professional. Service bureaus might also be able to help in this regard. (Trapping is actually a complex subject that spans both traditional and digital prepress. If you are interested in pursuing your own trapping, you might want to begin with Brian P. Lawler's *The Complete Guide to Trapping*.)

Color Separations

Although PageMaker's color separation ability is admirable, nothing compares to high-end color prepress systems, especially in their capability to compensate for dot gain (an undesirable increase in the size of halftone dots caused by a variety of factors both in the photographic prepress processes and on the printing press), undercolor removal, gray

615

component replacement, and other such image tweezes that can really make a difference. Your service bureau might also be able to do your color separations for you.

Imposition

Imposition was discussed at length in Chapter 14, so you are aware of how complex it can be. In many cases, you can do your own imposition on the desktop, either "solo" or using PageMaker's Build Booklet plug-in (also covered in Chapter 14). For longer or more complicated jobs, your service bureau might be able to do your imposition for you. However, because imposition has traditionally been the purview of the print shop and is dictated by the size of the paper and equipment the printer actually has, many printers prefer to do it themselves. Some, however, might give you a price break if you supply them with imposed pages. Either way, check with your printer before doing any imposition.

Haggling

The rates charged by service bureaus might not be carved in stone, and you might be able to negotiate deals with them, depending upon the volume and the complexity of the work you give them. If you do a long publication regularly and it gives them a minimum of trouble, you can probably get them to cut you a good deal. However, if you give them one long, shoddily-designed job that causes them all to pull out their hair, don't look for any special—or at least discounted—rates. Some people are better at haggling over costs than others. Service bureaus, like everyone else, like steady, loyal, and well-organized customers. If you have your service bureau perform any of the additional functions just outlined, you might also be able to get a special package deal.

Now that producing mechanicals and dealing with service bureaus has been covered, this chapter briefly looks at the world of proofing, before turning to the print shop.

PROOFING

The concept of proofing encompasses many different aspects and stages of the publishing process, from simple correction of typographical errors (typos) to verifying that process color will reproduce as you expect it to. Thus the following sections run though each of the various types of proofs and proofing processes.

Proofreading Copy

A long time ago, when the universe consisted of nothing more elaborate than typesetting machines and pasted-up copy, people actually read what was typed, and that time and effort, coupled with the ability to spell, ensured that many misspellings and typos were caught.

Spell-Checkers

Now we have spell-checkers, and the volume of typos that appears in books, magazines, and newspapers is astounding. PageMaker also has a spell-check feature. Here are the twin caveats about spell-checkers: They can foster laziness with regard to proofreading and, although sociological studies have yet to be done, some of us suspect that spell-checkers are diminishing our ability as a nation to spell properly. We all think, "Oh, I don't really need to know how to spell that. The spell-checker will catch it." Sure. When in doubt, look it up. The other caveat is: Spell-checkers only catch typos that form non-English words. Many typos become other—but wrong—words. One spell-checker in a popular word processing program used for a United States Patent Office application once failed to distinguish between "pumping" and "pimping," which certainly would have made for an interesting—if useless—patent. "Prostate" and "prostrate" also mean very different things.

In sum, it is okay to use spell-checkers so long as actual human eyes eventually look over what was typed. It is, as we all know, notoriously difficult to proofread one's own typing, which can be embarrassing when one spends a lot of time complaining about the prevalence of typos. Therefore, it is always a good idea to have someone else look over something you yourself typed. If you have the budget, hire professional freelance proofreaders. If you have to proof your own copy, do it slowly and carefully. One trick that can work is to read the copy backwards, from the end to the beginning. We miss typos because we know what it is *supposed* to say. We see what we want to see. By reading each word in the wrong order, we see each word independently of the context, which makes it easier to spot errors.

Typos and misspellings that turn up in published and printed documents look unprofessional, and give the impression of sloppiness, which can undermine the content of what it is you are writing. Given the content of many email messages, however, perhaps we are becoming more accepting of typos and bad spelling than we used to be, but I hope not.

Some people are just not very good spellers. This is okay; some of the most brilliant scientists and engineers have problems with basic spelling. It is really nothing to be ashamed of. The first step is to admit you have a problem, and to ensure that someone who *is* a good speller looks over typed material.

Grammar Checkers

Many word-processing programs also use grammar checkers, which many believe don't live up to their promise. They have their uses (they can spot things like the "to, too, two" confusion and other homonyms) but nothing can surpass human eyes and a knowledge of Strunk and White's *Elements of Style*. Professional proofreaders and copy editors can also spot garbled grammar with remarkable ease.

Some people think faster than they type, and tend to skip words. If you need to do your own copy checking and have some leeway in your production schedule, let some time pass between input and proofing. Let yourself "forget" what you typed. When you read it anew with "reset" eyes, you'll be more likely to catch grammatical mistakes, skipped words, and so on.

Signing Off

In many cases, the person who is financing the publication will be required to sign-off on, or approve, the copy. This generally means that a higher-up in the organization has checked the copy in some manner. Get approval in writing, such as a signature or initials. (Never get verbal approval for anything.) It doesn't guarantee that all errors have been caught, but it can shift responsibility elsewhere should an error be spotted at a stage in which such correction is expensive, or even found after printing.

It is perhaps a manifestation of Murphy's Law that the ability to catch errors increases in direct proportion to the expense of correcting them.

Laser-Printed Proofs

As you saw in the previous chapter, PageMaker allows for a variety of different types of proofs to be run on a laser printer. In addition to printing out text for copy checking, laser-proofs can be used to get approval on a layout.

Thumbnails, Reader's Spreads, and Proofs

You saw how PageMaker's Thumbnails printing option (in the Paper mode of the Print dialog box) can group together many rough pages on a single sheet of paper. This is useful in the early stages of page and publication design, as it provides a feel for the overall look and design of the publication. The Reader's Spreads function (in the Document mode of the Print dialog box) also allows for the evaluation of two-page spreads.

The Proof checkbox (in the Document mode of the Print dialog box), as mentioned, puts placeholder boxes in place of graphics. This function is useful if you just need to output a proof for checking the typography, such as spelling, kerning, hyphenation, and so on.

Composite Proofs

You'll have other opportunities further along in the process to proof color, but using the Composite (and Grayscale) option of the Color mode of the Print dialog box can also provide you with a general feel for the design of your pages. Text printed on a color background will print on a gray background, but if the text is unreadable, the problem will probably not resolve itself even when the actual color is used.

Composite proofs are also useful for getting approval on the design before moving to the color proofing stage.

LaserCheck

LaserCheck is a program created and marketed by Systems of Merritt, Inc., which can be used to turn your laser printer into a mock imagesetter. The program, essentially, is downloaded to your laser printer and resides in its memory. LaserCheck then intercepts any PostScript code sent to the printer and generates a proof page that looks exactly (albeit reduced and at a resolution equal to that of your laser printer) like the film you would get back from the service bureau. The film, for example, would be in reversed and in negative form. It also annotates the output in the same way an imagesetter would, by listing in the margins the font information, PostScript information for troubleshooting, error reports, and so on. If an error does turn up, LaserCheck will print out as much of the page as possible, perhaps allowing you to see exactly what went wrong.

LaserCheck is particularly useful for files you have printed to disk (such as saved as a PostScript file), as it is really the only way you can proof such pages after the file has been saved.

Run Laser Proofs *Before* Sending Out the Job

This was covered in the last chapter and in discussing the service bureau itself, but it bears repeating. Any complex page or document that fails to run on a laser printer is tempting fate if sent unrepaired to a service bureau. Any page missing crucial elements will also cause problems down the road. Would you *really* want to get 300 pages of film and be told by the printer that there are no crop marks? You would probably have to rerun all the film. This will take time (perhaps costing you a deadline), and at the very least you'll have to pay for the service bureau's output *twice*.

Look for Problems in Advance

Go back and consult the section in Chapter 14 on "Ensuring That Your Pages Print at All" for a list of problems that have traditionally snarled imagesetter output.

During the proofing phase, you can also use the PostScript error checking function (in the Options mode of the Print dialog box). If you have difficulty printing a page or document, this function might be able to tell you what the problem is. But check with the service bureau before keeping it enabled prior to file transmission. The service bureau might have their own more powerful PostScript error checking utilities.

Color Proofing at the Service Bureau

Although it seems simple enough, color proofing can be a remarkably complex subject. Whole books have been written on it. (See, for example, printing-industry guru Michael H. Bruno's *Principles of Color Proofing*, published in 1986 by GAMA Communications.) However, for your purposes, it doesn't need to be *that* complicated.

The basic difficulty with color proofing is that despite the remarkable array of films, papers, and devices available for color proofing, the only truly accurate way of seeing how color will print is to use the actual printing press, ink, and paper. This, of course, isn't the most feasible means of color proofing.

Laser-Printed Test Separations

As you saw in the discussion of the Color mode of the Print dialog box, you can print out sample color separations as grayscale images on a laser printer. This might seem kind of pointless, but it actually is useful in initially evaluating the respective color densities of spot and process colors. Is what should be dark actually dark? Is it *too* dark? Is it light enough for any overprinted text or other line art to be visible?

You can also print each color separation on a sheet of transparent acetate and create overlay color proofs. If you have the budget, you can even buy different color toner cartridges and print each color as a colored overlay. Registration will probably not be very good, and the color values themselves will not be very accurate, but there are many overt, egregious errors which can be spotted in this manner. Remember, the more varied the proofing you do, the more errors and problems you are likely to catch before it becomes too expensive to fix.

Color Printers

Ink-jet printers, as you saw in Chapter 14, are inexpensive and are increasing in quality, and are often useful for generating composite color proofs. These are, again, inaccurate in terms of representing what you will probably get on the printing press, but if used with care—and with a disclaimer—such printers can also be used to spot serious problems, and can even be used to get approval on the work up to that point. The primary hues will be correct, but it is the other, subtle color variations that will differ on press. So, for example, you can tell if something is blue when it should be red.

How Accurate the Colors Need to Be

Remember that colors don't always have to match the original perfectly. Especially with regard to spot color, the color might only need to be aesthetically palatable, not matched wavelength-by-wavelength to an original design or palette. However, if you are reproducing a company logo or product, you will have to keep accurate color representation in mind, especially if you are specifically supposed to be fostering the recognition of a product.

You will also need to watch your *memory colors*. There are certain colors found in nature and everyday life with which you are familiar and that become inconspicuous if reproduced inaccurately. Flesh tones need to look like flesh tones, for example, (according to the ethnicity of the subject), or at least the flesh tones of a healthy person. An apple should look as red as an apple typically looks. A blue sky should look like a blue sky, not turquoise. An orange should look like an orange, not an apple.

Lighting

As you might know from experience, color values change according to the lighting under which they are viewed. Professional color experts use specially prescribed standard lighting conditions. If you have access to a color evaluation booth, use it to evaluate color proofs in concert with an original photograph. The color evaluation booth attempts to replicate a constant condition corresponding to the light seen outdoors at midday.

Composite versus Laminate Color Proofs

There are basically two types of color proofs you can get from your service bureau. The first is known as a composite proof, and it is essentially what its name infers. The first is a single sheet containing all the color information, generated by digital data from the computer file. These are output from ink-jet printers, thermal dye-sublimation print-ers, or color copiers driven by a computerized front-end. What these proofs do is image all your color directly on the substrate, often on the substrate you'll be using (with the exception of thermal dye printers, which require special paper). These are quick and inexpensive to produce, but they also provide misleadingly accurate color trapping, and don't indicate if any moiré patterns are produced in your overlayed halftone screens.

The second type of proofs are more expensive and difficult to generate, but they are also the most accurate. These are laminate-based proofs, and are essentially created by printing or photographing individual color separations on transparent sheets and stacking them together. (If they are left as transparent overlays, they are called, not surprisingly, overlay color proofs; if they are laminated together into a single thick sheet, they are called, again not surprisingly, single-sheet color proofs. Examples of the latter are the so-called Cromalin and Matchprint proofs, names derived from the brand of photo paper used to produce them.) These usually produce the most accurate means of checking the color, the register, and the trapping.

Usually one of these proofs—preferably, the most accurate—is eventually signed-off on. In this case, it becomes the okay proof, and is sent along with the film to the print shop, where it is consulted during makeready and printing. If the press sheets match the proof very closely, and they are incorrect, it is the fault of whoever approved the proof.

Proofing doesn't end after the film is sent to the print shop. There are various additional checks and proofs the printer generates to ensure that the job is printed to your specifications. Those proofs are covered in the next section.

THE PRINT SHOP

Most people who have become desktop publishers have never worked in a print shop—they've never had ink on their hands, sniffed gum arabic, or spilled fountain solution all over their clothes. Printers have a great deal of experience in, well, printing and have probably seen more jobs in a year than you'll be likely to see or prepare in a lifetime. The printer, in addition to the service bureau, is there to help you prepare your job properly. After all, any step you have done incorrectly will eventually mean more work for them in the long run. In the high-tech world of desktop publishing, digital scanning, and so on, we forget the low-tech world of ink on paper. That's why the printer is there—to translate the high-tech to the low-tech. Listen to him carefully. He knows what he is talking about.

Preflight Considerations

Before you place a single byte in PageMaker, it is always a good idea to begin meeting with printers and soliciting bids. This won't always be the case, of course, but often meeting with a printer and finding out what a job is likely to cost will affect your layout and design. You might think several different spot colors on each page would be a neat idea, for example, until you actually find out what it would cost to do that. You might ultimately decide to go with a single spot color on only one page. If you need to begin the design and layout before meeting with a printer, try to keep your design reasonably flexible. By now, you should be aware of what is likely to increase the cost of a print job. Some of it is also quite intuitive; more colors means more money. Process color can be more expensive than spot color.

If you have been dealing with printers, you probably already know what kind of "preflight" work you need to do. Also, if your job is very simple—no colors beyond black or a standard paper size, for example—there is also not a *great* deal of preliminary work you need to do.

The Preflight Meeting

Regardless of how much initial design work has actually been accomplished prior to meeting with the printer, you naturally have *some* idea of what you want to do early in the process. The specific issues that should be dealt with in a preflight meeting include:

- **Raison d'être of the publication**   In other words, who is it for and what is its goal? Is it designed to sell or promote something? Provide information?

- **Rough sketches**   You will probably already have produced some sample designs, either on the computer, on paper, or even on cocktail napkins, as a means of illustrating the basic idea and layout of the publication. Is it a four-panel fold-out brochure, for example, an eight-page newsletter, or a perfect-bound book? This will also help you to glean accurate information concerning any bindery operations. Will it be perfect bound, for example, or saddle-stitched? Will it be a single folded piece? Will it be mailed to subscribers or other mailing list? Will it have any perforated coupons or other removable cards?

A mock-up of the piece itself—which need not consist of anything more elaborate than a sheet of paper folded in a way that is representative of the piece—also helps communicate your idea(s) accurately.

◆ **Print Run**   How many copies of your publication will you need? Keep in mind that the price per unit tends to decrease with increasing print run. Also keep in mind that printers don't often like to print very small runs. If you're dealing with a quantity of under 500 or even 1,000, prepare to pay a premium. You are likely to be able to negotiate better rates if you are planning a longer run. But then again, if you absolutely cannot *use* a large number of copies, that's a waste, and warehouse space might be scarce. If you're planning a regular publication, you might already have a mailing list. How many additional copies (for new subscribers and promotional mailings) would you want? Do you want to have any back issues kept on hand?

◆ **Budget**   Naturally, this will affect all the other considerations. But is your budget flexible? If you've never done this sort of thing before, your budget might be completely unrealistic. Or, for a slight expense beyond the budgeted amount you might be able to do something of much higher quality or quantity. Is it worth it? There is some degree of haggling and negotiation involved, so don't reveal what you are absolutely willing to pay at the outset.

◆ **Quality**   This is a vague term, admittedly, but how "slick" does the publication need to be? This will also be a function of budget and *raison d'être*. A sales brochure for a line of sports cars, for example, will obviously have a different level of targeted quality than a four-page Little-League bulletin.

- **Deadline**   As mentioned previously, the looser the deadline the less you'll end up paying. No one likes crash schedules, although sometimes they might be unavoidable. The questions to ask yourself and the printer include: When are the finished pieces needed? How soon would the printer need to get the job in order to make that date? Are you specifying inks or papers that need to be ordered specially and might not arrive in time? Also keep in mind that the service bureau needs to do its job before the printer can do his or hers. Do you have enough time in the production schedule for that?

- **Ink and Paper**   The printer knows what types of inks on what types of paper will yield the best results. But are there any special considerations in this area? Do you need spot color inks or process inks? Or both? Any special paper requirements, with regard to size or finish? Will you be needing cover stock in addition to body stock? Any special varnishes or lamination? Any unusual inks, such as high-gloss, metallic, and so on?

These are the basic considerations to which you'll need to give some thought before meeting with a printer. Having answers to all these questions will enable you to better explain to the printer what it is you want to do. But don't just stop here. Do you have any unusual ideas that could be implemented? Does your printer? Remember, if the production of the publication hasn't yet begun in earnest, it might be possible to indulge in a bit of brainstorming with the printer. Allowing the printer to get involved in the creative aspect of the project goes a long way toward forming a long-term relationship with him or her. Printers aren't mindless automatons (like your computer is). They can be just as creative as any designer or art director, and they've probably seen so many different types of jobs they might be able to recall something that they've seen before, which you hadn't thought of but which could work extremely well.

Also ask your printer for a reality check if you think your publication is getting out of hand. It is to the printer's advantage to keep you from going astray and designing something that can't be printed. Get advice.

At this stage you might not have yet chosen a printer. Therefore, the preflight meeting is not only an opportunity to explore the aspects of the job, but also to determine if a particular printer is the best one for the job. Does this printer even support desktop publishing? Have they heard of PageMaker? (You'd be surprised, but many printers in a place as purportedly "hip" and "with it" as New York City are not involved in desktop publishing or digital prepress at all. Many printers in New York still do manual paste-up—and prefer it. Go figure.) It makes no sense to design your pages in PageMaker only to have your printer not understand what to do with it.

A particular printer might also not be the type of printer that can handle your job. There are many "quick printers" who excel at letterhead, envelopes, business forms, labels, and so on, but not be able to do a full-color promotional brochure. This is no one's fault, of course; it's a function of the equipment the shop owns and what their experience and customer base comprises. It can even work the other way, too: a printer who specializes in hardcover books or glossy periodicals might not have the ability or inclination to do envelopes or letterhead. As in just about every other industry, many printers specialize in certain areas.

Coordinate Your Prepress Considerations

As you read the last chapter and the first half of this one, you might have noticed that you were often told to "check with your printer" to see what is required. Here are a few of the aspects you should discuss with the printer at the outset:

- ◆ **Color Matching Systems**   If there were a limited number of colors in the world, there would be no need to worry about color matching systems. But, there are literally tens of millions of colors that can be reproduced, and simply specifying "Oh, a kind of reddish orange" isn't going to yield expected results. Even the color you see on you computer screen is going to differ from what get on paper; thus, many color matching systems exist that attempt to quantify colors for the easy specification of different shades.

When specifying spot colors, most printers use—and PageMaker supports—the PANTONE Color Matching System. The PANTONE system essentially comprises a series of numbered color swatches which you specify by number. This needs to be done on paper and in person; colors vary from computer screen to paper, and from paper to paper (a colored ink printed on an uncoated paper will appear different than the exact same ink printed on a coated paper). Thus, PANTONE swatch books include swatches for different types of paper. Ask your printer which system they use. If you are using process color, these can differ from substrate to substrate as well. Also check with the service bureau to see what color management system they use. (A color management system, unlike a color matching system, keeps all colors used by all the devices in a system on the same wavelength—so to speak—ensuring that colors remain consistent from device to device.) PageMaker supports the Kodak Precision Color Management System.

Also discuss the printing order of the process inks. This helps with the design of knockouts, reverses, and overprinting. Black is usually the first color down, followed by, in order, cyan, magenta and yellow. This is a common printing sequence, but by no means universal. Double-check with the printer.

◆ **Line Screen** As you saw, the optimal line screen for halftones affects the resolution at which scans need to be made, and the optimal line screen itself depends upon the press and paper. Printers know this stuff cold; check with them to find out what the best screen frequency would be.

A good alternative is to not bother doing your own scans of continuous-tone images at all. Instead, do a low-resolution scan of an image and place it in PageMaker solely for position only (FPO). The printer can then strip the photo into the mechanical or the negative flat himself. This saves time and disk space, but if you have special photo manipulations in mind for a specific page, you might want more control over the image. In that case, you might have no choice but to scan it yourself.

- **Trapping** You've seen trapping before. Some printers would prefer to control the trapping themselves, some would prefer it be done by someone else. Ask the printer whether he or she sees any potential trapping problems in your proposed design. Ask if he or she knows of any modifications to a design that would render it unnecessary.

- **Imposition** You've also seen imposition before. During preflight, resolve the question of who will be doing the imposition. If you are dealing with a large number of pages, see if the printer will do it. If it's done incorrectly, you could run into big problems. Many print shops are now acquiring imagesetters and are doing direct digital imposition. Many still do it manually. Check.

- **What the Printer Needs** Digital prepress is still in the throes of transition. Some printers like imagesetter film, some prefer mechanicals. Some even like actual paste-ups. Does a printer need mechanicals? If so, will laser output be fine, or do you need to supply higher-resolution mechanicals, such as for halftones? Would the printer prefer film? If so, negatives? Positives? What orientation: right-reading or wrong-reading? Emulsion-up or -down?

  Will the printer be willing to work with the service bureau on such issues as trapping, dot gain compensation, and imposition? Does the printer also double as a service bureau? Some do. If the answer to this last question is yes, could you have them do both service bureau and print shop work? There are a good number of advantages to this system, as you can well imagine because there is a lot less coordination between different companies to worry about. If you can get them to do all service bureau work, what kind of package deal can you work out for the entire project?

- **Proofing** Some print shops will accept the color proofs generated by the service bureau. Others prefer to produce their own proofs, as they are better able to relate the appearance of the proofs to their own presses. Will they accept service bureau proofs that have been approved by you (or your superior)?

◆ **New Technologies**   It was mentioned in Chapter 14 that newer direct digital printing systems were emerging, such as direct-to-plate systems. Does your printer have the ability to image plates directly from your PageMaker or PostScript file? If so, what would the advantages and disadvantages be? Do you have access to a Xerox DocuTech, or any of a variety of direct digital presses, now capable of good-quality color reproduction? If so, what are the advantages and disadvantages to using them? Get and evaluate samples.

Bidding

The process of bidding is kind of like comparison shopping. You essentially submit a bid form (see Figure 15.8) to a printer, specifying all the various aspects of the job. The printer then returns an estimate of the amount the job will cost. Typically, you submit the same form to several different printers and compare and contrast the results. Usually, the bids will all fall within a certain narrow range. Keep in mind that it probably isn't always the best bet to accept the lowest bid, especially if it is significantly lower than the others. It might be the result of a cost-cutting technique the printer can implement. This would be fine, but there is the chance that it will compromise the quality of the job to some extent. It would be best to call and find out. Similarly, if there is a bid (or bids) that are much higher than the others, there might be a reason for it beyond the simple fact that they just might have higher rates. Perhaps they detected something problematic about the job that no one else did. Again, call them and ask.

By the way, it never hurts to solicit a bid from your regular printer, even if you get a significant price break from them as it is. (Retaining the same printer from job to job—especially a regular job, such as a newsletter— is always a good idea if they are doing a good and economical job, especially as they'll be likely to go to bat for you when difficult problems arise or when crash deadlines loom. Long-term relationships are beneficial to all parties involved.) Soliciting a bid from your regular printer, especially for a new job they've never seen before, leaves no doubt as to what is expected. It also never hurts to solicit bids from other printers once in a while, especially if you've been using the same printer for a long time. Who knows? Someone might be able to do your job at a lower cost. Even if you don't really want to go elsewhere, you can always use the new bid as leverage when negotiating with your printer.

Bid Request & Specification

Vitals
Job Name: _____
New Job ○ Exact Repeat ○ Repeat With Changes ○ Previous Job Number: _____
Type Of Publication: _____
Date Requested: _____ Date Quote Due: _____ Job Deadline: _____
Contact Info: _____
_____
_____
_____
_____

Printing
Size Of Run: _____
Number Of Pages: _____
Finish Size: _____
Body
Paper: _____
Inks/Varnish: _____

Cover
Paper: _____
Inks/Varnish: _____

Notes/Critical Elements/Quality: _____
_____
_____

PrePress
Service Bureau Specifications
Film ○ Repo Paper ○ Negative ○ Positive ○
Right Reading ○ Wrong Reading ○
UCR/GCR Coordination Required ○
Trapping Coordination Required ○
Imposition Coordination Required ○
Print Shop PrePress:
Halftoning/Stripping: B&Ws:_____ Duotones: _____ Color: _____
Screens/Reverses/Solids/Bleeds: _____
Trapping Required: _____
Bindery
Sewing ○ Stapling ○ Gluing ○ Comb ○ Spiral ○ Drilling ○ Padding ○ Carbonless ○
Perfing ○ Die Cutting ○ Embossing ○ Foil Stamping ○ Folding ○ Scoring ○
Inserting ○ Tipping ○ Stuffing ○
Fulfillment
Packing Instructions: _____
_____
Delivery Instructions: _____
_____

Figure 15.8

A sample bid form.

Bid Specifications

◆ **Deadlines**   Specify when the bid is due, and when the job would be due. Needless to say, it is probably not a good idea to actually put down a date that corresponds to the very last minute before you are late.

◆ **Print Run and Trim Size**   Natually, you'll have to indicate how many copies you need, as well as the total number of pages in each copy of the publication, and the trim size of the finished piece. This allows the printer to determine what size paper is needed and can be used.

◆ **Paper Specifications** The type of paper you choose is the single most important specification you can make, affecting as it does the line screen (for halftones), the type of ink that can be used, the specification of color, and the cost of the job. There are literally hundreds of different types of paper. Here is a quick guide to some important paper qualities and properties:

   ◆ **Basis Weight.** Essentially, basis weight is equal to the weight of one ream (500 sheets) of a paper at a specific size (called its *basic size*). If you look at the wrapper on your photocopier paper, for example, you'll probably see it classified as 20-lb. This means that one ream of that paper at its basic size (in the case of photocopier paper it is 17×22) equals 20 pounds. The thing to note about basis weight is that the larger the number, the thicker the paper. Cover papers start at about 50-pound, card stock starts at about 70-pound, and so on. (The important consideration with paper weight in general is whether you are going to mail the publication. If so, the thicker the paper, the heavier it is, and the more it will cost to mail it. In contrast, you might need a thicker stock, especially if you are going to be folding, scoring or perforating the pieces.) A printer will let you examine paper samples, but check your own photo-copier paper and its weight and use that as a starting point when beginning to think about your desired paper weight.

   In terms of paper size, that can be a bit more complicated. Check with your printer to see if your choice is available at a size the printer can use on the press.

   ◆ **Paper Type.** There are many types of paper. Bond paper is often used for writing and typing paper, letterhead, photo-copiers, and so on. (It was originally used for stocks and, as its name implies, bonds.) Book paper is often optimized for use on printing presses. Offset paper is a variety of book paper design-ed to run well on offset presses. Bristol and tag papers are thick stocks used for index cards, postcards, folders, and so on. Cover paper is not as thick as Bristol paper, but is thicker than book or bond paper and is often used for covers of reports or news-letters. There is also a seemingly endless number of specialty papers, from simulated parchment or vellum, to Bible papers.

◆ **Finishes.** How a paper is finished—or, in other words, what the texture of its surface is—will affect how well your pages print on them. The most common type of paper is wove finish, and is characterized by a plain or smooth finish. (It essentially has the smooth texture of the woven wire on the papermaking machine. Hence its name.) Laid paper is often used for bond paper or book paper. It has a slight, fabric-like texture to it. Smooth, machine-glazed, and enamel papers have undergone *calendering*, or a smoothing by a set of polished steel rollers called a *calender*. Calendered paper has a very smooth, polished finish. *Supercalendered* paper has an even smoother finish.

◆ **Coatings.** Paper is coated with a variety of materials, including clays, titanium dioxide, styrene-butadiene, and so on, primarily to increase its smoothness.

◆ **Opacity.** The thickness (related to basis weight) and other paper properties affect how easily one can see through a paper. A paper designed to have printing on both sides should be highly opaque, lest the problem of *show-through* (the visibility of the printing on the opposite side) occur.

◆ **Gloss.** Related to a finish is the concept of paper gloss, or how diffusely the paper surface reflects the light hitting it. Or, in other words, how shiny it is. Glossy paper appears very shiny, because most of the light rays hitting it are reflected back in a single direction. Glossy paper is often more difficult to read than matte paper, whose surface reflects incident light in a greater number of directions and thus appears much duller.

- **Grain.** A paper's grain is essentially the direction the paper fibers are running. Paper is easier to fold along the grain than across the grain. (There are also press considerations with which your printer is concerned with regard to grain.) Long-grain paper has grain that is parallel to the longer dimension of a paper sheet. Short-grain paper has a grain that is parallel to the shorter dimension of a sheet.

- **Color.** Paper is available in a wide variety of colors. Be certain, however, that the color of the paper will not interfere with any colors or designs (or the basic legibility thereof) that will be printed on it.

- **Ink Holdout and Setoff.** Ink holdout is a function of the surface properties of a paper and describes how well the ink fails to penetrate the paper surface. In some cases, inks dry by having the liquid portion of their vehicle soak into the paper. Other inks dry by oxidizing or evaporating the liquid portion of the ink and polymerizing the remaining portion. In the former case, paper with a low degree of ink holdout is desirable (newsprint and newsinks take advantage of that situation), while in the latter case a high degree of ink holdout is desirable. *Ink setoff* is a condition in which the ink does not dry quickly or properly causing a transfer of a printed ink film to the back of the sheet lying on top of it. In extreme cases the phenomenon of *blocking* causes the sheets to stick together.

- **Inks and Varnishes.** There are also many types of inks, which differ primarily in their drying mechanisms. The type of ink that is chosen will be a function of the paper chosen, the color ink required, and the desired characteristics of the dried ink film (such as high-gloss, and so on). Your printer will let you know the best ink to use for your job. A varnish is a type of lacquer applied to a printed piece to increase gloss or water resistance and protection. Spot varnish, often used on book jackets, involves the localized application of a varnish on a matte surface. Specify whether you would like a varnish of some kind.

- **Cover.** What type of cover is the publication going to use? You need to select a paper and ink for the cover, as well as for the body.

- **Bindery.** You also need to specify what binding and finishing operations you are going to require. Will you require folding? Stapling? Adhesive (called perfect) binding? Case binding (*à la* hardcover books)? Spiral binding? Three-hole punching? Embossing? Die-stamping? Die-Cutting? Foil-Stamping? Perforating? Scoring? Inserting? Tipping in? Stuffing? Mailing?

Those are most of the specifications and issues you will probably encounter. If you have preexisting examples of what you're after, by all means present it. Printers, binders, papermakers, and everyone else in the industry have thousands upon thousands of terms that get bandied around, which can be quite bewildering to those not acquainted with most of them. Describe specifically what you want if you don't know the term for it. (Accidentally specifying die-cutting rather than die-stamping will set you up for a big surprise.)

Preflight versus Bidding

Preflight essentially refers to a preliminary consultation with a printer (or other expert) to determine what the best design and layout based on your budget will be. Some people prefer to do preflight after the design process has been initiated, some before. Everyone also has his or her own strategy for when to begin shopping around a print job. Some prefer to start preflight and design meetings with printers before soliciting bids, some prefer to do it afterward.

Regardless of your preference, these things will need to be done at *some* point in the process. Just keep in mind the advantages and disadvantages of each strategy: You might be on a very tight deadline and might have needed to begin design and layout after (or at the same time as) doing preflight and bidding. You might have done all your layout and design already and discovered in your talks with printers that the design exceeds your budget, or that a different layout could reduce the cost significantly. You might find that another printer has a press setup that would provide a less expensive way of doing something.

Proofing and Inspecting During and After Printing

Depending on the print shop and the complexity of the job, you might get a variety of proofs and double-checks from the print shop that you might need to sign-off on.

Ink Swatches

Nothing is better for proofing color than seeing the actual page printed with the actual ink on the actual paper. This isn't usually possible very far in advance, but you can ask to see the actual ink smeared on the actual paper. (The combination of ink and paper structure and chemistry can produce very different results.) The technique of *draw down* involves taking a sample of the ink to be used and applying a bit of it to the stock you have specified. This allows you to verify that the ink and paper combination will yield the desired color and shade.

Film Inspection

If your printer is not doing your prepress work, you might want to have the printer inspect the films output by the service bureau. They will probably be better at spotting any errors or problems than will you.

Blues

A type of proof generated by the printer is called a *blueline*, or collectively, *blues*. They are photographically-produced proofs generated from your stripped films. (The images are in blue, the color of the dye used in the paper; some use brown dye and are called, unsurprisingly, *brownlines*.)

Press Check

On occasion you might be asked (or you can invite yourself) to conduct a press check, which is essentially showing up in the pressroom and seeing your job come off press at the start of the run. (This is more often done during multicolor jobs rather than simple black-and-white jobs.) During makeready, the setting up of the press involving inking, regulating the dampening system, mounting plates, and so on, many tries will be made, and when the press is up to speed, the press operator will stop the press and hand you a copy of the press sheet for your approval. If the color balance is correct (this is no time whatsoever to find a typo or suddenly hate the design), you'll approve it and this sheet is the one that will be used as a guide for the rest of the pressrun. What should you pay attention to?

◆ **Printer's Marks**   In particular, the color control bars and the registration marks. Do they all line up? For the images themselves, does everything appear to register properly? Is the quality up to the level that you and the printer agreed upon?

◆ **Accurate Color**   Make sure you have color swatches of PANTONE colors or other samples with you and compare the print with the samples, preferably in as close to a standard viewing condition as possible. Don't rely on memory.

◆ **Press Defects**   Are there wrinkles, show-through, strike-through, hickeys (undesirable spots caused by foreign particles on the plate or blanket), or other stray marks? Is the ink density dark enough and consistent?

Go to a press check with as many samples and other checks as possible. Take your time (but don't waste the printer's time unduly) and examine the press sheet carefully. If you sign off on a press sheet, you will be responsible for any defects or problems not caught. You will have no recourse if you approve a press sheet that eventually turns out to have defects. (If defects turn up that were not on what you approved, that's another matter.)

Inspection of the Finished Job

When your job is finished, inspect it before accepting it. Check it against the press check sheet, if you did one. Take random samples from various spots in the pressrun, to ensure that it is not only the top few copies that were printed properly. Make sure all colors and images are in register, and that all the colors are as specified. (In sum, do everything you did during the press check.) Also check to ensure that all binding and finishing operations were performed as specified, and that the approximate number copies requested is there. (Don't count each piece, however.) There will usually be some amount of over- or underrun. The printing contract that you signed prior to the job usually specifies some degree of variation in the total number of pieces delivered versus the number that was ordered.

ACROBAT AND PDF

In prepress, the PDF has a variety of uses and is beginning to catch on. One problem with the PageMaker/PostScript file dichotomy that we have concentrated on in this chapter and in Chapter 14 is that you either have a completely editable PageMaker file (requiring the application itself to run) or you have a nonviewable PostScript file that is sent directly to the output device. No more, however. With Acrobat, you can transmit your pages and documents from place-to-place as essentially PostScript files, but PostScript files that are viewable.

Why PDF?

Creating a portable document format file is a useful thing to do in two different scenarios: First, you want to distribute the files on the Web or through email, Lotus Notes, network file servers, or CD-ROM, for viewing or downloading; or second, you want a convenient, foolproof way to prepare a file for output at another location, such as a service bureau or a print-on-demand system. In all cases, your color, graphics, and fonts are included (in the case of fonts, you have the option to include them or not).

The advantages of PDF are as follows:

◆ The file, especially if you embed your fonts (see the "Font Issues" section later in this chapter for an explanation of how to do that), is totally self-contained—hence the portable appellation.

- The only software anyone else needs to read your PDF file is the free Acrobat Reader, available to anyone in many places, both online and off.

- The file is not editable by the recipient, which might be of importance to you in your distribution strategy. Actually, if you don't choose to protect your PDF using Acrobat Exchange (which is not included with PageMaker), your PDF is editable to a minor extent by anyone who has Acrobat Exchange; but if you select one checkbox, it's protected from anyone without the password you've assigned to it. With Acrobat Exchange, PDFs can be edited in terms of creating links and bookmarks, moving things around, and merging two PDFs, but not in terms of changing the text.)

- The file represents a PostScript rendition of your PageMaker file. The implication of this is that after you've successfully made your PageMaker file into a PDF file, you know it will image correctly to any PostScript output device. This makes PDF useful to you as a PostScript proofing, or preview, device in and of itself.

Before You Start

Before you can begin the process, you must make sure Adobe Acrobat Distiller is installed. The Export Adobe PDF plug-in really is just a way for PageMaker to run Acrobat Distiller by remote control. Distiller is a program that comes with PageMaker. It takes the PostScript output of PageMaker (as if PageMaker was printing to a PostScript printer) and "distills" it into a PDF file.

You cannot make a PDF file without Distiller; therefore, you must install it. (It's on your PageMaker CD.) (By the way, Distiller is a separate commercial product; it is not available for free downloading anywhere online. Adobe is nice enough to include it in the PageMaker package, otherwise you'd have to pay for it.)

Creating an Adobe Acrobat File

To create an Adobe Acrobat file out of a PageMaker file, choose Export from the File menu and then select Adobe PDF from the Export pop-up menu. You open the dialog box shown in Figure 15.9. The remainder of this chapter walks through this dialog box, with side excursions to the sub-dialog boxes that are brought up by clicking on the various buttons.

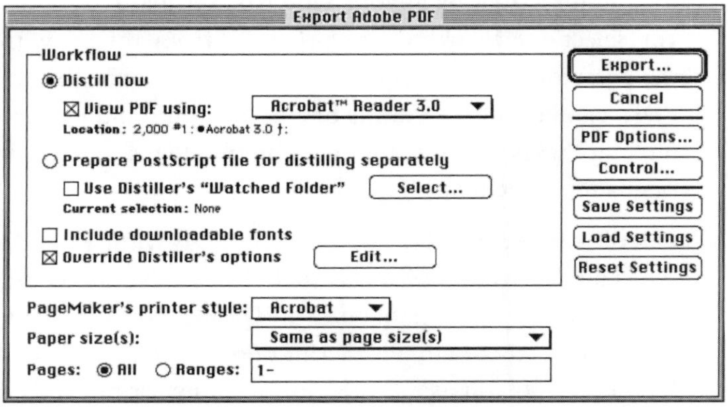

Figure 15.9

The Export Adobe PDF dialog box.

Note

You can't have Reader's Spreads (that's where you print pages 2 and 3 together on one sheet of paper or film, pages 4 and 5 together, and so on), set in PageMaker's Print dialog box at the time you use the Export Adobe PDF function. This will make Acrobat function incorrectly.

The safest way to avoid reader's spreads is to use the Acrobat printer style, which you can choose in the Export Adobe PDF dialog box.

Your PageMaker document can begin on any page number; Acrobat won't choke on it. You will even still see your PageMaker page numbers (if you had them printing on the pages in your PageMaker document). However, what Acrobat *will* do is to impose its own page-numbering system once the document becomes a PDF. Acrobat considers "page numbers" as logical symbols only: In other words, the first page in a PDF is, by definition, Page One, the second page is Page Two, and so on.

If you are making a PDF of a book with a separately numbered front-matter section, for example, and you want to retain your PageMaker page numbering, your best course of action is to *not* include the front matter in the same PDF as the rest of the book; instead, make a separate PDF out of it and then hyperlink it to the rest in Acrobat Exchange. (You have to purchase Exchange and read its documentation to learn how to do this).

Managing Distiller Options

Because the Export Adobe PDF plug-in has such intimate contact with Distiller, it can set some Distiller options from within PageMaker. Click the Override Distiller's options checkbox to open the dialog box shown in Figure 15.10. Here you can set compression on text and line art, store the file as raw ASCII text, store as an Acrobat 2.1 or 3.0 file, and decide whether to embed fonts or not.

And just what, you say, does that "Subset fonts below xx%" option do? Only this: Say you're embedding fonts, and you've used only a couple of characters from a certain pi font. Wouldn't it be nice if you didn't have to embed the whole font (of roughly 200 characters) just so you could use one or two characters? This option enables you to do that. You can set the number to whatever percentage you want. Then, if you've used fewer than that many characters from any particular font, *only* those characters will be embedded. Obviously, this slows down the distilling process a little, but again for the tradeoff of smaller file size.

Distill Now or Delay

Now, you need to decide whether to distill your PDF file out of PageMaker immediately or enable PageMaker to make a PostScript file that can be distilled later. Refer to the Export Adobe PDF dialog box in Figure 15.9.

Why would you want to delay? One major reason could be the amount of RAM you don't have. Many computer systems just don't have enough memory to handle both programs simultaneously. PageMaker needs at least 8MB, and Distiller needs another 6MB. If your System uses a lot of RAM because of extensions and fonts, you could easily need in excess of 20MB. At any rate, if you don't have enough RAM, you have to distill later.

Another reason to choose to distill later is speed. If you have many files to distill, it's probably faster (because then Distiller only has to launch the one time) for you to make your PostScript file from PageMaker and Distill later at your leisure—rather, at Distiller's leisure. You can send the PostScript file to Distiller's watched folder (set from within Distiller), and then Distiller calmly takes care of processing the files while you take a nap, have supper, or go out for coffee.

Figure 15.10

*Override Distiller's Options
dialog box.*

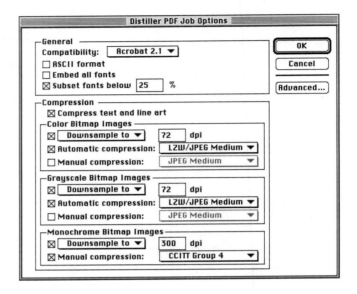

If you want to make your file as small as possible (while still embedding fonts), set the percentage to 100%.

In this same dialog box, you also can set preferences for working with graphics embedded in PDFs by Distiller. You can put graphics on a diet with downsampling or subsampling, or by choosing to compress them. The choices are self-explanatory.

In addition, you can click the Advanced button to open the dialog box you see in Figure 15.11, where you can set advanced printing (prepress, really) options. This is only applicable for color jobs that will be color-separated for commercial printing. If you are only printing to a desktop printer, even a color one, then this doesn't affect you.

The subject of prepress is way too complex to even begin to cover it in a short chapter like this; it rates a book of its own. Basically, if you don't know what these things are, you really shouldn't be fooling with them; conversely, if you are conversant with them, then you won't need any further explanation here.

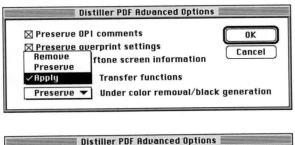

Figure 15.11

The Distiller Advanced Options dialog box, with the two pop-up menus open.

To read up on such things, the following series of digital color prepress booklets from AGFA are recommended: *Intro to Digital Color Prepress*; *A Guide to Color Separation*; *Working With Prepress and Printing Suppliers*; *Introduction to Digital Scanning*; and *Introduction to Digital Photo Imaging*. They're available from: Agfa Prepress Education Resources, P.O. Box 7917, Mount Prospect, IL 60059-7917. Phone 800-935-7007 or 708-296-6703; fax 708-296-4805.

Font Issues

Maybe the most important reason to even have PDF files has to do with fonts. "After all," you're probably asking, "how can I possibly share files with someone unless we both have the same fonts?" PDF gives you two choices:

◆ **Embed fonts.** You can actually include a copy of the font right inside the PDF document (see the checkbox about halfway down the "Export Adobe PDF" dialog box). If you include fonts, the file will be bigger (the size of a full font varies, but 50K is a decent average estimate), a particular issue for Web distribution, but generally not a problem at all if you are

643

distributing through CD-ROM. If you don't include fonts, Acrobat's approximation of the font may conceivably not please you. And don't even think about not including fonts if you are using symbol or pi fonts.

◆ **Local fake fonts.** You can depend on the viewer's local copy of Acrobat to try to make up the fonts on-the-fly. This does an adequate job as long as your font is fairly generic in look, because that's the kind of look Acrobat's made-up fonts have.

If you want to test your document both ways (to see whether Acrobat's fake fonts will serve your purposes), you have to create two PDF's, one with fonts included and one without; then close your fonts so they're not available (in Suitcase or whatever font management utility you use), and open each PDF. If the difference is alarming to you, you might decide to go with the one with fonts included; if the difference doesn't bother you at all, then it probably won't bother anyone else either.

One thing you should do is go into Distiller's setup and show it where you have your fonts stored if they are in a customized folder setup. (Distiller is looking for both your screen and printer fonts.)

If the *exact* look of your document—down to the exact fonts and line breaks—isn't 100 percent important to you, do not embed your fonts. This will keep your PDF file size down (again, the size of a full font varies, but 50K is a decent average estimate). Again, though, you'll be at the mercy of the Acrobat substitution fonts (generic-looking serif and sans-serif fonts) and their line breaks. The choice is yours. The bottom line is that, even without embedding your fonts, you still get a *lot* more control over the look of your documents than you do by going the HTML route described in Chapter 16, "HTML and the World Wide Web."

Tip

If you're running PageMaker on one computer and Distiller on a second computer, and you're embedding your fonts in the PDF, you need to make sure the fonts are available on the second computer. If the fonts are installed on the second computer in the normal way, you're fine, of course.

If the fonts are not installed on the second computer, you need to select "Include downloadable fonts" in the main Export Adobe PDF dialog box. This will include the fonts in the PostScript file that Distiller then uses.

Managing Automatic Hypertext Links

For a description and explanation of hypertext links and why you want them, see Chapter 16.

PageMaker can automatically make all the cross-references you'll probably need, right in the PDF file. That means you can provide your reader with an easy-to-navigate structure by putting to work the structure you've already developed for the PageMaker document. Just set up a table of contents and an index in the normal PageMaker way, prior to running the Export Adobe PDF command, and they will be translated intact into your PDF file.

Then when the person reading the PDF (onscreen, of course) clicks an item in the table of contents or index, he'll be immediately transported to the appropriate spot on the page of the document that contains the text that's referenced by the TOC or index entry. In other words, when you create your PageMaker TOC or index, you're creating not only the internal PageMaker link, which PageMaker uses to insert the correct page number into the TOC or index itself; but you're also setting up links that will automatically become, if you want, hypertext links when you create your PDF. You don't have to do more than create the TOC or index.

You turn on these automatic links by clicking the PDF Options button in the Export Adobe PDF dialog box. This opens the PDF Options dialog box, which is shown in Figure 15.12.

Figure 15.12

The PDF Options dialog box, showing hyperlink and bookmark options.

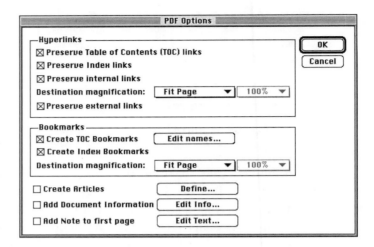

The checkboxes for Preserve Table of Contents (TOC) links and Preserve Index links (in the Hyperlinks section of the dialog box) create hypertext links between the items in the table of contents and index (the sources) and the locations referred to by those sources (anchors).

The checkboxes for Create TOC Bookmarks and Create Index Bookmarks (in the Bookmarks section) create bookmarks (the narrow strip of hypertext links you see in the left margin in some PDFs; see the sample PDF in Figure 15.10) between the table of contents or index and the locations. The difference between these two check boxes is that you can edit the TOC bookmarks; the reason you would want to do this is that the default name might be too long for the width of the bookmark strip in the PDF (again, see figure 15.13; many of the bookmarks are really too long and could have been shortened).

You can also preserve any internal hypertext links you've created manually, using PageMaker's Hyperlinks palette. (For information on creating these links, see Chapter 16.

The Preserve TOC, Index, and internal links checkboxes are all checked by default.

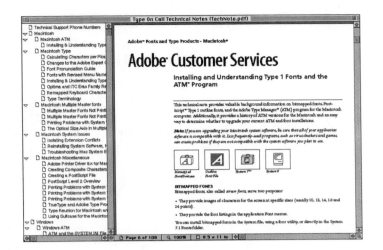

Figure 15.13

A sample PDF, showing bookmarks in the left-hand column.

As with the HTML language, you can perform your PDF conversion on the basis of PageMaker stories instead of pages. Remember that story is a very basic PageMaker term; it means "all text that's threaded together," or, in other words, "all text that becomes highlighted when you click an insertion point with the text tool and Select All." A story can be one character or hundreds of pages; the only criterion is "Is this text threaded to other text?"

Perform your conversion on the basis of stories by clicking the Create Articles checkbox (it's near the bottom of the PDF Options dialog box). What this does is to keep threaded PageMaker stories (stories that consist of more than one text block or frame) threaded in the PDF.

Document Information is text that appears in the Acrobat viewer's Document Info box; it gives useful information to the reader, consisting of a Title, a Subject, an Author (by default the name that appears in the Owner Name field in the Sharing Setup Control Panel), and Keywords. Use these if you want; they're not essential, but they can be useful.

You can type a note to appear on the first page of your PDF document by clicking the Add Note to first page checkbox. You can choose whether the note is displayed opened or closed when the PDF is opened.

There are three more items in the main Export PDF dialog box that have not been discussed yet:

The PageMaker's printer style pop-up menu gives you the default Acrobat printer style that comes built in to the program, and any other printer styles you've created. Be smart and use the Acrobat printer style (unless, of course, you've created your own printer style dedicated to Acrobat).

The Paper size(s) pop-up menu gives you Same as page size(s), Apply settings of each publication, and Apply printer style's setting. Normally you'll probably want to go with the default, Same as page size(s).

And then there's the Control... button (see Figure 15.14). This is actually preferences for the Export PDF dialog box:

Figure 15.14

The Control (preferences) dialog box.

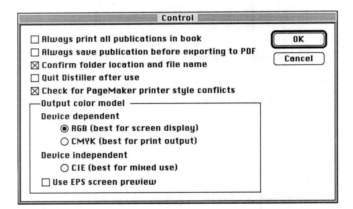

These choices are all pretty self-explanatory; you just need to know they exist. You probably have a consistent workflow and will want to set these preferences up to be consistent with that.

The choices in the Output color control section, just in case they *aren't* self-explanatory, mean this:

If you know you're targeting your PDF for onscreen display only, then choose RGB; if you know your PDF is destined for printing, and not screen display, choose CMYK; if you're not sure, or you know it's going to be used both ways, then choose CIE. There's not room here to go into why, but those choices work best.

And you would want to check the Use EPS screen preview checkbox if, and only if, your PDF will be viewed on screen only, not printed. The reason for this is that the message in the dialog box should really read Use EPS screen previews *ONLY*. Because that's what will happen: Any EPS graphics in your PageMaker document will retain their screen-resolution preview only; when the document is exported to PDF, they will lose the actual PostScript code that makes up the high-resolution EPS.

So if you have EPS graphics and you want them to print nicely, *don't* check this checkbox. If you don't care how they print (which should only be the case if the PDF will only be viewed onscreen), then go ahead and check it; thus the file size of the PDF will be smaller.

Bundling Book Publications

You can bundle together book publications into one PDF by opening, and making a PDF out of the document that contains the book list (see Figure 15.15).

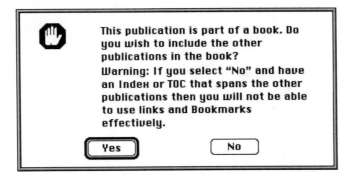

Figure 15.15

Booklist alert.

Minimizing Your PDF File Size

To make your PDF file as small as possible, make the following choices in the appropriate dialog boxes:

- ◆ Don't use the ASCII format option

- ◆ Use one of the available compression options for all text and graphics

- ◆ Downsample files for low-resolution and online use

- ◆ Convert CMYK images to RGB for onscreen use

- ◆ Embed only the fonts you need

SUMMARY

That's it. Simple, isn't it? There's really nothing to it. By far this is the easiest way to publish your documents electronically. You get to retain your formatting, fonts, line breaks, everything. About the only disadvantage, again, is file size: PDFs, especially with embedded fonts, can be just a little big for optimal online use.

This chapter and Chapter 14 have been concerned with "traditional" prepress, and how PageMaker can be used in those processes. The world of the Internet, especially the World Wide Web (the graphics- and multimedia-based "region" of the Internet) is increasingly usurping documents and publications that have traditionally been produced and disseminated on paper. There are those who predict that some day soon all information will be delivered online and that the printed page will be obsolete. This disheartens some of us (especially those who like to read in the bathtub!), but regardless of whether it is desirable or not, or whether it even happens, it should be prepared for. After all, "he who hesitates is lost."

Chapter •••••••• **16**

HTML AND THE
WORLD WIDE WEB

This chapter covers preparing PageMaker files for publishing on the World Wide Web. The Web is the graphically oriented portion of the Internet; the Internet, which also includes non-graphical areas, is a world-wide network of computer locations that contain various kinds of electronic information.

PUBLISHING ELECTRONICALLY: THE WEB

A Web site, which is the location you visit on the Web (for example, the Adobe Web site), is composed of documents called "pages," which consist of text and graphics, along with what are called "hypertext links" to other places in the same Web document, other Web documents (pages) on the same Web site, and pages on other Web sites.

The foundation that most Web pages are built on is called *hypertext*. The "hyper" part of that word refers to the fact that links can be created between various locations, as described in the previous paragraph. To use a link, the user clicks on the link (called the "source") onscreen, and is magically transported to the "anchor," which is the destination referred to by the source. An anchor represents a specific spot, a location on a page.

Each source can point to only one anchor (which makes sense, when you think about it because you are transported to the anchor when you click the source, that's the only way it *could* work), but each anchor can have as many sources as you want pointing to it.

Hypertext is implemented in a language called HTML (HyperText Markup Language). HTML is a text-only language with visible codes; any hypertext file can be created, viewed (as text and codes; not "viewed" graphically), and edited in any text editor or word processor. Of course, you have to know the codes and their syntax, and what they mean and what they do, before you can do any editing on this level. The point is that it doesn't take a special program to do the creating and editing.

Alternatively, Web pages can be based on PDF instead of HTML. That format is discussed in Chapter 14; this chapter is about HTML specifically, with the exception that the feature shared by the two formats (hyperlinks) is covered in this chapter only.

It is far beyond the scope of this book to either list or explain all the HTML codes. There are books that do this; in fact, there are dozens, scores, probably hundreds of such books. Visit your local book store and pick one up. A few are mentioned in the "It Doesn't Look Like You Expected It To?" section later in this chapter. The HTML language is not particularly difficult to learn, but it is extensive and, like all languages, does have considerable syntax requirements. This chapter touches on some examples of HTML coding, but you won't really learn how to write it here.

Getting back to the subject of Web sites themselves for a moment, note that you need a physical location for your Web site. That's obvious. (Such a location, by the way, is provided by what's known as an ISP [Internet Service Provider]). What might not be so obvious is that there's going to be someone at that ISP in charge of Web sites: he or she is called the Webmaster.

Here's the important thing: Before you do *anything* in terms of determining what the content of your Web site is going to be, or exactly how you're going to do anything at all, talk to your Webmaster. There are specific requirements that you must follow; you'll probably also pick up a lot of common-sense tips. Do what your Webmaster says to do. Enough said.

HTML AND WEB BROWSERS

An HTML document is composed of plain text and codes. The codes do three main things:

- ◆ Format the text
- ◆ Point to graphic files to be included in the document
- ◆ Point to anchors for hyperlinks

The text-formatting codes are of two main varieties: paragraph formatting and character formatting.

The paragraph codes include such styles as six different levels of heads, several different kinds of lists (bulleted, numbered, and so on), and body copy, among many others; and such attributes as text alignment (left or centered).

The character formats include such attributes as point-size changes, bold, and italic, among many others.

There are a few other codes that fall slightly outside the three main categories: just for a few examples, there are codes for objects such as horizontal rules; information about site indexes; frames; and HTML tables.

Here is an example of some HTML code from the Library of Congress home page. You can see how this same code looks graphically later in this chapter.

```
<html>
<head>
<title>Library of Congress World Wide Web (LC Web) Home
➥Page</title>
<base href="http://lcweb.loc.gov/homepage/lchp.html">
</head>

<body bgcolor="#ffffff">

<a href="http://lcweb.loc.gov/homepage/
➥lchp_txt.html">[text-only]</a>

<!--begin imagemap for head-->
<p align=center>
<a href="http://lcweb.loc.gov/homepage/lchp.html">
<img src="/homepage/images/homehead.gif"
     border="0" alt="[Library of Congress World Wide Web
          (LC Web) Home Page - Header]"></a><br>
<!--end imagemap-->

<!--begin imagemap for bar-->
<a href="http://lcweb.loc.gov/cgi-bin/imagemap/homepage/
➥homebar.map">
<img src="/homepage/images/homebar.gif" border="0"
     alt="[Library of Congress World Wide Web (LC Web)
          Home Page - Button Bar]" ISMAP></a><br>
<!--end imagemap-->
```

```
<!--begin imagemap for body-->
<a href="http://lcweb.loc.gov/cgi-bin/imagemap/homepage/
➥homebod3.map">
<img src="/homepage/images/homebod3.gif"
      border="0" alt="[Library of Congress World Wide Web
            (LC Web) Home Page - Main Body Image]"
➥ISMAP></a>
</p>
<!--end imagemap-->


<h3 align=center><a
href="http://lcweb2.loc.gov/frd/cs/cshome.html">Library
➥of Congress
Country Studies - Area Handbook Program</a></h3>


➥<h3 align=center><a href="./more.html"> <em>MORE</em>
Databases and
Resources</a></h3>
<p align=center>
<strong>
<a href="http://lcweb.loc.gov/homepage/
➥more.html#locis">Library of
Congress Information System (LOCIS)</a><br>
<a href="http://lcweb2.loc.gov/pow/powhome.html">Vietnam
➥War Era POW/MIA
Database</a> ¦
<a href="gopher://marvel.loc.gov/">LC MARVEL (Gopher)</a>
➥<br>
<a href="http://lcweb.loc.gov/z3950/
➥gateway.html#other">Access to
Catalogs at Other Libraries</a> ¦
<a href="http://lcweb.loc.gov/loc/pubftp.html">Public FTP
➥Site</a> </strong>
</p>
```

```
<h3 align=center><a href="http://lcweb.loc.gov/loc/
➥infopub/">Information for Publishers</a> ¦
<a href="http://lcweb.loc.gov/loc/standards/">Standards</
➥a></h3>
</strong>


<h3 align=center><a href="/global/explore.html">Explore
➥the Internet</a></h3>
<hr>
<p>

<strong>Library of Congress</strong><br>
<address>Comments: <a
➥href="mailto:lcweb@loc.gov">lcweb@loc.gov</a>
(10/31/96)</address>


</body>
</html>
```

Why Use HTML? How Does It Work?

To answer the second question first, when you view an HTML document, what you see is very dependent on your setup. In other words, if you and someone else both view the same HTML document, you on your computer and he on his, you will probably see two differently formatted documents onscreen.

Note that this refers to the appearance, the formatting, the layout, of the document, not the actual content (the text and graphics).

First, you tell your Web browser (or, if you don't, it uses its defaults) what fonts, and what sizes of those fonts, you want it to use for various things such as the six head styles, the list styles, and the body style mentioned earlier.

Keep in mind that an HTML document doesn't specify its own width; rather, that is dependent on the size of the window you give it on your screen, which is obviously at least partially dependent on the size of your screen.

The implications of the unknown or unfixed width of an HTML document are as follows:

1. In conjunction with the unknown fonts and sizes, the line breaks of the text cannot be specified by the author of the document.

2. The exact locations and positioning of graphic items are also not truly specifiable.

Other things over which the author or designer has no control are the color depth of the viewer's monitor and what Web browser the viewer will be using.

What this means to you as a designer of a Web page is that you have to allow for any and all possible variations in the setup of the viewer of the document. You have to allow for different background colors (color is covered in detail in the "Starting From Scratch" section), different fonts, wide windows, narrow windows; you have to allow for any possible line break in your text; you name it, you have to allow for it. You cannot, in other words, specify very much at all: you can specify the text content itself, the paragraph styles (heads, lists, and so on), and the graphics, but that's about all.

HTML Text

One good analogy with the text and its unknown line breaks is one you're bound to understand as a PageMaker user. Think of your HTML text as having been typed in a word processor, and the viewer of the HTML document as being a designer and PageMaker operator who is pouring your text onto a page. You, the author, and typist have no idea what font, point size, and column width the designer/ PageMaker operator is going to use, and therefore you cannot possibly have any idea where your line breaks are going to happen; and it's the same between you as the HTML author and the person who's viewing your HTML document on his screen.

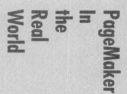

PageMaker In the Real World

So, with all these drawbacks, why use HTML at all? There are several good reasons.

1. It's still almost the only way to go. As you can see in the PDF section in Chapter 14, Adobe Acrobat's PDF (Portable Document Format) is becoming an alternative for Web publishing; however, it's not really prevalent enough at the time of this writing to be considered totally mainstream. (And to the extent that PDF is an alternative at all, it's the only alternative.)

2. It's being improved. The HTML spec is constantly being updated; at this writing, the next version of the spec is expected soon, and the next one beyond that is already being hotly debated among the powers that be. And it looks like a lot more control than was described earlier is coming in the future: for example, font control. You'll be able to specify a list of fonts, in order of precedence; only if the viewer has none of those fonts installed on his computer will you lose that control.

3. It's small. HTML creates vastly smaller file sizes than PDF does (because HTML files are just text-only files with a few codes).

4. It's simple. You can create an entire HTML document, an entire Web site, in a freeware text processor. You have to know the codes, and you have to buy a book or two to do that, but you don't necessarily have to have any expensive software (or hardware, for that matter).

5. It's very useable. There's nothing intrinsically wrong with not being in full control of exactly how your document will look to each individual viewer. After all, it's the content that's important, isn't it? I mean, I'm typing this chapter in a word processor, and I have no idea how it will look when it's finished. That doesn't keep me from saying what I want to say.

In addition, all the previous caveats notwithstanding, you *can* really be creative in HTML. If you've ever seen more than one or two Web pages, you certainly know what I mean. There's more variety in the Web pages I've seen, design-wise, than there is in all the books I've ever seen. Not knowing where the line breaks are going to fall does *not* prevent you from making beautiful, creative, highly informative Web pages.

Web Browsers

To view a Web page graphically (as opposed to viewing the code in a word processor), and to navigate its hyperlinks, you need a piece of software called a Web browser. There are several browsers available; the principal ones (as of this writing, of course; these things can change faster than you can sneeze) seem to be Netscape's Navigator, Microsoft's Internet Explorer, and a program called NCSA Mosaic that originated at the University of Illinois at Urbana/Champaign. Web browsers are fairly inexpensive as software goes, and can sometimes even be obtained for free (for example, Netscape had pre-release versions of Navigator 3.0 available for free download from their Web site). Figure 16.1 is a screen shot of the same HTML code that was listed earlier in this chapter, the Library of Congress home page, viewed in the Web browser Netscape Navigator.

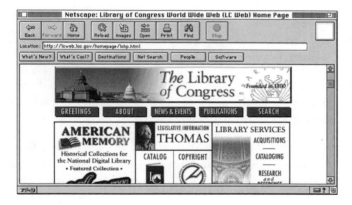

Figure 16.1

The Library of Congress home page, viewed in Netscape Navigator 3.0.

By the way, you'll continually see Netscape Navigator referred to simply as "Netscape." But really Netscape is the name of the company, and Navigator is the name of the software package. It's a bit like calling Adobe Illustrator "Adobe," or Lotus 1-2-3 "Lotus," to mention two other instances where this happens all the time. It'd be like calling this book "Hayden." It's even more confusing because Navigator seems to call itself "Netscape" onscreen, as you can see in Figure 16.1.

If you have an HTML document on disk (called a local document), you can view it in your Web browser, normally by using the Open command (depending on which browser you have). You can't do any editing (make any changes) to HTML files in your Web browser. All browsers can do is view Web files and execute hyperlink jumps, in addition to a few things like printing, remembering where you've been online, downloading files, and handling your email for you. (These things are not covered because that's not the subject of this book, and, furthermore, every browser is different.)

Web Addresses

To view a Web site (such as a remote HTML document) with your Web browser, you need its online address. When talking about the Web, addresses are called URLs (Universal Resource Locators). Here's Netscape Corp.'s URL, for example: `http://www.netscape.com`. This is a very typical, garden-variety URL. Dissecting its various parts, we have:

- `http://` This is the "prefix." http stands for HyperText Transfer Protocol.

- `www` World Wide Web. Not *all* Web sites have this as part of their URL, but most do, or something very similar.

- `.netscape` The most site-specific part of a URL. It doesn't always match the name of the organization as closely as this, but the URLs for major organizations usually do.

- `.com` This stands for "commercial." Some of the other possibilities are gov, edu, and org, for government, educational, and organization (normally a non-profit organization).

Here are a few more URLs, demonstrating some of the potential diversity:

- Carnegie Hall: `http://www.carnegiehall.org`

- The Baseball Server: `http://www4.nando.net/SportServer/baseball/`

This one has something new: more items, with slashes between. These indicate sub-areas (subdirectories, actually) on the same Web site: in other words, `nando.net` has one directory called SportServer, along with other directories; and the SportServer directory has one subdirectory called baseball. A trailing slash means you'll first see the "default" document for that site or directory, which is normally an index-type page. And this URL also has www4 instead of www.

Here's one that doesn't have anything remotely resembling www:

♦ SportsLine USA's Baseball area: `http://ps1.sportsline.com/u/baseball/`

So, you can see that URLs are *pretty* standardized in format, but you still can't assume anything. The only thing you *can* assume is that they all start with `http://`.

To visit a Web site, launch your Web browser, open your connection to your ISP (Internet Service Provider), find a menu command called (depending on which browser you're using) something like "Open Location" or "Open URL," and type the Web site's complete URL in the dialog box.

PAGEMAKER'S HTML TOOLS

Now I need to talk about how to accomplish some of this HTML stuff in PageMaker. (Much of this is also useful for the PDF processes described in Chapter 14, and this section is referenced there. If you're reading this with PDF in mind, just substitute the word "PDF" when you see the word "HTML" here.)

PageMaker has the following HTML-related tools:

♦ Importing external links (such as URLs from existing HTML documents)

♦ Creating internal links (such as from a source in your PageMaker document to an anchor in the same document)

♦ Creating links from an internal source to an external anchor (such as a Web URL)

♦ The 216-color Web-safe color palette, so you can ensure that you don't use a color that won't work in someone else's browser

Hyperlink Tools

Importing external links is very easy. There are two ways to do it:

1. Place an entire HTML document into your PageMaker document, using the Place command in the File menu; the hyperlinks that exist in the HTML document will follow it into PageMaker.

2. To import a hyperlink only, drag it from your browser window into your PageMaker window.

Creating internal links is a much more complex process, but it's still quite easy to do once you get the hang of it. This is, obviously, something you do entirely in your PageMaker document. You don't need your Web browser open at all.

1. First, you need to have your Hyperlinks palette showing. (It's in the Window menu.)

2. You have to set up an anchor (the destination the hyperlink from the source will jump to) before you can set up the source (the spot you click). To set up an anchor, select the text or graphic object (either imported graphic or PageMaker-drawn object) you want to serve as the anchor, and click the "New Anchor" button, which is at the bottom right of the Hyperlinks palette, to the left of the trash can icon (see Figure 16.2).

Figure 16.2

The Hyperlinks palette.

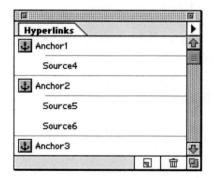

Clicking the New Anchor button gives you a new anchor with a suggested default name (see Figure 16.3), and it immediately gives you a dialog box where you can change that name. (If you hold down the Option key while you click, you'll bypass this dialog box and your anchor will be assigned that default name.) You'll probably want to change the default name to something meaningful, because later, when you're adding sources, you need to know which anchor you're looking at in the palette. (The default names were not changed in the figures here, but you should do so when you're doing real work.)

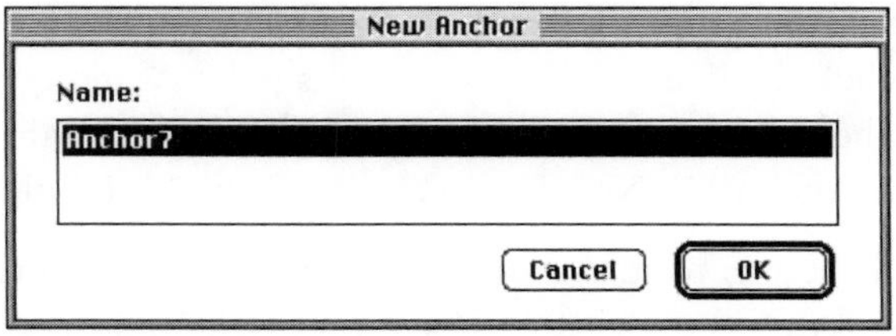

Figure 16.3

The New Anchor dialog box. The New Source dialog box looks the same except for the title in the title bar.

Note the black arrow in the upper-right corner of the Hyperlinks palette (Figure 16.2). When you press that arrow, you get a pop-up menu that gives you several choices, among which is "New Anchor." This is an alternative, although less convenient, way to add an anchor.

You can, of course, either set up all your anchors first, before you begin adding sources at all; or you can do an anchor, then its sources, then another anchor, then its sources, and so on; or you can mix and match. The only rule is that an anchor has to be defined before any sources that point to it can be defined.

3. To define a source, select the text (with the text tool) or the graphic object (with the pointer tool) you want people to click; and then, in the Hyperlinks palette, click the anchor icon to the left of the appropriate anchor's name. Again, you get a dialog box allowing you to change the default name of the new source. And again, if you press the Option key while clicking, you bypass that dialog box; so if you really *want* the default names instead of meaningful "real" names, this is a great way to save time.

Again, alternatively, the pop-up menu at the upper right of the Hyperlinks palette contains a "New Source" item.

To create an external anchor, you need first to know the URL you want to refer to (of course); then simply deselect all text and graphics, and click the "New Anchor" button just like you did for an internal anchor; then type (or paste) the URL into the resulting "New URL" dialog box, which looks just like the "New Anchor" dialog box in Figure 16.3.

The pop-up menu at the upper right of the Hyperlinks palette also contains a "New URL" item.

If you want to change the name of a source or anchor later, it's easy. Double-click the name in the Hyperlinks palette, and type your new name in the resulting dialog box. This dialog box is again identical to the "New Anchor," "New Source," and "New URL" dialog boxes.

That's all there is to it. Again, perhaps the most important thing to remember is that one anchor can have as many sources as you want, but each source can point to only one anchor.

Previewing Your Hyperlinks

Before you export to HTML, you can preview the functionality of your hyperlinks right in PageMaker. This is a handy, time-saving way to make sure your links work the way you want them to without having to export and re-export while you test things in your Web browser.

Click the Grabber tool in the Tool palette; then you see your hyperlink sources outlined or framed in blue. Position your cursor over the source you want to test; the cursor changes to a pointing hand. Click the source to jump to its anchor.

While you're in preview mode, there's also a Go Back command, and Go Forward too, in the Layout menu. How these work is that after you've followed a link, Go Back takes you back to where you jumped from. And then after you've Gone Back, Go Forward takes you back— or forward (terminology becomes so very confusing)—to where you just Went Back from.

The Web-Safe Color Library

All graphically oriented programs (which includes all Macintosh and Windows programs) either have their own color scheme (such as only certain colors can be used and viewed in the program) or have an editable color scheme where the user can define new colors and perhaps new colors can be imported from other sources. PageMaker, for example, qualifies on both these latter points: its color scheme is editable, and new colors in an EPS graphic are automatically imported.

Web browsers have non-editable color schemes. They handle color; they show color; the user can even specify colors in certain instances, like the color of hyperlink sources both before and after they've been followed; but their color scheme, or color palette, is fixed, unchangeable.

The implication of this for you, the creator of a Web page, is that you need to restrict yourself to colors that the common Web browsers can use. If you don't, then you don't know what the viewer will see and the possibility exists that you'll have created a color background, for example, that makes your colored text unreadable.

Fortunately, a compilation has been made of the colors that are supported in common by the Macintosh and Windows versions of the three main Web browsers: Netscape Navigator, Internet Explorer, and Mosaic. There are 216 such colors. And the great news is that PageMaker 6.5 comes with these 216 colors as a color library you can use.

Here's how you use this color library to add one of these colors to your color palette in the current PageMaker document: In the Utilities menu, choose Define Colors/New/Library/Online. You'll go through the following dialog box sequence to get there (see Figures 16.4 through 16.6):

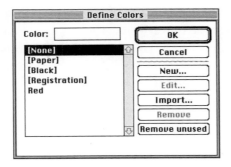

Figure 16.4

The Define Colors dialog box. Click the "New" button.

Figure 16.5

The Color Options dialog box. Press the pop-up arrow to the right of the word "Libraries." Choose "Online " from that pop-up menu.

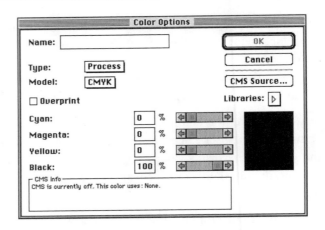

Figure 16.6

The Online color library dialog box. Click a color here and click OK; the color is added to your Color palette, ready for you to use.

Adding the Web-Safe Colors to your Color Palette

If you want to add all 216 colors to your PageMaker color palette, create a new document and then do this in the Define Colors process as described: select all the colors at once

Online Page Sizes

As already stressed, your page doesn't really *have* an intrinsic size or shape; that's all dependent on the setup at the viewer's end. The arrangement of graphics, however, is a design topic that needs to be addressed. The question must be asked: What size and shape do you make your page?

If you have many graphics, or large graphics, or if the look of your page and where things are located is important to you, then you need to consider this topic. If your Web page's emphasis is text, with a few small graphics at most and you don't choose to have PageMaker's HTML Export process retain your layout, then this is of lesser importance.

One thing that you should assume is that the viewer is very likely to be seeing your "page" in landscape rather than portrait orientation—that is, the window on the viewer's screen is likely to be wider than it is tall. (This is the case with most windows on most computer screens, of course.)

What you should therefore do is to take advantage of that knowledge. You have to assume something for your page size, so start with the smallest common computer screen: the screen on a laptop computer. Make your own estimate as to the exact size discussed here (my two laptops have screens of 7-1/2×4-3/4 inches and 7×5 inches).

On the other hand, you might want to assume a larger window. At any rate, make a minimum assumption about the size of screen your document will be viewed on, and work with that as the width of your document.

After you have determined what size to make your pages, you might want to make yourself a PageMaker template of that page size.

Note

A good example of a Web site that makes an assumption about the width of the viewer's window, and tries to control

continues

by pressing the Shift key and clicking the colors (or, if you're clever, make sure no color is selected, scroll all the way to the left, hold down your shift key, point without clicking at the upper-left color swatch, and, holding your mouse button down now, drag your cursor from the upper-left swatch down and to the right until your cursor is to the right of the scroll bar, at which point the swatches will scroll past you and they'll all become selected); then click OK to all dialog boxes until you're out of the Define Colors sequence.

Then either create an EPS graphic out of that dummy PageMaker document (Print/Options/Write PostScript to File) and later import that EPS into any other PageMaker document where you want to have the 216-color palette available; or simply Import the colors from the PageMaker document you created in the previous paragraph (Utilities/Define Colors/Import).

Remember if you go through the Define Colors process to add all 216 colors to your color palette when you have no PageMaker document open, you'll be adding those colors to your application defaults and they'll be present whenever you create a new PageMaker document in the future. If that's what you want, fine; otherwise, make sure you have a document open when you do this.

*what the viewer will see, is the New York Times site (http://
www.nytimes.com). There's a message at the beginning that says you
should open your window to a certain width, which it shows to you onscreen.
I think this is a "good" example because that width fits easily on my laptops,
and therefore will fit easily on almost anyone's screen.*

You don't know what font the viewer will use, or at what size; but you
do know the size of your graphics. So you need to make your layout fit
in whatever size screen you assume your viewer will have available.

Type Online

As emphasized throughout this chapter, you have no control over the
fonts and sizes your viewers will be using.

Here is an example of the control the viewer has: the Font dialog box
in the Netscape Navigator 3.0 General Preferences menu (see Figure
16.7).

Figure 16.7

*The font preferences from
Netscape Navigator 3.0.*

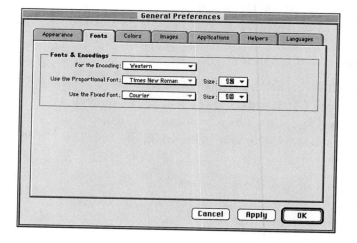

As you can see, the viewer can set the font for two usages: "proportional" (proportionally spaced fonts, like the one you're reading in this
book), and "fixed" (monospaced fonts, like the Courier font you've
certainly seen many times). These usages are determined by HTML

codes: heads and text are proportional; some codes, usually used for tabular material, call for a monospaced font.

The viewer can also set the base size for each font; the base size is used in determining other sizes, like for the six head styles; the user has no control over how that works.

Internet Explorer has fairly analogous controls over font and size; Mosaic also has some control, although not as much as Netscape Navigator.

So the upshot is that you, the creator of the Web page, have absolutely no idea as to what font, and no exact idea as to what size, the viewer will be seeing your document in; therefore you should make no assumptions.

You can say that the viewer will probably choose a text size that makes sense—in other words, probably somewhere between 10-point and 14-point. And you'll *probably* be right if you say that. It's probably a fairly safe assumption. But you obviously can't bet the house on it.

If you need to guarantee that a particular font is used for a very short run of text (for example, a title), your only choice is to create a graphic that uses that font, and then use the graphic instead of text in your document. Don't forget that your graphic has to be in GIF format.

Graphics in HTML

The HTML language only accepts, or allows you to use or link to, graphics in two formats:

- GIF (which stands for Graphics Interchange Format), primarily for line-art graphics

- JPEG (which stands for Joint Photographic Experts Group), for compressing color images

Note

The DOS filename extensions for these two formats are .GIF and .JPG.

The PageMaker export process *automatically* converts your graphics to GIF and JPEG for you. You don't even have to ask it to: it just does the conversion when you export to HTML. There are no controls or switches for you to set.

HTML Tables

One important feature of the current version of HTML, which is supported by most Web browsers and used extensively by PageMaker when it exports HTML, is HTML "tables." HTML tables relate *somewhat* to the kind of table you can create in PageMaker and in other programs, but they really mean much more than that.

In PageMaker, a table is essentially a set of tab columns. You know, the kind where each column has a number or a few words or so; the columns line up vertically, either flush left, centered, or flush right on each other; and the purpose of the table is to present data in a comprehensible, readable way.

HTML tables, again, *can* be used for exactly the same purpose and in exactly the same way; but they are potentially much more powerful than simple tab columns. HTML tables are more like computer spreadsheets, because each intersection of a row and a column (I will call it a "cell") can contain as much text as you want it to, and the text can "word-wrap" inside that cell. So an HTML table *could* be composed of columns of numbers; but it also could be composed of cells of paragraphs of text. In addition, HTML table cells can even contain graphics—so, in short, they can contain just about anything you want.

With an HTML table, you can specify, or control, its total width; or the width of any or all columns (individually, that is); or nothing at all (the viewer's browser determines how wide to make things). If you do decide to specify any widths, you can do it in absolute (so many inches wide) or percentage (a certain percent of the full width) terms.

Little Men Studio

With PageMaker's capability to act as a design environment for Web pages, it is important to have resources at hand that provide Web-ready graphic elements. The CD from Little Men Studio can suffice to do just that. It contains over 1,150 Web graphics images for background tiling, arrows, buttons, rules, headers, banners, bars, and more in both GIF and JPEG formats. As an extra, they also offer Web-Ready Talk Bytes, 110 useful vocal phrases in both male and female voices.

PageMaker actually doesn't use HTML tables to convert tabbed tables that exist on your PageMaker page. The next version of PageMaker might add this capability, but 6.5 doesn't have it. This is PageMaker 6.5's greatest weakness in converting documents to HTML: it just converts tabbed tables to text with spaces between the columns.

I am actually looking—and have been for some time—for an acceptable way to perform this conversion, because I have a client who wants to convert a 120-page catalog (which is, of course, full of tables) to HTML for his Web site; I have yet to find any utility that works in any kind of a fully automated way.

How PageMaker *does* use HTML tables is in approximating your page geometry when you convert your PageMaker document to an HTML document. We'll talk more about how to do this later; but what PageMaker does is to put everything on your PageMaker page into an HTML table cell. You have a 4×2-inch text block in the upper-left corner of your page? PageMaker will put that text (again, with no control over line breaks) into a 4-inch-wide HTML table cell (obviously, the cell's depth is determined by the point size and line breaks). You have a graphic to the right of that text block? It is put into its own HTML table cell in the appropriate location.

HTML tables, and their cells, are totally transparent to the viewer of the HTML document—especially when they're used like this. The creator of the document can specify a border between/around each cell; but if there's no border specified, there's no indication to the viewer that a table is present at all.

Exporting Documents to HTML

To convert your PageMaker document to HTML, you use the File/ Export/HTML command. This gives you the dialog box you see in Figure 16.8.

Figure 16.8

This is the dialog box you get when you choose the Export/ HTML command in the File menu.

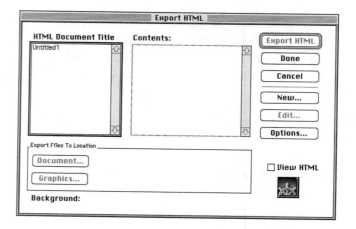

The first thing you should do is press the Options button, which opens the Options dialog box (see Figure 16.9).

In this dialog box, you make several important choices, some of which will have a huge impact on how your HTML document ends up looking.

Figure 16.9

The Options dialog box.

The first checkbox, Preserve approx. layout in HTML tables when exporting pages, needs to be explained. Notice that it says "HTML tables," not just "tables." What this refers to is using HTML tables, which was discussed earlier in this chapter, to retain the layout of your

PageMaker page, by putting elements, such as text blocks and graphics, in HTML table cells. This does *not* refer to material that is tabular in nature in PageMaker (columns of numbers and the like); in fact, such tables do *not* translate very usefully into HTML code at the current time.

Check this box if you want your layout retained (to the extent possible, of course). Fill in the number for Exported page width, which should match your assumption that we discussed above for the width of window your viewers will be viewing your HTML document in. A pixel is 1/72nd of an inch; 612 pixels is 8-1/2 inches. (There are three common sizes in the pop-up menu, or you can type your own number.)

Styles

Next, in the Options dialog box are the style assignments (see Figure 16.10). This is an extremely handy feature, in that you can continue using the same old PageMaker paragraph styles you've always used, and here you can map each one of them to an HTML paragraph style. Each PageMaker style, of course, can only map to one HTML style; but any HTML style can have many PageMaker styles mapping to it. The next figure illustrates the pop-up menu you get when you click one of the little arrows to the right of the HTML style names. Choose the HTML style you want the PageMaker style at the left to map to.

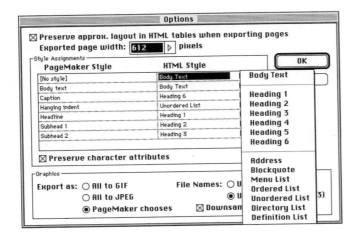

Figure 16.10

The Options dialog box with the HTML styles popped up to the right of the first PageMaker style/HTML style pair.

All the styles in your PageMaker document are contained in this scrolling list. If you make HTML style assignments for each of the PageMaker styles you've used, you'll have made your HTML conversion job much easier.

Character Attributes

The other text-based option here is Preserve character attributes. This means bold, italics, point-size changes, all that kind of thing. There's little reason, generally, not to accept this choice. If a viewer's Web browser doesn't support some of these attributes (and some definitely don't; in fact, no current browser reads all HTML codes), then that viewer will miss that character styling; therefore, it's best if you don't rely on boldfacing or italicizing or any other character styling for important contextual meanings. But then we're talking about rewriting your document if you've done that; it's not going to be fixed by choosing or not choosing this option. Again, in general, you normally can't be hurt by preserving the attributes; if you have a scenario where it *would* be a bad idea, then you definitely shouldn't choose it.

Graphics

The other options in the Options dialog box are for graphics. First, you can choose to have PageMaker convert all your graphics to GIFs, or all your graphics to JPEGs; or you can allow PageMaker to decide which is best on a case-by-case basis. Unless you have a definite reason for choosing one of the first two choices, it seems by far the easiest and most prudent to let PageMaker decide. Line art should normally get translated to GIF, and bitmaps (photographs) to JPEG; PageMaker does this for you.

PageMaker assigns filenames to these converted graphics based on the original filename of the graphic at the time it was imported into PageMaker. Use Long Names means, essentially, Macintosh- or Windows 95-compatible filenames. You shouldn't do this, unless you know your HTML documents will be viewed only by Macintoshes or PCs running Windows 95, which is certainly not the case on the Web.

You should, rather, choose the Use Short Names (8.3) option, because 8.3 means DOS-compatible eight-character filenames with three-character extensions. The extension for a GIF file is .gif; the extension for a JPEG file is .jpg. PageMaker will do the best it can to shorten your Macintosh filenames, if that's what they were, to eight characters. (Of course, if you're working on a PC that's not running Windows 95, you probably don't need to worry about this option in the first place because you're already using 8.3 filenames.)

The last option, Downsample to 72 dpi, means that PageMaker will take any bitmapped graphic that is more than 72 dots per inch (dpi) and make it into a 72-dpi graphic while converting it to JPEG format. You are wise to check this option if your HTML document is intended for onscreen viewing only, because graphic resolution more than about 72 dpi (the resolution of most monitors, and those that have better resolution are still in the neighborhood of 100 dpi at the most) is wasted on the screen anyway and therefore increases file sizes unnecessarily.

Now click OK in the Options dialog box and look back at the Export HTML dialog box (Figure 16.8).

You can use the same PageMaker document as the basis for more than one HTML file, and this is the reason for some of the other choices you are going to encounter in this dialog box.

Take, for example, a hypothetical PageMaker document that has two pages and four stories located somewhere on those two pages. (Remember that a "story," to PageMaker, is all text that is threaded together; another way to look at it is all text that is highlighted when you click an insertion point and Select All. A story could be one character, or hundreds of pages, or anything in between; the contents of one text block, or hundreds of text blocks, or anything in between. You know that all text that's together in one text box is all together in the same story; the question becomes whether two text boxes are separate stories or parts of the same story. The bottom line is: It's whether the text is threaded that makes the difference.)

Assigning Elements from PageMaker to HTML

You can assign the following "elements" of your PageMaker document to an HTML document: one or more pages, including the text that's on those pages and those pages only; *or* one or more stories, regardless of what pages the stories happen to flow onto. In other words, you can base your HTML document on either pages or stories.

To begin, click the New button in the Export HTML dialog box (see Figure 16.8); you'll get what you see in Figure 16.11.

Figure 16.11

The "New Contents" dialog box, as it first opens for a two-page PageMaker document.

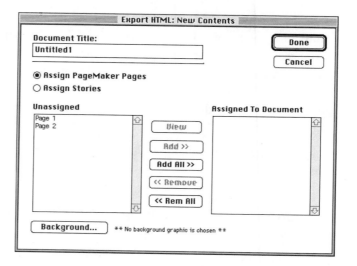

This dialog box, and its appearance in general, is what you first see when you click the "New" button. What you are going to do here is to assign the various pages and stories in your PageMaker document to one or more HTML documents.

What you see in this figure is a default HTML filename, the Assign PageMaker pages button selected, and two scrolling list boxes that together contain all the pages in your PageMaker document. Because this is the first time you are using this dialog box, all the pages (in this case, two pages) are on the Unassigned side.

If you click the Assign Stories button instead of the Assign PageMaker Pages button, you see the list of stories in this PageMaker document (see Figure 16.12), again split between unassigned (all the stories, because we're just beginning), and assigned. What you see is the first few words of each story: as much text as will fit in the window. Use the View button to identify different stories that begin with the same first few words, making them indistinguishable in this dialog box.

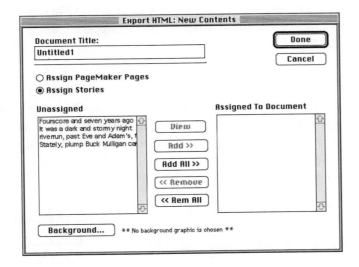

Figure 16.12

The New Contents dialog box, with stories shown for a PageMaker document that has four stories.

So, what you do with this New Contents dialog box is assign either pages or stories to a specific HTML document.

The first thing you should do is to give a real title to the first HTML document you want to set up. (Keep reading, you will set up another HTML document from the same PageMaker document later.)

By the way, remember than an HTML title is not at all the same thing as a filename. You will specify the filename in a bit, at the same time you are specifying what folder to save everything in. The Document Title here is the HTML title, a specific feature that all HTML documents must have, which will be displayed at the top of your HTML document when it's being viewed in a Web browser. (In Figure 16.1, for example, the title is at the top, after the word "Netscape.")

The next thing is obviously to decide whether to assign pages or stories to your HTML document. Remember that because the choice is made by radio button, you can only choose one or the other, not both.

Some of your decision-making on this score depends on the nature of your document. PageMaker stories help organize information no matter which pages that information happens to reside on. A newsletter or magazine that has stories jumping across many pages, for example, probably would best be broken up by stories rather than pages. On the other hand, you would most likely want to do a page-based conversion on a catalog of single-page sales sheets.

You want to set up a sample document based on stories. In Figure 16.13, you already clicked the Assign Stories button. You typed the title "Sample document #1" in the Document Title area. Then you chose the stories you wanted to include. You can move them from the unassigned area to the assigned area (or back, for that matter), by either selecting them and clicking the Add>> (or <<Remove) button, or by double-clicking the stories.

Figure 16.13

Edit Contents dialog box with some stories assigned to an HTML document named Sample document #1.

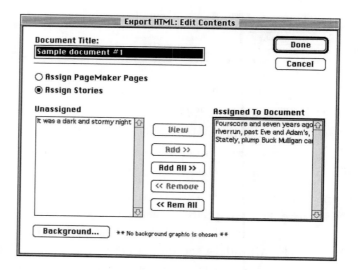

After you have all the stories assigned that you want, click Done to go back to the main Export HTML dialog box.

By the way, if you should ever need to change your page or story assignments, just click the Edit button in the Export HTML dialog box; you get a dialog box that looks exactly like the New Contents dialog box except it's called Edit Contents. In fact, many of the figures you're looking at right now are screen shots taken while in the editing process rather than the "new" process. Same difference.

Now you want to set up a second HTML document, and base it on pages this time. Click the New button again. Every time you click the New button, you're creating (or setting up) another HTML document.

This time, after typing in another document title (Sample document #2), and clicking Assign PageMaker Pages, do the same thing with the list of pages that we did with the list of stories for Sample document #1: assign the ones you want by adding them to the right-hand list box, as in Figure 16.14.

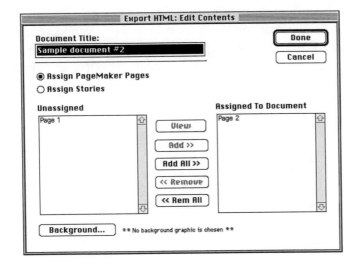

Figure 16.14

The Edit Contents dialog box with one page asigned to an HTML document named Sample document #2.

Here, you have assigned page 2 from the PageMaker document to the HTML document. Click Done again to go back to the main Export HTML dialog box, which you see a current version of in Figure 16.15.

Figure 16.15

The Export HTML dialog box after setting up the two HTML documents. The first document is selected.

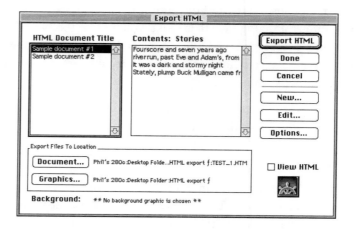

Saving HTML Files

Now you have set up two HTML documents for export. Select each HTML document in turn, and, by clicking the Document... and Graphics... buttons in the Export Files To Location section of the Export HTML dialog box, specify what folder it will be exported to and what filename you want to give it. Actually, that has already been done in Figure 16.15. Here are the dialog boxes where you specify this information (see Figures 16.16 and 16.17).

Figure 16.16

The dialog box you get when you click the Document... button in the Export HTML dialog box.

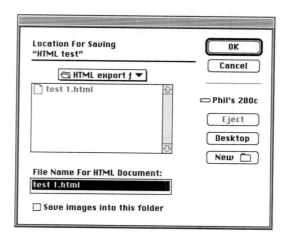

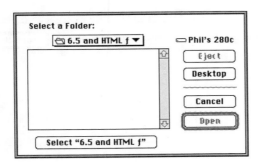

Figure 16.17

The dialog box you get when you click the Graphics... button in the Export HTML dialog box.

Simply navigate, using normal Macintosh or Windows navigation techniques for such dialog boxes, to the folder you want to use. Then type the filename you want to use for the HTML document. (Filenames for your graphics are automatically created by PageMaker.)

Actually, if you click the Save images into this folder checkbox at the bottom of the Document dialog box, then you don't have to click Graphics... at all. If, for some reason, you do want to save your graphics in a different folder, then you'll have to "do" both dialog boxes.

Do this process for each HTML document in the HTML Document Title scrolling list box in the upper left of the Export HTML dialog box: That is, select the HTML Document Title, and then click Document... (and perhaps Graphics...) in the Export Files to Location area.

Here's the Export HTML dialog box for our same PageMaker document, with Sample document #2 selected (Figure 16.18).

You can see that it is saved to the same folder as Sample document #1. There might be a reason to save your HTML documents to the same folder, or there might be a reason to save them to different folders. Depends on what you're trying to accomplish. One would assume that you'll normally—because these HTML documents appear to be related, coming from the same PageMaker document as they do—want to keep them together.

Figure 16.18

The Export HTML dialog box after setting up the two HTML documents. The second document is selected.

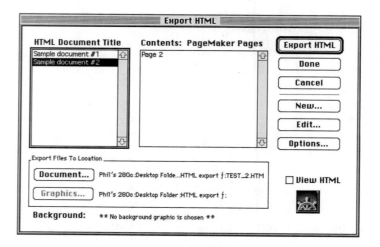

Inspecting Figure 16.18, you can also see the filenames, at the very end of the Document listing: Document #1's filename will be "TEST_1.HTM," and Document #2 will be "TEST_2.HTM." Again, you specified these filenames in the dialog box you reached when you clicked the "Document" button. For the same reason that it's good to give graphics 8.3 DOS-compatible filenames, it's also a very good idea to give your HTML documents themselves DOS-compatible filenames. And the 8.3 DOS version of the HTML filename extension is "HTM."

There remains only one more thing to do before you go ahead and click Export HTML, and that is to decide whether you want to view your new HTML document immediately in your Web browser. If you do, you have to first tell PageMaker where your browser is. If your Export HTML dialog box doesn't have an icon under the View HTML option (the figures in this chapter illustrate the icon for Netscape Navigator), go to File/Preferences/Online/Web Browser/ Browser, which gives you the dialog box in Figure 16.19. This is a preference-type setting that you'll only ever have to do once.

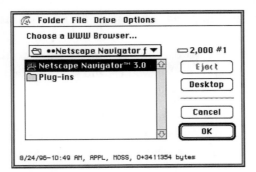

Figure 16.19

Use this dialog box to tell PageMaker where your Web browser is.

Viewing Exported HTML

Then, if you click the "View HTML" checkbox, your newly exported HTML document will launch your browser, if it's not already launched, and will open in it for your immediate viewing.

Ready? Click the HTML document you want to export (in the HTML Document Title list in the upper-left corner of the Export HTML dialog box), and click the Export HTML button in the upper-right corner of the same dialog box. You'll find your newly exported files in the location specified in the Export Files To Location section of the same dialog box.

It Doesn't Look Like You Expected It To?

If you need to do some fine-tuning after you see what you've done (and don't be embarrassed: we *all* do, most—or, more honestly, all—of the time), you'll have to appraise what you see in your browser and determine whether you can make your changes in PageMaker (and then re-export, of course), or whether you'll need to edit your HTML code in a word processor/text editor or perhaps one of the many HTML WYSIWYG (What You See Is What You Get) editors. (There are lots of the latter out there, and more appearing every week, so we hate to make a recommendation in a book that has to be written some time before you'll be reading it. But because this is a book about Adobe PageMaker, we'll mention that Adobe does make a WYSIWYG HTML editor, called Adobe PageMill.)

Some things are just going to be impossible to set up in PageMaker for export to HTML without any fine-tuning of the HTML code after exporting; in other words, you might well need to do your fine-tuning in both places: some in PageMaker, and some while dealing with the exported HTML code itself.

Again, this is not the book to teach you how to edit HTML code. There are plenty of books available on the subject; if you decide to make the plunge into HTML, consider a couple of other titles by Hayden Books:

- *Creating Killer Web Sites* by David Seigel
- *HTML Web Magic* by Ardith Ibañez and Natalie Zee

REPURPOSING PRINT-BASED DOCUMENTS FOR ONLINE

You could certainly use PageMaker and its HTML export process as a primary authoring tool for creating Web pages. I think you'll agree after you become familiar with the HTML export process that it isn't all that hard to do. The HTML language is so simple, in fact, that many people are writing Web pages in word processors, and plenty of special-purpose Web-authoring tools are out there.

However, it's quite likely, given the context of this chapter, that you are not using PageMaker to build Web pages from scratch. Rather, you are likely facing the more complicated challenge of "repurposing" existing paper-based documents so that they can be used on the Web. Maybe you've got a library of documents to convert, or perhaps you are designing new material and want to try to make it work in both distribution environments.

There are a series of steps to accomplishing the goal of converting a paper-based document to a Web page.

Consult with your Webmaster or Internet provider. As mentioned earlier, things are changing rapidly on the

---

Modify Your Styles to Match Browser Defaults

It's easier to evaluate how your page will look when it is on the Web, as you are redesigning it, if you modify all the styles to match browser defaults. Check out Netscape Navigator to see what those are likely to be (because it is the most popular browser at the moment). It usually comes supplied by providers with all the styles set to Times. You can do the same. Also while in preferences, set your Link Format to match browser defaults—probably blue and underlined in this case.

Web. Before doing anything else, you really must collaborate with whoever administers the network aspects of your Web site. Your pages must conform to that environment, or they won't function—or will otherwise embarrass you.

The issues range from the internal capabilities of the Web computer server, to the software your Webmaster supports, for example, will the server support lists, interactive forms, or image-mapped links? These terms might not mean much to you right now, but within a few weeks of getting set up on the Web, you will understand and want to use them. At the moment it's enough to simply know about these things.

One terribly important item—ask for precise instructions on how to set up your folder structure so that it mimics the structure of the Web server site. If you don't understand this issue, don't walk away until you do. Make whoever it is sit down with you and talk you through this part of it. It's the secret to being able to build documents on your computer that will easily transport to the server, with all your internal links intact and ready to go. It can't be covered adequately here, there are too many variables, but you need to know about this.

◆ **Make your layout Web-like.** It's unlikely that your paper-based document has been structured even remotely like a Web page. You'll need to make adjustments before using the HTML export process to get good results. See the sidebar "A Web Layout Survival Guide" elsewhere in this chapter.

A good paper-based layout has a certain visual complexity that engages the reader. Many layouts have multiple columns. However, a Web page generally must be much simpler. For one thing, it runs inline from top to bottom—one column only.

Web documents link to other locations—your own documents, graphics within your documents, and other locations on the Web. You'll need to plan out how to break down your PageMaker document so that it can take on this Web-like structure.

◆ **Run the HTML export process.** Converting the text in your document to HTML will be the easiest of all these tasks. It's PageMaker's HTML export's main purpose in life.

Hopefully, you've used paragraph styles throughout your document because HTML is a style-based way of describing documents.

◆ **Test your Web stuff.** There's nothing worse than logging on to a Web site and having to sit through a 100K download of some graphics that either could have been much smaller or a user option. Consult with your Webmaster about this topic; it's much too complex to cover fully here.

You've got to test the look and speed of your Web page design through a normal system to see what real users will experience. Otherwise, your page will be an instant first-impression bad experience, and all those surfers will head for a different and more friendly beach. Don't forget, also, to check that all the links are working correctly after your site has been constructed and installed on the Web. This is a very common failing; you're bound to discover it many times if you spend an hour or two surfing yourself. That doesn't forgive *you* for not checking *your* links, though. Do it!

Keep in mind that most folks are communicating through modems over phone lines. They aren't coming through ISDN high-speed data lines, and most of them aren't even coming on-line through dedicated networks like the ones that seem to be installed in virtually every newly constructed college dorm room these days. So anything you can do to speed up people's access to your Web page is a very good thing.

Auto Layout Adjustment

PageMaker now has an auto layout adjustment feature that is made to order for converting (often referred to as "repurposing") existing PageMaker documents to a format that works better for the Web, because, as discussed previously, print-based documents normally aren't the right shape for onscreen viewing. Your existing PageMaker documents will often have originally been print-based, but, they could have been created for any purpose at all. It doesn't matter because all that matters is that now you want them to look best on a computer screen.

Briefly, you employ the auto-adjustment feature by setting your preferences in the dialog box shown in Figure 16.20, and then by simply changing your page dimensions (and possibly margin settings) in the Document Setup dialog box.

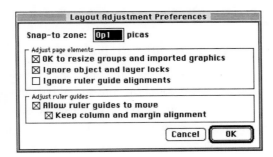

Figure 16.20

The Layout Adjustment Preferences dialog box.

So, set your preferences here and then change your PageMaker page dimensions like we discussed earlier in this chapter to fit the smallest screen you assume your viewers will be using.

Fine-tuning

You'll need to do some fine-tuning to your print-based documents before you try to export them. It's really impossible to even attempt here to cover all the possible problems you might run into. Read the sidebar "Do's and Don'ts" for a few major hints. Other than that, try cleaning up things you can see at first, then exporting a trial version, taking a look at that in your browser, all the time with the expectation that you'll be doing a lot of going back into PageMaker to make changes and re-exporting and continuing that loop until things look acceptable. If it doesn't work the first time, keep trying! You'll get it. And again, don't feel embarrassingly beginner-ish if you have to do this a few times:

Believe me, it's happened to all of us, more times than we'd probably like to admit.

PageMaker In the Real World

Copyrights and the Web

This topic is short and sweet: Everything you see on the Web is copyrighted by the person who put it there (if it's not actually copyrighted by someone even earlier in the process than that). You can *physically* download stuff from the Web, but you can't legally *use* it (or publish it) without permission. End of subject.

Dos and Don'ts

Here are some tips for things to do, to not do, and to watch out for when creating a PageMaker document that's destined to be converted to HTML.

◆ Avoid overlapping objects. HTML doesn't support things that overlap. If you want to overlap graphic elements, combine and overlap them in a graphic program and re-import into PageMaker.

◆ Don't rotate (or otherwise transform) things in PageMaker. Again, HTML doesn't support this; it will un-rotate rotated graphics. Again, do that in a graphic program and re-import.

◆ If there is an EPS graphic in your PageMaker document

A Web Layout Survival Guide

Here are some notes that may help get you through some of the most common conceptual barriers people face as they crawl out onto the Web—especially when they are trying to ease their way over from the paper-based publishing world.

◆ **Use styles.** If you use styles extensively in PageMaker, you have virtually all the conceptual information you need to understand HTML. The HTML codes are, more than anything else, a list of hierarchical styles—body copy, various levels of headlines, and so on.

◆ **HTML doesn't know from columns.** Because you can't tell whether someone will view your Web page on a 9-inch Windows laptop or compact Macintosh or a 21-inch two-page behemoth of a monitor, there's no way for HTML to allow you to work in columns. PageMaker's HTML export will convert your columns to a single column structure as long as the stories are threaded, giving you notice of the problem in the error analysis when you first begin the process.

◆ **Cross-the-fold graphics don't work.** Because there are no pages in the sense used for a magazine or book, HTML doesn't even begin to comprehend the idea of a graphic object crossing the fold in a two-page spread. So you need to edit those to one page or the other before converting to HTML.

◆ **Use long pages.** On the other hand, Web surfers are quite used to "pages" that are 6 inches wide and 30 or 40 inches long. On the Web, a page is a dynamic thing that people scroll through, so it's completely okay to think about making a "page" out of a PageMaker story that's 3, 5, or 7 pages long—even 70 or 700 (although the latter is definitely getting to be a bit on the long side, there's nothing intrinsically impossible about it). Do make sure you set up a table of contents with anchors to access the key points in this long "page," so your viewers don't need to scroll endlessly to get to their point of interest; obviously, the longer the "page," the more important this is.

◆ **Don't use big graphics.** Sorry for the repetition, but now we're getting a bit more specific. Your entire Web page, including all the graphics, should be under 50K for considerations of modem download time—and it's even better if it's more like 30K. It helps to think of a Web site as a fast food location for brain stimulation. Which fast food site do you think will get more customers? The one that takes 10 minutes to serve up the food, or the one that plunks it onto the consumer's tray in 30 seconds or less? If anything, competition for consumers on the Web is far more intense than in your average strip-zoned district on the outskirts of town.

being converted to HTML, only the screen image of the EPS will be converted to GIF or JPEG. If that isn't good enough for you (and well it shouldn't be), convert your EPS to TIFF, GIF, or JPEG in a graphic program and re-import.

◆ HTML ignores masks; so if you've masked anything in PageMaker, do that in a graphic program and re-import.

◆ PageMaker frames (but not their contents) will be ignored by HTML.

◆ Adobe Tables (tables created with the Adobe Table program and imported into PageMaker) will be converted to GIF graphics, where the text probably won't be sufficiently readable. You're better off doing tables as text in PageMaker: at least they will remain text after conversion.

◆ PageMaker-drawn graphics (lines, rectangles, ovals, polygons) will be ignored by HTML. If you need them, create them in a graphic program and import them.

continues

◆ Graphics that you've resized in PageMaker (as opposed to the other transformations like rotation, skewing, and so on) do retain their resizing in your HTML document, so you don't need to worry about that.

◆ **Do offer graphic download options.** At the top of the page, consider putting a line that gives the viewer an option to jump to a page with no graphics on it. Many people don't understand that they can turn off Auto Download Graphics in their browser, so you can do them a favor by offering the option onscreen.

◆ **Offer visual interest.** You don't need huge files to be visually interesting. Think of yourself as a Mark Rothko or Frank Stella instead of Sam Francis—they did pretty well with just a few colors and have managed to interest a few people along the way. Interesting shapes and subjects don't take up nearly as much file space as colors.

◆ **Test all monitoring conditions.** Run tests with various browsers and monitors. Look at your Web pages on a grayscale monitor, a laptop (Windows and Mac both, maybe even an Amiga), and a color monitor set to 16 colors instead of 256.

◆ **Test all browsing conditions.** Browsers are all over the map, and although Netscape Navigator might seem to have a lock on the market, it certainly would be a mistake to leave out the 30 percent or so (at last estimate) of the audience that doesn't use it. You need to stay abreast of changing browser feature sets and language extensions. Pretty much all browsers can read HTML 1.0; more can do 2.0; and 3.0 is getting to be fairly standard as this book goes to press. (Of course, if you read this book a year after it's placed on the shelf, it's likely we'll be talking about some other version or possibly a completely different hypertext language.)

RESOURCES

In addition to learning about the Web on the Web, a number of sites have been devoted to paper-based publishing, although because of their location, they tend to have a cyber-view consciousness as well. Try these for a start:

- `http://www.adobe.com` Adobe's World Wide Web stop for information on PageMaker and Acrobat, along with all Adobe's other products

- `http://the-tech.mit.edu/KPT/KPT.html` The place to get info from Kai Krause, world-famous guru of Photoshop filters

- `http://www.mccannas.com` Photoshop information

- `http://www.winternet.com` Newsletter on DTP Tips & Trips

- `http://www.prepress.pps.com` Site operated by PrePRESS Main Street

- `http://www.yahoo.com/` Of course, the ultimate way to find anything on the Web, the index called Yahoo!

Note

The DTP Forum on CompuServe (CompuServe is not the Web, of course, but it's definitely an important part of the on-line culture for many people) has, by way of cross-pollinating the electronic and paper publishing paradigms, a section on designing for on-line environments. To get there, after you've logged on to CompuServe, GO DTPFOR; then the information you're looking for is in Message Section 18 and Library 18.

SUMMARY

Publishing on the Web is not technically too difficult, but it does require a lot of forethought and planning—not to mention consultation with your Webmaster. PageMaker is probably not really the best tool with which to build an HTML Web document from scratch; but PageMaker's HTML Export feature is a very good way to repurpose existing print-based documents.

A p p e n d i x

KEYBOARD SHORTCUTS

Many keyboard shortcuts have been changed in the PageMaker 6.5 upgrade as Adobe tries to unify the interfaces of all its products so that, for example, PageMaker's Fit In Window command is the same one you'll use in Photoshop and Illustrator. In fact, it is said that Adobe was concerned that the interfaces for the various programs would get to be so similar that you might become confused about which program was currently active. That's the purpose of that smudgy looking thing at the top of the PageMaker toolbox. It's supposed to represent the initial PageMaker splash screen so you'll always be able to tell at a glance which program you are in.

There's also been a lot of work done to make the Macintosh and Windows version keyboard shortcuts more alike—although still not exactly the same. In more cases than not with this new upgrade the commands are the same if you keep in mind that the Mac's Command key is comparable to Windows' Control key. Likewise, the Option and Alt keys are used in similar ways on the two platforms.

However, there's one thing that Windows users will need to be especially watchful about. Some of the new keyboard shortcuts combine Control and Alt with other keys. That Control and Alt key combination is the standard set of keys used to create a custom keyboard shortcut for a shortcut file you have created on the Windows desktop. You could, for example, press Control-Alt-P expecting to get a page number marker and instead open Photoshop. Avoid setting a Windows desktop shortcut that uses one of these combinations.

As a major consolation to this problem, if you are a Windows users keep in mind that you have the shortcut of all time at your fingertips. Almost anywhere in the program you can click the right mouse button and get a short menu of appropriate commands you might want to use in that spot.

In addition to this appendix of some of the most often used shortcuts, you will want to keep close at hand the Quick Reference Card that came in your PageMaker box. Also, PageMaker's help system includes an elegantly constructed Shortcut reference guide, including special tabs that highlight shortcuts that have changed or been added with the PageMaker 6.5 upgrade.

In the following chart the Macintosh shortcuts have been listed on the first line and Windows shortcuts on the second line. In some cases, where there is only one line, the shortcuts are the same.

OVERALL PROGRAM AND FILE CONTROLS

Action	Keyboard Shortcut
New document	Command-N Control-N
Open document	Command-O Control-O
Place	Command-D Control-D
Print	Command-P Control-P

Action	Keyboard Shortcut
Rebuild PPD list	Shift-[Print]
Make printer style	Control-click-[Print] (menu goes to [Style])
Adopt print settings (no print, no style)	Shift-[Done]
Quit/Exit	Command-Q Control-Q
Save	Command-S Control-S
Save all open documents	Option-[Save] Shift-[Save] (menu goes to [Save all])
Save As	Command-Shift-S Control-Shift-S
Revert to last mini-save	Shift-[Revert]
Close document	Command-W Control-W
Close all open documents	Option-[Close] Shift-[Close] (menu goes to [Close all])
Open copy of document	Shift-[Recent Pubs]
Document setup	Command-Shift-P Control-Shift-P
General Preferences dialog box	Command-K Control-K
Installed filter list	Command-[About PageMaker] Control-[About PageMaker]
Layout/story editor toggle	Command-E Control-E
Close story editor	Command-W Control -W

continues

Action	Keyboard Shortcut
Links manager	Command-Shift-D Control-Shift-D
Add pages	Command-Option-Shift-G Control-Alt-Shift-G
OK/Cancel all open dialog boxes	Option-[OK/Cancel] Shift-[OK/Cancel]

PALETTE CONTROLS

Action	Keyboard Shortcut
Display/hide all palettes	Tab (use only when Text tool is not selected)
Display/hide all except tools	Shift-tab
Edit item in Palette list	Double click or Command-click Double click or Control-click
Minimize Palette size	Double click palette tab
Control palette	Command-' Control-'
Colors palette	Command-J Control-J
Styles palette	Command-B Control-B
Layers palette	Command-8 Control-8
Master pages palette	Option-Command-8 Shift-Control-8
Layers palette (Windows only)	Control-9

TOOL PALETTE

Tool	Keyboard Shortcut
Magnifying tool-(bigger)	Command-space bar-click or drag
Magnifying tool-(smaller)	Command-space bar-Option-click
Pointer	Command-space bar (slight tap toggle with current tool)

Left Side Tools

Tool	Keyboard Shortcut
Pointer	Shift-F1 F9 or Control-space bar toggle
Rotating tool	Shift-F2
Line tool	Shift-F3
Rectangle tool	Shift-F4
Ellipse (Oval) tool	Shift-F5
Polygon tool	Shift-F6
Grabber hand	Option-drag or Shift-F7 Alt-drag or Shift-F7
Grabber, constrained	Option-Shift-drag Alt-Shift-drag or Shift-F7

Right Side Tools

Tool	Keyboard Shortcut
Text tool	Option-Shift-F1 Alt-Shift-F1
Cropping tool	Option-Shift-F2 Alt-Shift-F2
Constrained Line tool	Option-Shift-F3 Alt-Shift-F3
Rectangle Frame tool	Option-Shift-F4 Alt-Shift-F4

continues

Action Tool	Keyboard Shortcut
Oval Frame tool	Option-Shift-F5 Alt-Shift-F5
Polygon Frame tool	Option-Shift-F6 Alt-Shift-F6
Magnifying tool	Option-Shift-F7 Alt-Shift-F7

Action	Keyboard Shortcut
Select all	Command-A Control-A
Front, Bring to	Command-] Control-]
Bring Forward	Command-Shift-] Control-Shift-]
Back, Send to	Command-[Control -[
Send Backward	Command-Shift-[Control-Shift-[
Copy	Command-C Control-C or Control-Insert key
Cut	Command-X Control-X or Control-Delete key
Paste	Command-V Control-V
Power Paste	Command-Option-V Control-Alt-V
Guides (toggle)	Command-; Control-;
Snap to Guides	Command-Shift-; Control-Shift-;
Rulers (toggle)	Command-R Control-R

Action	Keyboard Shortcut
Snap to Rulers	Command-Option-R Control-Alt-R
Text flow, Auto/Manual (toggle)	Command-flow text Control-flow text (toggle)
Text flow, Semi-automatic (toggle)	Shift-flow text Shift-flow text

POSITIONING/EDITING OBJECTS

Action	Keyboard Shortcut
Select multiple elements	Shift-click
Select subordinate item	Command-click (each click selects next element back on same layer)
Select multiple subordinates	Command-Shift-click (each click selects next element back on same layer)
Constrain move vertical or horizontal	Shift-drag item (first move sets constrained direction)
Nudge object	Use arrow keys or Control palette nudge buttons
Power nudge (10X)	Shift-arrow or Shift-nudge buttons
Edit original	Option-double click object Alt-double click object
Edit original (OLE)	Double-click object
Fill and Stroke (PageMaker object or frame)	Command-U Control-U
Lock	Command-L Control-L
Unlock	Command-Option-L Control-Alt-L

continues

Action	Keyboard Shortcut
Group	Command-G Control-G
Ungroup	Command-Shift-G Control-Shift-G
Mask and Group	Command-6 Control-6
Unmask and Ungroup	Command-Option-6 Control-Alt-6
Text wrap redraw, interrupt	Hold down Spacebar during adjustment
Align objects	Command-Shift-E Control-Shift-E
Rotate around center of object	Command-[Rotate tool] Control-[Rotate tool]
Rotate 45 degree increments	Shift-[Rotate tool]

FRAMES

Action	Keyboard Shortcut
Change to frame (toggles PageMaker object)	Command-Shift-Option-F Control-Shift-Alt-F
Attach/detach content and frame (toggle)	Command-F Control-F
Go to next frame (in Pointer tool mode)	Command-Option-] Control-Alt-]
Go to previous frame (in Pointer tool mode)	Command-Option-[Control-Alt-[
Text link tool (click windowshade)	Command-Shift-Control-click Control-Shift-Alt-click

IMPORTED GRAPHICS

Action	Keyboard Shortcut
Proportional stretch	Shift-drag corner handle
Proportions, restore	Shift-drag corner handle
Magic Stretch, regular (one-bit images only)	Command-drag handle of bitmap Control-drag handle of bitmap
Magic Stretch, proportional (one-bit images only)	Command-Shift-drag handle Control-Shift-drag handle

VIEW, LAYOUT

Action	Keyboard Shortcut
Layout/Story Editor (toggle)	Command-E
Edit story	Triple-click text block with pointer tool
Magnifying tool-(bigger)	Command-Spacebar-click or drag
Magnifying tool-(smaller)	Command-Spacebar-Option-click Control-Spacebar-Alt-click
50% Size	Command-5 Control-5
75% Size	Command -7 Control-7
Actual Size	Command-1 Control-1
200% Size	Command-2 Control-2
400% Size	Command-4 Control-4
Fit In Window	Command-0 (zero) Control-0 (zero)
Change page to fit in window	Shift-click page icon
Entire Pasteboard	Command-Option-0 (zero) Control-Shift-0 (zero)

continues

701

Action	Keyboard Shortcut
100%/Fit in window (toggle)	Command-Option-click Control-Alt-click
200%/100% (toggle)	Command-Option-Shift-click Control-Alt-Shift-click
Set all pages to same view	Option-[desired view] Alt-[desired view]
Trigger screen redraw	Command-Shift-F12 Control-Shift-F12
Redraw, high resolution	Control-[view] Control-Shift-[view]
Display/hide nonprinting	Command-Option-N Control-Alt-N
Display/hide hyperlinks	F10
Page turn (next)	Page Up
Page turn (previous)	Page Down
Go to page	Command-Option-G Control-Alt-G
Return to previous page	Command-Page Up or Command-Page Down Control-Page Up or Control-Page Down
Grabber hand, pan the view	Option-drag
Grabber hand, constrained	Option-Shift-drag pan

VIEW, STORY EDITOR

Action	Keyboard Shortcut
Story Editor/Layout (toggle)	Command-E
Close all open stories in current publication	Option-[Close story] Shift-[Close story]
Cascade all open stories	Option-[Cascade] Shift-[Cascade]

Action	Keyboard Shortcut
Tile all open stories	Option-[Tile] Shift-[Tile]
Close current story window	Command-W Control-W

CONTROL PALETTE

Action	Keyboard Shortcut
Display/hide (toggles palette on and off)	Command-' Control-~ (lower case tilde)
Activate (toggles between palette and publication)	Command-' Control-' (apostrophe)
Paragraph/character view	Command-Shift-' Control-Shift-~ (lower case tilde)
Go to next option	Tab or Arrow keys (in character styles)
Go to previous option	Shift-Tab or Arrow keys (in character styles)
Proxy control point	Numbers on numeric keypad or Arrow keys
Display last valid value for option	Esc
Apply change and return to layout	Return Enter
Apply change and stay at same option	Shift-Return Shift-Enter
On/Off selected button	Spacebar
Measurement system (cycle through choices)	Command-Option-M Control-Alt-M
Nudge, regular	nudge buttons
Nudge, power move (10X amount set in Preferences)	Command-[nudge] Control-[nudge]
Styles	Type first few characters (paragraph view only)

continues

Action	Keyboard Shortcut
Scaling/cropping	Arrow keys toggle (with scale/crop palette area selected)

Styles Palette

Action	Keyboard Shortcut
Display/hide Styles palette	Command-B
Edit style (on palette list item)	Double-click or Command-click Double-click or Control-click
Define new style	Command-click [No Style] Control-click [No Style]
Define styles	Command-3 Control-3
Select styles (Macintosh only)	Command-[F1-F12] (1st 12 styles) Shift-Command-[F1-F12] (next 12)

Hyperlinks Palette

Action	Keyboard Shortcut
Display/hide Hyperlinks palette (Windows only)	Control-9
Edit hyperlink	Double-click item
Display/hide hyperlinks	F10

Colors Palette

Action	Keyboard Shortcut
Display/hide Colors palette	Command-J Control-J
Edit color (on palette list item)	Double-click or Command-click Double-click or Control-click

Action	Keyboard Shortcut
Define new color	Double or Command-click [Registration] Double or Control-click [Registration]
Display Apple Color Picker (Macintosh only)	Command-Shift-click color

MASTER PAGES PALETTE

Action	Keyboard Shortcut
Display/hide Master Pages palette	Command Option-8 Control-Shift-8
Edit Master Page (on palette list item)	Double-click or Command-click Double-click or Control-click
Define New Master Page	Command-click [None]
Define New Master Page	Double-click or Command-click [None] Double-click or Control-click [None]
Remove all Master objects (single page)	Click-[None]
Remove objects only (both facing pages)	Option-Click-[None] Alt-Click-[None]
Remove objects and all guides (both facing pages)	Shift-Click-[None] Shift-Click-[None]
Remove objects and column guides (both facing pages)	Option-Shift-Click-[None] Alt-Shift-Click-[None]

TYPE FORMATTING

Action	Keyboard Shortcut
Increase one point size	Command-Shift-> Control-Option->
Increase to next standard size	Command-Shift-> Control-Alt->
Decrease one point size	Command Shift-<
Decrease to next standard size	Command-Option-Shift-< Control-Alt-Shift-<

Alignment

Action	Keyboard Shortcut
Align left	Command-Shift-L Control-Shift-L
Align right	Command-Shift-R Control-Shift-R
Align center	Command-Shift-C Control-Shift-C
Justify	Command-Shift-J Control-Shift-J
Force justify	Command-Shift-F Control-Shift-F

Leading, Width, Track

Action	Keyboard Shortcut
Auto leading	Command-Option-Shift-A Control-Alt-Shift-A
No track	Command-Shift-Q Control-Shift-Q

Case

Action	Keyboard Shortcut
All caps	Command-Shift-K Control-Shift-K
Small caps (Macintosh only)	Command-Shift-H
Subscript	Command-Shift-+ Control-\
Superscript	Command-Shift— Control-Shift-\

Action	Keyboard Shortcut
Bold	Command-Shift-B Control-Shift-B or F6
Italic	Command-Shift-I Control-Shift-I F7
Underline	Command-Shift-U Control-Shift-U
Strikethru	Command-Shift-/ Control-Shift-/
Outline (Macintosh only)	Command-Shift-D Control-Shift-D
Shadow (Macintosh only)	Command-Shift-W Control-Shift-W
Normal	Command-Shift-Spacebar Control-Shift-Spacebar or F5
Reverse	Command-Shift-V Control-Shift-V
Character Specifications dialog box	Command-T Control-T
Paragraph	Command-M Control-M
Indents/tabs (Layout view)	Command-I Control-I
Drag left indent marker only (in [Indents/tabs] dialog box)	Shift-drag indent
Define styles	Command-3 Control-3

TEXT EDITING

Selecting and Navigating in Text

Action	Keyboard Shortcut
Selection mode	Hold down Shift key while using a navigation shortcut
Left one character	Left arrow or Keypad 4
Right one character	Right arrow or Keypad 6
Left one word	Command-left arrow or Command-Keypad 4 Control-left arrow or Control-Keypad 4
Right one word	Command-right arrow or Command-Keypad 6 Control-right arrow or Control-Keypad 6
Click select word	Double-click with Text tool
Up one line	Up arrow or Keypad 8
Down one line	Down arrow or Keypad 2
To beginning of line	Keypad 7 Home or Keypad 7
To end of line	Keypad 2 End or Keypad 2
To beginning of sentence	Command-Keypad 7 Control-Keypad 7
To end of sentence	Command-Keypad 1 Control-Keypad 1
Up one paragraph	Command-up arrow or Command-Keypad 8 Control-up arrow or Control-Keypad 8
Down one paragraph	Command-down arrow or Command-Keypad 2 Control-down arrow or Control-Keypad 2
Click select paragraph	Triple-click with Text tool
Up one screen	Page Up or Keypad 9
Down one screen	Page Down or Keypad 3

Action	Keyboard Shortcut
To beginning of story	Command-Keypad 9 Control-Keypad 9
To end of story	Command-Keypad 3 Control-Keypad 3

SEARCH AND REPLACE

Action	Keyboard Shortcut
Find	Command-F Control-F
Find next	Command-G Control G
Change	Command-H Control-H
Reset Find/change text or paragraph attributes	(Option-click [Attributes])
Reset Find/change both attributes	(Shift-Option-click [Attributes])
Spelling	Command-L Control-L

INDEXING

Action	Keyboard Shortcut
Show index (for current publication only)	Command-[Show index]
Copy book list to all book publications	Command-[Book]
Create index entry	Command-Y Control-Y
Create fast index entry (highlighted text)	Command-Shift-Y Control-Shift-Y
Create proper name entry (highlighted text)	Command-Option-Y Control-Alt-Y

continues

Action	Keyboard Shortcut
Copy existing topics for new entry	Command-[OK] (in Topic dialog box)
Remove all entries	Command-Option-Shift-[Remove] Control-Alt-Shift-[Remove]
Remove all cross-references	Command-Shift-[Remove] Control-Shift-[Remove]
Remove all page references	Command-Option-[Remove] Control-Alt-[Remove]

KERNING

Action	Keyboard Shortcut
Kern apart .04 em	Command-Option-Right Arrow Control-Alt-Right arrow
Kern together .04 em	Command-Option-Left Arrow Control-Alt-Left Arrow
Kern apart .01 em	Option-Right Arrow Alt-Right Arrow
Kern together .01 em	Option-Left Arrow Alt-Left Arrow
Clear manual kerning	Command-Option-K

Appendix

SPECIAL CHARACTERS

This appendix will help you find special characters—everything from upside down question marks to foreign language characters or math symbols.

If you are doing a lot of work that requires special characters, you might want to print out your own cheat sheet for each font you are using. There are differences in font sets, not only between Macintosh and Windows, but also between different typefaces. PageMaker 6.5 comes with a special template that will help you create such a cheat sheet reference. The template includes directions for you to follow, so just open the file and follow the indicated steps.

◆ For Macintosh users, look for the file named Character Set, buried in the Typography folder, which is located inside the Extras folder, inside your PageMaker 6.5 folder.

◆ For Windows users, the file is called Charset.t65 and it is located in the Extras folder.

There are also some special utilities that help you find special characters for a given font set.

◆ The Macintosh comes with the Key Caps program, and in most installations you'll find it on your Apple menu. Also for Macintosh users, there's the popular shareware program Popchar.

◆ For Windows 95 users, there's a program called Charset.exe. One easy way to locate this file is to use the File/Find command in My Computer. After you locate the program the first time, take a moment to make a shortcut for it so it will be quickly available right on your desktop. Right click on the file, and then choose Shortcut. You can even right click on the Shortcut and choose a keyboard shortcut to the program for even quicker access.

If you swap files between platforms, there are some important differences between the way Macintosh and Windows machines handle font sets. In the following table, if a given item has two listings the Macintosh information is listed first, followed by the Windows info on the next line.

◆ One example of this difference is the fact that on the Macintosh the ligature characters have been built into most fonts but in order to get those same characters in Windows you will need to buy what's called an expert set for the font family you are using. Conversely, there are a few fractions built into most Windows fonts, but none are found in most Macintosh fonts unless you buy an expert set.

◆ Windows users need to use a special series of keys to get to many of these characters (although Macintosh users can access most special characters more directly through keyboard shortcuts). Whenever you see a reference like Alt-0999 in the following chart, that means to do the following. Hold down the Alt key while typing the four numbers on the **Numeric Keypad**. When you release the Alt key the character will appear in your text. You must use the numeric keypad and you must include the zero that begins the series of four numbers.

In the far right hand column of the following table we have listed PageMaker **metacharacters**. These special character combinations are what you type into the Find or Change dialog boxes, or any other PageMaker dialog boxes, when you need to specify certain special characters. As a general rule, if you can type the character directly into the dialog box, you don't need to worry about the metacharacters. But if you try to type the character in a dialog box and nothing happens, you need one of the metacharacters listed here. Notice that there are some differences in metacharacter requirements between the Macintosh and Windows versions of PageMaker 6.5.

All of the keystrokes listed in the following table apply to standard fonts. We tested with Times on both platforms, Macintosh and Windows. However, in the few cases in Windows where a character wasn't available in Times, the keystroke to get the character in the Symbol font is given instead.

Special Characters Chart

On Page	Description	Keystrokes	In Dialog Box
•	bullet	Option-8 Alt-8	same ^8
©	copyright symbol	Option-G Alt-G	same ^2
^	carat	Shift-6	^^
_	discretionary (soft) hyphen	Command-Shift -- (hyphen) Control-Shift-- (hyphen)	^-
...	ellipsis	Option-; Alt-0133	same

continues

SPECIAL CHARACTERS CHART, CONTINUED

On Page	Description	Keystrokes	In Dialog Box
—	em dash	Option-Shift--(hyphen) Alt-Shift--(hyphen)	^_ (underline)
	computer inserted hyphen	n/a	^c
	em space	Command-Shift-M Control-Shift-M	^m
–	en dash	Option-- Alt--(hyphen)	^=
	en space	Command-Shift-N Control-Shift-N	^>
↵	end of paragraph	Return Enter	^p
	forced line break	Shift-Return Shift-Enter	^n
	Index entry marker	n/a	^;
	proper name index entry	n/a	^z
	hyperlink	n/a	^:
	Inline graphic marker	n/a	^g
-	nonbreaking hyphen	Command-Option --(hyphen) Control-Alt--(hyphen)	^~
/	nonbreaking slash	Command-Option-/ Control-Alt-/	^/
	nonbreaking space	Option-Spacebar Control-Alt-Spacebar	^s
LM, RM	page-number marker	Command-Option-P Control-Alt-P	^# or ^3
¶	paragraph symbol	Option-7 Alt-7	same ^7
?	question mark	Shift-/	?

On Page	Description	Keystrokes	In Dialog Box
®	registered trademark	Option-R Alt-R	same ^r
§	section symbol	Option-6 Alt-6	same ^6
→	tab	Tab	^t
	thin space (1/4 em)	Command-Shift-T Control-Shift-T	^<
™	trademark symbol	Option-2 Alt-0153	same
"	typographers' open quotation marks	Option-[Alt-Shift-[	same ^{
"	typographers' close quotation marks	Option-Shift-[Alt-Shift-]	same ^}
'	typographers' single open quotation mark	Option-] Alt-[	same ^[
'	typographers' single close quotation mark	Option-Shift-] Alt-]	same ^]
	wild card (single character)	n/a	^?
	wild card (white space)*	n/a	^w
«	open guillemets (Fr. open quotation marks)	Option-\ Alt-0171	same
»	closing guillemets (Fr. close quotation marks)	Option-Shift-\ Alt-0187	same
‹	opening single guillemet	Option-Shift -3 Alt-0139	same
›	closing single guillemet	Option-Shift-4 Alt-0155	same

continues

SPECIAL CHARACTERS CHART, CONTINUED

On Page	Description	Keystrokes	In Dialog Box
¿	inverted question mark	Option-Shift-/ Alt-0191	same
¡	inverted exclamation point	Option-1 Alt-0161	same
À	uppercase A with grave accent	Option-'/Shift-A Alt-0192	same
Á	uppercase A with acute accent	Option-Shift-Y Alt-0193	same
Ã	uppercase A with tilde accent	Option-n/Shift-A Alt-0195	same
Ä	uppercase A with diaeresis	Option-u/Shift-A Alt-0196	same
Å	uppercase A with ring accent	Option-Shift-A Alt-0197	same
Ç	uppercase C with cedilla accent	Option-Shift-C Alt-0199	same
É	uppercase E with acute accent	Option-e/Shift-E Alt-0201	same
È	uppercase E with grave accent	Option-'/Shift-E Alt-0200	same
Ê	uppercase E with circumflex accent	Option-i/Shift-E Alt-0202	same
Ë	uppercase E with diaeresis accent	Option-U/Shift-E Alt-0203	same
Í	uppercase I with acute accent	Option-E/Shift-I Alt-0205	same
Ì	uppercase I with grave accent	Option-'/Shift-I Alt-0204	same
Î	uppercase I with circumflex accent	Option-Shift-D Alt-0206	same
Ï	uppercase I with diaeresis accent	Option-Shift-F Alt-0207	same

On Page	Description	Keystrokes	In Dialog Box
Ñ	uppercase N with tilde accent	Option-n/Shift-N Alt-0209	same
Ó	uppercase O with acute accent	Option-Shift-H Alt-0211	same
Ò	uppercase O with grave accent	Option-Shift-I Alt-0210	same
Ô	uppercase O with circumflex accent	Option-Shift-J Alt-0212	same
Ö	uppercase O with diaeresis accent	Option-u/Shift-O Alt-0214	same
Õ	uppercase O with tilde accent	Option-n/Shift-O Alt-0213	same
Ú	uppercase U with acute accent	Option-Shift-; Alt-0218	same
Û	uppercase U with circumflex accent	Option-i/Shift-U Alt-0219	same
Ü	uppercase U with diaeresis accent	Option-u/Shift-U Alt-0220	same
á	lowercase a with acute accent	Option-E/a Alt-0225	same
à	lowercase a with grave accent	Option-'/a Alt-0224	same
ä	lowercase a with diaeresis accent	Option-U/a Alt-0228	same
ã	lowercase a with tilde accent	Option-N/a Alt-0227	same
å	lowercase a with ring accent	Option-a Alt-229	same
ç	lowercase c with cedilla accent	Option-c Alt-0231	same
é	lowercase e with acute accent	Option-E/e Alt-0233	same
è	lowercase e with grave accent	Option-'/e Alt-0232	same

continues

SPECIAL CHARACTERS CHART, CONTINUED

On Page	Description	Keystrokes	In Dialog Box
ê	lowercase e with circumflex accent	Option-I/e Alt-0234	same
ë	lowercase e with diaeresis accent	Option-U/e Alt-0235	same
í	lowercase i with acute accent	Option-e/i Alt-0237	same
ì	lowercase i with grave accent	Option-'/i Alt-0236	same
î	lowercase i with circumflex accent	Option-i/i Alt-0238	same
ï	lowercase i with diaeresis accent	Option-u/i Alt-0239	same
ñ	lowercase n with tilde accent	Option-n/n Alt-0241	same
ó	lowercase o with acute accent	Option-e/o Alt-0243	same
ò	lowercase o with grave accent	Option-'/o Alt-0242	same
ô	lowercase o with circumflex accent	Option-i/o Alt-0244	same
ö	lowercase o with diaeresis accent	Option-u/o Alt-0246	same
õ	lowercase o with tilde accent	Option-n/o Alt-0245	same
ú	lowercase u with acute accent	Option-e/u Alt-0250	same
ù	lowercase u with grave accent	Option-'/u Alt-0249	same
û	lowercase u with circumflex accent	Option-i/u Alt-0251	same
ü	lowercase u with diaeresis accent	Option-u/u Alt-0252	same

On Page	Description	Keystrokes	In Dialog Box
ÿ	lowercase y with diaeresis accent	Option-u/y Alt-0255	same
Æ	uppercase AE diphthong	Option-Shift-' Alt-0198	same
æ	lowercase ae diphthong	Option-' Alt-0230	same
Œ	uppercase OE diphthong	Option-Shift-Q Alt-0140	same
œ	lowercase oe diphthong	Option-q Alt-0156	same
†	dagger symbol	Option-T Alt-0134	same
‡	double dagger symbol	Option-Shift-7 Alt-0135	same
°	degree symbol	Option-Shift-8 Alt-0176	same
¤	general currency symbol	Option-Shift-2 Alt-0164	same
¥	Japanese yen symbol	Option-Y Alt-0165 in Symbol font	same
£	British pound sterling symbol	Option-3 Alt-0163	same
¢	U.S. cent symbol	Option-4 Alt-0162	same
	Infinity symbol	Option-5 Alt-0165	same
ª	feminine ordinal indicator	Option-9 Alt-0170	same
º	masculine ordinal indicator	Option-0 (zero) Alt-0186	same
ß	German double s	Option-S Alt-0223	same
	diamond, lozenge symbol	Option-Shift-V Alt-0224 in Symbol font	same

continues

SPECIAL CHARACTERS CHART, CONTINUED

On Page	Description	Keystrokes	In Dialog Box
_ ´	accent	Option-e/Spacebar Alt-0180	same
¨	diaeresis accent,	Option-u /Spacebar Alt-0168	same
	does-not-equal symbol	Option-= Alt-0185 in Symbol font	same
	approximately equals symbol	Option-X Alt-0187 in Symbol font	same
	root symbol	Option-V Alt-0214 in Symbol font	same
ï	function symbol	Option-F Alt-0131	same
Ò	negation, logical NOT	Option-l Alt-0172	same
±	plus/minus symbol	Option-Shift-+ Alt-0177	same
	integral symbol	Option-B Alt-0242 in Symbol font	same
÷	division symbol	Option-/ Alt-0247	same
‰	salinity symbol	Option-Shift-R Alt-0137	same
fi	fi ligature	Option-Shift-5 Use expert set	same
fl	fl ligature	Option-Shift-6 Use expert set	same
Ø	uppercase O with slash	Option-Shift-o Alt-0216	same
ø	lowercase o with slash	Option-o Alt-0248	same
	less-than-or-equal-to symbol	Option-, Alt-0163 in Symbol font	same

On Page	Description	Keystrokes	In Dialog Box
	greater-than-or-equal-to symbol	Option-. Alt-0179 in Symbol font	same
	uppercase delta	Option-J Lowercase d in Symbol font	same
	uppercase omega	Option-Z Shift-W in Symbol font	same
	uppercase sigma, summation symbol	Option-W Alt-0229 in Symbol font	same
	uppercase pi	Option-Shift-P Alt-0213 in Symbol font	same
	lowercase pi	Option-P Alt-0112 in Symbol font	same
µ	lowercase mu, micron symbol	Option-M Alt-0181	same
	lowercase delta, differential symbol	Option-D Alt-0182 in Symbol font	same
^	circumflex	Option-i/Spacebar Alt-0136	same
~	tilde	Option-Shift-N Alt-0152	same
¯	macron (diacritical)	Option-Shift-, Alt-0175	same
˘	breve	Option-Shift-. n/a	same
·	dot	Option-H Alt-0215 in Symbol font	same
°	ring accent	Option-K n/a	same
·	vertically centered period	Option-Shift-9 Alt-0183	same

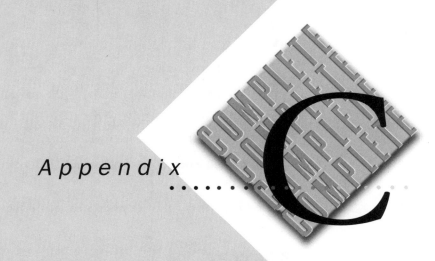

Appendix

PROOFING YOUR PUBLICATION

Proofing is necessary if you hope to get your job done correctly, on deadline, within budget—and approved by the client.

This appendix on proofing your publication covers the following topics:

- Checking for typos and other copy problems.

- Proofing the layout of your project—the way the graphics and type go together on the page.

- Checking whether the project will print at the service bureau.

- Determining whether your publication will be color-accurate off the press.

- Checking on your project while it's at the print shop.

CHECKING COPY

Some people (clients, especially) seem to go blank whenever they look at an easy-to-fix—and cheap—laser proof. But after the film is run by the service bureau, marking up and rewriting copy on the blueline seems to come easy. Maybe people feel that changing type is about the easiest thing you can correct; that's true enough, but the longer you wait, the more the correction costs. Late in the game, the costs to fix a typo are about the same as fixing a color graphic because by then, you've run the film or even gone to press.

This last-minute changing happens so often in the printing business that a name even exists for late copy changes, requested when the project already has arrived at the prepress bureau or the print shop. The changes are called AAs, for artist alterations.

These next few sections give you some down-to-earth—and easy—tips for fixing copy at the cheap and easy-to-fix stages, early in the process. Spell-checking software, professional proofers, indexing tools, sign-offs—these all can be part of a system for top-notch, money-saving copy proofing.

Run the Spelling and Grammar Check

Use PageMaker's spell check feature, naturally, to check spelling. However, you should check spelling in any document you import into PageMaker, before you ever place copy on the page.

Consider running a grammar check on the text, even if you are one of those folks who believe grammar checkers aren't smart enough yet to fulfill their promise. Sometimes a grammar checker just gives you a new look at your copy and unearths something you overlooked. For example, it's helpful to find what some call the too words—words that sound alike but are spelled differently, as in too, two, and to. The wrong too word is likely to trigger the grammar checker, but it won't even cause spell check to raise an eyebrow.

If you have done quite a bit of copy editing in PageMaker and still want to run a grammar check (which isn't possible inside PageMaker), export the text and run the check on the text file. Don't import the text back into PageMaker because you would destroy any kerning, inline graphics placement, and other typographical and special effects work you've done. Just use the grammar check on the exported text file as a means to spot problems and make the edits on the PageMaker version of the text.

Spot Check with an Index and a Table of Contents

The indexing and table of contents tools can give you a whole new view of your copy, possibly exposing mistakes you missed when proofing the text. A headline or a word on a page might look okay when it's cluttered with all that other copy, but when the item is isolated on a list, you are more likely to spot a problem.

Along this same line, if you are using the Sonar Bookends Plug-in to generate the initial index master topics list, put the tool to additional use. Sonar works by building lists of every unique word in a document and the word's page location. If you get all the similar words lined up in a list, a freak usage stands out right away.

Hire Professional Proofreaders

Consider hiring a professional proofreader or an editor. A few people on this planet love to find mistakes in copy—and are good enough to be right all the time. These professional nitpickers are worth whatever you have to pay them because they can save you money.

Keep in mind that proofreading charges depend on the nature of your need. Proofing always happens on the worst possible deadlines, and in that tension it's important to have a clear and specific agreement on what's to be accomplished and for what fee. Simple proofing for spelling errors and typos is less expensive and less time-consuming than a full-blown editing job, where your collaborator actually helps you do a rewrite.

Finding a pro can be tough, especially if you need the person on a project-by-project basis. Try hiring people who have worked the desk at the local newspaper, or legal secretaries who want to pick up some extra cash. Keyboarding services in larger cities often offer good proofreading work. Try putting a message on one of the online services, such as the Desktop Publishing Forum of CompuServe. Your local service bureau may know of someone. Also try your print shop, especially if it has a typesetting operation (desktop or otherwise), because some of the best proofers are people who have stared at type for the last couple of decades. They seem to be able to smell mistakes.

Use In-House Proofing Tricks

Never let the person who did the keyboarding do the proofing. They don't have fresh eyes—and fresh eyes are mandatory for proofreading.

If you must work alone, read the copy into a tape recorder. Let the whole thing sit for at least a few hours if you can and then come back to it. Proof the typeset copy as you listen to the original you read into the tape recorder.

Have two people do proofing of critical non-prose material such as scientific data tables or financial information. One person reads the original to the other person, who is checking each character in the typeset copy.

Get Formal Sign-Offs

Almost every project has an approval cycle of some kind. Ultimately, the sign-off probably comes from the person who's picking up the tab.

Make sure that everyone in the approval loop for your publication signs off formally. Do not accept a verbal approval. Ask the approver (the client or boss) to read the material carefully, and (if it's true) warn the person signing off that the expense of copy changes to the approved proof will be high—and will come out of his or her budget.

Making sure that the key approver signs off on the publication holds true for all proofs, not just copy proofs, and the further along you are in the project, the more important the approval is.

RUNNING PROOFS WITH A LASER PRINTER

You already own (or have access to) an extremely cheap tool for getting sign-offs on the layout of your publication—your laser printer. These next sections describe your laser printer layout proofing tools.

Thumbnails

Running thumbnails gives you an overall feel for your multipage project and how it all flows together from a visual point of view. If your publication is set up with facing pages, use PageMaker 6.5's capability to print out reader's spreads so you can evaluate pages as they will look when finally assembled at the bindery.

Composites

They might not be in full color, but gray-scale composites tell you a great deal about the basic design values of your pages, even if they are multicolor layouts. If text is unreadable because it doesn't have adequate contrast against a background, the problem will probably show up in gray-scale laser proofs. Composite laser proofs also are an important client sign-off step before going to expensive image setting and color proofs. You make gray-scale composites through the Color dialog box under the Print command.

The Proof Checkbox

If you need to print laser proof layouts for typesetting approval (to check kerning, line breaks, hyphenation, and so on), save time and visual clutter by clicking the Proof checkbox in the Print command's Document dialog box. PageMaker then runs placeholder boxes in the place of photos and other imported illustrations. This practice dramatically speeds up printing time, especially for a complex design or a long publication.

RUNNING PRE-SERVICE BUREAU PROOFS

About the worst thing you can have happen at the service bureau is to get one of the dreaded PostScript error codes. This message means your job won't run as is through the imagesetter. Another terrible fate—which you also can prevent—is to send a print to disk file to the bureau with the wrong settings. Ever pay for 211 useless pages of positive film with no crop marks? I guarantee, you won't like it.

At the very least, these kinds of troubles can cost you your deadline. Even worse, you can be out big bills for bad film or wasted time on the service bureau's system (they call it overtime, no matter the hour of the day). The best solution is to search out and cure this sort of thing early on, before taking your files to the service bureau. Take the following preventative proofing steps and your publication will fly right through the imagesetter.

Listen to Your Laser Printer

One service bureau tells about the client who sent in a complex design for film output. After four hours of trying to get the job to run, the technician called the client to talk about the trouble. Asked whether he had run a laser proof (one didn't come with the job), the client replied, "Well, I tried to run one, but it wouldn't print on my laser printer. It ran for half an hour and gave me a PostScript error." The trouble at the imagesetter suddenly became very clear—the file was unprintable. If your file burps in the laser printer, fix the file so it at least prints completely and correctly there. If your publication doesn't print at the laser printer's relatively low resolution of 300 or 600 dpi, it almost certainly won't print at 2,450 dpi in the imagesetter.

Check for Problems Onscreen

Look for potential problems such as complex graphics, cropping masks, embedded fonts, nested EPS files, excess use of graphics rotated in PageMaker rather than a graphics application, and so on. Buff that file, in other words, now that the frenzy of design has passed and you are getting ready to send it off to the service bureau.

Don't rely on the screen, however, to evaluate color—even with PageMaker's color management system capabilities.

Use a PostScript Error Checker

PageMaker has a PostScript error checker built right into it (see the Options dialog box of the Print command). During your proofing stages with the laser printer, you should use the PageMaker error checker if you are having trouble printing a file. The error checker might give you a clue as to what's going wrong.

If you are printing a file to disk, ask the service bureau before including the PageMaker error checker. The service bureau might be using something more robust at its end, such as Systems of Merritt's Advanced PostScript Error Handler.

Turn Your Laser Printer into an Imagesetter Proofer

LaserCheck is a special program that you download to your PostScript laser printer before you run your proof. The LaserCheck program then lives inside the memory of your laser printer, taking in whatever PostScript is being sent to it and formatting the information into a proof page.

LaserCheck makes a lot of sense if you submit print to disk files to the service bureau, because you can't otherwise double-check your PostScript output onscreen or on a laser printer. LaserCheck is about the only way you can actually proof the contents of your print to disk output.

Granted, you can use LaserStatus or any of the other PostScript downloaders to send the file to the laser printer, but that wouldn't solve the problem of fitting your 8½×11-inch page with crop marks and other printer's information onto a letter-sized page of printer paper. You also wouldn't be able to troubleshoot any of your problem files.

LaserCheck emulates the imagesetter by reducing the image down to the laser printer page and annotating it. By the way, if a PostScript error shuts down the job, LaserCheck doesn't blow off the entire page; it prints as much of the page as possible, stopping at the bad spot so you can see right where it is.

You get a fonts list for each page, the job information, information on what PostScript calls were made (for troubleshooting assistance), and complete details on page orientation, size, and the name of the printer.

One hot element is the printing time noted at the bottom of the page. The printing time—that shows how long processing the page through your laser printer took—is the biggest worry at the service bureau. The operators worry that your difficult-to-print page will tie up their equipment for hours when the file should take just a few minutes. Show the service bureau this proof, and you positively demonstrate that the file will output with no problem; you might even be able to negotiate a better rate on that basis.

Proofing Color at the Service Bureau

Ultimately, you won't know what your piece looks like until it runs off the press. You can get a good idea, but no test can beat the color accuracy of the final printed product, and the ultimate test of your project is a proof that comes back from the printer. So, in addition to the color proofing techniques discussed in the following sections, read the later section "Checking Your Publication at the Print Shop."

Test Separations on a Laser

One color-proofing technique that doesn't cost a bundle is testing your separations on your laser printer. Run non-composite laser proofs to see that spot color objects and type are going to the correct layer. Of course, evaluate the gray-scale composite for reality testing of your colors, just to see if things that ought to be dark are dark, and so on.

Running separated proofs to the acetate overlays used on overhead projects can help you see that everything is falling together properly. You can even invest in laser-printer cartridges of different colors and actually generate color overlay proofs. Registration probably will be terrible, so don't fool yourself into thinking this is a legitimate color evaluation technique. A laser printer just can't achieve real precision, but it is usually good enough to catch gross errors.

Inexpensive Color Printer Comps

Inexpensive color printers have been flooding the market. For a few hundred dollars, everyone can have color output. However, even with excellent color management systems, these printers can't possibly provide you with an accurate view of your color results on press.

Used with care, color printers still can play an extremely valuable role in the proofing process. Show color composites to your client. Then you have no question that the coat on the model is supposed to be red. The client sign-off proves it. However, consider putting some kind of disclaimer on your sign-off block indicating that the color comp is only an estimate and that considerable color variations may occur when the project goes to press.

Producing these color comps doesn't cost much, and they can be invaluable approval tools—as long as everyone understands that they don't represent 100 percent accurate color as it will appear on the printing press.

Set a Color Goal

To proof color, you need to set a goal. Do you need the color to be only pleasing to the eye, or must it precisely match the original subject? If you are producing a book full of art photos, for example, you might choose to go for art rather than accuracy. On the other hand, if you have a standard product color—like for a brand of soda pop, for example, the printed photos of that product better be an extremely close match.

When you have the goal defined as clearly as you can state it, get a sign-off from your client (or whomever the approver may be) and convey the goal in your conferences with the service bureau and the print shop.

Focus on the Memory Colors

Focus on the so-called memory colors when evaluating color proofs of scanned photographs. Some colors just stick out in a person's mind instantly if they seem wrong. Those colors are the memory colors.

Flesh tones are especially important memory colors. You need to pay particular attention to flesh tones if you have different races in the same shot, because that visual environment will make color accuracy problems even more glaring. The flesh tone memory colors may be the most important ones of all. Crayola even provides a variety of flesh tones for different races in these more aware times (although the old so-called flesh color, the pinkish/salmon one, never looked quite right anyway, did it?).

Other memory colors exist, too. Blue sky, oranges, apples, hamburgers, familiar brand-name products such as soft-drink cans—any objects that are really familiar also must look real and believable.

Evaluate Colors in Controlled Light

Actors have known about this fact for years, of course. The color of everything, including your skin, varies depending on the lighting. Your facial color is different if you're outside at dawn, under the incandescent lights in your dining room, or under fluorescent lighting at the office. If possible, evaluate proofs under standard lighting in a color evaluation booth. Most prepress service bureaus and print shops have such lighting or have rigged up the equivalent. The booths attempt to duplicate the color of daylight at midday.

Choose between Composite and Laminate Proofs

You can break color proof sheets down into two types: composites and laminates (or separation-based). The choice between composite and laminate proofing methods will probably be a money issue, so you need to understand the benefit that may cause you to buy into a laminate proofing technique (the more expensive of the two).

Using Composite Color Proofs

Composite proofs from color printers have become more and more common as color desktop publishing has grown. These proofs are generated digitally, straight out of the computer into a color desktop printer—usually a rather expensive one. Some people even refer to them as digital proofs. They are an alternative to traditional, laminate color proofs.

Keep in mind that much of this discussion relates to the proofing of process colors. Your color proofing method may not need to be so rigorous if you are printing in spot colors, because they come from premixed ink.

On the other hand, even with premixed spot colors, you may need to worry about proofing your trapping, if any, and about checking for moiré patterns in screens. Because composite proof printers don't build color in layers, a composite proof always looks like your document has been built with a perfect abutting of colors and blends. The lack of color build, however, means that the proof cannot show the problems caused by overlapping colors.

Three basic types of composite color printers are available:

- Color copiers are driven with special color controller boxes. You may see one of the Canon color laser copiers, for example, driven by EFI's Fiery unit or by ColorAge's ColorQ.

- Thermal dye sublimation printers, such as the 3M Rainbow and the SuperMac ProofPositive units, apply color to special glossy paper.

- High end inkjet printers spray ink on the paper in microscopic dots, not unlike the inexpensive color printer you may use for color comping. You may hear names at your service bureau such as Iris and Stork Bedford.

Your service bureau may offer one or two of these printer types on their price sheet.

Two of these printer types—the color copiers and the inkjets—can print to your actual paper, the stock you are using for your printed piece. The thermal dye sublimation printer requires special paper.

Using Laminate (Separation-Based) Color Proofs

The most expensive type of color proofing is the best. With laminate color proofs, the service bureau builds proofs from layers of colors, just like it is done on the printing press. This type of proof reveals any trapping or moiré flaws in your piece.

You can get overlay proofs where the color is built up from loose acetate sheets of each color, all bound together in register. If you are offered an overlay proof, it's likely to be a 3M Color Key or a DuPont Cromacheck.

The best proofs are bonded together in a lamination. Your film is shot to the layers of proofing materials, processed, and registered. Then the elements are sealed together in one solid sheet. Proofs don't get any better than this. Look for names like Cromalin (DuPont), Matchprint (3M), and ColorArt (Fuji).

CHECKING YOUR PUBLICATION AT THE PRINT SHOP

After all this talk about not believing the color you see on your screen, you can believe the color results at one place—the printing press.

But the press check isn't the only proofing service you can get from the print shop. The following sections explain other services.

Swatches of Ink and Varnish

The term proof doesn't strictly describe these two swatch techniques, but they help you predict results, and that's what a proof is supposed to do, isn't it? Both methods deliver color-accurate information from the inks you'll actually be using, on the paper you will be specifying for your job. Use these two ink trial methods for spot colors, although the spot colors can be mixed from CMYK inks.

First, you can ask the print shop just to smear some ink on your chosen paper for any given project. The ink is applied using a palette knife or rubber roller so you can see how it works on your paper stock. (You may sometimes hear this technique called a draw down.) You probably won't be charged for the sample unless the printer must special order the ink.

For day-to-day use in your designs, select your paper (or the papers you most commonly use for your projects) and run some swatches of your own instead of relying on commercial spot-color palette swatches. Make up a PageMaker document of the colors you need in various tints and run it through the service bureau imagesetter you commonly use. Then have your regular printer run it on the press. If you work with this printer quite a bit, it shouldn't charge you an arm and a leg for this calibration work. You may even be able to get it on press as shared work, taking up spare space on a flat.

Make sure that you understand how varnish will affect your job. If you'll be using varnish, try out the varnish on some swatches to see how much it darkens the color.

PRINTER INSPECTION OF FILMS

Nobody may be better qualified to inspect your imagesetter output than the person doing the printing. Even if the service bureau has checked the films, have the press people run another analysis with those experienced eyes that have been watching stuff come off the press for hundreds, maybe thousands, of print runs. The more eyes the better, and odds are high that your print shop folks have the best eyes of all.

Blueline

A blueline is, well, blue. It is made much the same way a blueprint is made. Light-sensitive paper is exposed to light in a one-to-one contact print with your actual stripped-together films—the flats about to be used to make up your printing press plates. The blueline is the most intimate and close to the press method of proofing—outside the press check itself—and tells you whether the print shop has properly collated all the separations for your job.

Dummy

If you are producing a multipage document, your print shop may provide you with an imposition proof—a dummied-up copy of how all the flats will be folded when they are printed to paper and then trimmed. The dummy shows you the spreads and how they will all fit together when bound.

Press Check

Do a press check at least once sometime in your life, even if you aren't working on color critical publications. Seeing your design coming to fruition is magic, and no better way exists to absorb into your gut the process of getting images onto paper from a printing press.

On the other hand, if you are one of those people who rejects the first two bottles of wine at a fancy restaurant, just to show you know your stuff, you might not enjoy the experience. And certainly the press crew won't enjoy the check if you cop an attitude. Remember, the goal is a collaboration between designer and print shop.

When you arrive (on time, right?), you go to the press room, where the press is ready to roll or close to it. When the crew hits the button, a lot of waste, called make ready, results. Sheet after sheet of paper (if the press is sheet-fed) or yards of paper (if it's a web press) roll along as the printing crew adjusts everything.

When the crew is satisfied, they shut down the press and bring a sample to you before rolling the press again to finish the job. This is no time to discover a typo. That should have been done long ago. You are there to see that the colors are accurate and that no obvious defects exist in the work. If you are happy, you sign the proof, and the crew uses it as a standard for evaluating the rest of the pieces off the press.

What do you look for at the press check?

- Ask the crew to share their technical check with you.

- How did dot gain look on the star targets? These wheel-like spoke patterns look a little like a miniature TV test pattern.

- What did the densitometer show about how the inks are laying down on the page? Have the printer explain what the crew discovered as they examined the color and gray-scale density bars.

- The press crew already should have done this, but take the extra care to double-check that all the registration marks are lined up.

- Go through the piece and check that colors are how you want them, suited to the accuracy goal that everyone agreed on. If the piece has critical items for color matching, such as product shots or color matching system swatches, make sure that those critical items are with you at the press check, and use the standard light table to make a comparison. Don't work from memory.

- Look for physical defects caused by the printing process. Wrinkles, print-through from the back side of the piece, impurities such as hair or dust sticking to the plate and printing on the piece, smudges, blotting from undried ink transferring between stacked sheets—these are the kinds of defects you need to look for.

The best approach to a press check is abject terror, moderated by pride and concentration. Be afraid you'll miss something. Focus all your energy on looking over the results of the effort you've put into the project, while remembering that a mistake now could waste all that work.

Tip

If color accuracy has major importance for the project, don't evaluate from memory. Bring the original, or have the prepress people bring it to the proofing session. If you are matching a product shot, bring the product. Bring your spot color swatches for comparison as well. If you are matching a previous press run, bring the signed press sheets.

SUMMARY

- Working with the printer involves more than doing a press check, and it begins when you do, at the start of a project.

- You cannot do a color proof without understanding the technology of color.

- Much of the proofing suggested in this chapter relies on your laser printer. You can't proof without the Print command.

- Likewise, the process of getting a project into the service bureau has much to do with the proofing results you get from your prepress collaborators.

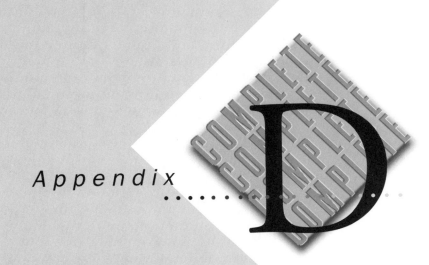

Appendix

MASTER CHECKLIST

Sometimes it seems that desktop publishing would be more logical if it ran in reverse—from printing press back to the first thumbnails. How many things would you change in the construction of a publication if you only knew the unanticipated problems you'd face down the road to the print shop? Try to figure out where you want to end up—then think about the best way to get there.

Tip

Desktop publishing involves many kinds of publications and hundreds of variables of budget, technique, and deadline. So, many items in these lists won't apply directly and precisely to your current job. Rather, in many instances, the items have been designed as reminders and brainstorming tools. Many of the items ask, "Did you think of this area of concern?" as opposed to the kind of detailed step-by-step approach that says, "Now do this, followed by that."

PLANNING

As you might expect, making a plan means starting with the goal. How can you make a plan to get where you want to go if you don't know the final destination?

Defining the Goal and Audience

Try to write down a description of the audience and the specific communication objective for the publication. Use the suggestions in the following sections to help you.

Audience

You can usually define the audience in terms of some common factors or characteristics. As many possible factors exist as there are people on this planet, so your options are broad, and your intent should be to narrow them down. For example, consider the demographics of your audience.

- Age
- Sex
- Family role (spouse, parent, sibling, child, and so on)
- Home location (urban, rural, suburban)
- Geographic location (Southwest, Northeast, foreign country)
- Income bracket
- Education level

Keep in mind that the census bureau doesn't have a lock on describing an audience. Think about what some marketing types call the "psychographic" or sociological profile of your target audience:

- Use of recreational time (for example, hobbies)

- Possessions (pets, cars, stereos, size of home, style of home decoration)

- Membership in organizations (fraternal order, bridge club, church, alumni group)

- Political (special interest group, Democrat, Republican)

Most of all, you must spend some time thinking about the reader's relationship to your publication and the topic:

- How is the reader involved in the topic? Is the reader reading it for work, for a hobby, or from a need to accomplish a certain goal?

- Where does the reader's knowledge of the topic begin? Is the user beginning, average, or advanced?

- Can you expect the reader to understand certain jargon and terms specific to the topic?

- How will the publication be used? Will the reader be using the material as a reference (book), a tutorial (syllabus or course outline), or the latest news (newsletter)?

Goal

Your publication—whether it's a magazine, newsletter, book, or brochure—has a purpose. After you define your audience, there's a good chance that the purpose will be crystallized in your mind. You might start with an idea about your objective, but it is almost always easier to state an objective in the context of the target audience.

Generally, your goal already exists in your head. You just need to turn those vague churnings of thought into a written goal statement that a client or a boss or you can sign off on before you move ahead with planning.

If you are doing a series of publications (an ad campaign or a newsletter), you will want to define a broad goal and then a specific goal for each element of the series. Of course, if you are creating a one-time piece (a brochure, for example) you only need to define the goal once.

Try these ways of focusing your thoughts:

◆ What are you selling?

It might be toothpaste, a thesis, or a business plan; but regardless of whether you realize it, you are probably selling some thing or some idea.

◆ What are you telling?

Even if you don't think you are selling a point of view, you are at least trying to give someone some information.

◆ What is the competition saying?

If you are in some competitive arena, such as retail point of purchase or advertising, your competition probably has a very good idea of what you are selling or telling. That's a good clue on which to center your thinking about your goal.

◆ What have you already been saying?

Look through back issues or other previous publications for your target audience and ask yourself what they were trying to say. If you are doing an in-house newsletter for a company, that company's advertising campaign can give you clues for your goals in the newsletter, although you need to filter your ideas through the target audience.

◆ What would you say?

Quite literally, say your message out loud. If possible, do it in the context of the delivery method for your piece. If it's a newsletter that will be delivered by mail, literally stand at the mailbox and talk to an imaginary member of your target audience. If it's a sales sheet handout, role play with yourself (and someone you feel comfortable around) on a pretend trade show floor. Just say what you feel—that gives you a good start on focusing your thoughts about the goal.

Setting a Budget, Deadline, and Schedule

There's no magic to this. You need to have at least some idea, formally or informally, of when the publication must be ready and how much you can spend to produce it.

Budget

Unfortunately, unless you have an unlimited budget, there's no way you can let your creativity range freely on the execution of your project. Most of us have budget limits, so here are some questions to help you get to the bottom line:

◆ What's the project worth?

What you spend may depend on what you will make. It makes sense to spend more per printed piece on a brochure to sell cars than it does to spend that same amount on a weekly supermarket flyer.

◆ What are the client's expectations and what will the market bear?

Sometimes it's true that the emotions of the client and the client's pocketbook dictate the budget. If the client is enthusiastic and wants to spend the money, you can go all out.

◆ How many do you need of what?

One dominant budget factor has to be the number of copies you need. After that, a rough vision of the format of the publication should at least get you some ballpark budget information.

◆ What's the minimum cost?

You might base the budget on the concept of minimums. (Can you say the word "cheap?")

◆ What has the project cost in the past?

Don't overlook the track record—yours and those of the publication. If a newsletter has been published every week for a year, you can get a good idea of the cost of the next one. If you have been doing similar jobs for other folks, you probably have a good idea of the costs involved.

◆ Should you come back to the budget?

So what if these guidelines say that you should have a budget before you develop the concept? You probably have some idea of where the budget stands, so maybe you should just take the gamble, move on to concept development, and come back to the budget. You can do a great budget after you finish a preliminary planning session with the printer, for example. You should certainly revise your preliminary budget after you meet with the printer.

◆ Are time factors involved that affect the budget?

Consider the deadline and ask yourself if the project demands extra funds to be completed on time. Overtime can be expensive, and rush orders at the service bureau cost plenty; but if the deadline is immutable, you may not have a choice.

Deadline and Schedule

Here's another situation in which you start from where you want to end up. The concert happens on the date the auditorium is booked, regardless of whether you think you can finish the playbill and program. If you are creating an annual report, there are often legally proscribed filing deadlines. What's the newsletter mailing date or the submission deadline for the advertisement?

Get out a calendar, maybe one of those desk planners. Sometimes print shops put out special calendar forms designed to help you plan print jobs. Begin with the last possible date you need the job, allow a bit of leeway, and count backwards, providing time for each of the functions in this chapter full of checklists. Only experience—yours or that of a collaborator—can help you fill in the blanks for how much time each element will take. Printing and bindery schedules are generally very reliable. The time to allow for writing the copy (accounting for writer's block), well, that's between you and your keyboard.

For each one of the following steps, plot the length of time for the task as well as the "by when" date—the deadline by which the task must be completed so that the next task can follow and be completed for its "by when" date:

- Allow time for approvals after each one of these steps—a variable that depends on your client relationship, assuming that the client isn't just you.

- For each of the steps, plan who will be responsible. (In many cases, it will probably be you.) You want someone to coordinate the project, and you need to know the writer for the copy, the layout artist, and the production services you need (illustrator, proofreader, probable service bureau, probable print shop, and so on).

- Estimate the time it will take to sketch out and further develop the core creative concept.

- How long will it take to test the concept and refine it further after the testing? Be especially certain to allow time for conceptualizing the structure of the publication, including the text styles and the color scheme.

- A planning session with the print shop and service bureau won't take long, but allow time for it. It's a must.

- Leave plenty of time to perfect the text and graphic elements of the design, including time to write the copy and create the illustrations.

- Executing the layout steps will bring the design to fruition, so don't shirk on time needed for that. Set up the publication's geometry, place all the text and graphics, and then fine-tune and elaborate the layout with special effects and color.

- For a table of contents and index, leave extra time at the end of layout.

- Develop a sense of the time that it takes to do the prepress steps of trapping, separating, and then outputting the mechanicals. Whether you send material to the laser printer or an image-setter, you need time to do this output step.

- Final proofing and approvals pay back the time investment in saved money and a better product, but these steps won't happen instantaneously. You will need an elapsed time estimate and a "by when" date for each of the proofing and approval stages.

- Manufacturing time varies, depending on whether you use a photocopier or a six tower web press. This time also depends on the way the publication will be folded and bound.

Developing Your Core Creative Concept

Developing your core creative concept means fleshing it out and bringing it to life with details. Development is the major sweat factor for the creative process. The rest of the effort to complete is the execution. Based on the target audience, design how you'll accomplish the goals of your publication. Some of your core creative concept can be doodled out right in PageMaker. Use the following thought-starters to help you prime your creative pump:

- Driving Force and Dominant Design Item

  In almost every case, some single element comes to the front in the design. It's a good place to start. As you stare at the screen or cradle that sketch pad in your lap, mulling over how to tackle the design, ask yourself what that element might be. Maybe you can use some slogan or logo to focus the eye. How about a product shot? Or maybe you want to use the title of a report or the masthead of a newsletter.

- Organizational Structure

  Applying a structure to your concept primarily concerns the written part of a publication design, but it can also be useful when you organize a concept visually on the page.

Try an outline. Look at your subject matter using journalism's big five: who, what, when, where, and why. Apply some hierarchy of thought to the idea or ideas you are trying to convey.

You can also try the age old saw about expository writing: Tell 'em what you're going to tell 'em. Tell 'em. Tell 'em what you told them. To say it more formally, state a proposition. Expand on it with factual detail and discussion. End by summarizing the proposition in its supported and elaborated state.

◆ Overall Style

You need to come up with an overall style that plays to your target audience and the purpose of the piece. When you hit this style, you can almost always sum it up in a single image or word. The word might be as vague as the word "formal" or "informal," but you'll be best served by words that evoke some sort of picture in your mind. Think about style names like Deco, antique, garden, sand painting, English, French, Japanese, impressionist, metallic, furry animal, and so on. Your goal will be to find a kernel around which you can accrete a pearl inside that oyster-like brain of yours.

◆ Graphics Style

You don't want to hop all over the map with your illustrations. Your publication will look most cohesive and purposeful if you select an approach to your illustrations and stick to it. Do you plan to use illustrations, and will they be realistic, line drawings, or abstract? Maybe you need photos to tell your story. Will you add charts and tables?

◆ Writing Style

Get an idea of the way your target audience speaks, which will put you on the trail of the writing style for your publication. But keep in mind that lawyers speak with one style in court in front of a jury, and quite another when they hang out at the swimming pool. So if you target your brochure to market a high-end golf club to a special mailing list that reaches lawyers in their homes, you'll want to take that point into account.

◆ Paper Style

Paper says a lot about the style of your publication. Stately royal blue covers that would work well for a business plan probably wouldn't be as appropriate for the covers of a fun-filled brochure selling cruises to the Bahamas.

◆ Type Style

You don't sell colonial pine furniture with art deco type, and you don't usually sell computers with a country and western style theme—that is, unless you are Borland, which did it very successfully. Remember the program Sidekick? In that case, the name was the dominant element for the core concept; it dictated all the other design choices, including the western style type and the cartoon sidekick character.

Think about the type style in light of all the other conceptual creative factors. You will probably want to link your type style to the imagery evoked by your overall style and by your dominant design element.

◆ Size and Format

It may seem obvious, but you do need to decide what kind of publication you are doing, and it needs to be suited to the audience and goals for the project. More than anything else, that means making the size and format suitable for the delivery method. If the publication is in the mail, for example, it may need to fit an envelope or at least conform to postal regulations. Brochures in "take-one" pockets at counter point-of-purchase displays must fit the pockets.

So, will it be a newsletter, brochure, calling card, or book? What form will the publication take? How big will it be? How many pages? What will be the trim size, and how much of the page will be margins and how much will be "live" area?

◆ Visual Structure of a Page

Given all these other creative elements, can you conceptualize the column grid yet? How will graphics and text fit together? How will headlines (which sort of straddle the line between type and graphics) occupy their prominent position on the page?

Testing the Concept and Getting Preliminary Approvals

It goes without saying that your designs sell a million of those widgets and always have those subscribers hugging the mailbox (or the postal carrier) waiting for the arrival of your bimonthly newsletter on Peruvian corn cultivation. Of course you're the world's most insightful and perceptive designer, but deep down inside, are you really sure? Here's how you can test your new concept:

◆ Dummy It Up

Make a mockup version of the publication. There's no other way to test your concept. Repeat that. To test your concept, you must mock it up. Describing it won't work, even if you wave your arms a lot.

Also, the dummied up publication will help you crystallize your thinking and show you whether it physically will work. Did you ever hear about the designer who produced 50,000 resort promotion brochures for travel agents and specified an oversized job that would be different and stand out in the crowd? It was different all right, but nobody saw it because the brochure wouldn't fit in the distributor's standard display rack.

◆ Use Informal Testing

Imagine cold water, reality check, horse sense—think of all these good things about an informal test. Some people call it a "grandma survey." Try out the dummy publication on anyone you can find who might have a point of view, including consumers, sales people, and distributors.

If you are thinking about informally testing a video sleeve design, for example, try it out on some potential viewers of the genre. Don't just ask them how they like it. Give the product to them and watch to see whether they handle it. Do you think they would really pick it up off the shelf and rent it?

◆ Use Formal Audience Research

If the project has enough importance and budget, maybe you should get some professional testing. The marketing pros test out product packaging ideas and concepts for new magazines by using focus groups and shopping mall intercepts.

◆ Make Adjustments

Why test your concept? So you can change it, of course, and make it better. The feedback from all these people who see a mockup will show you how to refine your approach. Be emotionally prepared to make adjustments to your great idea based on your research.

◆ Build a Consensus and Get a Sign-Off

So, all this testing leads to one thing—consensus. In addition, you can get a formal sign-off on the mockup, plus any written analysis you did based on the checklists up to this point.

Communications make—or break—a project. The better the job you do of bringing the client and everyone else on the team on board, the easier time you'll have from this point on. Those people who actually held a sketch of the end result in their hands and who experienced your mock-up concept are less likely to second-guess the refinements when you begin to execute the project. People like to own the things they are involved in, and your dummied up publication and concept testing will help the folks you are trying to please, including yourself, achieve that feeling of ownership and involvement. Sometimes it's called "emotional buy in."

Collaborating with the Printer and Service Bureau

At this point, you establish your prepress strategy and finalize your bid specifications. Precisely when you perform each of these steps in relation to your design process will vary, depending on your working style and your approach to getting the bid. Also, the print shop and service bureau issues get mingled together in real life (as opposed to checklist life), so think about your specific project needs when you apply this reminder list.

What To Bring to the Preliminary Meeting

Bring these items to the print shop or service bureau preliminary meeting:

◆ Purpose and audience for your publication

◆ Your rough sketch, comp, or mock-up

◆ Samples of other publications showing what you like

◆ Size of run and budget

◆ Quality expectations

◆ Deadline and schedule estimate

◆ Estimate of ink and varnish needs

◆ Thoughts on paper

◆ Special sensitivities regarding the project

◆ Crazy thoughts and brainstorms

Answers, Decisions, and Feedback for You To Get at the Preliminary Meeting

Before you do extensive layout work, you should resolve these production and prepress issues:

◆ Determine the method of reproduction (photocopy, sheet fed, web press, roto, screen printing, and so on).

◆ Finalize paper choice.

◆ Determine line screen frequency for scans.

- Identify items for service bureau prepress work and items that are less expensively or otherwise better handled with traditional prepress approaches at the print shop.

- Work out a trapping strategy (PageMaker internal, design to avoid the need, have service bureau do it). If you won't be doing the trapping, determine who will—the print shop or the service bureau. If you decide to use PageMaker trapping, be sure it can handle your specific design challenges.

- Discuss strategy for inks (process CMYK, number of spot colors, varnish).

- Coordinate implementation of a color management system or a color matching system such as one of the PANTONE libraries.

To get the most out of your collaboration with the printer and the service bureau, these additional points will help you:

- Reality—test your creative concepts and how you plan to execute them.

- Suggest ways to improve the quality of your piece.

- Determine ways to save money, perhaps by making acceptable adjustments to the design concept.

- Make suggestions regarding efficiency to cut down production and manufacturing time.

- Make recommendations for proofing (laser comps, composite color, laminate color, and so on).

- Discuss the probable approach for imposing the piece, based on the printer's particular press size and the probable size of the paper to be used.

- Determine whether it makes sense to submit imposed film, or whether the printer should strip together the flats.

- Discuss ideas for bindery (need for scoring, foil stamping or embossing, die cutting, loose-leaf, perfect bound, case bound, spiral, comb).

- Determine the best way to package the job for shipment and use.

The following issues have to do with your work with the service bureau in producing mechanicals:

- Will you need imagesetter output, or would laser printer output be just fine?

- If you need them, what are the specifications for imagesetter mechanicals (film or paper, right or wrong reading, negative or positive, emulsion up or down)?

- Do you need dot gain compensation on black and white halftones or on color scans?

- Do you need under color removal (UCR) and gray component replacement (GCR)?

- What strategy will you use for handling the large files produced by high resolution color scans?

- How will the service bureau manage your Photo CD scans, if you decide to take that approach?

- Should you print to PostScript or submit native PageMaker files?

Bidding

You will probably want to develop a bid and specifications form for the project. The form should cover these items:

- Contact information

- Indication of whether this is a new job or a repeat, or a repeat with changes

- Type of publication

- Dates (request date, quote due date, art ready date, date for completing the job)

- Size of run

- Number of pages in the piece

- Final trim size of the pages

- For text pages: paper, ink, and varnish

- For cover stock: paper, ink, and varnish

- Notes on critical issues in production and quality expectations

- Specifications for mechanicals to be provided by service bureau

- Specific needs for traditional prepress to be provided by print shop

- Bindery needs (sewing, stapling, gluing, comb, spiral, drilling, padding, carbonless, perfing, die cutting, embossing, foil stamping, folding, scoring, inserting, tipping, stuffing)

- Instructions for packing

- Shipping and delivery instructions

MAKING UP YOUR PAGES

After all that planning, here's the execution phase, which puts to work all the PageMaker power described throughout this book.

Perfecting Your Elements

Before you actually place the elements into your layout, you need to perfect all the elements of your publication. In most cases, you will probably begin by forming a strategy for word processing.

Managing Your Text

How will you get those words created so that they can then be put on pages? Of course, this question assumes that you actually took care of the writing, which may be the biggest challenge of all. As for the logistics of managing the text, consider these points:

◆ Choose a word processor, or perhaps use the PageMaker Story Editor.

◆ Plan ahead to make sure that conversion problems will not occur when you import your text into PageMaker.

◆ If an outside writer is involved, find out whether that person's word processor allows for styles, or if you need to plan for the use of style tags.

◆ If the files come from a PC, determine how to get them onto your Mac and how to convert them to a format that's PageMaker readable.

Planning and Setting Up Your Style Sheet

You need to form a strategy for your style sheet arrangements and, preferably, set up the same style sheet names in both your word processor and PageMaker.

◆ First, remove from the Style palette the PageMaker default styles, which are unlikely to match your own needs.

◆ Name styles so that the most-used ones are at the top of the Style palette and ad hoc special purpose styles are alphabetized at the bottom.

◆ Decide on your work style. Will you design the style sheet in advance, create it as you go, or use a combination of both methods?

◆ Create base definitions for the common denominator styles (body text, headlines, bullet indents) that share a common typeface.

◆ Define the rest of your styles to cascade from the base definitions, using the Based On style attribute.

◆ For easy reference while you're working, list your styles in writing, probably using one of the plug-ins or third-party utilities provided for the purpose (for instance, CheckList or PageMaker's Pub Info plug-in).

Style Sheet Formatting Options

As you set up your styles here are all the factors you may want to consider including in your style definitions, beginning with the ones in the Type Specifications dialog box:

◆ Typeface

◆ Size of type

◆ Leading

◆ Set automatic kerning

◆ Set tracking

◆ Set width

◆ Line break option

◆ Subscript, superscript, baseline shift

The paragraph level definition possibilities are contained in three commands: Paragraph Specifications, Hyphenation, and Indents/Tabs.

◆ Alignment

◆ Word and letter spacing for justified text

◆ Hyphenation

◆ Tabs

◆ Leaders

◆ Indents

◆ Keep together

◆ Widow and orphan control

◆ Page and column forced breaks

◆ Space before and after

◆ Rules

◆ Leading method

Cleaning Up Your Text

Before you can put your text into the publication, you need to do a good copy cleaning job:

- Decide which kinds of edits should be done in PageMaker, probably those that aren't feasible in your word processor because they involve some special PageMaker characteristic such as kerning.

- Run spell check again.

- Build a custom dictionary, or import it from your word processor.

- Translate word processor formats.

- Remove flaws.

- Code the text for importation if you have some special moves you need to make inside PageMaker.

- Apply mass formatting, using text processing utilities.

- Make a decision about whether to hire an outside proofreader and implement any of the other text proofing steps in the proofing checklist.

Assembling Your Graphics

Produce your graphics. As with text material, keep a wary eye on how your graphics will ultimately be brought into PageMaker:

- Will you do tabletop scanning in black and white, or will you have high resolution scans (corrected and proofed) at a service bureau?

- Will you rely on PageMaker drawn objects?

- Will you create original illustrations or hire outside illustration help?

- Remember to find sources for and gather your clip art.

- Scope out your sources for Photo CD processing.

- How will you generate graphs?

- Does your table formatting strategy involve clipboarding material into PageMaker as graphic images?

- Consider any graphics conversion issues. If you are working between Macs and DOS machines, for example, stick to TIFF and EPS files.

- You need to know if you'll be working in spot or process color so that you can ultimately share color definitions among all your different graphics sources.

- Create custom Color palettes to share among all those working on the project.

- Plan for sizing and manipulating (rotating, skewing, and so on) your images before you import them into PageMaker.

- Consider how the items will work as inline graphics, if that's your plan.

Setting Up Your Publication

This checklist boils down all the information for setting up your publication into a short list.

- Determine whether you will be working from a template or building your publication from scratch.

- Set up your Style, Color, and Library palettes, removing the default styles and colors.

- Plan your page numbering, including your numbering style (in Page setup).

- Plan your master pages and set up your Master Pages palette, including your design grid.

Setting the Master Page and Design Grid

Your master page design grids require the following:

◆ Set up your page geometry using Page setup (page size, margins, print on both sides, and facing pages).

◆ Plan your columns.

◆ Set up any ruler guides that you want to have on every page.

◆ Set your zero point if you want it somewhere other than the default (upper-left corner of a single page and the common edge of facing pages).

◆ Set your vertical ruler measurement and leading grid if you'll be using the Baseline alignment and Snap to rulers features.

Working with Books and Other Long Form Publications

The following are some special considerationsif you are working on a long form document:

◆ Set up your chapter breakdowns, using the Book feature to pull together each chapter file.

◆ In your style sheet planning, provide for automatic generation of your table of contents.

◆ You'll probably want to produce an index.

◆ If you need page cross-referencing, you want to use the index-based technique.

◆ Footnotes need special handling.

◆ Consider whether you want to use bleeder tabs or some other visual indexing method.

◆ Along those same lines, your style sheet planning will have a lot to do with how you use the PageMaker Plug-in for creating dictionary style running footers and headers.

Setting Preferences

Using the Preferences command, you'll probably want to consider setting preferences for all the following items, although your working style may differ from some of these specific recommendations:

◆ Set your measurement system to picas, unless you prefer one of the other systems, such as inches.

◆ Set the Preferences command to pinpoint layout problems by highlighting violations to your settings for spacing and line breaks.

◆ Most people work with graphics set at Standard resolution. Keep in mind that you can always turn graphics on to High resolution using the redraw trick.

◆ To prevent accidentally grabbing guides as you work with objects, set guides to the back.

◆ It's generally a good idea to keep file size down by setting the Smaller option, especially when you are working with very large documents.

◆ Set your personal preferences for Control palette nudge amounts and Snap to characteristics.

◆ Turn Autoflow off. You may prefer the opposite, depending on your workflow and the circumstances of your project, but it is important to keep in mind its effects. Autoflow must be off before using Build Booklet. Also, Autoflow could cause you to accidentally pour out a bunch of pages when you just wanted to set one text block.

◆ The internal image size defaults are pretty good, but with PageMaker's capability to store all graphics outside the publication, some people link all graphics, storing them outside PageMaker.

◆ Turn on typographer quotes unless you are setting type for a math or computer programming text, where you need the straight quotes.

♦ Set the greeking level, usually 4 pixels or below.

♦ Set your Story Editor preferences to show paragraph and other symbols and to display your text in a typeface and size of your choice.

♦ Work your way through all the menus, with nothing selected, setting your personal preferences for each item that's not grayed out. You'll probably want to particularly focus on the settings in the Type, Element and Window menus.

Placing Text and Graphics

Using the Place command becomes pretty anti-climactic, if you've done all the advance planning. Here are some thoughts to guide you through:

♦ Depending on the nature of the piece and your personal working style, you'll want to decide whether it's best to place text or graphics first.

♦ Do a couple of pages first to see how things are working; then make any adjustments to your styles and such before finishing.

♦ You may want to adjust the mini-default for the Text Wrap command, as you see how the layout gels during the first part of the Place process.

♦ As you bring inline graphics into the pages, you'll learn how the graphics and the text formatting work together, and you may need to make some style sheet adjustments.

♦ As you import graphics, you may want to compress any TIFFs to save disk space.

♦ In particular, you need to experiment as you bring in tables to be formatted using PageMaker's tabs and styles functions. Start with the toughest table and develop the basic form of your layout before you move on to the rest. If your tables will be limited to a single page, it may make sense to use the Table Editor.

- Keep the various positioning techniques at the front of your mind as you work.

- In most situations, you will want to save disk space by linking graphics as much as possible, keeping the original outside your publication.

Fine-Tuning, Producing Special Effects, and Coloring Your Pages

Next go through each page and fine-tune, putting into place any special effects and assigning element colors. It's a page-by-page tweak process where you check and adjust each of the following page elements:

- Hanging indents

- Headline treatments

- Fractions, formulas, weird type

- Text wrap

- Initial caps

- Rotate, skew

- Vertical rules

- Rules above and below

- Screens and drop shadows

In addition to checking those items, be sure to take care of the following tasks:

- Perform any kerning that's needed.

- Check picture captions for placement and line breaks.

- Adjust page breaks and column breaks.

- Look for ungainly line breaks.

- Be certain that all objects have their proper color assignments.

Generating Contents and Index

Implement the final stages of building your long form document by doing the following:

- Generate the master table of contents.

- Run the chapter level table of contents pages.

- Using the table of contents facilities, create any other specialized lists you'll need, such as tables of illustrations.

- Generate the index.

PUBLISHING

You made all the decisions when you did your preliminary and bid specification work. Now it's time to implement those decisions.

Submitting Files to the Service Bureau

It might be a drag, but you need to fill out the service bureau work order form. It's the only way to be sure that your job is done right. To complete the form, you need to be prepared with this information:

- Contact information (24 hours)

- Deadline

- A clear statement that indicates whether you are providing PostScript print to file data, or native PageMaker files

- A list of all files being transmitted

- A list of fonts

- A list of programs used to create your work

- Specific line screen setting

- Selection of the type of imagesetter

- Film or paper specifications (for example, negative or positive, right or wrong reading, emulsion up or down)

- Specific list of printer's marks

- Description of the number of pages

- A list of the number of high-resolution scans to be performed

- Specific colors (and therefore, separations needed)

In addition to gathering all that data, check on these items:

- Determine whether you should include PostScript error checking code if you are submitting PostScript files.

- Consider trapping issues—whether you should do it yourself or, if not, provide any needed trapping directions.

- Request imposed film, if that's needed.

- Order proofs to be provided with output.

- Give delivery or pick up instructions.

Bundling Up Your Files for the Service Bureau

Gather those files and organize them for minimal confusion. Here are some suggestions:

- Fine-tune your files, following the checklist provided in this section.

- Submit files with laser proofs (composites or LaserCheck).

- Use the PageMaker Save As command with Files For Remote Printing to gather your files.

- Include all files to be run as well as linked files and original art files (for example, original of EPS export graphic).

- Provide fonts not supported by service bureau.

- Include "spare" folder backup.

Buffing Your Files for Optimum Laser or Imagesetter Output

Prevent problems at output time by buffing your files for the best possible output:

- Calculate your blend steps.

- Make sure that there are no spot color to spot color blends.

- Outlaw white boxes.

- You may want to replace some graphics, sizing and cropping them in their originating programs for faster output results.

- Rotate graphics before placement.

- Search out and see if you can eliminate nested EPS file problems.

- Adjust the flatness of complex clipping paths.

- Search for TrueType text that may choke the imagesetter.

- Likewise, see whether any PICT graphics have crept in and determine whether you need to replace them.

- Hairlines can disappear down to nothing in the imagesetter.

Proofing and Final Approvals

Here's a list of all your proofing options. Make sure that you get a written sign-off on any proofs for client approval; otherwise, you may end up paying for a botched job where there's no proof of your proofing.

Copy Proofing

Checking for typos, misspellings, and other problems with text is your first line of defense against errors in your publication. Use the following list to make sure that you don't miss even one of your possible copy-proofing tools:

- Use spell check—more than once, even.

- Note that indexing and table of contents lists often reveal bad word usage and spelling problems.

◆ You may want to hire a professional proofreader—it might be worth the investment.

◆ Read into a tape recorder and listen back while scanning the printed copy, or have two people do the check with one reading and the other proofing. You can also, believe it or not, try reading backwards. That way the material is out of context and errors might stand out better.

Pasteup Checking with a Laser Printer

Before spending money on expensive imagesetter film or color proofs, run laser proofs on the following items to be sure that your layout works:

◆ Thumbnails

◆ FPO proofs with gray boxes using the Print command

◆ Composites

Proofing Prior to the Service Bureau

All the preceding proofs will be next to worthless if you end up wasting a lot of money on mistake-ridden film at the service bureau. Perform the following proofing steps before going to the imagesetting stage:

◆ Laser printer reality check: the law is, if it won't go through the laser printer, it almost certainly won't run on the imagesetter. Naturally, to be an effective reality check, it must be a PostScript laser printer.

◆ Run a visual inspection of what you see on-screen, particularly in relation to the hot spots named in the earlier checklist, "Buffing Your Files for Optimum Laser or Imagesetter Output."

◆ Use a PostScript error checker.

◆ Run a LaserCheck proof.

If your job will be in color and it's only a couple of pages long, print out a set of color separated lasers for all pages. Make sure all the colors are falling on the right layers. If you're producing a longer piece, print out at least a couple of the more complex pages to color separated lasers to confirm that your color definitions are working correctly.

Color

Producing good quality color can be pretty intimidating, unless you have the security of good quality control steps like the ones in this list:

◆ Work toward a quality goal. (Do you want accuracy, or do you simply desire pleasing-to-the-eye color results?)

◆ Naturally, coordinate with your printer and service bureau on the use of PageMaker's color management system.

◆ Check color using a standard color evaluation booth.

◆ Test separations on a laser printer.

◆ Check memory colors, such as flesh, familiar objects, blue sky.

◆ Composite color proofs.

◆ Laminate (separation-based) proofs if you need to check trapping.

Print Shop Proofing

Until you've actually seen your publication come off the press, you have no way to be sure what you'll get—especially for a color publication—no matter how much proofing you've done. To improve your chances of getting from the press what you designed on the computer, have your print shop help you to implement the following proofing tools and steps:

◆ Create your own swatch system.

◆ Ask for a draw down so that you can see your ink on your paper.

◆ Have the printer inspect the mechanicals.

◆ Get and check blueline proofs.

♦ Ask for a print shop-created dummy of how the project will be imposed.

♦ Request a press check inspection.

Going To Press, Imposing, Folding, and Binding

Now the print shop runs the job based on your bid specifications, as revised during the long process of putting together the finished project. The last job you have is to inspect the results.

♦ Pull random samples through the job for inspection.

♦ Satisfy yourself that the random samples show consistent results, including consistent color matching.

♦ Look for wrinkles.

♦ Inspect to see whether there's print through—where the ink shows through from the other side of the paper.

♦ Look for foreign material, such as lint, hairs, or dust, stuck in the ink.

♦ See whether there's any blotting of ink from the front of one piece to the back of the next.

♦ Sometimes you find smudging from the paper feed mechanism.

♦ This is the first time you've seen your project since it's been through the bindery, so look for physical registration problems, for example, across spreads.

♦ See that the packing instructions have been followed.

♦ Satisfy yourself that you received the full count on your order.

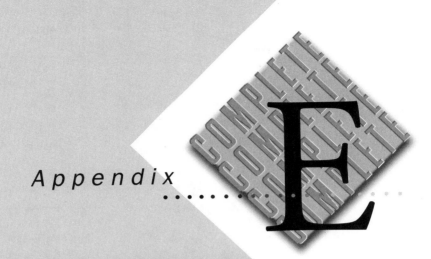

Appendix

PAGEMAKER RESOURCE GUIDE

Product	Manufacturer	Address
AA Celler AA Shadow	Integrated Software Inc.	475 Park Avenue S. New York, NY 10016 212-545-0110
Access PC	Insignia Solutions	1300 Charleston Rd. Mountain View, CA 94043 415-335-7100
Add/Strip	(shareware)	Jon Wind 2374 Hillwood Dr. Maplewood, MN 55119 612-731-4840 CIS: 70167,3444 AOL: Jwind
Adobe Type Reunion ATM Illustrator Photoshop PostScript Fonts PageMaker PageMill SiteMill	Adobe Systems	1585 Charleston Road Mountain View, CA 94039 800-833-6687 415-961-4400
StuffIt Lite	Aladdin Systems	165 Westridge Dr. Watsonville, CA 95076 408-761-6200
AlkiSeek Alki MasterWord	Alki Software Corporation	300 Queen Anne Ave. N Suite 410 Seattle, WA 98109 206-286-2600
America Online	America Online	8619 Westwood Center Dr. Vienna, VA 22182 800-227-6364

Product	Manufacturer	Address
Before & After (magazine)	Before & After	1830 Sierra Gardens Dr. Suite 30 Roseville, CA 95661-2912 916-784-3880 sub. $36 per year
BlackBox	Alien Skin Software	322 Chapanoke Suite 101 Raliegh, NC 27603 919-832-4124 www.alienskin.com
Bookends Pro 3.1	Westing Software	134 Redwood Ave. Corte Madera, CA 94925 415-435-9343
CanOpener RescueTxt	Abbott Systems	62 Mountain Road Pleasantville, NY 10570 800-552-9157 914-747-4171
Capture	Mainstay	591-A Constitution Ave. Camarillo, CA 93012 805-484-9400
Compact Pro	(shareware)	Bill Goodman 109 Davis Ave. Brookline, MA 02146
CompuServe	CompuServe	5000 Arlington Centre Blvd. Columbus, OH 43220 800-848-8199 614-457-8600

continues

Product	Manufacturer	Address
Conflict Catcher	Casady & Greene	22734 Portola Dr. Salinas, CA 93908 408-484-9228
CREF (Computer Ready Electronic Files Booklet)	Scitex Graphic Arts Users Assn.	750 Old Hickory Blvd. Ste. 264, Brentwood TN 37027 800-858-0489
DeBabelizer	Equilibrium	475 Gate Five Road #225 Sausalito, CA 94965
DesignKit	Logic Arts	11475 Chickahominy Branch Dr. Glen Allen, VA 23060 804-266-7996
DocuComp	MASTERSOFT	8737 E. Via de Commercio Scottsdale, AZ 85258 800-624-6107
DOS Mounter	Dayna Communications	50 S. Main St., 5th Floor Salt Lake City, UT 84144 801-531-0600
DTP Forum	(see CompuServe)	GO DTPFORUM
DTP Journal	(magazine)	462 Old Boston St. Topsfield, MA 01483 800-887-7900 www.nadtp.com

Product	Manufacturer	Address
File Fanatic	(shareware)	Roby Sherman P.O. Box 63-04 Miami, FL 33163 rsherman@nthvax.- cs.miami.edu
Flash	BlackLightning, Inc.	Riddle Pond Road West Topsham, VT 05086 800-252-2599
FreeHand Fontographer	Macromedia (formerly Altsys)	600 Townsend St. Suite 310W San Francisco, CA 94103 415-252-2000
Fraemz, Arrowz Starz	ShadeTree Marketing	5515 N. 7th St. Suite 5-144 Phoenix, AZ 85014 602-279-3713
GalleyOops Get Info	Sundae Software (shareware)	Robert Gibson Carrying Place RR#1 Ontario, Canada K0K 1L0 CIS: 71261,2236
Graphics Suite LaserCheck	HiJaak Systems of Merritt	2551 Old Dobbin Dr. E. Mobile, AL 36695-3732 205-660-1240
TransVerter Pro	TechPool Studios	1463 Warrensville Road Center Cleveland, OH 44121 216-382-1234

continues

773

Product	Manufacturer	Address
Conversions Plus	DataViz Inc.	55 Corporate Dr. Trumbull, CT 06611 203-268-0030
KPT 3	MetaTools	6303 Carpentaria Ave.. Carpentaria, CA 93013 805-566-6289 www.metatools.com
Multimedia Dimensions Potpourri Marble and Granite	Artbeats	P.O. Box 709 Myrtle Creek, OR 97457 503-863-4429
Suitcase II Norton Utilities	Symantec	10201 Torre Ave. Cupertino, CA 95014 408-253-9600
Now Utilities	Now Software	921 SW Washington St. Ste. 500, 11th Floor Portland, OR 97205 503-274-2800
PageTools	Extensis Corporation	55 S. W. Yamhill St. 4th Floor Portland, OR 97204 800-796-9798 503-274-2020 extensis@aol.com Compuserve: 70242,33
PIXymbols Shadowkey	Precision Type	47 Mall Dr. Commack, NY 11725-5703 516-864-1067 800-248-3668

Product	Manufacturer	Address
PopChar	(shareware)	Gunther Blascheck Petzoldstrasse 31 A-4020 Linz Austria
POSTools	Azalea Software	P.O. Box 16745 Seattle, WA 98116-0745 800-48A-SOFT 206-937-5919
Professional Series (Photo CD Image Pacs)	Digital Stock	400 S. Sierra Ave. Suite 100 Solana Beach, CA 92075 800-545-4514 619-794-4040
Publish Americas (magazine)	Integrated Media Communications	1290 Avenue of the Americas New York, NY 10104 800-707-5173 sub. $39.90 per year
QuarkXPress	Quark, Inc.	300 S. Jackson Suite 100 Denver, CO 80209 800-778-7835 303-934-2211
RAM Doubler	Connectix	2655 Campus Dr., Suite. 100 San Mateo, CA 94403 415-571-5100

continues

Product	Manufacturer	Address
QuicKeys LaserStatus Mockpackage	CE Software	1801 Industrial Circle P.O. Box 65580 West Des Moines, IA 50265 515-224-1995
Resolution Trapping (disk-based tutorials)	Pixel Ink, Inc.	San Francisco, CA
SonarBookends 3.5 Sonar TOC 2.1	Virginia Systems, Inc.	5509 West Bay Court Midlothian, VA 23112 804-739-3200
Step-by-Step (newsletter)	Step-by-Step Publishing (division of Dynamic Graphics)	6000 N. Forest Park Dr. Peoria, IL 61614-3592 800-255-8800 sub. $48 per year
ThePage (newsletter)	The Cobb Group	P.O. Box 35160 Louisville, KY 40232 800-223-8720 sub. $65 per year
Techtures	Andromeda Software	699 Hampshire Rd. Westlake Vil, CA 91361 800-379-4109 www.andromeda.com
Tint Effects ColorSuite PRINT Casebooks	R.C. Publications	3200 Tower Oaks Blvd. Rockville, MD 20852-9789 800-222-2654

Product	Manufacturer	Address
Torquemada Mark My Words		Greg Swann 1006 West Main Street #101 Mesa, AZ 85201 CIS: 70640, 1574 gswann@mailhost.primenet.com
Word Excel	Microsoft Corporation	One Microsoft Way Redmond, WA 98052 206-882-8088
WordPerfect	Corel Corporation	1600 Cerling Way Ottowa, Ontario Canada K1Z 8R7 613-728-0826 www.corel.com
Zephyr Specs DisBatch SuperSnap	Zephyr Design	600 Fifth Avenue Suite 296 Seattle, WA 98104 206-545-0319
Zipit	(shareware)	Tommy Brown 110-45 Queens Blvd. #716 Forest Hills, NY 11375 CIS: 70314,3342 AOL: Tommy6 tbrown@minerva.cis.yale.edu
Object Series (and other digital stock photo art)	PhotoDisc	2013 Fourth Avenue Suite 402 Seattle, WA 98121 206-441-9355

continues

Product	Manufacturer	Address
[T-26]		361 West Chestnut Street First Floor Chicago, IL 60610
Treacyfaces		P.O. Box 26036 West Haven, CT 06516-8036 203-389-7037
GraphicConverter	(shareware)	Thorsten Lemke CIS: 100102,1304 thorsten_lemke@pe.maus.de
epsConverter	(shareware)	Sam Weiss Artemis Software P.O. Box 11488 Bainbridge Island, WA 98110-5488 AOL: ArtemisSW
Web Weaver	(shareware)	Robert C. Best III 118 Leroy St., Apt. N2 Potsdam, NY 13676 Robert.Best@potsdam.edu

PAGEMAKER 6.5
PLUG-INS

ADDING FUNCTIONALITY TO PAGEMAKER
WITH PLUG-INS

Extensibility is an important term when it comes to talking about software. It means that an application can do more than its designers intended, because it is open to the incorporation of other programmer's ideas and products. PageMaker ships with its own list of plug-ins, but users of any professional software always discover things they wish the software could accomplish, but can't. By incorporating plug-ins, PageMaker allows you to extend its infinite possibilities even further. You may find only an item or two in the following list that suits your present expansive creative needs, but a designer never knows what challenges tomorrow may hold. Here then is a short list of additional plug-ins and utilities that can add depth and functionality to your PageMaker compositions.

Adding Map Art to a PageMaker Document (Windows and Macintosh)

Whether you are doing serious cartographic work within PageMaker or just need to incorporate a map graphic, one of the most valuable reference CD-ROM libraries you can own is from Cartesia software (see Figure F.1). The CDs include geopolitical maps of both the U.S. and the World, as well as other map types. Because PageMaker enables you to import Illustrator files directly with the release of version 6.5, Cartesia's Designer Series of maps is useful. The Designer Series contains maps in Vector format that can be imported and edited in Illustrator, FreeHand, CorelDRAW!, or other vector drawing applications.

Figure F.1

Cartesia's MapArt Globes utility is perfect for PageMaker map needs.

Cartesia Map Types

The Cartesia Map CD-ROMs include several mapping types, any of which can be imported into a PageMaker document. All of the maps are either physical terrain maps, political boundary maps, or some combination of the two. Generally, they are separated into U.S. specific maps and maps for non-U.S. geography. Some of the collections are vector based while others address pixelated graphics (bitmaps). In all cases, different levels of detail are involved (Low-resolution for Web and video use, High-resolution for publishing applications). In many cases, grayscale maps are included for use as Alpha maps or other texturing and layering uses. The maps come with both text callouts and no text.

Cartesia Maps include the MapArt Designer Series-U.S.A. (with maps at the state and county levels), MapArt Designer Series-World (Regions, Countries, Oceans and Seas, and land-Water boundaries), and the MapArt Cartographic Data Bank-U.S.A. and world (with dozens of possible layers including Small to large cities, airports, roads and highways, railroads, islands and lakes, rivers, metro areas, and much more). The MapArt Globes series features 15 global perspectives of the Earth, with 13 possible overlays for each perspective in both Photoshop and Illustrator formats. Twelve color tables are also included along with 30 High-Resolution TIFF globes and 180 Low-Resolution globes. Grayscale maps are an anticipated future release that will be perfect for bump mapping features for multimedia use.

Cartesia's MapArt-Globes is part of the MapArt Terrain series of products. These maps show both physical and political features of different areas of the world from different perspectives and levels of detail. You can create customized and layered globes, or simply import and place finished global art into a PageMaker document in low or high resolution. The maps also work as grayscale images.

Where to use Cartesia Maps

◆ Other than producing a PageMaker generated Atlas, Cartesia Maps can be used in a number of ways in your PageMaker designs.

◆ Use a map to indicate your place of business, either globally or to actually direct others to your location. This is a common way to use map data, especially on the back of a brochure or within a mailer. When you are moving to a new place of business, it's always wise to send out a flyer with an included map that details the way to your new location.

◆ Use a map as part of your logo heading, giving your publication a more global look. Use a regional, national, or even global map as a background for your logo. This immediately pumps up the importance of your organization without saying one extra word.

continues

- Use a map as a hot spot on a PageMaker generated Web page so that when users click it (or image mapped parts of it) they are transported to that location for data or multimedia interaction. If you label a Web map to give users a hint about what they might find there, or what the next page they're transported to will contain, you get much more Web mileage (and surfers) out of your page design.

- Use a map as a ghosted out background for appropriate text overlay. Maps are just plain interesting, so even a ghosted map image invites elongated perception.

WORKING WITH NATIVE PAGEMAKER PLUG-INS AND EXTERNAL DRAWING FX

Unless you use PageMaker as a type-only application, you are going to encounter situations that demand either image processed graphics or new graphics altogether. Your PageMaker documents are going to need both Vector and Bitmap graphics at one time or another and most times stock images will not do. PageMaker users come from two separate camps of thought. One segment of the PageMaker community leans toward the publishing end of the spectrum, whereas the other part of the PageMaker population approaches PageMaker as an artist's extension. It takes both artistic and publishing savvy to create PageMaker documents that stand the test of time and usability. If you stay with PageMaker long enough, even if your background experience focuses more on publishing than graphics design, you will encounter the need to stretch your talents towards creating graphic content. At that point, unless you simply decide to farm out all of your graphics to established professionals, you will be forced to learn applications that have the tools you require.

If you are an experienced and successful PageMaker user, you have already accumulated a good amount of graphics design training, even though you may lack an academic degree in design. After using PageMaker long enough, you'll have a better idea of how to compose elements in a document so that they look balanced, serving both your clients and readership.

If you are a design professional using PageMaker, you constantly realize that design education never ends. You are forever on the lookout for new and better (up-to-date and economical) ways of generating interesting images and compositions. PageMaker 6.5 has some special gifts for you, no matter what end of the spectrum you call home.

For the desktop publisher needing a gentle invitation into image processing and effects, PageMaker can address Photoshop plug-ins from within PageMaker. Four specific Photoshop plug-ins that you will find useful to your creative endeavors can be accessed from within PageMaker. Even professional designers unaware of these applications and what they offer will find this section of potential value because it contains both explanatory text and copious illustrations.

To open the proper effects in PageMaker after placing your selected image, go to the Element/Image/Photoshop Effects menu item (see Figure F.2). The effects are located in PageMaker's RSRC folder under Plug-ins/Effects.

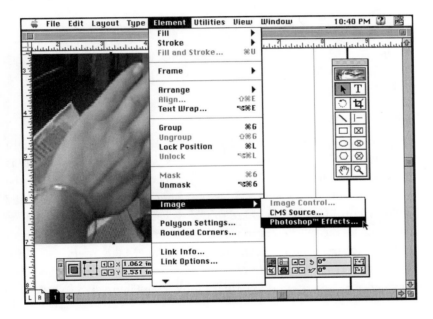

Figure F.2

The Element/Image/Photoshop Effects menu.

A SELECTION OF INTERNAL PAGEMAKER PLUG-IN EFFECTS

Four effects questions a PageMaker user should ask:

1. How useful is the effect to PageMaker needs?

2. Does the effect emulate "looks" commonly associated with the printing tradition?

3. Can the effect produce unique and startling results?

4. Does the effect have a range of options, so that it doesn't become too "noticeable"?

Note

Photoshop plug-in effects work best when the image has a fairly high contrast. This allows the image to be seen more clearly through the effect.

Gallery Effects

These effects were developed originally by Aldus. When Adobe bought Aldus, they were renamed Gallery Effects, and now they come as resident plug-ins inside Photoshop 4.0. because of this, they can be accessed from PageMaker's Photoshop plug-ins menu (Element/Image/ Photoshop Effects). These are in a class called media effects because they make the selected graphic look as if it were created in the media chosen (charcoal, watercolor, and so on). PageMaker users can utilize them to best advantage on nondescriptive technical images that need to evidence a "softer" and "warmer" look. (See Figures F.3 to F.26).

Gallery Effects: Volume 1. Charcoal

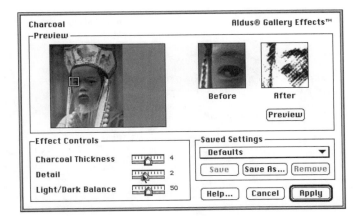

Figure F.3

The original photo in the Charcoal dialog box.

Figure F.4

Charcoal Settings: Thickness=1, Detail=0, Light/Dark=50.

Figure F.5

Charcoal Settings: Thickness=5, Detail=4, Light/Dark=24.

Gallery Effects: Volume 1. Fresco

Figure F.6

The Original Photo in the Fresco dialog box.

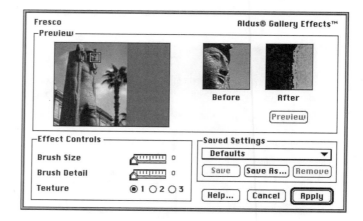

Figure F.7

Fresco Settings: Brush Size=1, Brush Detail=5, Texture=2.

Figure F.8

Fresco Settings: Brush Size=2, Brush Detail=10, Texture=3.

Gallery Effects: Volume 1. Graphic Pen

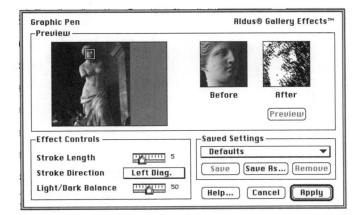

Figure F.9

The Original Photo in the Graphic Pen dialog box.

Figure F.10

Graphic Pen settings: Stroke Length=5, Direction=Left, Light/Dark=50.

Figure F.11

Graphic Pen settings: Stroke Length=15, Direction=Left, Light/Dark=60.

Gallery Effects: Volume 2. Colored Pencil

Figure F.12

The Original Photo in the Colored Pencil dialog box.

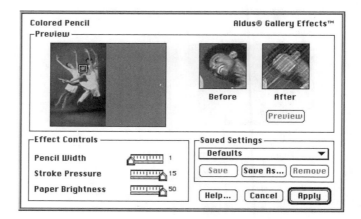

Figure F.13

Colored Pencil Settings: Pencil Width=24, Stroke Pressure=15, Paper Brightness=50.

Figure F.14

Colored Pencil Settings: Pencil Width=13, Stroke Pressure=10, Paper Brightness=0.

Gallery Effects: Volume 2. Photocopy

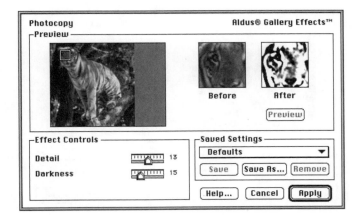

Figure F.15

The Original Photo in the Photocopy dialog box.

Figure F.16

Photocopy Settings: Detail=13, Darkness=15.

Figure F.17

Photocopy Settings: Detail=4, Darkness=48.

Gallery Effects: Volume 2. Patchwork

Figure F.18

The Patchwork settings dialog box with the original image.

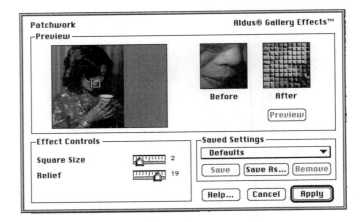

Figure F.19

Patchwork Settings: Square Size=2, Relief=18.

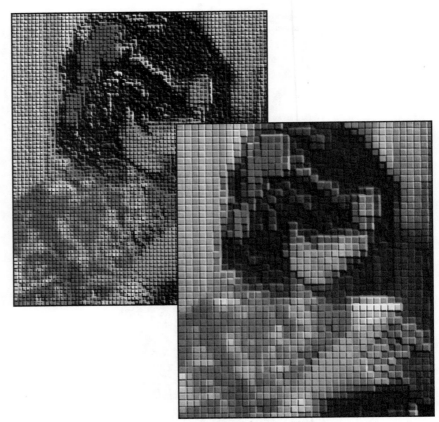

Figure F.20

Patchwork Settings: Square Size=8, Relief=15.

Gallery Effects: Volume 3. Conté Crayon

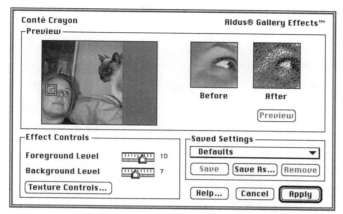

Figure F.21

The Conté Crayon dialog box displaying the original image.

Figure F.22

Conté Crayon Settings: Foreground Level=10, Background Level=7.

Figure F.23

Conté Crayon Settings: Foreground Level=14, Background Level=5.

Gallery Effects: Volume 3. Halftone Screen

Note

When using the Dot type, it's best to use a high-contrast setting, effectively making the image black-and-white. Otherwise, you run the risk of getting moires on the printout due to a PageMaker screen of a screen when the graphic is printed!

Figure F.24

The Halftone dialog box with the original image.

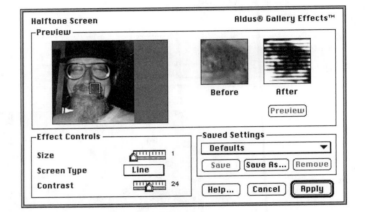

Figure F.25

Figure F.26

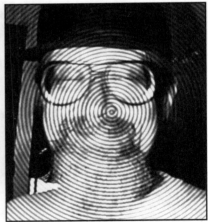

Halftone Settings: Size=2, Contrast=36, Type=Line.

Halftone Settings: Size=2, Contrast=15, Type=Circle.

Gallery Effects: Volume 3. Water Paper

Water Paper has three controls: Fiber Length, Brightness, and Contrast (see Figures F.27 to F.29). The higher you push the Fiber Length, the more blurred the image gets. For PageMaker projects, you should stay at 10 or below. The final result of this effect is a dreamy image, just right for hazy and romantic topics and projects.

Figure F.27

Water Paper settings: Fiber Length=10, Brightness=88, Contrast=72.

Figure F.28

Water Paper settings: Fiber Length=14, Brightness=62, Contrast=72.

Figure F.29

Water Paper settings: Fiber Length=4, Brightness=100, Contrast=100.

Andromeda Effects Volumes

Andromeda Software produces five volumes of unique Photoshop Effects plug-ins that can be accessed and applied from within PageMaker. Described here are the first three volumes. Volume 1 deals with more standard plug-ins, including reflection and rainbow effects, for example. Volume 2 is a full 3-D effects application, allowing you to wrap selected image areas around or on 3-D shapes. Volume 3 is a wonderful collection for PageMaker DTP use because it centers upon the application of diverse line and Mezzotint screens.

Andromeda cMulti

Figure F.30

The cMulti dialog box showing original image and controls.

Figure F.31

cMulti Settings: Area=Radial, SpokeTran=On, Width=100%, Number Areas=5, Transition=100%, Intensity=100%.

Figure F.32

cMulti Settings: Area= Square, SpokeTran=On, Width=75, Number Areas=10, Transition=100%, Intensity=75%.

Andromeda Effects Reflection

Figure F.33

*Andromeda Effects Reflection
Filter dialog box and the
original image.*

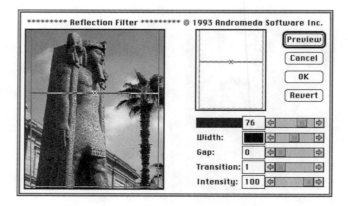

Figure F.34

*Andromeda Effects Reflection
settings: Width=35, Gap=0,
Transition=11, Intensity=100%.*

Figure F.35

*Andromeda Effects Reflection
settings: Width=100,
Gap=100, Transition=20,
Intensity=40%.*

Andromeda Effects 3-D Volume 2

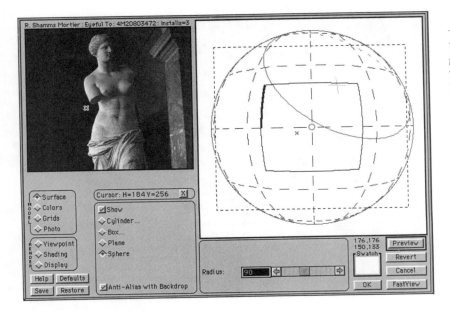

Figure F.36

The Andromeda Effects 3-D plug-in dialog box, showing the variety of controls and switches for customizing the output.

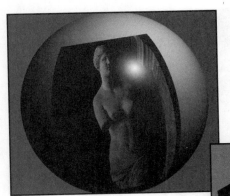

Figure F.37

The image wrapped on a 3-D sphere.

Figure F.38

The image wrapped on a 3-D cube.

Andromeda Effects: Screens Volume 3

Figure F.39

The Andromeda Effects Screens dialog box, showing the original graphic.

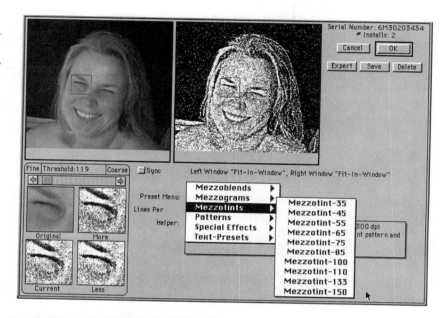

Figure F.40

A 55 lpi Mezzogram.

Figure F.41

A 35 lpi Mezzotint.

Figure F.42

A 20 lpi Circles pattern.

Figure F.43

A 20 Spokes pattern at 30 lpi.

Figure F.44

A 20 lpi Wavy and Sharp Star pattern.

Figure F.45

A Swirl 20 pattern at 30 lpi.

Figure F.46

A Wavy Circle pattern at 20 lpi.

Figure F.47

Special Effects: Butterflyeeeee.

Figure **F.48**

A 20 lpi Intaglio Etching Special Effect

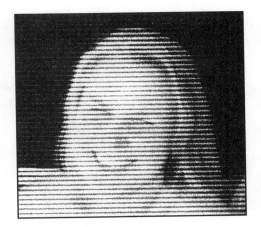

Figure **F.49**

A 20 lpi Intaglio Woodblock Special Effect.

Figure **F.50**

A selection of Type Effects: (top down) Capital Corrosion, Ribbon Stack, Rose Vine, and Serrated Swirl.

MetaTool's KPTools

Kai's Power Tools is a group of image effects responsible for much of the marketplace lust for new Photoshop effects. The most startling aspect of these tools is the design of their collective interfaces, making the application of effects more similar to an addictive game environment than to a mere professional application. Version 3.0 of KPTools lists dozens of exquisite image processing effects, only a few of which are listed here. As Photoshop plug-ins, they can all be accessed and applied from PageMaker 6.5.

KPTools Page Curl

Figure F.51

The Page Curl dialog box is a small Control panel that sits above the selected graphic.

Figure F.52

A curl that reveals the same image underneath.

Figure F.53

This effect is almost an optical illusion. The Page Curl seems to be transparent and reveals a subtle clone of the same photo beneath.

KPTools Planar Tiling

Figure F.54

The KPTools Planar Tiling interface sits on top of the selected graphic.

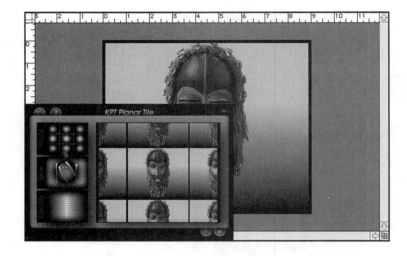

Figure F.55

A Perspective Planar Tiling with clouds added in the sky backdrop.

Figure F.56

A Perspective Planar Tiling made 50% transparent enabling the original image to shine through.

KPTools Vortex Tiling

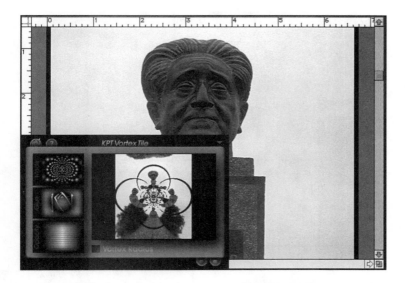

Figure F.57

The KPTools Vortex Tiling dialog box sits on top of the selected graphic.

Figure F.58

A Pinch Vortex can be moved anywhere on the image, often producing some bizarre results.

Figure F.59

Using the "Difference" setting with an 85% opacity on a Pinched Vortex produces a dream-like quality.

KPTools Gradient Designer

Figure F.60

The KPTools Gradient Designer interface takes over the screen and enables you to choose from a library of gradients or customize your own.

Figure F.61

This circular Burst Gradient was applied as a Positive Procedural at a 50% Saturation.

Figure F.62

This circular Burst Gradient was applied as a Negative Procedural at a 50% Saturation.

AlienSkin's BlackBox Effects

AlienSkin Software calls its Photoshop plug-ins collection Blackbox Effects. Version 3 is the present one. The BlackBox effects are both media effects and also emulate natural phenomena (fire, smoke, atmospheric swirls, and more). The Blackbox effects offer organic options for image processing.

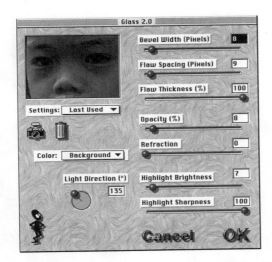

Figure F.63

The BlackBox Glass effect dialog box allows you to preview all command set alterations.

Figure F.64

Glass Settings: Bevel Width=10, Flaw Space=10, Flaw Thickness=50%, Opacity=50%, Refraction=10, Hilight Brightness=10, Hilight Sharpness=50, Light Direction=135 degrees.

Figure F.65

Glass Settings: Bevel Width=5, Flaw Space=10, Flaw Thickness=60%, Opacity=50%, Refraction=40, Hilight Brightness=60, Hilight Sharpness=100, Light Direction=45 degrees.

807

Figure F.66

The Swirl dialog box enables you to see an instant preview of any changes you make to the parameters.

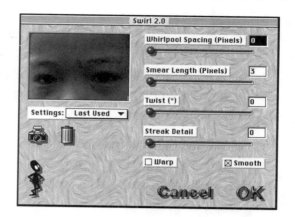

Figure F.67

Swirl Settings: Whirlpool Spacing=10, Smear Length=10, Twist=10, Streak Detail=10, Warp and Smoothing=ON.

Figure F.68

Swirl Settings: Whirlpool Spacing=50, Smear Length=10, Twist=50, Streak Detail=50, Warp and Smoothing=ON.

Illustrator/FreeHand Plug-Ins

PageMaker 6.5 now enables you to place Illustrator files as native rather than as EPS files only. The primary benefits of allowing this include file maintenance and the elimination of version control issues, with a side benefit of saving disk space, because Adobe Illustrator files take less space than EPS graphics. This emphasizes the connection between Illustrator and PageMaker and means that the effects applications usable from within Illustrator have a more direct effect on the graphics that PageMaker can utilize. To that end, it is important for the designer to be aware of Illustrator plug-ins, especially those that can shape and alter text blocks that a PageMaker design could benefit from. Three very high-end Illustrator plug-ins can be used to produce text blocks for PageMaker and are vital for the designer: DrawTools from Extensis, Stylist from BlackBox, and KPT VectorFX from MetaTools. It is important to keep in mind that using these Illustrator tools and exporting the resulting graphics to PageMaker can give you text looks that are impossible to achieve in PageMaker alone.

It should be noted that except Stylist from BlackBox, the plug-ins mentioned here also work with Macromedia FreeHand. Macromedia FreeHand is a favorite drawing application for many PageMaker users, Stylist is an Illustrator 6+ only plug-in, because of the way that Illustrator works with Styles.

Extensis DrawTools

DrawTools consists of three effects plug-ins that address different parameters in Adobe Illustrator: DrawTools Color, DrawTools Move, and DrawTools Shape (for Macromedia FreeHand users, DrawTools Move is not applicable). DrawTools Color is a collection of five filters that enhance your ability to control the colors in an Illustrator graphic. With DrawTools Color, you can edit color ramps, mix and replace colors, convert objects to grayscale, and create duotones, tritones, and multitones. DrawTools Move contains five filters that give you discreet control over object positions within and between layers. DrawTools Move also enables you to resize objects and extend your control over complex object structures within a single layer or between layers. DrawTools Shape is a collection of seven filters that enable you to apply three-dimensional effects to objects by constraining them to specific geometric shapes. You can project objects onto a sphere, cylinder, cone, or diamond. Freeform projection onto a waveform is also allowed for creating pseudo three-dimensional art. As far as exporting the finished objects into PageMaker and their importance to the PageMaker user (especially for Text FX), the three DrawTools plug-ins can be prioritized in the following order: Shape, Color, Move.

Extensis DrawTools Shape

There are seven DrawTools Shape effects: Amplified Waves, Cone, Cylinder, Diamond, Free Projection, Globe, and Water. Each has its own dialog box where numeric parameters are entered (see Figure F.69). No visual preview feedback is provided. All of the DrawTools Shape effects produce pseudo 3-D results, as if the selected graphics were wrapped on 3-D objects. The finished graphics can be saved in a number of formats, with the most common ones for PageMaker use being either EPS or Illustrator itself. PageMaker 6.5's capability to import the smaller Illustrator files directly makes this the best choice for PageMaker users.

Figure F.69

Extensis DrawTools Shape is accessed from the Adobe Illustrator Filter menu.

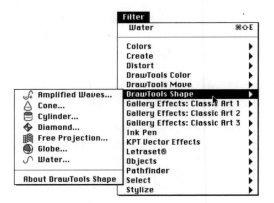

Amplified Waves

Amplified Waves produces an effect similar to a wave bubble that moves toward the viewer. Two main controls, Frequency and Amplitude, determine the shape of the 3-D Wave (see Figure F.70). *Frequency* is defined as one complete wave, expressed as a percentage of the rectangle that covers the selected graphic. *Amplitude* is defined as the height of each successive wave (which is perceived as a bubble that the selected graphic is wrapped around). To appreciate what this means visually, look at the examples in Figure F.71. The caption to this figure lists the Frequency/Amplitude parameters for each of the four samples, from top to bottom.

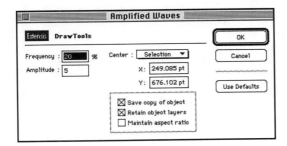

Figure F.70

The Shape/Amplified Wave effect is determined by the Frequency and Amplitude menu options.

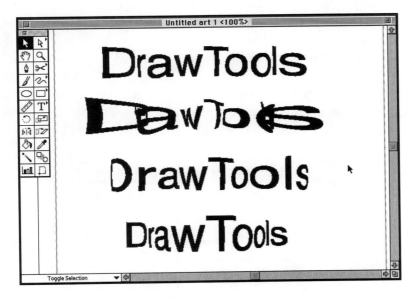

Figure F.71

The Frequency/Amplitude parameters entered into the Amplified Waves dialog box to produce the previous samples (top to bottom) are: 20/5, 20/25, 30/10, 60/20.

Cone

Cone produces an effect similar to wrapping the selected graphic on a 3-D cone. The controls that determine the shape of the cone are: Height (the percentage of the selection rectangle), Base Diameter (percentage of selection rectangles width), Top Diameter (also percentage of selection rectangles width), Interpolation (if the cone is viewed from the top or bottom, with positive numbers equal to top views and negative numbers to bottom views), and Angle (the angle of the graphic on the page). (See Figure F.72.)

Figure F.72

The Shape/Cone effect is determined by the Height, Base Diameter, Top Diameter, Interpolation, and Angle menu options.

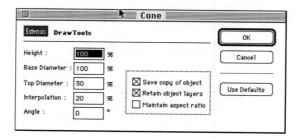

Cylinder

Cylinder produces an effect similar to wrapping the selected graphic on a 3-D cylinder and is a great tool for creating labels on 3-D cans for PageMaker designs. The controls that determine the shape of the cylinder are: Height (the height as determined by a percentage of the selection rectangle), Diameter (as determined by the width of the selection rectangle), Interpolation (whether the view is positive, from the top, or negative, from the bottom), and Angle (the angle of the graphic on the page). (See Figure F.73.)

Figure F.73

The Cylinder effect is determined by the Height, Diameter, and Interpolation menu options.

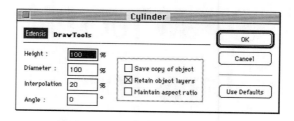

Diamond

The Diamond effect creates a parallelogram out of the chosen selection. This effect is not very useful for text blocks or single letters because it makes the text unreadable. The Diamond effect can create some interesting patterns from single letters, however, which can in turn be used as decorative elements in PageMaker designs (see Figure F.74).

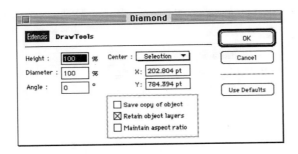

Figure F.74

The Diamond effect is determined by the Height, Diameter, and Angle menu options.

Free Projection

This is the most variable effect for text blocks in the Extensis DrawTools kit. The effect is as if the text block is pasted on a rubber sheet. By adjusting the sheet's control points, you affect the text block's appearance. This enables you to shape text to fit the confines of objects in PageMaker and the resulting shapes can be imported onto a specific layer (see Figure F.75).

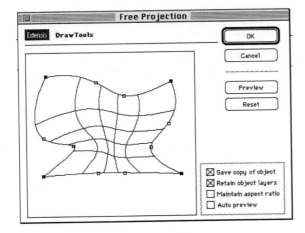

Figure F.75

The Free Projection effect is determined by your interactive manipulation of an onscreen grid.

Globe

With the Globe effect, your selected graphic acts as if it were wrapped on the face of a 3-D globe. In PageMaker, this effect is best applied when the text is placed over a spherical surface, like a ball. In PageMaker 6.5, the text can be placed on a layer over another layer that holds the textured ball or sphere (see Figure F.76).

Figure F.76

The Globe effect is determined by the Height, Diameter, and Angle settings.

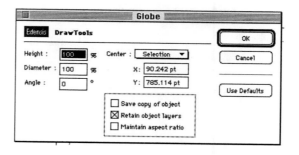

Water

The difference between this effect and Amplified Waves is that the Water effect seems to take place on a flat plane while Amplified Waves gives more of a sense of a 3-D volume. The idea is the same. Using this effect with a text block produces interesting variance in the shapes of the letters (see Figure F.77). Look at the results of some samples in Figure F.78.

Figure F.77

The Extensis Water effect is determined by setting the Frequency (quantity) and Amplitude (strength) of the observed "ripples."

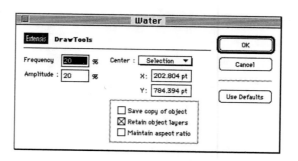

Note

Multiple lines of text can also be treated with Extensis DrawTools Shapes. This can be effective for PageMaker posters and mailers, especially when the occasion calls for a radical approach to make the text stand out. (See Figure F.78.)

Figure F.78

Shape option examples.

Multiple lines of text in Figure F.78 show the effects of various Extensis DrawTools Shape options (left to right, and top to bottom): Normal, Amplified Waves, Amplified Waves #2, Cone, Cylinder, Free Projection #1, Free Projection #2, Globe, Water.

Tip

There are times when your topmost text lines can disappear or get too squashed to read when you use Extensis DrawTools Shapes. If this happens, do the following:

1. *When you type in your text, include an extra top and bottom line.*

2. *Turn the text into outlines by selecting Create Outlines from the text menu as usual.*

3. *Select the top and bottom lines, and color them the hue of the paper (usually white), so that they disappear.*

4. *Select all of the lines, even the invisible white ones, as targets for a Shape effect.*

5. *When a Shape effect is applied, the invisible lines will act as a buffer, making all of the needed text more visible and readable. This is especially valuable when treating text with the Extensis DrawTools Globe Shapes plug-in.*

PROFESSIONAL PAGEMAKER SOLUTIONS PROVIDED BY EXTENSIS DRAWTOOLS SHAPE

Need: To design a headline that looks as if rippling waves were applied to it.

Solution: Use DrawTools Shape/Amplified Wave or Water in Illustrator to apply the effect, save the work in Illustrator format, and import into PageMaker. Place the text on a separate layer in PageMaker "over" a rippling liquid graphic background.

Need: To design a text block that takes on the appearance of a label for a can.

Solution: Use DrawTools Shape/Cylinder to get the look in Illustrator. Save the design and import it into PageMaker. Place the text on a separate layer in PageMaker, "over" the graphic background shape.

Need: To design a text block that is wrapped on a sphere or globe.

Solution: Use DrawTools Shape/Globe in Illustrator to achieve the effect. Make sure to include blank (invisible) beginning and ending lines above and below the text block so that the top and bottom text can still be read. Refer to the text on DrawTools/Shape/Globe to refresh your memory on this action if you need to.

Need: To give a text block or headline a unique "hand-drawn" appearance, or to produce what is called Beatnik text styles.

Solution: Use the DrawTools Shape/FreeForm Projection effect to warp the text to your liking. Save and import into PageMaker for placement on a separate layer.

Need: To design unique graphic ornaments that will be placed within a PageMaker project (perhaps for use as bullets, or just floaters).

Solution: Consider using the DrawTools Shape/Diamond module in Illustrator to target single letters, transforming them into ornaments. The best letters to use are those capitals with either bilateral or single axis symmetry: H, M, O, S, T, U, V, W, X, Z.

DRAWTOOLS COLOR

This Extensis DrawTools plug-in is useful if you want to manipulate the color in a graphic before importing it to PageMaker. It must be emphasized that DrawTools Color can be used only on Vector artwork, not on placed EPS graphics or imported bitmap graphics. Although no plug-ins or filters can create Spot Colors, DrawTools Color can replace and edit selected Spot Colors with Process Colors. A Color List in DrawTools Colors displays all of the Spot Colors used in a document and also all of the Spot Colors present but not currently used. This makes selecting and editing Spot Colors easier. Fill Patterns used in targeted DrawTools Color work are omitted from all operations. DrawTools Color supports editing CMYK Process Colors, Spot Colors, and Gray Gradients. RGB, CMY, IHS, K, and CMYK color models are supported. When a color model is not supported, it is converted to CMYK first. DrawTools Color does support UCR (Under Color Removal) to allow for precise conversions.

Six distinct color options are in DrawTools Color: Color Mixer/Replace Colors, Edit Curves, Gradient Settings, Grayscale Mode, Multitone, Random Color Replace. Each has its use in preparing a graphic for use in PageMaker. (See Figure F.79.)

Figure F.79

The six Color options are listed in the Filters/DrawTools Color menu.

Color Mixer/Replace Colors enables you to select any color in your artwork and change it by a system of CMYK color sliders (see Figure F.80). The Color Mixer enables you to play with new colors to add to the selected graphic. The color files can be saved and loaded to be applied to another graphic selection. It's easier to adjust the artwork's palette before you place the graphic in PageMaker, than to attempt to adjust it after it's placed.

Figure F.80

The DrawTools Color Color Mixer/Replace Colors dialog box.

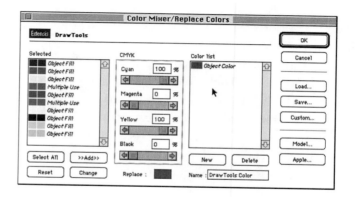

The Grayscale Mode operator converts your artwork to grayscale in one easy step. It can be applied to a whole page or a selected graphic. You can select or exclude the following options from the grayscale conversion: Object Fills, Object Strokes, Text Fills, Text Strokes, Custom Colors. Random Color Replace is an absolute gem and you should find it highly suitable to PageMaker imported graphics. A perfect PageMaker use for Random Color Replace is to target cloned graphics that need separate palette looks (poster art would be a good choice for this effect). This plug-in randomly replaces colors on color objects and adds colors to black-and-white art. The Gradient Settings option is a toggle on/off plug-in. If set to on, it tells the Color filters that it's okay to edit Illustrator gradients.

Edit Curves

This plug-in enables you to alter the Brightness and Contrast values of each of the CMYK channels by adjusting the curve that represents the CMYK low, mid-range, and high-end values. You can also enter numerical data that distinguishes input values from output values (see Figure F.81).

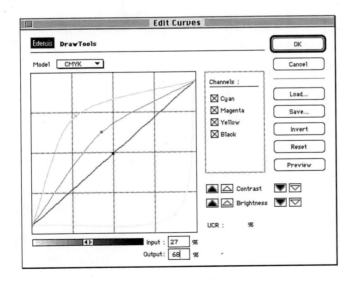

Figure F.81

The Edit Curves dialog box gives you delicate control over each CMYK channel in the Image palette.

819

Multitone

The DrawTools Color/Multitone plug-in gives you perfect duotone, tritone, and multitonal artwork every time (see Figure F.82). You can control the hues in the palette as well as the quantity of tones.

Figure F.82

The Multitone plug-in prepares instant duotones, tritones, and multitones for export to PageMaker.

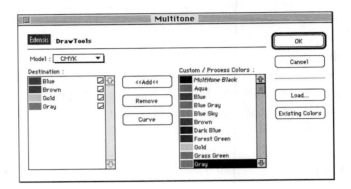

A Professional PageMaker Solution by Extensis DrawTools Color

Need: To design a page that displays six different graphic elements, all from the same graphic, and all with variations on a single Color palette.

Solution: This is definitely a task for DrawTools Color in Illustrator. Proceed in the following manner:

1. Draw or import your graphic (not an EPS file, but a Vector Drawing save).

2. Clone the graphic as many times as needed and separate the clones in whatever manner desired.

3. Use the DrawTools Color/Random Color Replace to alter the images so their palettes differ widely.

4. Use the DrawTools Color/Mulitone effect to apply a single palette to all of the cloned images. The result will be the same palette, but with widely different graphic looks. You can even transform this finished image into grayscale if the needs of the job demand a noncolor design.

BLACKBOX STYLIST FOR ADOBE ILLUSTRATOR 6.X+

If you are a devoted PageMaker user and also own Illustrator, the BlackBox Stylist application can help you add hundreds of style effects to PageMaker text. Stylist is an Illustrator plug-in especially designed to create text effects. After the text is created and the needed effects applied, the finished work can be exported to PageMaker for placement. The numerous effects possible with Stylist make it an essential utility for PageMaker as far as professional text effect options are concerned (see Figure F.83).

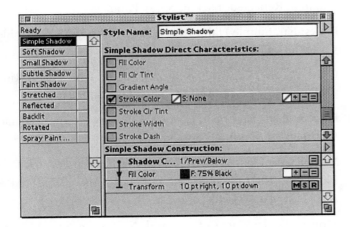

Figure F.83

The Stylist dialog box displays all of the loaded style libraries and their construction parameters.

Styles in Illustrator 6 and above are characteristics that can be applied to selected graphics. Styles can be saved and loaded for use as needed. Designing a style and saving it makes it available for use by Stylist. The parameters that can be utilized to form a specific style in Stylist are limitless and can include: Glows, Neons, Web, Halos, Patterns (for both fills and edges), and many more. Stylist comes with 11 Style Libraries, each of which holds groups of separate styles. You can design your own styles as you become accustomed to the process; amassing your specific styles for targeted clients is possible. A listing of the 11 style libraries that ship with Stylist and their style contents is as follows:

- **City Planner:** Highway, Single Lane, Dirt Road, Residential, and Commercial.

- **Dashes:** Plus, Plus-Minus, Hollow Dash, New Mexico, Circle Plus, Equals, Weaves, Circle, Bullseye, Pacman, Klingon.

- **Dividers:** Simple Row/Column, Squeezed Row/Column, Swollen Row/Column, Tumble Row/Column, Flip Row/Column.

- **Drop Shadows:** Simple, Soft, Small, Subtle, Faint, Stretched, Rotated, Reflected, Backlit, Spray Paint.

- **Edges:** Fat, Simple Halo, Rings, Faded Rings, Web, Stubble, Caffeine, Gnats.

- **Glows:** Fuzzy, Fuzzy Halo, Inverse, Metal Rim, Metal Rim Outline, Neon, Neon Offset, Neon Stripes, Stencil.

- **Hipster Text:** Artsy 1-4, Relax 1-3, Sloppy Sharp, Scale Down, Outline Left, Outline Top, Outline Only.

- **Map:** Ruler, Double Line, Triple Line, Thin and Thick Divider, Holes, Railroad, Body of Water, Creek, Toxic, Wildlife Reserve, City Park, Trails, and Dots.

- **Motion Trails:** Blast Off, General, No Stroke, Shrink, Over the Hole, Twist, Flying Logo.

- **Specialized:** Railroad Track, Millipede, Chain, Worm, Pearls, Button.

- **Utility:** Pop to Top, Ghost on Top, Do Not Print, 0.1 and 1 Point Black Outline, 0.1 and 1 Point White Outline.

Note

The advantage of using Stylist to add styles to text in Illustrator is that the targeted text need not be turned into outlines first. Stylist works best when it is the last effect applied in a chain.

Stylist enables you to load in as many style libraries as your allocated memory will accommodate. Any number of selected styles can be applied to the same selection in a style sandwich. When applying multiple styles, members in the list can be moved around so that different overlaps can be employed. Styles can be deleted and copied, so that separate libraries of your favorite styles can be constructed and saved. The elements that make up any styles construction are shown in the bottom portion of the Stylist dialog box and can be customized to create personal styles and style libraries. If you have to correct spellings after a style is applied, Stylist remembers the parameters and your corrections take on the selected style immediately. Four figures follow, giving you a visual appreciation for how Stylist works, what it can do, and how your PageMaker creations might benefit by its use.

Figure F.84

Stylist Glow styles applied from top to bottom: Fuzzy Glow, Fuzzy Halo, Neon, Metal Rim, Neon Stripes, Inverse Glow.

Stylist

Stylist

Stylist

Stylist

Stylist

Stylist

Stylist Shadow styles applied from top to bottom: Simple Shadow, Subtle Shadow, Stretched Shadow, Reflected Shadow, Backlit Shadow.

Figure F.86

Stylist Hipster styles applied from top to bottom: Artsy 2, Relax Pastel, Artsy 4, Sloppy Sharp, Scale Down.

Stylist Motion Trail styles applied from top to bottom: BlastOff, General, Shrink, Twist.

Professional PageMaker Solutions Provided by BlackBox Stylist

Need: To design a page that displays speed lines emanating from a text block.

Solution: Use the Stylist Motion Trail library and apply one of the motion styles to your selected text. Export the graphic to PageMaker.

Need: To design a page that displays a text block sitting on a reflective surface.

Solution: Use the Stylist Shadow library and select the reflected Shadow style. Go into the construction menu in the Stylist dialog and recolorize the "shadow" the same as the text color but about 50% lighter. Export the graphic to PageMaker.

Need: To design a simple map for a PageMaker mailer.

Solution: Use the Stylist map styles to create basic map symbols for the map. You can target the styles to simple shapes such as rectangles and ovals. Export the finished map to PageMaker and use the Text tools to add descriptive data to the map on a separate layer.

MetaTools VectorFX Overview

Unlike the other two Illustrator FX applications mentioned, VectorFX presents you with a visual display including full interactive previews. The interface to VectorFX (or rather the interfaces of each module) enable you WYSIWYG control over all of the modification parameters, including 3-D transformations of the selected graphics. VectorFX can be applied to both artwork and type, but for PageMaker users, it's the type specific effects that are most important. PageMaker users who also work in Illustrator will want to utilize VectorFX for headlines and subheads. Applying these effects to body type content is not suggested because it makes all but a small text block appear too busy and hard to read. For major headlines and subheads, however, VectorFX can add unique effects. It contains a total of 13 VectorFX plug-ins, including: 3-D Transform, ColorTweak, Emboss, Flare, Inset, Neon,

Point Editor, Resize&Reposition, Shadowland, ShatterBox, Sketch, Vector Distort, and WarpFrame. Each offers important creative options for Illustrator users who need to develop alternative looks for PageMaker projects.

3-D Transform

The 3-D Transform plug-in turns your selected graphic into 3-D, complete with your choice of extrusion depth and rotational angle. Rotation in 3-D space, beveling of the front face of the type, Perspective view angle, Color, Light direction and color, and the perceived "metalicity" of the text (how it reflects light), are all customizable here. You can zoom in on the text block for a closer look, and the complexity (number of points in the drawing) can be adjusted. Higher complexity means smoother looking output. The effect can be viewed as a wireframe or as a fully rendered drawing. (See Figure F.88.)

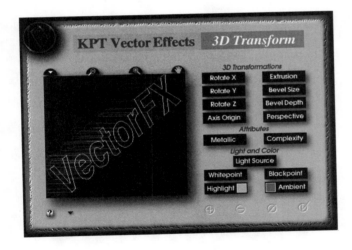

Figure F.88

The VectorFX/3-D Transform interface.

ColorTweak

This plug-in addresses color on all CMYK channels, allowing an instant preview of any alterations. You can also adjust the brightness and contrast, as well as take advantage of a list of presets. The interface can be minimized so that you can work with a smaller menu of choices and see your Illustrator screen at the same time. (See Figure F.89.)

Figure F.89

*The VectorFX/ColorTweak
interface.*

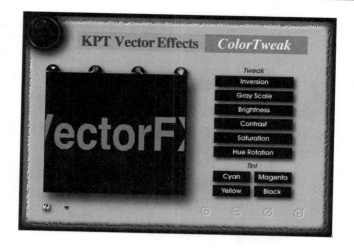

Emboss

Embossed text is often used to denote a classical or higher order message. This plug-in can add embossing to any selected text block and lets you control the Contrast, Angle, and Amount of the embossing. (See Figure F.90.)

Figure F.90

*The VectorFX/Emboss
interface.*

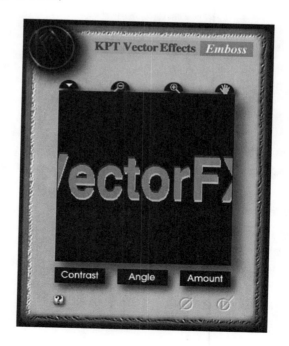

Flares

In computer graphics, a flare of light is usually associated with bitmap and 3-D applications, but the VectorFX flares are designed to address vector graphics. Although the finished flare comes in as an object, it remains invisible. Its effects, however, are visible and display as a lighter color on the selected graphic. VectorFX Flares can be multiplied and placed in the interactive interface with their size, halo, and flare spokes customized. (See Figure F.91.)

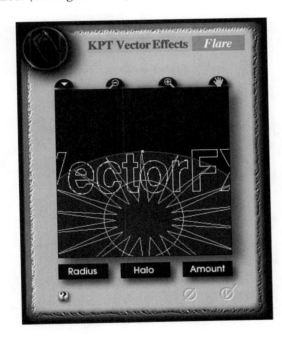

Figure F.91

The VectorFX/Flare interface.

Note

If you need to create multiple flares, keep their arms (or spokes) at a minimum and compose the graphic all at once by duplicating the flares in the first interface that's opened. Flare computation is intense and consumes a lot of memory in the process.

Inset

An Inset is a duplicate of the selected graphic that is sized smaller and placed over the original. This Inset plug-in enables you to control the size of the Inset (Amount) and the way it is chiseled out of the original selection (Round, Beveled, Mitered). Chiseled is the keyword because the final graphic looks like a text block carved out of granite in the classical style. Insets can also be colorized, producing a multicolored outline text block. (See Figure F.92.)

Figure F.92

The VectorFX/Inset interface.

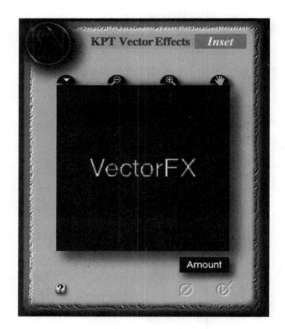

Neon

The best thing about the Neon glows is that you can customize and preview them in real time from the VectorFX/Neon interface. Only the Amount and Brightness of the Neonized text can be altered, which looks more like outlined text than neon. If you need more variable and professional neon effects, Blackbox Stylist software is recommended. (See Figure F.93.)

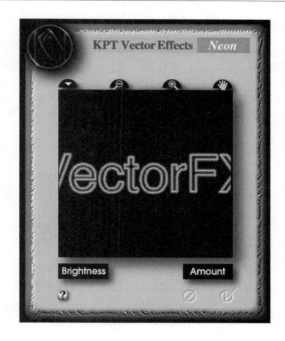

Point Editor

Just as PageMaker enables you to align blocks of text, VectorFX/Point Editor enables you to align selected points in a vector drawing. A headline can be altered by moving selected points so that they line up with each other, allowing you to create original-looking font effects for your PageMaker compositions. (See Figure F.94.)

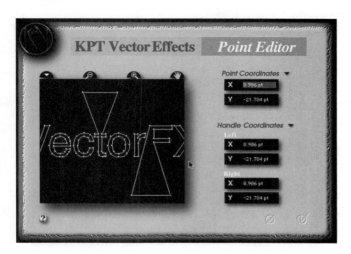

Figure F.94

The VectorFX/Point Editor interface.

Resize and Reposition

No mystery here, because this plug-in does exactly what it says. The only purpose it might have for PageMaker is to alter groups of graphics that you export to PageMaker after the fact. (See Figure F.95.)

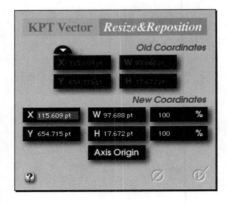

Shadowland

This is an exquisite plug-in for Illustrator that can give you loads of original content for PageMaker. Everything can be interacted with in real time as the preview updates in front of your eyes. All manner of special effects shadows can be generated, as well as the expected varieties. Shadowland enables you to set the Color, Halosity, Zoom, Rotation, Scale, Distance, gradation Steps, and Angle of the shadow. PageMaker users will appreciate the quality and variety of these shadows. (See Figure F.96.)

Figure F.96

The VectorFX/Shadowland interface.

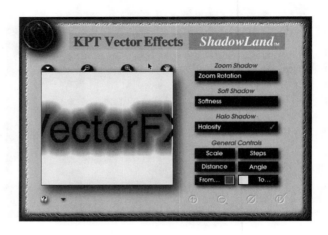

ShatterBox

This is another unique effect for text blocks, enabling you to literally shatter the selected text. How about using this on text used to advertise a sale on the Fourth of July? You can alter this dynamite effect by controlling the Radial Shatter, Random Lines, Random Curves, Fragment Offset, Radial Disruption, Lightness, Darkness, and Global Intensity. You have to play with this effect to get the hang of it, and unless you are out to create some unreadable chaos when it comes to text blocks, it must be used sparingly with very low settings. (See Figure F.97.)

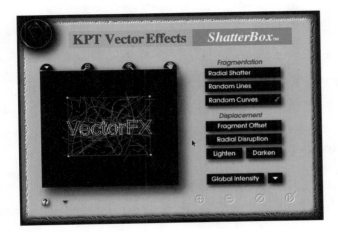

Figure F.97

The VectorFX/ShatterBox interface.

Sketch

Controls with this effect are minimal, enabling you to adjust the Stroke types and the Amount. The result on text is like a hand-lettered Zen poem at the low setting end and meaningless Klingon expletives at the high end. Use it with caution and your PageMaker compositions will take on a whole new look (see Figure F.98).

Figure F.98

The VectorFX/Sketch interface.

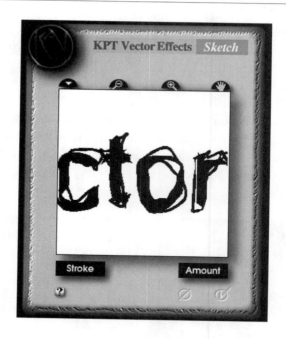

Vector Distort

Vector Distortions can be applied to an entire selection or to any specific part. You can manipulate the text by using several options: Swirl, Spherize, Rotate, Magnify, Zig, Zag, ZigZag, Warp Frame, and the Global Intensity of the effect. The number of possible effects is close to infinite and the results often lend a warmer organic look to the text block. PageMaker projects that address human topics would be the best place to use these effects. (See Figure F.99.)

Figure F.99

The VectorFX/Vector Distort interface.

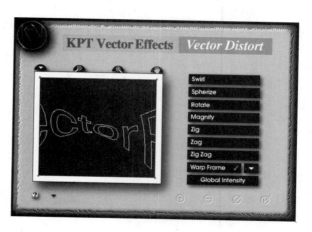

Warp Frame

This effect places your selection on a virtual rubber sheet whose corners can be stretched and manipulated with Bézier handles. An added feature is that there are over 100 presets to explore, helping you find the right look. PageMaker users will love these effects and their variability. (See Figure F.100.)

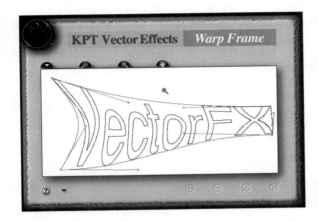

Figure F.100

The VectorFX/Warp Frame interface.

Professional PageMaker Solutions by VectorFX

Need: You are working on a PageMaker project that requires a metallic-looking, 3-D headline.

Solution: Open Illustrator, create your text block in the desired font, and go to the Filter/VectorFX/3-D Transform item. Boost the "metallic" indicator to a high setting and preview the result with full rendering preview turned on. Export the finished text block to PageMaker and set it in place.

Need: You are working on a PageMaker project that requires a backdrop of stars. You have to create it as a vector drawing and not as a bitmap.

Solution: Use VectorFX in Illustrator, and import the finished work in one piece to PageMaker.

Here's how to create the stars backdrop and place it in PageMaker:

1. In Illustrator, create a rectangle whose dimensions equal your requirements. Color it as desired (dark blue, black, magenta, or even with a gradated fill).

2. Open the VectorFX/Flare interface.

3. Compose a group of flare objects that mimic your vision of the cosmos.

4. Click the "Check" (OK) symbol and watch as your flares are drawn on the rectangular background.

5. Save the graphic for importation to PageMaker.

Need: You are working on a PageMaker project that requires that the text look like the scrawls of a child, perhaps a mailer for the neighborhood daycare center.

Solution: Create the text in Illustrator, and use fairly low settings with VectorFX Sketch to generate the effect. Export your artwork to PageMaker. (See Figures F.101, F.102, and F.103.)

Figure F.101

From top to bottom, VectorFX 3-D Transform with metallic reflectivity, alternate 3-D Transform, Emboss, Neon.

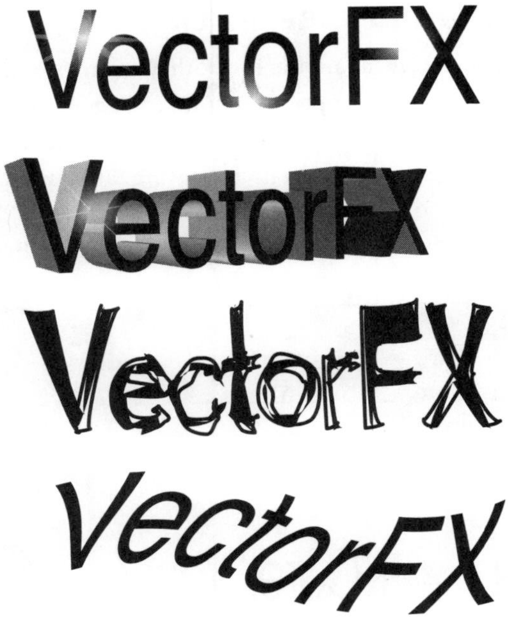

Figure F.102

From top to bottom, VectorFX Flares, Flares applied over a 3-D Transform, alteration with Point Editor and Sketch, Vector Distorted.

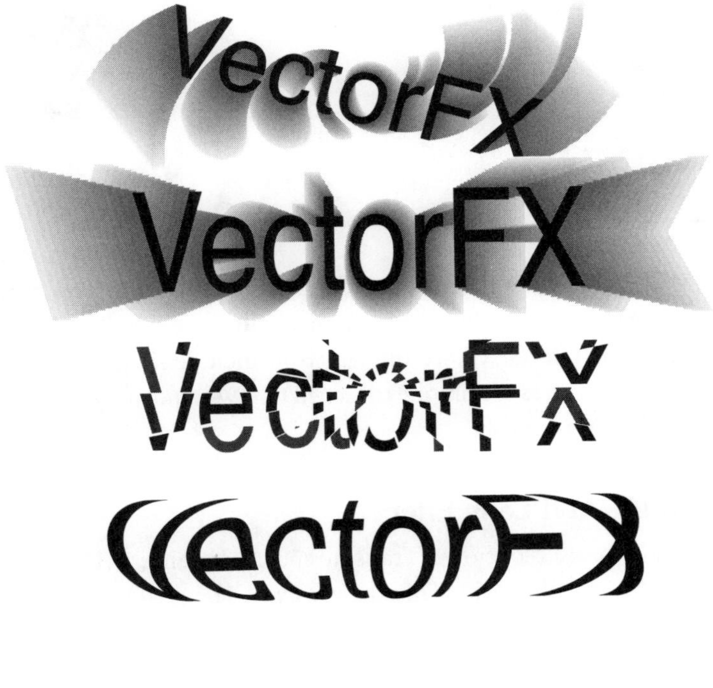

Figure F.103

From top to bottom, VectorFX Shadowland 1, Shadowland 2, radial Shatterland, Warp Frame "Sausage Bomb."

CORELDRAW! 6 AND PAGEMAKER

CorelDraw! 6 is now available for both Windows and Mac users and has a long list of creative options helpful to PageMaker pros who want to use it as a preparatory drawing environment. Its text modification and effects features are worth investigating, as finished CorelDRAW! work can be exported to PageMaker 6.5 as either EPS or Illustrator graphics (or bitmap formats if desired). (See Figure F.104.)

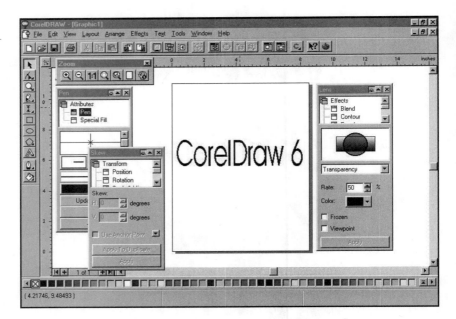

CorelDRAW! users should open the Effects Roll-Up Group menu as a first step in applying the effects that we will target for PageMaker use. The specific effects we are interested in include: Lens, and Extrude. These two features are unique to CorelDRAW!, and are also very useful to the PageMaker user.

The CorelDRAW! Lens Effect

The Lens has 12 options: Transparency, Magnify, Brighten, Invert, Color Limit, Color Add, Tinted Grayscale, Heat Map, Custom Color Map, Wireframe, Fisheye, and None. Any option that deals with color will expect that the artwork has a color fill or gradient to act upon.

Lens How-To

1. Place a line of text on the CorelDRAW! page. You do not have to transform it into curves for this effect.

2. Create any desired shape. Ovals and Rectangles work well, but you can create any closed shape desired. You can have a lot of fun applying these effects to a star polygonal shape.

3. Go to the Effects/Lens item in the Roll-Up, and with the polygon selected, click on the Fish Eye option. Click on Apply.

4. Move the polygon over the text block. Magic! Wherever you move it, the text underneath evidences a warp as if the polygon was a real Fish Eye Lens.

5. Create another polygon. This time, select Magnify from the menu. Select Apply. Now move the Magnify polygon over the text. Notice that it enlarges the text below, but without the warp effect. Now for some real magic...

6. Move both the Magnify and the Fish Eye polygons over the same text, and overlap one on the other. Not only can you effect the text, but you can effect the effect as well. See how the areas that overlap are effected by both Magnify and Fish Eye.

7. Now make a third polygon (the shape choice is yours, as long as it's a closed shape). Select Custom Color Map from the Roll-Up and choose two colors from the palette tags. Move the Color Mapped polygon over the text. Voila! Multicolored text on a color backdrop wherever you move the polygon.

8. Repeat this same step for another polygon, using two different colors. Now move both Custom Color Polygons over the text block, and let them overlap each other. Note that the colors act like transparent sheets, in that the overlap produces other colors.

9. As a final experiment, move the Magnify, the Fish Eye, and the two Custom Color polygons over the same text, and allow them to overlap each other. Play with these effects until you achieve something you like, and export the results to PageMaker.

Tip

If you make the edges (strokes) of the polygons invisible or None, all that you will have showing is the effects on the text.

Figure F.105

Any polygon can act as a lens in CorelDraw!, allowing you to develop unique text effects for your PageMaker projects.

Extrude How-to

CorelDraw's extrusion routine is also accessed from the Effects Roll-Up. When accessed, it brings up five options that can be customized: Color Choices from the Library, Extrusion Depth, Rotation, Lights (three), and user Set Colors. For most endeavors, you'll probably select to use the color choices from the library. They represent optional materials and reflections, and apply quickly to the text. After you have applied them, export the results to PageMaker. (See Figures F.103, F.104, and F.105.)

Figure F.106

CorelDRAW! can produce extruded text from library default settings (top) or customized results (bottom).

   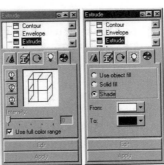

Figure F.107

There are five options to be set in the CorelDRAW! 6 Extrusion Effects dialog box.

843

PageMaker Text Effects with FreeHand

PageMaker users who also work in Macromedia FreeHand have access to a number of plug-ins and effects that can customize type. Three native FreeHand effects that are secreted away in the Window/Other/ Xtra Tools dialog box are very useful for PageMaker warped text purposes. They include: Smudge, Fisheye Lens, and 3-D Rotation. After these effects are applied, export the finished work to PageMaker as an EPS file.

Smudge

The FreeHand Smudge effect adds a pseudo-3-D extrusion to the text in the direction set by the user. The extrusion direction is set visually, with the farthest point being in the direction set. An attached dialog box, opened by double clicking the Smudge icon, allows you to set both the Fill and Stroke colors. Save the finished artwork (export it from FreeHand) as an EPS file.

Fisheye Lens

After your Type is selected in FreeHand, choose the Fisheye Lens in the Window/Other/Xtra Tools dialog box. With Fisheye Lens and your Text Object selected, you can draw an oval over the text block. The text then reshapes itself according to the dimensions of the oval, as if the oval was a bubble refracting the light. An attached dialog box, brought up by double-clicking on the Smudge icon, allows you to set either the concavity or convexity degree of the warping effect. Save the finished artwork (export it from FreeHand) as an EPS file.

3-D Rotation

FreeHand's 3-D Rotation Tool adds a 3-D perspective look to selected text or single letters. PageMaker users might want to explore the possibility of using Perspective letters for drop caps. Open the Window/ Other/Xtra Tools dialog box, and select 3-D Rotation. As you move your mouse over the selected text block or letter (or any vector graphic), you can see its perspective change. When satisfied, release the mouse. An attached dialog box, brought up by double-clicking the Smudge icon, enables you to set the point the rotation is calculated from (mouse click, center of the object, center of gravity, or the origin) and the perceived distance of the observer from the perspective object. Save the finished artwork (export it from FreeHand) as an EPS file.

FreeHand's Text to Path Tool

Experienced FreeHand users might want to use the Text to Path tools before exporting their text block to PageMaker. FreeHand's Text to Path options are simple to master, and curved text always looks good in a layout when the job is suitable. FreeHand enables you to wrap text on either a free-standing curve or a closed curve. Simply select both the curve and the text block, and select the Type/Bind to Path option. You do not have to transform the text to paths first. A special effect that PageMaker users might be interested in however, does require that you change the text block to paths after the curve operation is complete. This is to utilize the 3-D Rotation effect mentioned previously after the text has been written to a curve. A perspective curved text block is the result, a multiple effect hard to achieve by other methods. Save the finished artwork (export it from FreeHand) as an EPS file.

FreeHand's Effects

FreeHand offers a collection of image processing effects unique to vector drawing applications. FreeHand's Smudge tool (see Figure F.108) creates a diminishing series of cloned images, giving text a 3-D extrusion look. The Fisheye Lens (see Figure F.109) reshapes the text as if it were refracted through a transparent bubble. The 3-D Rotation option (see Figure F.110) allows you to add perspective to a text block.

Figure F.108

FreeHand's Smudge Tool.

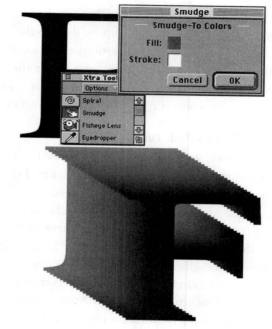

Figure F.109

FreeHand's Fisheye Lens effect.

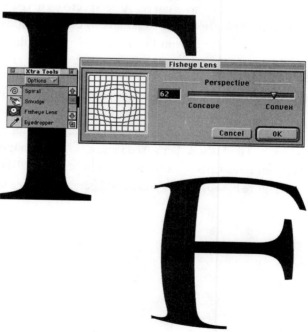

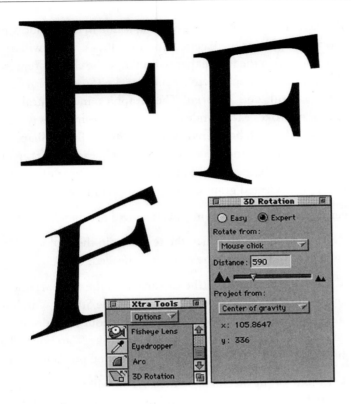

Fractal Expression and PageMaker

Fractal Expression is available for both Windows and Mac users, and it is the most useful drawing software dedicated to natural media output. Its text modification and effects features are worth investigating if you are looking for a softer graphic look. Fractal Expression enables the PageMaker user to create and incorporate artwork that looks more hand drawn than the colder more precise and mechanical output usually associated with Vector drawing applications. In addition, Fractal Expression's effects can be applied to text blocks as well as illustrations. It was difficult to get Vector art to emulate realistic pen-and-ink or wash media before Expression was introduced, but no more. Finished Fractal Expression work can be exported to PageMaker 6.5 as either EPS or Illustrator graphics (or bitmap formats if desired).

The Expression Stroke Warehouse menu, found in the Window menu, is the focus of applying media effects to text blocks. There will be more libraries released in the future that will enlarge the choices represented here, but even at this stage, there are three packed Stroke library groups: Graphic, Natural, and Tutorial. The Graphics and Natural Groups hold a dozen Strokes each, while the Tutorial Group holds two dozen. Each Stroke effect can be altered as to Size, Shear, Twist, Shape, Brush Nib, Randomization, and the way that ends Join each other, giving the user infinite possibilities. In addition, fills and colorizations may be targeted to the selected graphic (see Figures F.111 and F.112).

The general method for applying an effect to a text block is as follows:

1. Open Expression and click the text icon in the toolbar. Write your text to the screen, resizing it as needed.

2. Click the selection icon (the top arrow in the toolbar) and move the text where you want it. Open the Stroke Warehouse and Paint Style dialog boxes. Make sure your text block is selected. Click the Outline Tab in the Stroke Warehouse dialog box, and open all of the libraries by clicking on their names.

3. Click one of the Stroke Style items. You will notice an immediate response as the text takes on that specific Stroke attribute. For text, you have to play with the resizing option (Width) listed in the Paint Style dialog box (under the Stroke tab). Move the width dimension down until you can read the text block (unless you want an unreadable but interesting graphic as a result).

4. Export or Save the graphic in the desired format, and import or place the graphic in a PageMaker layout.

Use this same procedure to develop natural media looks for PageMaker headlines.

Note

It's a good idea to save out a group of text blocks that you have experimented with as a separate Expression file. This will enable you to develop a "looks" visual journal that can serve as a portfolio for your PageMaker clients.

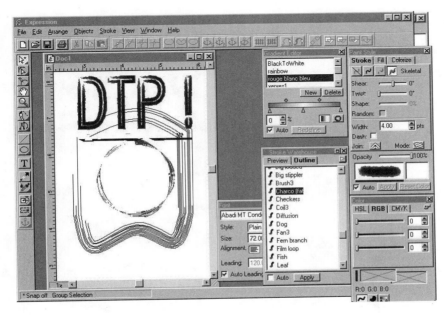

Figure F.111

Fractal Expression is the best application when you need to create looser more handmade text looks for your PageMaker documents.

Figure F.112

The number of unique text block styles that Expression can help you create is limitless.

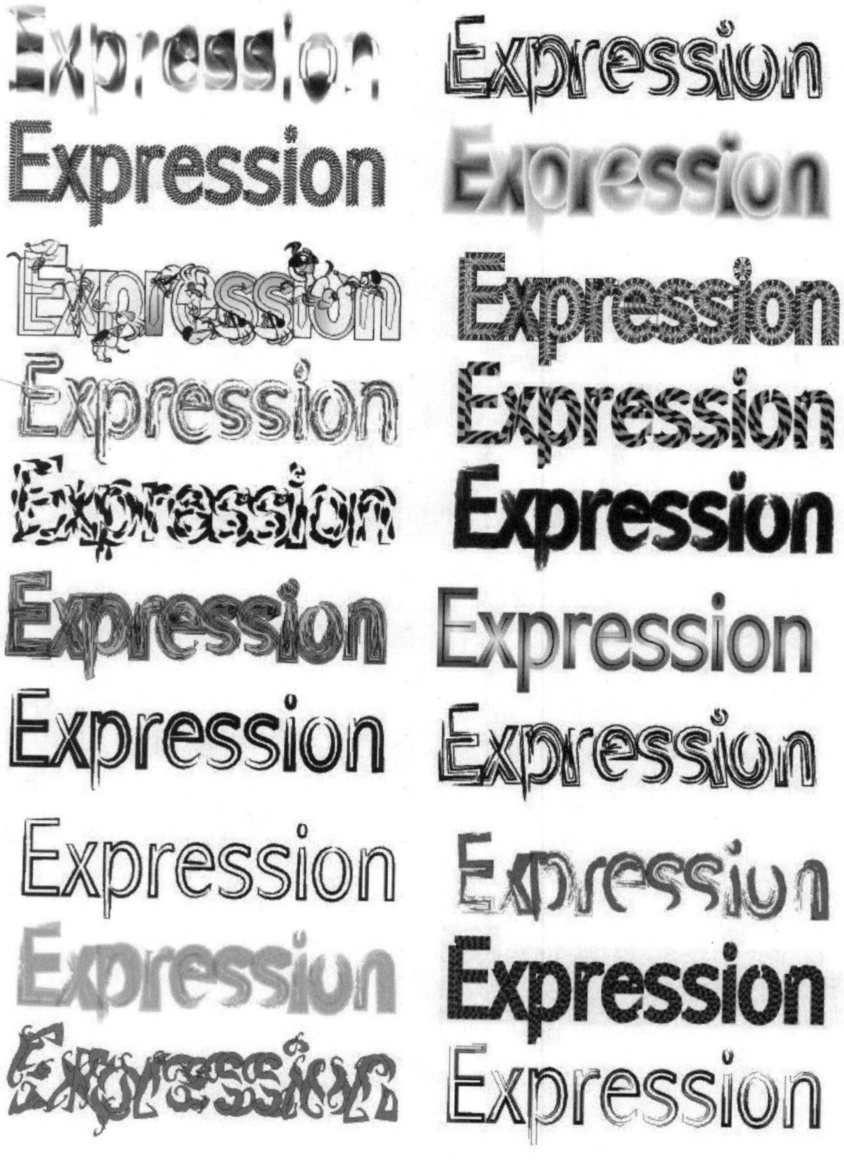

Using Tables in Your Documents

Tables are one of the most common ways to display comparative data. PageMaker 6.5 includes Adobe Table 3.0, an intuitive table creation utility that runs as a stand-alone application. Using Adobe Table, you can design and fine tune all of your table needs. You can have as many Tables open at the same time as are allowed by the amount of RAM you have available. The names of all open Tables are listed in the Window Menu.

Adobe Table Overview

Adobe table is run as a separate application. It resides in the PageMaker 6.5 folder. Just find its icon and double-click to launch the application. The New Table dialog box appears, allowing you to configure the global parameters of the table, including: table height and width (up to 40×40 inches), number of rows and columns (up to 100 each), and gutter dimensions (see Figure F.113). If the settings have to be changed later, that can be accomplished from within Adobe Table. You can also select a preset line weight, or select None to make the border invisible. You can set the line weight for each outside edge of the table, and for the vertical or horizontal lines between rows and columns within the table. If you want a uniform border throughout the table, use the All option. It is suggested that if you need to create tables with over 200 cells, you consider dividing the table into two files, and join them together after they are imported into PageMaker. This ensures the optimal and smooth performance of Adobe Table.

Figure F.113

The Adobe Table New Table dialog box opens when you start a new Table project.

If you need to open a previously saved Table document instead of creating a new Table, choose Open from the File menu. Select the table file you want, and specify whether you want to open the Original version or a Copy. (You can open the original version or a copy of Adobe Table 2.5 files as well), and click OK. You can open the following files in Adobe Table:

◆ Tables saved in the Adobe Table 2.5 native file format. You can open Adobe Table files created on the Windows platform directly from the Macintosh platform, and vice versa.

◆ Tables created with Table Editor version 2.x (included with earlier versions of PageMaker for Windows) and version 1.01 (included with PageMaker 4.x for the Macintosh).

◆ Table Editor files open as untitled copies of the original. All the table formatting is converted, including grouped cells and number formats, with the exception of dashed or dotted lines, which are converted into solid lines.

◆ If you also own Adobe Table 1.0, included with Adobe Persuasion 3.0 for Windows and Macintosh (or Aldus Table 1.0 if you own Aldus Persuasion 3.0), you must use that version of the application to open the tables it created. Adobe Table 3.0 does not open them.

If the fonts included in the table you are opening are not available on your system, Adobe Table alerts you and asks if you want to continue opening the file. If you click Continue, Adobe Table opens an untitled copy of the table. On the Macintosh, Adobe Table substitutes the application default font for the missing font. Adobe Table for Windows substitutes the Windows default font (Arial, in most instances) for the missing font.

Setting Adobe Table Defaults

You can set two types of defaults in Adobe Table:

◆ **Application defaults.** You set Application Defaults when no table is open, and they are then applied to all new tables you create. Choose Table Setup from the Adobe Table File menu before you open a table. In the Table Setup dialog box, for example, you can change the number of rows to your desired setting. All of the future new tables created will have that number of rows.

◆ **Cell-range defaults.** These apply to one or more cells you have selected. For example, if you select all of the cells in Row 1 and choose Center paragraph alignment from the Adobe table Text palette, then any new text you type in Row 1 is aligned to the center of the cell without you having to set each individual cell to that specification separately.

Adobe Table Preferences

The Preferences command also controls the various parameters of Adobe Tables.

To set preferences:

1. Choose Preferences from the File menu.

2. Set the options you want, including:

   ◆ **The Type options**   These are identical to the type settings in PageMaker.

   ◆ **Text Format option**   Select the default delimiter you want to use when importing text.

   ◆ **Language option**   Select the version of English you want to appear in Adobe Table dialog boxes, messages, and palettes. When you start Adobe Table for the first time, you are prompted to select the language interface. This preference setting enables you to reset that choice.

   ◆ **Export EPS option (in the File/Export/Graphic menu)** Specify the default setting you want to use when saving EPS—with or without fonts.

3. Click OK. These settings stay in effect until you change them.

Several options for formatting text (the Autoleading percentage, Super/Subscript size and position), are available in the Preferences dialog box.

If you choose Preferences command with no Table open, you will change the attributes for all the new Tables you create. These type options are identical to the options in PageMaker itself.

The full Adobe Table interface contains access to the table you're working on as well as the Text palette and the Table palette. Additional commands are accessed by selecting items from the menus in the top menu bar (see Figure F.114). The Adobe Table Text palette contains intuitive controls for altering the typeface, size, leading, kerning, baseline adjustment, style, and justification of any selected Table text blocks (see Figure F.115). The Table palette gives you easy access to altering any selected cell border size and color, cell color, and cell dimensions (see Figure F.116). Mastering the Cell (see Figure F.117) and Table Format (see Figure F.118) menu options is vital when creating customized tables in Adobe Table.

Figure F.114

The Adobe Table interface.

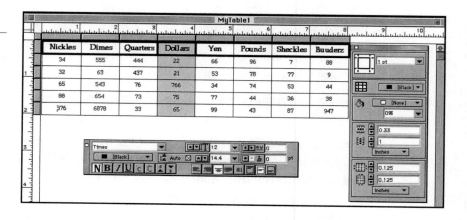

Figure F.115

The Adobe Table Text palette.

Figure F.116

The Adobe Table palette.

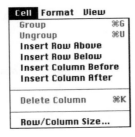

Figure F.117

The Cell menu gives you control over all of a Cell's parameters.

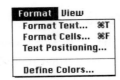

Figure F.118

The Adobe Table Format menu.

Typing, Editing, and Formatting Text in Adobe Table

Nothing is easier than creating your needed data in Adobe Table. Just Click in a cell to type, edit, and format the text to be entered within it. Formatting changes can also affect all text in a selected range of cells if you click and drag to select more than one cell. As you type, the text automatically wraps to fit within the width of the column. When necessary, the height of the row expands to accommodate the maximum text you add to a cell.

Instead of manually clicking in a cell each time you want to edit it or add text, use the following keys and key combinations as a shortcut:

- Press Tab to move to the next column to the right. If you press Tab with the insertion point in the last cell in the table, another row appears.

- Press Shift-Tab to move to the next column to the left.

- Press (Option-Tab) [Control-. (period)] to insert a tab at the insertion point.

- Press (Return) [Enter] to create a new paragraph in the cell.

- Press the arrow keys to move line-by-line (up or down arrows) or character-by-character (left and right arrows) through text in the cell, or to the next cell in the row or column.

Note

To view nonprinting markers representing tabs and other invisible characters:

Choose View/Show ¶.

Formatting Text in a Table

You should first be familiar with text formatting in PageMaker itself before using Adobe Table to format text. The Vertical and Decimal alignment are the only formatting options unique to Adobe Table where no counterpart is found in PageMaker.

Vertical Alignment

You can position the top line of text along the top of the cell's text block, position the bottom line of text along the bottom of the cell's text block, or center text vertically within the cell's text block. Vertical alignment is a specific cell attribute.

Decimal Alignment

In columns that contain numbers with decimals, you can ensure that the decimals align regardless of the number of digits before or after the decimal point. This feature is similar to the Decimal tab stop in PageMaker.

Text Attributes

Adobe Table is very similar to PageMaker in the methods it provides for applying text attributes. When formatting text, you have two options: use the Type and Paragraph Specifications command, or use the Text palette. The Text palette is similar to PageMaker's Control palette in Character or Paragraph view. To open it, choose Show Text from the Window palette. The state of the palette changes to reflect the text attributes of selected cells.

To format text, proceed as follows:

1. Select the range of text, or one or more cells containing text you want to format.

2. Choose Show Text palette from the Windows menu, or Type and Paragraph Specifications.

3. Specify the settings you want.

To set text defaults for all new tables you create:

1. Close any open tables.

2. Choose Format/Format Text to set the Application Text Defaults.

3. Specify the exact settings you want, and click OK.

To align numbers in a column:

1. Apply the Decimal Horizontal alignment attribute to the paragraphs that contain the numbers you want to align.

2. Insert a single tab—(Option-Tab) or [Control-. (period)]— immediately before each number you want to align by decimal point.

Note

If you want to override the default position of the tab stop (the place where the decimal point is positioned within the column), complete steps 3 and 4.

3. Make sure the Show Tab Markers and Show Selection Buttons commands are selected.

4. In the Select Button of the column containing the numbers you are formatting, drag the tab marker to where you want the decimals to appear.

Note

The position of the decimal point is a column-level setting, so that all paragraphs with the Decimal alignment attribute have the same tab position within a column.

Exporting and Saving Adobe Tables

Adobe Table is a separate utility, so the tables you create must be saved to a file or exported in order for other applications to be able to use them (see Figure F.119).

Figure F.119

Adobe Tables can be exported as EPS graphics, PICT (Mac) or WMF/EMF (Windows) files.

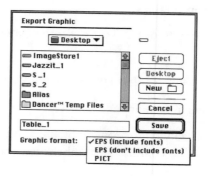

Exporting Tables from Adobe Table

The Export command enables you to export a table as a text or graphics file that other applications can import. When exporting text, you can export the entire table or only a selected range of cells. When you export an Adobe Table as a graphic, you must export the entire table. When you export a table as a graphic, you can format the file as an EPS graphic (with or without fonts), as PICT (Macintosh only) or WMF/EMF (Windows only). The EPS format is the best choice if you are going to print the Table on a Postscript printer, because it is supported on both Windows and Macintosh platforms and offers the best printing results. If you are certain your printer (or service bureau) has the fonts you used to create the table, you can save the EPS without fonts. If you choose to include fonts (to avoid font substitution problems), the file size of the exported graphic will be much larger than the same file saved without fonts.

If you export a table as a text-only (ASCII .TXT) file, the borders, fills, and text attributes applied in Adobe Table are not retained. When you place an exported table into PageMaker, PageMaker does not link its internal version of the table to the original Adobe Table file (the table from which you created the exported file). Instead, PageMaker links its placed version of the table to the external text or graphic file you exported from Adobe Table.

Exporting a Table as Text

Select an insertion point or a range of cells and go to File/Export/Text. Select the delimiter format you want, and click OK.

Exporting a Table as a Graphic

The entire table is exported regardless of what is selected when you choose to Export as a Graphic. Select the file format you want for the graphic and click OK.

Adobe Table supports OLE embedding, but not OLE linking. You can Import an OLE-embedded version of a Table into PageMaker. To use this option you do not create a native file on the hard disk or an exported version of the file. You must, however, have enough RAM for PageMaker and Adobe Table to run simultaneously.

To save a table opened as an embedded OLE document from within PageMaker, first make the needed changes. The changes appear automatically in PageMaker. If you use Adobe Table to embed a table in an application that only supports OLE 1.0, you can choose Update from the File menu to apply the changes to the version of the table stored in the application file. You can also choose Save Copy As to save the OLE document to disk (the version of the Table in PageMaker is not updated). In the dialog box that appears, specify a name for the file and a folder in which to save it, and whether you want to save the table as a Template or as a Table.

Saving Adobe Tables

To save a table opened from within Adobe Table, first complete the changes you want to make. Next, use either of the following options:

◆ Choose Save from the File menu if the table has been saved previously.

◆ Choose Save As if the file is being saved for the first time or if you want to change how the file is saved.

If you chose Save As, specify a name for the file and a folder in which to save it, and whether you want to save the table as a template or as a table. Adobe Table templates work just like they do in PageMaker; they enable you to create new, untitled documents using the content and formatting of the template as a starting point.

Importing and Updating a Table

If you import an object by placing, OLE linking or embedding, or subscribing (Macintosh only), you might be able to update the object in PageMaker each time the original document changes. In addition, you might be able to start the application in which you created an object directly from PageMaker, if the application is on your computer.

Importing and updating that can update a link:

◆ Place

◆ Paste link/Paste Special

- Insert object
- Subscribe (Macintosh)

These methods convert Imported text so you can edit it using PageMaker:

- Place
- Paste
- Subscribe (Macintosh)

These choices can open an imported object directly in its original application, if that application is installed on your computer:

- Place
- Paste link/Paste Special
- Insert object
- Subscribe (Macintosh)

These methods can simultaneously update multiple instances of an object in one or more publications:

- Place
- Paste link/Paste Special
- Subscribe (Macintosh)

These choices can import a portion of a saved file:

- Paste
- Paste link/Paste Special
- Subscribe (Macintosh)

File management and Version Control

Stores an imported graphic inside a publication:

- Place
- Paste
- Paste link/Paste Special

- Insert object

- Subscribe (Macintosh)

Note

You can save disk space by storing imported EPS and TIFF files outside a publication with a link by using the Place method.

You can include an option to update a linked file automatically or manually by using these methods:

- Place

- Paste link/Paste Special

- Subscribe (Macintosh)

Note

You can edit and update an imported graphic without an external saved file by selecting the Insert Object command.

The ExecuTable Plug-In

There might be times when you need to stay within PageMaker, and still have the capacity for generating a table aside from using Adobe Table. One alternative that gives you that option is to use the ExecuTable plug-in from ExecuStaff Composition Services. ExecuTable does not generate table cells as such, because it does not allow for vertical rules. It also separates each column/row text block into an individual component, cutting the grouping involved. If neither of these attributes are important to you, ExecuTable might provide an answer for some of your table needs (see Figure F.120).

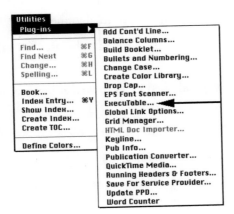

Figure F.120

After installing ExecuTable, it can be found in the PageMaker Plug-ins list.

ExecuTable addresses three table types:

- **Table Type I**—automatically calculates both the table columns and gutters based upon the longest line in each column. Gutters may be set with a minimum and maximum width specification. This Table Type simultaneously allows for both program and user generated column/gutter specifications.

- **Table Type II**—enables the user to define the gutter space, and the program then automatically distributes the remaining space evenly across the columns.

- **Table Type III**—enables the user to define the width of each column. The program then automatically distributes the remaining space evenly between gutters.

ExecuTable has the following features:

- Automatic text wrap, which formats tables containing paragraphs of text

- Automatic decimal alignment for decimal tables

- The number of columns is automatically generated by the program

- Automatic Straddle Heads

- All paragraph and type specifications are maintained

- Independent column and head alignment

- A "Don't Align" feature that can be used for table footnotes, and so on

- Text vertically aligned in its row to either top, middle, or bottom

- A variety of column alignment choices

- User specified hanging indents

- Automatic resizing of table width when the table is narrower than the type page

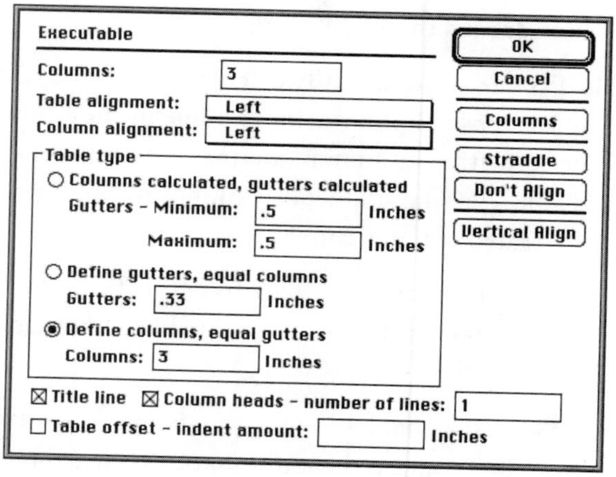

Figure F.121

The ExecuTable main dialog box automatically calculates the number of columns involved in your table from the selected PageMaker data.

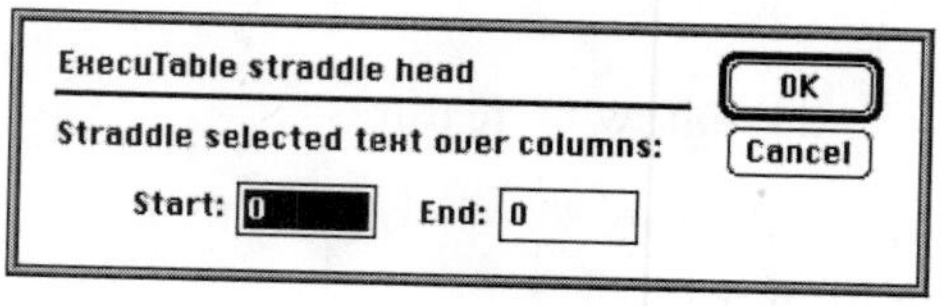

Figure F.122

ExecuTable allows you to customize the table's straddle heads.

ExecuTable allows you to apply very precise attributes to PageMaker Table creation, so it is a favorite plug-in for professionals in the publishing community, with a central focus upon book publishers. Though ExecuTable offers less creative options than Adobe Table 3, it might be perfect for specific targeted uses. As a plug-in, it is always easily accessible.

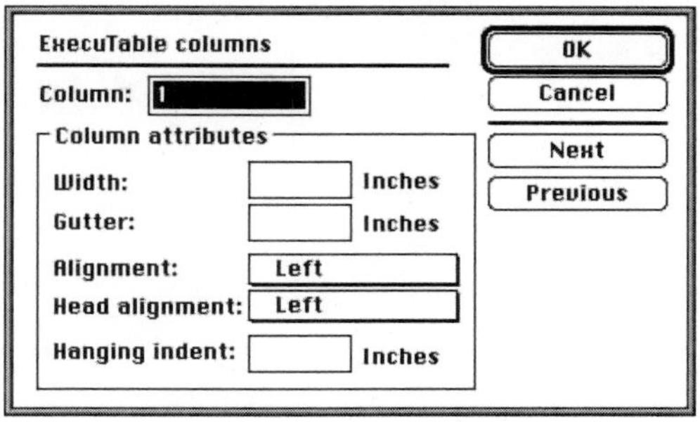

Figure F.123

You can customize column dimensions and override ExecuTable's automatic features.

ExecuStaff Composition Services also has one of the most useful PageMaker Web sites online. The site features ExecuTable tips and tricks, a "Table of the Month" display, and numerous pages dedicated to PageMaker specific help topics. You can access the ExecuStaff Web site at: `http://www.execustaff.com` (see Figure F.124).

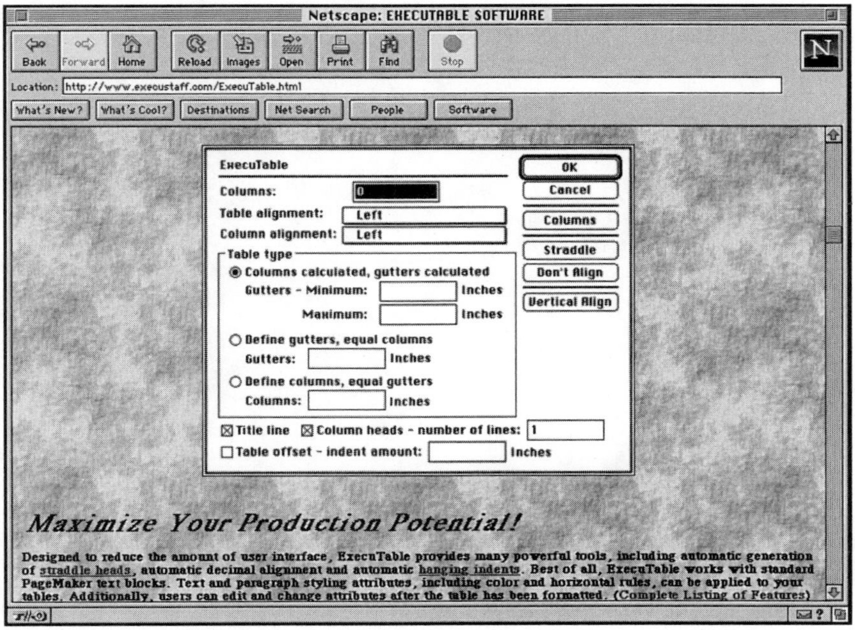

Figure F.124

ExecuStaff's Web site features online tips for using ExecuTable.

Index

Symbols

A

B

C

Q

T

W

X-Y-Z

MACMILLAN COMPUTER PUBLISHING USA

A VIACOM COMPANY

Technical Support:

If you need assistance with the information in this book or with a CD/Disk accompanying the book, please access the Knowledge Base on our Web site at **http://www.superlibrary.com/general/support**. Our most Frequently Asked Questions are answered there. If you do not find the answer to your questions on our Web site, you may contact Macmillan Technical Support **(317) 581-3833** or e-mail us at **support@mcp.com**.